Computer Science

Volume 1

Computer Science

Volume 1

J. Stanley Warford

Pepperdine University

D. C. Heath and Company
Lexington, Massachusetts / Toronto

Address editorial correspondence to:

D. C. Heath
125 Spring Street
Lexington, MA 02173

Acquisitions Editor: Carter Shanklin
Developmental Editor: Katherine Pinard
Production Editor: Jennifer Brett
Designer: Judith Miller
Production Coordinator: Lisa Merrill
Photo Researcher: Ann M. Barnard

Cover Image: Digital Art/Los Angeles

Photo Credits: p. 5—Franklin D. Murphy Sculpture Garden, University of California, Los Angeles, Grey Crawford, Photographer; p. 52—Culver Pictures; p. 98—Eidgenossische Technische Hochschule (ETH), Zurich, Switzerland; p. 136—ACM, Association of Computing Machinery; p. 190—Culver Pictures; p. 323—Herb Bethoney; p. 472—MIT Museum Collections.

Published simultaneously in Canada.

Printed in the United States of America.

International Standard Book Number: 0-669-24976-9

Library of Congress Catalog Number: 90-84807

10 9 8 7 6 5 4 3

This book is dedicated to
Ann
(and Moose and Goose).

Preface

This book is the outgrowth of an introductory computer science course taught at Pepperdine University, where the book has been class-tested for five years. The course, as well as the book, is primarily for majors in computer science who intend a more in-depth study later, and secondarily for nonmajors who desire a strong background in computers so that they can deal with them effectively in their chosen fields. The book is designed for a two- or three-semester course.

The Physics Model

The approach taken in this book is unique. The idea is best illustrated by looking at the typical curriculum in physics, a much older discipline. Like computer science, physics is a broad area. Over the years a traditional introductory physics course, which is uniform in content from school to school, has evolved. Physics educators realize that the first course should teach some problem-solving techniques and give the student some laboratory experience. In addition, they realize the importance of introducing the student to all the main areas of study, including mechanics, thermodynamics, electricity, magnetism, and modern physics. In-depth mastery of the subfields of physics is postponed for later courses in which the instructor can assume that the student has already been exposed to the main concepts.

The traditional design of the introductory computer science sequence lacks the breadth of the typical physics sequence. Computer science includes the study of hardware, language theory, algorithms, data structures, architecture, and operating systems. Although the recent trend is to incorporate more topics from data structures into the introductory course, most introductory sequences in computer science neglect hardware, language theory, architecture, and operating systems.

The physics curriculum generally recognizes that the concepts of motion, force, and energy as developed in classical Newtonian mechanics are the foundation on which all the other topics can be presented. However, physics books rarely present just mechanics—they develop the concepts in mechanics first and then move on to the other topics.

Similarly, this introductory computer science text begins with algorithm design in a high-order language, but is not be confined to it. Although Pascal programming accounts for much of the content, a substantial portion of the text is devoted to computer organization down to the logic gate level. Students should get an overall picture of the discipline of computer science in their first year of study. Indeed, if they do not get a unified picture of the discipline then, when will they get it later?

Summary of Contents

Computers operate at several levels of abstraction; programming in Pascal at a high level of abstraction is only part of the story. This book presents a unified concept of computer systems based on the level structure of Figure P.1.

The book is divided into six parts corresponding to six of the seven levels of Figure P.1:

Level 7   Applications

Level 6   High-order languages

Level 3   Machine

Level 5   Assembly

Level 4   Operating system

Level 1   Logic gate

Volume 1 of the two-volume edition covers Levels 7 and 6, and Volume 2 covers Levels 3, 5, 4, and 1. Microprogramming, Level 2, is beyond the scope of this book.

The text generally presents the levels top-down, from the highest to the lowest. Level 3, the machine level, is discussed before Level 5, the assembly level, for pedagogical reasons. In this one instance, it is more natural to revert temporarily to a bottom-up approach so that the building blocks of the lower level will be in hand for construction of the higher level.

Level 7 is a single chapter on applications programs. It presents the idea of levels of abstraction and establishes the framework for the remainder of the book. A few concepts of relational databases are presented as an example of a typical computer application. It is assumed that students have experience with text editors or word processors.

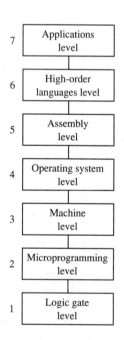

Figure P.1

The level structure of a typical computer system.

Level 6 consists of 10 chapters on algorithm design and data structures in Pascal (Chapters 2–11). The treatment of Pascal is fairly complete and includes separate chapters on recursion and pointers. Some topics, such as passing procedures as parameters, are not included.

Students learn best by studying and imitating complete programs, so the Pascal chapters present the material in a case-study format. Generalizations then follow the examples. As much as possible, Pascal language features are discussed in the context of the specific programs.

Two design methodologies are integrated into the Pascal chapters—stepwise refinement and top-down design. Although these two techniques are closely related (some would say they are identical), they are treated separately. Stepwise refinement is a tool for developing a single main program or a single module. Top-down design is a tool for partitioning a program into modules. (In this book, a module is defined as a main program or a procedure or a function.) The design methodologies and associated terminology are simplified to avoid intimidating the student.

Two other topics integrated throughout the Pascal chapters are assertions and statement execution counts. Assertions are introduced with nested `if` statements as a tool for reasoning about the behavior of executable code. Formal proofs of correctness are left for a later course, but the book lays the groundwork by giving the students the ability to formulate a strong assertion. Statement execution counts are introduced with loops. Given the execution time of a program with a small amount of data, the student is shown how to estimate the execution time of the program with a large amount of data. The numerical exercises included in these chapters give the student a feel for the usefulness of time-complexity results.

Level 3 is the machine level. Its two chapters describe Pep/5, a hypothetical computer designed to illustrate computer concepts. The Pep/5 computer is a classical von Neumann machine. The CPU contains an accumulator, an index register, a base register, a program counter, a stack pointer, and an instruction register. It has four addressing modes—immediate, direct, indexed, and stack relative. The Pep/5 operating system, in simulated read-only memory (ROM), can load and execute programs in hexadecimal format from students' text files. Students run short programs on the Pep/5 simulator and learn that executing a store instruction to ROM does not change the memory value.

Students learn the fundamentals of information representation and computer organization at the bit level. Because a central theme of this book is the relationship of the levels to one another, the Pep/5 chapters show the relationship between the ASCII representation (Level 3) and Pascal variables of type `char` (Level 6). They also show the relationship between two's complement representation (Level 3) and Pascal variables of type `integer` (Level 6).

Level 5 is the assembly level. The text presents the concept of the assembler as a translator between two levels—assembly and machine. It introduces Level 5 symbols and the symbol table.

The unified approach really pays off here. Chapters 14 and 15 present the compiler as a translator from a high-order language to assembly language. In previous chapters students learned a specific Level 6 language, Pascal, and a specific von Neumann machine, Pep/5. These chapters continue the theme of relationships between the levels by showing the correspondence between (a) assignment statements at Level 6 and load/store instructions at Level 5, (b) loops and `if` statements at Level 6 and branching instructions at Level 5, (c) arrays at Level 6 and indexed addressing at Level 5, (d) procedure calls at Level 6 and the run-time stack at Level 5, (e) function and procedure parameters at Level 6 and stack-relative addressing at Level 5, and (f) `case` statements at Level 6 and jump tables at Level 5.

The beauty of the unified approach is that the text can implement many of the examples from the Pascal chapters at this lower level. For example, the run-time stack illustrated in the recursive examples of an earlier chapter corresponds directly to the hardware stack in Pep/5 main memory. Students gain an understanding of the compilation process by translating manually between the two levels.

This approach provides a natural setting for the discussion of central issues in computer science. For example, the book presents structured programming at Level 6 versus the possibility of unstructured programming at Level 5. It discusses the goto controversy and the structured programming/efficiency tradeoff, giving concrete examples from languages at the two levels. As in the Pascal chapters, the style of presentation involves drawing general conclusions from specific examples.

Chapter 16, Language Translation Principles, introduces students to computer science theory. Now that students know intuitively how to translate from a high-level language to assembly language, we pose the fundamental question underlying all of computing, What can be automated? The theory naturally fits in here because students now know what a compiler (an automated translator) must do. They learn about parsing and finite state machines—deterministic and nondeterministic—in the context of recognizing Pascal and Pep/5 assembly language tokens. This chapter includes an automatic translator between two small languages, which illustrates lexical analysis, parsing, and code generation. The lexical analyzer is an implementation of a finite state machine. What could be a more natural setting for the theory?

Level 4 consists of two chapters on operating systems. Chapter 17 is a description of process management. Two sections, one on loaders and another on interrupt handlers, illustrate the concepts with the Pep/5 operating system. Four instructions have unimplemented opcodes that generate software interrupts. The operating system stores the process control block of the user's running process on the system stack while the interrupt service routine interprets the instruction. The classic state transition diagram for running and waiting processes in an operating system is thus reinforced with a specific implementation of a suspended process. The chapter concludes with a description of concurrent processes and deadlocks. Chapter 18 describes storage management, both main memory and disk memory.

Level 1 uses two chapters to present combinational networks and sequential networks. Chapter 19 emphasizes the importance of the mathematical foundation of computer science by starting with the axioms of boolean algebra. It shows the relation between boolean algebra and logic gates, then describes some common SSI and MSI logic devices. Chapter 20 again illustrates the fundamental concept of a finite state machine through the state transition diagrams of sequential circuits. It concludes with the construction of the data section of the Pep/5 computer. The same machine model is thus used from the Pascal level to the logic gate level, providing a complete, unifying picture of the entire system.

 Unifying Themes

In physics, fundamental concepts of motion, force, and energy are developed in one area of study and carried over into other areas, thus providing a unifying framework. Unifying themes of this book include abstraction, languages, and finite state machines.

The fundamental space/time tradeoff is another recurring theme. Execution-time analysis begins with the first `while` loop in Chapter 5 and continues throughout the text. The tradeoff occurs in software when the availability of extra memory may permit a faster algorithm, and in hardware when a two-level network may require more gates to implement a binary function than a multilevel one.

 The Denning Report

This text reflects the recent recommendations of the Denning Report, "Computing as a Discipline."[1] That report identifies the following nine subareas of computer science on which the introductory sequence should be based:

1. Algorithms and data structures
2. Programming languages
3. Architecture
4. Numeric and symbolic computation
5. Operating systems
6. Software methodology and engineering
7. Databases and information retrieval
8. Artificial intelligence and robotics
9. Human-computer communication

---

1. Peter J. Denning et al., "Computing as a Discipline," *Computer* 22 (February 1989): 63–70. © 1989 by IEEE.

This book emphasizes five areas (1, 2, 3, 5, 6), touches on two others (4, 7), and admits that two areas are beyond its scope (8, 9). Even with the omissions, I believe that this book achieves the goal enunciated in the Denning Report that the "introductory sequence should bring out the underlying unity of the field and should flow from topic to topic in a pedagogically natural way."

 ## Additional Features

Exercises and Programming Assignments In a course based on this book, homework assignments consist of exercises, which are handwritten, and problems, which are programming assignments for computer execution. There are an average of nearly 40 exercises and programming assignments in each chapter. These two types of assignments reflect the difference between analysis and design. Neglecting analysis is like trying to teach children to write (design) before they can read (analyze). At the introductory level, analysis is just as important as design. If students do not get explicit practice in reasoning about control structures, it is more difficult for them to locate logical errors in the loops they write. After all, debugging is analysis, not design.

Software Tools One goal of this text is to give the student useful software tools. Accordingly, I have tried to present the "best" known algorithms. The sequential search algorithm installs the search key after the last item in the list, so the loop has only one test. The binary search algorithm is free of the subtle errors described by Pattis.[2] The random number generator is based on that recommended by Park and Miller.[3] The sequential file update algorithm is the balanced-line algorithm as described by Levy.[4] The section on sorting uses the taxonomy of sort algorithms from Merritt.[5] The version of quick sort is one that executes in time $n \log n$ even in the case when the original array is approximately in order.

Use in the Curriculum

With such broad coverage, some instructors may wish to omit some of the material when designing their introductory sequence. To provide maximum flexibility for

2. Richard E. Pattis, "Textbook Errors in Binary Searching," *ACM SIGCSE Bulletin* 20 (February 1988): 190–94.
3. Stephen K. Park and Keith W. Miller, "Random Number Generators: Good Ones Are Hard to Find," *Communications of the ACM* 31 (October 1988): 1192–1201.
4. Michael R. Levy, "Modularity and the Sequential File Update Problem," *Communications of the ACM* 25 (June 1982): 362–67.
5. Susan M. Merritt, "An Inverted Taxonomy of Sorting Algorithms," *Communications of the ACM* 28 (January 1985): 96–98.

curriculum design, the model is again the traditional introductory physics textbook, which usually contains many topics and applications that may be omitted depending on the interest of the instructor.

Students are introduced to the concept of an abstract data type as applied to the stack in Chapter 9. Although other data structures topics are normally included in the introductory sequence, it is possible to omit half of Chapter 10 (Dynamic Storage Allocation) and all of Chapter 11 (Data Structures), trading off this depth for the breadth that comes by studying the lower levels. Later material in the book is not dependent on these omitted topics, which can be left to a more advanced data structures course.

In the remainder of the book, Chapters 12–14 must be covered sequentially. Chapters 15 (Compiling to the Assembly Level) and 16 (Language Translation Principles) can be covered in either order. I often skip ahead to Chapter 16 to initiate a large software project, writing an assembler for a subset of Pep/5 assembly language, so students will have sufficient time to complete it during the semester. Chapter 20 (Sequential Networks) is obviously dependent on Chapter 19 (Combinational Networks), but neither depends on Chapter 18 (Storage Management), which may be omitted. Figure P.2, a chapter dependency graph, summarizes the possible chapter omissions.

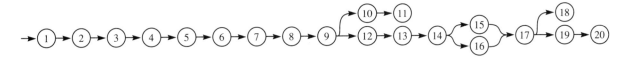

In addition to possible chapter omissions, some sections within chapters may be omitted; examples include sections 6.4 (Scope of Identifiers), 6.5 (Random Numbers), 13.5 (Some Typical Architectures), 15.4 (Data Types at Level 5), 17.3 (Concurrent Processes), and 17.4 (Deadlocks). Selected topics within sections may also be omitted; examples include specific algorithms such as matrix multiplication and recursive merge sort.

Figure P.2

A chapter dependency graph.

Support Materials

Pep/5 Assembler/Simulator Disk Machine-readable source code for the Pep/5 system is available to adopters from the publisher or the author (Bitnet address: warford@pepvax). The package, complete with assembler and trace facilities, is written in Pascal and runs on MS-DOS, MacOS, or UNIX systems. (Please specify which system you use.) The software may be copied freely without express permission.

Instructor's Guide An Instructor's Guide containing solutions to exercises and overhead transparency masters of the figures and program listings is available to adopters. Teaching hints and suggestions on how to structure the course, based on classroom experience teaching computer science from a unified perspective, are also included.

Test Disk The exercises and problems in the book have been combined with additional test items and are available on disk in ASCII format. These can be imported into your word processor to facilitate the printing of exams.

Test Item File A printed Test Item File contains the same questions that are available on the Test Disk.

Program Disk All the programs from the book and the data files necessary to test the programming problems are available on disk.

Acknowledgments

The nroff document-preparation utility on Pepperdine's VAX UNIX system was valuable for preparing early versions of the manuscript. I was able to design most of the figures with MacDraw on a Macintosh. I commend the folks at Apple Computers for such a great desktop graphics system. I believe the quality of the book is significantly better than it would have been without these tools.

Pep/1 had 16 instructions, one accumulator, and one addressing mode. Pep/2 added indexed addressing. John Vannoy wrote both simulators in ALGOL W. Pep/3 had 32 instructions and was written in Pascal as a student software project by Steve Dimse, Russ Hughes, Kazuo Ishikawa, Nancy Brunet, and Yvonne Smith. In an early review Harold Stone suggested many improvements to the Pep/3 architecture that were incorporated into Pep/4 and carried into Pep/5. Pep/4 had special stack instructions, simulated ROM, and software interrupts. Pep/5 is a more orthogonal design, allowing any instruction to use any addressing mode. John Rooker wrote the Pep/4 system and an early version of Pep/5. Gerry St. Romain implemented a MacOS version and an MS-DOS version.

More than any other book, Tanenbaum's *Structured Computer Organization* has influenced this text.[6] This text extends the level structure of Tanenbaum's book by adding the high-order programming level and the applications level at the top.

The following reviewers of the manuscript in its various stages of development shaped the final product significantly:

Wayne P. Bailey
Northeast Missouri State University

Fadi Deek
New Jersey Institute of Technology

William Decker
University of Iowa

---

6. Andrew S. Tanenbaum, *Structured Computer Organization* (Englewood Cliffs, N.J.: Prentice-Hall, 1984).

Gerald S. Eisman
San Francisco State University

Victoria Evans
University of Nevada at Reno

David Garnick
Bowdoin College

Ephraim P. Glinert
Rensselaer Polytechnic Institute

Dave Hanscom
University of Utah

Michael Hennessy
University of Oregon

Michael Johnson
Oregon State University

Robert Martin
Middlebury College

Richard H. Mercer
Pennsylvania State University—Berks Campus

Randy Molmen
Baldwin-Wallace College

Peter Ng
New Jersey Institute of Technology

Bernard Nudel
University of Michigan

Carolyn Oberlink
Western Michigan University

Wolfgang Pelz
University of Akron

James F. Peters III
Kansas State University

James C. Pleasant
East Tennessee State University

Eleanor Quinlan
Ohio State University

Glenn A. Richard
State University of New York at Stony Brook

David Rosser
Ramsey, N.J.

Scott Smith
State University of New York at Plattsburgh

Harold S. Stone
The Interfactor, Inc.

J. Peter Weston
Daniel Webster College

Norman E. Wright
Brigham Young University

Don Thompson, Don Hancock, Carol Adjemian, Chelle Boehning, and Janet Davis taught sections of the course on which this book is based. They contributed suggestions and exercises. Thanks especially to Gerry St. Romain, who provided, based on his experience, literally hundreds of ideas that were incorporated into the text. Those who typed early drafts of the manuscript include Julie Teichrow, Russ Hughes, and Janet Davis. Joe Piasentin provided artistic consultation.

It has been a pleasure to work with the publisher of this book, D. C. Heath. Karin Ellison provided constant enthusiasm and encouragement from the beginning. Carter Shanklin guided the project on to completion. Thanks to Kitty Pinard for suggesting the sidebars and to Scott Smith of SUNY Plattsburgh for writing them. Judy Miller did a magnificent job designing the book, and Jennifer Brett did a superb job producing it, no small feat for a technical book of this length.

I am fortunate to be at an institution that is committed to excellence in undergraduate education. Pepperdine University in the person of Ken Perrin provided the creative environment and the professional support in which the idea behind this project was able to evolve. My wife, Ann, provided endless personal support. To her I owe an apology for the time this project has taken, and my greatest thanks.

Stan Warford

Brief Contents

Contents

xxiv *Contents*

3.4 Case Statements 109
Summary 112
Exercises 113
Problems 120

Chapter 4   File Input/Output and Stepwise
Refinement   125

4.1 Text Files 125
4.2 Nontext Files 133
Professional Computing Organizations:
ACM and IEEE 136
4.3 Stepwise Refinement 137
Summary 142
Exercises 143
Problems 146

Chapter 5   Repetition   149

5.1 While Statements and Loop Invariants 149
5.2 Repeat Statements 172
5.3 For Statements 175
5.4 Enumerated and Subrange Types 184
Ada: The Lady and the Language 190
5.5 Nested Loops 196
Summary 204
Exercises 204
Problems 210

Chapter 6   Functions and Procedures   223

6.1 Functions with Value Parameters 223
6.2 Procedures with Value Parameters 235
6.3 Procedures with Variable Parameters 241
Computer Viruses Are No Laughing Matter 251
6.4 Scope of Identifiers 255
6.5 Random Numbers 265
Summary 274
Exercises 275
Problems 278

Chapter 7   Arrays and Top-Down Design   285

7.1 One-Dimensional Arrays 285
7.2 Fixed Length Strings 305
7.3 Two-Dimensional Arrays 321
The Ethical and Legal Use of Software 323

Computer Science

Volume 1

Applications

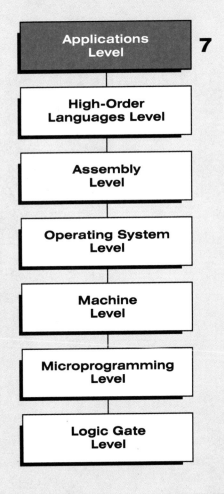

| Applications Level | 7 |

High-Order Languages Level

Assembly Level

Operating System Level

Machine Level

Microprogramming Level

Logic Gate Level

Chapter

Computer Systems

The fundamental question of computer science is, What can be automated? Just as the machines developed during the Industrial Revolution automated manual labor, computers automate the processing of information. When electronic computers were developed in the 1940s, their designers built them to automate the solution of mathematical problems. Since then, however, computers have been applied to problems as diverse as financial accounting, airline reservations, word processing, and graphics. The spread of computers is so relentless that new areas of computer automation seem to appear almost daily.

The fundamental question of computer science

The purpose of this book is to show how the computer automates the processing of information. Everything the computer does, you could do in principle. The major difference between computer and human execution of a job is that the computer can perform its tasks blindingly fast. However, to harness its speed, people must instruct, or program, the computer.

The nature of computers is best understood by learning how to program the machine. Programming requires that you learn a programming language. Before plunging into the details of studying a programming language, this chapter introduces the concept of abstraction, the theme on which this book is based. It then describes the hardware and software components of a computer system and concludes with a description of a database system as a typical application.

Programming languages

1.1 Levels of Abstraction

The concept of levels of abstraction is pervasive in the arts as well as in the natural and applied sciences. A complete definition of abstraction is multifaceted and for our purposes includes the following parts:

- Suppression of detail to show the essence of the matter
- An outline structure
- Division of responsibility through a chain of command
- Subdivision of a system into smaller subsystems

Definition of abstraction

3

The theme of this book is the application of abstraction to computer science. We begin, however, by considering levels of abstraction in areas other than computer science. The analogies drawn from these areas will expand on the four parts of our definition of abstraction and apply to computer systems as well.

Three common, graphic representations of levels of abstraction are (a) level diagrams, (b) nesting diagrams, and (c) hierarchy or tree diagrams. We will now consider each of these representations of abstraction and show how they relate to the analogies. The three diagrams will also apply to levels of abstraction in computer systems throughout this book.

A *level diagram*, shown in Figure 1.1(a), is a set of boxes arranged vertically. The top box represents the highest level of abstraction, and the bottom box represents the lowest. The number of levels of abstraction depends on the system to be described. This figure would represent a system with three levels of abstraction.

Figure 1.1(b) shows a *nesting diagram*. Like the level diagram, a nesting diagram is a set of boxes. It always consists of one large outer box with the rest of the boxes nested inside it. In the figure, two boxes are nested immediately inside the one large outer box. The lower of these two boxes has one box nested, in turn, inside it. The outermost box of a nesting diagram corresponds to the top box of a level diagram. The nested boxes correspond to the lower boxes of a level diagram.

In a nesting diagram, none of the boxes overlaps. That is, nesting diagrams never contain boxes whose boundaries intersect the boundaries of other boxes. A box is always completely enclosed within another box.

The third graphic representation of levels of abstraction is a *hierarchy* or *tree diagram,* as shown in Figure 1.1(c). In a tree, the big limbs branch off the trunk, the smaller limbs branch off the big limbs, and so on. The leaves are at the end of the chain, attached to the smallest branches. Tree diagrams such as Figure 1.1(c) have the trunk at the top instead of the bottom. Each box is called a *node,* with the single node at the top called the *root.* A node with no connections to a lower level is a *leaf.* This figure is a tree with one root node and three leaves. The top node in a hierarchy diagram corresponds to the top box of a level diagram.

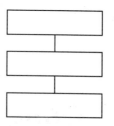

(a) A level diagram.

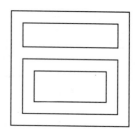

(b) A nesting diagram.

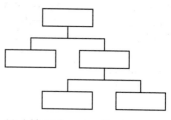

(c) A hierarchy or tree diagram.

Figure 1.1

The three graphic representations of levels of abstraction.

 **Abstraction in Art**

Henri Matisse was a major figure in the history of modern art. In 1909, he produced a bronze sculpture of a woman's back entitled *Bas Relief I*. Four years later, he created a work of the same subject but with a simpler rendering of the form, entitled *Bas Relief II*. After four more years, he created *Bas Relief III*, followed by *Bas Relief IV* 13 years later. The four sculptures are shown in Figure 1.2.

A striking feature of the works is the elimination of detail as the artist progressed from one piece to the next. The contours of the back become less distinct in the second sculpture. The fingers of the right hand are hidden in the third. The hips are barely discernible in the fourth, which is the most abstract.

Bas Relief I
1909

Bas Relief II
1913

Bas Relief III
1917

Bas Relief IV
1930

Figure 1.2

Bronze sculptures by Henri
Matisse. Each rendering becomes
successively more abstract.
(**Source:** Franklin D. Murphy
Sculpture Garden, University of
California, Los Angeles.)

Matisse strove for expression. He deliberately suppressed visual detail in order
to express the essence of the subject. In 1908, he wrote:[1]

> In a picture, every part will be visible and will play the role conferred upon it,
> be it principal or secondary. All that is not useful in the picture is detrimental.
> A work of art must be harmonious in its entirety; for superfluous details
> would, in the mind of the beholder, encroach upon the essential elements.

Suppression of detail is an integral part of the concept of levels of abstraction
and carries over directly to computer science. In computer science terminology,
Bas Relief IV is at the highest level of abstraction and *Bas Relief I* is at the lowest
level. Figure 1.3 is a level diagram that shows the relationship of these levels.

Like the artist, the computer scientist must appreciate the distinction between
the essentials and the details. The chronological progression of Matisse in the *Bas
Relief* series was from the most detailed to the most abstract. In computer science,
however, the progression for problem solving should be from the most abstract to
the most detailed. One goal of this book is to teach you how to think abstractly, to
suppress irrelevant detail when formulating a solution to a problem. Not that detail
is unimportant in computer science! Detail is most important. However, in computing problems there is a natural tendency to be overly concerned with too much
detail in the beginning stages of the progression. In solving problems in computer
science, the essentials should come before the details.

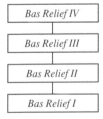

Figure 1.3

The levels of abstraction in the
Matisse sculptures. *Bas Relief IV* is
at the highest level of abstraction.

1. Alfred H. Barr, Jr., *Matisse: His Art and His Public* (New York: The Museum of Modern Art,
1951).

Abstraction in Documents

Levels of abstraction are also evident in the outline organization of written documents. An example is the United States Constitution, which consists of seven articles, each of which is subdivided into sections. The article and section headings
shown in the following outline are not part of the Constitution itself.[2] They merely
summarize the contents of the divisions.

Outline structure

Article I.	Legislative Department	*United States Constitution*
Section 1.	Congress	
Section 2.	House of Representatives	
Section 3.	The Senate	
Section 4.	Elections of Senators and Representatives—Meetings of Congress	
Section 5.	Powers and Duties of Each House of Congress	
Section 6.	Compensation, Privileges, and Disabilities of Senators and Representatives	
Section 7.	Mode of Passing Laws	
Section 8.	Powers Granted to Congress	
Section 9.	Limitations on Powers Granted to the United States	
Section 10.	Powers Prohibited to the States	
Article II.	Executive Department	
Section 1.	The President	
Section 2.	Powers of the President	
Section 3.	Duties of the President	
Section 4.	Removal of Executive and Civil Officers	
Article III.	Judicial Department	
Section 1.	Judicial Powers Vested in Federal Courts	
Section 2.	Jurisdiction of United States Courts	
Section 3.	Treason	
Article IV.	The States and the Federal Government	
Section 1	Official Acts of the States	
Section 2.	Citizens of the States	
Section 3.	New States	
Section 4.	Protection of States Guaranteed	
Article V.	Amendments	
Article VI.	General Provisions	
Article VII.	Ratification of the Constitution	

---

2. California State Senate, J. A. Beak, Secretary of the Senate, *Constitution of the State of California,
the Constitution of the United States, and Related Documents* (Sacramento, 1967).

The Constitution as a whole is at the highest level of abstraction. A particular article, such as Article III, Judicial Department, deals with part of the whole. A section within that article, Section 2, Jurisdiction of United States Courts, deals with a specific topic and is at the lowest level of abstraction. The outline organizes the topics logically.

Figure 1.4 shows the outline structure of the Constitution in a nesting diagram. The big outer box is the entire Constitution. Nested inside it are seven smaller boxes, which represent the articles. Inside the articles are the section boxes.

This outline method of organizing a document is also important in computer science. The technique of organizing programs and information in outline form is called *structured programming.* In much the same way that English composition teachers instruct you to organize a report in outline form before writing the details, this book will direct you to organize your programs in outline form before filling in the programming details. This design technique, called *stepwise refinement,* is introduced in Chapter 4.

Abstraction in Organizations

Corporate organization is another area that uses the concept of levels of abstraction. For example, Figure 1.5 is a partial organization chart in the form of a hierarchy diagram for D. C. Heath and Company, the publisher of this book. The president of the company is at the highest level and is responsible for the successful operation of the entire organization. The four vice presidents report to the president. Each vice president is responsible for just one major part of the operation. There are more levels, not shown in the figure, under each of the managers and vice presidents.

Levels in an organization chart correspond to responsibility and authority in the organization. The president acts in the best interest of the entire company. She delegates responsibility and authority to those who report to her. They in turn use

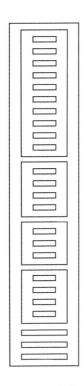

Figure 1.4

A nesting diagram of the United States Constitution.

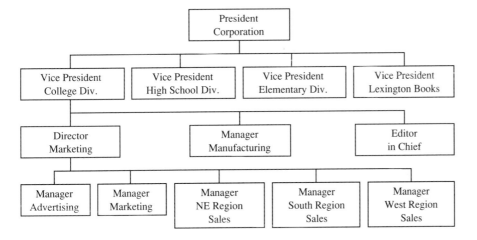

Figure 1.5

A simplified organization chart for D. C. Heath and Company.

their authority to manage their part of the organization and may delegate responsibilities to their employees. In businesses, the actual power held by individuals may not be directly reflected by their position on the official chart. Other organizations, such as the United States Army have a rigid chain of command. Figure 1.6 is a level diagram that shows the line of authority in the U.S. Army and the units for which each officer is responsible.

There is a direct relationship between the way an organization functions, as reflected by its organization chart, and the way a computer system functions. Like a large organization, a large computer system is typically organized as a hierarchy. Any given part of a computer system takes orders from the part immediately above it in the hierarchy diagram. In turn, it issues orders to be carried out by those parts immediately below it in the hierarchy.

Abstraction in Machines

Another example of levels of abstraction that is closely analogous to computer systems is the automobile. Like a computer system, the automobile is a man-made machine. It consists of an engine, a transmission, an electrical system, a cooling system, and a chassis. Each part of an automobile is subdivided. The electrical system has, among other things, a battery, headlights, and a voltage regulator.

People relate to automobiles at different levels of abstraction. At the highest level of abstraction are the drivers. Drivers perform their tasks by knowing how to operate the car: how to start it, how to use the accelerator, and how to apply the brakes, for example.

At the next lower level of abstraction are the backyard mechanics. They understand more of the details under the hood than the casual drivers do. They know how to change the oil and the spark plugs. They do not need this detailed knowledge to drive the automobile.

At the next lower level of abstraction are the master mechanics. They can completely remove the engine, take it apart, fix it, and put it back together again. They do not need this detailed knowledge to simply change the oil.

In a similar vein, people relate to computer systems at many different levels of abstraction. A complete understanding at every level is not necessary to use a computer. You do not need to be a mechanic to drive a car. Similarly, you do not need to be an experienced programmer to use a word processor.

Abstraction in Computer Systems

Figure 1.7 shows the level structure of a typical computer system. Each of the seven levels shown in the diagram has its own language:

  7 Language depends on applications program

  6 Machine-independent programming language

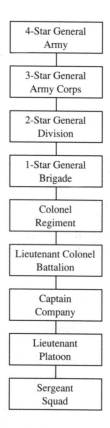

Figure 1.6

The chain of command in the United States Army. The 4-Star General is at the highest level of abstraction. (**Source:** Henry Mintzberg, *The Structuring of Organizations,* © 1979, p. 27. Adapted by permission of Prentice-Hall, Inc., Englewood Cliffs, New Jersey 07632.)

5 Assembly language

4 Operating system calls

3 Machine language

2 Microinstructions and register transfer

1 Boolean algebra and truth tables

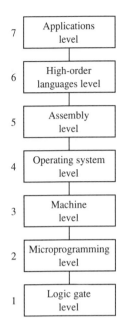

7	Applications level
6	High-order languages level
5	Assembly level
4	Operating system level
3	Machine level
2	Microprogramming level
1	Logic gate level

Figure 1.7

The level structure of a typical computer system. Some systems do not have Level 2.

Programs written in these languages instruct the computer to perform certain operations. A program to perform a specific task can be written at any one of the levels of Figure 1.7. As with the automobile, a person writing a program in a language at one level does not need to know the language at any of the lower levels.

When computers were invented, only Levels 1 and 3 were present. A human communicated with these machines by programming them in *machine language* at the machine level. Machine language is great for machines but is tedious and inconvenient for a human programmer. *Assembly language*, at Level 5, was invented to help the human programmer.

The first computers were large and expensive. Much time was wasted when one programmer monopolized the computer while the other users waited in line for their turn. Gradually, *operating systems* at Level 4 were developed so many users could access the computer simultaneously. With today's microcomputers, operating systems are still necessary to manage programs and data, even if the system services only one user.

In the early days, every time a company introduced a new computer model, the programmers had to learn the assembly language for that model. All their programs written for the old machine would not work on the new machine. *High-order languages* at Level 6 were invented so programs could be transferred from one computer to another with little modification and because programming in a high-order language is easier than programming at a lower level. Some of the more popular Level 6 languages that you may be familiar with are

- *COBOL* Common Business Oriented Language
- *FORTRAN* Formula Translator
- *BASIC* Beginner's All-purpose Symbolic Instruction Code
- *Pascal* Named after Blaise Pascal
- *LISP* List processing

The widespread availability of computer systems spurred the development of many applications programs at Level 7. An *applications program* is one written to solve a specific type of problem, such as printing payroll checks, typing documents, or statistically analyzing data. It allows you to use the computer as a tool without knowing the operational details at the lower levels.

Level 1, the lowest level, consists of electrical components called *logic gates*. Along the way in the development toward higher levels, it was discovered that a level just above the logic gate level could be useful in helping designers build the Level 3 machine. *Microprogramming* at Level 2 is used on some computer systems today to implement the Level 3 machine. Level 2 was an important tool in the invention of the hand-held calculator.

Your goal in studying this book is to communicate effectively with computers. *The goal of this book* To do so, you must learn the language. Languages at the higher levels are more human-oriented and easier to understand than languages at the lower levels. That is precisely why they were invented.

Most people first learn about computers at Level 7 by using programs written by others. Office workers who prepare input for the company payroll program fall into this category, as do the video game fans. Descriptions of applications programs at Level 7 are generally found in user's manuals, which describe how to operate the specific program.

As you study this book, you will gain some insight into the inner workings of a computer system by examining successively lower levels of abstraction. The lower you go in the hierarchy, the more details will come to light that were hidden at the higher levels. As you progress in your study, keep Figure 1.7 in mind. You must master a host of seemingly trivial details; it is the nature of the beast. Remember, however, that the beauty of computer science lies not in the diversity of its details but in the unity of its concepts.

1.2   Hardware

We build computers to solve problems. Early computers solved mathematical and engineering problems, while later computers emphasized information processing for business applications. Today, computers also control machines as diverse as automobile engines, robots, and microwave ovens. A computer system solves a problem from any of these domains by accepting input, processing it, and producing output. Figure 1.8 illustrates the function of a computer system.

Figure 1.8

The three activities of a computer system.

Computer systems consist of hardware and software. *Hardware* is the physical part of the system. Once designed, hardware is difficult and expensive to change. *Software* is the set of programs that instruct the hardware and is easier to modify than hardware. Computers are valuable because they are general-purpose machines that can solve many different kinds of problems, as opposed to special-purpose machines that can solve only one kind of problem. Different problems can be solved with the same hardware by supplying the system with a different set of instructions, that is, with different software.

Every computer has four basic hardware components:

- Input devices
- Output devices
- Main memory
- Central processing unit (CPU)

Components of hardware

Figure 1.9 shows these components in a block diagram. The lines between the blocks represent the flow of information. The information flows from one component to another on the *bus,* which is simply a group of wires connecting the components. Processing occurs in the CPU and main memory. The organization in Figure 1.9, with the components connected to each other by the bus, is common. However, other configurations are possible as well.

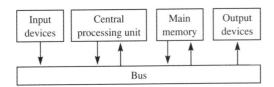

Figure 1.9

Block diagram of the four components of a computer system.

Computer hardware is often classified by its relative physical size:

- *Small* microcomputer
- *Medium* minicomputer
- *Large* mainframe

Just the CPU of a mainframe often occupies an entire cabinet. Its input/output (I/O) devices and memory might fill an entire room. Microcomputers can be small enough to fit on a desk or in a briefcase. As technology advances, the amount of processing previously possible only on large machines becomes possible on smaller machines. Microcomputers now can do much of the work that only minicomputers or mainframes could do in the past.

The classification just described is based on physical size as opposed to storage size. A computer system user is generally more concerned with storage size, since that is a more direct indication of the amount of useful work that the hardware can perform. Speed of computation is another characteristic that is important to the user. Generally speaking, users want a fast CPU and large amounts of storage, but a physically small machine for the I/O devices and main memory.

When computer scientists study problems, therefore, they are concerned with space and time—the space necessary inside a computer system to store a problem and the time required to solve it. They commonly use the metric prefixes of Table 1.1 to express large or small quantities of space or time.

Example 1.1 Suppose it takes 4.5 milliseconds, also written 4.5 ms, to transfer some information across the bus from one component to another in Figure 1.9. (a) How many seconds are required for the transfer? (b) How many transfers can take place during one minute?

(a) A time of 4.5 ms is 4.5×10^{-3} from Table 1.1, or 0.0045 s. (b) Since there are 60 seconds in one minute, the number of times the transfer can occur is (60 s)/(0.0045 s/transfer) or 13,300 transfers. Note that since the original value was given with two significant figures, the result should not be given to more than two or three significant figures. ∎

Multiple	Prefix	Abbrev.
10^9	giga-	G
10^6	mega-	M
10^3	kilo-	K
10^{-3}	milli-	m
10^{-6}	micro-	μ
10^{-9}	nano-	n

Table 1.1

Prefixes for powers of 10.

Table 1.1 shows that in the metric system the prefix kilo- is 1000 and mega- is 1,000,000. But in computer science, a kilo- is 2^{10} or 1024. The difference between 1000 and 1024 is less than 3%, so you can think of a computer science kilo- as being about 1000 even though it is a little more. The same applies to mega- and giga-, as in Table 1.2. This time, the approximation is a little worse, but for mega- it is still within 5%. The reason for these seemingly strange conventions has to do with information representation at the machine level (Level 3).

▭ Input Devices

Input devices transmit information from the outside world into the memory of the computer. Figure 1.10 shows the path the data takes from an input device to the memory via the bus. There are many different types of input devices, including

- Keyboards
- Disk drives
- Magnetic tape drives
- Mouse
- Bar code readers

The *keyboard* looks like a standard typewriter keyboard. If you press a key on a typewriter, you place the character permanently on paper, but if you press a key on a computer keyboard, you send the character to main memory.

The character is stored in memory as a sequence of eight electrical signals. Each signal in the sequence is called a *binary digit* (bit). A signal can have a high value, represented by the symbol 1, or a low value, represented by 0. The sequence of eight signals that make up the character is called a *byte* (pronounced bite), as shown in Figure 1.11.

Office workers typing on a computer keyboard are at the applications level (Level 7), the highest level of abstraction in the organization of a computer system. They do not need to know the bit pattern for each character they type. Programmers at the machine level (Level 3) do need to know about bit patterns. For now, you should just remember that a byte of data corresponds to one keyboard character.

Example **1.2** A typist is entering some text on a computer keyboard at the rate of 35 words per minute. If each word is 7 characters long on the average, how many bits per second are being sent to main memory? A space is a character. Assume that each word is followed by one space on the average.

Including the spaces, there are 8 characters per word. The number of characters per second is (35 words/min) × (8 characters/word) × (1 min/60 s) = 4.67 characters/s. Since it takes one byte to store a character, and there are eight bits in a byte, the bit rate is (4.67 characters/s) × (1 byte/character) × (8 bits/byte) = 37.4 bits/s. ∎

Prefix	Computer science value
giga-	2^{30} = 1,073,741,824
mega-	2^{20} = 1,048,576
kilo-	2^{10} = 1,024

Table 1.2

Computer science values of the large prefixes.

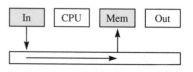

In   input devices
CPU central processing unit
Mem main memory
Out output devices

Figure 1.10

The data path for input. Information flows from the input device on the bus to main memory.

(a) Storage for an eight-bit byte.

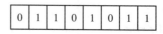

(b) The bit pattern for the character 'k'.

Figure 1.11

A byte of information. When you press 'k' on the keyboard, the signal 01101011 goes on the bus to main memory for storage.

There are two basic kinds of disk drives—floppy disk drives and hard disk drives. A *disk drive* is the part of a computer that extracts data from or writes it onto a disk. The drive includes a motor that makes the disk spin, a spindle or hub clamp that secures the disk to the motor, and one or more read/write heads that detect individual bits on the surface of the disk itself.

Floppy disks, primarily used for microcomputers, are so called because of their flexibility. They range from 8 inches in diameter down to $3\frac{1}{2}$ inches. As of the time of this writing (1990), a single floppy disk can store from about 500 Kbytes to 1 or 2 Mbytes of information, depending on the drive. Technology has advanced rapidly in this field, however. Early floppy disks were 8 inches in diameter and could store only 400 Kbytes, while some $3\frac{1}{2}$-inch floppy disks today can store 1.5 Mbytes. Soon, disks may be even smaller and their capacity greater.

In contrast to floppy disks, *hard disks* are rigid. Some are permanently sealed inside the disk drive and cannot be removed. Others, usually used with mainframe computers, are removable. Hard disks store much more information than floppy disks. Typically, storage capacities range from 20 to 100 Mbytes for microcomputers, 500 Mbytes to 10 Gbytes for minicomputers, and more than 10 Gbytes for mainframes. One way hard disk drives achieve their high capacity is by stacking several disk platters on a single spindle. A separate read/write head is dedicated to each disk surface. Hard drives also provide much faster access to their information than floppy drives.

Example **1.3**   Your 20 Mbyte hard disk is full of information that you want to transfer to a set of 800 Kbyte floppy disks. How many floppies are required?

The exact number of bytes on the hard disk is $20 \times 1,048,576$, and on each floppy it is 800×1024. However, if you are content with approximate values you can estimate $20 \times 1,000,000$ bytes for the hard disk and 800×1000 bytes for each floppy. The number of floppies required is $(20 \times 1,000,000)/(800 \times 1000) = 20,000/800 = 25$ floppies.   ∎

Figure 1.12 is a comparison of the two types of disk drives. Floppies are slower and have a smaller capacity than hard drives, but are less expensive.

Magnetic tape drives for computers are similar to the tape drives in a stereo system. On computers, they can be the open reel type, typically used on mainframes, or the cassette type, typically used on microcomputers and minicomputers. In a stereo, the tape stores music, but in a computer, the tape stores information as bits.

The major advantage of tapes compared to disks is cost. Tapes are much less expensive per byte than disks. The disadvantage of tapes is that they are accessed sequentially and, therefore, they are slower than disks. If you need some information near the beginning of a tape and the read/write head happens to be near the end, you must rewind the tape, sequentially passing over all the information in-between. The access method for magnetic tape versus disks is analogous to stereo cassettes versus audio compact discs. You can change selections on a compact disc much faster than on a cassette because of the access method. Because of their slow

Disk drive

Magnetic tape drive

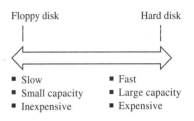

Figure **1.12**

The spectrum of price and performance for disk drives.

access, tapes are usually used for backup or archival storage. A typical reel of tape is 2400 feet long and can store about 200 Mbytes of data.

The *mouse,* which is moved on a desk top, is becoming a popular hand-held input device. As the mouse is moved on the desk, it gives a small arrow on the computer screen the identical motion. You can move the mouse to point the arrow at command selections or objects on the screen, then make the selection by pressing a button on the mouse. A mouse is especially valuable for graphic input because the arrow can be used to draw figures on the screen. Most of the figures in this book were produced with a mouse.

The *bar code reader* is another efficient input device. Perhaps the most common bar code is the Universal Product Code (UPC) on grocery store items (Figure 1.13). Each digit in the UPC symbol has seven vertical data elements. Each data element can be light or dark. Photocells inside the bar code reader detect the light and dark regions and convert them to bits. Light elements are read as zeros, and dark elements as ones. Figure 1.14 shows the correspondence between light and dark regions and bits for two digits from the right half of the UPC symbol in Figure 1.13.

Table 1.3 shows the UPC correspondence between decimal and binary values. The code is different for the characters on the left half and those on the right half. A dark bar is composed of from one to four adjacent dark regions. Each decimal digit has two dark bars and two light spaces. The characters on the left half begin with a light space and end with a dark bar, while the characters on the right half begin with a dark bar and end with a light space. Each left character has an odd number of ones, while each right character has an even number of ones.

Checkout clerks at the supermarket work at the highest level of abstraction. They do not need to know the details of the UPC symbol. They only know that if they try to input the UPC symbol and they do not hear the confirmation beep, an input error has occurred and they must rescan the bar code. Programmers at a lower level, however, must know the details of the code. Their programs, for example, must check the number of ones, or dark elements, in each left character. If a left character has an even number of ones, the program must not issue the confirmation beep.

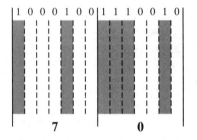

Figure 1.13

The UPC symbol from a package of cereal. The left five digits identify the manufacturer. The right five digits identify the product. The Quaker company code is 30000, and the 100% Natural Cereal code is 06700.

Figure 1.14

Part of the UPC symbol from the Quaker cereal box. Visually, groups of adjacent dark regions look like thick bars.

▄ Output Devices

Output devices transmit information from the memory of the computer to the outside world. Figure 1.15 shows the path that the data takes from main memory to an output device. On output, data flows on the same bus used by the input devices. Output devices include

- Disk drives
- Magnetic tape drives
- Screens
- Printers

Notice that disk and tape drives can serve as both input and output devices. This is similar to a stereo cassette, which can both record and play back music. When disks and tapes are used for input, the process is called *reading*. When they are used for output, the process is called *writing*.

The *screen* is a visual display similar to the picture screen of a television set. It can be either a cathode ray tube (CRT) or a flat panel. The picture tube in a television set is a CRT. Flat panel screens are found mostly in portable microcomputers. A monitor is a CRT packaged separately from the keyboard and the CPU. A standard-sized screen holds 24 lines of text with a maximum of 80 characters in a line.

A *terminal* is a monitor together with a keyboard. It is not a self-contained, general-purpose microcomputer, although it may resemble one. Terminals communicate with minicomputers and mainframes and are useless without them. Microcomputers, on the other hand, are self-contained and can process information without being connected to larger machines. Microcomputers can also behave like terminals and communicate with other machines, however.

Individual characters on a screen are actually composed of a rectangular grid of dots. Each dot is called a *pixel,* which stands for picture element. In a black and white screen, a pixel can be either bright or dark. The pattern of bright pixels in the rectangular grid forms an image of the character. Figure 1.16 shows a grid of pixels with five columns and seven rows that forms an image of the character 'B'. Higher-quality screens have more pixels in the rectangular grid to form a smoother image of the character. See how much clearer the image of the 'B' is in the field of 9×13 pixels.

Printers range widely in performance and cost. Dot matrix printers operate on the same basis as the pixels in a screen. A print head with a single column of pins scans the paper. The pins strike a typewriter ribbon that is between the print head and the paper at just the right moment, to produce the image of the character on the paper.

As with the screen, the greater the number of dots for an individual character, the higher the quality of the print. Many printers have several modes of operation, ranging from lower quality but faster to higher quality but slower. Typical speeds range from 50 to 300 characters per second.

Letter quality printers are more expensive than dot matrix printers, but they have certain advantages. They operate like electric typewriters, and their output is almost indistinguishable from a hand-typed document. They are slow compared with dot matrix printers, with typical speeds of 15 to 50 characters per second.

Decimal value	Left chars.	Right chars.
0	0001101	1110010
1	0011001	1100110
2	0010011	1101100
3	0111101	1000010
4	0100011	1011100
5	0110001	1001110
6	0101111	1010000
7	0111011	1000100
8	0110111	1001000
9	0001011	1110100

Table 1.3

Bit patterns for the decimal digits in the UPC symbol.

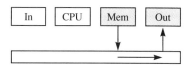

Figure 1.15

The data path for output. Information flows from main memory on the bus to the output device.

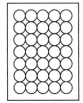 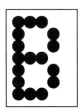 

(a) A 5×7 pixel grid.   **(b)** An image of a 'B' in a 5×7 pixel grid.   **(c)** An image of a 'B' in a 9×13 pixel grid.

Figure 1.16

Picture elements (pixels) on a rectangular grid. The pixels in (b) have the same diameter as the ones in (c).

Line printers are fast. They have a separate print element for each column of output, usually 132 columns in all. Each print element can print every character in the alphabet and every numerical digit and punctuation character. To print a line, all 132 print elements must align with their proper character positions simultaneously. Then the printer can print all the characters on the whole line in one step. No scanning from one end of a line to the other is necessary. A common line printer speed is 600 lines per minute.

The page printer is a high quality output device. Many page printers use a laser beam to form the image on the page. Page printers also use pixels for their imaging systems, but the pixels are spaced closely enough to be unnoticeable. A typical desktop laser printer has 300 pixels per inch, which is $300 \times 300 = 90,000$ pixels per square inch. Commercial typesetting machines have 1200 to 2400 pixels per inch.

Main Memory

Main memory stores both the data being processed and the programs processing the data. As with disk and tape, its capacity is measured in bytes. Small microcomputers usually have about 640 Kbytes of main memory. Larger micros can have up to 10 Mbytes, minicomputers usually have 50 to 100 Mbytes, and mainframes have several hundred Mbytes of main memory.

An important characteristic of main memory is that it is volatile. That is, if the power source to the computer is discontinued, whether intentionally or unintentionally, the information in main memory is lost. That is not true with disks or tapes. You can eject a floppy disk from a computer, turn off the machine, come back the next day, and the information will still be on your disk.

Another important characteristic of main memory is its access method, which is random. In fact, the electronic components that make up main memory are often referred to as RAM circuits, for *random access memory*. Unlike magnetic tape, if you have just fetched some information from one end of main memory, you can immediately get information from the other end at random without passing over the information in-between. Disk drives are part sequential and part random. They are accessed more quickly than tapes but more slowly than main memory (Figure 1.17). Tape and disk drives are called *peripheral memory devices* to distinguish them from main memory.

Central Processing Unit

The *central processing unit* (CPU) contains the circuitry to control all the other parts of the computer. It has its own small set of memory called *registers*. The CPU also has a set of instructions permanently wired into its circuitry. The instructions do such things as fetch information from memory into a register, add, subtract, compare, store information from a register back into memory, and so on. What is not permanent is the order in which these instructions are executed. The order is determined by a program written in machine language at Level 3.

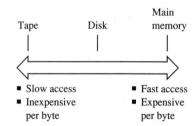

Figure 1.17

The spectrum of price and performance for three types of memory. Tape and disk are called peripheral or secondary memory.

A single machine instruction is fast by human standards. CPU speeds are commonly measured in millions of instructions per second (MIPS).

Example 1.4 Suppose a CPU is rated at 2 MIPS. What is the average length of time needed to execute one instruction?

Two MIPS is 2.0×10^6 or 2,000,000 instructions/s. That is 1/2,000,000 = 0.5 us/instruction. ∎

To process data stored in main memory, the CPU must first bring it into its local registers. Then the CPU can process the data in the registers and send the results back to main memory. Eventually, to be useful to the user, the data must be sent to an output device. Figure 1.18 shows the data flow for a complete job.

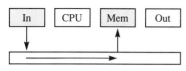

(a) First data flows from the input device into main memory.

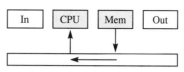

(b) Next the CPU brings the data into its registers for processing.

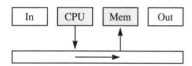

(c) Then the CPU sends the processed data back to memory.

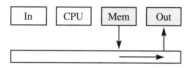

(d) Finally the results go to the output device.

Figure 1.18

The data flow for a complete job. Steps (b) and (c) usually repeat many times.

1.3 Software

An *algorithm* is a set of instructions that, when carried out in the proper sequence, solves a problem in a finite amount of time. Algorithms do not require computers. The following recipe is an algorithm in English that solves the problem of making six servings of stirred custard.

Adapted from *Better Homes and Gardens* New Cook Book[3]
Ingredients
3	slightly beaten eggs
$\frac{1}{4}$	cup sugar
2	cups milk, scalded
$\frac{1}{2}$	teaspoon vanilla

An algorithm for making stirred custard

Algorithm
 Combine eggs, sugar, and $\frac{1}{4}$ teaspoon salt.
 Slowly stir in slightly cooled milk.
 Cook in double boiler over hot, not boiling, water, stirring constantly.
 As soon as custard coats metal spoon, remove from heat.
 Cool at once—place pan in cold water and stir a minute or two.
 Add vanilla.
 Chill.

This recipe illustrates two important properties of algorithms—the finite number of instructions and execution in a finite amount of time. The algorithm has seven instructions—combine, stir, cook, remove, cool, add, and chill. Seven is a finite number. An algorithm cannot have an infinite number of instructions.

Even though the number of instructions in the custard algorithm is finite, there is a potential problem with its execution. The recipe instructs us to cook until the custard coats the metal spoon. What if it never coats the spoon? Then, if we strictly followed the instructions, we would be cooking forever! A valid algorithm must never execute endlessly. It must provide a solution in a finite amount of time. Assuming that the custard will always coat the spoon, this recipe is indeed an algorithm.

The finite requirement for an algorithm

A *program* is an algorithm written for execution on a computer. Programs cannot be written in English. They must be written in a language for one of the seven levels of a computer system.

Definition of a program

General-purpose computers can solve many different kinds of problems, from computing the company payroll to correcting a spelling mistake in a memorandum. The hardware gets its versatility from its ability to be programmed to do the different jobs. Programs that control the computer are called software.

Software is classified into two broad groups:

■ Systems software

■ Applications software

Systems software makes the computer accessible to the applications designers. *Applications software,* in turn, makes the computer system accessible to the end user at Level 7. Generally speaking, a systems software engineer designs programs at Level 6 and below. These programs take care of the many details of the computer system with which the applications programmer does not want to bother.

Systems software versus applications software

Operating Systems

The most important software for a computer is the operating system. The *operating system* is the systems program that makes the hardware usable. Every general-purpose computer system includes both hardware and an operating system.

Practical Uses of Computers

Although this text as a whole attempts to provide a comprehensive introduction to the broad and diverse field known as computer science, many people use computers for their own applications, without understanding much, if any, of the theory. In fact, you probably first became interested in computers because of what you heard you could do with them, not because of a theoretical interest in how they function.

Because of its affordability and attractive price/performance ratio, the microcomputer is the primary workhorse for much of the computing community. There are three generic categories of software, often integrated into easy-to-use packages, that are found on most general-purpose microcomputers. These categories are, of course, word processing, spreadsheets, and database systems.

Within the last decade, large corporations and small businesses, as well as authors, salespeople, and others, have gone from regarding a microcomputer equipped with the "big three" software packages as an expensive frill or luxury to regarding it as a managerial necessity.

Desks, chairs, filing cabinets, staplers, and telephones have been relegated to second-class status for many of us—our status in the workplace is now measured not by whether the office chair has arms or not, but by what version of Lotus 1-2-3 we have, or by the capabilities of our word processor.

Sometimes, the software is used as a substitute for existing technology, as when a word processor replaces a typewriter, or when a database system replaces a Rolodex or manual filing system. Yet a word processor is more than just a fast typewriter on which typos don't show up—it can enable writers to improve their writing by allowing them to develop a document through several drafts. Likewise, a

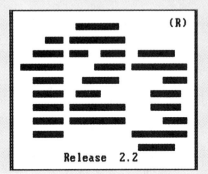

Release 2.2

database system with a mailing-label generator can allow a small business to quickly target a new product announcement for the subset of its customers that is most likely to buy that item.

Is a spreadsheet fundamentally different from a pencil-and-paper accounting system? In theory, one might think it to be equivalent because one can record the same mathematical calculations on paper that one can store in the spreadsheet grid. Yet the speed with which one can engage in "what if?" business forecasting—experimenting with different columns of balance sheets according to different volumes of possible sales—allows managers and entrepreneurs to make more informed decisions.

Thus, although computers demonstrate their power and utility as the ultimate *quantificational* tool devised by mankind, the effects of our use of computers are *qualitatively* significant. Applied wisely, general-purpose word processors, spreadsheets, and database systems can be embedded in the information-processing core of many organizations, helping to support more effective decision making.

To study this text effectively you must have access to a computer with an operating system. Some common commercial operating systems are MS-DOS, MacOS, UNIX, and VMS. Unfortunately, each operating system has unique commands. This book cannot explain how to use all of the different operating systems. You must learn the specifics of your operating system from your instructor or from another source.

An operating system has three general functions:

- File management
- Memory management
- Processor management

Of these three functions, file management is the most visible to the user. The first thing a new computer user must learn is how to manipulate the files of information on the operating system.

Files in an operating system are analogous to files in an office. They contain information to be retrieved and processed on request. In an office, the filing cabinet stores files. In an operating system, peripheral memory devices store files. Although tapes and disks can store files, the following discussion concentrates on disks.

In an office, an individual file is in a file folder. The office worker names each file and places the name on the tab of the folder. The name indicates the contents of the folder and makes it easy to pick out an individual file from the cabinet. In an operating system, every file also has a name. The name serves the same purpose as the name on a folder—to make it easy to pick out an individual file from a disk.

When a computer user creates a file, the operating system requests a name for the file. Depending on the system, there are usually some restrictions on the length of the name and the allowable characters in the name. Sometimes the system will automatically attach a prefix or a suffix to the name. Other files are created by the system and automatically named by it.

Files can contain three types of information:

- Documents
- Programs
- Data

Documents may be company memoranda, letters, reports, and the like. Files also store programs to be executed by the computer. To be executed, first they must be loaded from disk into main memory. Input data for an executing program can come from a file, and output data can also be sent to a file.

The files are physically scattered over the surface of the disk. To keep track of all these files of information, the operating system maintains a directory of them. The directory is a list of all the files on the disk. Each entry in the directory has the file's name, its size, its physical location on the disk, and any other information the operating system needs to manage the files. The directory itself is also stored on the disk.

The operating system provides the user with a way to manipulate the files on the disk. Some typical operating system commands include

- List the names of the files from the directory.
- Delete a file from the disk.
- Change the name of a file.

- Print the contents of a file.
- Execute an applications program.

These are the commands you need to learn for your operating system in order to work the problems in this book.

Your operating system is a program written for your computer by a team of systems programmers. When you issue the command to "delete a file from the disk," a systems program executes that command. You, the user, are using a program that someone else, the systems programmer, wrote.

Software Analysis and Design

A major portion of this book is devoted to software. Its goal is to teach you how to design good programs. Most of your problems will not be systems programs, such as the program to delete a file from the disk, but applications programs.

Software, whether systems or applications, has much in common with literature. Human authors write both. Other people read both, although computers can also read and execute programs. Both novelists and programmers are creative in that the solutions they propose are not unique. When a novelist has something to communicate, there is always more than one way to express it. The difference between a good novel and a bad one lies not only in the idea communicated, but also in the way the idea is expressed. Likewise, when a programmer has a problem to solve, there is always more than one way to program the solution. The difference between a good program and a bad one lies not only in the correctness of the solution to the problem, but also in other characteristics of the program, such as clarity, execution speed, and memory requirement.

As a student of literature, you participate in two distinct activities—reading and writing. Reading is analysis; you read what someone else has written and analyze its contents. Writing is design or synthesis; you have an idea to express, and your problem is to communicate that idea effectively. Most people find writing much more difficult than reading, because it requires more creativity. That is why there are more readers in the general population than authors.

Analysis versus design

Similarly, as a student of software you will analyze and design programs. Remember that the three activities of a program are input, processing, and output. In analysis, you are given the input and the processing instructions. Your problem is to determine the output. In design, you are given the input and the desired output. Your problem is to write the processing instructions, that is, to design the software. Figure 1.19 shows the difference between analysis and design.

(a) Analysis—The input and processing are given. The output is to be determined.

(b) Design—The input and desired output are given. The processing is to be determined.

Figure 1.19

The difference between analysis and design.

As in reading and writing English literature, designing good software is much more difficult than analyzing it. A familiar complaint of computer science students is "I understand the concepts, but I can't write the programs." This is a natural complaint because it reflects the difficulty of synthesis as opposed to analysis. Our ultimate goal is for you to be able to design software as well as analyze it. The following chapters will give you specific software design techniques.

But first you should become familiar with these general problem-solving guidelines, which also apply to software design:

- Understand the problem.

- Outline a solution.

- Solve each part of your outlined problem.

- Test your solution by hand.

- Test your solution on the computer.

General problem-solving guidelines

When faced with a software design problem, test your understanding of the problem by writing down some sample input and the corresponding output. You cannot solve a problem by computer if you do not know how to solve it by hand. To outline a solution, you must break down the problem into several subproblems. Since the subproblems are smaller than the original problem, they are easier to solve. If you have doubts about the correctness of your program, you should test it by hand before entering it on the computer. You can test it with the sample input you wrote in the first step.

Many students find these steps unnecessary for the small programs found in an introductory textbook. If the problem is easy for you, it is all right not to organize your thoughts on paper this way before programming your solution to the problem. In that case, you are mentally following these steps anyway. On the other hand, you may eventually encounter a large design problem for which these problem-solving steps will be indispensable.

1.4   Database Systems

Database systems are one of the most common applications at Level 7. A *database* is a collection of files that contain interrelated information, and a *database system* (also called a database management system or DBMS) is a program that lets the user add, delete, and modify records in the database. A database system also permits queries of the database. A *query* is a request for information, usually from different parts of the database.

An example of a database is the information a furniture manufacturer maintains about his inventory, parts suppliers, and shipments. A query might be a request for a report showing the number of each part in storage that is required to manufacture a particular sofa. To produce the report, the database system combines the information from different parts of the database, in this case from an inventory file and from a required-materials file for the sofa.

Database systems come in three main varieties: hierarchical systems, network systems, and relational systems. Of these three types of database systems, the hierarchical is the fastest but the most restrictive for the user. This system is appropriate if you can naturally organize the information in the database into the same structure as a hierarchy chart. The network system is more flexible than the hierarchical system but more difficult for a user than the relational database system.

Three types of database systems

The relational system is rapidly becoming the most popular of the three. It is the most flexible and easiest to use at Level 7. But in computer science, nothing is free. This high flexibility comes at the cost of low speed compared to the other database systems. This section describes the basic idea behind a relational DBMS.

Relational database systems

Relations

Relational database systems store information in files that appear to have a table structure. Each table has a fixed number of columns and a variable number of rows. Figure 1.20 is an example of the information in a relational database. Each table has a name. The table named `Sor` contains information about the members of a sorority, and the one named `Frat` contains information about the members of a fraternity. The user at Level 7 fixed the number of vertical columns in each table before entering the information in the body of the tables. The number of horizontal rows is variable so that individuals can be added to or deleted from the tables.

Sor

S.Name	S.Class	S.Major	S.State
Beth	Soph	Hist	TX
Nancy	Jr	Math	NY
Robin	Sr	Hist	CA
Allisôn	Soph	Math	AZ
Lulwa	Sr	CompSci	CA

Frat

F.Name	F.Major	F.State
Emile	PolySci	CA
Sam	CompSci	WA
Ron	Math	OR
Mehdi	Math	CA
David	English	AZ
Jeff	Hist	TX
Craig	English	CA
Gary	CompSci	CA

Figure 1.20

An example of a relational database. This database contains two relations—`Sor` and `Frat`.

In relational database terminology, a table is called a *relation*. A column is an *attribute,* and a row is a *tuple* (rhymes with couple). In Figure 1.20, `Sor` and `Frat` are relations, (Nancy, Jr, Math, NY) is a 4-tuple of `Sor` because it has four elements, and `F.Major` is an attribute of `Frat`. The *domain* of an attribute is the set of all possible values of the attribute. The domain of `S.Major` and `F.Major` is the set {Hist, Math, CompSci, PolySci, English}.

Relations, attributes, tuples, and domains

Queries

Examples of queries from this database are requests for Ron's home state and for the names of all the sophomores in the sorority. Another query is a request for a list of those sorority and fraternity members who have the same major, and what that common major is.

In this small example, you can manually search through the database to determine the result of each of these queries. Ron's home state is OR, and Beth and Allison are the sophomores in the sorority. The third query is a little more difficult to tabulate. Beth and Jeff are both history majors. Nancy and Ron are both math majors, as are Nancy and Mehdi. Robin and Jeff are both history majors, and so on.

It is interesting that the result of each of these queries can be written in table form (Figure 1.21). The result of the first query is a table with one column and one row, while the result of the second is a table with one column and two rows. The result of the third is a table with three columns and eight rows. So the result of a query of a relational database, which is a collection of relations, is itself a relation!

Result1
F.State
OR

Result2
S.Name
Beth
Allison

Result3		
S.Name	**F.Name**	**Major**
Beth	Jeff	Hist
Nancy	Ron	Math
Nancy	Mehdi	Math
Robin	Jeff	Hist
Allison	Ron	Math
Allison	Mehdi	Math
Lulwa	Sam	CompSci
Lulwa	Gary	CompSci

Figure 1.21

The result of three queries from the database of Figure 1.20. Each result is a relation.

The fact that the result of a query is itself a relation, is a powerful idea in relational database systems. The user at Level 7 views the database as a collection of relations. Her query is a request for another relation that the system derives from the existing relations in the database.

Remember that each level has a language. The language of a Level 7 relational DBMS is a set of commands that combines or modifies existing relations and produces new relations. The user at Level 7 issues the commands to produce the

Query as a relation result

Input — Processing — Output
Database → Query → Result

desired result. Figure 1.22 shows the relationship between the database, a query, and the result. As it does in every level in the computer system, the relationship takes this form: input, processing, output.

This chapter cannot describe every language of every relational database system on the market. Instead, it describes a simplified language typical of such systems. Most relational DBMS languages have many powerful commands. But three commands are fundamental—`select`, `project`, and `join`.

The `select` and `project` statements are similar because they both operate on a single relation to produce a modified relation. The `select` statement takes a set of rows from a given table that satisfies the condition specified in the statement. The `project` statement takes a set of columns from a given table according to the attributes specified in the statement. Figure 1.23 illustrates the effect of the statements

```
select Frat where F.Major = English giving Temp1
```

and

```
project Sor over S.Name giving Temp2
```

The `project` statement can specify more than one column, in which case the attributes are enclosed in parentheses and separated by commas. For example,

```
project Sor over (S.Class, S.State) giving Temp3
```

selects two attributes from the `Sor` relation.

Note in Figure 1.23(c) that the pair (Sr, CA) is common from both 4-tuples (Robin, Sr, Hist, CA) and (Lulwa, Sr, CompSci, CA) in relation `Sor` (Figure 1.20). But the pair is not repeated in relation `Temp3`. A basic property of relations is that no row in any table may be duplicated. The `project` operator checks for duplicated rows and does not permit them. Mathematically, a relation is a set of tuples, and elements of a set cannot be duplicated.

`join` differs from `select` and `project` because its input is two tables, not one. A column from the first table and a column from the second table are specified as the `join` column. The `join` column from each table must have a common domain. The result of a `join` of two tables is one wide table whose columns are duplicates of the original columns, except that the `join` column only appears once. The rows of the resulting table are copies of those rows of the two original tables that have equal elements in the `join` column.

For example, in Figure 1.20 the columns `S.Major` and `F.Major` have a common domain. The statement

```
join Sor and Frat over Major giving Temp4
```

specifies that `Major` is the `join` column and that the relations `Sor` and `Frat` are

Figure 1.22

The relationship between the database, a query, and the result. The database is the input. The query is a set of commands in the Level 7 language.

Temp1

F.Name	F.Major	F.State
David	English	AZ
Craig	English	CA

(a) `select Frat where F.Major = English giving Temp1`

Temp2

S.Name
Beth
Nancy
Robin
Allison
Lulwa

(b) `project Sor over S.Name giving Temp2`

Temp3

S.Class	S.State
Soph	TX
Jr	NY
Sr	CA
Soph	AZ

(c) `project Sor over (S.Class, S.State) giving Temp3.`

Figure 1.23

The `select` and `project` operators.

Temp4

S.Name	S.Class	S.State	Major	F.Name	F.State
Beth	Soph	TX	Hist	Jeff	TX
Nancy	Jr	NY	Math	Ron	OR
Nancy	Jr	NY	Math	Mehdi	CA
Robin	Sr	CA	Hist	Jeff	TX
Allison	Soph	AZ	Math	Ron	OR
Allison	Soph	AZ	Math	Mehdi	CA
Lulwa	Sr	CA	CompSci	Sam	WA
Lulwa	Sr	CA	CompSci	Gary	CA

Figure 1.24

The `join` operator. The relation is from the statement `join Sor and Frat over Major giving Temp4`.

to be joined over it. Figure 1.24 shows that the only rows included in the `join` of the two tables are the ones with equal majors. The 4-tuple (Robin, Sr, Hist, CA) from `Sor` and the 3-tuple (Jeff, Hist, TX) from `Frat` are joined in `Temp4` because their majors, Hist, are equal.

Structure of the Language

The statements in this Level 7 language have the following form:

```
select relation where condition giving relation
project relation over attributes giving relation
join relation and relation over attribute giving relation
```

The reserved words of the language are

select	project
join	and
where	over
giving	

Reserved words

Each reserved word has a special meaning in the language, as the previous examples demonstrated. Words to identify objects in the language, such as `Sor` and `Temp2` to identify relations and `F.State` to identify an attribute, are not reserved. They are created arbitrarily by the user at Level 7 and are called *identifiers*. The existence of reserved words and user-defined identifiers is common in languages at all the levels of a typical computer system.

Do you see how to use the `select`, `project`, and `join` statements to generate the results of the query in Figure 1.21? The statements for the first query, which asks for Ron's home state, are

```
select Frat where F.Name = Ron giving Temp5
project Temp5 over F.State giving Result1
```

The statements for the second query, which asks for the names of all the sophomores in the sorority, are

```
select Sor where S.Class = Soph giving Temp6
project Temp6 over S.Name giving Result2
```

The statements for the third query, which asks for a list of those sorority and fraternity members who have the same major and what that common major is, are

```
join Sor and Frat over Major giving Temp4
project Temp4 over (S.Name, F.Name, Major) giving Result3
```

SUMMARY

The fundamental question of computer science is, What can be automated? Computers automate the processing of information. The theme of this book is levels of abstraction in computer systems. Abstraction includes suppression of detail to show the essence of the matter, an outline structure, division of responsibility through a chain of command, and subdivision of a system into smaller systems. The seven levels of abstraction in a typical computer system are

7 Applications

6 High-order languages

5 Assembly

4 Operating system

3 Machine

2 Microprogramming

1 Logic gate

Each level has its own language, which serves to hide the details of the lower levels.

A computer system consists of hardware and software. Four components of hardware are input devices, the central processing unit, main memory, and output devices. Programs that control the computer are called software.

An algorithm is a set of instructions which, when carried out in the proper sequence, solves a problem in a finite amount of time. A program is an algorithm written for execution on a computer. A program inputs information, processes it, and outputs the results.

Database systems are one of the most common applications at Level 7. Relational database systems store information in files that appear to have a table structure; this table is called a relation. The result of a query in a relational database system is itself a relation. The three fundamental operations in a relational database system are `select`, `project`, and `join`. A query is a combination of these three operations.

EXERCISES

At the end of each chapter in this book is a set of exercises and problems. Work the exercises on paper by hand. Answers to the starred exercises are in the back of the book. (For some multipart exercises, answers are supplied only for selected parts.) The problems are programs to be entered into the computer. This chapter contains only exercises.

Section 1.1

1. **(a)** Draw a hierarchy diagram that corresponds to the United States Constitution. **(b)** Based on Figure 1.5, draw a nesting diagram that corresponds to the organization of D. C. Heath and Company.

2. Genghis Khan organized his men into groups of 10 soldiers under a "leader of 10." Ten "leaders of 10" were under a "leader of 100." Ten "leaders of 100" were under a "leader of 1000." * **(a)** If Khan had an army of 10,000 soldiers at the lowest level, how many men in total were under him in his organization? **(b)** If Khan had an army of 5763 soldiers at the lowest level, how many men in total were under him in his organization? Assume that the groups of 10 should contain 10 if possible, but that one group at each level may need to contain fewer.

3. In the Bible, Exodus Chapter 18 describes how Moses was overwhelmed as the single judge of Israel because of the large number of trivial cases that were brought before him. His father-in-law, Jethro, recommended a hierarchical system of appellate courts where the lowest-level judge had responsibility for 10 citizens. Five judges of 10 sent the difficult cases that they could not resolve to a judge of 50 citizens. Two judges of 50 were under a judge of 100, and 10 judges of 100 were under a judge of 1000. The judges of 1000 citizens reported to Moses, who had to decide only the most difficult cases. * **(a)** If the population were exactly 2000 citizens (excluding judges) draw the three top levels of the hierarchy diagram. **(b)** In part (a), what would be the total population including Moses, all the judges, and citizens? **(c)** If the population were exactly 10,000 citizens (excluding judges), what would be the total population including Moses, all the judges, and citizens?

4. A full binary tree is a tree whose leaves are all at the same level, and every node that is not a leaf has exactly two nodes under it. Figure 1.25 is a full binary tree with three levels. * **(a)** Draw the full binary tree with four levels. * **(b)** How many nodes total are in a full binary tree with five levels? **(c)** With six levels? **(d)** With *n* levels in general?

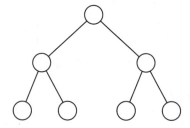

Figure 1.25

Exercise 4. The full binary tree with three levels.

Section 1.2

*5. A typist is entering text on a keyboard at the rate of 40 words per minute. If each word is 5 characters long on the average, how many bits per second are being sent to main memory? A space is also a character. Assume that each word is followed by one space on the average.

6. A typist is entering text on a keyboard at the rate of 30 words per minute. If each word is 6 characters long on the average, how many bits per second are being sent to main memory? A space is also a character. Assume that each word is followed by one space on the average.

7. A town has a population of 800,000. Assume that on the average a resident's name is 15 characters, his address is 20 characters, and his phone number is 7 characters. *(a) If no spaces are stored with the characters, how many 600 Kbyte floppy disks are required to store the phone book for the town? *(b) How many 20 Mbyte hard disks are required? (c) All the data will fit on a 1 Gbyte hard disk. What percentage of the disk is left for other purposes?

8. A typical cooking recipe contains 400 characters of text. How many recipes can you store on a 500 Kbyte floppy disk?

*9. A screen has an 8×10 rectangular grid of pixels for each character. It can display 24 rows by 80 columns of characters. (a) How many pixels in total are on the screen? (b) If each pixel is stored as one bit, how many Kbytes does it take to store the screen?

10. A screen has a 5×7 rectangular grid of pixels for each character. It can display 24 rows of 80 columns of characters. (a) How many pixels are on the screen? (b) If each pixel is stored as one bit, how many Kbytes does it take to store a screen image?

11. A desktop laser printer has a 300-pixel-per-inch resolution. If each pixel is stored in one bit of memory, how many bytes of memory are required to store the complete image of one $8\frac{1}{2}$-by-11-inch page of paper?

12. A medium-sized book has about a million characters. *(a) How many hours would it take to print it on a letter quality printer at 15 characters per second? (b) Assuming an average of 55 characters per line, how many hours would it take on a 600-line-per-minute line printer?

13. What two decimal digits does the UPC symbol in Figure 1.26 represent?

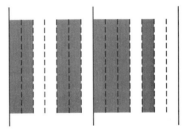

Figure 1.26

Exercise 13. The digits are characters on the right half of the UPC symbol.

Section 1.3

14. Answer the following questions about file names for your operating system. (a) Is there a limit to the number of characters in a file name? If so, what is the limit? (b) Are certain characters not allowed or, if allowed, problematical? (c) Does your operating system distinguish between uppercase and lowercase characters in a file name?

15. Determine how to perform each of the following procedures with your operating system. (a) Sign onto the system if it is a mainframe or minicomputer, or start up the system if it is a microcomputer. (b) List the names of the files from the directory. (c) Delete a file from the disk. (d) Change the name of a file. (e) Duplicate a file. (f) Print the contents of a file.

Section 1.4

*16. Write the relations `Temp5` and `Temp6` from the discussion of Section 1.4.

17. Write the statements for the following queries of the database in Figure 1.20. *(a) Find Beth's home state. (b) List the fraternity members who are English majors. (c) List the sorority and fraternity members who have the same home state, and indicate what that home state is.

18. (a) Write the statements to produce `Result2` in Figure 1.21, but with the `project` command before the `select`. (b) Write the statements to produce `Result3` in Figure 1.21, but with `join` as the last statement.

High-Order Languages

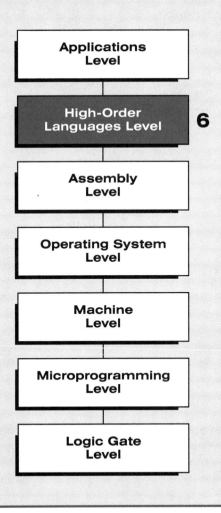

Chapter

2

Interactive Input/Output

A program inputs information, processes it, and outputs the results. The processing part of a program is usually its most complex part. This chapter shows how a Pascal program inputs and outputs values, leaving processing for the next chapter. The programs illustrated here may not seem useful, since their only purpose is to introduce the Pascal language. Nevertheless, they are an important illustration of how the computer handles input and output.

Input devices in a computer system include disk drives, keyboards, and mice. Output devices include disk drives, screens, and printers. This chapter presents interactive input/output (I/O), in which the input device is the keyboard and the output device is the screen. Chapter 4 will introduce I/O with other devices.

Interactive I/O

2.1 Pascal

Pascal, a Level 6 language, was developed in the early 1970s by the European computer scientist Niklaus Wirth. It is named after the French mathematician Blaise Pascal, who invented the first mechanical calculating machine.

Niklaus Wirth

Many Level 6 languages in the 1960s were unnecessarily complex. Wirth wanted a language that was simple and concise, but powerful enough to solve non-trivial problems. His two goals were for Pascal to be a language that would be

- Suitable for teaching programming as a systematic discipline, with fundamental concepts clearly and naturally reflected by the language

Goals of the Pascal language

- Efficient to execute on the computers of the day

Wirth's language succeeded beyond these two modest goals. In keeping with his first goal, Pascal is widespread as a teaching language in most colleges and universities in the United States. But people discovered that clarity and efficiency in a programming language were good qualities for nonacademic problems as well. Pascal is now used extensively in scientific and business applications as well.

Compilers

A computer can directly execute statements in machine language only at Level 3, the machine level. So a Level 6 statement must first be translated to Level 3 before executing. Figure 2.1 shows the function of a *compiler,* which performs the translation from a Level 6 language to the Level 3 language.

To execute the programs in this book you will need access to a Pascal compiler. Running a program is a three-step process:

- Write the program in Pascal, called the *source program*, with a text editor.
- Invoke the compiler to translate, or compile, the source program from Pascal to machine language. The machine language version is called the *object program.*
- Execute the object program.

Some systems allow you to specify the last two of these steps with a single command, usually called the "run" command. Whether you specify the compilation and execution separately or not, some translation is required before a Level 6 program can be executed.

When you write the source program, it will be saved in a file on disk just like any other text document would be. The compiler will produce another file for the object program called a *code file*. Depending on your compiler, the object program may be visible on your file directory after the compilation.

If you want to execute a program that was previously compiled, you do not need to translate it again. You can simply execute the object program directly. If you ever delete the object program from your disk you can always get it back from the source program by compiling again. But the translation can only go from a high level to a low level. If you ever delete the source program you cannot recover it from the object program.

Your Pascal compiler is software, not hardware. It is a program that is stored in a file on your disk. Like all programs, the compiler has input, does processing, and produces output. Figure 2.2 shows that the input to the compiler is the source program and the output is the object program.

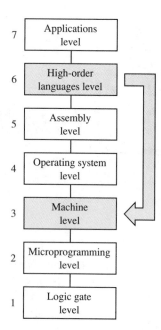

Figure 2.1

The function of a compiler, which translates a program in a Level 6 language to an equivalent program in a language at a lower level. This figure shows translation to Level 3. Some compilers translate from Level 6 to Level 5, which then requires another translation from Level 5 to Level 3.

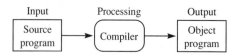

Figure 2.2

The compiler as a program.

Machine Independence

Level 3 languages are *machine dependent*. If you write a program in a Level 3 language for execution on a Brand X computer, it cannot run on a Brand Y computer. An important property of the languages at Level 6 is their *machine independence*. If you write a program in a Level 6 language for execution on a Brand X computer, it will run with only slight modification on a Brand Y computer.

Figure 2.3 shows how Pascal achieves its machine independence. Suppose you write an applications program in Pascal to do some statistical analysis. You want to sell it to people who own Brand X computers and to others who own Brand Y. The statistics program can only be executed if it is in machine language. Since machine language is machine dependent, you will need two machine language versions, one for Brand X and one for Brand Y. Since Pascal is a common high-order language, you will probably have access to a Pascal compiler for the Brand X machine and a Pascal compiler for the Brand Y machine. If so, you can simply invoke the Brand X Pascal compiler on one machine to produce the Brand X machine language version and invoke the Brand Y Pascal compiler on the other machine for the other version. You need to write only one Pascal program!

The key to machine independence is the quality of the compilers. Since the Brand X Pascal compiler and the Brand Y Pascal compiler might be from different manufacturers, their input requirements may differ slightly. When Niklaus Wirth designed Pascal, he specified the rules for writing valid statements in the language. The problem is that many other people are responsible for constructing the compilers, and each one is slightly different from all the others.

To encourage compiler writers to minimize their differences, the International Standards Organization (ISO) and American National Standards Institute (ANSI) examined Wirth's language rules. They clarified some of them and slightly modified others. The result is ISO/ANSI Standard Pascal, on which this book is based. The goal of the ISO and ANSI organizations is to encourage compiler writers to conform to the standard. If everyone conformed 100%, then Pascal programs would be 100% machine independent.

Unfortunately, conformance is more like 95%. Rather than discuss the differences between the various Pascal dialects, this book describes the ideal standard. You should keep in mind that your Pascal compiler may differ somewhat from the standard described in this book.

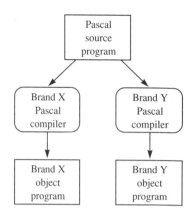

Figure 2.3

The machine independence of a Level 6 language.

Standard Pascal

2.2 String Output

Recall that, in general, a program receives input, processes it, and produces output. The examples in this section have no input, do no processing, and only produce output.

Program 2.1

Program 2.1, outputs a name and address on the screen. The first part is the *program listing*, which starts with the line

```
{  Stan Warford                        }
```

and ends with the line

```
end.
```

The second part is the output produced when the program executes.

```
{   Stan Warford                        }
{   March 22, 1990                      }
{   This program illustrates the writeln }
{   statement.                          }

program Address (output);
   begin
   writeln (output, 'Mr. K. Kong');
   writeln (output, 'Suite 8572');
   writeln (output, 'Empire State Building');
   writeln (output, 'New York, NY 10019')
   end.
```

Output

```
Mr. K. Kong
Suite 8572
Empire State Building
New York, NY 10019
```

Program 2.1

Illustration of the writeln statement.

To run this program, first create a file with your text editor containing the listing. Then compile the source program, producing the object program. When you execute the object program, the four lines shown under Output in Program 2.1 will appear on the screen.

Program 2.1 illustrates five features of the Pascal language:

- Comments
- Reserved words
- Identifiers
- The standard output device
- writeln statements

The following discussion describes each of these features plus a special kind of diagram called a *syntax chart,* which specifies in graphic form the rules of the Pascal language.

Comments

The *documentation section* at the beginning of the program is enclosed in *comment braces,* { }. The compiler ignores everything between the braces. The only purpose of the documentation section is to explain the program to a human reader. This documentation section lists the programmer's name, the date the program was written, and a brief description of the program's purpose.

All of your programs should contain a documentation section with at least your name and the date you wrote the program. In addition, your instructor or employer should have documentation standards for you to follow. For example, your instructor may require you to place the assignment number in the documentation section of your programming problems. Even if the program is only for your personal use, you should still document it with at least your name and the date you wrote it. Documenting programs is a good habit to cultivate.

The importance of comments

Although the documentation section of Program 2.1 is at the beginning of the listing, you can write a comment anywhere that a blank space can occur and not affect the program execution. If you ever write a Pascal program on a keyboard without the { } symbols, you can use the two symbols, (* for the left brace and *) for the right brace.

Reserved Words

Program 2.1 has three reserved words—program, begin, and end. *Reserved words* have special meaning to the Pascal compiler. The reserved word program indicates to the compiler the start of a Pascal program. The reserved word begin indicates the start of a list of Pascal statements, and the reserved word end indicates the end of the list. Pascal has 35 reserved words. They are

Pascal's reserved words

and	end	nil	set
array	file	not	then
begin	for	of	to
case	function	or	type
const	goto	packed	until
div	if	procedure	var
do	in	program	while
downto	label	record	with
else	mod	repeat	

Identifiers

The name of Program 2.1 is Address. Address is a Pascal *identifier* determined arbitrarily by the programmer. You could just as easily call the program Mail instead of Address. In that case, the first line of the listing after the documentation section would be

```
program Mail (output);
```

Objects other than programs can be named by Pascal identifiers. Regardless of the object named, you must follow certain rules for devising an identifier. Pascal identifiers may contain only letters and digits, and they must start with a letter. An

Rules for identifiers

identifier can consist of more than one word, but the words may not be separated by a space. For readability you should capitalize the first letter in each word and write all other letters in lowercase.

Example **2.1**   Here are five legal Pascal identifiers:

```
NewYork  DC9  QuantityOnHand  i  HoursWorked
```

Notice how much easier it is to read the identifier `QuantityOnHand` instead of `quantityonhand`. The identifier `i` is legal in Pascal, but since our style convention is to capitalize the first letter, that identifier should be written `I`. ∎

Although there is practically no limit to the length of a name, only the first eight characters are recognized by some compilers, usually those that are older. Also, standard Pascal does not distinguish between uppercase and lowercase characters in identifiers or reserved words. Reserved words may not be used as Pascal identifiers.

Example **2.2**   In a compiler that recognizes only the first eight characters, the names `HoursWorked` and `HoursWorking` will refer to the same object, the one the compiler knows as `HoursWor`. ∎

Example **2.3**   In standard Pascal, `Hours` and `HOURS` refer to the same object. Even though it would be legal to use these two identifiers in different parts of the program to refer to the same object, that practice would be confusing to a human reader. You should be consistent in your capitalization, even though the compiler will accept the inconsistency. ∎

Example **2.4**   Here are some illegal Pascal identifiers:

```
7Eleven  Tax%  Home-Address  Packed
```

The first is illegal because it does not begin with a letter. The second and third have characters other than letters or digits. The last is illegal because it is a reserved word. ∎

To write a Pascal program you must make up identifiers to name objects. You should get in the habit of using mnemonic identifiers, that is, identifiers that remind the human reader about the meaning of the object. `Address` is a good name for Program 2.1 because the program prints an address on the screen. The program would execute exactly the same if you wrote

Mnemonic identifiers

```
program Xyz (output);
```

as the first line after the documentation section. But that would be horrible style, since the identifier indicates nothing about what the program does. Even worse would be

```
program Payroll (output);
```

for Program 2.1, since that would indicate to the human reader that the program has something to do with a payroll problem, which it does not. When you use a program from this book as a model for your own program, do not blindly copy the identifiers if they are not appropriate to your problem. Instead, make up your own mnemonic identifiers.

Syntax Charts

The syntax of a language is the set of rules you must follow to write correct phrases in the language. *Syntax charts* are diagrams that show the rules of the Pascal language. Figure 2.4 is the syntax chart that defines a valid Pascal identifier. Imagine that the chart represents the tracks of a model railroad. A train enters the diagram on the single incoming arrow from the left. It drives around the tracks, always going in the direction of the arrows. When it comes to a fork, it can take either path it chooses. Finally, after driving around, it exits on the single outgoing arrow to the right.

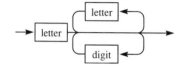

Figure 2.4

The syntax chart for a valid Pascal identifier.

In the course of its travels, the train runs over the boxes labeled *letter* and *digit*. Imagine writing a letter on a piece of paper every time the train runs over a letter box and a digit every time it runs over a digit box. Then, when the train exits from the diagram, you will have written a valid Pascal identifier!

An identifier must begin with a letter. Accordingly, the train must run over the first letter box in Figure 2.4 before going anywhere else. All other characters must be letters or digits, in any order. Thus, the train can loop back over the letter box or digit box any number of times, in any order, before exiting.

For Figure 2.4 to produce valid identifiers, you must write a valid digit on the paper each time the train runs over the digit box. What is a valid digit? It is one of the characters 0, 1, 2, 3, 4, 5, 6, 7, 8, or 9. Figure 2.5 shows the corresponding syntax chart for a valid digit. The syntax chart for a valid letter would be similar, but there would be 26 circles instead of 10, one for each letter in the English alphabet.

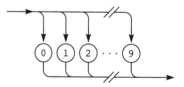

Figure 2.5

The syntax chart for a valid digit.

Syntax charts cannot specify all of the rules for a valid Pascal object. For example, the syntax chart for identifiers of Figure 2.4 does not forbid the word `Packed` from being an identifier. But we know that `Packed` cannot be an identifier because it is a reserved word. The syntax chart does not specify the rule forbidding identifiers from being reserved words.

The Standard Output Device

Program 2.1 contains the word `output` in several places. Remember that a computer system can have many different kinds of output devices. Disks, magnetic tape, printers, and screens are all output devices. Your operating system maintains one of these as the *standard output device*. The word `output` in a Pascal program

The screen as standard output device

listing specifies the standard output device. The most common standard output device maintained by an operating system is the screen. We will assume in this program, and throughout this book, that the system's standard output device is in fact the screen.

After the identifier `Address` in this program, comes the word `output` enclosed in parentheses. It is a program parameter. *Program parameters* specify to the operating system from where the program will get its input, and to where the program will send its output. So the word `output` as a program parameter specifies to the operating system that the program will send some results to the screen.

Writeln Statements

Program 2.1 has four `writeln` statements between the `begin` and `end` reserved words. `writeln` stands for "write line." When executed, the `writeln` statement sends text to an output device as shown in Figure 2.6.

A pair of parentheses follows each `writeln`. Between the parentheses are two items separated by a comma. The first item is called the *file variable,* and the second item is called the *write parameter.* The file variable tells the computer where to send the text. In this program, the file variable is `output`, which in a Pascal program signifies the standard output device. So the `writeln` statements in Program 2.1 send text to the screen.

The write parameter of the first `writeln` statement

```
'Mr. K. Kong'
```

is a string. *Strings* are sequences of characters enclosed in apostrophes. When you put a string in a `writeln` statement as a write parameter, the computer outputs the sequence of characters without the apostrophes. When the `writeln` statement

```
writeln (output, 'Mr. K. Kong')
```

executes, the computer outputs the sequence of characters

```
Mr. K. Kong
```

to the output device.

If you want to include an apostrophe within the string, you must put two apostrophes next to each other. Otherwise, the compiler will mistake the internal apostrophe for the terminating apostrophe.

Example **2.5**   The `writeln` statement

```
writeln (output, 'Let''s go out')
```

will send the sequence of characters

```
Let's go out
```

to the standard output device.

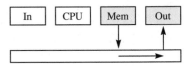

Figure 2.6

The execution of `writeln`. It is an output statement.

Strings

Apostrophes within strings

Figure 2.7 is the syntax chart for a `writeln` statement. You can see from the chart that the write parameter may be omitted. That possibility lets you send a blank line to the output device. Also, more than one write parameter is allowed if separated by a comma from the previous write parameter. In that case, the parameters are output in the same order on the same line.

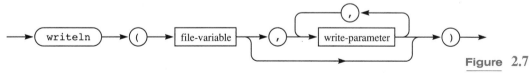

Figure 2.7

The syntax chart for a `writeln` call.

Example **2.6**   When executed, the `writeln` statements

```
writeln (output, 'Mr. K. Kong');
writeln (output);
writeln (output, 'Suite 8572');
writeln (output, 'Empire State Building')
```

send the following text to the screen:

```
Mr. K. Kong

Suite 8572
Empire State Building
```

■

The four `writeln` statements between `begin` and `end` in Program 2.1 are called *executable statements*, because they perform an operation when the program executes. Namely, they send some text to the screen. Pascal has the following 10 executable statements:

assignment	goto	while
case	if	with
compound	procedure	
for	repeat	

The statements of Pascal

We will consider them in later chapters. The `writeln` statement is an example of a procedure statement, or procedure call. We will see later that large portions of Pascal program listings can be nonexecutable.

Syntax for a Pascal Program

How do all these elements—reserved words, identifiers, references to the standard output, `writeln` statements, and strings—come together to make a program? The answer is in Figure 2.8, the syntax chart for a valid Pascal program. In English, a Pascal program is a program heading followed by a block. A semicolon separates the program heading from the block. A period terminates the program.

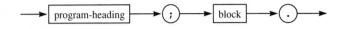

Figure 2.8

The syntax chart for a Pascal program.

What is a program heading? Figure 2.9 shows that a *program heading* is the reserved word **program**, followed by an identifier, followed by one or more identifiers enclosed in parentheses separated by commas. You can see how much easier it is to specify the syntax with a syntax chart instead of with English!

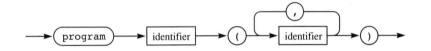

Figure 2.9

The syntax chart for a program heading.

The boxes in Figure 2.9 have two shapes; the boxes with rounded corners contain terminals, while those with sharp corners contain nonterminals. *Terminals* are items that appear literally in the program listing, while *nonterminals* are items that do not.

Terminals and nonterminals

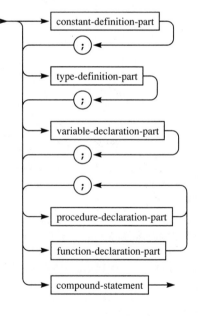

Example 2.7   Figure 2.9 indicates that **program**, (,), and , are all terminals. They appear literally in the first line of the program listing. *Identifier* is not a terminal. If it were, the program heading of Program 2.1 would look like

```
program identifier (identifier)
```

instead of like

```
program Address (output)
```

■

Figure 2.10 is the syntax chart for a *block*. It consists of five parts, any or all of which may be omitted, followed by a compound statement. In Program 2.1, all five parts are omitted. When a program contains some of the five parts, semicolons separate them from each other and from the compound statement.

Finally, Figure 2.11 is the syntax chart for a *compound statement*. You may have noticed in Program 2.1 that a semicolon appears after each **writeln** statement except for the last one. Figure 2.11 shows that semicolons are used to separate two statements.

For example, use the semicolon after the first **writeln** statement to separate it from the second **writeln** statement. Then use the semicolon after the second statement to separate it from the third. The reserved word **end**, however, is not a statement. Therefore, you do not need a semicolon separator after the last

Figure 2.10

The syntax chart for a block.

`writeln`. The general rule to remember is

- Do not place a semicolon before an `end`.

Figure 2.11

The syntax chart for a compound statement.

Program 2.2

When you try to execute a program, two types of errors are possible:

- *Syntax error* The program does not compile.
- *Logical error* The program compiles but produces incorrect results.

The syntax charts can only indicate possible sources of syntax errors, not logical errors. Remember that they are not even perfect at specifying all the syntax rules of the Pascal language.

Program 2.2 illustrates a syntax error. When a program does not compile, no object program can be generated, and it is impossible to test for logical errors. Errors, whether syntax or logical, are called *bugs*. Getting the errors out of your program is called *debugging*. Can you spot the bug in Program 2.2?

```
{  Stan Warford            }
{  March 22, 1990          }
{  This program has a bug. }

program Address (output)
   begin
   writeln (output, 'Mr. K. Kong');
   writeln (output, 'Suite 8572');
   writeln (output, 'Empire State Building');
   writeln (output, 'New York, NY 10019')
   end.
```

Output

```
Syntax error
Semicolon expected
```

Program 2.3

Some computer languages are line-oriented, that is, each statement must be written on a separate line. Program 2.3 shows that Pascal is not line-oriented. The behavior of the object program does not depend on the spacing or indentation style of the source program.

```
{   Stan Warford                              }
{   March 22, 1990                            }
{   This program is the same as Program 2.1  }
{   except for its spacing and indentation    }
{   style.                                    }

program Address (output      );
begin writeln (output,'Mr. K. Kong');writeln
(output,    'Suite 8572');
writeln(output    ,'Empire State Building')
;writeln
(output,'New York, NY 10019')end.
```

Program 2.3

A program identical to Program 2.1 except for its spacing and indentation style. Its output is identical to the output of Program 2.1.

Output

```
Mr. K. Kong
Suite 8572
Empire State Building
New York, NY 10019
```

One good habit to cultivate when learning to program is to adhere to a consistent standard of style. You should follow either the style of the programs in this book, the style specified by your instructor or employer, or a consistent style from some other source.

In this book, a comma is always followed by a single space. The reserved word `begin` is indented the same amount (three spaces) as the reserved word `end`. The statements enclosed by `begin` and `end` line up with them vertically.

The computer does not require such neatness for the program to work. However, just getting the program to work correctly is not sufficient. Good style is necessary because people, as well as computers, must read your programs. You would not write a business letter without the paragraphs indented consistently. Nor should you write a program that way.

The importance of good style

Although you may want to rebel at first against such seemingly trivial details, you will find in the long run that they are not restrictive at all. In fact just the opposite is true—these rules are liberating.

The situation is similar to that of a new driver on the road for the first time. Think of how many restrictive rules there are—speed limits, yield signs, stop signals, and so on. New drivers may feel hampered and may worry about all the rules they need to remember. But experienced drivers do not even consciously try to remember the rules. They know them subconsciously. What's more, the rules liberate them from fear of an accident. Programming standards will liberate your mind to think constructively. The standards will take care of the details, freeing you to take care of the problem.

Program 2.4

Program 2.4 illustrates the difference between `write` and `writeln`. The Pascal `write` statement does one thing:

Write versus writeln

- It outputs the write parameters.

But the `writeln` statement does two things:

- It outputs the write parameters.
- Then it positions the output device at the beginning of the next line.

The point to understand is that `writeln` does not necessarily put its output on the next line. Instead, it causes the following output statement to put its output on the next line.

```
{  Don Thompson                          }
{  March 22, 1990                        }
{  This program shows the difference between  }
{  write and writeln.                    }

program ApostropheTest (output);
   begin
   writeln (output, 'How are you?');
   write (output, 'I am fine.  ');
   writeln (output, 'Let''s go out.')
   end.
```

Output

```
How are you?
I am fine.  Let's go out.
```

Program 2.4

The difference between `write` and `writeln`.

In program `ApostropheTest` the first `writeln` outputs 'How are you?'. Then, since it is a `writeln` and not a `write`, it sends the cursor to the start of the next line. When the `write` statement executes, it outputs 'I am fine. '. But since it is a `write` and not a `writeln`, the cursor does not go to the start of the next line. When the last `writeln` executes, it starts where the cursor was left by the previous statement. That is, it starts at the end of the line containing 'I am fine. '. It outputs 'Let's go out.' Then, since it is a `writeln`, the cursor goes to the start of the next line. Next, the program execution ends.

If the last statement of program `ApostropheTest` were changed from `writeln` to `write`, as follows:

```
writeln (output, 'How are you?');
write (output, 'I am fine.  ');
write (output, 'Let''s go out.')
```

then the output would not be noticeably different. The cursor would just end up at the end of Let's go out. instead of at the start of the next line.

▮ Programs 2.5 and 2.6

Programs 2.5 and 2.6 introduce the concept of a programmer-defined *procedure*, which will be discussed in more detail in Chapter 6. Procedures are useful when your program has a task that it needs to perform more than once. Programmers working with procedures must first define the task in the *procedure declaration part* (see the syntax chart of Figure 2.10), then invoke or *call* the procedure when the task needs to be executed.

Introduction to procedures

```
{   Don Hancock                     }
{   March 30, 1990                  }
{   This program outputs a pattern of }
{   asterisks.                      }

program Pattern (output);
   begin
   writeln (output, '*');
   writeln (output, '**');
   writeln (output, '***');
   writeln (output, '****');
   writeln (output, '*');
   writeln (output, '**');
   writeln (output, '***');
   writeln (output, '****');
   writeln (output, '*');
   writeln (output, '**');
   writeln (output, '***');
   writeln (output, '****')
   end.
```

Program 2.5

The output of a repetitious pattern of asterisk characters.

Output

```
*
**
***
****
*
**
***
****
*
**
***
****
```

Program 2.5 outputs a pattern of asterisks without using a procedure. The pattern is a repetition of three smaller patterns in the shape of a triangle.

Program 2.6, on the other hand, collects the statements that print a single triangle into a procedure. The programmer declared the procedure and gave it the name `PrintTriangle`. He then called the procedure three times to produce the final pattern.

In Program 2.6, `procedure` is a reserved word and `PrintTriangle` is an identifier that names the procedure. Figure 2.12 shows that procedure `PrintTriangle` is nested in program `Pattern`. The `writeln` statements in region (1) belong to the procedure declaration. The procedure call statements in region (2) belong to the main program. The term *main program* means the entire program, excluding the procedure declaration. The punctuation rules for semicolons in the procedure are identical to the punctuation rules in the main program.

Pattern

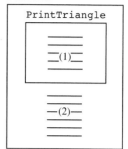

Figure 2.12

Procedure `PrintTriangle` nested in program `Pattern`.

Program 2.6

A procedure that is called three times from the main program. Its output is identical to that of Program 2.5.

```
{  Don Hancock                      }
{  March 30, 1989                   }
{  This program uses a procedure to print}
{  a triangle pattern three times.}

program Pattern (output);

   procedure PrintTriangle;
      begin
      writeln (output, '*');
      writeln (output, '**');
      writeln (output, '***');
      writeln (output, '****')
      end;

   begin
   PrintTriangle;
   PrintTriantle;
   PrintTriangle
   end.
```

Output

```
*
**
***
****
*
**
***
****
*
**
***
****
```

Region (1) in the inner block is the declaration of the procedure. After the compiler translates the program, the first statement to execute is not the first statement in region (1), but the first statement in region (2).

The first statement in region (2) is `PrintTriangle`. It is a call to procedure `PrintTriangle` defined earlier in the listing, and causes execution to jump to the first statement of region (1). The computer then executes all the statements of region (1). After it executes the last statement of region (1), it transfers execution to the statement in the main program after the one that called the procedure. At this point the first triangle has been printed.

Next, the computer executes the second statement in region (2), which is another call to procedure `PrintTriangle`. So the statements in region (1) execute again. Similarly, the third statement in region (2) makes them execute a third time.

Since `PrintTriangle` is an identifier, the programmer determined it arbitrarily. The program would produce the exact output if the programmer wrote

```
procedure WriteTriangle
```

in the definition of the procedure, and then called it with

```
WriteTriangle
```

in the main program. The only requirement is that the name in the procedure definition match the name in the procedure call. Of course, the identifiers you choose for the names of your procedures should be mnemonic.

Figure 2.13 shows the order in which statements are executed when a main program has two procedure calls.

Figure 2.13

The order of execution when a program has two procedure calls.

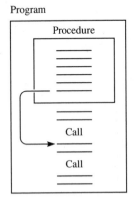

(a) The first call transfers control to the procedure. The procedure executes.

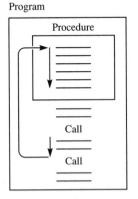

(b) The procedure returns control to the statement following the call.

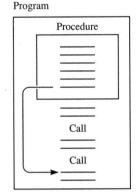

(c) The second call transfers control to the procedure. The procedure executes again.

(d) The procedure returns control to the statement following the second call.

Procedures are useful when you need to perform the same task at several different points in a program. They are also useful in structuring a program into levels of abstraction, even if the task is only performed once. Although this program uses a procedure to output text to the screen, later programs will use procedures to input or process data as well.

The `write` and `writeln` statements are really procedure calls. They differ from `PrintTriangle` in two respects. First, they are standard procedures as opposed to user-defined procedures. Their declaration part is hidden from the programmer at Level 6. This is in contrast to a user-defined procedure, which must be declared within the main program.

Second, `write` and `writeln` calls include a file variable and write parameters enclosed in parentheses. The declaration part (hidden from us at Level 6) needs this information to do its task. It needs the file variable to know where to send the output and the write parameter to know what to output. User defined procedures can also have parameters. Chapter 6 will explain how to define procedures with parameters.

2.3   Numeric Input/Output

The programs in the previous section illustrated the basic structure of a Pascal program and showed how to output strings to the screen. They also gave us a preview of programmer-defined procedures. This section begins by demonstrating how to transfer numeric values to the screen and then how to input numeric values from the keyboard.

Program 2.7

Program 2.7 outputs two values to the screen that represent the dimensions of a rectangle. It illustrates the following Pascal features:

- Variables
- Assignment statements
- Real output formats

Trace tables are introduced with this program as an analysis tool to help visualize the behavior of the program when it executes.

```
program Rectangle (output);
   var
      Width:  real;
      Length: real;
   begin
   Width := 3.6;
   Length := 12.4;
   writeln (output, Width, Length)
   end.
```

Output

```
3.60000000000000e+00  1.24000000000000e+01
```

Program 2.7

Output of real values. This program illustrates the assignment statement.

To conserve space in the remainder of this book, documentation sections will no longer appear at the beginning of the program listings. Instead, documentation will be in the program captions in the margin. We emphasize that documentation sections in comment braces at the beginning of your program listings are still important, however.

Variables

Every Pascal variable has three attributes:

- A name
- A type
- A value

The three attributes of a Pascal variable

A variable's *name* is an identifier determined arbitrarily by the programmer. A variable's *type* specifies the kind of *values* it can have. Variable names and types are declared in the *variable declaration part,* which must be placed before the executable statements as shown in the syntax chart for a block in Figure 2.10. As Program 2.7 shows, the variable declaration part begins with the reserved word `var` and contains a list of all variables used in the program. `Width` is the first variable's name, and `real` is its type. The type `real` means the variable's value will be a *real* number, with a fractional part indicated by a decimal point. The name and type of a variable are separated by a colon.

Figure 2.14 shows the syntax chart for the variable declaration part. After the colon you have two options, either a type identifier or a new type. The word `real` in Program 2.7 is a type identifier.

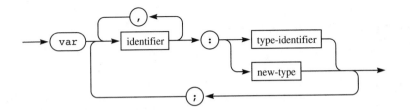

Figure 2.14

The syntax chart for the variable declaration part.

Notice how semicolons serve to separate the variables in the variable declaration part. The semicolon after the last variable,

```
Length: real
```

separates the variable declaration part from the compound statement. That semicolon is shown in Figure 2.10 and not in Figure 2.14.

Assignment Statements

Unlike names and types, the values of the variables are usually not visible in the program listing (although they are in this example). Instead, they exist in main memory during program execution. An *assignment statement* sets the value of a variable. The assignment statement

```
Width := 3.6
```

sets the value of the variable `Width` to 3.6. The `:=` symbol is called the *assignment operator.* You should read this statement in English as

> Width gets 3.6.

Do not say "Width equals 3.6." The equals operator, `=`, has a different meaning in Pascal from the assignment operator, `:=`.

Figure 2.15 is the syntax chart for an assignment statement. The name of a variable must be on the left side of the assignment operator, and an expression must be on the right side. A numeric value such as 3.6 is an example of an expression. The next chapter discusses more complex expressions that allow you to process values before making the assignment.

Figure 2.15

The syntax chart for an assignment statement.

Real Output Formats

The `writeln` statement

```
writeln (output, Width, Length)
```

does not have apostrophes around `Width` or `Length`. If they were enclosed in apostrophes they would be strings, and the text "`Width`" and "`Length`" would be output on the screen. When you use the name of a variable as a write parameter in a `writeln` statement, the computer sends the value of the variable, not the name of the variable, to the output device.

The `writeln` statement sent the values 3.6 and 12.4 to the screen, but it wrote them as

```
3.60000000000000e+00 1.24000000000000e+01
```

which is scientific notation. The letter `e` means "times 10 to the." So the second number is 1.24 times 10 to the 1, or 1.24×10^1, which is 12.4. The number of zeros printed after the decimal point varies from one computer to the next and depends on the accuracy with which it can store real values. Negative exponents are allowed.

Scientific notation

Blaise Pascal

Blaise Pascal, a French religious thinker, mathematician, and physicist who lived from 1623 to 1662, was one of the greatest minds of the seventeenth century. When Pascal's mother died in his infancy, his father moved the boy and his two sisters to Paris and undertook their education himself. By the time the boy was 12, his father could no longer keep the secrets of mathematics from him, and by 16, Pascal had written his "Treatise on Conic Sections," which includes Pascal's theorem, his famous theorem of hexagons. He was dealing, at this young age, on equal terms with some of the greatest scientific minds of his day.

Pascal was an early contributor to probability theory, a branch of mathematics. He wrote on scientific subjects, as well. One of his most significant early scientific works was "A Treatise on Vacuum." Though this work was never published and was found in fragmentary form only after his death, it provided the basis for his invention of the hydraulic press and the syringe and for his perfection of the barometer.

Another invention of Pascal's was the Pascaline, a calculating machine that was a dismal financial failure. This mechanical calculator operated rather like a complex mechanical clock, using gears and dials to represent and manipulate numeric values. Although it offered an improvement over having to perform time-consuming manual calculations, it had several drawbacks, one of which was that Pascal was the only person who could repair it. Another problem was that using the Pascaline was more expensive than using people to manually complete calculations. The device was also rejected by those in fear of losing their jobs to a machine. However, Pascal's gear-driven decimal-counting wheel was replaced only by the invention of the electronic calculator more than two centuries later.

Pascal's family history is almost as interesting as his mathematical and scientific career

Known for their wit and culture, his entire family moved in the highest social circles. Pascal's father, Étienne, was an eminent civil servant and mathematician and was appointed by the king of France to a high position in the government, representing Upper Normandy. But it was in Normandy that Étienne Pascal sustained an injury that was to change the lives of the whole family. He was tended by a local order of Jansenite priests, who were somber followers of Cornelius Jansen, and through this family involvement with the Jansenites, Blaise Pascal "got religion," which was to influence him until his death. It is said that on the night of November 23, 1654 he received a mystical vision of God and from that day forward he turned his life over to Jesus Christ. Accordingly, many of Pascal's writings were on religious subjects; these works included "Provincial Letters," "Prayer to Ask of God the Good Use of Maladies" (written from his sickbed), and "Pensées sur la religion."

Pascal was known during his lifetime, as he is known today, for his conviction that reason in the study of nature is totally subordinated to fact. He never relied on theory alone and felt compelled to transform it into something palpable.

Example **2.8** The text 8.7000e+02 represents a value of 870, the text 8.7000e-02 represents 0.087, the text −8.7000e+02 represents −870, and the text −8.7000e-02 represents −0.087. ∎

If you do not want the output to be in scientific notation you can format the output like this:

```
writeln (output, Width: 10: 2, Length: 10: 2)
```

The writeln statement would then produce

```
      3.60      12.40
```

The 10 and 2 separated by colons are the format specification. The 10 indicates the field width allocated for displaying the value of the variable. The value will occupy 10 spaces, right justified in the field and padded with leading blanks. The 2 indicates the number of places displayed past the decimal point as shown in Figure 2.16. Note in the figure that the decimal point occupies one of the 10 spaces in the field. This format is called *fixed point,* in contrast to scientific notation, which is called *floating point.*

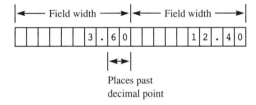

Figure 2.16

The output from a format specification of 10:2.

Table 2.1 shows the output for some real values in memory with various format specifications. The vertical bars in the output column mark the beginning and the end of the field position. Values are rounded properly if necessary.

The table illustrates two characteristics of format specifications for real values. First, if the value is too large to fit in the field, the field width is expanded to accommodate the display. For example, it is impossible to output the value −43152.7 with a field width of seven and with one place past the decimal point, since eight characters are required. In this situation, the write statement uses eight characters to display the value instead of seven as specified in the field width.

Second, if only one number is in the format specification for a real variable, the specification indicates the field width, and the number is printed in scientific notation. Here is the algorithm to determine how the value is displayed in scientific notation:

- The fourth character from the right is the letter e.
- The third character from the right is + or −.
- The last two characters are the exponent (power of 10).

Value in main memory	Format specification	Output
61.483	8: 3	61.483|
61.483	8: 2	61.48|
61.483	8: 1	61.5|
−52.7	7: 1	−52.7|
−152.7	7: 1	−152.7|
−3152.7	7: 1	−3152.7|
−43152.7	7: 1	−43152.7|
3.141593	12	3.14159e+00|
3.141593	11	3.1416e+00|
3.141593	10	3.142e+00|

Table 2.1

Some formatted real values.

- If the number is negative, the first character is −.
- If the number is nonnegative, the first character is blank.
- The third character from the left is a decimal point.
- The rest of the characters are the digits of the number.

One deficiency of Program 2.7 is that it simply outputs the values of the variables without any explanation of their meaning. A better way to display the values is with the following statements:

```
writeln (output, 'Width is ', Width: 3: 1);
writeln (output, 'Length is ', Length: 3: 1)
```

which produce the output

Identifying your output

```
Width is 3.6
Length is 12.4
```

Note that the field width for 12.4 was expanded from three to four. This style of output is preferred because it tells the program user the meaning of the values. Always identify your output when sending values to the screen.

You can use floating point notation in assignment statements. For example, replacing the first executable statement in Program 2.7 by

```
Width := 0.36e1
```

would not change the execution or output of the program.

Figure 2.17 is the syntax chart for a signed real number in a Pascal program listing. You should be able to tell from the chart that a signed real number requires either a decimal point, or the letter e, or both. If it does contain a decimal point, there must be at least one digit before and after the decimal point.

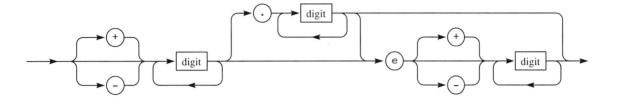

Figure 2.17

The syntax chart for a signed real number.

Example 2.9 Both 37. and .37 are invalid if written in a Pascal program listing. They should be written 37.0 or 0.37. ∎

Trace Tables

A *trace table* helps visualize the values of variables during execution. It is a picture of the contents of main memory. The heading of a trace table contains the names of the variables, and the body of the table shows the value of each variable at each point during program execution.

Table 2.2 is a trace of Program 2.7. The first column lists the statement executed, the second shows the value of variable `Width`, and the third shows the value of variable `Length`. To conserve space under the first column, if an executable statement is too long, only its first part will be shown in the trace table.

Statement executed	Width	Length
begin	?	?
Width := 3.6;	3.6	?
Length := 12.4;	3.6	12.4
writeln (output, W	3.6	12.4
end.		

Table 2.2

A trace of Program 2.7.

At every point in time during program execution, each variable has some value. However, before the first statement executes it is impossible to predict the values of any of the variables. If you execute Program 2.7 one time, the initial value of `Width` before the first assignment statement might be 920.8403. The next time you execute the same program, the initial value might be something completely different, such as −0.000017482. We will call such values that are impossible to predict *undefined* and indicate them in trace tables by question marks.

Undefined values

Table 2.2 shows `Width` and `Length` with undefined values before the first statement executes. Note that an assignment statement changes the value of a variable in main memory, but a `writeln` statement does not. A `writeln` statement merely sends a copy of the value of a variable from main memory to an output device, as Figure 2.6 illustrates.

▉ Program 2.8

Integer variables differ from real variables in that they do not have fractional parts. Program 2.8 shows how to declare an integer variable and output an integer value to the screen.

<table>
<tr><td>

```
program Change (output);
   var
      Cents: integer;
   begin
   Cents := 39;
   writeln (output,
   'You have ', Cents: 1, ' cents in change.')
   end.
```

Output

```
You have 39 cents in change.
```

</td><td>

Output of an integer value.

</td></tr>
</table>

▉ Integer Output Formats

The variable declaration part of Program 2.8 declares `Cents` to have type `integer`. During execution the assignment statement gives the value 39 to `Cents`. Then the `writeln` statement outputs the value to the screen. The format specification in a `writeln` for an integer value specifies only the field width, since there is no fractional part. This `writeln` specifies a field width of one because the value displayed on the screen will appear in the middle of a sentence. Since the field width will expand, if necessary, to fit all the digits into the display, this technique guarantees proper spacing within the sentence.

For example, suppose you specify a field width of two, anticipating that the value of the variable will require exactly two digits to display. If the value is 39, as in Program 2.8, the output will be unchanged. But if the value is 8 instead of 39 and you still specify a field width of two, the output would be

```
You have  8 cents in change.
```

with an extra space before the 8. If you specify a field width of one, the spacing will always be correct in the sentence regardless of how many digits are required to display the value.

Figure 2.18 is the syntax chart for a signed integer in a program. It shows that a positive or negative sign is optional and that an integer must contain one or more digits.

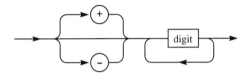

Figure 2.18

The syntax chart for a signed integer.

Program 2.9

Computers store integer values in main memory differently from real values. Remember that at the machine level (Level 3) information is stored as a sequence of bits. To store an integer, the computer uses one bit to indicate the sign of the value and a group of bits for its magnitude. However, to store a real value, the computer uses binary scientific notation with one bit to store the sign of the exponent (the power of 10), a group of bits for the exponent, one bit for the sign of the value, and a group of bits for the magnitude.

   Because of this difference in the way the computer stores integer and real values at Level 3, Pascal puts some restrictions on how you use them in a program. Program 2.9 illustrates the fact that you cannot assign a real value to an integer variable. You can, however, assign an integer value to a real variable.

```
program Error (output);
   var
      I: integer;
   begin
   I := 2.7;
   writeln (output, 'The value of I is ', I)
   end.
```

Output

```
Syntax error
Type conflict of operands
```

Program 2.9

A program that tries to assign a real value to an integer variable. This program has a bug.

Example 2.10 If you declare X to be a real variable then

```
X := 7
```

is a valid assignment statement, even though 7 is an integer. In this case, the computer automatically converts the integer 7 to the real number 7.0 before assigning it to X. ■

Automatic conversion from integer to real

Program 2.10

One shortcoming of the previous programs is that they produce the same output each time you execute them. Program 2.8 will always output the sentence

```
You have 39 cents in change.
```

If you wanted to output a different value, say 8, you would need to change the assignment statement

```
Cents := 39
```

in the program listing to

```
Cents := 8
```

You could then recompile the program and execute the resulting object program to get the different output.

Input statements allow programs to perform the same processing with different values, but without program modification and recompilation. Like assignment statements, input statements give values to variables. But unlike assignment statements, the values do not appear in the program listing. The programmer writes the source program not knowing the values that will be input by the user during execution of the object program.

Input statements

Program 2.10 is identical to Program 2.7, except that it gets its input interactively. It illustrates the standard input device and `readln` statements.

```
program Rectangle (input, output);
   var
      Width:  real;
      Length: real;
   begin
   write (output, 'Enter width: ');
   readln (input, Width);
   write (output, 'Enter length: ');
   readln (input, Length);
   writeln (output);
   writeln (output, 'The width is ', Width: 4: 2,
   ' and the length is ', Length: 4: 2, '.')
   end.
```

Program 2.10

Getting input from the keyboard. This program prompts the user to type in values, then pauses to receive the values.

Interactive Input/Output

```
Enter width: 3.6
Enter length: 12.4

The width is 3.60 and the length is 12.40.
```

The Standard Input Device

Program 2.10 contains the word `input` in several places. Of all the input devices on your computer, the operating system maintains one as the *standard input device*. The word `input` in a Pascal program specifies the standard input device. The

The keyboard as the standard input device

most common standard input device maintained by a computer system is the keyboard. We will assume from now on that the standard input device is in fact the keyboard.

The program parameter in Program 2.10 contains the words `input` and `output`. `input` tells the operating system that the program will be getting some input from the keyboard, and `output` tells it that the program will be sending some output to the screen.

Readln Statements

The `readln` statement

```
readln (input, Width)
```

has `input` for its file variable and `Width` as a variable identifier. As a file variable, `input` indicates that values will be entered from the keyboard. As a variable identifier, `Width` will receive the value entered. Figure 2.19 shows the execution of `readln`, which is an input statement.

The `readln` statement does two things:

- It makes the computer pause and wait for a response from the keyboard.
- It gives the variable the value typed at the keyboard.

The first `write` statement is a prompt that asks the user to type some input. The `readln` stops execution momentarily, so the user can enter the value. After typing the value the user must press the return key to make the program continue its execution.

Table 2.3 is a trace of Program 2.10. A significant difference between reading and writing illustrated by the trace is that writing does not change the value of a variable, but reading does. In contrast to Program 2.7, the values 3.6 and 12.4 are not in the program listing. This same program will execute for different values entered at execution time and, therefore, is more general.

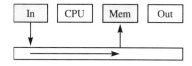

Figure 2.19

The execution of `readln`. It is an input statement.

Changing the value of a variable with a read statement

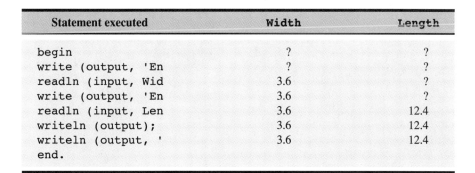

Statement executed	Width	Length
begin	?	?
write (output, 'En	?	?
readln (input, Wid	3.6	?
write (output, 'En	3.6	?
readln (input, Len	3.6	12.4
writeln (output);	3.6	12.4
writeln (output, '	3.6	12.4
end.		

Table 2.3

A trace of Program 2.10.

Figure 2.20 is the syntax chart for a `readln` statement. It is similar to the syntax chart for a `writeln` statement, except that in a `readln` statement a variable identifier follows the file parameter, while in a `writeln` statement a write parameter follows the file parameter (Figure 2.7).

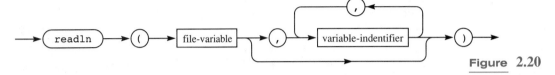

Figure 2.20

The syntax chart for a `readln` call.

2.4 Character Input/Output

The most common application when computers were first invented was the solution of numerical problems. Eventually, people realized that computers could solve nonnumeric problems as well.

Program 2.11

Variables of type `real` or `integer` are numeric, while variables of type `char`, which means *character,* are nonnumeric. Program 2.11 illustrates how to input and output character values.

```
program Echo (input, output);
   var
      Char1: char;
      Char2: char;
      Char3: char;
   begin
   write (output, 'Please type three characters: ');
   readln (input, Char1, Char2, Char3);
   writeln (output, 'The characters were ', Char1, Char2, Char3)
   end.
```

Program 2.11

Input and output of values with type `char`.

Interactive Input/Output

Please type three characters: Joy
The characters were Joy

Interactive Input/Output

Please type three characters: %/$
The characters were %/$

Interactive Input/Output

Please type three characters: 7.6
The characters were 7.6

Table 2.4 is a trace of Program 2.11 for the first sample execution. `Char1`, a variable of type `char`, gets the value 'J' from the keyboard. The table shows the value enclosed in quotation marks, although the user does not type the value in apostrophes during program execution.

Statement executed	Char1	Char2	Char3
`begin`	?	?	?
`write (output, 'Pl`	?	?	?
`readln (input, Cha`	'J '	'o'	'y'
`writeln (output, '`	'J '	'o'	'y'
`end.`			

Table 2.4

A trace of Program 2.11.

Every computer system has its own character set, a set of values that variables of type `char` can get. The character set may vary somewhat from one computer to the next, but it always includes the uppercase and lowercase letters, digits, and common punctuation characters. The second sample execution shows that symbols other than letters are in the character set. In this sample execution, `Char1` gets the value '%'.

Character sets

The third time the program was executed the user typed `7.6`. Each variable got the following values:

Char1	Char2	Char3
'7'	'.'	'6'

Note that `Char1` has type `char` and value '7'. It does not have type `integer` with value 7, which would be a different situation altogether.

One reason for enclosing the values of character variables in quotation marks in a trace table is to distinguish them from integer values. Furthermore, in a Pascal program, a character value is a single character enclosed in apostrophes. In that respect, character values look like strings, except that they can have only one character between the apostrophes.

Example 2.11 If `Ch` is a variable of type `char` then the statement

```
Ch := 'y'
```

gives the value 'y' to the variable `Ch`. ∎

Example 2.12   The statement

```
Ch := 'yes'
```

is illegal if `Ch` is of type `char`, because the value has more than one character between the apostrophes.   ■

SUMMARY

Pascal is a Level 6 language designed by Niklaus Wirth for teaching programming as a systematic discipline. A program written in Pascal must be translated into machine language before it can be executed on a computer. A compiler translates a program in a high-order (Level 6) language into an equivalent program in a language at a lower level.

In interactive input/output (I/O), the input is from the keyboard and the output is to the screen. The Pascal `write` statement is used for output, and the `read` statement is used for input. When you use a procedure, you define a task in a procedure declaration part, then invoke or call the procedure when the task needs to be executed.

Every Pascal variable has three attributes: a name, a type, and a value. A variable's name is an identifier determined arbitrarily by the programmer. A variable's type specifies the kind of values it can have. Three Pascal types are `real`, for real numeric values with fractional parts; `integer`, for integer numeric values without a decimal point; and `char`, for single character values. Unlike names and types, the values of variables exist in main memory only during program execution. A trace table is a device that shows how the values of the program variables change in main memory during execution. Two Pascal statements that change the value of a variable are the assignment statement and the `read` statement.

Two kinds of errors are possible when you write a program. If your program has a syntax error, it will not compile. If it has a logical error, it compiles but produces incorrect results. Syntax charts show the syntax rules of the Pascal language.

EXERCISES

Section 2.2

*1. State whether each of the following Pascal identifiers is valid. For those that are not valid, explain why they are not.

(a) `HourlyWage`   (b) `Last 1`   (c) `Function`
(d) `One Name`   (e) `1stOne`   (f) `%Profit`
(g) `Acme-Tool`   (h) `A`

2. State whether each of the following Pascal identifiers is valid. For those that are not valid, explain why they are not.

(a) `AmountOnHand`   (b) `2Day`
(c) `SuperCallifragillistic`   (d) `Procedure`
(e) `Soc-Sec-Num`   (f) `John Smith`
(g) `Tools/Bolts`   (h) `I`

*3. Find all the syntax errors in the following Pascal program.

```
program Wrong; (output)
   begin
   writeln (output, 'Is this wrong?');
   writeln (output, 'Maybe it's right')
   end.
```

4. Find all the syntax errors in the following Pascal program.

```
program WrongAgain (output);
   begin
   writeln (output, 'This can''t be wrong!')
   writeln (output, 'Or can it')
   end
```

*5. Predict the output of the following Pascal program.

```
program Crazy (output);
   begin
   write (output, 'The company''s name is ');
   writeln (output, 'Gigantic Ant Control. ');
   writeln (output, 'Their business is ');
   write (output, 'controlling ants.')
   end.
```

6. Predict the output of the following Pascal program.

```
program SeriousStuff (output);
   begin
   writeln (output, 'Smith-Jones Company ');
   write (output, '2121 Adam''s Blvd. ');
   writeln (output, 'Los Angeles, CA ');
   write (output, '(213) 342-3987')
   end.
```

*7. Predict the output of the following Pascal program.

```
program Turn (output);

   procedure Warp;
      begin
      writeln (output, 'xoo');
      writeln (output, 'oxo');
      writeln (output, 'oox');
      writeln (output, 'oxo')
      end;

   begin
   Warp;
   Warp
   end.
```

8. Predict the output of the following Pascal program.

```
program Pretty (output);

    procedure Fun;
        begin
        writeln (output, '+++');
        writeln (output, ' +');
        writeln (output, '+++')
        end;

    begin
    Fun;
    Fun;
    Fun
    end.
```

9. Refer back to Figure 2.10, the syntax chart for a block, to answer the following questions: *(a) Can you have more than one variable declaration part in a block? (b) Can
you have more than one procedure declaration part in a block? (c) If you have a type
definition part and a variable declaration part, is it legal to put the variable declaration
part first? (d) If you have a procedure declaration part and a function declaration part,
is it legal to put the function declaration part first?

Section 2.3

*10. A real variable has a value of −396.784 in main memory. What is the output of the val-
ue with each of the following format specifications?

(a) `10: 3`   (b) `10: 2`   (c) `10: 1`
(d) `10: 0`   (e) `8: 1`   (f) `10`

11. A real variable has a value of −487.663 in main memory. What is the output of the value with each of the following format specifications?

(a) `10: 3`   (b) `10: 2`   (c) `10: 1`
(d) `10: 0`   (e) `8: 1`   (f) `10`

PROBLEMS

Section 2.2

12. Write a Pascal program to output the following message on the screen:

```
Hi there.
What's up?
```

13. Write a Pascal program to output to the screen your name and address suitable for use
as a mailing label.

14. Write a Pascal program to output the following pattern on the screen:

```
   *
  ***
 *****
*******
```

15. Write a Pascal program to output the following pattern on the screen:

```
*******
* 0  0 *
*   -   *
*******
```

16. Using a procedure, write a Pascal program to output the following pattern on the screen:

```
   *
  ***
 *****
*******
   *
  ***
 *****
*******
   *
  ***
 *****
*******
```

17. Using a procedure, write a Pascal program to output the following pattern on the screen:

```
*******
* 0  0 *
*   -   *
*******
*******
* 0  0 *
*   -   *
*******
```

Section 2.3

18. Write a program to input an integer and a real value that represent the number of Frisbees purchased and the price of each. Output the values read as shown.

Sample Input/Output

```
How many Frisbees do you want to buy? 3
How much does each cost? 4.75

That is 3 Frisbees at 4.75 each.
```

19. Write a program to input a real value and output it to one place past the decimal point with proper rounding. Output the value read as shown.

Sample Input/Output

```
Please enter a real number: 47.2816

Value to the nearest tenth: 47.3
```

20. Write a program to input a real value and output it in scientific notation with two places past the decimal point. Output the value as shown.

Sample Input/Output

```
Please enter a real number: 47.2816

In scientific notation that is:  4.73e+01
```

Section 2.4

21. Write a program that asks the user to input a single character, and then echoes it twice on the next line.

Sample Input/Output

```
Enter a character: R
RR
```

22. Write a program that asks the user to input two characters on the same line, then echoes them in reverse order on the next line.

Sample Input/Output

```
Enter two characters: up
pu
```

23. Write a program that asks the user to input a three-letter name and then outputs a nice message with that name in it.

Sample Input/Output

```
What is your name? Bob
Hello, Bob.  How are you today?
```

Chapter

3

Selection

Some problems can be solved by a fixed computation. For example, to compute the area of a rectangle you always multiply the length by the width. Many problems, however, cannot be solved by a fixed computation. For instance, some businesses sell their products at a price that depends on the quantity of the order. They charge a lower price per ball for an order of 200 golf balls than for an order of 10 golf balls. A program to calculate the total dollar amount of an order cannot simply multiply the quantity by a fixed unit price if the unit price itself depends on the quantity.

This chapter describes expressions, which process information with fixed computations, and `if` statements, which allow for the selection of different computations within a program.

3.1 Expressions

Pascal expressions are similar to the mathematical expressions that you learned in algebra, but they have one important difference. Algebra usually makes no distinction between expressions for real values and expressions for integer values. However, since computers store integer values and real values with different binary codes, Pascal makes an important distinction between real and integer expressions.

Furthermore, nonnumeric expressions are just as important in programming as numeric expressions. In addition to expressions of type `real` and `integer`, which are numeric, this section presents nonnumeric expressions of type `char` and `boolean`.

Distinction between real and integer expressions

Real Expressions

The four *real operations* in Pascal are addition, subtraction, multiplication, and division, indicated symbolically by +, −, *, and / as summarized in Table 3.1. They have the same precedence you are familiar with from algebra. The operators * and / have a higher precedence than + and −. When parentheses are present in the expression, the contents of the parentheses are evaluated first.

Operator	Meaning
+	Addition
−	Subtraction
*	Multiplication
/	Division

Table 3.1

The real operators.

67

Example **3.1** Two examples of expressions and their evaluations without parentheses are

```
4.0 * 5.5 + 6.0        4.0 + 5.5 * 6.0
```
22.0 + 6.0   4.0 + 33.0
28.0   37.0

The multiplication operation is performed first because it has higher precedence than addition. ∎

Example **3.2** An example with parentheses is

```
4.0 * (5.5 + 6.0)
```
4.0×11.5
46.0

The addition is performed before the multiplication because the addition is within parentheses. ∎

If two operators of the same precedence are adjacent, the evaluation is done from left to right.

The left-to-right rule

Example **3.3** Two examples of the left-to-right rule are

```
11.5 - 3.0 - 4.5        25.0 / 10.0 / 5.0
```
8.5 − 4.5   2.5 / 5.0
4.0   0.5

Notice the difference that this rule makes in the second example. If you first divide 10.0 by 5.0 to get 2.0, and then divide 25.0 by 2.0, you get 12.5, which is quite different from the correct value of 0.5. ∎

Program 3.1

Program 3.1 shows how to use a real expression in a Pascal program. The program prompts the user for the values of the width and length of a rectangle. It then computes the area and perimeter of the rectangle and outputs them on the screen.

Table 3.2 is a trace of Program 3.1. The first assignment statement gives the product of `Width` and `Length` to `Area`. The second assignment statement computes the perimeter of the rectangle and gives it to `Perim`. As you recall from Figure 2.15, an expression must be on the right side of the assignment operator. Accordingly, this program has real expressions on the right of the assignment operators.

```
program Rectangle2 (input, output);
   var
      Width:  real;
      Length: real;
      Area:   real;
      Perim:  real;
   begin
   write (output, 'Enter width: ');
   readln (input, Width);
   write (output, 'Enter length: ');
   readln (input, Length);
   Area := Width * Length;
   Perim := 2.0 * (Width + Length);
   writeln (output);
   writeln (output, 'Area = ', Area: 4: 2);
   writeln (output, 'Perimeter = ', Perim: 4: 2)
   end.
```

Program 3.1

Real expressions on the right side
of assignment statements.

Interactive Input/Output

```
Enter width: 3.6
Enter length: 12.4

Area = 44.64
Perimeter = 32.00
```

The `writeln` statements output the results of the computations. Figure 2.7
showed that a write parameter must go between the parentheses of a `writeln`
call. The `writeln` statement

```
writeln (output, 'Area = ', Area: 4: 2)
```

Statement executed	Width	Length	Area	Perim
begin	?	?	?	?
write (output, 'En	?	?	?	?
readln (input, Wid	3.6	?	?	?
write (output, 'En	3.6	?	?	?
readln (input, Len	3.6	12.4	?	?
Area := Width * Le	3.6	12.4	44.64	?
Perim := 2.0 * (Wi	3.6	12.4	44.64	32.0
writeln (output);	3.6	12.4	44.64	32.0
writeln (output, '	3.6	12.4	44.64	32.0
writeln (output, '	3.6	12.4	44.64	32.0
end.				

Table 3.2

A trace of Program 3.1.

has two write parameters, namely `'Area = '` and `Area: 4: 2`. The first write parameter is a string, and the second is a variable with a format specification. In Pascal, the write parameter can be an expression.

Example 3.4 You could omit the variable `Area` in Program 3.1 and simply output the following expression directly:

```
writeln (output, 'Area = ', Width * Length: 4: 2)
```

Operator	Meaning
+	Addition
−	Subtraction
*	Multiplication
div	Division
mod	Modulo

Table 3.3

The integer operators.

Integer Expressions

Integer values, which do not have fractional parts, are used for counting whole objects. For example, if you need to keep track of the number of employees who work for your company, you could have a variable, `NumEmpl`, of type `integer` whose value represents the number of workers the company has. `NumEmpl` could never have a value like 234.6, since you cannot have 0.6 of an employee.

Addition, subtraction, and multiplication for integer values are similar to the same operations for real values, but division is different. In *integer division,* denoted by the operator `div`, a fractional part cannot be included in the result. Instead, the fractional part is discarded, or truncated.

Example 3.5 The real expression `14.0 / 3.0` evaluates to 4.667, but the integer expression `14 div 3` evaluates to 4.

Another integer operator related to integer division is the `mod` operator. `mod` stands for *modulus,* which is the remainder when you divide one integer by another.

Example 3.6 The expression `14 mod 3` evaluates to 2, since you get a remainder of 2 when you divide 14 by 3.

Table 3.3 summarizes the integer operators, and Table 3.4 shows some evaluations of integer expressions.

Expression	Value
2 + 3 * 4	14
(2 + 3) * 4	20
15 div 3	5
14 div 3	4
13 div 3	4
12 div 3	4
11 div 3	3
12 mod 3	0
11 mod 3	2
10 mod 3	1
9 mod 3	0
8 mod 3	2

Table 3.4

Values for some integer expressions.

Program 3.2

Program 3.2 uses integer expressions to compute the change in dimes, nickels, and pennies for a given number of cents. Integer variables are appropriate for this problem, since you cannot have a fraction of a coin.

```
program Change (input, output);
   var
      Cents:   integer;
      Dimes:   integer;
      Nickels: integer;
      Pennies: integer;
   begin
   write (output, 'How much change do you have? ');
   readln (input, Cents);
   Dimes := Cents div 10;
   Cents := Cents mod 10;
   Nickels := Cents div 5;
   Pennies := Cents mod 5;
   writeln (output);
   writeln (output, 'That is');
   writeln (output, Dimes: 5, ' dimes');
   writeln (output, Nickels: 5, ' nickels');
   writeln (output, Pennies: 5, ' pennies')
   end.
```

Program 3.2

The number of dimes, nickels, and pennies required for a given amount of change. This program illustrates the mod and div operators.

Sample Input/Output

```
How much change do you have? 39

That is
    3 dimes
    1 nickels
    4 pennies
```

Table 3.5 is a trace of Program 3.2. The first assignment statement computes the number of dimes by dividing the amount of change by 10 with the div operator. Notice that div does not round off the value to 4, which would be the incor-

Statement executed	Cents	Dimes	Nickels	Pennies
begin	?	?	?	?
write (output, 'Ho	?	?	?	?
readln (input, Cen	39	?	?	?
Dimes := Cents div	39	3	?	?
Cents := Cents mod	9	3	?	?
Nickels := Cents d	9	3	1	?
Pennies := Cents m	9	3	1	4
writeln (output);	9	3	1	4
writeln (output, '	9	3	1	4
writeln (output, D	9	3	1	4
writeln (output, N	9	3	1	4
writeln (output, P	9	3	1	4
end.				

Table 3.5

A trace of Program 3.2.

rect number of dimes for the change. The second assignment statement gives
`Cents` a new value, the remainder of the change after the three dimes have been
accounted for. The values for `Nickels` and `Pennies` are computed similarly.

When writing a trace table by hand, it is convenient to omit the statements that
cause the values in the trace table to change. When a value is assigned to a variable, you should cross out the old value lightly. Figure 3.1 shows a handwritten
trace of Program 3.2. You should observe the following two rules when making a
trace table by hand:

- Begin every variable with an undefined value denoted by '?'.
- Cross out a value when an assignment is made.

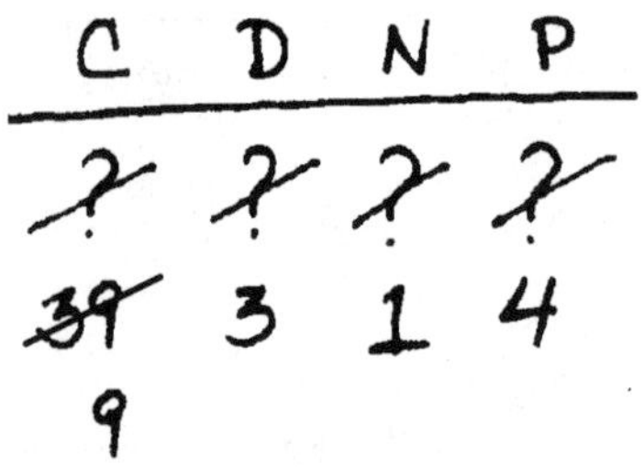

Figure 3.1

A handwritten trace of Program
3.2. You do not need to show the
statements causing the change.

Mixed Expressions

Pascal permits you to use integer values in real expressions, though it does not permit you to use real values in integer expressions. This feature is another example
of automatic conversion from integer to real values, as described in the discussion
of Program 2.9. When you use an integer value in a real expression, the compiler
converts it to the equivalent real value before translating the expression to machine
language.

Example 3.7 Suppose `Dollars` is a real variable and `Cents` is an integer
variable. The assignment

```
Dollars := Dollars + Cents / 100.0
```

is legal even though `Dollars` and `100.0`, which are real, are in the same expression as `Cents`, which is integer. Since the division operator is `/`, not `div`, the
compiler expects both operands to be real. Though the 100.0 operand is already
real, the `Cents` operand is integer, so the compiler converts it to real. Then the
addition takes place between the two real operands. ∎

*Automatic conversion from integer
to real values*

Example 3.8 The expression

```
Dollars mod 100
```

would be illegal if `Dollars` is a real variable, since `mod` expects its operands to
be integers. There is no automatic conversion from real to integer, only from integer to real. ∎

These ideas may be a little confusing at first because the symbols for addition,
subtraction, and multiplication are the same for real expressions as they are for
integer expressions. (However, the symbols for division are different.) Whether an
expression with +, −, or * is an integer expression or a real expression depends on
its operands. If one or both of its operands is real, the result is real. If both
operands are integers, the result is integer. Table 3.6 summarizes the types of
results for the arithmetic operations.

Table 3.6

Types of results for the arithmetic operations.

Operator	Operation	Type of operands	Type of result
+	Addition	Both integer	Integer
		At least one real	Real
–	Subtraction	Both integer	Integer
		At least one real	Real
*	Multiplication	Both integer	Integer
		At least one real	Real
/	Real division	Integers or reals	Real
div	Integer division	Integers	Integer
mod	Modulus	Integers	Integer

Example 3.9   Here are two examples of legal mixed expressions:

```
14.0 / (12 div 5)      98 / 3
14.0 / 2               98.0 / 3.0
14.0 / 2.0             32.667
7.0
```

In each example, Pascal recognizes that / is a real operator and converts the operands to real values if necessary. ∎

If you ever have a real value that you need to use in an integer expression, Pascal provides two type-transfer functions—`trunc`, which stands for truncate, and `round`, which stands for round off.

The trunc and round functions

Example 3.10   If `Dollars` is a real variable and `Bills` is an integer variable, then

```
Bills := trunc (Dollars)
```

truncates the value of `Dollars`, converts it to an integer, and assigns it to `Bills`. If `Dollars` has the value 4.95, then `Bills` gets 4. ∎

Example 3.11   The statement

```
Bills := round (Dollars)
```

would give 5 to `Bills` if `Dollars` has the value 4.95. ∎

The quantity in parentheses, `Dollars` in these examples, is called the *parameter* of the function. The concept and the notation of a Pascal function are the same as in mathematics, where $f(x)$ usually means a function of x. If you supply a value for x, the function will return a value for $f(x)$. In Example 3.11, you supply the value of 4.95 for the parameter x, and the function returns the value 5

Function	Meaning	Type of parameter *x*	Type of function
abs (*x*)	Absolute value	Integer or real	Same as *x*
sqr (*x*)	Square	Integer or real	Same as *x*
sqrt (*x*)	Square root	Integer or real	Real
sin (*x*)	Sine	Integer or real	Real
cos (*x*)	Cosine	Integer or real	Real
arctan (*x*)	Arc tangent	Integer or real	Real
exp (*x*)	Exponentiation	Integer or real	Real
ln (*x*)	Natural logarithm	Integer or real	Real

Table 3.7

The arithmetic functions of standard Pascal.

for round (*x*). The transfer functions are of type integer, since that is the type of the value they return. They take real types for their parameters.

Standard Pascal provides the eight arithmetic functions listed in Table 3.7. Table 3.8 shows some examples of their use. The angles of the trigonometric functions are always expressed in radians, not degrees. The exp function raises the base of the natural logarithms, *e*, to the power specified by the parameter.

Loosely speaking, an arithmetic expression is a combination of real values, integer values, variable identifiers, operators, functions, and parentheses. The syntax charts for making a valid expression are a bit involved and will not be given here. However, your experience from mathematics is probably sufficient to recognize an illegal expression.

Example 3.12 The following examples are valid expressions, assuming that A and B are real variables, and I and J are integer variables.

```
A * (B + 4.7)        2 * (3 + 4 * (I + 1))
2.1                  -3.4 * sin (abs (B))
J                    cos (3.1416 / 4.0)                    ∎
```

Function	Value	Type
abs (5)	5	Integer
abs (-5)	5	Integer
abs (-5.0)	5.0	Real
sqr (3)	9	Integer
sqr (3.0)	9.0	Real
sqrt (2)	1.414	Real
sin (3.14)	0.0	Real
exp (0)	1.0	Real
ln (1.0)	0.0	Real

Table 3.8

Some examples of the use of the arithmetic functions.

Example 3.13 An example of an illegal expression is

```
A * ((B + 4.7)
```

since one of the left parentheses does not have a matching right parenthesis. ∎

▮ Character Expressions

Different computers have different *character sets*. A common character set is the American Standard Code for Information Interchange, abbreviated ASCII (pronounced *as-key*). Another one common on IBM mainframes is the Extended Binary Coded Decimal Interchange Code, abbreviated EBCDIC (pronounced *ebseedick*).

Whatever the character set of your computer, every character has some position on the number line. The particular position a given character has on the number line varies from one character set to the next. Figure 3.2 shows part of the number line for the ASCII character set.

Figure 3.2

Part of the number line for the ASCII character set.

Each character in a character set corresponds to a nonnegative integer on the number line. The corresponding integer value of a character is called its *ordinal value*. The *successor* of a character is the character immediately to its right on the number line, and its *predecessor* is the character to its left.

Example 3.14 In the ASCII character set, the ordinal value of the character 'B' is 66. Going the other way, the character value of 58 is ':'. Notice that the decimal digits are part of the character set. For example, the character value of 56 is '8'. ∎

Example 3.15 The successor of 'A' is 'B', and the predecessor of 'A' is '@'. ∎

Pascal provides four ordinal functions to process variables of type `char`. The functions in Table 3.9 assume that `I` is of type `integer` and `Ch` is of type `char`.

Function	Meaning	Type of function
`succ (Ch)`	Successor	`char`
`pred (Ch)`	Predecessor	`char`
`ord (Ch)`	Ordinal value	`integer`
`chr (I)`	Character value	`char`

Table 3.9

The four ordinal functions.

▭ **Program** 3.3

Program 3.3 illustrates some of the ordinal functions. If you run this program on your computer, the values printed for the ordinal values may not be the same as the ones printed here, because the values depend on the particular character set of your computer.

Program 3.3

Illustration of some ordinal functions.

```
program Characters (input, output);
   var
      Letter: char;
   begin
   write (output, 'Please type a letter: ');
   readln (input, Letter);
   writeln (output);
   writeln (output,
   'The following letter is: ', succ (Letter));
   writeln (output,
   'The preceding letter is: ', pred (Letter));
   writeln (output,
   'The letter''s ordinal value is: ', ord (Letter): 1)
   end.
```

Interactive Input/Output

```
Please type a letter: R

The following letter is: S
The preceding letter is: Q
The letter's ordinal value is: 82
```

Interactive Input/Output

```
Please type a letter: g

The following letter is: h
The preceding letter is: f
The letter's ordinal value is: 103
```

■ **Program** **3.4**

Suppose you have a variable of type **char** whose value is a lowercase letter and you want to convert it to the corresponding uppercase letter. You need to shift the value on the number line. In algebra, you shift values to the right by adding and to the left by subtracting. The problem in this case is that you cannot add an integer to a character in Pascal.

Figure 3.3 shows part of the number line for the ASCII character set. The lowercase letters are to the right, and the uppercase letters are to the left. In this situation, the conversion is a four-step process.

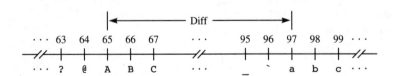

Figure 3.3

The uppercase and lowercase characters on the ASCII number line.

- Find the length of that part of the number line between an uppercase character and its corresponding lowercase character. That is how much you will need to shift the value.
- Find the ordinal value of the lowercase character.
- Shift the ordinal value to the left by subtracting the length calculated in the first step.
- Take the character value of that result.

Program 3.4 converts a character from lowercase to uppercase. The integer variable `Diff` is the length of the number line between an uppercase character and its corresponding lowercase character.

```
program LowerToUpper (input, output);
   var
      Diff:  integer;
      Lower: char;
      Upper: char;
   begin
   write (output, 'Please enter a lowercase letter: ');
   readln (input, Lower);
   Diff := ord ('a') - ord ('A');
   Upper := chr (ord (Lower) - Diff);
   writeln (output, 'The uppercase letter is: ', Upper)
   end.
```

Program 3.4

Conversion of a lowercase letter to an uppercase letter.

Interactive Input/Output

```
Please enter a lowercase letter: j
The uppercase letter is: J
```

Interactive Input/Output

```
Please enter a lowercase letter: b
The uppercase letter is: B
```

Tradeoffs

If your computer uses the ASCII character set, you know that the value of `Diff` will be $97 - 65$, which is 32. You could simply eliminate the variable `Diff` from the program, and compute `Upper` as

```
Upper := chr (ord (Lower) - 32)
```

This approach has two advantages over Program 3.4. It is shorter, because there are fewer variables and fewer executable statements. It also runs faster, because it does not take the time to compute `Diff`.

But Program 3.4 has the advantage of portability. It will run correctly on any computer regardless of the character set. Remember that the placement of a specific character on the number line will vary from one computer to the next. For your computer ord ('A') may be 65, but it could be some other value, such as 193. Therefore, the value computed for Diff may vary from one computer to the next.

Regardless of the specific character set, however, Diff will be consistent within the alphabet. That is, a given computer will have

```
ord ('a') - ord ('A') = ord ('b') - ord ('B')
                      = ord ('c') - ord ('C')
                      = ord ('d') - ord ('D')
```

and so on. For this reason, Program 3.4 works on any computer, regardless of the specific ordinal value of the characters.

Program 3.4 has the advantage of portability, but at the cost of size and speed. In design terminology, this situation is called a *tradeoff*. It occurs when you want two characteristics in your software but you must sacrifice one to obtain the other. The old cliche "You can't have your cake and eat it, too" applies here. In this case you cannot have portability and maximum speed, too. You must trade off one characteristic for the other.

So which program is better—Program 3.4 or the program without Diff in it? It is impossible to make this judgment without knowing how important each characteristic is in a given situation. The importance of the characteristics is determined by considerations external to the program that are relative, not absolute. In one situation, portability may be of paramount importance. In another, speed of execution may be the primary goal.

Good software design requires that you understand your goals before programming a solution to the problem. Since design always permits different solutions to the same problem, it is important that you consider more than one approach. Then you should recognize what tradeoffs are possible and follow the approach that trades the less desirable characteristic for the more desirable one according to your goals.

Generally speaking, people tend to underestimate the importance of portability. Frequently they write software for the particular hardware they have at the time, thinking that they will never need to run it on a different computer system. A number of years later when the hardware needs to be upgraded, they realize that portability should have been a more important goal in the beginning. The algorithms in this textbook were developed with portability as a major goal.

Boolean Expressions

Another Pascal type, which is important in the if statements described in the next section, is the boolean type. *Boolean expressions* always have one of two values, either true or false. The simplest boolean expressions use the *relational operators* of Table 3.10. In mathematics notation, the "less than or equal to" operator is $\leq$. This symbol is not available on most keyboards, so Pascal programs require that you write "less than or equal to" as the two symbols <= without a space between

Operator	Meaning
=	Equal to
<	Less than
<=	Less than or equal to
>	Greater than
>=	Greater than or equal to
<>	Not equal to

Table 3.10

The relational operators.

them. The same idea applies to the "greater than or equal to" operator and the "not equal to" operator.

Example 3.16 An example of a boolean expression is

```
Income > 2400
```

where `Income` is an integer variable. This expression is either true or false, depending on the value of `Income`. If `Income` has the value 2500, the expression is true. If it has the value 2300 or even 2400, the expression is false.   ■

Example 3.17 In contrast to the previous example, the expression

```
Income >= 2400
```

evaluates to true if `Income` has the value 2400.   ■

Variables of type `boolean` are declared in the variable declaration part similarly to the way numeric and character variables are declared. A boolean variable can have one of two values, true or false.

Example 3.18 The following variable declaration part declares `Rich` to be a boolean variable.

```
var
   Rich: boolean;
```

The assignment statement

```
Rich := (Income > 2400)
```

gives `Rich` the value true if `Income` has value greater than 2400, and gives the value false otherwise.   ■

The relational operators can compare expressions of type `char` as well as real and integer values. Characters to the right on the number line of the character set are greater than characters on the left. All character sets, regardless of the computer, have the characters in proper alphabetical order.

Example 3.19 Suppose that `Ch` is a variable of type `char` that has value 'k'. The boolean expression

```
Ch < 'j'
```

is a legal Pascal expression whose value is false, because 'k' lies to the right of 'j' on the number line of the character set.   ■

The `odd` function is a built-in Pascal function that takes an integer parameter and returns true if the value of the integer is odd. There is no corresponding even function.

The odd function

Example *3.20* Suppose that I is a variable of type `integer` that has the value 14. Then the boolean expression

`odd (I)`

has the value false, and the expression

`odd (I + 1)`

has the value true.   ∎

Boolean expressions may contain the AND operator. Suppose *p* is the statement "The sky is green," which is obviously false, and *q* is the statement "Computer science is fun," which is obviously true. Then, *p* AND *q* is the statement "The sky is green and computer science is fun," which is false. For the entire statement *p* AND *q* to be true, *p* must be true apart from *q,* and *q* must be true apart from *p.* If either or both are false, then the entire statement is false. Table 3.11, the truth table for the AND operator, summarizes these ideas.

Boolean expressions may also contain the OR operator. With *p* and *q* representing the same statements about the sky and computer science, *p* OR *q* is the statement "The sky is green or computer science is fun." This time, the entire statement is true. *p* OR *q* is true if *p* is true, if *q* is true, or if they are both true. Table 3.12, the truth table for the OR operator, summarizes these ideas.

One other boolean operator is the NOT operator. If *p* is the statement "The sky is green," which is false, then NOT *p* is the statement "The sky is not green," which is true. Table 3.13 is the truth table for the NOT operator.

Example *3.21* Suppose that I is a variable of type `integer` that has the value 8. Then the boolean expression

`not odd (I)`

has the value true.   ∎

Sometimes it is possible to simplify a boolean expression that contains the NOT operator with a relational operator.

Example *3.22* The boolean expression

`not (NumSides > 8)`

first evaluates the boolean expression (`NumSides > 8`). If `NumSides` has the value 10, then (`NumSides > 8`) is true, and not (`NumSides > 8`) is false. A simpler way to write an equivalent boolean expression is

`NumSides <= 8`

Suppose again that `NumSides` has the value 10. Then `NumSides <= 8` is false, as it was in the previous expression. The two boolean expressions are the same regardless of the value of `NumSides`.   ∎

p	*q*	*p* AND *q*
true	true	true
true	false	false
false	true	false
false	false	false

Table *3.11*

The truth table for the AND operator.

p	*q*	*p* OR *q*
true	true	true
true	false	true
false	true	true
false	false	false

Table *3.12*

The truth table for the OR operator.

p	NOT *p*
true	false
false	true

Table *3.13*

The truth table for the NOT operator.

This example demonstrates that the <= operator is the inverse of the > operator. Table 3.14 shows the relational operators and their inverses.

Example 3.23 You could write the expression

```
not (NumTrials = MaxTrials)
```

more simply as

```
NumTrials <> MaxTrials
```

since the <> operator is the inverse of the = operator. ∎

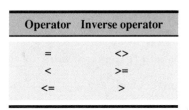

Operator	Inverse operator
=	<>
<	>=
<=	>

Table 3.14

The inverses of the relational operators.

A common mistake you should avoid is putting the NOT operator next to a relational operator. A relational operator must be placed between two integers, reals, or characters and cannot be next to a NOT.

A common mistake in boolean expressions

Example 3.24 The compiler will not accept the expression

```
NumTrials not = MaxTrials
```

because the equals operator cannot have the NOT operator to its left. ∎

Another error you should avoid is combining two relational operators with one variable, as is frequently done in mathematics. The mathematical expression

$$5 \le n < 10$$

means that n is greater than or equal to 5 and less than 10. Such expressions are common in mathematics. However, they are illegal in Pascal.

Example 3.25 To test if the variable NumTrials is greater than or equal to 5 and less than 10, you may be tempted to write the boolean expression as

```
5 <= NumTrials < 10
```

This expression is illegal, since the same operand, NumTrials, is used by both operators. You should write it with the AND operator as follows:

```
(5 <= NumTrials) and (NumTrials < 10)
```

If NumTrials has the value 6, this boolean expression evaluates to true AND true, which is true. ∎

Two other rules, known as *De Morgan's laws*, can sometimes help to simplify boolean expressions. Suppose that p and q are boolean expressions. De Morgan's laws are

De Morgan's laws

NOT (p OR q) = (NOT p) AND (NOT q)
NOT (p AND q) = (NOT p) OR (NOT q)

Example 3.26   As an example of the first of De Morgan's laws, you can write the boolean expression

```
not ((Slope >= 1.0) or (Length <= 0.0))
```

more simply as

```
(Slope < 1.0) and (Length > 0.0)
```

because < is the inverse of >=, and > is the inverse of <=.   ■

How can we prove that De Morgan's laws are true? The simplest way is to look at the expressions in De Morgan's laws for all possible combinations of *p* and *q* in a table. To prove the first of De Morgan's laws

NOT (*p* OR *q*) = (NOT *p*) AND (NOT *q*)

construct Table 3.15, which tabulates the boolean expression NOT (*p* OR *q*) for all possible combinations of *p* and *q*. Then construct Table 3.16, which tabulates the boolean expression (NOT *p*) AND (NOT *q*) for all possible combinations of *p* and *q*. The fact that these two tabulations are the same proves the first of De Morgan's laws.

p	*q*	(*p* OR *q*)	NOT (*p* OR *q*)
true	true	true	false
true	false	true	false
false	true	true	false
false	false	false	true

Table 3.15

A table of NOT (*p* OR *q*) for all possible combinations of *p* and *q*.

p	*q*	(NOT *p*)	(NOT *q*)	(NOT *p*) AND (NOT *q*)
true	true	false	false	false
true	false	false	true	false
false	true	true	false	false
false	false	true	true	true

Table 3.16

A table of (NOT *p*) AND (NOT *q*) for all possible combinations of *p* and *q*. The last column of this table is the same as the last column of Table 3.15, which proves the first of De Morgan's laws.

When the Pascal compiler encounters a boolean expression in your program, it gives the NOT operator the highest precedence, the AND operator the next highest precedence, and the OR operator the lowest precedence of the three. Table 3.17 summarizes these precedence rules and also compares the precedence of the boolean operators to the relational and arithmetic operators.

Example 3.27 The Pascal compiler interprets the boolean expression `not P and Q` as (NOT *p*) AND *q* rather than NOT (*p* AND *q*). ∎

Example 3.28 If `Alpha`, `Beta`, and `Gamma` are integer variables, the boolean expression

`Alpha < Beta and Gamma = 0`

is illegal because the compiler groups `Beta and Gamma` first. The AND operator expects boolean operands, but `Beta` and `Gamma` are integers. You should write the expression as

`(Alpha < Beta) and (Gamma = 0)`

which is now a legal boolean expression. ∎

You can output the value of a boolean expression with a Pascal output statement. But you cannot input a boolean value into a variable from the keyboard.

Example 3.29 The `writeln` statement

`writeln (output, 'Qualified is ', Qualified)`

would produce the output

`Qualified is true`

if `Qualified` is a boolean variable with value true. ∎

Example 3.30 The input statement

`readln (input, Qualified)`

is illegal if `Qualified` is a boolean variable. ∎

Operator	Precedence
`not`	Highest
`and, div, mod, /, *`	____
`or, +, –`	____
`=, <>, <, >, <=, >=`	Lowest

Table 3.17

Precedence of the Pascal operators.

Boolean input/output

3.2 If Statements

`if` statements allow you to solve problems that are not based on fixed computations. The idea is to evaluate a boolean expression, and if that expression is true, perform a computation. The following programs illustrate the `if` statement.

Program 3.5

Program 3.5 solves the problem of computing the wages for an employee who may have worked overtime. Customarily, weekly wages are computed as the hourly rate times the number of hours worked, as long as the employee does not work more

```
program Payroll1 (input, output);
   var
      Hours: real;
      Rate:  real;
      Wages: real;
   begin
   write (output, 'Enter hours worked: ');
   readln (input, Hours);
   write (output, 'Enter hourly rate: ');
   readln (input, Rate);
   Wages := Hours * Rate;
   if Hours > 40.0 then
      Wages := Wages + (Hours - 40.0) * 0.5 * Rate;
   writeln (output);
   writeln (output, 'Total wages are $', Wages: 4: 2)
   end.
```

Interactive Input/Output

```
Enter hours worked: 35
Enter hourly rate: 10


Total wages are $350.00
```

Interactive Input/Output

```
Enter hours worked: 50
Enter hourly rate: 10


Total wages are $550.00
```

Program 3.5

A payroll calculation program. This program uses an **if** statement without an **else** part.

than 40 hours. If the employee works more than 40 hours, then the number of hours in excess of 40 are paid at time and a half. That is, the hourly rate for those hours beyond 40 is 1.5 times the normal rate.

Table 3.18 is a trace of this program when the input is 35 for the hours worked and 10 for the hourly rate. The readln statements get the values for Hours and Rate from the keyboard. The assignment statement computes Wages as the product of Hours and Rate assuming no overtime.

The words if and then are Pascal reserved words. When an if statement executes, it first evaluates the boolean expression following the reserved word if. If the boolean expression is true, then it executes the statement following the reserved word then. Otherwise, it skips the statement following the reserved word then.

In this program, after Wages is computed as Hours * Rate, the if statement evaluates the boolean expression

```
Hours > 40.0
```

which is false, since 35.0 is not greater than 40.0. So the assignment statement fol-

Statement executed	Hours	Rate	Wages
begin	?	?	?
write (output, 'En	?	?	?
readln (input, Hou	35.0	?	?
write (output, 'En	35.0	?	?
readln (input, Rat	35.0	10.0	?
Wages := Hours * R	35.0	10.0	350.00
if Hours > 40.0 th	35.0	10.0	350.00
writeln (output);	35.0	10.0	350.00
writeln (output, '	35.0	10.0	350.00
end.			

Table 3.18

A trace of Program 3.5 when the body of the if statement is not executed.

lowing the `if` statement is not executed. Instead, it is skipped, and `Wages` maintains its value of 350.00.

Table 3.19 is a trace of Program 3.5 when the input is 50 for the hours worked and 10 for the hourly rate. This time, when `Wages` is computed as `Hours * Rate` it gets the value 500.00. This value is not yet correct because the 10 hours beyond 40 were computed at straight time, not time and a half. Now the boolean expression

```
Hours > 40.0
```

is true since the value of `Hours` is 50. So the assignment statement following the `if` statement

```
Wages := Wages + (Hours - 40.0) * 0.5 * Rate
```

executes. The value of `Wages` is increased to reflect the extra amount (at half time) earned in overtime.

Statement executed	Hours	Rate	Wages
begin	?	?	?
write (output, 'En	?	?	?
readln (input, Hou	50.0	?	?
write (output, 'En	50.0	?	?
readln (input, Rat	50.0	10.0	?
Wages := Hours * R	50.0	10.0	500.00
if Hours > 40.0 th	50.0	10.0	500.00
Wages := Wages + (	50.0	10.0	550.00
writeln (output);	50.0	10.0	550.00
writeln (output, '	50.0	10.0	550.00
end.			

Table 3.19

A trace of Program 3.5 when the body of the if statement is executed.

Figure 3.4 is the syntax chart for an `if` statement. You can see from the chart that there are two kinds of `if` statements—one with an `else` part and one without an `else` part. The `if` statement in Program 3.5 does not have an `else` part.

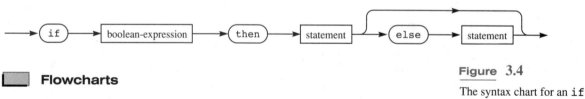

Figure 3.4

The syntax chart for an `if` statement.

▮ Flowcharts

You can visualize the action of an `if` statement with a *flowchart*. Figure 3.5 shows some of the more common flowchart symbols. The start symbol corresponds to the reserved word `begin`, which starts the executable statements of a Pascal program. The stop symbol, which is the same shape as the start symbol, corresponds to the reserved word `end`. The parallelogram corresponds to input or output statements, the Pascal `read` and `write` statements. Rectangles correspond to processing, performed by the assignment statement in Pascal. The hexagon is a symbol that indicates the test of some condition. It is used in several Pascal statements, including the `if` statement. The half ellipses are the symbols for the Pascal `case` statement, another selection statement discussed later in this chapter. The small circle is the collector symbol for joining lines from other flowchart symbols.

Figure 3.5

The flowchart symbols.

Figure 3.6 is the flowchart for an `if` statement without an `else` part. The incoming arrow from the top points to the test condition box, which represents the boolean expression of the `if` statement. If the boolean expression is true, control branches to the left to the processing box, which represents the statement after the reserved word `then`. If the boolean expression is false, control branches to the right, skipping execution of the statement after the reserved word `then`. The two branches of the `if` statement join at the collector symbol. Figure 3.7 is Program 3.5 in flowchart form.

Flowcharts are useful for visualizing the logic of a program. They used to be considered helpful in software design, but have fallen out of favor recently for several reasons. Flowcharts are fine for small programs but they require huge pages of paper for large programs. They also require artwork and are consequently more difficult to modify than the programs they represent.

This book presents flowcharts to help you visualize the behavior of some Pascal statements. As you gain experience writing Pascal programs, however, you will not need to rely on flowcharts to design your software.

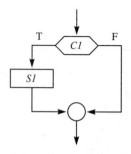

Figure 3.6

The flowchart for an `if` statement without an `else` part. T stands for true, and F stands for false. C1 is a boolean expression and S1 is a statement.

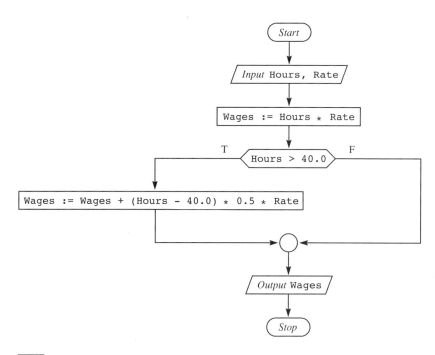

Figure 3.7

The flowchart for Program 3.5.

Program 3.6

Program 3.6 presents a different way to compute the wage correctly. Its output is identical to the output of Program 3.5.

```
program Payroll2 (input, output);
   var
      Hours: real;
      Rate:  real;
      Wages: real;
   begin
   write (output, 'Enter hours worked: ');
   readln (input, Hours);
   write (output, 'Enter hourly rate: ');
   readln (input, Rate);
   if Hours <= 40.0 then
      Wages := Hours * Rate
   else
      Wages := 40.0 * Rate + (Hours - 40.0) * 1.5 * Rate;
   writeln (output);
   writeln (output, 'Total wages are $', Wages: 7: 2)
   end.
```

Program 3.6

A payroll calculation program that uses an `if` statement with an `else` part. It performs the same processing as Program 3.5.

Interactive Input/Output

Identical to Program 3.5

The program uses an `if` statement with an `else` part. If the boolean expression in the `if` statement is true, the `then` part

```
Wages := Hours * Rate
```

executes. After it executes, the statement after the reserved word `else`

```
Wages := 40.0 * Rate + (Hours - 40.0) * 1.5 * Rate
```

is skipped.

If, on the other hand, the boolean expression in the `if` statement is false, the `then` part is skipped, and the `else` part executes. The effect of the `if` statement is to select one of the two statements to execute.

There is no semicolon after the statement following the reserved word `then`. You can see in Figure 3.4 that there are no semicolons in the syntax chart for an `if` statement. Then why is there a semicolon after the statement following the reserved word `else`? That semicolon is there to separate the entire `if` statement from the following `writeln` statement as Figure 2.11 showed. We now have two general rules for placing semicolons:

- Do not place a semicolon before an `end`.
- Do not place a semicolon before an `else`.

Figure 3.8 shows the flowchart for an `if` statement with an `else` part. It is similar to the flowchart for an `if` statement without an `else` part in two respects. Both flowcharts have exactly one collector, and both have exactly one arrow coming in at the top and one arrow going out at the bottom.

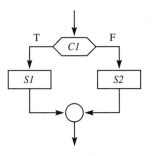

Figure 3.8

The flowchart for an `if` statement with an `else` part.

Rules for semicolons

 ## Program 3.7

Program 3.7 determines whether a customer qualifies for a 15% airline discount. If the customer qualifies, it computes the discounted fare. Otherwise, it states that the customer does not qualify. A customer qualifies by having made more than 10 flights during the previous 12 months and being 18 years of age or older. The program illustrates the constant definition part and the compound statement as an alternative of an `if` statement.

 ## Constant Definition Part

Figure 2.10, the syntax chart for a block, showed that if there is a constant definition part, it must be before the variable declaration part. The *constant definition part* is similar to the variable declaration part, except that an equal sign follows the identifier instead of a colon. Another difference is that in the variable declaration part a type is associated with each identifier, while in the constant definition part a value is associated with each identifier. Figure 3.9 is the syntax chart for the constant definition part.

```
program FlightDiscount (input, output);
   const
      Discount    = 0.15;
      FlightLimit = 10;
   var
      Fare:       real;
      NumFlights: integer;
      Response:   char;
      Qualified:  boolean;
   begin
   write (output, 'Amount of fare: ');
   readln (input, Fare);
   write (output, 'Number of flights in previous twelve months: ');
   readln (input, NumFlights);
   write (output, 'Are you 18 years of age or older? (y or n): ');
   readln (input, Response);
   writeln (output);
   Qualified := (NumFlights > FlightLimit) and (Response = 'y');
   if Qualified then
      begin
      writeln (output, 'You qualify for discount.');
      writeln (output, 'Fare: $', (1.00 - Discount) * Fare: 4: 2)
      end
   else
      writeln (output, 'You do not qualify for discount.')
   end.
```

Program 3.7

A program to compute a discount on an airline ticket.

Interactive Input/Output

```
Amount of fare: 200
Number of flights in previous twelve months: 13
Are you 18 years of age or older? (y or n): y

You qualify for discount.
Fare: $170.00
```

Interactive Input/Output

```
Amount of fare: 200
Number of flights in previous twelve months: 13
Are you 18 years of age or older? (y or n): n

You do not qualify for discount.
```

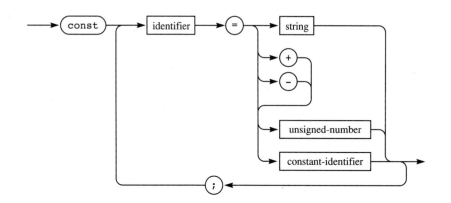

Figure 3.9

The syntax chart for the constant definition part.

Constants are similar to variables in that you refer to them by their names, which are Pascal identifiers. However, you cannot change the value of a constant the way you can the value of a variable.

Example **3.31**   The assignment statement

```
Discount := 0.20
```

would be illegal in this program, because `Discount` is a constant.   ∎

Program 3.7 defines the identifier `Discount` to be the constant 0.15 and `FlightLimit` to be 10. The program would produce exactly the same result without the constant definition part and with the expression for `Qualified` changed from

```
(NumFlights > FlightLimit) and (Response = 'y')
```

to

```
(NumFlights > 10) and (Response = 'y')
```

and the `writeln` statement changed from

```
writeln (output, 'Fare: $', (1.00 - Discount) * Fare: 4: 2)
```

to

```
writeln (output, 'Fare: $', 0.85 * Fare: 4: 2)
```

So, what is the advantage of a constant definition part? One advantage is the ease with which you can modify the program. This program is short, and it is easy to locate the `writeln` call where it computes the discount. If you wanted to modify the program to change the discount to 20% instead of 15%, you could find the `writeln` statement with your text editor and change the `0.85` to `0.80`. But in a

The advantage of constant definitions

large program, the statement that performs the computation may be difficult to locate. Also, more than one computation may need to be modified to make one change.

For example, suppose you write a big tax computation program in which a tax rate for both businesses and individuals is 20%. These rates are used in many different computations. You do not use a constant definition part, so that the value 0.20 is scattered in various expressions throughout the program. Now suppose that a new tax law changes the rate for businesses to 30% but leaves the rate for individuals unchanged. To modify the program you cannot simply use your text editor to change every occurrence of 0.20 to 0.30, since that would change the rate for individuals as well.

On the other hand, suppose you write the program with a constant definition part that defines

```
const
   BusRate = 0.20;
   IndRate = 0.20;
```

and use these identifiers in the appropriate expressions in the program. Then, if the tax law changes the business rate to 30% you only need to change one value at the beginning of the program to modify it correctly.

Another advantage of constants is the increased readability that identifiers provide. In this program, the expression

```
(1.00 - Discount) * Fare
```

represents the meaning of the computation better than the expression

```
0.85 * Fare
```

The presence of identifier `Discount` tells the reader explicitly that a discounted fare is being computed.

Compound Statements

The syntax chart for an `if` statement, Figure 3.4, showed that a single statement follows the reserved word `then`. If you want more than one statement to execute when the boolean expression of the `if` statement is true, you must combine them into a single *compound statement*. Program 3.7 combines the two `writeln` statements into a single compound statement. The syntax chart for a compound statement was shown in Figure 2.11.

Table 3.20 is a trace of Program 3.7 that corresponds to the first sample I/O. In this trace, the boolean variable `Qualified` gets the value true. Both parts of the compound statement execute, and the statement in the `else` part is skipped.

Statement executed	Fare	NumFlights	Response	Qualified
begin	?	?	?	?
write (output, 'Amo	?	?	?	?
readln (input, Fare	200.00	?	?	?
write (output, 'Num	200.00	?	?	?
readln (input, NumF	200.00	13	?	?
write (output, 'Are	200.00	13	?	?
readln (input, Resp	200.00	13	'y'	?
writeln (output);	200.00	13	'y'	?
Qualified := (NumF1	200.00	13	'y'	true
if Qualified then	200.00	13	'y'	true
writeln (output, 'Y	200.00	13	'y'	true
writeln (output, 'F	200.00	13	'y'	true
end.				

Table 3.20

A trace of Program 3.7.

▢ Using If Statements

This section concludes by pointing out some aspects of if statements that tend to give beginning programmers problems. Some are style guidelines that have been mentioned previously, while others are unique to if statements.

In the following discussion and throughout the remainder of the book, we will sometimes use the word *code* in a different sense. Previously the word *code* meant the binary sequence at the machine level to store information, as in the Universal Product Code. Another meaning for code is what a programmer writes in a program listing. Coding an algorithm means writing a program in some programming language that will execute the algorithm on a computer. A *code fragment* is a few lines of code from a program listing.

Another definition of code

A common tendency with boolean variables is to use a redundant computation with the equals operator. A boolean variable is a special case of a boolean expression, and so can be used alone as a boolean expression in an if statement.

Example **3.32**   In Program 3.7, you could write the test for the if statement as

```
if Qualified = true then
```

With this test the program still works correctly, because the expression Qualified = true evaluates to true when Qualified has the value true and to false when Qualified has the value false. But this is bad style because it contains a redundant computation. The more straightforward test

```
if Qualified then
```

presented in Program 3.7 is better.   ■

Boolean variables are useful because they allow Pascal `if` statements to be written similar to English phrases whose meaning is close to the effect of the Pascal statement. In the previous example, `if Qualified then` is much like an English phrase. You should name your boolean variables so that the test of an `if` statement corresponds to the way you would phrase the test in English.

Example 3.33 Suppose that `Exempt` is a boolean variable that indicates whether a taxpayer is exempt from a tax. Instead of writing the test

```
if Exempt = false then
```

you should write the equivalent test

```
if not Exempt then
```

since this corresponds more closely to the way you would state the test in English.
■

It is worth repeating a point here that was made in the previous chapter: do not save typing time by choosing extremely short identifiers at the expense of program readability.

Example 3.34 In the previous example, if you choose `E` for the identifier instead of `Exempt`, the test of the `if` statement becomes

```
if not E then
```

which would be more difficult for a human reader to understand.
■

When you design a program with interactive I/O, you should consider the various possibilities for the user's input from the keyboard. One difficult problem occurs when the user enters letters when the computer has requested a numeric value. For example, in Program 3.7 if the user enters the text `what?` in response to the request for the fare, the program will terminate immediately with an error message, because the computer expects digits instead of letters. This premature termination of a program is called a *crash*.

Another input problem occurs when the user inputs an uppercase letter even though the program requests a lowercase letter. In Program 3.7, if the user enters an uppercase 'Y' in response to the question about his age, the program will interpret the response as a no, because an uppercase 'Y' does not equal a lowercase 'y'. To remedy this shortcoming of the program, you could write the computation for qualified as

Definition of a program crash

```
Qualified := (NumFlights > FlightLimit)
           and ((Response = 'y') or (Response = 'Y'))
```

The AND and OR operators must be between two boolean expressions. They cannot be between numeric or character expressions.

Example 3.35   You might be tempted to write the preceding expression for
Qualified as

```
Qualified := (NumFlights > FlightLimit)
             and (Response = ('y' or 'Y'))
```

Even though the last test sounds reasonable when you say it in English (Response
equals 'y' or 'Y'), it is illegal because the OR operator is not between two boolean
expressions.   ∎

   Our last problem area concerns the unnecessary duplication of code. Suppose
you write an `if` statement with an `else` part that has the following form:

```
if Condition 1 then
    begin
    Statement 1;
    Statement 2
    end
else
    begin
    Statement 3;
    Statement 2
    end
```

where Statement 2 is the same statement in both alternatives of the `if` statement.
Condition 1 is a boolean expression. If it is true, Statement 1 executes, followed by
Statement 2. Otherwise, Statement 3 executes, followed by Statement 2. Regardless of whether Condition 1 is true or false, Statement 2 executes. It is simpler
to write

```
if Condition 1 then
    Statement 1
else
    Statement 3;
Statement 2
```

which executes like the previous code but is shorter.

3.3   **Nested If Statements
and Assertions**

Figure 3.8 showed that an `if` statement selects one of two alternative statements,
depending on the value of a boolean expression. Pascal allows either of those alternative statements to contain another `if` statement. An `if` statement contained in
one of the alternatives of another `if` statement is called a *nested* `if`.

Program 3.8

Program 3.8 inputs a salary and calculates an income tax from it. There is no tax at all if the salary is less than or equal to $10,000. Otherwise, the tax is 20% of the salary for a salary of up to $30,000 and 30% if the salary is more than $30,000. The program performs its computation with a nested `if` statement.

After `Salary` gets its input value from the keyboard, the outer `if` statement executes. If its boolean expression,

```
Salary > MinTaxable
```

```
program IncomeTax (input, output);
   const
      LowRate     = 0.20;
      HighRate    = 0.30;
      MinTaxable = 10000.00;
      MaxTaxable = 30000.00;
   var
      Salary: real;
      Tax:    real;
   begin
   write (output, 'Annual salary: ');
   readln (input, Salary);
   if Salary > MinTaxable then
      begin
      if Salary <= MaxTaxable then
         Tax := Salary * LowRate
      else
         Tax := Salary * HighRate;
      writeln (output, 'Your tax is $', Tax: 4: 2)
      end
   else
      writeln (output, 'No tax.')
   end.
```

Program 3.8

An income tax computation with a nested `if` statement.

Interactive Input/Output

```
Annual salary: 50000
Your tax is $15000.00
```

Interactive Input/Output

```
Annual salary: 20000
Your tax is $4000.00
```

Interactive Input/Output

```
Annual salary: 8000
No tax.
```

is false, which it will be if the value of `Salary` is less than or equal to 10,000.00, the compound statement containing the nested `if` statement is skipped, and the "no tax" message is output. If the boolean expression is true, the nested `if` executes, followed by the "tax is" output statement.

Table 3.21 is a trace of Program 3.8 when the salary is 50,000. The boolean expression of the outer `if` is true and the boolean expression of the nested `if` is false. The tax is computed with `HighRate` instead of `LowRate`.

Statement executed	Salary	Tax
begin	?	?
write (output, 'Ann	?	?
readln (input, Sala	50000.00	?
if Salary > MinTaxa	50000.00	?
if Salary <= MaxTax	50000.00	?
Tax := Salary * Hig	50000.00	15000.00
writeln (output, 'Y	50000.00	15000.00
end		

Table 3.21

A trace of Program 3.8 when the input is 50000.00.

Figure 3.10 is the flowchart for Program 3.8. It shows the compound statement nested in the true alternative of the outer `if` statement.

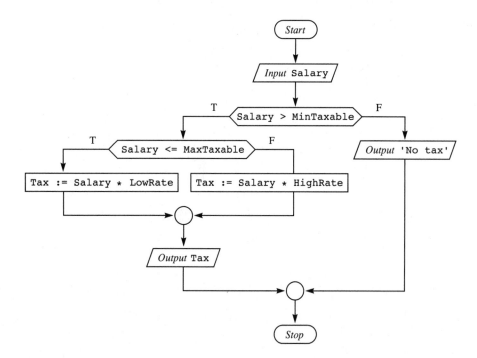

Figure 3.10

The flowchart for Program 3.8.

Program 3.9

The previous program had the nested `if` statement in the true alternative of the outer `if` statement. Program 3.9 has the nested `if` in the false alternative. It computes the letter grade from an integer score according to the traditional 10-point criteria. This means a score of 90 or more is an A, between 80 and 89 is a B, and so on.

```
program TestScore (input, output);
   var
      Score: integer;
   begin
   write (output, 'Enter test score: ');
   readln (input, Score);
   if Score >= 90 then
      writeln (output, 'Grade is A.')
   else
      if Score >= 80 then
         writeln (output, 'Grade is B.')
      else
         if Score >= 70 then
            writeln (output, 'Grade is C.')
         else
            if Score >= 60 then
               writeln (output, 'Grade is D.')
            else
               writeln (output, 'Grade is F.')
   end.
```

Program 3.9

Conversion of an integer test score to a letter grade. This indentation style is consistent with Program 3.8, but is not the preferred style.

Interactive Input/Output

```
Enter test score: 70
Grade is C.
```

Interactive Input/Output

```
Enter test score: 38
Grade is F.
```

You can nest `if` statements to any level. The last `if` statement in this program is nested three levels deep. Each `if` statement is nested in the `else` part of its outer `if` statement.

Suppose the value of `Score` is 93. The boolean expression of the outer `if` statement

```
Score >= 90
```

would be true, and the "Grade of A" message would be output. The `else` part of the outer `if` statement would be skipped. Since the `else` part is a single large nested `if` statement, none of the other boolean expressions is ever tested.

It would be quite appropriate to call Niklaus Wirth the "father of structured programming." In fact, Wirth (pronounced "*Veert*") was so convinced of the need to emphasize better programming style that he developed a programming language built on this principle. That language is Pascal, the high-level programming language emphasized in this book.

Niklaus Wirth teaches at the Eidgenossische Technische Hochschule, a Swiss equivalent of MIT or Cal. Tech., in Zurich, Switzerland. He has had a long and interesting career and is widely recognized as one of the leading contributors to the field of computer science.

Wirth contributed to the development of the ALGOL family of programming languages during the 1960s. ALGOL, an acronym for Algorithmic Language, achieved widespread use in Europe and praise, at least, in North America, and was recognized for its inclusion of higher-level control structures. Before that time, the goto control structure common to early versions of FORTRAN often led to the "spaghetti code" phenomenon—attempting to follow a thread of logic through a program was like trying to discern where a strand of spaghetti led to amidst all the other strands on your plate. ALGOL provided a richer set of language primitives for the programmer, helping to lift programming out of the dark ages of unstructured, monolithic programs and transform it into a more organized, engineering discipline.

The ALGOL-60 language was expanded by a committee (have you ever seen a committee make something smaller?) into the ALGOL-68 standard. Although the underlying concepts from the parent language were still visible, Wirth felt that the direction the committee was taking was inappropriate. ALGOL-68 was a large language, sharing some similarities with its North American counterpart, PL/I. Although applauded by many for their innovative features, both ALGOL and PL/I have been likened by some to the Swiss army knife, which is either a fantastic collection of tools or a dangerous gadget, depending on who is handling the device and upon your definition of a good tool.

In any case, Wirth recognized a need for an elegant instructional language for students of computer science, and he devised Pascal with this in mind. Pascal is a relatively neat and tidy collection of carefully chosen language primitives that

constitutes a powerful programming language, but that also encourages the programmer to adhere to the structured programming principles advocated by Wirth. As a "strongly typed" language, Pascal requires the programmer to declare the categories of variables in advance, and then prohibits nonsensical operations, such as trying to add a number and an alphabetic character. Earlier programming languages often allowed such operations, yielding bizarre program bugs that were difficult to locate and could lead to expensive errors if the program was delivered to a customer as "completed" software.

To push our analogy with the Swiss army knife a bit further, we might say that Pascal is to its predecessors as a 10-gizmo knife is to the 25-gizmo knife; it does just about everything you could possibly want, while reducing the chances that you'll hurt yourself due to unnecessary complexity. Wirth helped to blaze the way for structured programming—Pascal has been adopted as the primary language of introductory instruction at many universities over the last 10 or 12 years.

After devising Pascal, Wirth developed the Modula-2 programming language, an extension of Pascal, which supports even more rigorous software engineering principles. For his efforts in helping to develop the field of computer science, Wirth was awarded the ACM's prestigious A. M. Turing Award in 1984.

Suppose the value of `Score` is 70. The boolean expression of the outer `if` statement would be false, and the `else` part of the outer `if` statement would execute. Now the boolean expression

```
Score >= 80
```

of the second `if` statement would be tested as false. So the `else` part of the second `if` statement would execute. This time, the boolean expression

```
Score >= 70
```

would be true, and the "Grade of C" message would be output. The `else` part of the third `if` statement is skipped. Therefore, the D and F messages are not output.

This pattern of a succession of `if` statements nested in the false alternatives occurs frequently in practice. If the nesting level is deep, our indentation style will cause the statements in the program listing to be placed too far to the right of the page. The following alternative pattern is recommended in this situation:

```
readln (input, Score);
if Score >= 90 then
   writeln (output, 'Grade is A.')
else if Score >= 80 then
   writeln (output, 'Grade is B.')
else if Score >= 70 then
   writeln (output, 'Grade is C.')
else if Score >= 60 then
   writeln (output, 'Grade is D.')
else
   writeln (output, 'Grade is F.')
```

The preferred indentation style of Program 3.9

You can think of `else if` and the last `else` as a list of conditions that starts with the first `if` statement. The boolean expressions in the list are evaluated in order, starting with the first. When a boolean expression is false, the next one in the list is tested. The first boolean expression that tests true causes its alternative to execute and the rest of the `else` alternatives in the list to be skipped.

When using this style of indentation, you must be careful to distinguish between nested `if` statements and sequential `if` statements, which are not nested. The following `if` statements are sequential:

```
readln (input, Score);
if Score >= 90 then
   writeln (output, 'Grade is A.');
if Score >= 80 then
   writeln (output, 'Grade is B.');
if Score >= 70 then
   writeln (output, 'Grade is C.');
if Score >= 60 then
   writeln (output, 'Grade is D.')
else
   writeln (output, 'Grade is F.')
```

Sequential if statements

In this code fragment, suppose that `Score` gets the value 70 from the `readln` statement. The first two boolean expressions would be false and the third one would be true. But after the C message is output, the next `if` statement would execute. Since `Score >= 60` is true, the D message would also be output. The net result would be an output of

```
Grade is C.
Grade is D.
```

Figure 3.11 shows the difference in flow of control between three sequential `if` statements and three `if` statements with nested `else` parts.

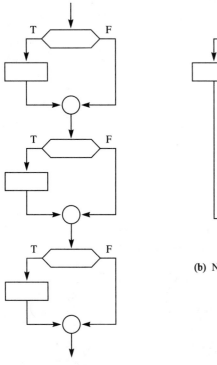

(a) Sequential `if` statements.

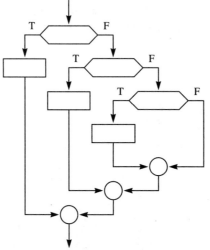

(b) Nested `if` statements.

Figure 3.11

Flowcharts for sequential `if` statements versus nested `if` statements.

Program 3.10

Program 3.10 illustrates a potential problem with nested `if` statements. Notice that the program is not indented which, of course, presents no problem to the compiler. But a human reader of the program may have trouble interpreting its meaning.

```
program DanglingElse (input, output);
   var
      Num: integer;
   begin
   write (output, 'Type an integer: ');
   readln (input, Num);
   if Num > 5 then
   if Num < 10 then
   write (output, 'A')
   else
   write (output, 'B');
   write (output, 'C')
   end.
```

Program 3.10

The dangling else problem. To which `if` statement does the `else` belong?

Interactive Input/Output

```
Type an integer: 12
BC
```

Interactive Input/Output

```
Type an integer: 7
AC
```

Interactive Input/Output

```
Type an integer: 2
C
```

There are two `if` statements but only one `else`. To which `if` does the `else` belong? If it belongs to the first `if` statement, the correct indentation is Possibility (a), which follows. If it belongs to the second `if` statement, the correct indentation is Possibility (b).

Possibility (a)

```
if Num > 5 then
   if Num < 10 then
      write (output, 'A')
else
   write (output, 'B');
write (output, 'C')
```

Possibility (b)

```
if Num > 5 then
   if Num < 10 then
      write (output, 'A')
   else
      write (output, 'B');
write (output, 'C')
```

This is called the "dangling else" problem. The rule in Pascal is that an `else` belongs to the most recent `if` that does not have an `else` clause. Hence, the compiler interprets the program as in (b).

This interpretation is confirmed by the sample I/O. Suppose the compiler interpreted the program according to Possibility (a). If the input were 12, the boolean expression in the outer `if` statement would be true, so the `else` part would be skipped. The boolean expression in the nested `if` statement would also be false, so the output would be C. If the input were 2, the boolean expression in the outer `if` statement would be false, the `else` part would execute, and the output would be BC. The sample I/O, however, shows that the actual output is just the opposite—BC for an input of 12 and C for an input of 2. Can you work out the execution of Possibility (b) to see that this output is to be expected?

Even if you write the indentation as in (a), the compiler will still interpret the program as in (b). The execution of a Pascal program never depends on the indentation style.

Execution does not depend on indentation.

Suppose that you want to write code that behaves as implied by the indentation of Possibility (a). You can make the true alternative of the outer `if` statement a compound statement with a `begin`/`end` pair:

```
if Num > 5 then
   begin
   if Num < 10 then
      write (output, 'A')
   end
else
   write (output, 'B');
write (output, 'C')
```

The compound statement hides the nested `if` statement from the `else`, which now must refer to the outer `if`.

Another way to achieve the same effect is to supply every `if` with an `else` part, even if the `else` alternative does nothing:

```
if Num > 5 then
   if Num < 10 then
      write (output, 'A')
   else
      begin
      end
else
   write (output, 'B');
write (output, 'C')
```

Yet another way is to use the inverse of the outer boolean expression and switch the alternatives:

```
if Num <= 5 then
   write (output, 'B')
else if Num < 10 then
   write (output, 'A');
write (output, 'C')
```

You can see that this code is equivalent to Possibility (a) by working out the execution for inputs 12, 7, and 2.

Assertions

Sometimes it is helpful to write special comments in complex nested if statements to keep track of what is happening at each point in the program. A comment that is particularly helpful in analyzing program logic is an *assertion*. An
assertion is a comment describing a condition that is always true at a given point in
a program.

Definition of an assertion

For example, the following code fragment is the nested if statement of
Program 3.8 with assertions.

```
if Salary > MinTaxable then
   begin
   if Salary <= MaxTaxable then
      { Assert: MinTaxable < Salary <= MaxTaxable }
      Tax := Salary * LowRate
   else
      { Assert: Salary > MaxTaxable }
      Tax := Salary * HighRate;
   writeln (output, 'Your tax is $', Tax: 4: 2)
   end
else
   { Assert: Salary <= MinTaxable }
   writeln (output, 'No tax.')
```

*The nested if statement of Program
3.8 with some assertions*

To see how assertions are formulated, we will begin with the simplest assertion, which can be found just before the statement

```
writeln (output, 'No tax.')
```

What condition must be true at this point in the program? In other words, what
condition must be true for this writeln statement to execute? The boolean
expression of the outer if statement must be false. But if the expression

```
Salary > MinTaxable
```

is false, the expression

```
Salary <= MinTaxable
```

must be true, which is the assertion shown in the code fragment.

The next assertion we will consider is the one just before the statement

```
Tax := Salary * LowRate
```

Why must Salary be greater than MinTaxable and less than or equal to
MaxTaxable at that point in the program? Because to arrive at that point, the
boolean expression of the outer if statement must be true. Then the boolean
expression of the nested if statement also must be true. The assertion

```
{ Assert: MinTaxable < Salary <= MaxTaxable }
```

is simply reflecting those two conditions.

The remaining assertion is just before the statement

```
Tax := Salary * HighRate;
```

To arrive at this point, the boolean expression of the outer `if` statement must be true and the boolean expression of the nested `if` statement must be false. Therefore, to get to this point in the program, `Salary` must satisfy

```
(Salary > MinTaxable) and (Salary > MaxTaxable)
```

So why does the assertion in the code fragment

```
{ Assert: Salary > MaxTaxable }
```

seem to ignore the fact that `Salary` must be greater than `MinTaxable`?

The answer to this question involves the concept of strong versus weak assertions. One assertion is stronger than another if it places greater limits on the possible values of a variable. In general, stronger assertions are more helpful in analysis of logic than weaker ones, because they give you more information. Suppose you ask your teacher for your score on an exam. If she says, "You scored between 50 and 80," she is not giving as much information as if she says, "You scored between 73 and 75." The second statement places a greater limitation on the possible values of your exam score and, therefore, gives you more information.

In this example,

Strong assertions

```
{ Assert: Salary > MinTaxable }
```

is a valid assertion, because it is a condition guaranteed to be true at this point in the program. However,

```
{ Assert: Salary > MaxTaxable }
```

is stronger because it places a greater limitation on the possible values of `Salary`.

One way of visualizing strong assertions is with the number line. Figure 3.12 shows the regions of the real number line corresponding to each of the preceding conditions. Recall from mathematics that the AND operation corresponds to the intersection of the regions, while the OR operation corresponds to the union of the regions. The intersection of these two regions is simply the region for

Using the number line to formulate strong assertions

```
Salary > MaxTaxable
```

by itself, which is the stronger assertion.

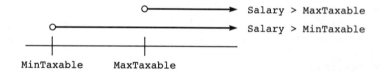

Figure 3.12

The real number line showing the two conditions `Salary > MaxTaxable` and `Salary > MinTaxable`.

To write programs that work correctly, you must be able to analyze the logic of the statements you write. Assertions will help you to think through the logic of your programs. In the beginning, it may seem that assertions make things more complicated than necessary. But after some practice, you will find that you can formulate assertions in your mind as you write your programs. That ability will make it easier for you to write correct programs. Occasionally, it may help to write an assertion as a comment in a program to make the program easier to understand.

Usefulness of assertions

Example 3.36 Consider the following code fragment, where `Age` is a variable of type integer.

```
if Age > 65 then
    Statement 1
else if Age > 21 then
    Statement 2
else
    Statement 3
```

The logic in this code is identical to that in Figure 3.11(b), where the nesting was consistently in the false part of the `if` statements. What are the strongest assertions you can make before each statement?

For Statement 1, the condition `Age > 65` must be true. That is the strongest assertion you can make at this point of the program.

For Statement 2, the boolean expression of the outer `if` statement, `Age > 65`, must be false. In other words, `Age <= 65` must be true. Furthermore, the boolean expression of the nested `if` statement, `Age > 21`, also must be true. So the strongest assertion at this point is

```
{  Assert: 21 < Age <= 65  }
```

which corresponds to the intersection of the two regions in Figure 3.13.

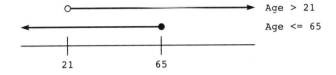

Age > 21
Age <= 65

Figure 3.13

The number line showing the two conditions `Age > 21` and `Age <= 65`.

For Statement 3, both boolean expressions must be false; that is, `Age <= 65` and `Age <= 21` must be true. The strongest assertion is

```
{  Assert: Age <= 21  }
```

which corresponds to the intersection of the two regions in Figure 3.14. The final code fragment including the strongest assertions is

```
if Age > 65 then
    {  Assert: Age > 65  }
    Statement 1
else if Age > 21 then
    {  Assert: 21 < Age <= 65  }
    Statement 2
else
    {  Assert: Age <= 21  }
    Statement 3
```

■

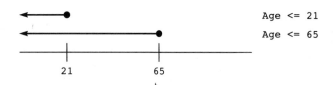

Age <= 21
Age <= 65

21   65

Figure 3.14

The number line showing the two conditions `Age <= 21` and `Age <= 65`.

Dead Code

Something to avoid when you write nested `if` statements is dead code. *Dead code* is a statement that cannot possibly execute. If you ever discover dead code in your own program or in a program that someone else wrote, you can be sure that it was unintentional. Since dead code never executes, there is never a reason to put it in a program except by mistake. Assertions can help you discover dead code.

Example **3.37**   Consider the following code fragment:

```
if Quantity < 200 then
    Statement 1
else if Quantity >= 100 then
    Statement 2
else
    Statement 3
```

Statement 3 can never execute regardless of the value of `Quantity`.

To see why, try to formulate a strong assertion at the point just before Statement 3. To get to that point in the program, you must have `Quantity >= 200` because the first boolean expression must be false. You must also have `Quantity < 100` because the second boolean expression also must be false. But it is impossible to have `Quantity` greater than or equal to 200 and less than 100 at the same time. So Statement 3 can never execute and is considered dead code.   ■

Do not conclude from this example that dead code is always the last statement in a sequence of nested `if` statements. You must analyze each situation afresh. The general strategy to determine the strongest assertion at a given point is to list the boolean conditions that must be true. This may involve taking the NOT of some expressions if the nesting is in the false part of an `if` statement. The intersection of the corresponding regions represents the strongest assertion. If the intersection at a given point is empty, the statement at that point is dead code.

Example 3.38 Consider the following code fragment, where `Ch` has type `char`.

```
if (Ch >= 'o') and (Ch < 'y') then
    if (Ch > 'j') then
        Statement 1
    else
        Statement 2
else
    Statement 3
```

What is the strongest assertion you can make at each statement? The first step is to draw a sketch of the number line with the character values in their proper order, as in Figure 3.15.

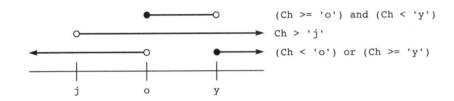

Figure 3.15

The number line for Example 3.38.

For Statement 1, you can see from the figure that the intersection of the top two lines corresponds to both boolean expressions being true. The strongest assertion is

```
{  Assert:  'o' <= Ch < 'y'  }
```

For Statement 2, `Ch` must be less than or equal to 'j' and between 'o' and 'y', which is impossible. So Statement 2 is dead code.

For Statement 3, the first boolean expression must be false. From De Morgan's law it follows that the assertion is

```
{  Assert: (Ch < 'o') or (Ch >= 'y')  }
```

This corresponds to the third region of Figure 3.15, which is that part of the number line not included in the first region.   ∎

Using Nested If Statements

One of the most common problems beginning programmers have is a failure to recognize the appropriateness of the logic characterized by Program 3.9, which contained `if` statements nested in the false alternatives.

Example 3.39 Suppose you need to perform three different computations depending on the value of `Weight`, a real variable. The following code:

```
if Weight > 150.0 then
    Statement 1;
if (Weight > 50.0) and (Weight <= 150.0) then
    Statement 2;
if (Weight <= 50.0) then
    Statement 3
```

is not as efficient as the equivalent nested `if` sequence:

```
if Weight > 150.0 then
    Statement 1
else if Weight > 50.0 then
    Statement 2
else
    Statement 3
```

For example, suppose `Weight` has a value of 200.0. In the first code fragment, every boolean expression must be evaluated because the `if` statements are sequential. But in the second fragment, only the first boolean expression is evaluated because the nested `if` statement is skipped. ∎

Another tendency when programming with "else if" logic is to include a redundant test at the end.

Example 3.40 The following code fragment has a redundant test.

```
if Price > 2000 then
    Statement 1
else if Price > 1000 then
    Statement 2
else if Price <= 1000 then
    Statement 3
```

The last boolean expression is redundant. In the following code fragment, you can assert that `Price <= 1000` when Statement 3 executes.

```
if Price > 2000 then
    Statement 1
else if Price > 1000 then
    Statement 2
else
    Statement 3
```

This code fragment executes exactly the same as the previous one, but without the extra test. ∎

| 3.4 | Case Statements

A single `if` statement selects between two alternatives, depending on the value of a boolean expression. A single **case** statement, however, can select between more than just two alternatives. The corresponding expression can be of type `integer` or `char`.

◻ **Program 3.11**

Program 3.11 poses a multiple choice question to the user. It asks for an integer between 1 and 4 and outputs one of four messages depending on the value input for `Response`. The **case** statement selects among the four alternatives to output the appropriate message.

```
program PresidentQuiz (input, output);
   var
      Response: integer;
   begin
   writeln (output, 'Who was the first U.S. president?');
   writeln (output, '(1)  Abraham Lincoln');
   writeln (output, '(2)  Albert Einstein');
   writeln (output, '(3)  George Washington');
   writeln (output, '(4)  Franklin Roosevelt');
   writeln (output);
   write (output, 'Enter response: ');
   readln (input, Response);
   case Response of
      1: writeln (output, 'Abraham Lincoln is not correct.');
      2: writeln (output, 'Albert Einstein is not correct.');
      3: writeln (output, 'That is correct.');
      4: writeln (output, 'Franklin Roosevelt is not correct.')
   end {case}
   end.
```

Program 3.11

A multiple choice question that illustrates the **case** statement.

Interactive Input/Output

```
Who was the first U.S. president?
(1)  Abraham Lincoln
(2)  Albert Einstein
(3)  George Washington
(4)  Franklin Roosevelt

Enter response: 2
Albert Einstein is not correct.
```

The words `case` and `of` are reserved and must contain an expression between them. In this program, the `case` expression is `Response`. Following the word `of` is a list of possible values that the expression might have, each one followed by a statement to execute if the expression has that value. A possible value and its corresponding statement are separated by a colon. In this program, the possible values are 1, 2, 3, and 4, and each corresponding statement is a `writeln`. Figure 3.16 shows the syntax chart for a `case` statement.

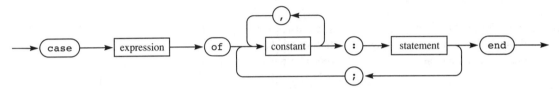

Figure 3.16

The syntax chart for a `case` statement.

Every `case` statement terminates with the reserved word `end`. Unfortunately, so does the compound statement. This book will note that an `end` belongs to a `case` statement with a comment:

```
end {case}
```

This style helps the reader identify whether an `end` matches a `case` or a `begin`.

The program begins by prompting the user to enter a response to a history question. The `readln` statement gives the value 2 to `Response`, and then the `case` statement executes. Since the value of the `case` expression is 2, control is passed directly to the statement following 2 in the list of possible values, and the Einstein message is output. All the statements after the other constants are skipped.

Figure 3.17 is the flowchart for Program 3.11. The `case` symbol depicts the fact that a single test achieves a four-way selection of alternative statements.

Using Case Statements

In Program 3.11 if the user enters 6, a response that is not listed as one of the `case` values, the result is not defined in standard Pascal but will vary depending on the particular compiler. In some systems, none of the alternatives execute and control is passed to the following statement. In others, however, an execution error occurs and the program crashes. A good programming technique that will guarantee correct execution on any Pascal compiler is to nest the `case` statement within an `if` statement, which guards against the undefined possibility.

Example 3.41   The code fragment that follows is a variation of Program 3.11. If the user enters 6, the `case` statement never executes, and an "invalid input" message is output.

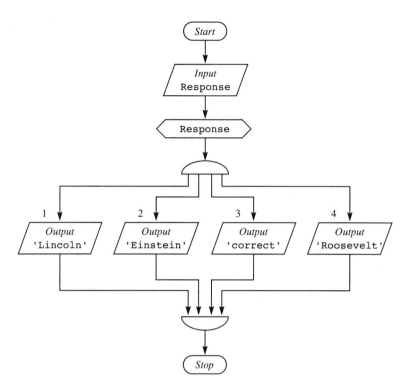

Figure 3.17

The flowchart for Program 3.11.

```
readln (input, Response);
if (1 <= Response) and (Response <= 4) then
   case Response of
   1, 4:
      begin
      writeln (output, 'He was a president,');
      writeln (output, 'but not the first one.')
      end;
   2:
      writeln (output, 'He was not a president.');
   3:
      writeln (output, 'That is correct.')
   end {case}
else
   writeln ('Invalid response.')
```

If you want more than one statement to execute when one alternative is select-ed by the case, the statements must be written as a single compound statement. This code fragment shows a compound statement as the first alternative. It also shows that one case alternative can be selected by more than one value, namely 1 and 4. ∎

Although the `case` expression can have type `integer` or `char`, it is not allowed to have type `real`.

Example 3.42 Suppose you present the user with a list of three options and ask for an input of the letter 'G,' 'B', or 'Q' to select a particular option. What follows is a `case` statement that will test what the user entered and will allow an uppercase or lowercase response. It assumes that `Response` has type `char`.

```
readln (Response);
case Response of
'G', 'g':
    Statement 1;
'B', 'b':
    Statement 2;
'Q', 'q':
    Statement 3
end {case}
```

■

Strictly speaking, the `case` statement is not a necessary part of the Pascal language. Any program logic that you design with a `case` statement can always be designed with a nested `if` statement.

Example 3.43 The following code fragment performs processing identical to that of the previous example:

```
readln (Response);
if (Response = 'G') or (Response = 'g') then
    Statement 1
else if (Response = 'B') or (Response = 'b') then
    Statement 2
else if (Response = 'Q') or (Response = 'q') then
    Statement 3
```

This code has the disadvantage of being longer than the previous code, but the execution is well defined if the user enters a letter other than those requested. If you want to output an error message for invalid input, you can include an `else` at the end of this code. The `case` statement, however, has no `else` part in standard Pascal. ■

SUMMARY

Pascal expressions can be real, integer, mixed, character, or boolean. Pascal makes a distinction between real and integer expressions because computers store real values and integer values with different binary codes. Real expressions contain the operators +, −, *, and / for addition, subtraction, multiplication, and division. Integer expressions contain the `div` and `mod` operators instead of the real division operator. In a mixed expression, Pascal converts values automatically from integer to real, but not from real to integer. The `trunc` and `round` functions convert a value from real to integer. Each character value has a place on the integer number line. Two character functions are `succ` and `pred`, which stand for successor and predecessor. The `ord` function converts from character to integer, and the `chr` function converts from integer to character. Boolean expressions have values true or false. The three boolean operators are AND, OR, and NOT. The boolean function `odd` takes an integer parameter and returns true if the value of the integer is odd.

An `if` statement tests a condition, which is a boolean expression. If the condition is true, the `if` statement executes the `then` alternative. Otherwise it executes the `else` alternative, if there is an `else` alternative. Pascal allows you to place an `if` statement within the `if` alternative or the `else` alternative of another `if` statement. This construction is called a nested `if` statement. The indentation style shown in this chapter reflects the nesting—each level of indentation corresponds to a level of nesting. The principle that resolves the problem of a dangling `else` with nested `if` statements, is that an `else` belongs to the most recent `if` that does not have an `else` clause.

An assertion is a comment that describes a condition that is always true at a given point in a program. Assertions are helpful in analyzing program logic. One assertion is stronger than another if it places greater limits on the possible values of a variable. Stronger assertions are more helpful in analysis of logic than weaker ones because they give you more information. Assertions can help you discover dead code, which is a statement that cannot possibly execute.

A `case` statement can select between more than two alternatives. In contrast to the boolean expression of an `if` statement, the expression tested by a `case` statement can be of type `integer` or `char`.

EXERCISES

Section 3.1

*1. Evaluate the following expressions. Indicate real results in your answer with a decimal point and integer results by not including a decimal point. If the expression is illegal, explain why.

(a) `5.0 / 2.0` (b) `5 / 2` (c) `5 div 2`
(d) `5.0 div 2.0` (e) `5 mod 2` (f) `5.0 mod 2`
(g) `round (8.7)` (h) `trunc (8.7)` (i) `abs (-6.8)`
(j) `abs (6)` (k) `sqr (3)` (l) `sqr (3.0)`
(m) `sqrt (16.0)` (n) `sqrt (16)` (o) `sin (0.0)`
(p) `exp (1.0)` (q) `ln (exp (4.7))`

2. Evaluate the following expressions. Indicate real results in your answer with a decimal point and integer results by not including a decimal point. If the expression is illegal, explain why.

(a) `7.0 / 3.0` (b) `7 / 3` (c) `7 div 3`
(d) `7.0 div 3.0` (e) `7 mod 3` (f) `7.0 mod 3`
(g) `round (7.9)` (h) `trunc (7.9)` (i) `abs (-4.6)`
(j) `abs (4)` (k) `sqr (4)` (l) `sqr (4.0)`
(m) `sqrt (9.0)` (n) `sqrt (9)` (o) `sin (0.0)`
(p) `exp (1.0)` (q) `ln (exp (5.1))`

3. I and J are integer variables, and X is a real variable. Construct a handwritten trace like that of Figure 3.1 for the following sequences of assignment statements. Indicate real values in your table with a decimal point and integer values by not including a decimal point.

(a)	(b)	(c)
begin	begin	begin
I := 18;	J := 14;	I := 3;
J := I div 7;	I := J mod 5;	J := 18;
X := 4.5;	X := 2.7;	X := 7.9;
I := I + 1;	J := J + 1;	I := J;
X := X + I * 2	X := X + J * 2	J := I
end	end	end

*4. Evaluate the following expressions.

    (a) succ ('C')   (b) pred ('Z')
    (c) succ ('2')   (d) pred ('9')
    (e) ord ('C') - ord ('A')   (f) chr (ord ('A'))
    (g) ord (chr (41))
    (h) chr (ord ('D') - ord ('A') + ord ('a'))

5. Evaluate the following expressions.

    (a) succ ('d')   (b) pred ('h')
    (c) succ ('8')   (d) pred ('6')
    (e) succ (pred ('?'))   (f) pred (succ ('!'))
    (g) ord (chr (45))
    (h) chr (ord ('e') - ord ('a') + ord ('A'))

*6. State whether the boolean expression

    odd (Num1) and (Num2 <= 10)

is true or false for each of the following sets of values for the integer variables Num1 and Num2.

    (a) Num1 = 6,   Num2 = 10
    (b) Num1 = 5,   Num2 = 11
    (c) Num1 = 5,   Num2 = 10

7. State whether the boolean expression

    (Char1 > 'm') or (Char2 <= 'R')

is true or false for each of the following sets of values for the character variables Char1 and Char2.

    (a) Char1 = 'm',   Char2 = 'R'
    (b) Char1 = 'j',   Char2 = 'T'
    (c) Char1 = 't',   Char2 = 'T'

8. Suppose that Num is an integer with the value 5, Ch is a character with the value 'D', and Cond is a boolean with the value false. What is the value of each of the following boolean expressions?

    *(a) Cond or ((Ch < 'G') and (Num >= 5))

(b) `Cond or ((Ch < 'G') and (Num > 5))`
(c) `(not Cond) or (Cond and (Num < 10))`

*9. Prove the second of De Morgan's laws

$$\text{NOT } (p \text{ AND } q) = (\text{NOT } p) \text{ OR } (\text{NOT } q)$$

by constructing one table that tabulates NOT (p AND q) for all possible combinations of p and q, and another table that tabulates (NOT p) OR (NOT q).

10. Prove the distributive law

$$r \text{ OR } (p \text{ AND } q) = (r \text{ OR } p) \text{ AND } (r \text{ OR } q)$$

by constructing one table that tabulates r OR (p AND q) for all possible combinations of p, q, and r, and another table that tabulates (r OR p) AND (r OR q). There are eight possible combinations of p, q, and r.

11. Prove the distributive law

$$r \text{ AND } (p \text{ OR } q) = (r \text{ AND } p) \text{ OR } (r \text{ AND } q)$$

by constructing one table that tabulates r AND (p OR q) for all possible combinations of p, q and r and another table that tabulates (r AND p) OR (r AND q). There are eight possible combinations of p, q, and r.

Section 3.2

12. Write the equivalent of the following `if` tests without using the NOT operator.

*(a) `if not (Ch < 'z') then`
(b) `if not ((Num1 < 20) or (Num2 >= 10)) then`
(c) `if not ((Num1 = 20) and (Num2 > 10)) then`

13. Write a trace table and predict the output of Program 3.5 for the following inputs.

*(a) `38.0  4.75`   (b) `50.0  5.00`   (c) `-2.0  10.00`

14. Write a trace table and predict the output of Program 3.6 for the following inputs.

(a) `36.0  5.00`   (b) `48.0  6.00`   (c) `-1.0  10.00`

15. Write a trace table and predict the output of Program 3.7 for the following inputs.

*(a) `100.00  9  N`   (b) `100.00  19  y`   (c) `100.00  14  Y`

16. Draw the flowcharts for (a) Program 3.6 and (b) Program 3.7.

17. Draw the flowcharts for the following code fragments.

*(a)
```
if Condition 1 then
    Statement 1
else
    begin
    Statement 2;
    Statement 3
    end
```

(b)
```
if Condition 1 then
    Statement 1
else
    Statement 2;
Statement 3
```

18. Simplify the following code fragment. Assume that none of the statements change the variables in Condition 1.

```
if Condition 1 then
    begin
    Statement 1;
    Statement 2
    end
else
    begin
    Statement 1;
    Statement 3
    end
```

19. Rewrite the following code fragments with the correct indentation and draw their flowcharts.

*(a)
```
Statement 1;
if Condition 1 then
Statement 2
else
Statement 3;
Statement 4;
Statement 5
```

(b)
```
Statement 1;
if Condition 1 then
Statement 2
else
begin
Statement 3;
Statement 4
end;
Statement 5
```

Section 3.3

20. Draw the flowchart for Program 3.9.

21. Draw the flowcharts for the following code fragments.

*(a)
```
if Condition 1 then
    if Condition 2 then
        Statement 1
    else
        Statement 2
else
    Statement 3
```

(b)
```
if Condition 1 then
    begin
    if Condition 2 then
        Statement 1
    else
        Statement 2;
    Statement 3
    end
else
    Statement 4
```

(c)
```
if Condition 1 then
    begin
    Statement 1;
    if Condition 2 then
        Statement 2
    end
else
    Statement 3
```

(d)
```
if Condition 1 then
    Statement 1
else
    begin
    if Condition 2 then
        Statement 2;
    Statement 3
    end
```

22. Rewrite the following code fragments with the correct indentation and draw their flowcharts.

*(a)
```
if Condition 1 then
if Condition 2 then
Statement 1
else
Statement 2
```

(b)
```
if Condition 1 then
begin
if Condition 2 then
Statement 1
end
else
Statement 2
```

23. Rewrite the following code fragments with the correct indentation and draw their flowcharts.

(a)
```
if Condition 1 then
if Condition 2 then
if Condition 3 then
Statement 1
else
Statement 2
else
Statement 3
```

(b)
```
if Condition 1 then
Statement 1;
if Condition 2 then
Statement 2
else
Statement 3
```

(c)
```
if Condition 1 then
Statement 1
else if Condition 2 then
Statement 2
else
Statement 3
```

24. Rewrite the following equivalent code fragment with only one `if` statement.

```
if Condition 1 then
    if Condition 2 then
        Statement 1;
Statement 2
```

*25.** Simplify the following code fragment so that fewer comparisons are needed. `Age` is a variable of **type integer**.

```
if Age > 64 then
    write (output, 'Social security');
if Age < 18 then
    write (output, 'Exempt');
if (Age >= 18) and (Age < 65) then
    write (output, 'Taxable')
```

26. Simplify the following code fragment so that fewer comparisons are needed. `Earnings` and `Bonus` are variables of type `integer`.

```
if Earnings > 10 then
    Bonus := 1;
if Earnings > 20 then
    Bonus := Bonus + 1;
if Earnings <= 10 then
    Bonus := 0
```

*27. Determine the output, if any, of the following code fragment. `H`, `M`, and `W` are variables of type `integer`. Hint: Rewrite with correct indentation first.

```
if H > M then
if W > M then
writeln (output, M)
else
writeln (output, H)
```

(a) Assume H = 10, M = 3, and W = 4.
(b) Assume H = 10, M = 20, and W = 15.
(c) Assume H = 10, M = 5, and W = 3.

28. Determine the output, if any, of the following code fragment. `X`, `Y`, `Z`, and `Q` are variables of type `integer`. Hint: Rewrite with correct indentation first.

```
if X > Y then
write (output, Y)
else if X > Z then
if X > Q then
write (output, Q)
else
write (output, X)
```

*(a) Assume X = 10, Y = 5, Z = 0, and Q = 1.
(b) Assume X = 10, Y = 20, Z = 5, and Q = 1.
(c) Assume X = 10, Y = 10, Z = 12, and Q = 5.
(d) Assume X = 10, Y = 5, Z = 20, and Q = 15.

29. In Program 3.10, what would be the output of Possibility (a) if the input is 7?

30. Write the strongest possible assertion just before each statement in the following code fragments. Assume that `Num` is a variable of type `integer`.

*(a)
```
if Num < 23 then
    if Num >= 15 then
        Statement 1
    else
        Statement 2
else
    Statement 3
```

(b)
```
if Num >= 50 then
    Statement 1
else if Num >= 25 then
    Statement 2
else
    Statement 3
```

(c)
```
if Num >= 60 then
    Statement 1
else if Num < 80 then
    Statement 2
```

(d)
```
if (Num < 30) or (Num > 40) then
    Statement 1
else if Num < 35 then
    Statement 2
else
    Statement 3
```

31. Which of the following statements are dead code, if any? Write the strongest possible assertion just before each statement that is not dead code in the code fragment. Assume that Num is a variable of type `integer`.

*(a)
```
if Num < 70 then
    if Num >= 80 then
        Statement 1
    else
        Statement 2
else
    Statement 3
```

(b)
```
if Num >= 45 then
    Statement 1
else if Num <= 35 then
    Statement 2
else if Num >= 55 then
    Statement 3
else
    Statement 4
```

(c)
```
if Num > 35 then
    Statement 1
else if Num > 45 then
    Statement 2
else
    Statement 3
```

(d)
```
if (Num < 5) or (Num > 9) then
    Statement 1
else if (Num > 5) and (Num < 9) then
    Statement 2
else
    Statement 3
```

(e)
```
if (Num < 40) or (Num > 50) then
    Statement 1
else if Num > 30 then
    Statement 2
else
    Statement 3
```

(f)
```
if (Num >= 40) and (Num <= 50) then
    Statement 1
else if (Num < 42) or (Num > 48) then
    Statement 2
else
    Statement 3
```

Section 3.4

＊32. Assuming that `I` is an integer variable whose value is between 2 and 6 inclusive, rewrite the following code with a `case` statement.

```
if (I = 2) or (I = 5) then
    Statement 1
else if (I = 3) then
    Statement 2
else
    Statement 3
```

33. Assuming that `J` is an integer variable whose value is between 1 and 5 inclusive, rewrite the following code with a `case` statement.

```
if J mod 2 = 1 then
    Statement 1
else if J = 2 then
    Statement 2
else
    Statement 3
```

34. In Pascal, the `case` expression may be of type `boolean` (although this fact is not very useful). Write an `if` statement equivalent to the following Pascal `case` statement.

```
case Condition 1 of
true:
    Statement 1;
false:
    Statement 2
end {case}
```

PROBLEMS

Section 3.1

35. Write a program to compute the price per ounce of a box of laundry detergent. Get the number of ounces the box contains and the cost of the box in dollars from the keyboard. Show the result to the nearest tenth of a cent (that is, to the nearest thousandth of a dollar) as the following shows.

Sample Input/Output

```
Number of ounces of detergent: 22
Cost of one box (dollars): 1.89

The price per ounce is $0.086
```

36. Write a program to convert feet and inches into meters. Get the number of feet and inches from the keyboard. Show the result to the nearest hundredth of a meter with the value identified appropriately.

37. Write a program to convert a temperature in Fahrenheit to Celsius. Get the temperature from the keyboard. Show the result to the nearest tenth of a degree with the value identified appropriately.

38. Write a program to compute the length of the hypotenuse of a right triangle. Get the length of the two sides from the keyboard. Show the result to the nearest tenth with the value identified appropriately.

39. Write a program to compute the area of a circle. Get the radius from the keyboard. Show the result to the nearest hundredth with the value identified appropriately.

40. Write a program to convert an uppercase letter to a lowercase letter. Use interactive input/output.

41. The following program should convert two character values into a single integer value. Finish the program.

```
program Convert (input, output);
   var
      Char10: char;
      Char1:  char;
      Int:    integer;
   begin
   write ('Please type two digits: ');
   readln (Char10, Char1);
   {  Supply statements here  }
   writeln ('The integer value is: ', Int: 1)
   end.
```

Sample Input/Output

```
Please type two digits: 27
The integer value is: 27
```

Section 3.2

42. A salesperson's commission is computed as 15% of the sales that exceed $1000. Write a Pascal program to input a sales figure and output the salesperson's commission. Use an `if` statement without an `else` part.

43. In a bowling tournament, participants bowl three games and receive a consolation prize of $5 regardless of their score. Those bowlers whose three-game average exceeds 200 get an additional prize of $30. Write a program to input a bowler's three scores and output his prize earnings.

44. Write a Pascal program to input two real numbers and output the smaller of the two, as shown in the following sample. Your program must contain only one output statement.

Sample Input/Output

```
Enter two real numbers: 8.9   3.6
The smaller is 3.6
```

45. Write a Pascal program to input two lowercase characters and output them in alphabetical order, as shown in the following sample.

Sample Input/Output

```
Enter two lowercase characters: up
In alphabetical order they are pu
```

46. Write a program that asks the user to enter a character, and outputs whether the character is a lowercase letter.

47. A student gets on the dean's list if her grade point average (GPA) is at least 3.5 (based on a scale of 4.0 for an A). Write a program to input the number of A's, B's, C's, D's, and F's a student earned during a given semester and to print her GPA and a message telling whether she made the dean's list, as shown in the following sample.

Sample Input/Output

```
How many A's? 1
How many B's? 2
How many C's? 1
How many D's? 0
How many F's? 0


Grade point average is 3.00.
You did not make the dean's list.
```

Section 3.3

48. Write a program to input three lowercase characters and print them in alphabetical order, as shown in the following sample.

Sample Input/Output

```
Enter three lowercase letters: bad
In alphabetical order, they are abd
```

49. Write a program to input three real numbers and print them in descending order.

Sample Input/Output

```
Enter three real numbers: 3.9 2.0 7.1
In descending order, they are 7.1 3.9 2.0
```

50. Write a program to input three real numbers and output the number that is neither the smallest nor the largest. Assume that none of the numbers are equal.

51. Write a program to input two integers and output either the larger integer or a message stating that they are equal.

52. A salesperson gets a 5% commission on sales of $1000 or less, and a 10% commission on sales in excess of $1000. For example, a sale of $1300 earns him $80; that is, $50 on the first $1000 of the sale and $30 on the $300 in excess of the first $1000. Write a program that inputs a sales figure and outputs the commission.

53. The fine for speeding in a 45 MPH zone is $10 for every mile per hour over the speed limit for speeds from 46 to 55 MPH. It is $15 for every additional mile per hour between 56 and 65 MPH. It is $20 for every additional mile per hour over 65 MPH. For example, the fine for driving 57 MPH is $100 for the first 10 MPH plus $30 for the 2 MPH in excess of 55 MPH, for a total of $130. Write a program that inputs the speed as an integer and outputs the fine, if any.

54. Write a program that performs the same processing as described in the previous problem, but inputs the speed limit as well, as shown in the following sample.

Sample Input/Output

```
Enter speed limit (integer): 50
Enter defendant's speed: 65
The fine is $175
```

55. Write a program to read the temperature (integer value), then print the appropriate message for a given value of temperature, as Table 3.22 shows.

56. The price per Frisbee depends on the quantity ordered, as Table 3.23 indicates. Write a Pascal program to print the total cost of an order, including a 6.5% sales tax, from the quantity requested.

Temperature, T	Message
$T \geq 90$	Go swimming
$90 > T \geq 80$	Play tennis
$80 > T \geq 70$	Study
$70 > T \geq 60$	Go to sleep
$60 > T$	Go to Hawaii

Quantity	Price per Frisbee
0 – 99	$5.00
100 – 199	3.00
200 – 299	2.50
300 or more	2.00

Table 3.22

The table for Problem 55.

Table 3.23

The table for Problem 56.

57. You are eligible for a tax benefit if you are married and have an income of $30,000 or less, or unmarried and have an income of $20,000 or less. Write a program that asks for the user's marital status (character input) and income (real input), then prints a message stating whether the user is eligible for the tax benefit.

58. The following statements are from the Department of Internal Revenue Instructions for Form 1040 for 1987:

Use this schedule if you checked Filing Status Box 2 or 5 on Form 1040.

If the amount on line 36 is over $28,000 but not over $45,000, enter on line 37 $4080 + 28% of the amount over $28,000.

If the amount on line 36 is over $45,000 but not over $90,000, enter on line 37 $8840 + 35% of the amount over $45,000.

Assuming the declarations

```
var
   FilingStatusBox: integer;
   Line36:          real;
   Line37:          real;
```

write a program that inputs the values for the filing box and line 36, and outputs the value for line 37. If the values input are not covered by the instructions, output an appropriate message.

59. Table 3.24 shows the interpretation of a letter grading system. Write a Pascal program that reads a letter grade and prints the appropriate phrase from the table.

Section 3.4

60. Rewrite Program 3.9 using a `case` statement. Hint: First divide the score by 10 with the `div` operator.

61. A person's last initial determines her registration period, as Table 3.25 shows. Write a program using a `case` statement that asks a user to input her last initial (uppercase) then outputs her registration hour. If the user enters a character that is not an uppercase letter, the program should output an appropriate error message.

62. Write a program using a `case` statement that inputs an integer representing the baseball "scorecard code" and outputs the position as indicated in Table 3.26. Issue an error message if the value input is not between 1 and 9.

Grade	Meaning
A	Excellent
B	Good
C	Average
D	Below average
F	Failing

Table 3.24

The table for Problem 59.

Last initial	Registration period
A, B, C	9:00
D, E, F, G	10:00
H, I, J, K, L	11:00
M, N	12:00
O, P, Q, R, S	1:00
T, U, V, W	2:00
X, Y, Z	3:00

Table 3.25

The table for Problem 61.

Code	Position
1	Pitcher
2	Catcher
3	First base
4	Second base
5	Third base
6	Short stop
7	Left field
8	Center field
9	Right field

Table 3.26

The table for Problem 62.

Chapter

File Input/Output and Stepwise Refinement

All the programs we have studied so far have used interactive input/output (I/O). That is, the input was taken from the keyboard, and the output was sent to the screen. Many applications, however, require the input to come from a file. Take, for example, a company that maintains records on its financial operations in a file in its computer. Programs read values from the file, process them, then send the results to another file for storage. Obviously it would be impractical for the company's financial programs to prompt the user for vast amounts of information to be processed. Accessing a file is much more efficient.

This chapter describes how to read values from a file (input) and write values to a file (output). There are two kinds of files—text files and nontext files—each with its own set of advantages and disadvantages. Following a description of both kinds of files, the chapter concludes with an important design technique called stepwise refinement.

4.1 Text Files

By now, you are familiar enough with your operating system to know how to create a text file, name it, and save it to disk. The programs you write are all created and stored on disk with your text editor, which is an example of an applications program. It is also possible for a program to create a text file and save it on disk.

Programs can create files.

Program 4.1

Program 4.1 behaves like Program 2.1, except that the output is sent to a file instead of to the screen. When this program executes, no output appears on the screen! To verify that it worked correctly, you must examine the newly created file with your text editor or with some suitable operating system command.

```
program Address2 (AddrFile);
   var
       AddrFile: text;
   begin
   rewrite (AddrFile);
   writeln (AddrFile, 'Mr. K. Kong');
   writeln (AddrFile, 'Suite 8572');
   writeln (AddrFile, 'Empire State Building');
   writeln (AddrFile, 'New York, NY 10113')
   end.
```

Output—AddrFile

```
Mr. K. Kong
Suite 8572
Empire State Building
New York, NY 10113
```

Program 4.1

A program that creates a text file. Its output is identical to the output of Program 2.1 except that it is sent to the newly created file instead of to the screen.

In this program, AddrFile is the program parameter instead of output. Remember that the program parameter tells the compiler where the program will be sending its output. In Program 2.1, the word output as a program parameter told the compiler that output would be going to the standard output device, which is usually the screen. In this example, AddrFile as the program parameter tells the compiler that output will be going to a file named AddrFile instead of to the screen.

Every program parameter, except for input and output, must be declared in the variable declaration part of the main program. In this program, AddrFile is declared to be of type text. The word text, as a type, means *text file*. Text files are the same kind of files you create and modify with your text editor.

The statement

```
rewrite (AddrFile)
```

is a procedure call to a standard Pascal procedure. Its parameter must be a variable declared as some kind of file. rewrite creates a new file and prepares it for possible writing later in the program. If there is already a file called AddrFile in your directory, its contents will be erased in the process of preparing the file for output.

The rewrite statement

In Program 2.1, the file parameter of the writeln statements was output. In this program, the writeln call

```
writeln (AddrFile, 'Mr. K. Kong')
```

has AddrFile as the file parameter. In English, this writeln call means, "Write to disk file AddrFile the string 'Mr. K. Kong'."

Anything that can be sent to the screen can be sent to a text file. The formatting rules for numeric output all apply without change.

Example 4.1   If `EmplFile` is a text file and `Wages` is a real variable, the statement

```
writeln (EmplFile, 'The wages are: $', Wages: 4: 2)
```

sends the string followed by the value of `Wages` to the file. The format specification works exactly the way it would if sent to the screen—with a field width of four with two places past the decimal point. The only difference is that nothing appears on the screen when the statement executes.   ■

Compiler Differences for File Output

The `rewrite` statement is one of the greatest areas of difference between standard Pascal and its various implementations. Your compiler may differ somewhat from the `rewrite` statement shown here. Many operating systems have rules for naming the files in their disk directories that are different from the rule for naming a Pascal variable. Some systems require file names to be in uppercase letters, and some require a period in the name followed by a special suffix indicating the type of the file. Others may limit the file name length to being shorter than a Pascal identifier. For example, operating system rules may require that the file in the disk directory be named `ADDR.TXT`.

Differences in naming rules

Some compilers reconcile the difference between the naming rules for the operating system and the rule for Pascal identifiers by requiring two parameters in the `rewrite` statement instead of one. Such a compiler would expect the rewrite call to look like

```
rewrite (AddrFile, 'ADDR.TXT')
```

In this example, two names are associated with the same file—`AddrFile`, the internal Pascal file name, which is a Pascal identifier, and `ADDR.TXT`, the external file name recognized by the operating system. With these compilers the `rewrite` call links these two names. `AddrFile` is still the file parameter in the `writeln` calls, and when the values are output they are sent to the file known as `ADDR.TXT` by the operating system.

Another common compiler requirement that is not specified by the Pascal standard is the execution of a `close` statement before ending the program. In this case, such a compiler would require the statement

The close statement

```
close (AddrFile)
```

just before the last `end` of the program.

This requirement can cause subtle problems if it is not met. On some compilers, the `close` statement is equivalent to the save command, so if `close` is not executed the file is not saved. On other compilers, omitting the `close` statement may not appear to cause a problem at first, because the file is saved. However, it is saved in an "open" state, which may lead to problems later. Your compiler documentation has the details about these differences from the standard.

Program 4.2

Program 4.2 gets its input from a previously created text file. The numbers 3.6 and 4.0 were placed in a file using a text editor. Instead of the word `input`, which would indicate that the input comes from the keyboard, this program has the identifier `SizeFile`, which indicates the name of the file containing the input data.

```
program Rectangle (SizeFile, output);
   var
      SizeFile: text;
      Width:    real;
      Length:   real;
      Area:     real;
      Perim:    real;
   begin
   reset (SizeFile);
   read (SizeFile, Width, Length);
   Area := Width * Length;
   Perim := 2 * (Width + Length);
   writeln (output, 'Width: ', Width: 4: 2);
   writeln (output, 'Length: ', Length: 4: 2);
   writeln (output);
   writeln (output, 'Area: ', Area: 4: 2);
   writeln (output, 'Perimeter: ', Perim: 4: 2)
   end.
```

Program 4.2

Getting input from a previously created text file.

Input—SizeFile

3.6   4.0

Output

Width: 3.60
Length: 4.00

Area: 14.40
Perimeter: 15.20

Before a program can get data from a file, it must open the file with a `reset` statement. `reset` is similar to `rewrite` in that they both prepare the file for I/O operations. When `rewrite` executes, it creates a new file that did not exist previously. When `reset` executes, it assumes the file already exists on disk and search-

The reset statement

es the directory for its name. If the file name is not in the directory, an execution error occurs, and the program crashes.

The `rewrite` statement prepares the file for writing later in the program, but `reset` prepares it for reading. You cannot have a file prepared for both reading and writing simultaneously.

The computer reads from a file the same way it reads from the keyboard. The only difference is that when you place the name of a file before the variables instead of the word `input` to indicate the keyboard, the computer does not pause and wait for a response from the user. It goes immediately to the file to get the data. In Program 4.2 you should think of the statement

```
read (SizeFile, Width, Length)
```

as "Read from `SizeFile` into `Width` and `Length`." In the file the values for `Width` and `Length` must be separated by at least one space.

Figure 4.1 is a system flowchart for this program, and shows the input coming from a file instead of the keyboard.

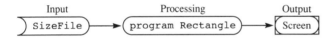

Input	Processing	Output
SizeFile	program Rectangle	Screen

Figure 4.1

A system flowchart for Program 4.2.

Compiler Differences for File Input

The `reset` statement is another area of difference between standard Pascal and many compilers. The difference, which is similar to the difference in the `rewrite` statement between standard Pascal and the compilers, comes from the different naming rules imposed by operating systems.

For example, if you named the file `BOX.TXT` when you saved it in the text editor, then your compiler might require the `reset` statement to be

```
reset (SizeFile, 'BOX.TXT')
```

This `reset` statement makes the connection between the internal Pascal name `SizeFile` and the external operating system name `BOX.TXT`.

As with the `rewrite` statement, many compilers require a `close` statement just before the end of the program. The problems encountered if you omit the `close` statement are similar to those encountered when you omit it with the `rewrite` statement.

Using Text Files

A common mistake that beginning programmers make when creating text files of data is typing a documentation section at the beginning of the file.

Example 4.2   In Program 4.2, `SizeFile` must contain only the two numeric values at the beginning, nothing else. If the file contains

```
{  Stan Warford  }
{  May 20, 1990  }
3.6   4.0
```

the program will crash when it tries to read the numeric values because it expects the first character to be a digit instead of a comment brace. ∎

If there are not enough values in the file for the program, it will crash with an "attempt to read past end of file" message. If there are more values in the file than the program needs, the remaining values are simply ignored. You can use this feature to document an input file by simply placing the documentation after the last value that the program needs.

When the number of values in the file differs from the number required

Example 4.3   Suppose in Program 4.2 that `SizeFile` contains only the value 3.6. When the program executes, `Width` will get 3.6, but then the program will crash because there is no value for `Length`. ∎

Example 4.4   In Program 4.2, if `SizeFile` contains

```
3.6   4.0   5.9
```

the output would be identical to the sample output shown after the listing. After the `read` statement gets 3.6 and 4.0, no other statements request input, so when the program ends, 5.9 has simply been ignored. ∎

Example 4.5   You could document `SizeFile` by putting your comments after the data values as follows:

```
3.6   4.0
Data for program Rectangle
```

Note that comment braces are not required if you document your text file this way because the program never attempts to read anything after the 4.0. ∎

When inputting values from a text file into a list of variables, you must be careful to distinguish the difference between `read` and `readln`. The Pascal `read` statement does one thing:

The difference between read and readln

- It inputs values from the file into the variables in parentheses.

But the `readln` statement does two things:

- It inputs values from the file into the variables in parentheses.
- Then it sets the input device to the start of the next line, possibly skipping over some values at the end of the line.

Example 4.6 Suppose `DataFile` is declared to be a text file, and it contains

```
26   17   4
12
```

Then if `I`, `J`, and `K` are declared to be integers, the statements

```
read (DataFile, I, J)
read (DataFile, K)
```

produce the values

I	J	K
26	17	4

But the statements

```
readln (DataFile, I, J)
read (DataFile, K)
```

produce the values

I	J	K
26	17	12

In the latter case, the `readln` statement inputs the values 26 and 17 into the variables `I` and `J`, then sets the input device to the start of the next line, skipping the value of 4 in the process. Then the `read` statement inputs the value of 12 into K. ∎

Another property of both the `read` and `readln` statements with text files is their behavior when they get to the end of a line and there are still more variables that need values. In that case, they are forced to go to the start of the next line to pick up the remaining values.

Reaching the end of a line with more values required

Example 4.7 If `L` is also declared to be an integer, then the single statement

```
read (DataFile, I, J, K, L)
```

produces the values

I	J	K	L
26	17	4	12

when `DataFile` is unchanged from the previous example. The `read` statement inputs the values 26, 17, and 4 into `I`, `J`, and `K`. At this point it is at the end of the line, but it still needs another value for `L`. It is forced to the start of the next line, where it picks up the value 12 for `L`.   ∎

You can omit the variable parameters of a `readln` call. The effect is to position the input device at the beginning of the next line, possibly skipping over some values.

Omitting the variable parameters

Example **4.8**   If `DataFile` contains

```
60   40
20   30
50   90
```

and the following input statements execute:

```
readln (DataFile, I, J)
readln (DataFile)
readln (DataFile, K, L)
```

the integer variables will get the following values:

I	J	K	L
60	40	50	90

After the first `readln` executes, the input device is positioned at the start of the second line, just before the 20. The second `readln` positions the device at the start of the third line, skipping the 20 and 30.   ∎

Example **4.9**   The statement

```
readln (DataFile, I, J)
```

is always equivalent to the pair of statements

```
read (DataFile, I, J);
readln (DataFile)
```

This equivalence shows explicitly that a `readln` advances to the start of the next line after getting its values.   ∎

4.2   **Nontext Files**

Text files have three advantages over nontext files:

- You can create a text file with a text editor.

  Advantages of text files

- You can examine the contents of a text file with a text editor or with an appropriate operating system command.

- You can modify a text file with a text editor.

Nontext files have none of these features. You cannot manipulate them with text editors. However, they do have two advantages over text files:

- Large amounts of data, especially numeric data, can be stored in smaller physical space compared to the equivalent text file.

  Advantages of nontext files

- Reading and writing between the file and the program are faster than with equivalent text files.

Nontext files are often used with large amounts of data to conserve disk storage and to speed execution of programs.

Program 4.3

Text editors cannot create nontext files. They must be created with programs. Program 4.3 creates a nontext file containing a single integer value. It asks the user to type an integer value, then outputs that value to the nontext file.

```
program NonText (input, output, CentsFile);
   var
      CentsFile: file of integer;
      Number:    integer;
   begin
   write (output, 'Enter an integer: ');
   readln (input, Number);
   writeln (output, 'Number entered: ', Number: 1);
   rewrite (CentsFile);
   write (CentsFile, Number);
   writeln (output, 'Number stored in CentsFile.')
   end.
```

Program 4.3

A program that creates a nontext file.

Interactive Input/Output

```
Enter an integer: 42
Number entered: 42
Number stored in CentsFile.
```

Output—CentsFile (nontext)

Program 4.3 has three program parameters—input, output, and CentsFile. input and output tell the operating system that the program will be using the keyboard and screen. CentsFile tells the operating system the name of an additional file to be used for input or output.

In the variable declaration part, the code fragment

```
CentsFile: file of integer
```

declares CentsFile to be a nontext file containing integer values. The words file and of are reserved.

file of integer in Program 4.3 is an example of a new type in the syntax chart for a variable declaration part in Figure 2.14. It is called a *type constructor* because it constructs a new file type from the previously defined integer type. Figure 4.2 is the syntax chart for a file type.

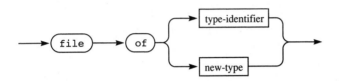

Figure 4.2

The syntax chart for a file type, which is an example of a new type.

Figure 4.3 is a system flowchart for this program. It shows the input coming from the keyboard and the output going to the screen and to the newly created nontext file.

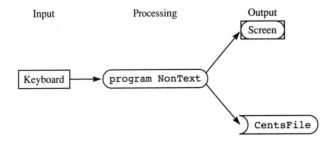

Figure 4.3

A system flowchart for Program 4.3.

Program 4.4

Program 4.4 inputs data from a previously created nontext file. It is similar to programs that input data from text files, except that in the variable declaration part CentsFile is declared to be a nontext file.

```
program Change (CentsFile, output);
   var
      CentsFile: file of integer;
      Cents:     integer;
      Dimes:     integer;
      Nickels:   integer;
      Pennies:   integer;
   begin
   reset (CentsFile);
   read (CentsFile, Cents);
   writeln (output, 'You have ', Cents: 2, ' cents in change.');
   Dimes := Cents div 10;
   Cents := Cents mod 10;
   Nickels := Cents div 5;
   Pennies := Cents mod 5;
   writeln (output, 'That is');
   writeln (output, Dimes: 5, ' dimes');
   writeln (output, Nickels: 5, ' nickels');
   writeln (output, Pennies: 5, ' pennies')
   end.
```

Program 4.4

Getting input from a previously created nontext file.

Input—`CentsFile` (nontext)

42

Output

```
You have 42 cents in change.
That is
4 dimes
0 nickels
2 pennies
```

The statement that inputs from the nontext file

```
read (CentsFile, Cents)
```

is indistinguishable from one that reads from a text file. The compiler knows this is to be read from a nontext file because of the earlier declaration of `CentsFile` as such.

The previous two programs do not process enough data to show the advantages of nontext files over text files. Remember that the advantages of nontext files are low storage requirements and high speed. A file with only one value in it will not be noticeably smaller or faster than the equivalent text file. However, if you have tens of thousands of values to store, using a nontext file could make a significant difference in the performance of your program. Nontext files are used routinely in business applications that process large amounts of data.

Founded in 1947, the Association for Computing Machinery (ACM) is a leading professional organization for computer scientists. Although the organization's name now sounds a bit dated, we should recall that in the 1940s the enthusiasm about computing was largely about the machines themselves. As the equally important realm of software research has been recognized, the ACM has broadened its scope to address the entire spectrum of computing. The ACM is dedicated to the development of information processing as a discipline and to the promotion of responsible computer use in increasingly diverse applications.

The Institute of Electrical and Electronic Engineers (IEEE) is a much older professional organization whose members are active in many different fields of electrical engineering. The IEEE contains several specialized societies, the largest of which is the Computer Society. The IEEE is interested in computer circuitry, of course, but many of its members are software engineers and theoretical computer scientists.

Members of the ACM and the Computer Society of the IEEE include faculty members, graduate and undergraduate students, business professionals, and others who wish to keep abreast of both research developments and policy issues in the ever-changing field of computing. Basic membership in the organizations entitles members to receive the monthly publications *Communications of the ACM* and *IEEE Computer*. These flagship journals publish articles of general interest to the computing community, often arranging the articles into special "theme" issues. They also contain lively dialogue in the "Letters to the Editor" column; announcements of international, national, and regional conferences; notices of student programming contests; and job postings.

Members may also choose to join one or more of the special interest groups (SIGs) that organize conferences and publications on more specialized topics, such as software engineering or artificial intelligence. Both organizations publish additional specialty journals of interest to researchers keeping abreast of the latest developments in the active subfields of computing.

In addition to publishing journals and organizing several annual conferences, the ACM publishes an annual directory of universities offering graduate programs. Undergraduates considering pursuing a master's or doctorate degree can find out about the size and research specialties of departments they are considering, as well as the amount of financial support available for graduate students.

The ACM also sponsors a speaker's bureau consisting of interesting professionals who can be invited to give talks at student chapters of the ACM; this program exposes students to job ideas and professional perspectives beyond the scope of their everyday experience. Since the aims of both the ACM and the IEEE Computer Society are so similar, there have been suggestions from time to time that they merge in order to avoid the costs of duplicating services and take advantage of a unified membership base. For the moment, the organizations remain distinct, but they recognize the overlap, providing discounted joint memberships.

Student members can join the ACM or IEEE at substantially reduced membership rates. If you are interested in membership information, you can write to the following addresses:

ACM Inc.
P.O. Box 12114
Church St. Station
New York, NY 10249

IEEE Computer Society
10662 Los Vaqueros Circle
P.O. Box 3014
Los Alamitos, CA 90720-1264

Alternatively, you may find your school already has a student chapter of the ACM, with membership brochures and a faculty advisor already in place. If not, you might consider organizing one—it could be a rewarding experience, and besides, it would look great on your resume!

Using Nontext Files

You can construct a nontext file to contain values of any type, but all the values in the file must be of the same type. In general, the type of the file must be compatible with the type of the input variable.

Example 4.10 You can declare a nontext file of real values like this:

```
SomeFile: file of real
```

If `Wage` is a real variable, then

```
read (SomeFile, Wage)
```

gets the next value from the file and assigns it to `Wage`. ∎

Example 4.11 If `SomeFile` is declared, as in the previous example, and `I` is an integer variable, then

```
read (SomeFile, I)
```

is illegal, because you are trying to give a real value to an integer variable. ∎

When you view a text file with a text editor, the values appear as separate lines of text on the screen. However, there are no lines in a nontext file. Instead, the values are stored in binary notation, packed together in one long unbroken sequence. Consequently, although you can use `read` and `write` statements with nontext files, you can never use `readln` or `writeln`.

Example 4.12 If `DataFile` is a file of integers and `I` is a variable of type integer then both

```
readln (DataFile, I)
```

and

```
writeln (DataFile, I)
```

are illegal, because `DataFile` is not a text file. ∎

4.3 Stepwise Refinement

To program effectively you must develop two distinct skills. First, you need to understand how each statement in the language works. For example, you need to understand how the `read` statement works, as well as how it differs from `readln`.

Second, given the problem to be solved, you need to be able to put together combinations of statements that will produce the correct output from the input. This skill is far more difficult than the first one—it involves design as opposed to analysis.

Stepwise refinement is one technique that aids the design effort. Basically an outline method, it is related to the concept of levels of abstraction. You know that the first step in writing a report is constructing an outline. The outline gives a concise overall description of the various parts of the report at the highest level of abstraction. After the outline is complete, you can go back and fill in the details of each part when you write the report.

Similarly, stepwise refinement is a way of organizing your program in outline form. You write your program in several passes in an informal language called *pseudocode*. Each time you make another pass at the program you add more detail, converting the pseudocode to Pascal.

Pseudocode

▪ Program 4.5

Program 4.5 illustrates stepwise refinement. The problem is to calculate a tax from an Internal Revenue schedule according to the following rule:

> The tax is 5% of the larger of Income A and Income B, with the provision that neither income can be negative, and the total tax cannot exceed $400. The input values are in a text file.

For example, if the input file contains

```
3000.00   5000.00
```

then the output should be

```
First income: $3000.00
Second income: $5000.00

Tax: $250.00
```

When faced with an algorithm design problem, always ask yourself three questions:

- What is the input?
- What processing needs to be done?
- What is the output?

These three questions can help you decide how to construct your variable declaration part.

In this problem two numbers are in the input file. That suggests two real variables, say `IncomeA` and `IncomeB`. One value needs to be output, suggesting the real variable `Tax`.

The first pass, written in pseudocode, is

```
begin
Input IncomeA, IncomeB
Output IncomeA, IncomeB
Compute Tax
Output Tax
end
```

First pass of Program 4.5

This is the program in outline form. The next step is to go back and fill in the details, converting each pseudocode statement into Pascal.

You are free to add the detail in any order you wish. For example, you could work on the compute statement first. But if you do, how should you handle the requirement that neither income is to be negative? If that case does arise, an error message should be output instead of tax. The second pass, therefore, might look something like the following:

Second pass of Program 4.5

```
begin
Input IncomeA, IncomeB
Output IncomeA, IncomeB
if (IncomeA < 0.0) or (IncomeB < 0.0) then
   Output an error message.
else
   begin
   Compute Tax
   Output Tax
   end
end
```

The essence of stepwise refinement is to divide the problem into subproblems that can be solved separately. The second pass solved the subproblem of how to treat the case of negative incomes without considering the subproblem of how to compute the tax when the incomes are both nonnegative. Instead, the pseudocode statement

Compute `Tax`

was written at the point where the computation will eventually occur, but without bothering with the details of the computation. Stepwise refinement is an example of levels of abstraction. This pseudocode statement hides the details of the computation that will become visible at a lower level of abstraction.

The third pass attacks the problem of computing `Tax` from `IncomeA` and `IncomeB` assuming they are both nonnegative. The problem statement says the tax is 5% of the larger, with a provision that puts a maximum on the dollar amount. The computation can be broken down into two subproblems—computing the tax, then applying the maximum provision. The third pass might choose to solve the subproblem of applying the maximum provision as follows:

Third pass of Program 4.5

```
begin
Input IncomeA, IncomeB
Output IncomeA, IncomeB
if (IncomeA < 0.0) or (IncomeB < 0.0) then
   Output an error message.
else
   begin
   Compute Tax without regard to maximum.
   if Tax > 400.00 then
      Tax := 400.00
   Output Tax
   end
end
```

If the tax based on the two incomes is above the maximum, the algorithm simply gives `Tax` the maximum allowed amount.

There are several ways to approach the subproblem of computing the tax without regard to the maximum. One possibility is to determine the larger of the two incomes, then compute the tax on that amount.

```
if IncomeA > IncomeB then
    LargerInc := IncomeA
else
    LargerInc := IncomeB
Tax := 0.05 * LargerInc
```

This code assumes that `LargerInc` is another real variable. The code gives `LargerInc` the larger value of the two incomes, then computes the tax on that amount. Another technique for computing the larger value that is a bit more compact is to give it the value from `IncomeB`, then change it to the value of `IncomeA` if necessary.

```
LargerInc := IncomeB
if IncomeA > IncomeB then
    LargerInc := IncomeA
Tax := 0.05 * LargerInc
```

Still another approach is to dispense with `LargerInc` altogether and have two computations for `Tax` in the code, depending on which income is larger.

```
if IncomeA > IncomeB then
    Tax := 0.05 * IncomeA
else
    Tax := 0.05 * IncomeB
```

This seems the most straightforward approach. When placed in the pseudocode developed so far, you get the fourth pass:

Fourth pass of Program 4.5

```
begin
Input IncomeA, IncomeB
Output IncomeA, IncomeB
if (IncomeA < 0.0) or (IncomeB < 0.0) then
    Output an error message.
else
    begin
    if IncomeA > IncomeB then
        Tax := 0.05 * IncomeA
    else
        Tax := 0.05 * IncomeB
    if Tax > 400.00 then
        Tax := 400.00
    Output Tax
    end
end
```

At this point, the program is still part pseudocode and part Pascal, but the logic has been completely worked out. The last step is to convert the input and output statements to Pascal. The original problem stated that the two incomes were in a file. To complete this step you must use the **reset** statement. The finished program is shown as Program 4.5.

```
program IRSComputation (IncFile, output);
   const
      Rate    = 0.05;
      MaxTax = 400.00;
   var
      IncomeA: real;
      IncomeB: real;
      Tax:     real;
      IncFile: text;
   begin
   reset (IncFile);
   read (IncFile, IncomeA, IncomeB);
   writeln (output, 'First income: $', IncomeA: 4: 2);
   writeln (output, 'Second income: $', IncomeB: 4: 2);
   writeln (output);
   if (IncomeA < 0.0) or (IncomeB < 0.0) then
      writeln (output, 'Error: neither income can be negative.')
   else
      begin
      if IncomeA > IncomeB then
         Tax := Rate * IncomeA
      else
         Tax := Rate * IncomeB;
      if Tax > MaxTax then
         Tax := MaxTax;
      writeln (output, 'Tax: $', Tax: 4: 2)
      end
   end.
```

Program 4.5

The finished Pascal program from a stepwise refinement process. All the pseudocode has been eliminated.

Input—IncFile

3000.00 5000.00

Output

First income: $3000.00
Second income: $5000.00

Tax: $250.00

Notice that the program uses constants for the tax rate and the maximum tax. Even though stepwise refinement did not bother with such details, the inclusion of constants for these values is important in the finished product. It makes the program easier to read and to modify.

Using Stepwise Refinement

This program is fairly short. Perhaps you could have written the complete Pascal program immediately without resorting to a preliminary outline. If so, you may be asking, Why bother with pseudocode?

One purpose of pseudocode is to show the logic of the program while ignoring irrelevant details. It helps you concentrate on the actual design of the algorithm. For example, when you write

Input `IncomeA, IncomeB`

you can assume that the variables will get their values from the file. You do not have to worry about the name of the file, whether it is text or nontext, and so on. All those input details can be postponed until later, allowing you to concentrate on the logic of the program. Pseudocode is especially timesaving when you experiment with different possibilities using pencil and paper.

As you begin to write larger programs, the importance of stepwise refinement and pseudocode will become more apparent. This short program only required four passes. Larger programs will require more passes to convert the algorithm to a complete Pascal program.

A system with levels of abstraction has details at the lower levels that are hidden at the higher levels. The series of bronze sculptures by Matisse (Figure 1.2) showed the details visually at the lower levels of abstraction. Just as Matisse stated that "superfluous details" would "encroach upon the essential elements," the superfluous details of input/output and Pascal syntax often detract from the essential problem in an algorithm design.

Stepwise refinement as an application of levels of abstraction

See how many details are in Program 4.5. There are numerous semicolons and colons, `reset` statements, program parameters, and so on. Now compare that with the second pass of the same algorithm. All those details are hidden, showing the essence of the algorithm.

Eventually the details of input/output and Pascal syntax must be supplied. Compilers demand the details. Stepwise refinement, on the other hand, recognizes that it is best for you to think in global terms before getting enmeshed in specifics.

SUMMARY

Files contain values that can be used for input or output. Two types of files are text and nontext. Text files are created with a text editor and can be inspected and modified with a text editor. Nontext files cannot be manipulated with a text editor, but have the advantage of smaller physical size and faster input/output as compared to equivalent text files. Nontext files must be created, inspected, and modified with programs.

The `rewrite` statement prepares a file for output with the `write` statement. It is a standard Pascal procedure whose parameter is a file variable; it creates a new file with a name identical to the file variable. If there is already a file with that name in the disk directory, its contents will be erased in the process of preparing the file for output. The `reset` statement prepares a file for input with the `read` statement. It assumes a file already exists on the disk and searches the directory for its name. If the file is not on the disk, the program crashes.

Stepwise refinement is a software design technique that helps you organize your program in outline form. It is based on the concept of levels of abstraction and consists of writing a program in several passes in an informal language called pseudocode. On each pass, you successively fill in more levels of detail, gradually transforming pseudocode into Pascal code until the program is completely written.

EXERCISES

Section 4.1

*1. Suppose `DataFile` is a text file that contains the values

```
2   8   6
1
3   5   9
```

What are the values of the integer variables I, J, and K after the following input statements execute?

(a) read (DataFile, I, J, K)   (b) readln (DataFile, I, J, K)

(c) readln (DataFile, I, J);   (d) readln (DataFile, I);
     read (DataFile, K)   read (DataFile, J, K)

(e) readln (DataFile, I);   (f) readln (DataFile, I, J, K);
     readln (DataFile, J);   readln (DataFile, I, J, K)
     readln (DataFile, K)

(g) read (DataFile, I);   (h) read (DataFile, I);
     read (DataFile, J);   read (DataFile, J);
     read (DataFile, K)   read (DataFile, I)

2. Complete Exercise 1 for the following text file.

```
4   1   7
5
9   2   3
```

Section 4.3

*3. Develop a stepwise refinement solution to the following problem. Include the last pass before the Pascal program, but do not include the program itself.

The problem is to input three integers corresponding to the day, month, and year of a person's birthdate, followed by three integers corresponding to today's date. Then output the person's age in years. Note that the computation depends on whether the person has had a birthday yet this year.

Sample Input/Output

```
Enter birthdate (day, month, year): 16 10 1970
Enter today's date (day, month, year): 14 10 1989
You are 18 years old.
```

Sample Input/Output

```
Enter birthdate (day, month, year): 16 10 1970
Enter today's date (day, month, year): 18 10 1989
You are 19 years old.
```

4. Develop a stepwise refinement solution to the following problem. Include the last pass before the Pascal program, but do not include the program itself.

   The problem is to input two integers corresponding to the hours and minutes of a time, and a character that indicates whether the time is A.M. or P.M. The same information is also input for a later time. Then output the number of hours and minutes that elapse between the first and later time.

Sample Input/Output

```
Enter first time (Hr, Min): 3   15
AM or PM (a or p): p

Enter later time (Hr, Min): 4   17
AM or PM (a or p): a

Elapsed time is 13 hours and 2 minutes.
```

The convention is that 12:00 P.M. is midnight and 12:01 A.M. is one minute later. Similarly, 12:00 A.M. is noon and 12:01 P.M. is a minute past noon. Assume that the later time is less than 24 hours from the first time. You may find it useful to sketch a time line with alternating A.M. and P.M. regions.

5. Develop a stepwise refinement solution to the following problem. Include the last pass before the Pascal program, but do not include the program itself.

   Most years divisible by four are leap years. For example, 1988 was a leap year because 1988 is divisible by four. An exception to the rule is for years that are divisible by 100. Even though these years are divisible by four, they are not leap years unless they are divisible by 400. For example, 1900 was not a leap year, but 2000 will be. The problem is to input a year as an integer and output a message stating whether it is a leap year.

6. Develop a stepwise refinement solution to the following problem. Include the last pass before the Pascal program, but do not include the program itself.

   The two real solutions of the quadratic equation

   $$ax^2 + bx + c = 0$$

   are given by the quadratic formula

   $$\frac{-b \pm \sqrt{b^2 - 4ac}}{2a}$$

   when the coefficient a is not zero, and when the quantity under the square root (called the discriminant) is positive. When a is zero, the equation becomes linear instead of quadratic and has the one solution $x = -c/b$ (providing b is not zero, in which case there would be no solution). When the discriminant is zero, the one solution is $x = -b/2a$

(providing *a* is not zero, in which case there would be no solution). When the discriminant is negative, there is no solution, since the square root of a negative number is not real. Read three integer coefficients for *a*, *b*, and *c*. Output either one or two real numbers that are the solutions to the equation, or a statement that the equation has no real solution.

7. Develop a stepwise refinement solution to the following problem. Include the last pass before the Pascal program, but do not include the program itself.

   The problem is to input the integer (*x*, *y*) coordinates of a point and output one of three messages, depending on the location of the point (Figure 4.4). If it lies within a quadrant, state the quadrant in which it lies. If it lies on a boundary between two quadrants, state which quadrants it is between. If it lies on the origin, so state.

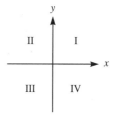

Figure 4.4

The four quadrants for Exercise 7.

   Sample Input/Output

```
Enter x and y coordinates (integers): -3 0
The point lies between quadrants II and III.
```

8. Develop a stepwise refinement solution to the following problem. Include the last pass before the Pascal program, but do not include the program itself.

   The problem is to input the integer (*x*, *y*) coordinates of two points and output a message that tells whether the line between the two points crosses the *x*-axis or *y*-axis. If a point is exactly on an axis, the line does not cross that axis. Figure 4.5 corresponds to the following sample input/output:

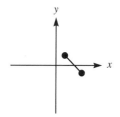

Figure 4.5

The sample input/output of Exercise 8.

   Sample Input/Output

```
Enter x and y coordinates of first point: 3 -1
Enter x and y coordinates of second point: 1 1

The line between the points crosses the x-axis.
The line does not cross the y-axis.
```

9. Develop a stepwise refinement solution to the following problem. Include the last pass before the Pascal program, but do not include the program itself.

   The problem is to input the end points of two line segments and output whether the line segments overlap, and if they do, state the overlap region. The two end points of a line segment are integers and can be entered in either order. If two line segments only touch each other at a common end point, the segments do not overlap. Figure 4.6 corresponds to the following sample input/output:

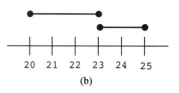

(a)

(a) Sample Input/Output

```
Enter the end points of the first segment: 4  1
Enter the end points of the second segment: 3  6

The segments overlap from 3 to 4.
```

(b) Sample Input/Output

```
Enter the end points of the first segment: 20  23
Enter the end points of the second segment: 23  25

The segments do not overlap.
```

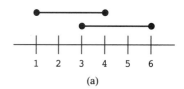

(b)

Figure 4.6

Number lines for the sample input/output of Exercise 9.

PROBLEMS

Section 4.1

10. For Problem 2.13, write the program to output your name and address, but send the results to a text file.

11. For Problem 2.16, write the program to output a pattern with a procedure, but send the results to a text file.

12. For Problem 3.35, write the program to compute the price per ounce, but get the number of ounces and cost from a text file.

Sample Input (text file)

```
22   1.89
```

Sample Output

```
The price per ounce of a 22 ounce box that
costs $1.89 is $0.086.
```

13. For Problem 3.47, write the program to compute the grade point average, but get the number of A's, B's, C's, D's, and F's (in that order) from a text file.

Sample Input (text file)

```
1   2   1   0   0
```

Sample Output

```
Grade point average is 3.00.
You did not make the dean's list.
```

Section 4.2

14. Write a program to compute a wage similar to Program 3.5, but get the hours worked followed by the hourly rate from a nontext `file of real`.

15. For Problem 3.36, write the program to convert feet and inches into meters, but get the values for the number of feet followed by the number of inches from a nontext `file of real`.

16. For Problem 3.37, write the program to compute the Celsius temperature, but get the Fahrenheit temperature from a nontext `file of real`.

17. For Problem 3.47, write the program to compute the grade point average, but get the five integers from a nontext `file of integer`.

Section 4.3

18. Use your stepwise refinement solution from Exercise 3 to complete the Pascal program that computes the age from the day, month, and year of a person's birthdate.

19. Use your stepwise refinement solution from Exercise 4 to complete the Pascal program that computes the elapsed time.

20. Use your stepwise refinement solution from Exercise 5 to complete the Pascal program that determines if a given year is a leap year.

21. Use your stepwise refinement solution from Exercise 6 to complete the Pascal program that computes the solution to a quadratic equation.

22. Use your stepwise refinement solution from Exercise 7 to complete the Pascal program that determines in which quadrant a point lies.

23. Use your stepwise refinement solution from Exercise 8 to complete the Pascal program that detects whether a line segment crosses the *x*- or *y*-axis.

24. Use your stepwise refinement solution from Exercise 9 to complete the Pascal program that determines if two line segments overlap.

Chapter

5

Repetition

A powerful feature of all computer systems is their ability to perform repetitious tasks. Most people dislike monotonous, mechanical jobs that require little thought. Computers have the marvelous property of executing monotonous jobs without tiring or complaining.

A group of statements that executes repetitively is called a *loop*. This chapter examines the three Pascal loop statements—the `while` statement, the `repeat` statement, and the `for` statement. It also introduces enumerated and subrange types, as well as nested loops.

Loops

5.1   While Statements and Loop Invariants

`while` statements are similar to `if` statements because they both evaluate boolean expressions and execute a "body statement" if the boolean expression is true. The difference between them is that after the body executes in a `while` statement, control is automatically transferred back up to the boolean expression for evaluation again. Each time the boolean expression is true, the body executes and the boolean expression is evaluated again. The following programs illustrate the use of the `while` statement.

Action of the while loop

Program 5.1

Program 5.1 computes the sum of a list of numbers in a text file. Each number represents the dollar balance in a customer's account.

The program shows a file with four real values, but the same program would work with any number of real values. The last value, `2e30`, does not represent an amount to be added to the others. It is a special value called a *sentinel,* which comes after the balance values and signifies that no more numbers are in the file to add. Since the last number is much greater than even a billion times a billion, you can be sure that everyone's balance will be less than the sentinel value.

Program 5.1

A program to find the total of all the data values in a text file. It uses the sentinel technique.

```
program TotalAccounts1 (AcctFile1, output);
   var
      Balance:   real;
      Sum:       real;
      AcctFile1: text;
   begin
   reset (AcctFile1);
   Sum := 0.00;
   read (AcctFile1, Balance);
   {  Assert: Sum is the sum of all the values  }
   {  input except for the value in Balance.    }
   while Balance < 1e30 do
      begin
      Sum := Sum + Balance;
      read (AcctFile1, Balance)
      end;
   writeln ('Total is $', Sum: 4: 2)
   end.
```

Input—AcctFile1

```
54.00   20.40   76.50   2e30
```

Output

```
Total is $150.90
```

When the program executes, the **reset** statement prepares **AcctFile1** for reading. Then the assignment statement sets the value of **Sum** to 0.00. The **read** statement gives the value of 54.00 from the file to variable **Balance**. Then, the **while** test

```
while Balance < 1e30 do
```

executes. The words **while** and **do** are Pascal reserved words. The boolean expression

```
Balance < 1e30
```

is true since the value of **Balance**, 54.00, is less than 1e30. Because the boolean expression is true, the next statement to execute is the compound statement

```
begin
Sum := Sum + Balance;
read (AcctFile1, Balance)
end
```

called the *body* of the loop. If the boolean expression were not true, the compound statement would be skipped.

The compound statement adds the values of **Sum** and **Balance** and gives the result, 54.00, to **Sum**. Then **read** gives the next value in the file, 24.00, to **Balance**.

At this point, the computer automatically transfers control back to the test after the reserved word `while`. The boolean expression is true again, since 24.00 is less than 1e30. So the compound statement executes again. Table 5.1 is a trace of the execution.

Statement executed	Balance	Sum
`begin`	?	?
`reset (AcctFile);`	?	?
`Sum := 0.00;`	?	0.00
`read (AcctFile1, B`	54.00	0.00
`while Balance < 1e`	54.00	0.00
`Sum := Sum + Balan`	54.00	54.00
`read (AcctFile1, B`	20.40	54.00
`while Balance < 1e`	20.40	54.00
`Sum := Sum + Balan`	20.40	74.40
`read (AcctFile1, B`	76.50	74.40
`while Balance < 1e`	76.50	74.40
`Sum := Sum + Balan`	76.50	150.90
`read (AcctFile1, B`	2e30	150.90
`while Balance < 1e`	2e30	150.90
`writeln ('Total is`	2e30	150.90
`end.`		

Table 5.1

A trace of Program 5.1 with three data values and a sentinel value as input.

Control keeps transferring back to the test at the top of the loop after the compound statement executes. Eventually, the `read` statement in the body of the loop gives the value 2e30 to `Balance`. Then the boolean expression is false, since 2e30 is not less than 1e30. The `writeln` statement outputs the value of `Sum`, and the program terminates.

This program illustrates a feature of Pascal that we will use throughout the remainder of the book. The `writeln` statement omitted the `output` file parameter. Whenever a `write` or `writeln` omits the file parameter, `output` is assumed and the values are sent to the screen. Similarly, whenever a `read` or `readln` omits the file parameter, `input` is assumed and the values come from the keyboard.

Omitting the file parameter

Figure 5.1 is the syntax chart for the `while` statement. The boolean expression can contain the AND, OR, or NOT operators. The statement after the reserved word `do` in this example was a compound statement. It can be any Pascal statement including an `if`, a `case`, or even another `while` statement.

Figure 5.1

The syntax chart for a `while` statement.

Figure 5.2 shows the general form of the flowchart for a `while` statement. It tests condition C1 first. If C1 is false, it skips statement S1. Otherwise, it executes statement S1 and transfers control up through the collector to the test again.

The flowchart shows several important properties of the `while` statement. First, there are two ways to reach the condition C1—from the statement immediately preceding the `while` statement or from the body of the loop. If C1 is true the first time, it will be tested again after S1 executes. S1 must eventually do something to change the evaluation of C1. Otherwise, C1 would be true always, and the loop would execute endlessly.

Figure 5.3 is the flowchart for Program 5.1. The input statement in the body of the loop affects the evaluation of the test condition. For the loop to terminate properly, the file must contain a sentinel value greater than 1e30. If it does not, the program will eventually try to read a real value from the file when no values are remaining. When that happens, the program will crash with an "attempt to read past end of file" error.

Figure 5.2 also shows that it is possible for statement S1 to never execute. It does not execute if C1 is determined to be false the first time. Table 5.2 is a trace of Program 5.1 when the input file, `AcctFile1`, has only the sentinel value, `2e30`. The body of the loop never executes, and the output is 0.00, as it should be with no data values that represent dollar amounts.

The file processing technique that Program 5.1 illustrates is called the *sentinel technique*. It requires that the sentinel in the file be compatible with the test in the `while` loop. You must select a value for the sentinel that is distinguishable from the values to be processed and test for it accordingly. Program 5.1 used 2e30 because it is well within the range of real numbers, even on small microcomputers.

Example 5.1 Suppose the sentinel value is –2e30. An appropriate test would be

```
while Balance > -1e30 do
```

since –2e30 is less than –1e30. (–2e30 is to the left of –1e30 on the number line.) ∎

Example 5.2 Suppose you choose a sentinel value of 1e–30 and a `while` test of

```
while Balance > 2e-30 do
```

Although this choice of sentinel and `while` test will work correctly with the previous data values of

```
54.00   20.40   76.50   1e-30
```

it will not work correctly if any of the data values are zero or negative. ∎

 Execution Counts

As consumers, we are familiar with the process of evaluating products. When you choose between two automobiles to purchase, what factors influence your choice?

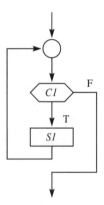

Figure 5.2

The flowchart for the `while` statement.

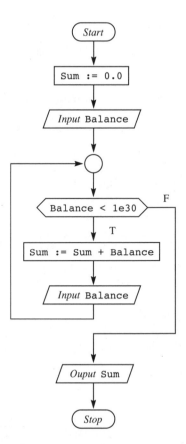

Figure 5.3

The flowchart for Program 5.1.

Statement executed	Balance	Sum
begin	?	?
reset (AcctFile1)	?	?
Sum := 0.00;	?	0.00
read (AcctFile1, B	2e30	0.00
while Balance < 1e	2e30	0.00
writeln ('Total is	2e30	0.00
end.		

Table 5.2

A trace of Program 5.1 with only the sentinel value in the input file.

For some people, speed and road handling may be the most important factors. Others may care about fuel economy. Some may be looking for luxury and a smooth ride. Most people are also concerned about price.

These factors usually compete with one another in the car buyer's mind. A car with much power and speed typically does not have good fuel economy. One that is luxurious does not come with a low price. In design terminology, that is a trade-off. The buyer may wish to trade off fuel economy to gain speed and power.

Tradeoffs

The same type of problem emerges when we evaluate algorithms. Several competing factors are present. Usually, a gain of one property in an algorithm comes at the expense of another.

Two important properties of an algorithm are the memory space required to store the program and its data, and the time necessary to execute the program. To compare several different algorithms that perform the same computation, we need a method of assessing these two properties. The following discussion presents a method for estimating the time necessary to execute a program.

Memory space and execution time

One way to estimate the time necessary for an algorithm to execute is to count the number of Level 6 statements that execute. If an algorithm has no if statements or loops, then the number of statements that execute is simply the number of executable statements in the program listing.

Execution time is related to statement execution count.

If the algorithm has a loop, however, the number of statements in the listing is not equal to the number of statements executed. This is because the statements in the body may execute many times, even though they appear only once in the program listing.

Program 5.1 has seven executable statements:

1. reset (AcctFile1)
2. Sum := 0.00
3. read (AcctFile1, Balance)
4. while Balance < 1e30 do
5. Sum := Sum + Balance
6. read (AcctFile1, Balance)
7. writeln ('Total is $', Sum: 4: 2)

The executable statements of Program 5.1

The declarations in the variable declaration part are not executable. Neither are the begin and end reserved words.

Even though the listing contains seven executable statements, more than seven statements execute. Statements 4, 5, and 6 are all part of a loop and may execute more than once. The trace in Table 5.1 shows that when the input file contains 3 data values and 1 sentinel value, a total of 14 statements execute. Table 5.3 shows

Statement	Three data values	*n* data values
`reset (AcctFile1);`	1	1
`Sum := 0.00;`	1	1
`read (AcctFile1, Balance);`	1	1
`while Balance < 1e30 do`	4	$n + 1$
`    begin`		
`    Sum := Sum + Balance;`	3	n
`    read (AcctFile1, Balance)`	3	n
`    end;`		
`writeln ('Total is $', Sum: 4: 2)`	1	1
Total:	14	$3n + 5$

Table 5.3

Statement execution count for Program 5.1.

the execution count for each of the executable statements. The `while` test executes once more than each statement in the body of the loop.

If `AcctFile1` contained *n* data values followed by the sentinel value, then a total of $3n + 5$ statements would execute. Substituting $n = 3$ into the formula $3n + 5$ produces 14, as expected. Also, substituting $n = 0$ into the formula produces 5, as expected from Table 5.2, the trace when there are no data values.

Execution Time Estimates

You can use the general expression for the statement count, $3n + 5$, to estimate the execution time for a large number of data values, given the execution time for a small number of data values.

Example 5.3 Suppose you execute Program 5.1 with 100 data values and it takes 140 ms (140 milliseconds, which is 0.140 seconds). The problem is to estimate how long it would take to execute the program with 1000 data values.

Assuming that each Level 6 statement takes the same amount of time to execute, simply form the ratio

$$\frac{140}{3 \times 100 + 5} = \frac{T}{3 \times 1000 + 5}$$

where *T* is the time to execute with 1000 data values. Solving for *T* gives

$$\frac{140}{305} = \frac{T}{3005}$$

or $T = 1379$ ms $= 1.38$ s. ∎

The time of 1.38 seconds is only an estimate. Each statement at Level 6 does not execute in the same amount of time. Remember that the compiler must translate the Level 6 statement to Level 3, the machine level, before it can execute. Typically, the compiler translates one Level 6 statement to more than one Level 3 statement. It may translate one Level 6 statement into three Level 3 statements and another Level 6 statement into five Level 3 statements. Furthermore, even the Level 3 statements do not execute in equal amounts of time.

Under these circumstances, it is unreasonable to expect each Level 6 instruction to execute in the same amount of time. Nevertheless, the estimate can still be a good indication of the execution time. To check the validity of the method, Program 5.1 was executed in 140 ms on one computer with 100 data values, as Example 5.3 assumed. It was then executed on the same computer with 1000 data values and took 1.31 seconds, which compares favorably with the 1.38 second estimate.

Assumptions in the estimate

The following example shows why the estimate works so well in practice. In dealing with large numbers of data, say hundreds or thousands for the value of n, the additive constants are insignificant to the final result and can be ignored.

Example 5.4 In the previous example, ignoring the additive constant, 5, in the expression can be justified because 305 is about equal to 300, and 3005 is about equal to 3000. Assuming that $3n + 5$ is approximately equal to $3n$, forming the ratio and solving for T then yields

$$\frac{140}{3 \times 100} = \frac{T}{3 \times 1000}$$

$$\frac{140}{100} = \frac{T}{1000}$$

or $T = 1400$ ms $= 1.4$ s, which is not too different from our original estimate. ∎

Notice that when you ignore the additive constant, the coefficient of n, which is 3, cancels in the ratio. Why is the coefficient of n unimportant in the estimate of the execution time for 1000 data values? Because for these large amounts of data, namely $n = 100$ and $n = 1000$, the number of statements executed is just about directly proportional to n. That implies that doubling the number of data values will double the number of statements executed, hence it will double the execution time. Or, as in this problem, multiplying the number of data values by 10 multiplies the execution time by 10.

When the coefficient of n is unimportant

Although the coefficient of n is unimportant in estimating the execution time for one algorithm with different amounts of data, it is important in comparing two different algorithms for the same job. If one algorithm requires $3n + 5$ statements to execute, and another algorithm to do the same processing requires $7n + 5$ statements to execute, the first will execute faster than the second with the same amount of data.

When the coefficient of n is important

Loop Invariants

Program 5.1 contains an assertion just before the `while` statement.

```
{  Assert: Sum is the sum of all the values  }
{  input except for the value in Balance.    }
```

The assertion is true before the loop executes the first time. It is also true after the loop executes each time. An assertion at the beginning of a loop that is also true after each execution of the loop is called a *loop invariant*. It is an invariant because its truth does not vary with each execution of the body.

The definition of a loop invariant

Like ordinary assertions, loop invariants can help you analyze the logic of your programs. Writing a correct loop generally involves two steps—initializing some variables before the loop and modifying those variables in the body of the loop. Formulating the right loop invariant is useful in getting these steps correct.

In this example, the initializing step

```
Sum := 0.00;
read (AcctFile1, Balance)
```

Making the loop invariant true the first time

makes the loop invariant true the first time. The sum of all the values so far is 0.00, since no values have been input, other than the current value in `Balance`.

Then, the modifying step

```
Sum := Sum + Balance;
read (AcctFile1, Balance)
```

Keeping the loop invariant true each time

keeps the loop invariant true each time the body of the loop executes. Suppose `Sum` is the sum of all the values input so far except the one in `Balance` (this is the loop invariant). If you add the value of `Balance` to `Sum` and get the next value from the file into `Balance`, then `Sum` will again be the sum of all the values input so far except the one in `Balance`. That is, the loop invariant remains true.

When the loop terminates, the loop invariant will therefore be true. Namely, `Sum` will contain the sum of all the values input except for the current value of `Balance`. Since the current value of `Balance` is the sentinel value, you do not want to add it to `Sum` anyway. Therefore, `Sum` contains the correct value.

Computing the Average

Suppose you want to compute the average of the balances in the accounts. You would need not only their sum, but the number of accounts as well. The following algorithm uses another integer variable, `NumAccts`, to count how many data values are in the file.

```
begin
Sum := 0.00
NumAccts := 0
Input Balance
while Balance < 1e30 do
   begin
   Sum := Sum + Balance
   NumAccts := NumAccts + 1
   Input Balance
   end
Output Sum / NumAccts
end
```

An algorithm to compute the average

This algorithm illustrates a common programming technique. To determine how many times a loop executes, initialize a counting variable, in this algorithm `NumAccts`, outside the loop to zero. Each time the loop executes, increment the counting variable by one. When the loop terminates, the value of the counting variable will be the number of times the loop executed.

Variables for counting

Finding the Largest

The following algorithm finds the largest number from a text file of quiz scores. It uses the sentinel technique with –1 as the sentinel value. If the input is

```
73   80   68   92   75   -1
```

then the output is 92. The two variables, `Score` and `MaxScore`, are integers.

```
begin
Input Score
MaxScore := Score
while Score >= 0 do
   begin
   if Score > MaxScore then
      MaxScore := Score
   Input Score
   end
if MaxScore >= 0 then
   Output MaxScore
else
   Output empty file message.
end
```

An algorithm to find the largest value

The algorithm contains an `if` statement nested inside a `while` loop. It works by getting the first value from the file, 73, and giving it to `MaxScore`. The first time the body of the loop executes, `Score` is not greater than `MaxScore`, since they both have the same value, 73. Then, `Score` gets the next value from the file, 80.

The second time through the loop, the true alternative of the `if` statement executes since the value of `Score`, which is now 80, is greater than the value of `MaxScore`, which is 73. `MaxScore` gets 80, which is the largest score input thus far. Had the value of `Score` been less than 73, `MaxScore` would have retained that value and would still be the largest score input thus far. When the loop terminates, `MaxScore` will contain the largest of all the data values input.

This algorithm illustrates another common programming technique. To save a value through successive loop iterations, declare a variable and initialize it appropriately. In the body of the loop, update the value with an assignment statement in the alternative of an `if` statement as needed.

Variables for saving values through successive loop iterations

◼ **Program 5.2**

Program 5.2 creates a nontext file by asking the user for input from the keyboard. It uses the sentinel technique with a sentinel value of n entered from the keyboard. Actually, since the test for continuing the loop is

```
(Response = 'Y') or (Response = 'y')
```

the sentinel value can be any character other than the letters Y or y.

AcctFile2 is a nontext file. The output with the listing in Program 5.2 shows the numbers in the file with two digits past the decimal point and with spaces between the values. That format is misleading because, in a nontext file

```
program MakeNonText (input, output, AcctFile2);
   var
      Num:       real;
      Response:  char;
      AcctFile2: file of real;
   begin
   rewrite (AcctFile2);
   write ('Enter a number? (y or n): ');
   readln (Response);
   while (Response = 'Y') or (Response = 'y') do
      begin
      write ('Type the number: ');
      readln (Num);
      write (AcctFile2, Num);
      writeln;
      write ('Enter another number? (y or n): ');
      readln (Response)
      end
   end.
```

Program 5.2

A program to create a nontext file. It uses the sentinel technique to get input from the keyboard. A sentinel value is not placed in the nontext file.

Interactive Input/Output

```
Enter a number? (y or n): y
Type the number: 54.00

Enter another number? (y or n): y
Type the number: 20.40

Enter another number? (y or n): y
Type the number: 76.50

Enter another number? (y or n): n
```

Output—AcctFile2 (nontext)

```
54.00   20.40   76.50
```

there is no format—no space characters and no lines. The computer stores all values in binary scientific notation with the same precision, which is determined by the particular hardware and compiler.

No lines in a nontext file

Since a nontext file has no lines, you cannot use `readln` with a nontext file parameter, nor can you use `writeln` with a nontext file parameter. It is also illegal to use the format specification with a nontext file.

Example 5.5 It may look like the output values listed with Program 5.2 were produced with

```
write (AcctFile2, Num: 7: 2)
```

However, this `write` statement is illegal because the format specification is used with a nontext file. ∎

The `while` loop in Program 5.2 terminates with the sentinel value n from the keyboard. But the program does not write a sentinel value to `AcctFile2`. If the user types n in response to the first question from the program, no values will be placed in the nontext file. `AcctFile2` will exist in the file directory of the operating system, but it will be empty.

Program 5.3

Program 5.3 performs the same computation as Program 5.1, except that the input comes from a nontext file instead of a text file. It illustrates a different file-processing technique that uses the `eof` function. The values to process are taken from the nontext file created by the previous program.

The Pascal boolean function `eof` stands for *end of file*. Two statements affect the `eof` function, the `reset` statement and the `read` statement. The statement

```
reset (AcctFile2)
```

does the following:

- It prepares the file `AcctFile2` for reading.
- It examines the contents of `AcctFile2`. If the file is empty, it sets `eof` (`AcctFile2`) to true. Otherwise it sets `eof` (`AcctFile2`) to false.

The effect of reset on eof

Similarly, the statement

```
read (AcctFile2, Balance)
```

does the following:

- It reads the next value from `AcctFile2` into the variable `Balance`.
- After reading the value, it examines the remaining contents of `AcctFile2`. If another value is in the file after the value just read, it sets `eof` (`AcctFile2`) to false. Otherwise it sets `eof` (`AcctFile2`) to true.

The effect of read on eof

```
program TotalAccounts2 (AcctFile2, output);
   var
      Balance:   real;
      Sum:       real;
      AcctFile2: file of real;
   begin
   reset (AcctFile2);
   Sum := 0.00;
   {  Assert: Sum is the sum of all the values  }
   {  input thus far.                           }
   while not eof (AcctFile2) do
      begin
      read (AcctFile2, Balance);
      Sum := Sum + Balance
      end;
   writeln ('Total is $', Sum :4: 2)
   end.
```

Program 5.3

A program to find the total of all the data values in a nontext file. It uses the eof technique.

Input—AcctFile2 (nontext)

54.00   20.40   76.50

Output

Total is $150.90

Statement executed	Balance	Sum	eof (AcctFile)
begin	?	?	?
reset (AcctFile2);	?	?	false
Sum := 0.00;	?	0.00	false
while not eof (Acc	?	0.00	false
read (AcctFile2, B	54.00	0.00	false
Sum := Sum + Balan	54.00	54.00	false
while not eof (Acc	54.00	54.00	false
read (AcctFile2, B	20.40	54.00	false
Sum := Sum + Balan	20.40	74.40	false
while not eof (Acc	20.40	74.40	false
read (AcctFile2, B	76.50	74.40	true
Sum := Sum + Balan	76.50	150.90	true
while not eof (Acc	76.50	150.90	true
writeln ('Total is	76.50	150.90	true
end.			

Table 5.4

A trace of Program 5.3 with three data values in the nontext file.

Table 5.4 is a trace of Program 5.3 with three data values in the file. Since `AcctFile2` is not empty, the `reset` statement sets `eof (AcctFile2)` to false. When the `while` statement executes, the boolean expression

```
not eof (AcctFile2)
```

is true, so the body of the `while` loop executes.

The `read` statement gives the value 54.00 to `Balance` and detects the presence of the next value, 20.40, in the file. Since there is another value after the one just read, it sets `eof (AcctFile2)` to false.

The next time the `while` statement executes, the boolean expression

```
not eof (AcctFile2)
```

is true again, so the body executes again.

The third time around, the `read` statement gives the value of 76.50 from `AcctFile2` to `Balance`. But this time it detects that no values are after the one just read, so it sets `eof (AcctFile2)` to true. The next time the `while` statement tests the `eof` function, the loop terminates.

Table 5.5 is a trace of the program when the input file is empty. The `reset` statement sets the `eof` statement to true. The body of the loop never executes, and the program outputs a sum of 0.00 as desired.

Statement executed	Balance	Sum	eof (AcctFile)
begin	?	?	?
reset (AcctFile2);	?	?	true
Sum := 0.00;	?	0.00	true
while not eof (Acc	?	0.00	true
writeln ('Total is	?	0.00	true
end.			

Table 5.5

A trace of Program 5.3 with an empty input file.

The loop invariant

```
{  Assert: Sum is the sum of all the values  }
{  input thus far.                           }
```

is true at the beginning of the loop because `Sum` is 0.00 and no values have been input yet. It is also true after each execution of the loop body, because after a value is input it is added to `Sum`. Therefore, `Sum` is the sum of all the values in the file when the loop terminates.

Remember that the two advantages of a nontext file are its small size and its fast I/O compared to the corresponding text file. Table 5.6 shows the size and I/O time for the text file of Program 5.1 compared with the nontext file of Program 5.3 on the same computer. Both files contained 1000 real data values. Although the

Type	Size (bytes)	I/O time (ms)
Text	11,022	1,310
Nontext	8,000	610

Table 5.6

An example of text file versus nontext file performance.

specific numbers in the table will vary from one computer to another, nontext files always perform better than text files. The disadvantage of nontext files is the inconvenience of not being able to manipulate them with text editors.

Sentinel Versus Eof Technique

A crucial difference between the sentinel technique and the `eof` technique is the placement of the `read` statement. With the sentinel technique, you must place an initial `read` statement before the `while` statement. Since the `while` statement tests the value of the input variable, that variable must have a value. The last statement in the body of a `while` loop should be another `read`, so the `while` statement will be able to test for the sentinel value again.

With the `eof` technique, however, the `while` statement does not test the value of the input variable. So you must *not* place an initial `read` statement before the `while` statement. Furthermore, the `read` statement in the body of the loop must be the *first* statement in the body, not the last statement. The `read` statement causes the `eof` function to look after the value just read to test for the end of the file so that the loop will terminate properly.

Real Expressions in Loops

You must be careful when you test real expressions in `while` statements. Unlike integer values, real values have fractional parts, which the computer can store only approximately in main memory. The approximate nature of real values can cause endless loops if you do not design your `while` tests properly.

Example 5.6   The following code fragment, where R is a real variable, is an endless loop:

```
R := 0.6;
while R <> 1.0 do
   R := R + 0.1
```
An endless loop

It would seem that after R is initialized to 0.6, the loop would increase it to 0.7, 0.8, 0.9, and 1.0, at which point the loop would terminate. The problem is that R is never exactly 1.0 after those calculations. After four executions of the loop the value of R will be approximately one, not exactly one. ∎

The problem in Example 5.6 is that R was tested for strict inequality. In general, you should use the following rule for testing real values:

An important rule for testing real values

- Never test a real expression for strict equality, =, or strict inequality, <>.

Tests for real values should always contain a *less than* or a *greater than* component. Note that the test for terminating the `while` loop in Program 5.1 is

```
while Balance < 1e30 do
```

with the *less than* operator, instead of

```
while Balance <> 2e30 do
```

which uses a strict inequality test.

Example 5.7   The previous example could be coded

```
R := 0.6;
while R <= 0.95 do
   R := R + 0.1
```

which would increase R to 0.7, 0.8, 0.9, and 1.0, at which point the loop would terminate.   ∎

Pascal does not have an operator that raises a value to a power. For example, the expression $7x^3$ where x is a real variable, must be written `7 * X * X * X`, which requires three multiplications. Multiplication of real values is one of the most time-consuming operations that the CPU can do. Polynomial expressions, which are sums of terms such as $7x^3$, are especially time consuming when they occur in loops that execute repeatedly. A common technique to minimize the computation time is to completely factor such expressions to reduce the number of real multiplications required. This technique will be used in Program 5.4.

Factoring for efficiency

Example 5.8   Suppose you need to evaluate

$$7x^3 + 2x^2 + 8x + 5$$

Without factoring, the corresponding Pascal expression is

```
7 * X * X * X + 2 * X * X + 8 * X + 5
```

which requires six multiplications and three additions. On the other hand, if you completely factor the expression as

$$((7x + 2)x + 8)x + 5$$

then the corresponding Pascal expression is

```
((7 * X + 2) * X + 8) * X + 5
```

which only requires three multiplications and three additions.   ∎

Program 5.4

A *numerical method* is an algorithm that calculates a value or set of values that approximates the solution of a mathematical problem. Program 5.4 is a numerical method that computes one root of the cubic equation

$$x^3 - 4x + 2 = 0$$

with the bisection algorithm.

Figure 5.4 is a graph of the function

$$f(x) = x^3 - 4x + 2$$

The roots of the cubic equation are the values of x for which $f(x) = 0$. Figure 5.4 shows that $f(x)$ is zero for three different values of x: (a) between -3.0 and -2.0, (b) between 0.0 and 1.0, and (c) between 1.0 and 2.0. Although this cubic equation has three roots, cubic equations in general can have from one to three roots. The program will determine the root of the equation that lies between $x = 1$ and $x = 2$.

In the bisection algorithm, the variable `Left` is a value of x that lies to the left of the root and the variable `Right` is a value of x that lies to the right of the root. This program initializes `Left` to 1.0 and `Right` to 2.0. Then, as Figure 5.5(a) shows, it calculates the variable `FLeft` as

```
FLeft := f(Left)
```

Figure 5.4

A graph of the function $f(x) = x^3 - 4x + 2$.

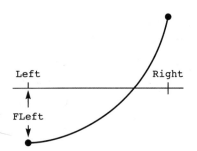

(a) Before the loop executes the first time.

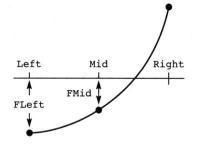

(b) Computation of `Mid` and `FMid`.

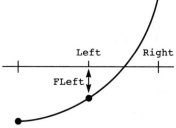

(c) Updating `Left` and `FLeft`.

Figure 5.5

The bisection method to find the root of $f(x)$ that lies between 1.0 and 2.0.

The next step is to compute the value of x that is the midpoint between `Left` and `Right`. As Figure 5.5(b) shows, the algorithm gives that value of x to the variable `Mid` and computes `FMid` as

```
FMid := f(Mid)
```

The value of `FMid` determines whether the root lies to the left or right of `Mid`. If `FLeft` and `FMid` have the same sign, then the root lies to the right of `Mid`.

```
program FindRoot1 (input, output);
   const
      A = 1.0;
      B = -4.0;
      C = 2.0;
   var
      Left, FLeft: real;
      Mid, FMid:   real;
      Right:       real;
      Tolerance:   real;
   begin
   write ('Enter tolerance: ');
   readln (Tolerance);
   Left := 1.0;
   FLeft := (A * Left * Left + B) * Left + C;
   Right := 2.0;
   {  Assert: Root is between Left and Right.  }
   while abs (Left - Right) > Tolerance do
      begin
      Mid := (Left + Right) / 2.0;
      FMid := (A * Mid * Mid + B) * Mid + C;
      if FLeft * FMid > 0.0 then
         {  Assert: Root is between Mid and Right.  }
         begin
         Left := Mid;
         FLeft := FMid
         end
      else
         {  Assert: Root is between Left and Mid.  }
         Right := Mid
      end;
   writeln ('Root is: ', (Left + Right) / 2.0: 6: 4)
   end.
```

Interactive Input/Output

```
Enter tolerance: 0.1
Root is: 1.6563
```

Interactive Input/Output

```
Enter tolerance: 0.01
Root is: 1.6758
```

Interactive Input/Output

```
Enter tolerance: 0.001
Root is: 1.6753
```

Program 5.4

Computation of the root of the equation $x^3 - 4x + 2$ that lies between 1.0 and 2.0 with the bisection algorithm.

Otherwise, the root lies to the left of `Mid`. In the figure, `FLeft` and `FMid` have the same sign, since both are negative. Therefore, the root lies to the right of `Mid`.

If the root lies to the right of `Mid`, the algorithm changes the value of `Left` and `FLeft` by

```
Left := Mid
FLeft := FMid
```

as Figure 5.5(c) shows. The root is still between `Left` and `Right`. Had the root lain to the left of `Mid`, the algorithm would have changed the value of `Right` by

```
Right := Mid
```

so that the root would still be between `Left` and `Right`.

The bisection algorithm continues to find the midpoint between `Left` and `Right`. Each time it updates `Left` or `Right`, it decreases the interval between them such that the root is still in the interval. The loop invariant is the assertion that the root is between `Left` and `Right`.

Program 5.4 implements the bisection algorithm in Pascal. The program inputs a real value into `Tolerance` that controls termination of the loop. As long as the length of the interval is greater than the tolerance entered by the user, the loop executes. Each time the loop executes, the program halves the interval, which guarantees that the loop will eventually terminate.

When the user enters 0.1, the bisection method calculates the root as 1.6563. It is accurate to the nearest tenth, so the last three digits, 563, are not significant. When the user enters 0.01, the loop executes more times and calculates the root as 1.6758, a more accurate value for the root than 1.6563. The smaller the tolerance, the more times the loop executes and the more accurate is the value for the root. But then the program runs longer. So there is a tradeoff between the accuracy of the solution and the execution time.

The tradeoff between accuracy and execution time

If the user enters zero for the tolerance, the loop will execute endlessly, since continually halving the interval never permits it to reach zero. If the user enters a negative tolerance, the loop will execute endlessly because the boolean expression in the `while` statement will always be true. The program could be improved by testing the tolerance for negative or zero values and not allowing them.

Program 5.5

The next example of the `while` loop illustrates stepwise refinement. The data consists of a nontext file of real values that represent the number of hours worked per week and the hourly pay rate. Program 5.5 must output a table with the hours worked, pay rate, and weekly pay with the possibility of overtime. The table indicates those entries that include overtime pay. It must also determine the average salary of all the employees as well as the number of employees who earned overtime. For example, if the input file contains the real values

Sample input for Program 5.5

```
35.0   13.00
45.0   10.00
40.0   12.50
40.0   11.00
50.0   10.00
```

then the output should be

Sample output for Program 5.5

```
-------------------------------
Hours worked  Pay rate   Wages
-------------------------------
     35.0       13.00   455.00
     45.0 *     10.00   475.00
     40.0       12.50   500.00
     40.0       11.00   440.00
     50.0 *     10.00   550.00
-------------------------------
Note: * indicates overtime.
Average wage: $484.00
Number with overtime: 2
```

The first step is to determine the variables in the `var` section. Remember that input, processing, and output are the three major parts of a program. That gives a hint of the variables required.

Determining the variables

Input   The input consists of a file of real values. Hence you will need two real variables, say `Hours` and `Rate`, for the input. `PayrollFile` will be the nontext file of reals.

Processing   To compute the average, you must compute each wage and divide the total wages by the number of employees. Hence you will need real variables, `Wages` and `TotalWages`, to store the computed wage for an individual and for the total of all the wages. An integer variable, `NumEmpl`, will count the number of employees. The integer variable `NumOvertime` will keep track of the number of employees who worked overtime.

Output   The three variables, `Hours`, `Rate`, and `Wages`, will be used to output a single line in the report. `AveWages` will be a real variable for outputting the average wage at the bottom of the report. The value of `NumOvertime` will also appear at the bottom.

The tentative variable declaration part now looks like this:

```
Hours:        real
Rate:         real
Wages:        real
TotalWages:   real
NumEmpl:      integer
NumOvertime:  integer
AveWages:     real
PayrollFile:  file of real
```

In this problem, the number of variables and their types were fairly easy to determine before writing the logic of the program. With some problems it is not always possible to determine the variables beforehand. In general, you should determine the principal variables of the program at an early stage of the stepwise refinement. Then, augment the variable declaration part with new variables as refinement progresses.

First Pass Program 5.3 showed the technique of processing from a nontext file. Use the `eof` boolean function and do not place a `read` before the `while` statement. In the body of the loop, first read, then process the data that was just read. Using this pattern, the first pass is the following:

The first pass of Program 5.5

```
begin
reset (PayrollFile)
Initialize variables
while not eof (PayRollFile) do
   begin
   read (PayrollFile, Hours, Rate)
   Process Hours, Rate
   end
Compute the average.
Output AveWages, NumOvertime
end
```

Second Pass Each pass in a stepwise refinement solution should concentrate on one aspect of the problem. This problem requires a table with a heading, a list of values, and a footing. The second pass will solve the table output part of the problem.

The heading appears once in the output. So the output statements for the heading must come before the `while` statement. Two kinds of lines appear in the body of the report, one with an asterisk for those who worked overtime, and one without an asterisk for those who did not. This requires an `if` statement in the body of the loop. The footing appears once at the bottom of the report. The output statement for the footing must therefore be after the `while` loop.

Here is the second pass:

```
begin
reset (PayrollFile)
```
Initialize variables.
Output heading.
```
while not eof (PayrollFile) do
   begin
   read (PayrollFile, Hours, Rate)
```
   Process `Hours, Rate`
```
   if employee did not work overtime then
       Output Hours, Rate, Wages
   else
       Output Hours, '*', Rate, Wages
   end
```
Output footing.
Compute the average.
```
Output AveWages, NumOvertime
end
```

Third Pass This pass will solve the problem of processing `Salary` and computing the output.

The average is the sum of the salaries divided by the number of employees. You can compute the sum by the technique of Program 5.3. That example initialized the variable `Sum` to 0.00 before the `while` loop. Each time the loop executed, `Sum` increased by the value input from the file. In this problem you can initialize and increase `TotalWages` the same way.

You can compute the number of employees using `NumEmpl` as a counting variable. Initialize `NumEmpl` to zero before the `while` loop. Each time the `read` statement is executed in the loop, increment `NumEmpl` by one. After the loop has terminated, the value of `NumEmpl` will equal the number of times the loop was executed.

Similarly, you can initialize `NumOvertime` to zero before the loop. But now you only want to increment `NumOvertime` by one if the employee worked overtime.

The third pass is

```
begin
reset (PayrollFile)
TotalWages := 0.00
NumEmpl := 0
NumOvertime := 0
```
Output heading.

```
while not eof (PayrollFile) do
    begin
    read (PayrollFile, Hours, Rate)
    if Hours <= 40.0 then
        begin
        Wages := Hours * Rate
        Output Hours, Rate, Wages
        end
    else
        begin
        Wages := 40.0 * Rate + (Hours - 40.0) * 1.5 * Rate
        Output Hours, '*', Rate, Wages
        NumOvertime := NumOvertime + 1
        end
    TotalWages := TotalWages + Wages
    NumEmpl := NumEmpl + 1
    end
Output footing.
AveWages := TotalWages / NumEmpl
Output AveWages, NumOvertime
end
```

Fourth Pass   This pass is the complete Pascal listing shown in Program 5.5.

Notice the format specifications for the real values in the body of the loop. Since these values appear in a table with their decimal points lined up, it is inappropriate to use the expanding field feature. `Hours` has a field width of 10, larger than that required for the largest value of `Hours` expected. The field widths for `Rate` and `Wages` are also large enough to accommodate their maximum expected values.

Stepwise Refinement

Stepwise refinement is a valuable technique for developing software. It is based on the principle of abstraction presented in Chapter 1. The idea is to proceed from the highest level of abstraction, with a minimum of details, to the lowest level of abstraction, with all the details of a complete Pascal program. Figure 5.6 is the level diagram of the stepwise refinement process for Program 5.5.

This program shows several common stepwise refinement characteristics. In every pass except the last one, all the irrelevant details of input and output should be suppressed. The first three passes of this example used the pseudocode statements *Input* and *Output*. Only on the last pass were they converted to Pascal `reads` and `writes` with formatting details.

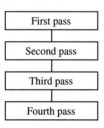

Figure *5.6*

The level diagram of the stepwise refinement process of Program 5.5.

```
program Payroll (PayrollFile, output);
   var
      Hours:        real;
      Rate:         real;
      Wages:        real;
      TotalWages:   real;
      NumEmpl:      integer;
      NumOvertime:  integer;
      AveWages:     real;
      PayrollFile:  file of real;
   begin
   reset (PayrollFile);
   TotalWages := 0.00;
   NumEmpl := 0;
   NumOvertime := 0;
   writeln ('-----------------------------');
   writeln ('Hours worked  Pay rate    Wages');
   writeln ('-----------------------------');
   while not eof (PayrollFile) do
      begin
      read (PayrollFile, Hours, Rate);
      if Hours <= 40.0 then
         begin
         Wages := Hours * Rate;
         writeln (Hours: 10: 1, Rate: 12: 2, Wages: 8: 2)
         end
      else
         begin
         Wages := 40.0 * Rate + (Hours - 40.0) * 1.5 * Rate;
         writeln (Hours: 10: 1, ' *', Rate: 10: 2, Wages: 8: 2);
         NumOvertime := NumOvertime + 1
         end;
      TotalWages := TotalWages + Wages;
      NumEmpl := NumEmpl + 1
      end;
   writeln ('-----------------------------');
   writeln ('Note: * indicates overtime.    ');
   AveWages := TotalWages / NumEmpl;
   writeln ('Average wage: $', AveWages: 4: 2);
   writeln ('Number with overtime: ', NumOvertime: 1)
   end.
```

Program 5.5

A payroll program that outputs the wage for each employee including the possibility of overtime. It computes the average wage and the number of employees who earned overtime pay.

Input/Output

See text.

Each pass should isolate and solve one specific part of the problem. In this program, the parts solved by each pass were the following:

- *First pass* input from the nontext file
- *Second pass* output of the table
- *Third pass* computation of output values
- *Fourth pass* Pascal details

The subproblems of Program 5.5

The strategy here is to divide and conquer. If you have a large problem that you do not know how to solve, divide it into smaller subproblems that you can solve. Stepwise refinement gives you a framework for dividing a problem into smaller parts.

Another tip with stepwise refinement is to work it out on your text editor if you have unlimited computer access, not on paper. With each pass you can expand one pseudocode statement into several statements that are closer to Pascal, a job more easily accomplished on a screen than on a piece of paper. At the end of the last pass, the Pascal program will be on your disk ready to compile.

A stepwise refinement tip

5.2   Repeat Statements

In the `while` statement the test is at the beginning of the loop. It is therefore possible for the body of a `while` loop to never be executed. The `repeat` statement is a loop whose test is at the end. The body of a `repeat` loop, therefore, always executes at least one time.

Program 5.6

A common situation in which you always want the body of the loop to be executed at least once is with interactive input. Program 5.6 repeatedly asks the user a question until the response is valid. Then it makes an appropriate reply.

The words `repeat` and `until` are Pascal reserved words. The word `repeat` signifies the start of the loop. When the executing program encounters the `repeat`, it simply enters the body of the loop. Program 5.6 asks the user a personal question and waits for the response. Unlike the `while` loop, the body of a `repeat` loop can have more than one statement without it being a compound statement enclosed with `begin` and `end`.

When the program encounters `until`, it evaluates the boolean expression

```
(Response = 'y') or (Response = 'n')
```

Since `Response` is '5', the boolean expression is false and the body of the loop repeats. When the user finally inputs a response that makes the boolean expression true, the loop terminates.

```
program Love (input, output);
   var
      Response: char;
   begin
   repeat
      write ('Do you love me? (y or n) ');
      readln (Response)
   until (Response = 'y') or (Response = 'n');
   if Response = 'y' then
      writeln ('I love you, too.')
   else
      writeln ('How sad.')
   end.
```

Interactive Input/Output

```
Do you love me? (y or n) 5
Do you love me? (y or n) ?
Do you love me? (y or n) y
I love you, too.
```

Program 5.6

A program that repeatedly asks the user a question until a valid response is entered.

Figure 5.7 is the syntax chart for the `repeat` statement. As with the `while` statement, the boolean expression can contain the AND, OR, or NOT operators. Any Pascal statement can be in the body of the `repeat`.

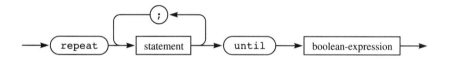

Figure 5.7

The syntax chart for a `repeat` statement.

Figure 5.8 shows the general form of the flowchart for a `repeat` statement. Statement S1 executes first, then condition C1 is tested. If it is true, the loop terminates. Otherwise, control transfers up through the collector to statement S1 again.

Repeat Versus While Loops

A comparison of the flowcharts of Figures 5.2 and 5.8 shows that the `while` and `repeat` loops differ in their termination conditions. In the `while` loop, if the boolean expression is true the loop continues. But in the `repeat` loop, if the boolean expression is true the loop terminates. It "repeats until" the boolean expression is true.

A `repeat` statement is more useful in this program than a `while` statement because the question always should be asked at least once. In fact, any algorithm written with a `repeat` statement can always be rewritten with a `while` statement

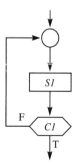

Figure 5.8

The flowchart for the `repeat` statement.

by duplicating the body of the repeat loop before the while test and changing the boolean expression for the test.

Example 5.9 The following code fragment produces exactly the same output as Program 5.6, but with a while loop.

```
write ('Do you love me? (y or n) ');
readln (Response);
while not ((Response = 'y') or (Response = 'n')) do
   begin
   write ('Do you love me? (y or n) ');
   readln (Response)
   end
```

If this code fragment were substituted into Program 5.6 in place of the repeat loop, the difference in execution would be indistinguishable to the user. ■

When confronted with a choice between using a repeat loop or a while loop, ask yourself the question, Do I want the body of the loop to always execute at least once? If so, use the repeat loop; otherwise, use the while loop.

In practice, the while loop is usually more convenient to use than the repeat loop. Most repetitive computations require the possibility that the body may not be executed. Both the sentinel technique and the eof technique are based on the while loop because of the possibility that the file may be empty.

Choosing between repeat and while loops

Example 5.10 Suppose you want Program 5.6 to output the error message that follows if the user enters invalid input.

```
Do you love me? (y or n) 5
Invalid response.  Try again.
Do you love me? (y or n) ?
Invalid response.  Try again.
Do you love me? (y or n) y
I love you, too.
```

The error message should be in the body of a while loop, as in the following code fragment:

```
write ('Do you love me? (y or n) ');
readln (Response);
while not ((Response = 'y') or (Response = 'n')) do
   begin
   writeln ('Invalid response.  Try again.');
   write ('Do you love me? (y or n) ');
   readln (Response)
   end
```

With this code, the body of the loop will not execute if the user enters a valid response the first time. ■

5.3 For Statements

Suppose you want to compute the sum of all the integers from 1 to 100. You could use a `while` loop, as in the following algorithm. Num, Sum, and I are variables of type integer. I is called the *control variable* of the loop because its value controls when the loop terminates.

```
begin
Input Num
Sum := 0
I := 1
while I <= Num do
   begin
   Sum := Sum + I
   I := succ (I)
   end
Output Sum
```

An algorithm to compute the sum of the integers from 1 to Num

The statement

```
I := succ (I)
```

is equivalent to the statement

```
I := I + 1
```

and is called incrementing variable I. The successor and predecessor functions work for integers the same as they do for characters.

If you input the value of 100 into Num, then the preceding algorithm will output 5050, which is the sum

$$1 + 2 + 3 + \cdots + 100$$

The sequence of steps

- Initialize a variable.
- Test the variable at the beginning of a loop.
- Execute the body of the loop.
- Replace the variable by its successor.

occurs frequently in programs. A special Pascal loop, the `for` statement, automatically initializes a control variable, tests it at the beginning of the loop, and replaces it with its successor after executing the body of the loop.

Program 5.7

Program 5.7 is the algorithm we just presented. It finds the sum of the first Num integers, but it is written with a for loop in place of the while loop.

```
program IntegerSum (input, output);
   var
      Num: integer;
      Sum: integer;
      I:   integer;
   begin
   write ('Enter an integer: ');
   readln (Num);
   Sum := 0;
   for I := 1 to Num do
      Sum := Sum + I;
   writeln ('Sum from 1 to ', Num: 1, ' is ', Sum: 1)
   end.
```

Program 5.7

Computation of the sum of all the integers from one to the number input. The for statement initializes, tests, and increments the control variable I.

Interactive Input/Output

```
Enter an integer: 100
Sum from 1 to 100 is 5050
```

When the program executes, the readln statement gives the value of 100 to Num. Sum gets 0. Then, the statement

```
for I := 1 to Num do
```

executes. The words for, to, and do are Pascal reserved words. The assignment statement between the reserved words for and to gives an initial value to the control variable of the for statement. In this statement, I, the control variable, gets the initial value of 1.

The for statement then compares the current value of I with the expression after the reserved word to. If the value of the control variable is greater than the expression, the loop terminates. Otherwise, the loop body executes. In this statement, the value of the control variable, 1, is not greater than the value of the expression, 100. The loop body executes, which adds 1 to Sum.

Control returns to the top of the loop. The for statement replaces the value of I, 1, by its successor, 2. It then compares the value of I with the expression after the reserved word to. Since the current value of I, 2, is not greater than the value of the expression, 100, the body of the loop executes again. Table 5.7 is a trace of Program 5.7.

The loop continues executing, with I getting the values 1, 2, 3, and so on, to 100. After it executes with I having the value 100, the loop terminates.

The value of the control variable is undefined when the loop terminates. Table 5.7 indicates the undefined value of I by '?' in the last two lines. It is undefined

The control variable is undefined on completion of the loop.

Statement executed	Num	Sum	I
begin	?	?	?
write ('Enter an i	?	?	?
readln (Num);	100	?	?
Sum := 0;	100	0	?
for I := 1 to Num	100	0	1
Sum := Sum + I;	100	1	1
for I := 1 to Num	100	1	2
Sum := Sum + I;	100	3	2
for I := 1 to Num	100	3	3
Sum := Sum + I;	100	6	3
.			
.			
.			
for I := 1 to Num	100	4851	99
Sum := Sum + I;	100	4950	99
for I := 1 to Num	100	4950	100
Sum := Sum + I;	100	5050	100
for I := 1 to Num	100	5050	?
writeln ('Sum from	100	5050	?
end.			

Table 5.7

A trace of Program 5.7 with an input value of 100 for Num.

because the value of I after the loop terminates will vary from one computer to another. On some computers, the `for` statement will leave the value of I at 100. On other computers, I will have the value 101. You should never assume a particular value of I after a `for` statement. Always treat it as undefined.

You should be able to determine the statement execution count for this program. A total of $2n + 5$ statements execute, where n is the value input for Num. That is $2(100) + 5$, or 205 statement executions for the computation of the sum of the first 100 integers.

Statement execution count for Program 5.7

The algorithm of Program 5.7 may be a good illustration of the `for` statement, but it is not a good solution to the problem. The formula, $m(m + 1)/2$, gives the sum of the first m integers directly, as will be shown later in Section 9.2. The following simpler algorithm solves the same problem with only two statement executions, regardless of the value input for Num.

```
begin
Input Num
Output Num * (Num + 1) / 2
end
```

A better algorithm than that in Program 5.7

■ Using For Statements

Figure 5.9 is the syntax chart for a `for` statement. If you put the reserved word `downto` in place of the reserved word `to`, then the value of the control variable is replaced by its predecessor instead of its successor, and the loop terminates when the value of the control variable is less than the expression instead of greater than the expression.

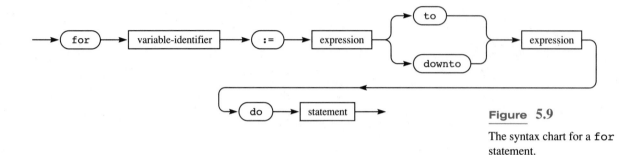

Figure 5.9

The syntax chart for a `for` statement.

Example 5.11   The following code fragment

```
for I := 1 to Num do
   write (I: 2)
```

where `Num` and `I` are variables of type integer, outputs

```
 1 2 3 4 5
```

if the value of `Num` is 5. But the code fragment

```
for I := Num downto 1 do
   write (I: 2)
```

outputs

```
 5 4 3 2 1
```

Since the test of a `for` statement is at the top of the loop, it is possible for the body to never execute. In this respect, the `for` statement is similar to the `while` statement.

The test in a for statement is at the top of the loop.

Example 5.12   In the two code fragments of the previous example, if the value of `Num` is zero, neither fragment will produce any output.   ■

In Figure 5.9, either expression can have any value—positive, negative, or zero.

Example 5.13 The code fragment

```
for I := Num to 5 do
   write (I: 3)
```

outputs

```
 -3 -2 -1  0  1  2  3  4  5
```

if the value of Num is –3. It outputs

```
 3  4  5
```

if the value of Num is 3. ∎

Standard Pascal imposes a restriction on the control variable. Although it is legal to use the control variable in an expression, you cannot change the value of the control variable in the body of a for loop. Two statements that change the value of a variable are the assignment statement and the read statement.

Illegal to change the value of the control variable in the body of the loop

Example 5.14 This code fragment

```
for I := 1 to Num do
   begin
   J := 2 * I - 1;
   write (J: 2)
   end
```

is legal and produces the output

```
 1 3 5 7 9
```

if the value of Num is 5. It is legal to use I in the expression on the right side of the assignment statement. ∎

Example 5.15 The code fragment

```
for I := 1 to Num do
   begin
   write (I: 2);
   I := I + 1
   end
```

is illegal because I is on the left side of an assignment statement in the body of the loop. A good compiler will detect this error, but some commercial compilers are deficient here and will let this error pass undetected with undefined results. Never do this, even if your compiler allows it! ∎

Example 5.16 The code fragment

```
for I := 1 to Num do
   begin
   write (I: 2);
   read (I)
   end
```

is illegal, because the read statement changes the value of the control variable, I.

◼

The expression whose value determines termination of the loop is evaluated only once at the start of the loop. If a statement in the body of the loop changes the expression, the new value is not used for the termination test. In practice, you should never want to change the value of the terminating expression.

Termination expression evaluated once at the beginning of the loop

Example 5.17 The code fragment

```
Num := 5;
for I := 1 to Num do
   begin
   Num := 4;
   write (I: 2)
   end
```

produces the output

```
 1  2  3  4  5
```

Even though the value of Num is changed from 5 to 4 in the body of the loop, the value of Num at the start of the loop, 5, is the one used to test for termination. ◼

The control variable is not limited to an integer, but can be of type char as well. The control variable cannot, however, be of type real.

Control variable can have type char

Example 5.18 In this code fragment, Letter is of type char.

```
for Letter := 'A' to 'Z' do
   write (Letter)
```

It produces the output

```
ABCDEFGHIJKLMNOPQRSTUVWXYZ
```

Each time through the loop, the for statement replaces the value of Letter with its successor. ◼

Example 5.19   The following code fragment

```
for Level := 0.5 to 6.5 do
   write (Level: 10: 1)
```

where `Level` is a real variable is illegal because the control variable cannot be real.   ∎

Now that we know how to program with three different kinds of loops—`while`, `repeat`, and `for`—the natural question is, when should you use the `for` loop instead of the others? The convenience of the `for` loop comes from the automatic incrementing and testing of the control variable, which acts like a counter. As a general rule, if you know before you enter the loop how many times it should execute, the `for` statement will be more convenient than the others.

When to use a for loop

For example, Program 5.1 added the total of all the balances in a file that had a sentinel value. Before entering the loop, you do not know how many values will be processed, so you do not know how many times the loop should execute. Program 5.4 computed the root of a cubic equation with the bisection algorithm. The termination condition was based on the value of `Tolerance`, so the number of times the loop will execute is unknown ahead of time. In both these programs, the `for` loop would be inappropriate. However, in Program 5.7 you know before entering the loop that it should be executed `Num` times, hence the appropriateness of the `for` statement.

Program 5.8

Program 5.1 used the sentinel technique to input and process data from a text file. Program 5.3 solved the same problem, but used the `eof` technique to input the data from a nontext file. Program 5.8 illustrates a third method, called the *count technique,* that is used with a text file. The first item in the file is an integer that tells how many data values are in the file.

Table 5.8 is a trace of the program. The first assignment statement gives `Sum` the value of 0.00. The `read` statement gives the first value in the file, 3, to `NumAccts`.

The `for` statement executes three times, once with `I = 1`, once with `I = 2`, and once with `I = 3`. Each time the body executes, it gets the next value from the file and adds it to `Sum`. After the loop executes the third time, the `for` statement terminates the loop. The control variable, `I`, gets an undefined value.

The count value in the file must be a true indication of how many data values follow. If the count value is less than the number of data values, the data at the end of the file will not be input and processed. If the count value is greater than the number of data values, the program will crash with an "attempt to read past end of file" error.

```
program TotalAccounts3 (AcctFile3, output);
   var
      Balance:   real;
      Sum:       real;
      NumAccts:  integer;
      I:         integer;
      AcctFile3: text;
   begin
   reset (AcctFile3);
   Sum := 0.00;
   read (AcctFile3, NumAccts);
   for I := 1 to NumAccts do
      begin
      read (AcctFile3, Balance);
      Sum := Sum + Balance
      end;
   writeln ('Total is $', Sum: 4: 2)
   end.
```

Program 5.8

A program that computes the total of all the values in a text file with the count technique.

Input—AcctFile3

3   54.00   20.40   76.50

Output

Total is $150.90

Statement executed	Balance	Sum	I	NumAccts
begin	?	?	?	?
Sum := 0.00;	?	0.00	?	?
read (AcctFile3, N	?	0.00	?	3
for I := 1 to NumA	?	0.00	1	3
read (AcctFile3, B	54.00	0.00	1	3
Sum := Sum + Balan	54.00	54.00	1	3
for I := 1 to NumA	54.00	54.00	2	3
read (AcctFile3, B	20.40	54.00	2	3
Sum := Sum + Balan	20.40	74.40	2	3
for I := 1 to NumA	20.40	74.40	3	3
read (AcctFile3, B	76.50	74.40	3	3
Sum := Sum + Balan	76.50	150.90	3	3
for I := 1 to NumA	76.50	150.90	?	3
writeln ('Total is	76.50	150.90	?	3
end.				

Table 5.8

A trace of Program 5.8 with one count value and three data values in the text file.

File-Processing Techniques

We have learned three basic techniques for inputting and processing a list of data:

- The sentinel technique
- The count technique
- The `eof` technique

Three file-processing techniques

Figure 5.10 summarizes the three techniques for file input. It shows the logic of each technique in pseudocode form. `DataIn` represents one or more input variables, and `FileIn` is a file. The input statements for the sentinel and count techniques represent `read` statements from the keyboard or a file.

```
Input DataIn
while DataIn is not the Sentinel do
   begin
   Process DataIn
   Input DataIn
   end
```

(a) The sentinel technique. Use with text files and interactive I/O.

```
Input NumItems
for I := 1 to NumItems do
   begin
   Input DataIn
   Process DataIn
   end
```

(b) The count technique. Use with text files and interactive I/O.

```
reset (FileIn)
while not eof (FileIn) do
   begin
   read (FileIn, DataIn)
   Process DataIn
   end
```

(c) The eof technique. Use with nontext files.

Figure 5.10

The three techniques for file input.

The sentinel technique inputs a value into the input variable before the `while` statement. The body of the loop processes the input value, then inputs the next value. The sentinel technique is useful for text files and interactive input. Although it is possible to use the sentinel technique with nontext files, the `eof` technique is preferred for those files.

The count technique assumes that an integer value will be the first item input. That value, which must be the number of data items that follow, is used in a `for` statement to control the number of times the loop executes. The body of the loop inputs the data value, then processes it.

The count technique is good for text files and interactive input. It is difficult to use with nontext files in general, since all the items in a nontext file must be of the same type. In the count technique the first item must be an integer. So if this technique were used in a nontext file, the file would be restricted to a file of integers.

The advantage of the count technique over the sentinel technique is that you do not need to devise some sentinel value that is distinguishable from a valid data value. The disadvantage is that with the count technique, it is more difficult to change the number of data values in the file. Each time you add or delete values in the file you must change the count value accordingly. With the sentinel technique, you simply insert the additional data values before the sentinel.

The `eof` technique is the easiest of the three techniques to program. It is better than the sentinel technique because the programmer does not need to know the details about the sentinel value in the file to write the program correctly. It uses the fact that the `reset` and `read` statements look ahead in the file and set the `eof` function appropriately. No input occurs before the `while` statement. The body of the loop inputs the data value, then processes it.

Pascal permits the `eof` function with text files, but this book does not recommend it for numeric data. The problem is with trailing spaces and blank lines at the end of the file. Since spaces and blank lines are not visible in text editors, they are difficult to detect and control. They cause problems because after the last data item is input, the file is still not empty. The `eof` function is set to false when it should be true for the program to terminate properly. Section 7.2 will describe a fourth technique, the basic character processing algorithm, that uses the `eof` function with text files.

The Pascal Statements

Figure 5.11 is a hierarchy diagram of every statement in the Pascal language. All statements fall into one of two groups, simple or structured. Each of these two categories is subdivided. For example, the `for` statement is a repetitive statement, which is a structured statement. You can see that we have now learned most of the Pascal statements.

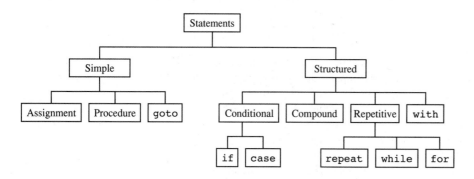

Figure 5.11

The Pascal statements.

5.4 Enumerated and Subrange Types

Figure 5.12 shows the classification of types in Pascal in the form of a hierarchy diagram. At this point, we have studied `real`, `integer`, `boolean`, `char`, and `file` types. This section introduces enumerated and subrange types, which are special cases of the ordinal type. `integer`, `boolean`, and `char` are the other ordinal types.

Pascal is strongly typed, compared to many other Level 6 programming languages. That is, in the variable declaration part of a Pascal program, the programmer must declare every variable to have a specific type before it can be used, and operators have strict rules for the types of their operands. Some older languages,

Pascal is strongly typed.

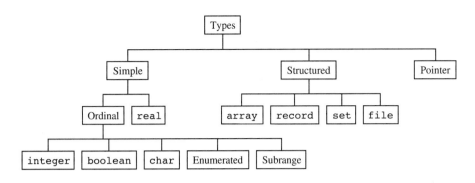

Figure 5.12

The Pascal data types.

such as FORTRAN and BASIC, do not have these requirements. Pascal's requirements force the programmer to be careful in the definition and use of the data.

Programmers sometimes need additional data types not supplied automatically by the language. The following type constructors allow you to construct new types, sometimes from previously defined types.

The Pascal type constructors

- File
- Enumerated
- Subrange
- Array
- Record
- Set

We have already used the file type constructor to construct nontext files. This section will show you how to construct enumerated and subrange types.

Recall that the constant definition part associates a name (Pascal identifier) with a constant value, and the variable declaration part associates a name and a type with a variable. It is convenient, and sometimes even necessary, to associate a name with a new type using the type definition part. Figure 2.10, the syntax chart for a block, showed that the type definition part must be after the constant definition part and before the variable declaration part.

The type definition part

Figure 5.13 is the syntax chart for a type definition part. It begins with the reserved word **type** and is followed by a list of identifiers. After each identifier is an equals symbol (=) and then a definition of the type named by the identifier.

Example 5.20 Program 4.3 declared a nontext file in the variable declaration part as follows:

```
var
   CentsFile: file of integer;
   Number:    integer;
```

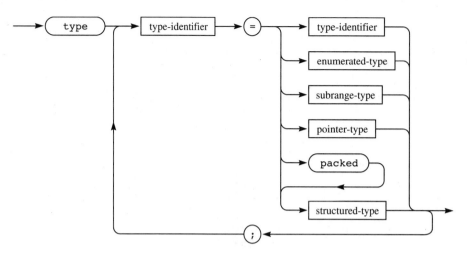

Figure 5.13

The syntax chart for a type definition part.

Another way to declare `CentsFile` as a file of integer is to name the type in a type definition part, then use the name in the variable declaration part.

```
type
   CentsFileType = file of integer;
var
   CentsFile: CentsFileType;
   Number:    integer;
```

The phrase `file of integer` in the type definition part defines a structured type in Figure 5.13.   ∎

Program 5.9

The purpose of Program 5.9 is to output the average of the numbers, which represent individual salaries, in a text file. If any of the salaries are greater than $50,000, the program computes the average and issues a warning message. If a value is negative, the program assumes it is erroneous and does not output the average, since the average would be meaningless under the circumstances.

In the type definition part

```
type
   ErrType = (None, Warning, Fatal)
```

`ErrType` is defined as an enumerated type. The possible values that a variable of type `ErrType` can have are enumerated between the parentheses. Each value is an identifier chosen by the programmer. The variable declaration part declares `Error` to be of type `ErrType`, so the possible values that `Error` can have are None, Warning, and Fatal. Figure 5.14 is the syntax chart for an enumerated type.

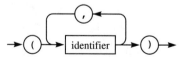

Figure 5.14

The syntax chart for an enumerated type.

```
program IncomeAverage (IncomeFile, output);
   const
      MaxIncome = 50000.00;
   type
      ErrType = (None, Warning, Fatal);
   var
      Income:     real;
      AveIncome:  real;
      NumIncomes: integer;
      I:          integer;
      Error:      ErrType;
      IncomeFile: text;
   begin
   AveIncome := 0.00;
   Error := None;
   I := 1;
   reset (IncomeFile);
   read (IncomeFile, NumIncomes);
   while (Error <> Fatal) and (I <= NumIncomes) do
      begin
      read (IncomeFile, Income);
      I := I + 1;
      if Income < 0.00 then
         Error := Fatal
      else
         begin
         AveIncome := AveIncome + Income;
         if Income > MaxIncome then
            Error := Warning
         end
      end;
   if Error = Fatal then
      writeln ('Negative income in file.  Processing terminated.')
   else
      begin
      AveIncome := AveIncome / NumIncomes;
      writeln ('Average income is $', AveIncome: 4: 2);
      if Error = Warning then
         writeln ('Warning--Individual income exceeded $', MaxIncome: 4: 2)
      end
   end.
```

Program 5.9

Computing the average of the values in a text file. `Error` is a variable of enumerated type that controls termination of the loop.

Input—IncomeFile

```
8
30000.00  40000.00  32000.00  26000.00
56000.00  30000.00  24000.00  38000.00
```

Output

```
Average income is $34500.00
Warning--Individual income exceeded $50000.00
```

Table 5.9 is the start of a trace of Program 5.9. Remember that the three attributes of a Pascal variable are its name, its type, and its value. In a trace table, the name of the variable is in the heading. Its current value during execution of the program is listed in the body of the table and is initially undefined.

Statement executed	AveIncome	Error	I
begin	?	?	?
AveIncome := 0.00;	0.00	?	?
Error := None;	0.00	None	?
I := 1;	0.00	None	1
.			
.			
.			

Table 5.9

The start of a trace of Program 5.9. None is a value that appears in the body of the table.

The table has the name AveIncome in the heading. Since it is a real variable, the values listed in the table under AveIncome must be real numbers with a fractional part. Similarly, Error is the name of a variable and appears in the heading of the trace table. But its type is not real, integer, char, or boolean. Its value cannot be a number, a character, or true or false, but must be either None, Warning, or Fatal. As Table 5.9 shows, the first value assigned to Error is None. Here is a summary of the three attributes of variable Error:

- *Name* Error
- *Type* ErrType
- *Possible values* None, Warning, Fatal

Beginners often have trouble with this concept because they are not used to Pascal identifiers being values.

Program 5.9 uses the count technique to process the real values from the text file. But it does not use the for statement because of the possibility of encountering a negative number in the file. Error is initialized to None, and I to one. Each time through the loop, I is incremented, and the value of Error may change depending on the value of Income. The test in the while statement causes the loop to terminate if Error equals Fatal or if I is greater than NumIncomes.

The first negative number to be read from the file will cause Error to get the value Fatal, and the loop will terminate immediately, even if more values remain in the file. The if statement after the loop will detect the fact that Error has value Fatal and it will print the fatal error message.

If Income ever gets a value greater than 50,000, Error is given the value Warning. The while test, however, permits the loop to continue executing, since Error does not have the value Fatal. The if statement after the loop will detect the fact that Error has the value Warning and it will print the warning message after outputting the average.

▭ **Program 5.10**

The file constructor allows you to define a nontext file of any type. Program 5.10 shows how to declare a file of enumerated values.

```
program Zoo (ZooFile, output);
   type
      AnimalType = (Monkey, Lion, Elephant, Giraffe);
   var
      ZooFile: file of AnimalType;
      Animal:  AnimalType;
   begin
   reset (ZooFile);
   while not eof (ZooFile) do
      begin
      read (ZooFile, Animal);
      case Animal of
      Monkey:
         writeln ('Monkey');
      Lion:
         writeln ('Lion');
      Elephant:
         writeln ('Elephant');
      Giraffe:
         writeln ('Giraffe')
      end {case}
      end
   end.
```

Program 5.10

Declaring a file of enumerated values. `ZooFile` is a nontext file.

Input—`ZooFile` (nontext)

Contents not shown.

Output

```
Lion
Elephant
Monkey
Lion
Giraffe
Monkey
Monkey
```

Since `Animal` is a variable of type `AnimalType`, its possible values are Monkey, Lion, Elephant, or Giraffe. `ZooFile`, which was created earlier by another program not shown, is a file of enumerated values.

The program uses the `eof` technique to input the enumerated values from the file. The processing consists of simply outputting the values to the screen.

Ada: The Lady and the Language

Augusta Ada Byron, Countess of Lovelace and a British mathematician, was born in London in 1815. The daughter of Lord Byron, one of England's greatest romantic poets, she led a life hampered by family scandals and personal illness. Her famous father confessed to his pregnant wife that he had had an incestuous relationship with his sister and several homosexual affairs. Annabella Byron stayed with her husband until Ada was two months old and then succeeded in separating herself from Byron's life. Annabella was an intelligent woman who gave Ada her first lessons in mathematics and oversaw the girl's education. By the age of eight, Ada was already building intricate model boats.

Ada grew up to be a scholarly and quiet young woman who abhorred high society life and frivolous pursuits. Far more interesting to Ada was her first visit to The Mechanics Institute in 1833 to hear Dr. Dionysius Lardner's lectures on the "difference machine," a calculating machine invented by Charles Babbage. Her interest in Babbage's machine led to an introduction to the great man, and a lifelong friendship ensued. It was for his prototype of a digital computer that Ada wrote a program, thus giving her the honorary title of "First Programmer."

Ada married Lord William Lovelace and had three children. However, she found motherhood far less exciting than mathematics, and she left the job of raising her children to her mother, Annabella. Lord Lovelace tolerated his wife's unusual intellect and, in fact, made himself useful to her by copying her writings.

If Lady Lovelace's place in the peerage afforded her a weakness, it was for betting on the horses. In fact, she ran up so many debts that she had to pawn the Lovelace jewels. Once again, Annabella came to the rescue, and when the jewels were back in Ada's possession, William was never the wiser.

By 1842, Ada had translated Luigi Menabrea's treatise on Babbage's analytical engine, a successor to the difference machine. Her translation and additional annotations were so expansive that the document grew to three times its original size. The final product, "The Sketch of the Analytical Engine," appeared in 1843, and critics proclaimed her annotations to be excellent. She wrote, "The analytical engine weaves algebraic patterns, just as the jacquard loom weaves flowers and leaves."

Lady Ada Lovelace died of cervical cancer at 36. Though she died prematurely, she lives on

through her writings and her name, which has been adopted for a computer programming language.

As a major software developer (or contractor thereof), the U.S. Department of Defense (DoD) realized in the 1970s that software costs were beginning to overtake hardware costs, and it organized an international language review committee to study the issue. The committee decided that although the existing languages, such as FORTRAN, COBOL, and Pascal, were suitable for certain applications, they were not capable of handling all of the DoD's applications, which ranged from finance to machine control. The committee also acknowledged that recent advances in software engineering and design had not yet been integrally coupled with any existing language standard.

The DoD decided it needed a new language to fit its needs, so it sponsored a language design contest. Eventually, a language was selected and tentatively dubbed DoD-1. The DoD realized that if the new language was to catch on commercially, it needed a name that didn't sound too militaristic. Recognizing that the elegant principles of the language would do honor to our programmer of the previous century, the DoD sought and received permission from Lady Ada Lovelace's heir to take her name for this new language standard, and Ada was born. We can only hope that Lady Lovelace would have been pleased with the mark she has made on programming, from its inception to its current advanced state.

Using Enumerated Types

Pascal has strict limitations on how you can use enumerated values. You cannot store enumerated values in text files, enter them from the keyboard, or output them to the screen.

Example 5.21 In Program 5.10, it would certainly be more convenient to write the loop without a `case` statement as

```
while not eof (ZooFile) do
   begin
   read (ZooFile, Animal);
   writeln (Animal)
   end
```

Unfortunately, the `writeln` statement is illegal, because `Animal` has enumerated type. ∎

Example 5.22 Similarly, if `Animal` is defined as in Program 5.10, the code fragment

```
write ('Enter an animal: ');
readln (Animal)
```

is illegal, because you cannot enter an enumerated value from the keyboard. ∎

Programmer-defined enumerated types are similar to the character type. Remember that a value of type `char` has an ordinal value corresponding to the position of the character on the number line. The values specified in an enumerated type also have positions on the number line. They follow the order enumerated in the type definition part and begin with zero.

Example 5.23 Figure 5.15 shows the number line for the values of `AnimalType`. Monkey, the first value enumerated in the definition of the type, has the ordinal value of zero. ∎

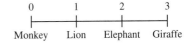

Figure 5.15

The number line for the values of `AnimalType` as defined in Program 5.10.

The `ord` function returns the ordinal value of an enumerated expression, but there is no function that corresponds to `chr` for characters. The predecessor and successor functions can be used with enumerated values and have the same meaning as with character values.

Example 5.24 Suppose `ColorType` is defined as follows, with `Color` a variable of type `ColorType`.

```
type
   ColorType = (Red, Orange, Yellow, Green, Blue, Purple);
var
   Color: ColorType
```

If `Color` has value Yellow, then `ord (Color)` is two, `pred (Color)` is Orange and `succ (Color)`is Green. ∎

The relational operators <, <=, =, <>, >=, and > can all be applied directly to enumerated expressions. The position on the number line determines the order. Beginning programmers have a tendency to use the `ord` function unnecessarily when comparing enumerated values.

Example 5.25 Suppose that `ColorType` is declared as in the previous example, and `MyColor` and `YourColor` each have type `ColorType`. The `if` test

```
if MyColor <= YourColor then
```

is legal. The boolean expression is true, for example, if `MyColor` is Red and `YourColor` is Blue. Although the test

```
if ord (MyColor) <= ord (YourColor) then
```

is also legal and performs the equivalent test, it is unnecessarily complicated. ∎

The boolean type shares many characteristics of enumerated types. Properties of the boolean type are as if `boolean` were defined as

```
type
   boolean = (false, true)
```

with the values of false and true on the number line as shown in Figure 5.16. Although the similarity of boolean and enumerated types is interesting and shows Pascal's underlying consistency, it is not too useful in practice.

Figure 5.16

The number line for boolean values.

Example 5.26 The value of `ord (false)` is zero and the value of `ord (true)` is one. False is less than true and `succ (false)` is true. ∎

The control variable of a `for` statement can be of any ordinal type, including the enumerated type.

Example 5.27 Suppose a program has the following type definition and variable declaration parts:

```
type
   DayType = (Sun, Mon, Tues, Wed, Thurs, Fri, Sat);
var
   Day: DayType
```

Then the code fragment

```
for Day := Sun to Sat do
```

is perfectly legal. Each time through the loop, the `for` statement replaces `Day` by `succ (Day)`.   ■

Although Pascal does not require it, this book will adhere to the style of ending every identifier that names a type with the string "Type," as in `DayType`. That convention will help the programs to be more readable.

A style convention for naming types

Subrange Types

In some programs it is important to limit the values of a variable to a specified range. For example, if you have an integer variable that represents the year, you might want to guarantee that its value is limited to the range 1900 to 1999. Subrange is a type constructor that is based on one of the other ordinal types shown in Figure 5.12. In the example of a subrange of integer values between 1900 and 1999, integer is called the *base type* of the subrange.

Variables of type subrange behave just like variables with their base type, except for one important characteristic. Every time a Pascal statement changes the value of a subrange variable, the new value is automatically checked to see if it lies within the allowed range. If it does, execution continues normally. But if it does not, the program crashes with a "range value error" message. The two Pascal statements that change the value of a variable are the assignment statement and the `read` statement.

Range checking during execution

Program 5.11

Program 5.11 shows how to define and use a subrange variable. It asks the user for his year of birth, echoes the year to the screen, adds 10 to the year, and outputs the year in which the user was 10 years old. Both variables are subranges of base type integer.

The type definition part declares `YearType` to be restricted to the integer values 1900 to 1999 inclusive. Note that the two adjacent periods must not have a space between them. Figure 5.17 is the syntax chart for a subrange type.

Figure 5.17

The syntax chart for a subrange type.

Since both `BirthYear` and `TenthYear` are `YearType`, neither one is allowed to have a value outside the subrange. They could have been declared with-

```
program Birthday (input, output);
   type
      YearType = 1900..1999;
   var
      BirthYear: YearType;
      TenthYear: YearType;
   begin
   write ('Enter year of birth: ');
   readln (BirthYear);
   writeln ('You were born in ', BirthYear: 1, '.');
   TenthYear := BirthYear + 10;
   writeln ('You were ten in ', TenthYear: 1, '.')
   end.
```

Program 5.11

A program that inputs and processes subrange values.

Sample Input/Output

```
Enter year of birth: 1970
You were born in 1970.
You were ten in 1980.
```

Sample Input/Output

```
Enter year of birth: 1870
Value of 1870 is out of range
```
Program crash

Sample Input/Output

```
Enter year of birth: 1995
You were born in 1995.
Value of 2005 is out of range
```
Program crash

out naming the type in a type definition part as

```
var
   BirthYear: 1900..1999;
   TenthYear: 1900..1999;
```

Such a type is called *anonymous* because it does not have a name.

Anonymous types

The first sample I/O in Program 5.11 shows that `BirthYear` and `TenthYear` behave like ordinary integers as long as their values are within the subrange. You can input values, use standard arithmetic operations, and output values with integer formats.

In the second sample I/O, the user entered a value that was outside the allowed subrange. As part of the `read` statement, the computer detected that 1870 is less than 1900 and caused the program to crash with an execution error message.

In the third sample I/O, the input value was within the range, but the assignment statement attempted to give a value that was out of the range of a subrange variable.

 **Using Subrange Variables**

Recall from Section 3.4 that the behavior of the `case` statement is undefined when the value of the `case` expression is not included in the list of `case` constants. You can use a subrange variable to ensure that the value of the `case` expression is included in the `case` list.

Example 5.28 Program 3.11, `PresidentQuiz`, asked the user to enter the response to a multiple choice question. A `case` statement selected the computer's reply depending on the value of input variable `Response`, which was declared as an integer. However, if you declare `Response` as

```
var
   Response: 1..4;
```

instead of as an integer, then the behavior is predictable when the user enters an invalid value. Namely, the program will crash with a range value error message. ■

Example 5.28 illustrates the behavior of subrange types, but it is hardly a convincing display of practical advantages. After all, rather than have the program crash if a value is out of the desired range, you can use an `if` statement as described in Example 3.41 to guard against invalid input. This is a much more user-friendly approach, and this technique could be used in Program 5.11.

The real advantage of subrange types will become apparent in Chapter 7, where they are used in conjunction with arrays. There we will see that subrange types are useful mainly as a debugging tool because of the information they give in the error message when a buggy program crashes.

The base type of a subrange type can be any ordinal type, including enumerated. The base type cannot be real.

Example 5.29 Suppose that `DayType` is defined as in Example 5.27. Then the declaration

```
var
   WeekDay: Mon..Fri
```

gives `WeekDay` a subrange type and restricts its values to Mon, Tues, Wed, Thurs or Fri. ■

Example 5.30 In the previous example, the subrange was anonymous. Another way to give `WeekDay` the same type is to name the subrange type in the type definition part along with the base type.

```
type
   DayType     = (Sun, Mon, Tues, Wed, Thurs, Fri, Sat);
   WeekDayType = Mon..Fri;
var
   WeekDay: WeekDayType
```

`WeekDay` has the same restriction on its values as in the previous example. ■

Example 5.31 The variable declaration

```
var
    Probability: 0.0 .. 1.0;
```

is illegal because the base type cannot be real. ■

5.5   Nested Loops

Any structured statement can be nested in any other structured statement. In the same way that an `if` statement can be nested inside another `if`, a loop statement can be nested inside another loop. Such a configuration is called a *nested loop*.

Program 5.12

Program 5.12 uses a nested loop to draw a box of asterisks with the same number of rows and columns. It prompts the user for the size of the box.

```
program Box (input, output);
   var
      NumAstr: integer;
      I, J:    integer;
   begin
   write ('How many rows? ');
   readln (NumAstr);
   writeln;
   for I := 1 to NumAstr do
      begin
      for J := 1 to NumAstr do
         write ('*');
      writeln
      end
   end.
```

Program 5.12

A nested `for` loop.

Interactive Input/Output

```
How many rows? 3

***
***
***
```

Table 5.10 is a trace of Program 5.12. The `for` loop with control variable `I` is called the *outer loop,* and the nested loop with control variable `J` is called the *inner loop*. The first time the outer `for` statement executes, it initializes `I` to 1. Then the inner loop gives the values 1, 2 and 3 in turn to `J`, causing the body of the inner loop to execute three times. Each time the body of the inner loop executes, it outputs a single asterisk to the screen. The fourth time the inner `for` statement executes, it detects that the loop should terminate and gives `J` an undefined value.

Statement executed	NumAstr	I	J
begin	?	?	?
write ('How many r	?	?	?
readln (NumAstr);	3	?	?
writeln;	3	?	?
for I := 1 to NumA	3	1	?
for J := 1 to NumA	3	1	1
write ('*');	3	1	1
for J := 1 to NumA	3	1	2
write ('*');	3	1	2
for J := 1 to NumA	3	1	3
write ('*');	3	1	3
for J := 1 to NumA	3	1	?
writeln	3	1	?
for I := 1 to NumA	3	2	?
for J := 1 to NumA	3	2	1
write ('*');	3	2	1
for J := 1 to NumA	3	2	2
write ('*');	3	2	2
for J := 1 to NumA	3	2	3
write ('*');	3	2	3
for J := 1 to NumA	3	2	?
writeln	3	2	?
for I := 1 to NumA	3	3	?
for J := 1 to NumA	3	3	1
write ('*');	3	3	1
for J := 1 to NumA	3	3	2
write ('*');	3	3	2
for J := 1 to NumA	3	3	3
write ('*');	3	3	3
for J := 1 to NumA	3	3	?
writeln	3	3	?
for I := 1 to NumA	3	?	?
end.			

Table 5.10

A trace of Program 5.12 with nested loops.

Then `writeln` executes, which places the cursor on the screen at the start of the next line. If the `writeln` statement were omitted from the program, all the asterisks would be printed on the same line. The `writeln` statement is outside the body of the inner loop, but inside the body of the outer loop.

The second time the outer `for` statement executes, it increments `I` to 2. The inner loop executes exactly as before, producing another row of three asterisks on the screen. The same thing happens after `I` gets the value of 3.

Statement Execution Count

What is the statement execution count for this program? From the trace table you can count 31 statements executed when `NumAstr` gets three from the keyboard. What if it gets *n* in general?

Statements in a nested loop are a little more difficult to count than those in a single loop. Consider the statements in the inner loop as if they were not nested in the outer loop.

```
for J := 1 to NumAstr do
   write ('*');
writeln
```

(1) The `for` statement executes $n + 1$ times, (2) the body executes *n* times, and (3) the `writeln` statement executes 1 time. But these statements are, in fact, the body of a loop that executes *n* times. So each one executes *n* times the amounts just mentioned. Namely, (1) the first statement executes $n(n + 1)$ times, (2) the body executes n^2 times, and (3) the `writeln` statement executes *n* times. Table 5.11 shows that the count for the whole program is $2n^2 + 3n + 4$, which is 31 when *n* is 3, as expected.

Statement	Executions
`write ('How many rows? ');`	1
`readln (NumAstr);`	1
`writeln;`	1
`for I := 1 to NumAstr do`	$n + 1$
`   begin`	
`   for J := 1 to NumAstr do`	$n(n + 1)$
`      write ('*');`	n^2
`   writeln`	n
`   end`	
Total:	$2n^2 + 3n + 4$

Table *5.11*

Statement execution count for Program 5.12.

The squared term in the expression for the number of statements executed is typical for nested loops. It causes an estimate for the execution time that is quite different from the case where the statement count is proportional to the first power of n.

Example 5.32 Suppose it takes 400 ms to execute Program 5.12 when `NumAstr` has the value of 35. If you double the value to 70, how long will it take to execute?

Setting up the precise ratio gives

$$\frac{400}{2(35)^2 + 3(35) + 4} = \frac{T}{2(70)^2 + 3(70) + 4}$$

As before, however, we can approximate by neglecting the lower-order terms in the statement execution count.

$$\frac{400}{2(35)^2} = \frac{T}{2(70)^2}$$

Again, the coefficient cancels, but this time solving for T yields $400(70/35)^2 = 400(4)$. That is 1600 ms, or 1.6 s, which is four times the original execution time, not just double the execution time. ∎

Such a result is expected when you think of the output. When you double the value given to `NumAstr`, you quadruple the number of asterisks that need to be output, since the program prints a figure in the shape of a box with an equal number of rows and columns.

Printing a Triangle

It is possible for the upper or lower limit of the control variable of the inner loop to depend on the control variable of the outer loop. Suppose you change the loops of Program 5.12 as follows:

```
for I := 1 to NumAstr do
   begin
   for J := 1 to I do
      write ('*');
   writeln
   end
```

A modification to Program 5.12

The control variable of the inner loop, `J`, now goes from 1 to `I`, where `I` is the control variable of the outer loop. Table 5.12 is a trace of Program 5.12 with this modification.

When `I` has the value 1, the inner loop gives `J` values from 1 to 1. That makes the inner loop execute once. When `I` has value 2, the inner loop gives `J` values from 1 to 2, for two executions of the inner loop. The last time, `J` goes from 1 to 3

Statement executed	NumAstr	I	J
begin	?	?	?
write ('How many r	?	?	?
readln (NumAstr);	3	?	?
writeln;	3	?	?
for I := 1 to NumA	3	1	?
for J := 1 to I do	3	1	1
write ('*');	3	1	1
for J := 1 to I do	3	1	?
writeln	3	1	?
for I := 1 to NumA	3	2	?
for J := 1 to I do	3	2	1
write ('*');	3	2	1
for J := 1 to I do	3	2	2
write ('*');	3	2	2
for J := 1 to I do	3	2	?
writeln	3	2	?
for I := 1 to NumA	3	3	?
for J := 1 to I do	3	3	1
write ('*');	3	3	1
for J := 1 to I do	3	3	2
write ('*');	3	3	2
for J := 1 to I do	3	3	3
write ('*');	3	3	3
for J := 1 to I do	3	3	?
writeln	3	3	?
for I := 1 to NumA	3	?	?
end.			

Table 5.12

A trace of a modification of Program 5.12. The upper limit of the inner loop depends on the control variable of the outer loop.

for three executions. The effect is to print a triangle of asterisks. If NumAstr has a value of 3, the output will be

```
*
**
***
```

Statement Execution Count

To determine the statement execution count of the modified program that prints the triangle, you need to use the fact that

$$1 + 2 + 3 + \cdots + m = \frac{m(m+1)}{2}$$

where *m* is positive. This fact was used in the discussion of Program 5.7 and will be proven in Section 9.2.

First, we will consider the statements in the body of the outer loop alone and determine their counts for given values of I. Table 5.13 summarizes the statement execution counts for values of I from 1 to *n*.

	Values of I					
Statement	1	2	3	4	. . .	*n*
`for J := 1 to I do`	2	3	4	5	...	*n* + 1
`write ('*');`	1	2	3	4	...	*n*
`writeln`	1	1	1	1	...	1

Table 5.13

Statement execution counts for the body of the inner loop for fixed values of I.

For example, when I has the value 3, the `for` loop gives J values from 1 to 3, so that the `write` statement in the body of the loop executes three times. The `for` test executes four times because of the extra last test necessary to terminate the loop. The `writeln` statement is outside the inner loop, so it executes once regardless of the value of I.

Since the outer loop executes with values of I from 1 to *n*, the statement execution count of each of the three lines in Table 5.13 is the sum of the counts listed in each line. Specifically, `writeln` executes *n* times and `write ('*')` executes $n(n + 1)/2$ times. The `for` test executes

$$2 + 3 + 4 + 5 + \cdots + (n + 1)$$

times. But this expression is 1 less than the expression

$$1 + 2 + 3 + 4 + 5 + \cdots + (n + 1)$$

which is the sum of the first *n* + 1 integers. Our formula says that the latter expression equals $(n + 1)(n + 2)/2$, so the `for` test must execute one less time, or $(n + 1)(n + 2)/2 - 1$. Table 5.14 summarizes the execution count for the complete algorithm.

Execution is quadratic in n.

Statement	Executions
`write ('How many rows? ');`	1
`readln (NumAstr);`	1
`writeln;`	1
`for I := 1 to NumAstr do`	*n* + 1
`  begin`	
`    for J := 1 to I do`	$(n + 1)(n + 2)/2 - 1$
`      write ('*');`	$n(n + 1)/2$
`    writeln`	*n*
`  end`	
Total:	$n^2 + 4n + 4$

Table 5.14

Statement execution count for the modification of Program 5.12.

The interesting conclusion to this analysis is that the execution time is still quadratic in *n,* just as with the algorithm to print a square.

Example 5.33   Suppose it takes 200 ms to execute this program when `NumAstr` has the value of 35. If you double the value to 70, how long will it take to execute?

Using the approximate ratio,

$$\frac{200}{(35)^2} = \frac{T}{(70)^2}$$

Solving for *T* yields $200(70/35)^2 = 200(4) = 800$ ms. So the quadratic nature of the statement execution count again predicts that the execution time is four times the original execution time when *n* is doubled.   ■

Program 5.13

Our last program in this chapter, Program 5.13, is a stepwise refinement problem that requires nested loops. The problem is to input two numbers and output a multiplication table for the values between the two numbers. For example, if the input is 5 8, the output should be

```
     5   6   7   8
 5   25  30  35  40
 6   30  36  42  48
 7   35  42  49  56
 8   40  48  56  64
```

Sample output for Program 5.13

First Pass   The input is a pair of numbers. That calls for two integer variables, `BeginNum` and `EndNum`.

The output consists of five rows for the input 5 8. The first row is different from the next four rows because it is the heading of the table. The other four rows contain the actual products. Regardless of the specific values input, the output will be one heading row and several rows of products. The integer variable, `I`, will represent the row number and will vary from `BeginNum` to `EndNum`.

```
begin
Input BeginNum, EndNum
Output the first row.
for I := BeginNum to EndNum do
    Output row with I as first number.
end
```

First pass of Example 5.13

Second Pass   The first row is a list of numbers from `BeginNum` to `EndNum`. It can be output with a single `for` statement.

Each row in the body of the multiplication table starts with the single value of `I`. The rest of the row is the product of the number, `I`, with another number, `J`, that varies from `BeginNum` to `EndNum`.

```
begin
Input BeginNum, EndNum
for J := BeginNum to EndNum do
    Output J
for I := BeginNum to EndNum do
    begin
    Output I
    for J := BeginNum to EndNum do
        Output I * J
    end
end
```

Third Pass   The third pass is Program 5.13. It has several output details not in the previous passes to make the numbers in the table line up properly. It prints each number in a field width of four. Four spaces must precede the first heading line so the numbers in the heading will line up with the proper columns. Values are output with a `write` instead of a `writeln`. So an extra `writeln` with no values must execute after printing each line.

```
program MultiplicationTable (input, output);
    var
        BeginNum: integer;
        EndNum:   integer;
        I, J:     integer;
    begin
    write ('Enter beginning number: ');
    readln (BeginNum);
    write ('Enter ending number: ');
    readln (EndNum);
    writeln;
    write ('    ');
    for J := BeginNum to EndNum do
        write (J: 4);
    writeln;
    for I := BeginNum to EndNum do
        begin
        write (I: 4);
        for J := BeginNum to EndNum do
            write (I * J: 4);
        writeln
        end
    end.
```

Program 5.13

Printing a multiplication table with nested **for** statements.

Input/Output

See text.

This program used a common programming convention for naming integer variables that are used to process a table. `I` is usually used as the control variable for the row loop, and `J` is usually used for the column loop. Chapter 7 continues this convention, and you should probably adopt it yourself.

SUMMARY

Pascal contains three loop statements—the `while` statement, the `repeat` statement, and the `for` statement. Each loop statement tests a boolean expression and, depending on whether it is true or false, either executes the body of the loop or exits the loop. The `while` and `for` statements test the condition at the beginning of the loop, and the `repeat` statement tests it at the end of the loop. It is possible for the body of a `while` loop or a `for` loop not to execute. The body of a `repeat` loop, however, always executes at least once. The `for` statement automatically initializes the control variable at the beginning of the loop and increments the control variable each time the body of the loop executes. It is useful when you know how many times the loop should execute.

Two important properties of an algorithm are the memory space required to store the program and its data, and the time necessary to execute the program. Statement execution counts enable you to predict the execution time of a program with a large amount of data from its execution time with a small amount of data. Typically, the statement execution count with a loop is proportional to n, the number of times the loop executes. n is, in turn, related to the size of the problem, such as the number of data values to process. Nested loops typically have statement execution counts that are proportional to n^2.

A loop invariant is an assertion that is true at the beginning of a loop and is also true after each execution of the loop. Loop invariants can help you analyze the logic of your programs. The initializing steps before the body of the loop make the invariant true the first time. The modifying steps in the body of the loop keep the invariant true each time the body executes. Identifying the loop invariant helps you write the initializing steps and the modifying steps correctly.

The three techniques for file input are the sentinel technique, the count technique, and the `eof` technique. The sentinel and count techniques are used with text files and with interactive I/O. The sentinel technique uses a special value, which is distinguishable from the normal data values, as the last value in the file. The count technique assumes that the first data value in the file is an integer that specifies how many data values follow. The `eof` technique is used with nontext files and is based on the boolean `eof` function.

An enumerated type allows you to define a list of identifiers that are the allowable values an enumerated variable can have. Each enumerated value has a place on the integer number line, as do character values. The same `pred` and `succ` functions that apply to character expressions apply to enumerated expressions. A subrange variable has values that are limited to a certain range. During program execution, the value is automatically tested each time it is changed, either by an assignment statement or by a `read` statement. If the value is out of the allowable range, the program terminates with an appropriate error message.

EXERCISES

Section 5.1

1. Look back at the algorithm on page 156 that computes the average of the accounts and do the following: *(a) Draw a flowchart. *(b) Construct a trace table if the input is `100.00 200.00 15.00 2e30`. (c) Construct a trace table if the input is `2e30`.

(d) Determine the total statement execution count if there are *n* data values followed by a sentinel value. **(e)** If the algorithm executes in 50 ms for 200 data values, estimate the execution time for 1000 data values from (c).

2. For the algorithm on page 157 that finds the largest quiz score, do the following: **(a)** Draw a flowchart. **(b)** Construct a trace table if the input is 73 80 68 92 75 −1. **(c)** Construct a trace table if the input is −1. **(d)** Determine the total statement execution count if there are *n* data values followed by a sentinel value, assuming that the body of the nested `if` statement executes every time. **(e)** Determine the execution count assuming that the first number in the list is the largest. **(f)** If the algorithm executes in 120 ms for 80 data values, estimate the execution time for 500 data values assuming the count in part (d). **(g)** Work part (f) assuming the count in part (e). **(h)** Give the percentage difference between your estimates from (f) and (g). Is the difference what you expected?

* 3. Construct a trace table for Program 5.4 if the input is 0.3.

4. Tell how many multiplication and addition steps are required to evaluate

$$ax^4 + bx^3 + cx^2 + dx + e$$

Factor the expression so that it only requires four multiplication and four addition steps.

5. Draw the flowchart for Program 5.5.

6. Write a trace table and determine the output of the code fragment.

```
read (A);
Sum := 0;
while A < 9 do
   begin
   Sum := Sum + A;
   A := A + 1
   end;
write (Sum)
```

for the following inputs.

* **(a)** 5   **(b)** 8   **(c)** 9   **(d)** 10

7. Answer these questions for each of the Pascal code segments. (1) What is the first value added to Sum? (2) What is the last value added to Sum? (3) What is the value of A at the termination of the loop? (4) How many times does the body of the loop execute?

* (a)	(b)	(c)
`Sum := 0;`	`Sum := 0;`	`Sum := 0;`
`A := 50;`	`A := 50;`	`A := 50;`
`while A < 100 do`	`while A < 100 do`	`while A <= 100 do`
`  begin`	`  begin`	`  begin`
`  A := A + 2;`	`  Sum := Sum + A;`	`  A := A + 2;`
`  Sum := Sum + A`	`  A := A + 2`	`  Sum := Sum + A`
`  end`	`  end`	`  end`

8. What is the value of Count after the statements are executed?

```
I := 15;
Count := 0;
while I <= 1000 do
   begin
   I := I + 2;
   Count := Count + 1
   end
```

9. A programmer writes the following algorithm to process data from a nontext file.

```
reset (SomeFile)
read (SomeFile, DataIn)
while not eof (SomeFile) do
   begin
   Process DataIn
   read (SomeFile, DataIn)
   end
```

* (a) What happens if the file is empty? (b) What happens if the file is not empty? (c) Will the program produce correct results under either of these two circumstances? Explain.

10. A programmer writes the following algorithm to process data from a file that has a sentinel.

```
Input DataIn
while DataIn is not the Sentinel do
   begin
   Input DataIn
   Process DataIn
   end
```

(a) What happens if the file has only the sentinel value? (b) What happens if the file has values before the sentinel? (c) Will the program produce correct results under either of these two circumstances? Explain.

Section 5.2

* 11. Draw the flowchart for Program 5.6.

12. A programmer uses the following algorithm to process data from a text file that has a sentinel.

```
repeat
   Input DataIn
   Process DataIn
until DataIn is the sentinel
```

Under what circumstances, if any, will the algorithm produce correct results? Explain.

13. A programmer uses the following algorithm to process data from a nontext file.

```
reset (FileIn)
repeat
   read (FileIn, DataIn)
   Process DataIn
until eof (FileIn)
```

(a) What happens if the file is empty? (b) What happens if the file is not empty? (c) Will the program produce correct results under either of these two circumstances? Explain.

14. A programmer uses the following algorithm to process data from a nontext file.

```
reset (FileIn)
read (FileIn, DataIn)
repeat
   Process DataIn
   read (FileIn, DataIn)
until eof (FileIn)
```

(a) What happens if the file is empty? (b) What happens if the file is not empty? (c) Will the program produce correct results under either of these two circumstances? Explain.

15. Write a trace table and determine the output of the code fragment

```
read (A);
Sum := 0;
repeat
   Sum := Sum + A;
   A := A + 1
until A > 9;
write (Sum)
```

for the following inputs.

*(a) 5   (b) 8   (c) 9   (d) 10

16. Answer the following questions for each of the Pascal code segments. (1) What is the first value added to Sum? (2) What is the last value added to Sum? (3) What is the value of A at the termination of the loop? (4) How many times is the body of the loop executed?

*(a)
```
Sum := 0;
A := 50;
repeat
   A := A + 2;
   Sum := Sum + A
until A > 100
```

(b)
```
Sum := 0;
A := 50;
repeat
   Sum := Sum + A;
   A := A + 2
until A > 100
```

(c)
```
Sum := 0;
A := 50;
repeat
   A := A + 2;
   Sum := Sum + A
until A >= 100
```

17. What is the value of Count after the following statements execute?

```
I := 15;
Count := 0;
repeat
   I := I + 2;
   Count := Count + 1
until I >= 1000
```

*18. Use the repeat statement to write Pascal code that has the same effect as

```
write ('Type an integer: ');
readln (A);
while (2 <= A) and (A < 15) do
   begin
   write ('Type an integer: ');
   readln (A)
   end
```

19. Use De Morgan's law to write the test for the while statement in Example 5.9 without the NOT operator.

Section 5.3

20. Write a trace table and determine the output of the code fragment

```
read (Num);
Sum := 0;
for I := 5 to Num do
   Sum := Sum + I;
write (Sum)
```

for the following inputs.

*(a) 10   (b) 6   (c) 5   (d) 4

21. Determine the total statement execution count of the code fragment in the previous exercise if Num has the value n. Assume that n is greater than or equal to 5.

22. Write a trace table and determine the output of the code fragment

```
read (Num);
Sum := 0;
for I := 10 downto Num do
   Sum := Sum + I;
write (Sum)
```

for the following inputs.

*(a) 5   (b) 9   (c) 10   (d) 11

23. If Program 5.7 takes 40 ms to execute when Num has the value of 100, how long does it take to execute if Num has the value of 150?

24. **(a)** Determine the total statement execution count for Program 5.8 assuming that `NumAccts` has the value n. **(b)** If the program takes 60 ms to execute when n is 200, how long does it take to execute if n is 300?

Section 5.4

25. If `Months` is defined in the type section as

    `Months = (Jan, Feb, Mar, Apr, May, Jun)`

    then what is the value of the following?

    *(a) `succ (Mar)`   (b) `ord (Feb)`   (c) `pred (Apr)`   (d) `Mar > Jun`

26. Assuming `Animal1` and `Animal2` have type `AnimalType` as in Program 5.10, write the trace table and determine the output of the following code fragment.

```
for Animal1 := Monkey to Giraffe do
   begin
   for Animal2 := Monkey to Animal1 do
      write ('*');
   writeln
   end
```

Section 5.5

27. Plot the statement execution counts for Program 5.12 and its modification to print a triangle on the same graph for values of n from 0 to 6. What shape does each graph have?

28. Verify the total at the bottom of Table 5.14 by adding the execution counts in the table.

29. What is the total statement execution count of the code fragment

    Statement 1
    ```
    for I := 1 to Num do
       begin
    ```
    Statement 2
    ```
    for J := 1 to I do
    ```
    Statement 3
    ```
       end
    ```

    if `Num` has the following values?

    *(a) 3   (b) 4   (c) n

30. What is the total statement execution count of the code fragment

    Statement 1
    ```
    for I := 1 to Num do
       begin
    ```
    Statement 2
    ```
    for J := -I to I do
    ```
    Statement 3
    ```
       end
    ```

if Num has the following values?

*(a) 3   (b) 4   (c) *n*

You may need to use this formula for the sum of odd integers.

$$1 + 3 + 5 + \cdots + (2n - 1) = n^2 \qquad \text{for positive } n$$

31. In Program 5.13, define

$$n = \texttt{EndNum} - \texttt{BeginNum} + 1$$

The value of *n* indicates the size of the problem. The larger *n* is, the bigger the multiplication table. In terms of *n* (not EndNum or BeginNum), what is the total statement execution count for Program 5.13?

| PROBLEMS |

An optional part of each problem in this chapter is to include the first pass of your stepwise refinement in the documentation part of the program at the beginning of the listing.

Section 5.1

32. Modify Program 5.4 so that it does not allow negative or zero values for the tolerance.

33. Modify Program 5.4 so that it also outputs the number of times the `while` loop executes. Run the modified program five times with the following tolerances: 1e–2, 1e–3, 1e–4, 1e–5, 1e–6. Graph the number of times the loop executes (*y*-axis) versus the tolerance (*x*-axis). What mathematical relationship did you discover between these two quantities? Hint: Use semilog graph paper or, equivalently, let each *x*-axis division be 10 times greater than the previous *x*-axis division. For what values of the tolerance, if any, will the loop never execute?

34. Write a program to compute and output the sum of all positive even integers less than or equal to a value entered by the user.

35. Write a program to compute and output the sum of all positive odd integers less than or equal to a value entered by the user.

36. A text file contains a list of positive integers followed by one negative integer as a sentinel. Write a program that counts how many even integers there are in the file.

Sample Input

```
5   38   1   45   21   7   12   5   -1
```

Sample Output

```
There are 2 even integers in the file.
```

37. A nontext file contains a list of integers. Write a program that counts how many positive integers are in the file.

```
5   38   1   −45   21   −7   12   5
```

Sample Output

```
There are 6 positive integers in the file.
```

38. A salesperson gets a 5% commission on sales of $1000 or less, and a 10% commission on sales in excess of $1000. For example, a sale of $1300 earns him $80—that is $50 on the first $1000 of the sale and $30 on the $300 in excess of the first $1000.

    A text file contains a salesperson's ID number (integer) and his sales amount (real) on each line. The last line has a sales figure of $2e30$, which serves as a sentinel.

    Write a program that outputs a report containing the ID number, the amount of sales, and the commission for each salesperson. At the bottom of the report, print the ID number of the salesperson who sold the most.

Sample Input

```
 134     580.00
1209     600.00
  30    1000.00
2238    1200.00
9411     800.00
2344    1150.00
   0       2e30
```

Sample Output

```
Commission Report
---------------------------
ID      Sales    Commission
---------------------------
 134     580.00      29.00
1209     600.00      30.00
  30    1000.00      50.00
2238    1200.00      70.00
9411     800.00      40.00
2344    1150.00      65.00
---------------------------
Highest sales: ID 2238
```

39. The price per Frisbee depends on the quantity ordered, as indicated in Table 5.15. A text file consists of a list of numbers that represent order quantities of Frisbees. The last integer, which is negative, serves as a sentinel. Write a program that prints a report of order quantities and the cost per order. At the bottom of the report print the total cost of all the orders.

Quantity	Price per Frisbee
0–99	$5.00
100–199	3.00
200–299	2.50
300 or more	2.00

Table 5.15

The price schedule for Problem 39.

Sample Input

```
50  150  20  200  300  1  250  100  -1
```

Sample Output

```
Order Report
--------------
Quant.    Cost
--------------
    50   250.00
   150   450.00
    20   100.00
   200   500.00
   300   600.00
     1     5.00
   250   625.00
   100   300.00
--------------
Total: 2830.00
```

40. An instructor determines the total score for each student according to the weights of Table 5.16. A total of 90 to 100 is a grade of A, 80 to 89 is a B, and so on for C, D, and F. Each line of a text file contains four real values that are the homework, exam, and final exam scores. The scores on the last line are all 2e30, any one of which may act as the sentinel. Write a program that prints a table with an appropriate heading, each line of which contains

   ■ The four values of each score
   ■ The weighted total
   ■ The letter grade

   At the bottom of the report print the average of the weighted totals.

41. A school computes the grade point average (GPA) according to the grade point scale of Table 5.17. A *plus* adds 0.3 points (except for A and F) and a *minus* subtracts 0.3 points (except for F) from the nominal grade value. Each line of a text file contains the letter grade (with no leading spaces) and the number of semester units (integer) for a course taken by a student. If a letter grade is not followed by a + or −, the second character input from the line will be the space character. The last line contains the letter Z as a sentinel. Write a program that computes the total number of units taken and the GPA.

Sample Input

```
B-   3
C    3
C+   5
A-   3
A    1
Z    0
```

Sample Output

```
Number of units: 15
Grade point average: 2.71
```

Score item	Percent toward total
Homework	15
Exam 1	25
Exam 2	25
Final exam	35

Table 5.16

The grading weights for Problem 40.

Grade	Points	Grade	Points
A	4.0	C	2.0
A−	3.7	C−	1.7
B+	3.3	D+	1.3
B	3.0	D	1.0
B−	2.7	D−	0.7
C+	2.3	F	0.0

Table 5.17

The grade point scale for Problem 41.

Section 5.2

42. Write a program that repeatedly asks the user to enter her age until she enters a number between 10 and 70 inclusive. Make an appropriate reply depending on her age. Use the repeat statement.

Sample Input/Output

```
Enter your age: 5
Enter your age: 75
Enter your age: 15
You are quite young.
```

43. Write a program that computes the sum of the squares of integer values up to the value entered by the user. For example, if the user enters 5, the program should compute

$$1 + 4 + 9 + 16 + 25$$

which is 55. Repeatedly ask the user to enter a positive value until he does so. Use the `repeat` statement for both the input and the computation.

Sample Input/Output

```
Enter a positive number: -3
Enter a positive number: 5
Sum of first 5 squares is 55.
```

44. Rework the previous problem with the output modified as follows. Use the `repeat` statement for both the input and the computation.

Sample Input/Output

```
Enter a positive number: -3
Enter a positive number: 5
1 + 4 + 9 + 16 + 25 = 55
```

45. Write a program that repeatedly asks the user to input a year from this century. Output a statement that tells whether the year is in the first half or last half of the century. Use the `repeat` statement.

Sample Input/Output

```
Enter a year from this century: 1776
Enter a year from this century: 2001
Enter a year from this century: 1917
1917 is in the first half of this century.
```

Section 5.3

46. A text file contains an integer that indicates how many real numbers follow. Write a program that counts how many negative numbers are in the file.

Sample Input

```
9   3.4   2.6   -4.1   0.0   -7.1   4.2   -3.9   -5.8   1.4
```

Sample Output

```
There are 4 negative numbers in the file.
```

47. A text file contains an integer that indicates how many integers follow. Write a program that counts how many even integers are in the file.

Sample Input

8   36   784   339   2   17   4973   8   555

Sample Output

There are 4 even integers in the file.

48. The factorial of an integer *n* is

$$n! = n \cdot (n-1) \cdot (n-2) \cdot \ \cdots \ \cdot 3 \cdot 2 \cdot 1$$

For example, the factorial of 4 is 24, since $4 \cdot 3 \cdot 2 \cdot 1 = 24$. Write a program that asks the user to input an integer, then computes the factorial of that number.

49. Suppose that *x* is a real nonzero number and *n* is an integer. Then *x* raised to the *n*th power, written mathematically as x^n, means

$x \cdot x \cdot \ \cdots \ \cdot x$	if *n* is positive
$1.0/(x \cdot x \cdot \ \cdots \ \cdot x)$	if *n* is negative
1.0	if *n* is zero

where there are *n* *x*'s in the first two expressions. Write a program that asks the user to enter a real number and an integer and raises the real number to the power indicated by the integer.

Sample Input/Output

Please enter a real number: 2.0
Raise to what power? -3
2.00 to the power -3 is 0.1250

50. The program for Problem 38 outputs a table of salespeople's commissions. Modify the program so that the text file has an integer on the first line that indicates how many lines of data follow.

Sample Input

```
6
 134     580.00
1209     600.00
  30    1000.00
2238    1200.00
9411     800.00
2344    1150.00
```

Sample Output

Same as Problem 38

51. The program for Problem 39 outputs an order report of Frisbee sales. Modify the program so that the first value of the text file is an integer that indicates how many data values follow.

Sample Input

8   50   150   20   200   300   1   250   100

Sample Output

Same as Problem 39

52. The program for Problem 40 outputs a table of class scores and grades. Modify the program so that the first value of the text file is an integer that indicates how many data values follow.

53. The program for Problem 41 computes the grade point average. Modify the program so that the first value of the text file is an integer that indicates how many data values follow.

Sample Input

```
5
B-   3
C    3
C+   5
A-   3
A    1
```

Sample Output

Same as Problem 41

54. The base of the natural logarithms, e, is approximated with four terms as

$$\frac{1}{1} + \frac{1}{1(1)} + \frac{1}{1(1)(2)} + \frac{1}{1(1)(2)(3)}$$

Notice that the fourth term is $\frac{1}{3}$ times the previous term. In general, the nth term is $1/(n-1)$ times the previous term. Write a program that asks the user to input the number of terms and outputs the approximation of e. Hint: You do not need to use nested loops. Use two variables, Sum, which represents the sum computed so far, and Term, which represents the value of the current term. Initialize Sum to the first term outside the loop, starting the loop with the second term.

Sample Input/Output

```
Number of terms in approximation of e: 4
Estimate of e with 4 terms: 2.66667
```

55. The average or mean of n numbers, $x_1, x_2, \ldots, x_n$, is

$$\bar{x} = \frac{x_1 + x_2 + \cdots + x_n}{n}$$

$$= \frac{1}{n} \sum_{i=1}^{n} x_i$$

The standard deviation, a measure of how scattered the n numbers are, is defined as

$$s = \sqrt{\frac{\sum\limits_{i=1}^{n} (x_i - \bar{x})^2}{n-1}}$$

If the numbers are all close to each other, they will all be close to the mean, their differences from the mean will be small, and the standard deviation will be small.

(a) The first item in a text file is an integer that indicates how many real values follow. Write a program that computes and outputs the standard deviation of the real numbers from the definition. You will need one loop to compute the mean, followed by a second reset of the file, followed by another loop for the squares of the differences from the mean.

(b) A mathematically equivalent formula for the standard deviation is

$$s = \sqrt{\frac{\sum\limits_{i=1}^{n} x_i^2 - n\bar{x}^2}{n-1}}$$

(Can you derive this formula from the definitions of the mean and standard deviation?) This formula only requires one loop, since you can accumulate the sum of the squares at the same time you are accumulating the sum for the mean. Write a program that computes the standard deviation from this formula using only one loop.

Section 5.4

56. Write a program to output the number of each kind of animal as well as the total in `ZooFile` as declared in Program 5.10.

Sample Input (nontext)

See Program 5.10 output

Sample Output

```
----------------
Animal    Number
----------------
Monkeys        3
Lions          2
Elephants      1
Giraffes       1
----------------
Total:         7
```

57. `EarthFile` is a file of `AnimalType` as declared in Program 5.10. An ark needs at least one pair each of the four types of animals from `EarthFile`. Write a program

that inputs animals, one at a time, from `EarthFile` and places them in the ark until the ark has a pair of each. If you reach the end of `EarthFile` before the ark gets a pair of each kind, output which animals do not have mates. Otherwise, stop loading the ark before the end of the file and output the number of each kind of animal in the ark.

58. `CardType` is defined in a type definition part as

```
type
    CardType = (Deuce, Three, Four, Five, Six, Seven,
                Eight, Nine, Ten, Jack, Queen, King, Ace)
```

and `DeckFile` is a file of `CardType` that has 52 values. The face cards—Jack, Queen, and King—count as 10 and the Ace counts as 11. Note that `ord (Three)` is not 3, although that card counts as 3 points in a card game. Write a program that inputs the first five cards from `DeckFile` and outputs the total of their point values. For example, if the first five cards in the file are

   Six   Queen   Deuce   Ace   Four

the output should be 33.

59. Modify Program 5.7, `IntegerSum`, to make `Num` have a subrange type whose values must lie in the range 1 to 1000. Test your program with some input values in range and some out of range.

60. Make the modification suggested in Example 5.28. Test the modified program with some input values in range and some out of range.

61. For Problem 3.40, write the program to convert an uppercase character to a lowercase character. Declare the input variable to have subrange type with a range between 'A' and 'Z'. Test your program with some input values in range and some out of range.

62. For Problem 3.45, write the program to output two lowercase letters in alphabetical order. Declare the input variables to have subrange type with a range between 'a' and 'z'. Test your program with some input values in range and some out of range.

63. For Problem 3.55, write the program to output a message depending on the value of the temperature. Declare the temperature to have subrange type with a range between 0 and 120. Test your program with some input values in range and some out of range.

Section 5.5

64. Write a program that asks the user to enter the number of rows and columns of a block of asterisks to be printed.

Sample Input/Output

```
How many rows? 3
How many columns? 5

*****
*****
*****
```

65. Write a program that asks the user to enter the number of rows and columns of an empty block of asterisks to be printed.

```
How many rows? 5
How many columns? 9

*********
*       *
*       *
*       *
*********
```

66. Write a program that asks the user to enter the number of asterisks on the base of a triangle, then prints the triangle as shown.

```
How many asterisks on the base? 5

    *
   **
  ***
 ****
*****
```

67. Write a program that asks the user to enter the number of asterisks on the base of a triangle, then prints the triangle as shown.

```
How many asterisks on the base? 7

   *
  ***
 *****
*******
```

```
How many asterisks on the base? 8

   **
  ****
 ******
********
```

68. Write a program that asks the user to input a lowercase character and prints a triangle of letters up to the one entered.

```
Enter a lowercase letter: d

a
bb
ccc
dddd
```

69. `RankType` and `SuitType` are defined in a type definition part as

```
type
    RankType = (Deuce, Three, Four, Five, Six, Seven,
                Eight, Nine, Ten, Jack, Queen, King, Ace);
    SuitType = (Clubs, Diamonds, Hearts, Spades)
```

Write a program with no input that outputs the 52 cards of a full deck of playing cards in the format of the sample output that follows. Use only two variables, `Rank` with type `RankType` and `Suit` with type `SuitType`. Do not simply use 13 `writeln` statements; instead use nested loops with `Rank` and `Suit` as the control variables.

Sample Output

```
Deuce of Clubs    Deuce of Diamonds    Deuce of Hearts    Deuce of Spades
Three of Clubs    Three of Diamonds    Three of Hearts    Three of Spades
Four of Clubs     Four of Diamonds     Four of Hearts     Four of Spades
etc.
```

All Sections

70. An integer greater than 1 is prime if the only positive integers that divide it are 1 and the number itself. For example, 13 is prime because it is divisible only by 1 and 13, while 15 is not prime since it is divisible by 1, 3, 5, and 15. Write a Pascal program that asks the user to input a positive integer and then outputs a message indicating whether or not the number is prime.

71. Write a program that asks the user to enter a positive integer, then outputs all the positive factors of that number. For example, if the input is 15 then the output should be 1, 3, 5, 15.

72. The first two Fibonacci numbers are 1 and 1. The third Fibonacci number is the sum of the first pair, 1 plus 1, which is 2. The fourth is the sum of the previous pair, 1 plus 2, which is 3. The first six Fibonacci numbers are

    1 1 2 3 5 8

each number being the sum of the two previous numbers. Write a program that asks the user to enter an integer, and outputs that many Fibonacci numbers.

73. A geometric series is a list of numbers, each of which is a constant multiple of the previous number. For example,

    3 6 12 24 48

is a geometric series because each number is two times the previous one. The constant multiple need not be two, however. Write a program that inputs a list of numbers from a nontext file of integers and states whether or not the series is geometric.

74. Table 5.18 shows the correspondence between the digits and the letters on a telephone. Some organizations have telephone numbers that spell words associated with their business. For example, a radio talk show host implores his listeners to "call 715-TALK," when the number they are to dial is 715-8255. A text file has seven consecutive characters, some of which may be letters. The dash is not included. Write a program that converts the file to all digits and outputs it with the dash between the third and fourth digit.

Digit	Letters
2	ABC
3	DEF
4	GHI
5	JKL
6	MNO
7	PRS
8	TUV
9	WXY

Table 5.18

The correspondence between the letters and digits on a telephone for Problem 74.

75. The number of runs for each team in each inning of a Dodgers versus Giants baseball game is in a text file. The file has no sentinel at the end and no count integer at the beginning. The Dodgers bat first. A complete game lasts nine innings.

    After the last Dodger out in the top of the ninth inning, if the Giants are ahead they do not bat in the bottom of the ninth. The game is over and the Giants win. In that case, no value is in the file for the number of Giants runs in the bottom of the ninth, not even a zero.

    If it is a tie game or if the Dodgers are ahead after their last out, the Giants bat in the bottom of the ninth. After the last Giant out, whoever is ahead wins. If it is a tie, the game goes into extra innings.

    Write a program that continues to input the runs for each inning until one team wins. Announce the winner and the score. Assume there are no input errors. The program must not attempt to read past the end of file. Do not use the **eof** function.

76. If a volleyball team serves the ball and wins the volley, they get 1 point and they get to serve again. If they serve the ball and lose the volley, the opposing team does not get a point. But the opposing team does win the right to serve next. The first team to get 15 points wins the game, except that they must win by at least 2 points. If the score is 15 to 14, play continues until one team is ahead by 2.

    A text file contains a sequence of 1's and 0's for a volleyball team that serves first in a game. A 1 represents winning the volley and a 0 represents losing the volley. There is no sentinel value at the end and no integer at the beginning to indicate the number of volleys. For example, the sequence at the beginning of the file

    ```
    1   1   0   1   0   0
    ```

    represents

    - Winning a volley and a point
    - Winning a volley and a point
    - Losing the serve
    - Winning the serve back
    - Losing the serve
    - Losing the volley and a point

    after which the team is ahead, 2 to 1.

    Write a program that continues to read from the file until the game is over. Output the score and state whether the team won or lost. Assume there are no input errors. The program must not attempt to read past the end of file. Do not use the **eof** function.

77. A businessman wants to claim depreciation of an asset with the straight line method. If the asset has a useful life of *n* years, then $1/n$ of its original value is subtracted each year. Write a program that asks for the asset's value and its useful lifespan, and outputs a depreciation schedule using the straight line method.

Sample Input/Output

```
Enter value of asset: 1000.00
Enter lifespan: 5
```

```
-------------
Year    Value
-------------
  0   1000.00
  1    800.00
  2    600.00
  3    400.00
  4    200.00
  5      0.00
-------------
```

78. A businessman wants to claim depreciation of an asset with the double declining balance method. If the asset has a useful life of n years, then $2/n$ times its current value is subtracted each year. Write a program that asks for the asset's value and its useful life-span, and outputs a depreciation schedule using the double declining balance method.

```
Enter value of asset: 1000.00
Enter lifespan: 5

-------------
Year    Value
-------------
  0   1000.00
  1    600.00
  2    360.00
  3    216.00
  4    129.60
  5     77.76
-------------
```

Chapter

Functions and Procedures

You will recall from our previous chapters that Pascal provides standard functions and procedures.

```
writeln (output, 'Mr. K. Kong')
```

from Chapter 3 is a procedure call, and

```
pred (Letter)
```

where `Letter` is of type `char`, is a function call. The objects between the parentheses are called *actual parameters*. In addition to using Pascal's predefined standard functions and procedures, you can define and use your own custom functions and procedures. This adds even greater flexibility to Pascal. In Program 2.6, for example, we defined the custom procedure `PrintTriangle`.

Unlike the `writeln` procedure and the `pred` function, the custom procedure `PrintTriangle` had no parameters. This chapter shows how to define custom functions and procedures with parameters, and explains the benefits of using them. The chapter concludes with an interesting application of procedures—random number generators.

 ## Functions with Value Parameters

Recall that a *syntax error* is an error that is detected by the compiler, while a *logical error* is an error in a syntactically correct program that produces incorrect results when the program executes. The *syntax* of a Pascal statement is the set of

Syntax and semantics

rules you must follow to write that statement in a program. The *semantics* of a statement is a description of how the statement behaves when it executes.

Program 6.1

Program 5.4, `FindRoot1`, computed one root of a cubic equation with the bisection algorithm. It calculated the value of the cubic function in two different places—once for `FLeft` and once for `FMid`. Program 6.1 solves the same problem with a programmer-defined function. The following discussion first describes the syntax of the function and then its semantics.

The function declaration part of this program consists of a function heading followed by a block and separated by a semicolon. In this program, the function declaration part is

```
function F (X: real): real;
   const
      A = 1.0;
      B = -4.0;
      C = 2.0;
   begin
   F := (A * X * X + B) * X + C
   end
```

The function heading is

```
function F (X: real): real
```

and the remainder of the declaration is the block. Figure 6.1 is the syntax chart for a function declaration part. The block of a function is identical to the block of a program, which was shown in Figure 2.10. The block of this function has a constant definition part followed by a compound statement, separated by a semicolon.

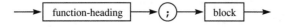

Figure 6.1

The syntax chart for a function declaration part.

Figure 6.2 is the syntax chart for a function heading. Every function has a type specified by the type identifier in the heading. This function has type `real`.

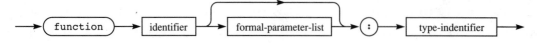

Figure 6.2

The syntax chart for a function heading.

The formal parameter list follows the name of the function. The formal parameter list of this function is

```
(X: real)
```

```
program FindRoot2 (input, output);
   var
      Left, FLeft: real;
      Mid, FMid:   real;
      Right:       real;
      Tolerance:   real;

   function F (X: real): real;
      const
         A = 1.0;
         B = -4.0;
         C = 2.0;
      begin
      F := (A * X * X + B) * X + C
      end;

   begin
   write ('Enter tolerance: ');
   readln (Tolerance);
   Left := 1.0;
   FLeft := F (Left);
   Right := 2.0;
   {  Assert: A root is between Left and Right.  }
   while abs (Left - Right) > Tolerance do
      begin
      Mid := (Left + Right) / 2.0;
      FMid := F (Mid);
      if FLeft * FMid > 0.0 then
         {  Assert: Root is between Mid and Right.  }
         begin
         Left := Mid;
         FLeft := FMid
         end
      else
         {  Assert: Root is between Left and Mid.  }
         Right := Mid;
      end;
   writeln ('Root is: ', (Left + Right) / 2.0: 6: 4)
   end.
```

Program 6.1

The bisection algorithm with a
programmer-defined function.

Interactive Input/Output

```
Enter tolerance: 0.001
Root is: 1.6753
```

Figure 6.3 is the syntax chart for a formal parameter list. The type of each parameter must be declared in the formal parameter list, just as variables are declared in the variable declaration part of a program. This function has one formal parameter, X, declared to have type `real`.

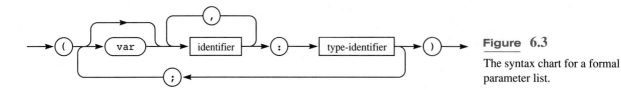

Figure 6.3

The syntax chart for a formal parameter list.

One of the statements that calls the function from the main program is

```
FLeft := F (Left)
```

`F (Left)` is a *function call*. Figure 6.4 is the syntax chart for a general function call. `F` is the function identifier.

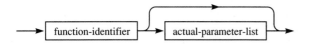

Figure 6.4

The syntax chart for a function call.

The actual parameter list of this function call is

```
(Left)
```

Figure 6.5 is the syntax chart for an actual parameter list. This function has one actual parameter, the expression `Left`.

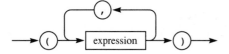

Figure 6.5

The syntax chart for an actual parameter list.

The syntax charts in Figures 6.1 to 6.5 describe the syntax of a function declaration and a function call. Now, we will turn to semantics to see what happens when the statements execute.

The first statements to execute are not the ones in the declaration of the function, but the statements in the main program.

```
write ('Enter tolerance: ');
readln (Tolerance);
Left := 1.0
```

The next statement

```
FLeft := F (Left)
```

calls the function, F. When the program calls the function, it gives the value of the actual parameter, in this case 1.0, to the formal parameter, in this case X. Then the function executes.

This function has one executable statement:

```
F := (A * X * X + B) * X + C
```

It uses the value for X that it received from the calling program to evaluate the expression on the right of the assignment operator. At this point in the execution, the value is

$$(1.0 \times 1.0 \times 1.0 - 4.0) \times 1.0 + 2.0$$

or −1.0. The function identifier, F, is on the left of the assignment operator. It acts like a variable with type `real` that gets the value −1.0. When execution reaches the `end` statement, the function turns control back to the statement that called it

Control returns to the function call statement.

```
FLeft := F (Left)
```

This calling statement gets the value of F, −1.0, from the function and assigns the value to FLeft.

The next statement in the main program

```
Right := 2.0
```

executes, giving the value 2.0 to Right.

After the `while` statement executes and Mid is computed, the statement

```
FMid := F (Mid)
```

calls the function a second time. This time the actual parameter, Mid, gives the value 1.5 to the formal parameter, X. When the statement in the function definition executes, it gives the value

$$(1.0 \times 1.5 \times 1.5 - 4.0) \times 1.5 + 2.0$$

which is −0.625, to F. That value is returned to the statement that called the function,

```
FMid := F (Mid)
```

and assigned to FMid.

Each time through the loop, FMid gets a different value from the function, depending on the value of Mid. The program is identical in behavior to Program 5.4.

Advantages of Functions

One advantage of this version of the bisection algorithm is the ability to easily modify the function. In Program 5.4, modifying the function would require changing the statement in two different places in the main program. In Program 6.1, you only need to modify the function definition once. That one modification affects the computation of the function from both calling points in the main program.

Ease of modification

Another advantage of this version is its readability. In the original version, the function was buried in the code of the main program, and the coefficients, A, B, and C, were separated from the function computation. In this version, the coefficients and the code for the function are all together. That makes the program easier to understand.

Readability

Program 6.2

To allocate a resource is to reserve it for someone's use. For example, you may allocate $30 from your paycheck to go to dinner with a friend on the weekend. When you call a function, Pascal *allocates*, or reserves, a portion of main memory for the function's use. Program 6.2 shows a function that computes the factorial of a number. It illustrates the allocation that takes place when the function executes.

Storage allocation

This function has its own variable declaration part that declares F and I to be integers. F and I are called *local variables* because they are declared locally within the function. F and I, along with function identifier Factorial and formal parameter N are all said to be local to the function.

The first statement executed is the prompt for input. The readln statement then gets a value from the standard input device for Num. The calling statement is

```
writeln ('Its factorial is: ', Factorial (Num): 1)
```

The function call

```
Factorial (Num)
```

is embedded in the writeln statement and causes function Factorial to execute.

When the function is called from the main program, Pascal allocates storage for all the local quantities. Table 6.1 is a trace of the program and depicts the storage allocation for the value returned, Factorial, the formal parameter, N, and the local variables, F and I.

Remember that the three attributes of a Pascal variable are its name, its type, and its value. A variable's name and type appear on the listing. But its value exists only in main memory during execution. Table 6.1 shows the values of the variables as they exist in main memory.

The function identifier, Factorial, is like a variable because it has a type and a value. So are the formal parameter, N, and the local variables, F and I. The difference between the formal parameter and the local variables is their initial values. When the main program calls the function, the formal parameter, N, gets the value of the actual parameter, Num. But the function starts with undefined values

Initial values of formal parameters and local variables

```
program FactFunction (input, output);
   var
      Num: integer;

   function Factorial (N: integer): integer;
      var
         F: integer;
         I: integer;
      begin
      F := 1;
      for I := 1 to N do
         F := F * I;
      Factorial := F
      end;

   begin
   write ('Enter an integer: ');
   readln (Num);
   writeln ('Its factorial is: ', Factorial (Num): 1)
   end.
```

Program 6.2

A program to compute the factorial of an integer with a function.

Interactive Input/Output

```
Enter an integer: 3
Its factorial is: 6
```

Statement executed	Num	Factorial	N	F	I
begin	?				
write ('Enter an i	?				
readln (Num);	3				
writeln ('Its fact	3				
Allocate					
begin	3	?	3	?	?
F := 1;	3	?	3	1	?
for I := 1 to N do	3	?	3	1	1
F := F * I;	3	?	3	1	1
for I := 1 to N do	3	?	3	1	2
F := F * I;	3	?	3	2	2
for I := 1 to N do	3	?	3	2	3
F := F * I;	3	?	3	6	3
for I := 1 to N do	3	?	3	6	?
Factorial := F	3	6	3	6	?
end;	3	6	3	6	?
Deallocate					
writeln ('Its fact	3				
end.					

Table 6.1

A trace of Program 6.2. Storage is allocated for `Factorial`, N, F, and I when the function is called.

for the local variables, F and I. Local variables begin with undefined values at the start of function execution, just as variables in the main program begin with undefined values at the start of program execution.

When the end of the function is reached, storage for the returned value, the formal parameter, and the local variables is "deallocated." You can see from the trace that storage for these objects only exists when the function is executing. Therefore, any statement referring to one of these objects, such as

Storage deallocation

```
write ('F = ', F: 1)
```

in the main program is illegal. The compiler would detect this statement as a syntax error with a message that F is undefined.

Program 6.3

Program 6.3 shows a function to compute wages with possible overtime pay. Note that it has more than one parameter in its parameter list.

After Hours and Rate get their values from the standard input device, the function Wage is called from within the writeln statement. The formal parameters, Rt and Hrs, get their initial values from the actual parameters, Rate and Hours. The order of the parameters determines which values go to the formal parameters. The first formal parameter gets the value of the first actual parameter, and the second formal parameter gets the value of the second actual parameter. Table 6.2 shows a trace of the program when the employee earns overtime.

Statement executed	Hours	Rate		Wage	Rt	Hrs	W
begin	?	?					
write ('Enter hour	?	?					
readln (Hours);	42.0	?					
write ('Enter hour	42.0	?					
readln (Rate);	42.0	10.00					
writeln;	42.0	10.00					
writeln ('Wages ar	42.0	10.00					
				Wage	**Rt**	**Hrs**	**W**
Allocate							
begin	42.0	10.00		?	10.00	42.0	?
W := Rt * Hrs;	42.0	10.00		?	10.00	42.0	420.00
if Hrs > 40.0 then	42.0	10.00		?	10.00	42.0	420.00
W := W + (Hrs - 40	42.0	10.00		?	10.00	42.0	430.00
Wage := W	42.0	10.00		430.00	10.00	42.0	430.00
end;	42.0	10.00		430.00	10.00	42.0	430.00
Deallocate							
writeln ('Wages ar	42.0	10.00					
end.							

Table 6.2

A trace of Program 6.3.

```
program Payroll3 (input, output);
   var
      Hours, Rate: real;

   function Wage (Rt, Hrs: real): real;
      var
         W: real;
      begin
      W := Rt * Hrs;
      if Hrs > 40.0 then
         W := W + (Hrs - 40.0) * 0.5 * Rt;
      Wage := W
      end;

   begin
   write ('Enter hours worked: ');
   readln (Hours);
   write ('Enter hourly rate: ');
   readln (Rate);
   writeln;
   writeln ('Wages are $', Wage (Rate, Hours): 4: 2)
   end.
```

Program 6.3

A program to compute wages with possible overtime with a function.

Interactive Input/Output

```
Enter hours worked: 42.0
Enter hourly rate: 10.00

Wages are $430.00
```

As always, Pascal allocates storage for the local quantities—in this case the returned value, `Wage`, the formal parameters, `Rt` and `Hrs`, and the local variable, `W`—when the function is called. Note that `Wage` and `W` begin with undefined values, but `Rt` and `Hrs` begin with the values of the actual parameters.

When the function terminates, storage is deallocated, and the the value of `Wage` at the time, in this case 430.00, is returned to the calling statement. The calling statement was `writeln`, which dutifully outputs the value returned.

Using Functions

Figure 6.5 shows that the actual parameter may be an expression.

Expression for the actual parameter

Example 6.1 The function call

```
DataValue := Factorial (2 * Num + 1)
```

where `DataValue` and `Num` are integer variables and `Factorial` is declared as in Program 6.2, is legal. If `Num` has the value of 3, then the formal parameter, `N`, would get the value of 7 at the start of function execution. ∎

Any number of parameters can be in the parameter list of a function. The number of parameters in the actual parameter list must equal the number of parameters in the formal parameter list. The types must correspond as well. The violation of these rules is a syntax error.

Rules for the number and types of formal and actual parameters

Example 6.2 The statement

`writeln ('Factorial is: ', Factorial (3.0): 1)`

where `Factorial` is declared as in Program 6.2, is illegal because the formal parameter, `N`, is an integer and the actual parameter, 3.0, is a real value. ∎

Example 6.3 With `Factorial` declared as before, the function call

`writeln ('Factorial is: ', Factorial (3, 5): 1)`

is illegal, because there are two actual parameters but only one formal parameter. ∎

Remember that if `X` is a real variable, the assignment `X := 7` is legal. The integer value, 7, is converted to a real value, 7.0, before being assigned to `X`. But if `I` is an integer variable, then `I := 2.7` is illegal. Similarly, integer values can be actual parameters for real formal parameters.

Automatic conversion from integer values to real values

Example 6.4 The function call

`writeln ('Wages are $', Wage (10, 42): 4: 2)`

where `Wage` is defined as in Program 6.3, is legal. The integer value, 10, is automatically converted to the real value, 10.0, before being given to the formal parameter, `Rt`. Similarly, 42 is automatically converted to 42.0. ∎

In general, a function call can be placed anywhere an expression is allowed. Program 6.1 has the function call, `F (Left)`, on the right side of an assignment statement, and Program 6.2 has the function call, `Factorial (Num)`, in a `writeln` statement. The function call can just as easily be part of a larger expression.

A function can be part of a larger expression.

Example 6.5 The statement

`Num := 3.1416 * sqr (X) / Factorial (I)`

is legal, where `Num` and `X` are real variables, `I` is an integer variable, and `Factorial` is declared as in Program 6.2. ∎

It would appear from the previous programs that the function identifier can be used just as any other variable. The only thing special about it seems to be the fact that the value of the variable named by the function identifier is the value returned when the function terminates. However, there is one restriction on the use of the function identifier as a variable. It can only appear on the left side of an assignment statement.

A restriction on the function identifier

Example 6.6   In Program 6.3, you might be tempted to dispense with the local variable, W, and use the function identifier in its place as follows:

```
function Wage (Rt, Hrs: real): real;
   begin
   Wage := Rt * Hrs;
   if Hrs > 40.0 then
      Wage := Wage + (Hrs - 40.0) * 0.5 * Rt
   end
```

This attempt is illegal because the function identifier, **Wage**, appears on the right of the assignment statement.   ∎

Example 6.7   On the other hand, the following function, which performs the same computation without W,

```
function Wage (Rt, Hrs: real): real;
   begin
   if Hrs <= 40.0 then
      Wage := Hrs * Rt
   else
      Wage := 40.0 * Rt + (Hrs - 40.0) * 1.5 * Rt
   end
```

is legal because the function identifier **Wage** only appears on the left of an assignment statement.   ∎

It is legal to have the actual parameter be a variable with the same name as the formal parameter. But you should realize that there are separate memory locations for each. To keep the distinction clear between the formal parameters and actual parameters, this book will generally avoid using the same name for both. The usual convention will have the formal parameter serve as an abbreviation of the actual parameter.

Giving the same name to the actual and formal parameters

Example 6.8   The function definition

```
function Wage (Rate, Hours: real): real;
   var
      W: real;
   begin
   W := Rate * Hours;
   if Hours > 40.0 then
      W := W + (Hours - 40.0) * 0.5 * Rate;
   Wage := W
   end
```

would be legal in Program 6.3, even though the formal parameters have the same name as the actual parameters in the main program. The trace of the program with this function would be identical to Table 6.2, with only the heading of the allocated table changed. The identifiers **Rate** and **Hours** would each appear twice when tracing the function execution.   ∎

▢ **Program 6.4**

Functions can return values of any simple type, including `real`, `integer`, `boolean`, `char`, and enumerated. The `eof` function is an example of a standard function that returns a value with `boolean` type. In Program 6.4, `Qualify` returns a value with enumerated type. The program determines whether a loan should be granted based on data entered by the applicant.

Any simple type for function value

```
program Loan (input,output);
   type
      RiskType = (Good, Risky, Bad);
   var
      LoanAmt:  real;
      Income:   real;
      Payments: real;

   function Qualify (Amt, Inc, Pmt: real): RiskType;
      begin
      if (Inc - Pmt) > (0.05 * Amt) then
         Qualify := Good
      else if (Inc - Pmt) > (0.04 * Amt) then
         Qualify := Risky
      else
         Qualify := Bad
      end;

   begin
   write ('Enter amount of desired loan: ');
   readln (LoanAmt);
   write ('Enter monthly income: ');
   readln (Income);
   write ('Enter current monthly payments: ');
   readln (Payments);
   case Qualify (LoanAmt, Income, Payments) of
   Good:
      writeln ('Your loan application is approved.');
   Risky:
      writeln ('We are investigating your loan application.');
   Bad:
      writeln ('Your loan is denied.')
   end {case}
   end.
```

Program 6.4

A function that returns a value of enumerated type.

Interactive Input/Output

```
Enter amount of desired loan: 55000
Enter monthly income: 3000
Enter current monthly payments: 500
We are investigating your loan application.
```

The function call is embedded in the `case` statement

```
case Qualify (LoanAmt, Income, Payments) of
```

which is legal. As we have seen, a function call can be placed anywhere an expression is allowed. Figure 3.16, the syntax chart for a `case` statement, showed an expression between `case` and `of`.

In this program, when the `case` statement executes, it triggers the function call. The values of `LoanAmt`, `Income`, and `Payments`, which came from the interactive input earlier, are given to `Amt`, `Inc`, and `Pmt` respectively. The function gives an enumerated value to `Qualify`, which is then returned to the `case` statement. The `case` statement then uses the returned value to select one of its alternatives to execute.

6.2   Procedures with Value Parameters

The purpose of a procedure is to perform a task for the calling program. Procedure `PrintTriangle` in Program 2.6 printed a single pattern and illustrated the flow of control for procedures. Each time the main program called the procedure, the pattern was printed, then control was passed back to the statement after the calling statement.

When a procedure has value parameters, its flow of control is similar to that of procedure `PrintTriangle`, and memory allocation and deallocation is similar to that of function calls. The only difference is that a procedure does not return a value, and hence does not have a type like a function does.

Program 6.5

Program 6.5 has a programmer-defined procedure, `PrintLine`, which the main program calls twice to print two lines of asterisks. The following discussion presents the syntax of the procedure declaration, followed by its semantics.

The structure of a procedure declaration is similar to the structure of a function declaration. Figure 6.6 is the syntax chart for a procedure declaration part. The block of a procedure is identical to the block of a function and a program.

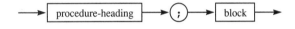

Figure 6.6

The syntax chart for a procedure declaration part.

The procedure heading in Program 6.5 is

```
procedure PrintLine (N: integer)
```

```
program AsteriskLines (output);

    procedure PrintLine (N: integer);
        var
            I: integer;
        begin
        for I := 1 to N do
            write ('*');
        writeln
        end;

    begin
    PrintLine (6);
    PrintLine (5)
    end.
```

Program 6.5

A procedure that prints a row of asterisks. The parameter specifies the number of asterisks in the row.

Output

```
******
*****
```

The syntax chart for a procedure heading, Figure 6.7, shows that a procedure heading is identical to a function heading except for the absence of a type. Unlike a function, the purpose of a procedure is not to return a single value, so you must not specify a type for the procedure itself.

Figure 6.7

The syntax chart for a procedure heading.

The formal parameter list for a procedure has the same syntax as the formal parameter list for a function (Figure 6.3). This procedure has one formal parameter, N.

Figure 6.8 is the syntax chart for a procedure call. The actual parameter list for a procedure has the same syntax as the actual parameter list for a function (Figure 6.5). In this program,

```
PrintLine (5)
```

is a procedure call, and 5 is the actual parameter.

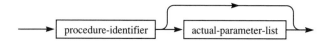

Figure 6.8

The syntax chart for a procedure call.

Turning now to semantics, the first statement of Program 6.5 to execute is the procedure call,

```
PrintLine (6)
```

Pascal allocates storage in main memory for the formal parameter, N, and the local variable, I. It gives the value of the actual parameter, 6, to the formal parameter, N. The procedure executes the `for` statement to print the first row of six asterisks. At the end of the procedure execution, the storage for N and I is deallocated.

Unlike a function, control does not return to the calling statement. Instead, control returns to the statement after the calling statement. In this case, that is the procedure call

Control returns to the statement after the procedure call.

```
PrintLine (5)
```

which calls the procedure again. Storage is reallocated for N and I, and the procedure prints a row of five asterisks.

Program 6.6

Program 6.6 uses a procedure to print a bar chart of data values. The input is a file of real values that the main program inputs with the count technique.

The program reads the first value into the integer variable NumPoints. The control variable of the `for` statement, I, counts the number of times the loop executes. With each loop execution a value is input into DataValue and the procedure PrintBar is called. Table 6.3 shows the beginning of a trace.

The first time through the loop, DataValue gets the value of 2.6. When procedure PrintBar is called, storage is allocated for the formal parameter, X, and local variables, I and N. X gets the value of the actual parameter, 2.6. I and N start with undefined values.

The local variable, I, in the procedure is not the same variable as I in the main program. I in the main program maintains its value of 1, while I in the procedure starts with an undefined value. As the procedure executes, the local variable, I, gets values 1, then 2, then 3, then becomes undefined. Throughout these changes to the local variable, I in the main program maintains its value of 1.

The same name for two different variables

The second time through the loop, I in the main program has the value of 2. Storage is again allocated for the formal parameter, X, and local variables, I and N. This time I in the main program maintains its value of 2, while the local variable, I, acquires several values in turn.

```
program BarChart (BarFile, output);
   var
      NumPoints: integer;
      DataValue: real;
      BarFile:   text;
      I:         integer;

   procedure PrintBar (X: real);
      var
         I, N: integer;
      begin
      write (X: 6: 1, ' |');
      N := round (X);
      for I := 1 to N do
         write ('*');
      writeln
      end;

   begin
   reset (BarFile);
   read (BarFile, NumPoints);
   for I := 1 to NumPoints do
      begin
      read (BarFile, DataValue);
      PrintBar (DataValue)
      end
   end.
```

Program 6.6

A program that prints a bar chart from data values in a file. The procedure prints a single bar.

Input—BarFile

```
12
 2.6   13.3   16.8   34.1   27.2   23.0   24.7
29.0   16.1    9.7    0.4    2.1
```

Output

```
  2.6 |***
 13.3 |*************
 16.8 |*****************
 34.1 |**********************************
 27.2 |***************************
 23.0 |***********************
 24.7 |*************************
 29.0 |*****************************
 16.1 |****************
  9.7 |**********
  0.4 |
  2.1 |**
```

Table 6.3

The beginning of a trace of Program 6.6.

Statement executed	NumPoints	DataValue	I		X	I	N
begin	?	?	?				
reset (BarFile);	?	?	?				
read (BarFile, Num	12	?	?				
for I := 1 to NumP	12	?	1				
read (BarFile, Dat	12	2.6	1				
PrintBar (DataValu	12	2.6	1				
					X	**I**	**N**
Allocate							
begin	12	2.6	1		2.6	?	?
write (X: 6: 1, '	12	2.6	1		2.6	?	?
N := round (X);	12	2.6	1		2.6	?	3
for I := 1 to N do	12	2.6	1		2.6	1	3
write ('*');	12	2.6	1		2.6	1	3
for I := 1 to N do	12	2.6	1		2.6	2	3
write ('*');	12	2.6	1		2.6	2	3
for I := 1 to N do	12	2.6	1		2.6	3	3
write ('*');	12	2.6	1		2.6	3	3
for I := 1 to N do	12	2.6	1		2.6	?	3
writeln	12	2.6	1		2.6	?	3
end;	12	2.6	1		2.6	?	3
Deallocate							
for I := 1 to NumP	12	2.6	2				
read (BarFile, Dat	12	13.3	2				
PrintBar (DataValu	12	13.3	2				
					X	**I**	**N**
Allocate							
begin	12	13.3	2		13.3	?	?
write (X: 6: 1, '	12	13.3	2		13.3	?	?
N := round (X);	12	13.3	2		13.3	?	13
for I := 1 to N do	12	13.3	2		13.3	1	13
.					.		
.					.		
.					.		

It is common for a local variable to have the same name as a variable in the main program. When a statement in a procedure refers to the variable with the common name, the Pascal compiler assumes the local variable, not the variable in the main program. When a statement in the main program uses the common name, the compiler must assume it is the variable in the main program because storage for the local variable will not be allocated at that point.

Program 6.7

In all our previous examples, the functions and procedures passed the values of actual parameters to formal parameters. This method of passing information from a main program to a function or procedure is known as *call by value*. The formal parameters are known as *value parameters*.

Call by value

Program 6.7 illustrates the fact that in call by value, the formal parameter gets a copy of the value of the actual parameter. If a subsequent statement in the procedure changes the value of the formal parameter, it does not affect the actual parameter.

```
program CallByValue (output);
   var
      I: integer;

   procedure PassVal (J: integer);
      begin
      J := J + 1;
      writeln ('J = ', J: 1)
      end;

   begin
   I := 6;
   writeln ('I = ', I: 1);
   PassVal (I);
   writeln ('I = ', I: 1)
   end.
```

Output

```
I = 6
J = 7
I = 6
```

Program 6.7

A procedure with a parameter called by value. A change of the parameter in the procedure does *not* change the value in the calling program.

In the main program, variable I gets the value of 6, which is verified by the output statement. Then the program calls procedure PassVal with the actual parameter, I.

As Table 6.4 shows, the formal parameter, J, gets a copy of the value of I. When the statement

```
J := J + 1
```

executes in the procedure, it changes the copy of the value to 7. The original value of 6 for I in the main program does not change, as verified by the last writeln call.

Statement executed	I		J
begin	?		
I := 6;	6		
writeln ('I = ', I	6		
PassVal (I);	6		
Allocate			
begin	6		6
J := J + 1;	6		7
writeln ('J = ', J	6		7
end;	6		7
Deallocate			
writeln ('I = ', I	6		
end.			

Table 6.4

A trace of Program 6.7. J is called by value.

When parameters are called by value, the procedure has access to the values of the formal parameters. If the value of the formal parameter is changed, the change is not reflected in the main program. Information flows from the calling program to the procedure—not in the other direction—via the value of the parameter. Figure 6.9 shows the information flow in procedure PassVal.

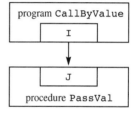

Figure 6.9

The information flow in procedure PassVal. In call by value, information flows from the calling program to the procedure.

6.3 Procedures with Variable Parameters

This section introduces the concept of *call by reference*, a technique by which a procedure can not only get values from the calling statement, but can give values back to it as well.

Program 6.8

The listing of Program 6.8 is identical to the listing of Program 6.7 except for one important detail. The programmer placed reserved word var before formal parameter J in the formal parameter list. The reserved word var in a formal parameter list has a different meaning from its meaning in the variable declaration part. In all our previous examples, var indicated the start of the variable declaration part. In a formal parameter list, var indicates that the parameter is called by reference instead of called by value. In Pascal, parameters that are called by reference are known as *variable parameters*.

Call by reference

```
program CallByReference (output);
   var
      I: integer;

   procedure PassRef (var J: integer);
      begin
      J := J + 1;
      writeln ('J = ', J: 1)
      end;

   begin
   I := 6;
   writeln ('I = ', I: 1);
   PassRef (I);
   writeln ('I = ', I: 1)
   end.
```

Output

```
I = 6
J = 7
I = 7
```

Program 6.8

A procedure with a parameter called by reference. A change of the parameter in the procedure *does* change the value in the calling program.

Table 6.5 is a trace of this program. When Pascal allocates memory for J, it does not give a copy of the value of the actual parameter, I, to J. Instead, it gives a reference to I. The table indicates the reference to I by the symbol <ref I> under the heading for J.

When J is used in the procedure, it is as though I has temporarily taken its place. The statement

```
J := J + 1
```

has the effect of

```
I := I + 1
```

since J, during execution of the procedure, refers to I. When control returns back to the calling program, the value of I has been modified. The purpose of call by reference is to change the value of the actual parameter in the calling statement.

When parameters are called by reference, the procedure has access to the values of the variables in the calling program referred to by the parameters. In this program, procedure **PassRef** had access to the value, 6, of I in the calling program. In that sense, information can flow from the calling program to the procedure.

When the procedure changes the value of a variable parameter, the value of a variable in the calling program changes. In this program, when procedure

Statement executed	I	J
begin	?	
I := 6;	6	
writeln ('I = ', I	6	
PassRef (I);	6	
		J
Allocate		
begin	6	< ref I>
J := J + 1;	7	< ref I>
writeln ('J = ', J	7	< ref I>
end;	7	< ref I>
Deallocate		
writeln ('I = ', I	7	
end.		

Table **6.5**

A trace of Program 6.8. J is called by reference.

`PassRef` assigned a value to J, the value of I in the calling program changed. In that sense, information can flow from the procedure to the calling program.

Figure 6.10 depicts the information flow in procedure `PassRef`. In contrast to Figure 6.9, the information flows both ways.

In call by value, the actual parameter could be an arbitrary expression. But in call by reference, the actual parameter must be a single variable.

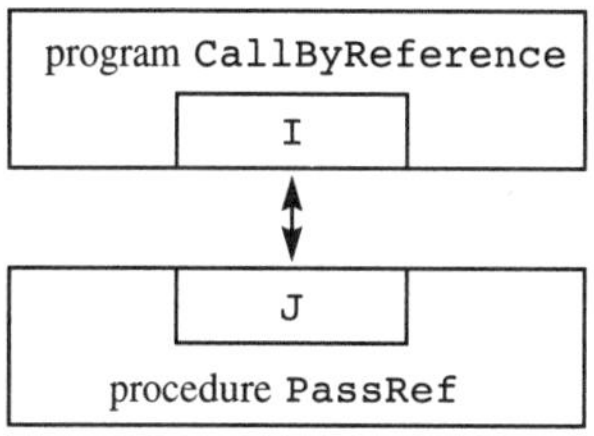

Example 6.9 The procedure call

`PassVal (I + 2)`

where `PassVal` is declared as in Program 6.7, is legal. The formal parameter, J, is called by value and can take the expression I + 2 as an actual parameter. ∎

Example 6.10 The procedure call

`PassRef (I + 2)`

where `PassRef` is defined in Program 6.8, is not legal, because I + 2 is not a single variable. ∎

Figure 6.10

The information flow in procedure `PassRef`. In call by reference, information can flow both ways.

The actual parameter must be a variable in call by reference.

Program 6.9

Program 6.9 uses a procedure to calculate the area and perimeter of a rectangle from its width and height. Procedure `CalcRect` has four formal parameters. Two of the parameters are called by value and two are called by reference.

```
program Rectangle2 (input, output);
   var
      Width:  real;
      Height: real;
      Area:   real;
      Perim:  real;

   procedure CalcRect (var Ar:  real;
                       var Per: real;
                           Wid: real;
                           Ht:  real);
      begin
      Ar := Wid * Ht;
      Per := 2.0 * (Wid + Ht)
      end;

   begin
   write ('Enter width: ');
   readln (Width);
   write ('Enter height: ');
   readln (Height);
   CalcRect (Area, Perim, Width, Height);
   writeln;
   writeln ('Area is ', Area: 3: 1);
   writeln ('Perimeter is ', Perim: 3: 1)
   end.
```

Program 6.9

Computing the area and perimeter of a rectangle with a procedure.

Interactive Input/Output

```
Enter width: 5.0
Enter height: 4.0

Area is 20.0
Perimeter is 18.0
```

Table 6.6 is a trace of program execution; the main program gets values for `Width` and `Height` from the keyboard. Then it calls procedure `CalcRect`. When the program calls the procedure, the actual parameters—`Area`, `Perim`, `Width`, and `Height`—correspond to the formal parameters—`Ar`, `Per`, `Wid`, and `Ht`. `Ar` and `Per` are called by reference. `Wid` and `Ht` are called by value. `Ar` refers to `Area`, and `Per` refers to `Perim`. `Wid` gets the value from `Width`, and `Ht` gets the value from `Height`.

Procedure `CalcRect` uses the values of `Wid` and `Ht` in its computation. That information flowed from the calling program to the procedure. When `CalcRect` assigns values to `Ar` and `Per`, it changes the values of `Area` and `Perim` in the calling program. That information flowed from the procedure to the calling program.

Statement executed	Width	Height	Area	Perim
begin	?	?	?	?
write {'Enter widt	?	?	?	?
readln (Width);	5.0	?	?	?
write ('Enter heig	5.0	?	?	?
readln (Height);	5.0	4.0	?	?
CalcRect (Area, Pe	5.0	4.0	?	?

	Ar	Per	Wid	Ht
Allocate				
begin	< ref Area>	< ref Perim>	5.0	4.0
Ar := Wid * Ht;	< ref Area>	< ref Perim>	5.0	4.0
Per := 2.0 * (Wid	< ref Area>	< ref Perim>	5.0	4.0
end;	< ref Area>	< ref Perim>	5.0	4.0

Combined trace:

Statement executed	Width	Height	Area	Perim
Allocate				
begin	5.0	4.0	?	?
Ar := Wid * Ht;	5.0	4.0	20.0	?
Per := 2.0 * (Wid	5.0	4.0	20.0	18.0
end;	5.0	4.0	20.0	18.0
Deallocate				
writeln;	5.0	4.0	20.0	18.0
writeln ('Area is	5.0	4.0	20.0	18.0
writeln ('Perimete	5.0	4.0	20.0	18.0
end.				

Table 6.6

A trace of Program 6.9.

Figure 6.11 shows the possible information flow in procedure `CalcRect`. In general, information can flow both ways when parameters are called by reference. In this program, `CalcRect` did not use the values of `Area` and `Perim`. With `Ar` and `Per` the information flowed one way, from the procedure to the calling program.

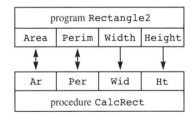

Figure 6.11

The possible information flow in procedure `CalcRect`. `Ar` and `Per` are called by reference. `Wid` and `Ht` are called by value.

Program 6.10

One common use of variable parameters is in procedures for input. Program 6.10 is a version of the bisection algorithm to find the roots of a cubic function. It uses two different procedures, `GetTolerance` and `GetLeftRight`, for input.

The original versions had several deficiencies that are corrected by this version of the program. If the user entered a negative or zero value for the tolerance, the program executed endlessly. Also, the previous versions only found one of the roots of the equation. Program 6.10 allows the user to find any of the three roots. The following pseudocode summarizes the logic of the main program:

```
begin
Input a value for Tolerance
Input values for Left and Right
Calculate the root of the equation.
Output the root.
end
```

The main program logic of Program 6.10

Program 6.10

Another version of the bisection program for finding the root of an equation. User-defined procedures get the input and validate it.

```
program FindRoot3 (input, output);
   var
      Left:      real;
      Right:     real;
      Tolerance: real;
      Root:      real;

   function F (X: real): real;
      const
         A = 1.0;
         B = -4.0;
         C = 2.0;
      begin
      F := (A * X * X + B) * X + C
      end;

   procedure GetTolerance (var Tol: real);
      begin
      write ('Enter tolerance: ');
      readln (Tol);
      while Tol <= 0.0 do
         begin
         writeln ('Tolerance must be greater than zero.');
         write ('Enter tolerance: ');
         readln (Tol)
         end
      end;

   procedure GetLeftRight (var Lft, Rt: real);
      begin
      write ('Enter left point: ');
      readln (Lft);
      write ('Enter right point: ');
      readln (Rt);
      while F (Lft) * F (Rt) > 0 do
         begin
         writeln ('A root may not lie between these points.');
         write ('Enter left point: ');
         readln (Lft);
         write ('Enter right point: ');
         readln (Rt)
         end
      end;
```

```
procedure CalcRoot (var R: real; Lft, Rt, Tol: real);
   var
      Mid:    real;
      FLeft:  real;
      FMid:   real;
   begin
   FLeft := F (Lft);
   { Assert: A root is between Lft and Rt.  }
   while abs (Lft - Rt) > Tol do
      begin
      Mid := (Lft + Rt) / 2.0;
      FMid := F (Mid);
      if FLeft * FMid > 0.0 then
         { Assert: Root is between Mid and Right.  }
         begin
         Lft := Mid;
         FLeft := FMid
         end
      else
         { Assert: Root is between Left and Mid.  }
         Rt := Mid;
      end;
   R := (Lft + Rt) / 2.0
   end;

begin
GetTolerance (Tolerance);
GetLeftRight (Left, Right);
CalcRoot (Root, Left, Right, Tolerance);
writeln;
writeln ('Root is ', Root: 6: 4)
end.
```

Program 6.10, continued

Interactive Input/Output

```
Enter tolerance: 0.001
Enter left point: -2
Enter right point: -1
A root may not lie between these points.
Enter left point: -3
Enter right point: -2

Root is -2.2144
```

The main program calls three procedures. These are `GetTolerance`, `GetLeftRight`, and `CalcRoot`. `GetTolerance` and `GetLeftRight` are input procedures. `CalcRoot` is a processing procedure. The procedures `GetLeftRight` and `CalcRoot` call function F. Figure 6.12 is a hierarchy diagram for this program. It shows the calling relationships between the main program, procedures and function.

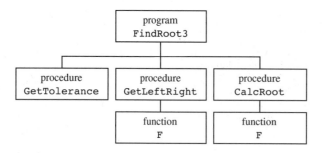

Figure 6.12

The hierarchy diagram for Program 6.10.

Figure 6.13 is a series of hierarchy diagrams that show the sequence of events when Program 6.10 executes. The box for the main program, which is at the root of the tree, contains the variables declared in the main program. Each part of the sequence shows the effect on the values of those variables.

`GetTolerance` prompts the user for a tolerance. If the user enters a value from the keyboard that is not positive, the procedure issues the message "Tolerance must be greater than zero" and asks the user to enter the tolerance again.

The formal parameter, `Tol`, is called by reference. Before the main program calls `GetTolerance`, the value of `Tolerance` is undefined. After `GetTolerance` returns control back to the main program, `Tolerance` has the last value entered by the user, 0.001 in this case. The procedure changes the value of a variable in the calling program from undefined to 0.001. So the formal parameter, `Tol`, must be called by reference.

`GetLeftRight` prompts the user for the starting points of *x* to the left and right of the root. It tests the two values to make sure a root lies between them by calling function F (Lft) and F (Rt). If F (Lft) and F (Rt) have the same sign, that is, if their product is positive, then a root may not lie between them. (Actually, either no roots or two roots may lie between them. Do you see why?) In that case, the procedure asks the user to enter the two values again.

The formal parameters, `Lft` and `Rt`, are called by reference. Before the main program calls `GetLeftRight`, the values of `Left` and `Right` are undefined. After `GetLeftRight` returns control back to the main program, `Left` and `Right` have the last values entered by the user, −3.0 and −2.0 in this case. The procedure changes the values of variables in the calling program from undefined to −3.0 and −2.0. So the formal parameters, `Lft` and `Rt`, must be called by reference.

Figure 6.13

The sequence of procedure calls in Program 6.10.

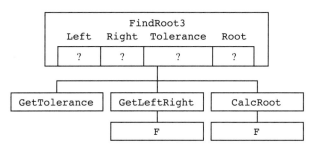

(a) At the beginning of the program.

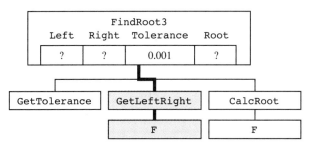

(b) During execution of `GetTolerance`.

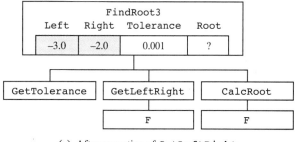

(c) After execution of `GetTolerance`.

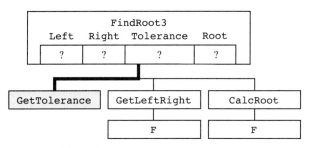

(d) During execution of `GetLeftRight`.

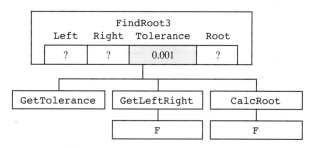

(e) After execution of `GetLeftRight`.

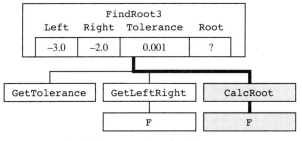

(f) During execution of `CalcRoot`.

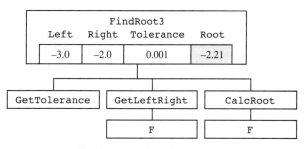

(g) After execution of `CalcRoot`.

CalcRoot gets values for Lft, Rt, and Tol from the main program. It uses the values to compute the root of the equation. Its purpose is not to change the value of Left, Right, or Tolerance in the calling program. Its purpose is to change the value of Root in the calling program. Therefore, Lft, Rt, and Tol are called by value, while R is called by reference.

Figure 2.10, the syntax chart for a block, showed that procedures and functions can be declared in any order. There is a restriction not shown in the syntax chart, however. If a procedure or function calls another procedure or function, the procedure or function that it calls must already have been declared. In Program 6.10, procedure GetLeftRight calls function F, so function F must be declared before procedure GetLeftRight. Accordingly, function F is before procedure GetLeftRight in the listing.

Functions and procedures must be declared before they are used.

 The Fundamental Space/Time Tradeoff

You could write procedure CalcRoot without the local variables FLeft and FMid. Rather than saving the values from the function call in those local variables, you could call the function directly whenever you need to. The following version of CalcRoot performs the same computation as the original version.

```
procedure CalcRoot (var R: real; Lft, Rt, Tol: real);
   var
      Mid: real;
   begin
   { Assert: A root is between Lft and Rt. }
   while abs (Lft - Rt) > Tol do
      begin
      Mid := (Lft + Rt) / 2.0;
      if F (Lft) * F (Mid) > 0.0 then
         { Assert: Root is between Mid and Right. }
         Lft := Mid
      else
         { Assert: Root is between Left and Mid. }
         Rt := Mid
      end;
   R := (Lft + Rt) / 2.0
   end
```

An alternate version of CalcRoot

Is this a better version of CalcRoot than the original one? The listing for this procedure is shorter than the original. It has two fewer variables in the variable declaration part. Three of the assignment statements in the original are missing here. The original listing was 24 lines of code compared to 17 for this version.

To execute a program, the computer must store both the program and the data in main memory. Since this version of the program is shorter, it will take less stor-

Space

Computer Viruses Are No Laughing Matter

Computer viruses were considered a curiosity when they first emerged a few years ago. But the first blush of benevolent curiosity faded quickly. Computer viruses, now documented on diverse mainframe and personal computers, have cost computer owners great time and expense in restoring their systems.

The name *virus* is very apt because of the way in which the computer virus spreads and the potential severity of an "infection." Just as with viruses that infect humans, the exact methods of transmission are diverse, and the severity of infection can range from a minor, short-lived nuisance to a "life-threatening" attack.

A virus may lie dormant for a period of time, until some calendar-date trigger or other counter is reached, at which time the virus attacks. The attack may be as harmless as the flashing of a humorous message on your monitor, or it may be as insidious as the gradual or sudden erasure of the contents of your hard disk.

Many universities and industries have their computers linked via telephone and other connections into a large network so that electronic mail and data can be easily transmitted and programs residing on one machine can be executed by another. The virus travels from computer to computer over such networks when users share programs and data.

Because of the complexity of getting a large network up and running, many of the systems programs for networking have been designed with special debugging options and/or *trap doors*, which allow a knowledgeable user to monitor the details of how remote connections are made. Trap doors also allow a program designer to use a hidden password or similar technique to break into software on another machine, even though the software may have been sold to the user as completed and secure. The original intent of such mechanisms was generally benign; software designers wanted to be able to have a quick way to get into a program to patch any bugs that might be discovered after the software was delivered. However, trap doors are now often used by malicious programmers to embed viruses.

In a well-documented case, a graduate student at Cornell, the son of a significant national security employee, wrote a complex program now known as the Internet Worm. Taking advantage of the trap doors designed by others, he designed a virus that invaded nationally networked computers on November 2 and 3, 1988, bringing many to a halt. Although this particular virus did not maliciously delete computer files or damage installations it attacked, it did bring a number of systems to a slowdown or halt, costing systems administrators many hours of work in purging the virus from their systems, and costing organizations many dollars in lost computer time. The author of this program has since been tried and convicted, which will bar him from many jobs. Rather than dignify the perpetrator by mentioning his name, we'll simply point you to the June 1989 edition of *Communications of the ACM* or to the *New York Times* coverage of the Internet Worm if you want to research the details of the case further.

There are several steps you can take to protect yourself against computer viruses. If it is absolutely critical that your computer remain virus-free, you can "quarantine" it so that it cannot be connected by telephone or computer network to any other machines, and so that no unknown software is ever loaded on the machine via tape or diskette. This is a very isolationist policy, however, and is only appropriate for very critical applications. Most users would be greatly inhibited in their work if their connections with other computers were severed.

Since electronic mail, remote data collection, off-site database queries, and the use of floppy disk file copies are daily activities for many computer users, how can users protect themselves from viruses? There are programs available to monitor your hard disk for suspicious changes, and these programs can be effective against certain kinds of viruses. Other ways to avoid problems include obtaining software only from reputable sources and testing new software on a safe machine for a while before loading it onto your regular system. Shareware, free software from bulletin boards, is far more likely to contain a virus than a program purchased from a legitimate software house.

Short of programming all your software yourself, there is no sure-fire way to avoid a computer virus, so the best you can do is to take reasonable precautions. As our legal system prosecutes more and more virus originators and as system designers build more secure systems, the likelihood of virus attacks may well diminish.

age space in main memory during execution. When the program calls the procedure, storage is allocated for local variables. Since this version has fewer local variables, it will take less storage space for them as well. So this version takes less space than the original version.

But storage space is only part of the story. What about execution time? In all computer systems, arithmetic operations on real quantities are slower than those on ordinal quantities. They are also much slower than simple assignments. At first glance these two versions seem to have the same number of real operations. The three statements with real operations in the original version produce one real division and multiplication inside the loop with

Time

```
Mid := (Lft + Rt) / 2.0
```

and

```
if FLeft * FMid > 0.0 then
```

and one real division outside the loop with

```
R := (Lft + Rt) / 2.0
```

Similarly, the three statements with real operations in this version produce one real division and multiplication inside the loop with

```
Mid := (Lft + Rt) / 2.0
```

and

```
if F (Lft) * F (Mid) > 0.0 then
```

and one real division outside the loop with

```
R := (Lft + Rt) / 2.0
```

In terms of the arithmetic operations in procedure `CalcRoot`, both versions seem to execute in approximately equal time.

But do not forget the function calls. Each time function `F` is called, it must perform three real multiplications and two real additions. This is a relatively simple function. To find the root of a different equation, function `F` could be much more complex. To compare the execution time of the two versions of `CalcRoot`, we should count how many times the function is called.

Including the time to execute the function calls

Suppose that the `while` loop executes *n* times. The original version has one function call outside the loop,

```
FLeft := F (Lft)
```

and one function call inside the loop,

```
FMid := F (Mid)
```

The total number of calls is *n* + 1. This version has no function calls outside the loop, but it does have two calls inside the loop:

```
if F (Lft) * F (Mid) > 0.0 then
```

The total number of calls is $2n$.

So if the loop executes 100 times, the original version would call the function $100 + 1$, or 101 times. This version would call the function 2(100), or 200, times, almost twice as many. This version is definitely slower than the original.

The original version takes more space but less time. This is a typical phenomenon in computer science problems. When you formulate several solutions to a problem you can usually trade off space for time. Generally speaking, if you can afford larger amounts of memory, you can design programs to run faster. The space/time tradeoff is one of the most fundamental tradeoffs in computer science.

The space/time tradeoff

Which version is better? Neither one is intrinsically better than the other. It depends on whether you have memory to spare or time to spare. If speed of execution is not a primary concern, as is typical with the small problems in this text, the second version is better. If speed becomes a concern with more complex functions, the first is better.

 ### Computing the Area Under a Curve

Another common mathematical problem is to compute the area under the curve of a function. The simplest numerical technique is the midpoint algorithm. Figure 6.14 shows the area, A, under the curve of an arbitrary function, $f(x)$, between the points `Lft` and `Rt`.

The midpoint algorithm approximates the area under the curve by dividing the x-axis between `Lft` and `Rt` into small intervals, as Figure 6.15(a) shows. It then computes the area under the curve as the sum of the areas of a series of rectangles. Each rectangle has a base equal to the length of the interval and a height equal to the function value at the midpoint. Figure 6.15(b) shows the approximation for five

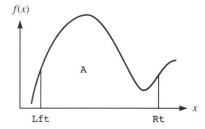

Figure 6.14

The area, A , under the curve of the function $f(x)$.

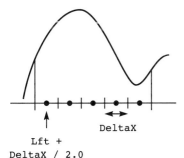

Lft + DeltaX / 2.0

(**a**) Calculation of `DeltaX` and the midpoint of the first interval.

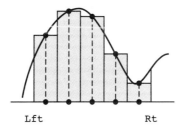

(**b**) The area of the rectangles that approximates the area under the curve.

Figure 6.15

The midpoint algorithm with five intervals.

intervals. The greater the number of divisions, the thinner the rectangles and the better the approximation to the true value of the area.

What follows is an algorithm that calculates the area under a curve with the midpoint algorithm.

```
procedure CalcArea (var A:       real;
                        Lft, Rt: real;
                        NumDivs: integer);
   var
      DeltaX: real;
      X:      real;
      I:      integer;
   begin
   DeltaX := (Rt - Lft) / NumDivs;
   X := Lft + DeltaX / 2.0;
   A := 0.0;
   for I := 1 to NumDivs do
      begin
      A := A + F (X) * DeltaX;
      X := X + DeltaX
      end
   end
```

A procedure to compute the area under the f(x) curve

The calling program supplies the procedure with values for `Lft` and `Rt`, the left and right boundaries of the area. It also supplies the procedure with an integer value for `NumDivs`, the number of divisions between `Lft` and `Rt`. The greater `NumDivs`, the better the approximation, but the longer the execution time.

The area, `A`, is called by reference. The procedure initializes `A` to 0.0. Each time through the loop it adds the area of one rectangle to `A`. The procedure will give the actual parameter in the calling program the value of the area.

This algorithm requires two additions and one multiplication each time the loop executes. Can you modify the algorithm to require fewer real multiplications?

Using Call by Reference

The key question to ask in deciding whether a parameter should be called by reference is, Do you want the procedure to change the value of the actual parameter in the calling program? If the answer is yes, use call by reference. If the answer is no, use call by value.

All the examples of call by reference so far have been with procedures instead of functions. Pascal permits functions to have variable parameters. However, variable parameters with functions are usually inappropriate. The purpose of a function is to return a single value. In mathematics, you give a function a value, *x*, and it returns a value *f(x)*. The function depends on *x* but does not change the value of *x*. Programs are easier to understand if functions behave as they do in mathematics. This book has no examples of functions with variable parameters.

When to use call by reference

Functions usually do not use call by reference.

6.4 Scope of Identifiers

A main program, a procedure, and a function each contain a block. You can declare an identifier within a block six ways:

- In the constant definition part
- In the type definition part
- In the variable declaration part
- In the formal parameter list
- As a function
- As a procedure

Six ways to declare an identifier

We have seen one example, Program 6.6, where it is possible to use the same identifier in two different blocks to name two different variables. This section will explore Pascal's naming and access rules that are based on the structure of the blocks within a program.

Program 6.11

Program 6.11 puts two integer values in numerical order and illustrates the block structure of Pascal.

Table 6.7 is a trace of Program 6.11. X and Y are called by reference. X refers to its actual parameter, A, and Y refers to its actual parameter, B.

Statement executed	A	B	X	Y	Temp
begin	?	?			
write ('Enter an i	?	?			
readln (A);	6	?			
write ('Enter an i	6	?			
readln (B);	6	4			
Order1 (A, B);	6	4			
Allocate					
begin	6	4	< ref A>	< ref B>	?
if X > Y then	6	4	< ref A>	< ref B>	?
Temp := X;	6	4	< ref A>	< ref B>	6
X := Y;	4	4	< ref A>	< ref B>	6
Y := Temp	4	6	< ref A>	< ref B>	6
end;	4	6	< ref A>	< ref B>	6
Deallocate					
writeln;	4	6			
writeln ('Ordered	4	6			
end.					

Table 6.7

A trace of Program 6.11.

```
program Arrange1 (input, output);
    var
        A, B: integer;

    procedure Order1 (var X, Y: integer);
        var
            Temp: integer;
        begin
        if X > Y then
            begin
            Temp := X;
            X := Y;
            Y := Temp
            end
        end;

    begin
    write ('Enter an integer: ');
    readln (A);
    write ('Enter an integer: ');
    readln (B);
    Order1 (A, B);
    writeln;
    writeln ('Ordered they are', A: 2, B: 2)
    end.
```

Program 6.11

The first version of a program to put two values in order. The procedure uses only local variables.

Interactive Input/Output

```
Enter an integer: 6
Enter an integer: 4

Ordered they are 4 6
```

Program 6.11 has two blocks, program `Arrange1` and procedure `Order1`. The main program declares three identifiers in its block—A and B in its variable declaration part, and `Order1` as a procedure. `Order1` declares three identifiers in its block, X and Y in its formal parameter list, and `Temp` in its variable declaration part. Figure 6.16 is a nesting diagram that shows the block structure of this program. Region (1) represents the statements of procedure `Order1`. The box surrounding the region is called a *contour line*. Region (2) represents the statements of the main program.

A, B, and `Order1` are local to the main program, `Arrange1`. A and B are local because they appear in the variable declaration part of the main program block. `Order1` is local because it is defined as a procedure in the main program block.

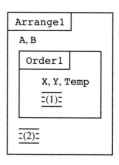

Figure 6.16

The block structure of Program 6.11.

Local identifiers always have meaning to the statements in the block in which they are declared. The statements in region (2) can refer to A, B, and Order1. For example,

```
readln (A)
```

is a legal statement in (2) because you can refer to A in that region.

The variables X, Y, and Temp are local to procedure Order1. X and Y are local to Order1 because they appear as formal parameters of that block. Temp is local to Order1 because it appears in the variable declaration part of that block. Since local identifiers always have meaning to the statements in their block,

```
X := Y
```

is a legal statement in (1).

But what about a statement that refers to an identifier that is not local? For example, would the statement

```
Temp := A
```

be legal in (1) since it refers to a nonlocal variable? The answer in this case is yes, the statement is legal.

Think of the contour line around Order1 as a one-way mirror. Statements in (1) can see out, but statements in (2) cannot see in. When the statement in (1) encounters the identifier A, it first looks at all its local identifiers to see if the A occurs there. Since it does not occur, the statement looks through the one-way mirror at the local identifiers of the next surrounding block. It spots the A in the variable declaration part of the main program. That is the A to which the statement refers. Similarly, statements in (1) can refer to B.

Identifiers that are not local to a block, but which can nevertheless be referred to by statements in the block, are called *global identifiers* to that block. In Figure 6.16, A and B are global to Order1.

How about the reverse situation? In Figure 6.16, can a statement in (2) refer to Temp? For example, would

```
Temp := A
```

be a legal statement in (2)? This time the answer is no, it would not be legal.

Again, the reason is the one-way mirror surrounding the block Order1. The statement in (2) cannot see in to look at the declaration of Temp.

The *scope* of an identifier is that set of regions in which statements can refer to the identifier. The scope of A, B, and Order1 is the set of regions (1) and (2). The scope of X, Y, and Temp is region (1).

Local identifiers

Contour lines as one-way mirrors

Global identifiers

Definition of scope

▐▌ Program 6.12

Program 6.12 performs the task of the previous program, but uses global variables to pass information between blocks.

```
program Arrange2 (input, output);
   var
      A, B: integer;

   procedure Order2;
      var
         Temp: integer;
      begin
      if A > B then
         begin
         Temp := A;
         A := B;
         B := Temp
         end
      end;

   begin
   write ('Enter an integer: ');
   readln (A);
   write ('Enter an integer: ');
   readln (B);
   Order2;
   writeln;
   writeln ('Ordered they are', A: 2, B: 2)
   end.
```

Program 6.12

The second version of a program to put two values in order. The procedure uses global variables.

Input/Output

Same as Program 6.11.

Table 6.8 is a trace of Program 6.12. Since `Order2` has no parameter list, the only storage that needs to be allocated when the procedure is called is for the local variable, `Temp`.

Figure 6.17 shows the block structure of Program 6.12. Since region (1) is in the scope of A, the statement

```
Temp := A
```

is legal. This statement in the procedure changes the value of the global variable, A, directly in the calling program.

Which program do you think is better, Program 6.11 or 6.12? Most beginning programmers think that Program 6.12 is better. After all, it is shorter. And when you write it, you do not need to bother with a parameter list. Why use a parameter list if you can do the same job without one?

Most software designers would contend that Program 6.11 is better. The general design rule for procedures is that you should avoid using global variables. For small programs, such as these examples, the problems created by using global variables are not as evident as they are with large programs.

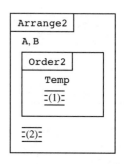

Figure 6.17

The block structure of Program 6.12.

Statement executed	A	B	Temp
begin	?	?	
write ('Enter an i	?	?	
readln (A);	6	?	
write ('Enter an i	6	?	
readln (B);	6	4	
Order2;	6	4	
Allocate			
begin	6	4	?
if A > B then	6	4	?
Temp := A;	6	4	6
A := B;	4	4	6
B := Temp	4	6	6
end;	4	6	6
Deallocate			
writeln;	4	6	
writeln ('Ordered	4	6	
end.			

Table 6.8

A trace of Program 6.12.

The advantage of using only parameters and local variables in a procedure is that the procedure is self-contained. Therefore, when compared to a procedure that uses global variables, it is

- Easier to read
- Easier to modify
- Easier to use in other programs

The advantages of avoiding global variables

Look at the two procedures in these examples, which are isolated from their surrounding blocks.

```
procedure Order1 (var X, Y: integer);    procedure Order2;
   var                                       var
      Temp: integer;                            Temp: integer;
   begin                                     begin
   if X > Y then                             if A > B then
      begin                                     begin
      Temp := X;                                Temp := A;
      X := Y;                                   A := B;
      Y := Temp                                 B := Temp
      end                                       end
   end                                       end
```

Suppose the program listing is 30 pages long, and these procedures are pages away from their calling programs. You are in the process of reading the code to find a bug and you come across these procedures.

`Order1` is completely self-contained. Its statements refer only to local variables. You can see from reading it that whatever the calling procedure supplies for the actual parameters, the procedure will put their values in order.

But `Order2` is not self-contained. What are `A` and `B`? They must be defined somewhere else in this long listing. You cannot even determine what their types are from reading this procedure alone.

Furthermore, `Order1` is more general than `Order2`. You can lift it out of this program and place it in another program with the assurance that it will work correctly.

`Order2` is not general-purpose. Its correctness depends on the environment of its surrounding blocks. You cannot place it in another program with a different environment and expect it to work. You may need to change its environment so that `A` and `B` are declared consistently and used properly with the procedure.

The most important skill for you to develop now is the ability to design good procedures and functions. In special situations, you can justify the use of global variables to pass information between blocks. But in general, you should not use global variables.

▆ Program 6.13

Pascal permits a procedure to call another procedure. In this program, procedure `Order3` calls procedure `Swap`. Program 6.13 performs the same processing as the two previous programs.

Table 6.9 (p. 262) is a trace of Program 6.13. When the main program calls `Order3`, `X` and `Y` are called by reference. `X` refers to `A`, and `Y` refers to `B`.

Then when `Order3` calls `Swap`, `R` and `S` are called by reference. `R` refers to `X`, but by the previous call `X` refers to `A`. Therefore `R` refers to `A`. Similarly, `S` refers to `Y`, which refers to `B`. Therefore `S` refers to `B`.

The trace table for this example has an interesting shape. Each time a procedure is called, the allocated storage is "stacked" onto the table on its right. Each time a procedure terminates, the storage is "unstacked" from the rightmost part of the table.

Figure 6.18 is a nesting diagram that shows the block structure of this program. Both `Swap` and `Order3` are nested in `Arrange3`. Both procedures use only local variables.

The identifiers declared in `Arrange3` are `A`, `B`, `Swap`, and `Order3`. Their scope is the set of regions (1), (2), and (3). For example, the calling statement in region (2)

`Swap (X, Y)`

can refer to `Swap` because region (2) is within the scope of `Swap`. The assignment statement

`A := B`

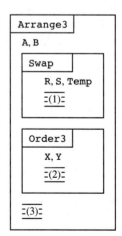

Figure 6.18

The block structure of Program 6.13.

```
program Arrange3 (input, output);
   var
      A, B: integer;

   procedure Swap (var R, S: integer);
      var
         Temp: integer;
      begin
      Temp := R;
      R := S;
      S := Temp
      end;

   procedure Order3 (var X, Y: integer);
      begin
      if X > Y then
         Swap (X, Y)
      end;

   begin {Arrange3}
   write ('Enter an integer: ');
   readln (A);
   write ('Enter an integer: ');
   readln (B);
   Order3 (A, B);
   writeln;
   writeln ('Ordered they are', A: 2, B: 2)
   end.
```

Input/Output

Same as Program 6.11.

Program 6.13

The third version of a program to put two values in order. One procedure calls another, passing the reference parameters.

would also be legal in region (2), since region (2) is within the scope of these variables. But it is not recommended, since A and B are global to Order3.

The identifiers declared in Swap are R, S, and Temp. Their scope is region (1). For example, the statement in region (1)

```
Temp := R
```

can refer to Temp and R, because region (1) is within their scope. That statement would not be legal in region (2), since region (2) is outside the scope of Temp and R. Considering the contours around Swap and Order3 to be one-way mirrors, from region (2) you can look out of the contour surrounding Order3. But you cannot look in through the contour surrounding Swap to see Temp and R. Temp and R are invisible from region (2).

Statement executed	A	B	X	Y	R	S	Temp
`begin`	?	?					
`write ('Enter an i`	?	?					
`readln (A);`	6	?					
`write ('Enter an i`	6	?					
`readln (B);`	6	4					
`Order3 (A, B);`	6	4					
Allocate							
`begin`	6	4	< ref A>	< ref B>			
`if X > Y then`	6	4	< ref A>	< ref B>			
`Swap (X, Y)`	6	4	< ref A>	< ref B>			
Allocate							
`begin`	6	4	< ref A>	< ref B>	< ref A>	< ref B>	?
`Temp := R;`	6	4	< ref A>	< ref B>	< ref A>	< ref B>	6
`R := S;`	4	4	< ref A>	< ref B>	< ref A>	< ref B>	6
`S := Temp`	4	6	< ref A>	< ref B>	< ref A>	< ref B>	6
`end;`	4	6	< ref A>	< ref B>	< ref A>	< ref B>	6
Deallocate							
`end;`	4	6	< ref A>	< ref B>			
Deallocate							
`writeln;`	4	6					
`writeln ('Ordered`	4	6					
`end.`							

Table 6.9

A trace of Programs 6.13 and 6.14.

Program 6.14

Program 6.14 is yet another version of the same problem. In its listing, procedure Swap is located in the procedure declaration part of `Order4`, not in the procedure declaration part of the main program.

The location of the heading of `Order4` in the listing changes the block structure of the program. Now `Swap` is nested inside `Order4`, as Figure 6.19 shows.

The identifiers declared in `Arrange4` are A, B, and `Order4`. Their scope is the set of regions (1), (2), and (3). For example, the input statement in region (1)

```
readln (A)
```

would be legal, because region (1) is within the scope of A. From region (1) you can look out through the one-way mirror to the `Order4` region, and then through that mirror to the `Arrange4` environment. A is visible from region (1). Since A is global to region (1), that statement is not recommended even though it is legal Pascal.

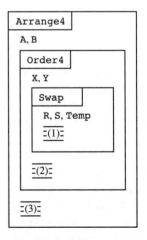

Figure 6.19

The block structure of Program 6.14.

```
program Arrange4 (input, output);
   var
      A, B: integer;

   procedure Order4 (var X, Y: integer);

      procedure Swap (var R, S: integer);
         var
            Temp: integer;
         begin
         Temp := R;
         R := S;
         S := Temp
         end;

      begin {Order4}
      if X > Y then
         Swap (X, Y)
      end;

   begin {Arrange4}
   write ('Enter an integer: ');
   readln (A);
   write ('Enter an integer: ');
   readln (B);
   Order4 (A, B);
   writeln;
   writeln ('Ordered they are', A: 2, B: 2)
   end.
```

Program 6.14

The fourth version of a program to put two values in order. One procedure is nested inside another.

Input/Output

Same as Program 6.11.

The identifiers declared in `Order4` are `X`, `Y`, and `Swap`. Their scope is the set of regions (1) and (2). That is why the procedure call

```
Swap (X, Y)
```

in region (2) is legal. Region (2) is within the scope of `X`, `Y`, and `Swap`. A call to `Swap` from region (3) would now be illegal, although it would be legal in Program 6.13.

The trace of Program 6.14 is identical to the trace of Program 6.13. The difference between the programs is not how they process the data. The only difference is in the scope of some of the identifiers. In Program 6.13 you could call `Swap` from region (3) if you wished. In Program 6.14 you could not.

When should you nest a procedure within another procedure? The effect of nesting procedures is to limit the scope of some identifiers. That limitation of scope is only appropriate in very large programs, typically ones that are designed by a team of programmers. Consequently, no program in this book other than those in this section contain nested procedures.

▣ Program 6.15

Two different variables can be named with the same identifier as long as they are declared in separate blocks. In Program 6.15, the variable A is declared in the main program and in procedure Alpha.

Figure 6.20 shows the block structure of this program. In region (3), A gets 7. The A in the assignment statement is the one declared in ScopeTest. The A declared in Alpha is not accessible to statements in (3).

```
program ScopeTest (output);
   var
      A: integer;

   procedure Alpha;
      var
         A: integer;

      procedure Beta;
         begin
         A := 8
         end;

      begin {Alpha}
      Beta
      end;

   begin {ScopeTest}
   A := 7;
   Alpha;
   write ('A =', A: 2)
   end.
```

Output

A = 7

Program 6.15

A program to illustrate the scope of an identifier when duplicate identifiers exist.

Then ScopeTest calls Alpha, but Alpha immediately calls Beta. Now in region (1), A gets 8. The question is, Which A gets 8? A is not local to Beta. And both A's are declared in a contour that surrounds Beta. To which A does the assignment statement refer?

It refers to the A that is closest to Beta. That is, it refers to the A declared in Alpha, not the one declared in ScopeTest. Consequently, the A declared in ScopeTest does not get 8.

Any time an identifier is defined in a block, it has the effect of keeping out other possible meanings for that identifier in blocks that are surrounded by the defining block. When a statement refers to an identifier that is not local, it first looks for the definition of the identifier in the block that immediately surrounds it. Only if it does not find the identifier there, does it search the next closest surrounding block.

This property is a valuable feature of block-structured languages such as Pascal. It helps to guarantee that a self-contained procedure will work correctly in any environment in which you place it. Recall procedure PrintBar in Program 6.6. It used the identifier, I, that was also used in the main program for a different variable. PrintBar uses X and N as well. You could put PrintBar in any environment and know that it will work correctly, even if X and N are defined somewhere else outside the PrintBar block. Since all the statements in PrintBar refer to local variables, they cannot accidently affect variables outside the block.

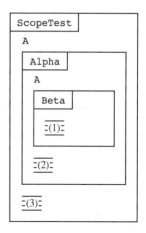

Figure 6.20

The block structure of Program 6.15.

6.5   Random Numbers

Many events in our lives are random. When you enter a full parking lot, for example, you drive around until someone pulls out of a parking space that you can claim. The event of someone pulling out of a parking space is random. You do not know when or where it will occur. Consequently, you cannot predict exactly how long you will drive before you find a place.

Random events in the real world

Computers are useful in part because they can behave like the real world. For example, the popular flight-simulator computer programs can give the illusion of piloting an airplane. Large, sophisticated flight simulators are even used to train airline pilots. But how can a computer behave like the real world when some events in the real world are random? Every algorithm you have encountered thus far in this book had no random element. Given the input and the processing statements, you could always predict the output. With random events, you cannot predict the outcome.

Program 6.16

The solution to the problem of random elements is to design an algorithm whose output appears random, even though it is not. Program 6.16 generates a list of real numbers between 0 and 1 that appear to be random.

The identifier UniformDistr stands for uniform distribution. It means that the actual parameter supplied by the calling program will get values that are uniformly distributed between 0.0 and 1.0.

The uniform distribution

```
program Random1 (input, output);
   var
      I:      integer;
      Seed:   integer;
      Result: real;

   procedure UniformDistr (var Rand: real; var Sd: integer);
      begin
      Sd := 28 * Sd mod 1013;
      Rand := Sd / 1013.0
      end;

   begin
   write ('Enter seed: ');
   readln (Seed);
   for I := 1 to 10 do
      begin
      UniformDistr (Result, Seed);
      writeln (Result: 5: 3, '   Seed = ', Seed: 4)
      end
   end.
```

Program 6.16

A random number generator that generates real values between 0.0 and 1.0.

Interactive Input/Output

```
Enter seed: 853
0.577   Seed =   585
0.170   Seed =   172
0.754   Seed =   764
0.117   Seed =   119
0.289   Seed =   293
0.099   Seed =   100
0.764   Seed =   774
0.394   Seed =   399
0.029   Seed =    29
0.802   Seed =   812
```

The procedure has two variable parameters, `Rand` and `Sd`. The first time the procedure is called, `Sd` refers to `Seed`, which has the value 853 from the keyboard. The procedure evaluates the expression

```
28 * Sd mod 1013
```

which is

$28 \times 853 \bmod 1013$
$23884 \bmod 1013$
585

and gives that value to `Seed` in the main program.

Then, it evaluates the expression

```
Sd / 1013.0
```

which is

585 / 1013.0
0.577

and gives that value to `Result` in the main program.

The next time the main program calls the procedure, it gets the value

28×585 mod 1013
16380 mod 1013
172

for `Seed`, and the value

172 / 1013.0
0.170

for `Result`.

Each time the procedure executes, it uses the current value of `Seed` from the program to compute a new value for `Seed`. Since the last step in the computation is a mod with 1013, every value of `Seed` is guaranteed to be between 1 and 1012. (`Seed` can never get 0, because 1013 is a prime number.) It computes the value for `Result` by dividing the new value of `Seed` by 1013.0. Therefore, the value of `Result` is guaranteed to be between 1/1013.0, which is 0.000987, and 1012/1013.0, which is 0.999013.

The upshot is that procedure `UniformDistr` gives values to `Result` that appear to be randomly generated between 0 and 1. `UniformDistr` is called a *random number generator*. The values generated are also called *pseudorandom* numbers because they are not really random.

Before `UniformDistr` can generate a sequence of random numbers, it needs an initial value for `Sd`. In this program, the user supplies the starting value. If the user supplies a different value, the procedure generates a different sequence of random numbers. Some Pascal compilers provide procedure calls that allow the programmer to access a clock in the computer hardware. These clocks typically keep time to the nearest millisecond or even microsecond. A common programming technique to make the sequence appear more random is to not request the starting value for `Seed` from the user. Instead, the program accesses the time from the internal computer clock and uses it to compute the first value for `Seed`. That way, each time the program runs it produces a different sequence of pseudorandom numbers.

The initial value of the random number seed

▭ Program 6.17

`UniformDistr` generates random real numbers. Program 6.17 contains a procedure that generates random integers with values between 1 and 10. It outputs a different list of random integers depending on the initial value for the seed.

```
program Random2 (input, output);
   var
      I:       integer;
      Seed:    integer;
      Result:  integer;

   procedure RandInt (var Rand:     integer;
                          Min, Max: integer;
                      var Sd:       integer);
      begin
      Sd := 28 * Sd mod 1013;
      Rand := trunc (Sd / 1013.0 * (Max - Min + 1)) + Min
      end;

   begin
   write ('Enter seed: ');
   readln (Seed);
   writeln;
   for I := 1 to 15 do
      begin
      RandInt (Result, 1, 10, Seed);
      write (Result: 3)
      end
   end.
```

Program 6.17

A random number generator that generates integer values between 1 and 10.

Interactive Input/Output

```
Enter seed: 853

  6  2  8  2  3  1  8  4  1  9  5  5  3  7  7
```

Interactive Input/Output

```
Enter seed: 557

  4  1  4  8  10  3  9  6  1  9  8  5  6  2 10
```

Procedure `RandInt` calculates `Sd` the same way `UniformDistr` does. But the value it gives to the actual parameter corresponding to `Rand` is an integer instead of a real value. The calling program in Program 6.17 gives the value of 1 to `Min` and 10 to `Max`, which indicates that `RandInt` is to generate a random integer between 1 and 10. As in the previous program, the random number generator computes `Sd` as 585. Then it computes `Rand` as

```
trunc (Sd / 1013.0 * (Max - Min + 1)) + Min
```

$\text{trunc}(585 / 1013.0 \times (10 - 1 + 1)) + 1$

$\text{trunc}(585 / 1013.0 \times 10) + 1$

$\text{trunc}(0.577 \times 10) + 1$

$\text{trunc}(5.77) + 1$

$5 + 1$

6

Any value of `Sd / 1013.0` that is between 0.500 and 0.599 will produce the integer value of 6 for `Rand`.

Figure 6.21 shows the transformation `RandInt` makes from `Sd / 1013.0`, which is what `UniformDistr` produces, to the integers. It transforms real values uniformly distributed between 0.0 and 1.0 into integer values uniformly distributed between 1 and 10.

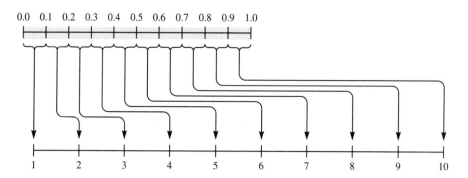

Figure 6.21

The transformation `RandInt` makes from the real number line to the integer number line.

◼ Program 6.18

Program 6.18 shows how `RandInt` can simulate a random event in the real world. Suppose you are playing a game with a pair of dice. Each die has six sides. When you roll one die, it will come to rest with some random integer between 1 and 6 showing on its top side. You can simulate the toss of a die by calling procedure `RandInt` with a `Min` of 1 and `Max` of 6. It will give the actual parameter a value that corresponds to the number showing on the die.

Here is an algorithm, written in pseudocode, that simulates the repeated toss of two dice until either 7 or 11 is rolled. `Seed`, `NumRolls`, `Die1`, `Die2`, and `Sum` are all integer variables.

```
begin
Input Seed
NumRolls := 0
repeat
    Simulate roll for Die1
    Simulate roll for Die2
    NumRolls := NumRolls + 1
    Sum := Die1 + Die2
    Output Die1, Die2, Sum
until (Sum = 7) or (Sum = 11)
Output NumRolls
end
```

Pseudocode outline of Program 6.18

Program 6.18 is the Pascal implementation of the algorithm. The two calls to procedure `RandInt` simulate one roll of the two dice.

This program calls `RandInt` with 1 and 6 as the actual parameters for `Min` and `Max`, because the number that appears on each die is between 1 and 6. To simulate other events requires appropriate values for `Min` and `Max`, either of which is allowed to be negative.

```
program Dice (input, output);
   var
      Die1, Die2: integer;
      Sum:        integer;
      NumRolls:   integer;
      Seed:       integer;

   procedure RandInt (var Rand:      integer;
                          Min, Max: integer;
                      var Sd:        integer);
      begin
      Sd := 28 * Sd mod 1013;
      Rand := trunc (Sd / 1013.0 * (Max - Min + 1)) + Min
      end;

   begin
   write ('Enter seed: ');
   readln (Seed);
   NumRolls := 0;
   writeln ('--------------------');
   writeln ('Die 1   Die 2    Total');
   writeln ('--------------------');
   repeat
      RandInt (Die1, 1, 6, Seed);
      RandInt (Die2, 1, 6, Seed);
      NumRolls := NumRolls + 1;
      Sum := Die1 + Die2;
      writeln (Die1: 5, Die2: 3, Sum: 8)
   until (Sum = 7) or (Sum = 11);
   writeln ('--------------------');
   writeln ('Number of rolls to get 7 or 11: ', NumRolls: 1)
   end.
```

Program 6.18

A simulation of several tosses of a pair of dice. The dice are rolled until a 7 or 11 appears.

Interactive Input/Output

```
Enter seed: 259
--------------------
Die 1   Die 2   Total
--------------------
    1       3       4
    4       6      10
    4       2       6
    1       5       6
    1       3       4
    6       1       7
--------------------
Number of rolls to get 7 or 11: 6
```

Example 6.11   To simulate the toss of a coin, you need random values with two possibilities, one for heads and one for tails. You could call

```
RandInt (Toss, 0, 1, Seed)
```

and let 0 represent heads and 1 represent tails. The sequence of 20 calls will produce

1 1 0 1 0 1 0 0 0 0 0 1 1 0 0 1 0 0 0 1

with an initial value of 351 for Seed.   ■

Example 6.12   One way to produce a sequence of random numbers with three possible values is to call

```
RandInt (Num, -1, 1, Seed)
```

The first 12 values of Num are

1 −1 0 0 0 −1 0 1 0 0 −1 −1

with an initial value of 933 for Seed.   ■

▨   Random Number Generators

The random number generators in the preceding programs are all based on the general computation

$$z_{n+1} = az_n \bmod m$$

The Lehmer pseudorandom number generator

where $z_1, z_2, z_3, \ldots$ are the successive values of Seed, m is the modulus, and a is the multiplier with $2 < a < m$. Generators of this form are called *Lehmer generators* after the person who proposed them. Our generators had (m, a) values of $(1013, 28)$. To design a different Lehmer generator you can use different values of (m, a).

Example 6.13   If you select values of $(17, 5)$ for (m, a), then 20 successive seed values from the Lehmer generator are

8 6 13 14 2 10 16 12 9 11 4 3 15 7 1 5 8 6 13 14

with an initial seed of eight.   ■

Example 6.14   The $(17, 13)$ Lehmer generator produces the sequence

4 1 13 16 4 1 13 16 4 1 13

starting from 4.   ■

These examples show an unavoidable feature of all pseudorandom number generators. Since each value is computed from the previous value, once the initial value reappears in the sequence, the sequence must repeat. The *period* of the generator is the maximum number of values before the sequence begins to repeat. The (17, 5) Lehmer generator has a period of 16, and the (17, 13) generator has a period of 4.

Random number cycles

A truly random sequence would contain no repeating cycles. But a pseudorandom sequence must repeat eventually, since there are only a finite number of values less than the modulus. The best you can do is to pick the modulus and multiplier to make the cycle as long as possible and to make the output appear random. The longest possible period with a modulus of m is $m - 1$. A generator with this period is known as a *full-period generator*. The (1013, 28) generator in the programs of this section is a full-period generator.

Full-period generators

Computer scientists have devised a set of statistical tests that measure the randomness of proposed generators. They have investigated the pseudorandom sequences generated by different choices of m and a in an effort to discover the best generators. One standard Lehmer generator that is among the best known is (2147483647, 16807), which is a full-period generator with good pseudorandom behavior. Both 1013 and 2147483647 are prime numbers.

The standard Lehmer generator

Unfortunately, you cannot simply put these large values of m and a into procedure `UniformDistr` and have a good generator. The problem is that all computers have some limit on the largest integer value they can store. The Pascal language has a built-in constant called `maxint` that you can output to determine the maximum integer value for your compiler. If you execute the statement

The built-in constant maxint

```
writeln ('Maximum integer value = ', maxint: 1)
```

you will probably get either 32767, which is $2^{15} - 1$, or 2147483647, which is $2^{31} - 1$ and happens to be the modulus of the standard Lehmer generator. The smaller value of `maxint` is common on microcomputers and the larger value is common on minicomputers and mainframes.

A system with a maximum integer value of 32767 obviously cannot directly implement the standard generator. Even a system with `maxint` 2147483647 cannot do so, because the seed is multiplied by a before the `mod` operation, and the computer will not be able to store the intermediate product.

Fortunately, an algorithm has been designed to implement the standard Lehmer generator on systems with a `maxint` of at least 2147483647. It is shown in the following example as a revised version of `UniformDistr`. You can see that `Hi` and `Lo` will always have values that are computed to be less than `Sd` so that the intermediate values will never exceed `maxint`. This algorithm is mathematically guaranteed to generate the same full-period sequence as (2147483647, 16807).[1]

---

1. Stephen K. Park and Keith W. Miller, "Random Number Generators: Good Ones Are Hard to Find," *Communications of the ACM* 31 (October 1988): 1192–1201.

```
procedure UniformDistr (var Rand: real; var Sd: integer);
   const
      A = 16807;
      M = 2147483647;
      Q = 127773;   {M div A}
      R = 2836;     {M mod A}
   var
      Lo, Hi: integer;
   begin
   Hi := Sd div Q;
   Lo := Sd mod Q;
   Sd := A * Lo - R * Hi;
   if Sd <= 0 then
      Sd := Sd + M;
   Rand := Sd / M
   end;
```

The standard Lehmer generator for systems with a maxint of at least 2147483647

If your system has a `maxint` of 32767, this version of the standard Lehmer generator will not work correctly. However, you can still implement the generator with the following version based on real values. The computation is analogous to the computation of the previous integer version.

```
procedure UniformDistr (var Rand, Sd: real);
   const
      A = 16807.0;
      M = 2147483647.0;
      Q = 127773.0;   {M div A}
      R = 2836.0;     {M mod A}
   var
      Lo, Hi: real;
   begin
   Hi := trunc (Sd / Q);
   Lo := Sd - Q * Hi;
   Sd := A * Lo - R * Hi;
   if Sd <= 0 then
      Sd := Sd + M;
   Rand := Sd / M
   end;
```

The real version of the standard Lehmer generator

The real value version is not guaranteed to work correctly unless it passes the following test, which is based on the fact that if you start with a `Seed` of 1 and call the generator 10,000 times, `Seed` should have a value of 1043618065. The code fragment

```
Seed := 1;
for I := 1 to 10000 do
   UniformDistr (X, Seed);
writeln ('Seed = ', Seed: 13: 1)
```

A test for the real version of the standard Lehmer generator

must produce the output

```
Seed =  1043618065.0
```

exactly, to the last digit. You can use the same code to test the integer version, but the value of `Seed` will obviously not have the decimal point.

If the real version of the standard generator does not pass the test, the real values that your compiler supplies are not accurate enough. You should then consult your compiler documentation, which will probably describe additional nonstandard real types that you can use for `Rand`, `Sd`, `Hi`, and `Lo`. A common nonstandard type is called `double`, which stands for double precision, and is usually sufficiently accurate to pass the test.

Although you can have fun trying to design your own generator, finding good values of *m* and *a* is not an easy task. If the modulus, *m*, is a prime number, then zero will never appear in the sequence, a desirable feature indeed. Even so, Example 6.14 shows that a prime modulus is no guarantee of a full-period generator. Actually, making a Lehmer generator full period is the easy part. It is much more difficult to find values of *m* and *a* that produce sequences that are sufficiently pseudorandom.

Designing a Lehmer generator

The (1013, 28) generator used in the programs of this section was designed for simplicity and portability. It will work even on systems with a `maxint` as low as 32767, and is good for simulating short games. For serious simulations, however, you should use one of the implementations of the (2147483647, 16807) generator. This standard Lehmer generator has been extensively tested and is known\to be one of the best.

SUMMARY

Functions and procedures let you define a task in the declaration part and then call the function or procedure when the task needs to be executed. Communication takes place by matching the actual parameters in the calling statement with the formal parameters in the declaration. The calling statement communicates to the function or procedure by giving values in an actual parameter list. A function communicates back to the calling statement by returning a single value. A procedure communicates back to the calling statement by changing the value of a formal parameter that is called by reference. The key question to ask in deciding whether a parameter should be called by reference is, Do you want the procedure to change the value of the actual parameter? If the answer is yes, use call by reference. When a function or procedure is called, the computer allocates storage for its formal parameters and local variables.

The space/time tradeoff is a fundamental principle of computer science. It means that you can usually make a program execute faster (time) if you use more main memory (space). This chapter illustrated the space/time tradeoff with procedure `CalcRoot` in the bisection algorithm. The version that conserved space by declaring fewer variables took longer to execute because of its additional calls to the function.

Pascal is a block-structured language; that is, it allows you to nest procedure and function declarations. The nesting defines regions of the program called blocks, which are denoted by contour lines in block structure diagrams. The scope of an identifier is that set of regions in which statements can refer to the identifier. A global variable is one that is used in a function or procedure, but is not declared in its formal parameter list or variable declaration part. In general, you should avoid the use of global variables. Procedures and functions that contain global variables are not self-contained and are more difficult to read than those that use only local variables.

A random number generator computes a sequence of numbers that appear to be random. Random number generators can simulate random events in the real world. The Lehmer generator computes each random number from the previous one by a multiplication operation followed by a mod operation. The design of a Lehmer generator consists of selecting the modulus, m, and multiplier, a, to give a good random sequence of integers. A generator with the longest possible period, $m - 1$, is called a full-period generator. A well-known standard generator has (m, a) values of (2147483647, 16807).

EXERCISES

Section 6.1

1. If the function `Exr1` is defined as

```
function Exr1 (A, B: integer): integer;
   begin
   if A < B then
      Exr1 := 2 * A
   else
      Exr1 := 2 * B
   end
```

then what is the output of each of the following code fragments?

```
*(a)                          *(b)
I := 12;                      I := 4;
J := 3;                       J := Exr1 (2 * I + 1, 10);
write (Exr1 (I, J))           write (J)

(c)
write (Exr1 (Exr1 (3, 2), Exr1 (4, 5)))
```

Section 6.3

* 2. Trace the following programs and determine the output.

(a)

```
program Exr2a (output);
   var
      Num: integer;

   procedure Pass2a (
         N: integer);
      begin
      N := N * 2;
      writeln (N)
      end;

   begin
   Num := 5;
   Pass2a (Num);
   writeln (Num)
   end.
```

(b)

```
program Exr2b (output);
   var
      Num: integer;

   procedure Pass2b (
          var N: integer);
      begin
      N := N * 2;
      writeln (N)
      end;

   begin
   Num := 5;
   Pass2b (Num);
   writeln (Num)
   end.
```

3. Trace the following programs and determine the output.

(a)

```
program Exr3a (output);
   var
      I, J: integer;

   procedure Pass3a (
          var I, J: integer);
      begin
      I := 1;
      J := 2
      end;

   begin
   Pass3a (I, J);
   writeln ('I = ', I: 1);
   writeln ('J = ', J: 1)
   end.
```

(b)

```
program Exr3b (output);
   var
      I, J: integer;

   procedure Pass3b (
          var J, I: integer);
      begin
      I := 1;
      J := 2
      end;

   begin
   Pass3b (I, J);
   writeln ('I = ', I: 1);
   writeln ('J = ', J: 1)
   end.
```

* 4. Suppose a calling program declares variables

```
A, B: real
```

and procedure Exr4 has the heading

```
procedure Exr4 (var C: real; D: real)
```

State whether each of the procedure calls is legal. For those that are not legal, explain why.

(a) Exr4 (A, B)   (b) Exr4 (A)   (c) Exr4 (A, 7.0)

    Exr4 (A, 7)   (e) Exr4 (7.0, B)   (f) Exr4 (7, B)

5. Suppose a calling program declares variables

   ```
   I, J: integer
   ```

   and procedure `Exr5` has the heading

   ```
   procedure Exr5 (var K: integer; L: integer)
   ```

   State whether each of the procedure calls is legal. For those that are not legal, explain why.

   (a) `Exr5 (I, J)`   (b) `Exr5 (I)`   (c) `Exr5 (I, 7)`
   (d) `Exr5 (I, 7.0)`   (e) `Exr5 (7, J)`   (f) `Exr5 (7.0, J)`

Section 6.4

6. Draw the block structure (corresponding to Figures 6.16 to 6.20) for the following program and determine the scope of every variable and formal parameter. Note the difference between the A in `Exr6` and the A in `Alpha`.

```
program Exr6 (output);
   var
      A, B: integer;

   procedure Alpha (C: integer);
      var
         A: integer;

      procedure Beta (D: integer);
         var
            E: integer;
         begin
         {Region (1)}
         end;

      begin {Alpha}
      {Region (2)}
      end;

   procedure Gamma (F: integer);
      var
         G: integer;
      begin
      {Region (3)}
      end;

   begin {Exr6}
   {Region (4)}
   end.
```

Section 6.5

7. When you toss two dice, the sum is a number between 2 and 12. Would it be a good idea to simulate the toss of two dice by calling `RandInt` once with a `Min` of 2 and `Max` of 12? Explain.

PROBLEMS

Section 6.1

8. Write the bowling prize program of Problem 3.43. Declare

   `function BowlingPrize (Scr1, Scr2, Scr3: integer): real`

   to compute the prize from the three scores, `Scr1`, `Scr2`, and `Scr3`.

9. For Problem 3.44, write the program to find the smaller of two values. Declare

   `function Minimum (R1, R2: real): real`

   to compute the minimum from the two values, `R1` and `R2`.

10. Write a program that asks the user to enter a character and outputs whether the character is a letter. Declare

    `function IsLetter (Ch: char): boolean`

    which should return true if `Ch` is a letter.

11. For Problem 3.47, write the program to find the grade point average. Declare

    `function GPA (NumA, NumB, NumC, NumD, NumF: integer): real`

    to compute the grade point average from the letter grades.

12. For Problem 3.52, write the program to find the sales commission. Declare

    `function Commission (Sales: real): real`

    to compute the commission from the amount of sales.

13. For Problem 3.53, write the program to determine the traffic fine. Declare

    `function TrafficFine (Speed: integer): real`

    to compute the traffic fine from the speed.

14. Write the Frisbee program of Problem 3.56. Declare

    `function OrderCost (NumFr: integer): real`

    to compute the cost of the order from the number of Frisbees ordered.

15. Write the schedule program of Problem 3.61. Declare

    `function RegPeriod (LastIntl: char): integer`

    to compute the registration period from the user's last initial. Check for bad input data in the main program, not in the function.

16. For Exercise 4.3, write the program to find the age of the user. Declare

    ```
    function Age (BDay, BMonth, BYear: integer;
                  TDay, TMonth, TYear: integer): integer
    ```

    to compute the age from the birth date and today's date.

17. For Exercise 4.5, write the program to determine whether a given year is a leap year.

Declare

```
function LeapYear (Year: integer): boolean
```

to determine the leap year from the year.

18. Write the quadrant program of Exercise 4.7. Declare

```
type
   QuadType = (Origin,
               One, Two, Three, Four,
               OneTwo, TwoThree, ThreeFour, FourOne);

function Quad (X, Y: integer): QuadType
```

to compute where the point lies from the integer coordinates of the point.

19. Write the axis-crossing program of Exercise 4.8. Declare

```
type
   CrossType = (Neither, XOnly, YOnly, Both);

function Cross (X1, Y1, X2, Y2: integer): CrossType
```

to compute which axes the line between the two points crosses.

20. For Problem 5.49, write the program to raise a number to a power. Declare

```
function Power (Base: real; Expon: integer): real
```

to compute the base raised to the exponent.

21. For Problem 5.54, write the program to estimate the value of the base of the natural logarithms, *e*. Declare

```
function EstE (NumTrm: integer): real
```

to compute the estimate from the number of terms.

22. For Problem 5.70, write the program to determine if a number is prime. Declare

```
function IsPrime (N: integer): boolean
```

to determine whether the number is prime.

23. Define `CardType` in the type definition part as

```
type
   CardType = (Deuce, Three, Four, Five, Six, Seven, Eight, Nine,
               Ten, Jack, Queen, King, Ace)
```

and declare `DeckFile` to be a file of `CardType`, which will contain 52 values. The face cards—Jack, Queen, and King—count 10 points and the Ace counts 11. Note that `ord (Four)` is not 4, although that card counts as 4 points in a card game. A single game consists of giving one card from the file to Player A, the second to Player B, the third to Player A, and the fourth to Player B. The winner is the player with the higher point total in his hand, with the possibility of a draw if the point totals are equal.

   Write a program that plays three games of cards from the file. Declare

```
function PointValue (Cd: CardType): integer
```

to compute the point value of a single card. For example, if `Card` is a variable and has the value `Four`, then `PointValue (Card)` should return 4. For each game, output the total number of points for each player and state which player won. For example, if the first few values in the file are

Queen, Ten, Five, Deuce, King, . . .

then Player A should win the first game with a score of 15 to 12.

24. Write a program that converts a lowercase character to an uppercase character. Declare

```
function Uppercase (Ch: char): char
```

to do the conversion. If the actual parameter is not a lowercase character, the function should return that character value unchanged. Test your function in a main program with interactive I/O.

Section **6.2**

25. Declare

```
procedure PrintRow (NumSpace, NumChr: integer; Ch: char)
```

that prints on one line `NumSpace` spaces followed by `NumChr` occurrences of Ch. For example, `PrintRow (5, 3, 'a')` should print one line with five spaces and three 'a's. Use your procedure to print the following pattern.

Sample Output

```
    *
   ***
  *****
 *******
   : : :
   : : :
```

Section **6.3**

26. For Problem 3.48, write the program to put three lowercase letters in order. Declare procedure `GetLetters` to get the values from the keyboard, Verify in the procedure that they are lowercase letters. Declare procedure `Order` to put the three values in order. Output the values from the main program, not from the procedure.

27. For Problem 3.49, write the program to put three real numbers in descending order. Declare procedure `Order` to put the three values in order. Output the values from the main program, not from the procedure.

28. For Problem 3.55, write the program to output a message depending on the temperature. Declare procedure `GetTemp` to get the temperature information from the keyboard. Verify in the procedure that the temperature is greater than −10 and less than 110. Declare procedure `PrintMesg` to print the appropriate message depending on the temperature.

29. For Problem 3.59, write the program to output a message depending on a letter grade. Declare procedure `GetGrade` to get the letter grade from the keyboard. Verify in the procedure that the grade is valid. Declare procedure `PrintMesg` to print the appropriate message depending on the grade.

30. Write the pattern program of Problem 5.64. Declare procedure `GetRowCol` to get the number of rows and columns from the keyboard. Verify in the procedure that the number of columns is between 0 and 79, and the number of rows is between 0 and 50. Declare procedure `PrintPattern` to print the appropriate pattern.

31. Write the pattern program of Problem 5.65. Declare procedure `GetRowCol` to get the number of rows and columns from the keyboard. Verify in the procedure that the number of columns is between 0 and 79, and the number of rows is between 0 and 50. Declare procedure `PrintPattern` to print the appropriate pattern.

32. Write the pattern program of Problem 5.66. Declare procedure `GetBase` to get the number of asterisks in the base from the keyboard. Verify in the procedure that the number of asterisks in the base is between 0 and 79. Declare procedure `PrintPattern` to print the appropriate pattern.

33. Write the pattern program of Problem 5.67. Declare procedure `GetBase` to get the number of asterisks in the base from the keyboard. Verify in the procedure that the number of asterisks in the base is between 0 and 79. Declare procedure `PrintPattern` to print the appropriate pattern.

34. Write the pattern program of Problem 5.68. Declare procedure `GetBaseChar` to get the base character from the keyboard. Verify in the procedure that the character is between 'a' and 'z'. Declare procedure `PrintPattern` to print the appropriate pattern.

35. For Problem 5.71, write the program to output all the factors of a positive integer. Declare procedure `GetPosInt` to get the positive integer from the keyboard. Verify in the procedure that the integer is positive. Declare procedure `PrintFactors` to print the factors.

36. Write the straight line depreciation program of Problem 5.77. Declare procedure `GetAsset` to get the asset value (real) and useful life (integer) from the keyboard. Verify in the procedure that both numbers are positive. Declare procedure `PrintDeprSched` to print the depreciation schedule.

37. Write the double declining balance depreciation program of Problem 5.78. Declare procedure `GetAsset` to get the asset value (real) and useful life (integer) from the keyboard. Verify in the procedure that both numbers are positive. Declare procedure `PrintDeprSched` to print the depreciation schedule.

Section 6.5

38. In the child's game of paper/scissors/rock, each child secretly chooses one of the objects. When the choices are revealed, paper loses to scissors, scissors loses to rock, and rock loses to paper. Equal choices are a draw. Write a program that asks the user to input a seed, then plays a series of games. In each game, ask the user for one object and compare it with a randomly selected object. Keep track of the score and play until the user wants to quit.

39. In Program 6.18, it took 6 rolls of the dice to get a 7 or 11. What do you think the average number of rolls would be? Can you calculate the average mathematically? Perform a computational experiment by writing a program to simulate 100 sequences of rolls. Output the fewest number of rolls, the greatest number of rolls and the average number of rolls, to get a 7 or 11.

40. The game of craps is played as follows. Roll a pair of dice. If you get a 7 or 11 on the first roll you win, and if you get 2, 3, or 12 (called craps) you lose. Otherwise, the number you rolled becomes your point. You then keep rolling until you roll your point again, in which case you win, or until you roll a 7 or 11, in which case you lose.

    For example, a roll of 9, then 2, then 10, then 9 is a win, since the point (9 in this case) was rolled again before 7 or 11. As another example, a roll of 5, then 2, then 10, then 7 is a loss, since a 7 was rolled before the point (5 in this case).

    Write a Pascal program to simulate a game of craps. Ask the user to input a seed for the random number generator. Output the result of each roll. In the end, announce if the user won or lost.

41. In Problem 40, what do you think the probability of winning a game of craps is? Can you calculate it mathematically? Perform a computational experiment by writing a program to simulate 100 games. Output the number of wins and losses, and an estimate of the probability of winning a single game as the ratio of the number of wins divided by the total number of games.

42. The local town drunk gets thoroughly inebriated, climbs to the roof of a skyscraper, steps out onto the center of the ledge, and begins to walk. Each time he takes a step, the probability is 1/3 that he will step to the right, 1/3 that he will step straight ahead, and 1/3 that he will step to the left. If he takes a total of two steps to the left, he will fall safely onto the roof. But if he takes a total of two steps to the right, he will fall to the sidewalk below. Write a program that asks the user for a seed value and simulates one walk of the drunk.

Sample Input/Output

```
Enter seed: 172

(  x  )
( x   )
( x   )
(  x  )
(   x )
(  x  )
(   x )
(   x )
(    x)

He fell to the sidewalk.
```

43. In Problem 42, suppose a whole army of drunks repeat the walk many times. Guess the average length of a walk. That is, how many steps on the average does a drunk take before he falls off one way or the other? Now perform a computational experiment by writing a program to simulate 100 walks. Output the number of times he fell to the sidewalk, the number of times he fell onto the roof, and the average number of steps he took before falling. How close is the computed value to your guess?

    The ideas in this problem form the basis of an important mathematical technique called the *Monte Carlo method*. The method has application to problems in statistical physics. The "army" of drunks is called an *ensemble*, and the average is called an *ensemble average*.

44. Figure 6.22(a) shows a graph of the equation $y = x^2$ between the points $x = 0.0$ and $x = 1.0$. The square of height 1.0 between these points has area 1.0. You can estimate the area under the curve by picking several points at random inside the square and counting

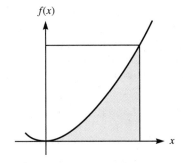

(a) The area under the curve.

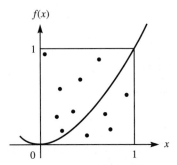

(b) Eleven random points for estimating the area.

Figure 6.22

The function $f(x) = x^2$ for Problem 44.

the points that are below the curve. The area is approximately the number of points below the curve divided by the total number of points. For example, the estimate from Figure 6.22(b) is $\frac{4}{11}$, or 0.3636.

Write a program that asks the user to enter a seed and the number of random points, then outputs the estimate of the area. Obtain the coordinates of a single point by calling procedure `UniformDistr` twice, once for the *x*-coordinate and once for the *y*-coordinate. What do you think is the relationship between the number of random points and the accuracy of the estimate? Can you illustrate that relationship with your program?

45. You can use a random number generator to compute the value of π based on the fact that the area of a circle is πr^2. Figure 6.23 shows the area of one fourth of a circle with radius 1.0 whose area is $\pi(1.0)^2/4 = \pi/4$. Write a program that asks the user to enter a seed and the number of random points, then computes the estimate of the area using the technique of the previous problem. Output the estimate of π as four times the area. What do you think is the relationship between the number of random points and the accuracy of the estimate? Can you illustrate that relationship with your program?

46. Write a program that outputs all the values of the multiplier that will produce a full-period Lehmer generator with a modulus of 1021. Remember that the multiplier is restricted to $2 < a < m$.

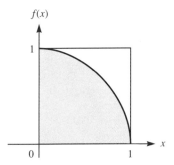

Figure 6.23

The quarter circle to estimate π for Problem 45.

Chapter

7

Arrays and Top-Down Design

Recall that abstraction involves the suppression of detail, an outline structure, division of responsibility through a chain of command, and subdivision of a system into smaller subsystems. The collection of a group of objects is generally the first step toward abstraction. The collection of troops into a squad and the collection of squads into a platoon, for example, is the first step toward the abstract concept of an entire army.

The previous chapter presented functions and procedures, which are collections of program statements executed when the program calls the function or procedure. Declaring a function or procedure creates a new statement that the calling program can use. One advantage of such declarations is that if different people design the calling program and called procedure, the person who writes the calling program does not need to know about the collection of statements in the procedure. The collection of statements is our first step toward program abstraction.

Program abstraction

Remember that Pascal has four structured data types: arrays, records, sets, and files. Each of these structures is a collection of values. Arrays will be our first step toward data abstraction.

Data abstraction

In this chapter, you will learn how to declare and manipulate arrays. You will see that arrays can help solve basic problems in character processing, searching, and sorting. The chapter concludes with a section that presents a method called top-down design, which is based on program abstraction and data abstraction, for solving software problems.

7.1 One-Dimensional Arrays

Arrays and files are similar because they are both collections of values. They are also similar because their values must all be of the same type. For example, a non-text file of real values cannot contain an integer value. Similarly, an array of real values cannot contain an integer value.

Similarities of files and arrays

You may be wondering about a text file that appears to contain several types. For example, the text file `AcctFile3` of Program 5.8 contains

3   54.00   20.40   76.50

The first value is read into an integer variable, `NumAccts`, while the remaining values are read into a real variable, `Account`.

But appearances are deceiving. A text file is similar to a file of `char`. `AcctFile3` does not contain integer or real values. It contains 22 values with type `char`. The first is the character value '3'. The second and third are the space character, ' '. The fourth is the character value '5', and so on. The read statement

Text files do not contain real or integer values.

```
read (AcctFile3, Account)
```

automatically converts the sequence of five characters '5', '4', '.', '0', and '0' into a real value before assigning it to `Account.` The conversion from a sequence of characters to a real value is time consuming. It is the reason text files are slower than nontext files.

The conversion from characters to a real value is an example of *parsing*, which is a basic problem in computer science. Parsing is an element in the translation that a compiler makes from a high-order language to a low-order language.

Arrays and files are different in two respects. First, the values are not stored in the same place. Remember that the four components of a typical computer system are an input device, a CPU, main memory, and an output device. File values are on disk or tape, which are I/O devices. Arrays, like all variables other than files, store their values in main memory.

Differences between files and arrays

Second, files are sequential, while arrays are random. You know that a file is a collection of values that you can access sequentially, that is, one after the other, with the `read` statement. An array is a collection of values that you can access randomly. To access the last value, you do not need to access all the previous values.

Program 7.1

Program 7.1 inputs four values from a file and outputs them in reverse order. It declares `List` to be an array of real values.

You could reverse the four values by declaring four variables, say `List1`, `List2`, `List3`, and `List4`. You could read them in with four input statements or one input statement with four parameters and write them out with four output statements. The disadvantage of this approach is that it is not feasibile for large data sets. Would you like to write a program with this approach to reverse 100 values?

Let's examine the syntax of arrays in Pascal using Program 7.1 as an example. As you recall, new type appeared in Figure 2.14, the syntax chart for the variable declaration part. The array type

```
array [1..4] of real
```

is an example of a new type. Figure 7.1 is the syntax chart of an array type. The quantity, between the square brackets is called the *index* and can be any ordinal

```
program Reverse1 (DataFile, output);
   var
      I:        integer;
      List:     array [1..4] of real;
      DataFile: text;
   begin
   reset (DataFile);
   for I := 1 to 4 do
      read (DataFile, List [I]);
   for I := 4 downto 1 do
      write (List [I]: 6: 1)
   end.
```

Input—DataFile

```
1.6    2.3   -1.0    5.1
```

Output

```
5.1   -1.0    2.3    1.6
```

Program 7.1

A program to reverse the numbers from an input file. It stores the numbers in an array.

type, including `boolean`, `char`, enumerated, and subrange. In this example the index is a subrange of integers.

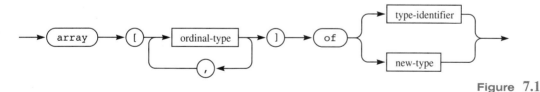

Figure 7.1

The syntax chart of an array type.

The declaration means that the array variable, `List`, contains four real values indexed from 1 to 4. The five values are referred to by `List [1]`, `List [2]`, `List [3]`, and `List [4]`. An element of the array, say `List [2]`, is also called a *subscripted variable* because of its similarity to subscripted variables in mathematics. In mathematical notation, if a variable L is subscripted, you refer to its values by L_1, L_2, L_3, and L_4. Pascal syntax calls for square brackets, since many text editors for program development cannot handle the small subscript style. An array variable is also called a *vector*, and the individual values are called the *components* of the vector. Figure 7.2 is the syntax chart of an indexed variable.

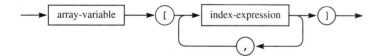

Figure 7.2

The syntax chart of an indexed variable.

Table 7.1, a trace of Program 7.1, shows the semantics of arrays. Note how you must keep track of four values for List, not just one.

The first time

```
read (DataFile, List [I])
```

executes, the value of I is 1. Therefore, the statement is equivalent to

```
read (DataFile, List [1])
```

The effect is to transfer 1.6 from the file to List [1]. But the second time it executes, the value of I is 2, and the statement is equivalent to

```
read (DataFile, List [2])
```

which transfers 2.3 from the file to List [2]. Figure 7.3 shows the action of this read statement.

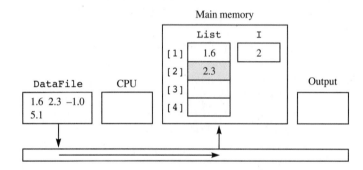

Figure 7.3

Reading a value from a file into an array in Program 7.1.

The first for loop reads the data values from the file into the array. The second for loop outputs the values in reverse order. It initializes I to 4 and decrements it down to 1. The trace table shows, as usual, that the read statement changes the value of its parameter but that the write statement does not.

Using Arrays

You must remember that an array like List contains a collection of values, not just one value. To assign a value to a component of an array you must specify which component gets the value.

An array is a collection of values.

Example **7.1**   The statement

```
List := -1.0
```

where List is declared as it is in Program 7.1 is illegal, even though −1.0 has type real. The problem is that the component of List is not specified. On the other hand,

```
List [3] := -1.0
```

Table 7.1

A trace of Program 7.1.

Statement executed	I	List [1]	[2]	[3]	[4]
begin	?	?	?	?	?
reset (DataFile);	?	?	?	?	?
for I := 1 to 4 do	1	?	?	?	?
read (DataFile, Li	1	1.6	?	?	?
for I := 1 to 4 do	2	1.6	?	?	?
read (DataFile, Li	2	1.6	2.3	?	?
for I := 1 to 4 do	3	1.6	2.3	?	?
read (DataFile, Li	3	1.6	2.3	−1.0	?
for I := 1 to 4 do	4	1.6	2.3	−1.0	?
read (DataFile, Li	4	1.6	2.3	−1.0	5.1
for I := 1 to 4 do	?	1.6	2.3	−1.0	5.1
for I := 4 downto	4	1.6	2.3	−1.0	5.1
write (List [I]: 6	4	1.6	2.3	−1.0	5.1
for I := 4 downto	3	1.6	2.3	−1.0	5.1
write (List [I]: 6	3	1.6	2.3	−1.0	5.1
for I := 4 downto	2	1.6	2.3	−1.0	5.1
write (List [I]: 6	2	1.6	2.3	−1.0	5.1
for I := 4 downto	1	1.6	2.3	−1.0	5.1
write (List [I]: 6	1	1.6	2.3	−1.0	5.1
for I := 4 downto	?	1.6	2.3	−1.0	5.1
end.					

is legal. The assignment statement gives the value of −1.0 to the third component of `List`. ∎

The index of `List` in Program 7.1 has subrange type

```
1..4
```

As with any subrange type, the computer checks whether the index is within the allowable range whenever a reference to a component of an array is made. If it is not, the program crashes with an appropriate error message. This feature of subrange types is especially valuable to the programmer who is tracking down bugs in a program that uses arrays.

Range checking with a subrange index

Example 7.2 With `List` declared as in Program 7.1, the assignment statement

```
List [6] := -1.0
```

causes the program to crash because the index, 6, is not between 1 and 4. ∎

Figure 7.2 shows that the index is not limited to a constant. It can be any arbitrary expression as long as it has the correct type.

The index can be an expression.

Example 7.3 The assignment statement

```
List [3 * I - 5] := 1.6
```

gives the value of 1.6 to `List [1]` if I has the value of 2. ■

Example 7.4 Suppose `List` has the same values that it was given in Program 7.1. The code fragment

```
for I := 2 to 5 do
   write (List [I mod 4 + 1]: 6: 1)
```

would output

```
  -1.0    5.1    1.6    2.3
```

These are the values of `List [3]`, `List [4]`, `List [1]`, and `List [2]`. ■

When the index is an integer subrange, it is not necessary for the lower limit to be 1.

The lower subscript limit need not be 1.

Example 7.5 The types

```
array [0..4] of real
array [-4..4] of real
```

are both valid. The first allocates storage for five real values, and the second allocates storage for nine real values. ■

In Program 7.1 the index had an anonymous type because it was not named. You can use the type section to give a name to the index type. You can also name the array type.

Naming the index type or the array type

Example 7.6 The type definition part and variable declaration part

```
type
   IndexType = 1..4;
var
   List: array [IndexType] of real;
```

name the subrange type for the index and give `List` the same structure as in Program 7.1. Similarly, you could declare `List` as

```
type
   ListType = array [1..4] of real;
var
   List: ListType;
```

which also has the same structure. ∎

Program 7.2

If you do not know exactly how many data items will be in the array, you must allocate more space than you would reasonably expect. Program 7.2 shows this technique. It allocates storage for 100 real values in List, even though the user may enter only 7 values.

Allocating extra memory when the problem size is unknown

```
program Reverse2 (input, output);
   const
      MaxLength = 100;
   var
      I:        integer;
      NumItems: integer;
      List:     array [1..MaxLength] of real;
   begin
   write ('How many numbers? ');
   readln (NumItems);
   write ('Enter the numbers: ');
   for I := 1 to NumItems do
      read (List [I]);
   writeln;
   writeln ('The numbers in reverse order are: ');
   for I := NumItems downto 1 do
      write (List [I]: 6: 1)
   end.
```

Program 7.2

Another program to reverse numbers. This program allows for up to 100 numbers to be input by allocating more storage than will be used.

Interactive Input/Output

```
How many numbers? 7
Enter the numbers: 6  2  9  7  1  2  8

The numbers in reverse order are:
   8.0    2.0    1.0    7.0    9.0    2.0    6.0
```

The trace table for this program would be very large indeed. It would have 102 values on each line—one for I, one for NumItems, and 100 for List, including List [1], List [2], and so on, to List [100]. In this example the user only entered 7 values. That means that the program did not use 93 values. They remained undefined throughout the program execution and represent wasted memory.

The subrange type, `1..MaxLength`, in the declaration of the array contained the constant `MaxLength`. You may be tempted to circumvent the problem of wasted memory by declaring `List` as

```
List: array [1..NumItems] of real
```

Variables not allowed in the index type

but this declaration is illegal because `NumItems` is a variable. You cannot have a variable in a subrange type. Storage allocation for variables in the main program occurs before the first statement executes. The program cannot wait until `NumItems` gets a value from

```
readln (NumItems)
```

before allocating memory.

Wasted memory is a common problem in array processing and does not have a simple solution. With some programs you will know ahead of time exactly how much data must be processed and exactly how large to declare your array to be. With other programs, however, you will not know. In this case, you must decide what is reasonable for the problem at hand and for the main memory size of your computer.

A Problem-Solving Technique

One skill you should develop is the ability to manipulate the elements of an array. Typically you will be confronted with a problem that requires the elements to be rearranged somehow, and you must write the statements that perform the rearrangement. Remember that *analysis* is determining the manipulation from given program statements, while *design* is determining the program statements from a given desired manipulation. We will now turn to design problems.

A useful problem-solving technique with arrays is to proceed from the specific to the general. Here are the steps of this technique:

A problem-solving technique based on generalization

- *Step 1* Write some specific initial values for the array in a trace table.
- *Step 2* Perform the manipulation by changing the values in the table, one at a time.
- *Step 3* For each change, write a specific assignment statement that will produce the change.
- *Step 4* Discover a pattern in the indices of the assignment statements you wrote. Generalize from the specific statements to a loop containing arrays with variables in the subscripts.

The last step is usually the hardest.

The following discussion presents a series of problems that require you to design a program or code fragment that manipulates the components of an array. Each problem is developed to show how you might use the generalizing technique.

Program 7.3

The first illustration of this problem-solving technique is to rotate the elements of an array to the left. The leftmost element will rotate to the rightmost spot. For example, suppose `List` and `NumItems` are declared as in Program 7.2, `NumItems` has the value 4, and `List` has the values

    5.0   −2.3   8.0   0.1

Then, after the rotation, `List` should have the values

    −2.3   8.0   0.1   5.0

Figure 7.4 shows a schematic of the left rotation operation.

Now you apply the four steps of the problem-solving technique.

Steps 1 and 2   In these steps, you write the values in a table and perform the changes one at a time.

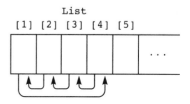

Figure 7.4

The left rotation operation.

	List			
	[1]	[2]	[3]	[4]
Original values	5.0	−2.3	8.0	0.1
Change List [1]	−2.3	−2.3	8.0	0.1
Change List [2]	−2.3	8.0	8.0	0.1
Change List [3]	−2.3	8.0	0.1	0.1
Change List [4]	−2.3	8.0	0.1	5.0

Step 3   For each change, you must write a specific assignment statement that will produce the change.

	List			
	[1]	[2]	[3]	[4]
Original values	5.0	−2.3	8.0	0.1
List [1] := List [2]	−2.3	−2.3	8.0	0.1
List [2] := List [3]	−2.3	8.0	8.0	0.1
List [3] := List [4]	−2.3	8.0	0.1	0.1
List [4] := ?	−2.3	8.0	0.1	?

But here you have a problem. You want `List [4]` to get the old value of `List [1]`. But if you write

```
List [4] := List [1]
```

then `List [4]` will get the current value of `List [1]`, which is –2.3, not 5.0. The solution is to employ a temporary real variable, say `Temp`, which saves the old value of `List [1]`. Here is a revised trace:

	Temp	List [1]	[2]	[3]	[4]
Original values	?	5.0	–2.3	8.0	0.1
Temp := List [1]	5.0	5.0	–2.3	8.0	0.1
List [1] := List [2]	5.0	–2.3	–2.3	8.0	0.1
List [2] := List [3]	5.0	–2.3	8.0	8.0	0.1
List [3] := List [4]	5.0	–2.3	8.0	0.1	0.1
List [4] := Temp	5.0	–2.3	8.0	0.1	5.0

Step 4 In this step, you discover a pattern in the indices of the assignment statements you wrote. The pattern in the indices just presented is

```
1    2
2    3
3    4
```

The index on the right of the assignment statement is one more than the index on the left. So the generalization is

```
Temp := List [1]
for I := 1 to 3 do
   List [I] := List [I + 1]
List [4] := Temp
```

in the case where the array has four elements. In the more general case where there are `NumItems` values, the statements are

```
Temp := List [1]
for I := 1 to NumItems - 1 do
   List [I] := List [I + 1]
List [NumItems] := Temp
```

Program 7.3 shows this algorithm implemented in a procedure called `RotateLeft`. Procedure `GetList` gets the values from a file, and procedure `PutList` puts the values on the screen. Procedure `RotateLeft` performs the rotation.

The program uses the count technique to input the data. When it calls procedure `GetList`, the program is requesting the procedure to change the values of `List` and `NumItems`. So those parameters are called by reference.

```
program Rotate (DataFile, output);
   const
      MaxLength = 100;
   type
      ListType = array [1..MaxLength] of real;
   var
      NumItems: integer;
      List:     ListType;
      DataFile: text;

   procedure GetList (var F:      text;
                      var L:      ListType;
                      var NumItm: integer);
      var
         I: integer;
      begin
      read (F, NumItm);
      for I := 1 to NumItm do
         read (F, L [I])
      end;

   procedure PutList (L: ListType; NumItm: integer);
      var
         I: integer;
      begin
      for I := 1 to NumItm do
         write (L [I]: 6: 1);
      writeln
      end;

   procedure RotateLeft (var L: ListType; NumItm: integer);
      var
         I:    integer;
         Temp: real;
      begin
      Temp := L [1];
      for I := 1 to NumItm - 1 do
         L [I] := L [I + 1];
      L [NumItm] := Temp
      end;

   begin
   reset (DataFile);
   GetList (DataFile, List, NumItems);
   PutList (List, NumItems);
   RotateLeft (List, NumItems);
   writeln;
   PutList (List, NumItems)
   end.
```

Program 7.3

A program with a procedure to rotate the elements in an array.

Input—`DataFile`

4
   5.0   -2.3   8.0   0.1

Output

   5.0   -2.3   8.0   0.1

   -2.3   8.0   0.1   5.0

Program 7.3, continued

It may appear strange that `DataFile` is called by reference also. After all, the program does not want the procedure to change the values in the file. But Pascal requires that all files be called by reference. The calling program can never give the values from a file to a procedure. The only way you can get values from a file is with a `read` statement. The `read` statements are in procedure `GetList` and refer to `DataFile` as F. Hence, `DataFile` must be called by reference. Table 7.2 shows the storage allocated when the program calls procedure `GetList`.

Files are always called by reference.

F	L	NumItm	I
<ref DataFile>	<ref List>	<ref NumItems>	?

Table 7.2

Storage allocated when the program calls procedure `GetList`.

Note that every reference to a variable in `GetList` is local. The procedure is completely self-contained.

When the program calls procedure `PutList`, the procedure does not change the values of the variables. It only outputs them. Therefore, the parameters are called by value. Table 7.3 shows the storage allocated when the program calls procedure `PutList` the first time.

L						NumItm	I
[1]	[2]	[3]	[4]	[5]	...		
5.0	-2.3	8.0	0.1	?	...	4	?

Table 7.3

Storage allocated when the program calls procedure `PutList` the first time.

Since `L` is called by value, all 100 values are allocated, even those that are undefined. Compare this situation with the previous table where `L` was called by reference. When an array is called by reference, only one reference to the entire array is necessary, not a reference to each component. So when an array is called by value it takes more memory. It also takes more time to make the allocation.

In practice, arrays are sometimes called by reference even when the procedure does not change any values in the calling program. The reason is to save both space and time during the call. Occasionally, the programs in this text will follow

Calling large arrays by reference to save space and time

that practice. It is somewhat misleading to call an array by reference when the actual parameter never changes. If an array is called by reference only for efficiency purposes, it should be so documented.

Recall that Figure 6.3, the syntax chart for a formal parameter list of a function or a procedure, showed that the type specified in the formal parameter list must be a type identifier. You cannot specify an anonymous type, but must name it in a type definition part.

The anonymous type is illegal in a parameter list.

Example 7.7 In Program 7.3 you may be tempted to dispense with the constant and type definition parts and declare the procedures like

```
procedure PutList (L: array [1..100] of real; NumItm: integer)
```

Such a declaration would be illegal, however, because the type specified for L is anonymous. ∎

Finding the Largest Element

The next illustration of this problem-solving technique involves finding the largest component of an array. For example, if List and NumItems have the same types and values as in Program 7.2, then the real variable, Largest, should have the value 8.0 after the processing.

The basic idea is the same as the algorithm, shown in Section 5.1, to find the largest value in a file. That algorithm saved the largest value found so far in a variable. Each time the loop executed, the algorithm read a new value from the file. If the new variable was greater than the largest found to that point, the algorithm updated the variable with the newly read value. The algorithm we will now discuss uses the same logic, but it compares Largest with the components of the array one at a time.

The first three steps of the problem-solving technique require you to write some specific initial values for the array in a trace table. Then change the values one at a time, and for each change, write a specific assignment statement that will produce the change. The following table shows one possibility.

	Largest	List [1]	[2]	[3]	[4]
Original values	?	5.0	−2.3	8.0	0.1
Largest := List [1]	5.0	5.0	−2.3	8.0	0.1
if List [2] > Largest then	5.0	5.0	−2.3	8.0	0.1
Update Largest	5.0	5.0	−2.3	8.0	0.1
if List [3] > Largest then	5.0	5.0	−2.3	8.0	0.1
Update Largest	8.0	5.0	−2.3	8.0	0.1
if List [4] > Largest then	8.0	5.0	−2.3	8.0	0.1
Update Largest	8.0	5.0	−2.3	8.0	0.1

You must now discover a pattern in the indices and generalize. The pattern in the indices in the comparisons is

2
3
4

So the statements, one of which is a loop, are

```
Largest := List [1]
for I := 2 to 4 do
   if List [I] > Largest then
      Largest := L [I]
```

in the case where the array has four elements. In the more general case where there are `NumItems` values, you should replace the constant 4 by `NumItems`. What follows is this algorithm in the form of a function.

```
function Maximum (L: ListType; NumItm: integer): real;
   var
      I:         integer;
      Largest: real;
   begin
   Largest := L [1];
   for I := 2 to NumItm do
      if L [I] > Largest then
         Largest := L [I];
   Maximum := Largest
   end
```

A function that returns the largest value in list L

Exchanging the Largest with the Last

The next problem is to switch the largest component of an array with the last component. For example, if `List` is declared as before with the same initial values

   5.0   –2.3   8.0   0.1

then, after the processing, the values should be

   5.0   –2.3   0.1   8.0

The first pass in a stepwise refinement approach would be

```
begin
```
Find the largest number.
Exchange the largest number with the last one.
```
end
```

Suppose you decide to find the largest number the same way as in the previous problem. Namely, suppose you have computed that `Largest` has the value 8.0. Now, how would you make the exchange? The following table shows the specific statements.

			List			
	Temp	Largest	[1]	[2]	[3]	[4]
Current values	?	8.0	5.0	−2.3	8.0	0.1
Temp := List [4]	0.1	8.0	5.0	−2.3	8.0	0.1
List [4] := Largest	0.1	8.0	5.0	−2.3	8.0	8.0
List [3] := Temp	0.1	8.0	5.0	−2.3	0.1	0.1

How do you generalize the last assignment statement in the table? Where did the 3 in `List [3]` come from? The problem is that we have the value of the largest element, when what we really need is the index of the largest element to make the exchange.

So we must be more precise in the first pass and revise it as follows:

```
begin
```
Find the index of the largest number.
Exchange the largest number with the last one.
```
end
```

An integer variable, say `MaxIndex`, will save the value of the index of the largest element found so far.

The following table shows the specific statements to compute `MaxIndex`.

		List			
	MaxIndex	[1]	[2]	[3]	[4]
Original values	?	5.0	−2.3	8.0	0.1
MaxIndex := 1	1	5.0	−2.3	8.0	0.1
if List [2] > List [MaxIndex] then	1	5.0	−2.3	8.0	0.1
Update MaxIndex	1	5.0	−2.3	8.0	0.1
if List [3] > List [MaxIndex] then	1	5.0	−2.3	8.0	0.1
Update MaxIndex	3	5.0	−2.3	8.0	0.1
if List [4] > List [MaxIndex] then	3	5.0	−2.3	8.0	0.1
Update MaxIndex	3	5.0	−2.3	8.0	0.1

The statements in the form of a loop are

```
MaxIndex := 1;
for I := 2 to 4 do
   if List [I] > List [MaxIndex] then
      MaxIndex := I
```

which is valid when there are four items in the list. In the general case, you must replace the 4 by `NumItems`. The algorithm is shown as the following procedure:

```
procedure LargestLast (var L: ListType; NumItm: integer);
   var
       I:          integer;
       MaxIndex:  integer;
       Temp:       real;
   begin
   MaxIndex := 1;
   for I := 2 to NumItm do
       if L [I] > L [MaxIndex] then
           MaxIndex := I;
   Temp := L [NumItm];
   L [NumItm] := L [MaxIndex];
   L [MaxIndex] := Temp
   end
```

A procedure to exchange the largest value with the last value in list L

Initializing in Decreasing Order

The previous problems were rearrangements of existing values in the array. Some problems call for initializing the values in the array. Here is an example. Suppose `List` is an array of integers. If `NumItems` has the value 5, you must initialize `List` to

    5   4   3   2   1

In general, the values should be in decreasing order, with the first value equal to the number of items and the last value equal to 1.

   The specific assignment statements for five elements are

```
List [1] := 5
List [2] := 4
List [3] := 3
List [4] := 2
List [5] := 1
```

You must discover the general relationship between the pairs

      1   5
      2   4
      3   3
      4   2
      5   1

   Each time the first integer in the pair increases by one, the second integer decreases by one. If you write the `for` loop

```
for I := 1 to 5 do
   List [I] := some expression
```

the expression must decrease as I increases.

An expression with -I satisfies that requirement. As I increases, -I decreases. Namely, the expression 6 - I works for five elements. When I has the value 1, 6 - I has the value 5. When I has the value 5, 6 - I has the value 1. For four elements the pattern is

1	4
2	3
3	2
4	1

and the expression is 5 - I.

For general values of NumItems, the expression is

```
NumItems + 1 - I
```

When I has the value 1, NumItems + 1 - I has the value NumItems. When I has the value NumItems, NumItems + 1 - I has the value 1. The algorithm in procedure form follows.

```
procedure Initialize (var L: ListType; NumItm: integer);
   var
      I: integer;
   begin
   for I := 1 to NumItm do
      L [I] := NumItm + 1 - I
   end
```

A procedure to initialize a list of integers in decreasing order

Another approach to the same problem is to note that the expression always starts with the value of NumItems and decreases by one. You can declare an integer variable, J, and initialize it to NumItems. Decrement the value of J each time through the loop and simply give the value of J to List [I]. The algorithm in procedure form follows.

```
procedure Initialize (var L: ListType; NumItm: integer);
   var
      I, J: integer;
   begin
   J := NumItm;
   for I := 1 to NumItm do
      begin
      L [I] := J;
      J := J - 1
      end
   end
```

Another version of the procedure to initialize a list of integers in decreasing order

Reversing the Elements of a List

The assignment operator is always legal between any two variables of the same type. For example, you can assign all the values from an array to another array with one assignment statement. An illustration of this feature is an algorithm that reverses the elements in array ListA. The idea is to create a second array, ListB, which is a copy of ListA but has the values in reverse order. Then the one assignment statement

```
ListA := ListB
```

copies all the values of ListB, even the undefined values, to the corresponding components of ListA. It is a valid assignment because ListA and ListB have the same type. Figure 7.5 shows the action of the algorithm. It is listed below as procedure Reverse.

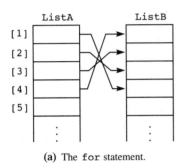

(a) The for statement.

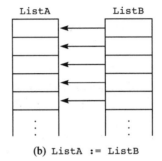

(b) ListA := ListB

Figure 7.5

The action of procedure Reverse when NumItm has the value 4.

```
procedure Reverse (var ListA: ListType; NumItm: integer);
   var
      I, J:  integer;
      ListB: ListType;
   begin
   J := NumItm;
   for I := 1 to NumItm do
      begin
      ListB [I] := ListA [J];
      J := J - 1
      end;
   ListA := ListB
   end
```

A procedure to reverse the items in ListA

This is not the best algorithm for reversing the elements of an array. Problem 38 suggests a more efficient algorithm.

Program 7.4

One common use of arrays is to store a collection of counts. In Program 7.4, GradeFile is a nontext file of grades. Each grade can be either A, B, C, D, F, Credit, or No Credit. GradeType is defined as an enumerated type with these values. The program totals the number of each kind of grade in the file.

Figure 7.1, the syntax chart of an array type, shows that the index can be any ordinal type. In Program 7.4, the declaration

```
GradeCount: array [GradeType] of integer
```

makes the index have the ordinal type GradeType. This means that there is a GradeCount [A], a GradeCount [B], and so on, up until a GradeCount [NC]. The fact that GradeCount is an array of integers means that each of these components will have an integer value. GradeCount [B], for example, is the number (an integer) of B's in GradeFile.

```
program GradeCount (GradeFile, output);
   type
      GradeType = (A, B, C, D, F, Cr, NC);
   var
      GradeFile:  file of GradeType;
      GradeCount: array [GradeType] of integer;
      Grade:      GradeType;
   begin
   for Grade := A to NC do
      GradeCount [Grade] := 0;
   reset (GradeFile);
   while not eof (GradeFile) do
      begin
      read (GradeFile, Grade);
      GradeCount [Grade] := GradeCount [Grade] + 1
      end;
   writeln ('   A   B   C   D   F   Cr   NC');
   writeln ('----------------------------');
   for Grade := A to NC do
      write (GradeCount [Grade]: 4)
   end.
```

Program 7.4

A program that counts the number of each grade in a file. An array stores the collection of counts.

Input—GradeFile (nontext)

C B F A B C Cr C B B D A C C A C Cr C

Output

A	B	C	D	F	Cr	NC
3	4	7	1	1	2	0

Table 7.4 is the start of a trace of Program 7.4. It assumes that the first two grades in GradeFile are C and B. The indices of GradeCount are enumerated values. The values of the components are integers.

The program initializes each component of GradeCount to zero with a for loop. It uses the standard eof technique to process the data sequentially from the file. Each time through the loop, it increments one of the counts with

```
GradeCount [Grade] := GradeCount [Grade] + 1
```

Statement executed	Grade	GradeCount							eof
		[A]	[B]	[C]	[D]	[F]	[Cr]	[NC]	(GradeFile)
begin	?	?	?	?	?	?	?	?	?
for Grade := A to	A	?	?	?	?	?	?	?	?
GradeCount [Grade]	A	0	?	?	?	?	?	?	?
for Grade := A to	B	0	?	?	?	?	?	?	?
GradeCount [Grade]	B	0	0	?	?	?	?	?	?
for Grade := A to	C	0	0	?	?	?	?	?	?
GradeCount [Grade]	C	0	0	0	?	?	?	?	?
for Grade := A to	D	0	0	0	?	?	?	?	?
GradeCount [Grade]	D	0	0	0	0	?	?	?	?
for Grade := A to	F	0	0	0	0	?	?	?	?
GradeCount [Grade]	F	0	0	0	0	0	?	?	?
for Grade := A to	Cr	0	0	0	0	0	?	?	?
GradeCount [Grade]	Cr	0	0	0	0	0	0	?	?
for Grade := A to	NC	0	0	0	0	0	0	?	?
GradeCount [Grade]	NC	0	0	0	0	0	0	0	?
for Grade := A to	?	0	0	0	0	0	0	0	?
reset (GradeFile);	?	0	0	0	0	0	0	0	false
while not eof (Gra	?	0	0	0	0	0	0	0	false
read (GradeFile, G	C	0	0	0	0	0	0	0	false
GradeCount [Grade]	C	0	0	1	0	0	0	0	false
while not eof (Gra	C	0	0	1	0	0	0	0	false
read (GradeFile, G	B	0	0	1	0	0	0	0	false
GradeCount [Grade]	B	0	1	1	0	0	0	0	false

Table 7.4

The start of a trace of Program 7.4.

If you want to exclude the Credit and No Credit grades from the count, you can declare the GradeCount array index with a subrange of GradeType. The declaration

```
GradeCount: array [A..F] of integer
```

allocates storage for five integers instead of seven integers. A reference to `GradeCount [Cr]` would produce a range value error during program execution. To avoid the error, you would need to test `Grade` to make sure it is in the range `A..F` before incrementing `GradeCount [Grade]`. The declaration

```
GradeCount: array [A..NC] of integer
```

is equivalent to the declaration in Program 7.4.

7.2   Fixed Length Strings

The examples in the previous section have all contained arrays of numbers. In Pascal, an array can have any type for its components. English words and sentences are stored in Pascal as arrays of characters.

 Program 7.5

Program 7.5 shows how to input and output a four-letter word. The declaration

```
Word: packed array [1..4] of char
```

makes `Word` an array with four components. Each component is of type `char`. Figure 5.13, the syntax chart for a type definition part, showed that the reserved word `packed` can be placed before any structured type.

```
program FourLetterWord (input, output);
   var
      Word: packed array [1..4] of char;
      I:    integer;
   begin
   write ('Type a four letter word: ');
   for I := 1 to 4 do
      read (Word [I]);
   readln;
   writeln;
   writeln ('You typed ', Word, '.')
   end.
```

Program 7.5

A program to input and output a four-letter word. The word is a packed array of `char`.

Interactive Input/Output

```
Type a four letter word: frog

You typed frog.
```

The difference between an `array of char` and a `packed array of char` is the way the values are stored in main memory. Remember that one byte can store one English character. In many computers it is easier for the hardware to access groups of bytes than individual bytes. Figure 7.6 shows the cells of main memory in a computer with four bytes per group. An array of four characters would be stored one character per group. But a `packed` array would be stored one character per byte.

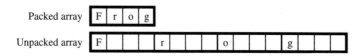

Figure 7.6

The difference between packed and unpacked arrays.

Why not declare every structured type to be `packed`? That would certainly save space. You may have guessed that the fundamental space/time tradeoff operates here. Typically, the system requires more time to access data that is packed than data that is unpacked.

In addition to the saving in space, Pascal allows the following special operations only when the array of `char` is `packed`.

- Output without a loop
- String assignment
- Alphabetical comparison without a loop

Advantages of packing an array of char

To take advantage of these special operations you must not only declare the array to be packed, but the first index must be 1.

Program 7.5 shows the advantage of output without a loop. The output statement

```
writeln ('You typed ', Word, '.')
```

Output without a loop

is equivalent to

```
write ('You typed ');
for I := 1 to 4 do
   write (Word [I]);
writeln ('.')
```

Since `Word` is a packed array, you do not need the `for` loop to output the components one at a time.

Program 7.6

Program 7.6 illustrates the advantage of string assignment. Variable `Word` is a packed array of seven characters.

```
program Farewell (output);
   var
      Word:       packed array [1..7] of char;
      FieldWidth: integer;
   begin
   Word := 'Goodbye';
   for FieldWidth := 9 downto 1 do
      writeln (Word: FieldWidth)
   end.
```

Program 7.6

String assignment to a packed array
of char.

Output

```
  Goodbye
 Goodbye
Goodbye
Goodby
Goodb
Good
Goo
Go
G
```

In this program the assignment statement

```
Word := 'Goodbye'
```

is equivalent to

String assignment

```
Word [1] := 'G';
Word [2] := 'o';
Word [3] := 'o';
Word [4] := 'd';
Word [5] := 'b';
Word [6] := 'y';
Word [7] := 'e'
```

Notice that on output the packed array is right-justified in the field. If the field width is smaller than the number of components in the packed array, the rightmost values are truncated.

When you assign a string to a packed array of characters, the number of character values in the string must exactly match the number of components in the packed array.

Example 7.8 If Word is declared as in Program 7.6, the assignment

```
Word := 'Good'
```

is illegal because the string `'Good'` has only four values, while packed array `Word` has seven components. ∎

Program 7.7

Program 7.7 illustrates the advantage of comparing a packed array without a loop. Single characters are ordered according to their position on the number line, as you recall from Figure 3.2. Thus, 'a' < 'b' and 'Z' > 'A' are both true boolean expressions. Packed arrays of characters are also ordered. In alphabetical order, the packed array `'bear      '` comes before `'berry     '`.

```
program Alphabetize (input, output);
   const
      StrLength = 10;
   type
      StrType = packed array [1..StrLength] of char;
   var
      Word1: StrType;
      Word2: StrType;
      Temp:  StrType;

   procedure GetString (var S: StrType);
      {  This procedure gets a string value for S from    }
      {  the keyboard.  It inputs characters until the    }
      {  user presses <return> and pads unused characters }
      {  on the right with spaces.  It assumes that StrType }
      {  is a packed array [1..StrLength] of char, where  }
      {  StrLength is a constant integer.                 }
      var
         I: integer;
      begin
      for I := 1 to StrLength do
         if eoln (input) then
            S [I] := ' '
         else
            read (input, S [I]);
      readln (input)
      end;
```

Program 7.7

A program to alphabetize two words. You do not need to compare individual letters in the packed arrays of `char`.

Program 7.7, continued

```
begin
write ('Please enter a word: ');
GetString (Word1);
write ('Enter another word: ');
GetString (Word2);
writeln;
if Word1 > Word2 then
    begin
    Temp := Word1;
    Word1 := Word2;
    Word2 := Temp
    end;
writeln ('In alphabetical order they are:');
writeln (Word1);
writeln (Word2)
end.
```

Interactive Input/Output

```
Please enter a word: berry
Enter another word: bear

In alphabetical order they are:
bear
berry
```

If the length of a word that will be entered from the keyboard is unknown, you must allocate more storage for it than you would reasonably expect. GetString inputs characters from the keyboard and pads the unused character components with blank spaces.

The eoln function detects the end of the input line the same way the eof function detects the end of the file. When the program begins, eoln (input) is false. Each time

The eoln function

```
read (input, S [I])
```

executes, it makes eoln true if the user presses the return key. If the user does press the return key, it gives S [I] the value ' ' (a single space). The

```
readln (input)
```

statement makes eoln false again in preparation for the next call to procedure GetString.

The comparison statement

```
if Word1 > Word2 then
```

considers all the values in the array. If Word1 [1] equals Word2 [1], then it compares Word1 [2] with Word2 [2]. If they are equal, it compares

Alphabetical comparison without a loop

`Word1 [3]` with `Word2 [3]`, and so on. This way, the words are placed in alphabetical order.

You must be careful when comparing string values that contain mixtures of uppercase and lowercase letters. In the ASCII character set, the uppercase letters are to the left of the lowercase letters on the number line. Therefore, any lowercase letter is less than any uppercase letter. Even though `'ape    '` is less than `'zebra'`, `'Zebra'` is less than `'ape    '` since 'Z' is less than 'a'. In the EBCDIC character set, the lowercase letters are on the left. Table 7.5 shows the order of four strings for both character sets.

ASCII	EBCDIC
`'Ape  '`	`'ape  '`
`'Zebra'`	`'zebra'`
`'ape  '`	`'Ape  '`
`'zebra'`	`'Zebra'`

Table 7.5

The order of four string values in the ASCII and EBCDIC character sets.

▢ The Character-Processing Algorithm

Programs that process character values get their input from the keyboard or from a text file. Section 5.3 recommended that programs with text files use only the sentinel or the count technique. That is a good recommendation when numbers are in the file, as was the case in previous examples. But when you want to analyze data in a text file one character at a time, the `eof` technique, in conjunction with `eoln`, is best.

There is a basic technique for character processing in Pascal. It is a fourth general file-processing technique to add to our first three, which are the sentinel, count, and `eof` techniques. Here is how it works.

Suppose you have a text file called `SomeFile` with several lines of characters, say

```
ab
cde
```

Although it appears in your text editor that five characters are in the file, there are really seven. Internally, the computer stores the sequence of characters as

a b <LF> c d e <LF>

The line feed marker <LF>

The character denoted <LF> is a special nonprintable marker that denotes the end of a line.

The letters LF stand for *line feed*. On a printer, the <LF> character would make the print carriage return to the start of the next line. On a screen it would send the cursor to the start of the next line. The particular marker used to separate lines depends on the computer system. Different computers use different markers.

When you reset a file, you affect not only `eof` but also `eoln`. If the file is empty, `reset` makes `eof` true, and `eoln` is undefined. If the file is not empty, `reset` makes `eof` false, and the value of `eoln` depends on the content of the first line in the file. If the first line has at least one character in it, `eoln` will be false. If the first line is empty, `eoln` will be true.

The effect of reset on eoln

When you read from a file, you affect `eoln` as well as `eof`. In the same way that reading the last element in a file sets `eof` to true, reading the character before

The effect of read on eoln

<LF> sets `eoln` to true. The `eoln` function looks ahead one character to see if the next reading would attempt to read past the end of the line. In the same way, the `eof` function looks ahead one item to see if the next reading would attempt to read past the end of the file.

The basic Pascal character-processing algorithm follows. `Ch` is a variable of type `char` and `SomeFile` is a text file.

```
reset (SomeFile)
while not eof (SomeFile) do
   begin
   while not eoln (SomeFile) do
      begin
      read (SomeFile, Ch)
      Perform character processing.
      end
   readln (SomeFile)
   Perform line processing.
   end
```

The basic Pascal character-processing algorithm

When `SomeFile` contains the above seven-character input stream, the `reset` statement makes `eoln (SomeFile)` and `eof (SomeFile)` false. The inner loop executes twice—once with `Ch` having the value 'a' and once having 'b'. The `read` that gives `Ch` the value 'b' sets `eoln (SomeFile)` to true, since the next character in the file is <LF>.

The statement

```
readln (SomeFile)
```

sets the input device to the start of the next line, skipping the <LF> marker. Since the next line is not empty, `eoln (SomeFile)` gets false.

The next time around, the inner loop executes three times, once each for 'c', 'd', and 'e'. This time the `readln` call skips the last <LF> and sets `eof (SomeFile)` to true. Whenever `eof (SomeFile)` gets true, `eoln (SomeFile)` gets undefined. That is acceptable in this algorithm, since the outer loop will terminate, and `eoln` will not be tested again.

Note that `Ch` will never have the value <LF>. You could process the file with the single loop

```
reset (SomeFile)
while not eof (SomeFile) do
   begin
   read (SomeFile, Ch)
   Perform character processing.
   end
```

The loop would terminate correctly. But at some points during execution of the loop, you would be executing

```
read (SomeFile, Ch)
```

when `eoln (SomeFile)` is true. The Pascal standard specifies that this operation should give `Ch` the value of ' ', a single space. But some compilers give `Ch` the value <LF> instead. At any rate, normally you will not want `Ch` to have an extra line-terminating value, whatever it would be.

You can solve most character-processing problems with this basic algorithm. Rarely will you need any other loop statements. You only need to determine the character-processing and line-processing statements, along with any initialization. Several algorithms that use this character-processing technique follow.

Algorithms to Echo and to Count

The simplest program is one that echoes the text file to the screen. The character processing is a simple `write (Ch)` and the line processing is a simple `writeln`, as shown in the following algorithm:

```
reset (SomeFile);
while not eof (SomeFile) do
   begin
   while not eoln (SomeFile) do
      begin
      read (SomeFile, Ch);
      write (Ch)
      end;
   readln (SomeFile);
   writeln
   end
```

An algorithm to echo a text file onto the screen

This code will copy the contents of one file to another file if you reset the new file and specify it in the output statements.

The following code fragment counts the total number of characters and lines in the file. Following execution of the code, `NumChars` will contain the number of characters in the file not including the <LF> line markers.

```
NumChars := 0;
NumLines := 0;
reset (SomeFile);
while not eof (SomeFile) do
   begin
   while not eoln (SomeFile) do
      begin
      read (SomeFile, Ch);
      NumChars := NumChars + 1
      end;
   readln (SomeFile);
   NumLines := NumLines + 1
   end
```

An algorithm to count the number of characters and lines in a text file

An empty line is a line that contains no characters, not even a space. For example, the text

ab

cde

has one empty line. The computer stores it internally as

a b <LF> <LF> c d e <LF>

In the algorithm just presented, `NumLines` will contain the number of lines, including the empty lines.

The following algorithm counts the number of empty lines in the file. An empty line causes the inner loop to be skipped. So to count the number of empty lines, you need to count how many times the outer loop executes without the inner loop executing.

```
NumEmptyLines := 0;
reset (SomeFile);
while not eof (SomeFile) do
   begin
   EmptyLine := true;
   while not eoln (SomeFile) do
      begin
      read (SomeFile, Ch);
      EmptyLine := false
      end;
   readln (SomeFile);
   if EmptyLine then
      NumEmptyLines := NumEmptyLines + 1
   end
```

An algorithm to count the number of empty lines in a text file

A counter variable, `NumEmptyLines` with type integer, will be incremented in the outer while loop only if the inner loop did not execute. The algorithm uses the boolean variable `EmptyLine` to detect whether the inner loop does not execute. `EmptyLine` is initialized to true just before the inner loop and set to false inside the inner loop. At the conclusion of the loop, if `EmptyLine` is still true, the loop never executed. This is a common programming technique used to detect whether a loop executes.

▭ Program 7.8

The final example of the basic Pascal character-processing algorithm is a problem that is simple to state but moderately difficult to solve. Program 7.8 must output the longest word from each line of the text file, `DataFile`. A space character or the end of the line terminates each word.

A problem to output the longest word on each line

The following discussion shows some typical problems that you might encounter solving this kind of problem. It also illustrates a problem-solving aid called a *decision table*.

Any algorithm that finds a maximum from some collection of items has the following general form:

A general approach to finding a maximum value

```
Initialize a MaxItem
while there are more items do
   begin
   Get the NextItem
   if NextItem is bigger than MaxItem then
      MaxItem := NextItem
   end
```

This form suggests that you need a variable, `LongWord`, that corresponds to `MaxItem`. It will be a packed array of `char`. A variable, `Word`, will also be a packed array of `char` and will correspond to `NextItem`. The `if` statement requires you to compare `NextItem` with `MaxItem` somehow. So you will need an integer variable, `LengthLongWord`, that tells how many characters are in `LongWord`.

The heart of the problem is how to perform the `while` loop and the processing to get the `NextItem`. Since the problem asks for the longest word on a line, you could write the `while` test as

```
while not eoln (DataFile) do
```

Then you could get the next word by

```
while Ch <> ' ' do
   begin
   I := I + 1;
   Word [I] := Ch;
   read (DataFile, Ch)
   end
```

where `I` is an integer variable initialized at the beginning of the line. At the termination of the loop, `I` would be the length of `Word`, which could be compared with `LengthLongWord`.

This approach would result in a loop nested two levels deep.

```
while not eof (DataFile) do
   while not eoln (DataFile) do
      while Ch <> ' ' do
```

One approach to constructing the loops for the longest-word problem

But the basic character-processing algorithm has a loop nested only one level deep.

```
while not eof (DataFile) do
   while not eoln (DataFile) do
```

The basic Pascal character-processing approach

How should you reconcile these two different approaches?

The answer is to stick with the basic Pascal character-processing algorithm. As a general rule you should nest loops as little as possible. In other words, do not nest a loop two levels deep when you can do the job with a loop nested only one level deep.

The general rule

The problem with excessive nesting of loops is their termination conditions. For example, the innermost loop in the first approach does not work correctly when the last word on a line has no trailing spaces. The condition must include an `eoln` test. But that test must be consistent with the `eoln` test of the middle loop. The situation gets unnecessarily complicated.

Here is the next stepwise refinement pass. It uses the basic Pascal character-processing algorithm.

A stepwise refinement pass for the problem to output the longest word on each line

```
begin
reset (DataFile)
while not eof (DataFile) do
   begin
   Word := '               '
   I := 0
   LongWord := '                '
   LengthLongWord := 0
   while not eoln (DataFile) do
      begin
      read (DataFile, Ch)
      If not at the end of a word,
         collect this character with I := I + 1
         and Word [I] := Ch.
      Otherwise,
         I is the length of the Word.
         Compare I with LengthLongWord
         and update LongWord if necessary.
         Initialize Word and I.
      end
   readln (DataFile)
   writeln (LongWord)
   end
end
```

This algorithm assumes that `Word` and `LongWord` are packed arrays of 20 characters.

Every statement is Pascal except the paragraph that describes how to process a character. The problem is complicated by the fact that there are two ways to detect the end of a word. You have detected the end of a word if `Ch` is ' ' or if `eoln (DataFile)` is true.

How do you proceed to write this paragraph in Pascal? Do you start with

```
if Ch = ' ' then
```

or with

```
if eoln (DataFile)
```

or with

```
if (Ch = ' ') or eoln (DataFile)
```

or with some other combination? The logic is complex, and there are many ways to go wrong.

One problem-solving technique that is helpful when you need to design complex `if` statements is the *decision table technique*. Using this technique, you would first, identify the operations that you know are involved in the computation. This problem has three operations. They are

The decision table technique

- Update `Word`
- Update `LongWord`
- Initialize `Word` and `I`

The code for the Update `Word` operation is

```
I := I + 1;
Word [I] := Ch
```

The code for the Update `LongWord` operation is

```
if I > LengthLongWord then
   begin
   LongWord := Word;
   LengthLongWord := I
   end
```

The code for Initialize `Word` and `I` operation is

```
Word := '                    ';
I := 0
```

The second step is to determine all possible combinations of the conditions. This problem has two conditions. They are

```
Ch = ' '
```

and

```
eoln (DataFile)
```

Each of these conditions can be true or false. So there are four possible combinations of the conditions—true/true, true/false, false/true, and false/false.

The third step is to construct a decision table that lists the operations that must be performed for each combination of the conditions. Figure 7.7 is the decision table for this problem.

	Ch = ' '	Ch <> ' '
eoln (DataFile)	*Update* LongWord	*Update* Word *Update* Longword
not eoln (DataFile)	*Update* LongWord *Initialize* Word *and* I	*Update* Word

Figure 7.7

The decision table for the longest-word problem.

To fill in each entry of the table, you must determine the processing that is required for each condition. For example, the upper right corner of the table lists the operations necessary when Ch is not a space character and it is the last character on the line. Since it is not a space character, it is a letter in the current Word, and you must update Word. Since it is the last character on the line, it completes the current Word, and you must update LongWord. Since eoln is true, you do not need to initialize Word and I. They will be initialized before the inner loop executes again.

The reasoning for each of the other entries in the decision table is similar. Be sure that you understand each entry in the decision table.

The fourth and final step in the decision table technique is to write the code from the decision table. The most straightforward way is with a nested if statement without regard to any possible economy of code. There are several possible orderings. For example, you could start with the outer if containing the eoln condition as follows:

```
if eoln (DataFile) then
   if Ch = ' ' then
      { Assert: At end of line and Ch = ' '.  }
      Update LongWord
   else
      { Assert: At end of line and Ch <> ' '.  }
      begin
      Update Word
      Update LongWord
      end
```

```
else
   if Ch = ' ' then
      {  Assert: Not at end of line and Ch = ' '.  }
      begin
      Update LongWord
      Initialize Word and I
      end
   else
      {  Assert: Not at end of line and Ch <> ' '.  }
      Update Word
```

Another possibility, equally long, would be to start with the outer `if` containing the test `Ch = ' '` and nest the `if` statements containing the `eoln` test.

But it is better to examine the decision table to see if there are common operations in any rows or columns. You can combine them to simplify the code. In the column with the `Ch = ' '` heading in Figure 7.7, a common operation is Update `LongWord`. In the column labeled `Ch <> ' '`, a common operation is Update `Word`. So a much simpler coding is the following:

```
if Ch = ' ' then
   begin
   Update LongWord
   if not eoln (DataFile) then
      Initialize Word and I
   end
else
   begin
   Update Word
   if eoln (DataFile) then
      Update LongWord
   end
```

Simplifying the code

You can simplify the code even further by considering the upper left entry of the decision table. If `Ch = ' '` and `eoln` are both true, you do not need to Initialize `Word` and `I`, because they will be initialized before the inner loop. But it would not hurt to initialize them here, even though it is unnecessary. Then each entry in the column for `Ch = ' '` would be identical, and you can eliminate one nested `if` statement. Here is the code:

```
if Ch = ' ' then
   begin
   Update LongWord
   Initialize Word and I
   end
else
   begin
   Update Word
   if eoln (DataFile) then
      Update LongWord
   end
```

Simplifying the code further

Program 7.8 is the Pascal program based on this algorithm. Since Update LongWord appears twice in the algorithm, it is declared as a procedure. The initialization operation appears in three places—twice with Word and once with LongWord. So it is performed with a procedure as well.

```pascal
program LongestWords (DataFile, output);
   type
      Str20Type = packed array [1..20] of char;
   var
      Word:            Str20Type;
      LongWord:        Str20Type;
      LengthLongWord:  integer;
      Ch:              char;
      I:               integer;
      DataFile:        text;

   procedure Initialize (var Str: Str20Type; var Len: integer);
      begin
      Str := '                    ';
      Len := 0
      end;

   procedure UpdateLongWord (var LongWd:    Str20Type;
                             var LenLongWd: integer;
                                 Wd:        Str20Type;
                                 LenWd:     integer);
      begin
      if LenWd > LenLongWd then
         begin
         LongWd := Wd;
         LenLongWd := LenWd
         end
      end;
```

Program **7.8**

A program to find the longest word in a line. This program uses the basic Pascal character-processing algorithm.

Program 7.8, continued

```
   begin
   reset (DataFile);
   while not eof (DataFile) do
      begin
      Initialize (Word, I);
      Initialize (LongWord, LengthLongWord);
      while not eoln (DataFile) do
         begin
         read (DataFile, Ch);
         if Ch = ' ' then
            begin
            UpdateLongWord (LongWord, LengthLongWord, Word, I);
            Initialize (Word, I)
            end
         else
            begin
            I := I + 1;
            Word [I] := Ch;
            if eoln (DataFile) then
               UpdateLongWord (LongWord, LengthLongWord, Word, I);
            end
         end;
      readln (DataFile);
      writeln (LongWord)
      end
   end.
```

Input—DataFile

```
It is for us the living, rather to be dedicated here
to the unfinished work which they who fought here
have thus far so nobly advanced.
```

Output

```
dedicated
unfinished
advanced.
```

Do you see that this program handles multiple spaces correctly? If the source file contains two consecutive spaces, the second one will cause `UpdateLongWord` to execute. But `LengthWd` will be zero, and the update will never occur. No matter how many spaces immediately follow the second consecutive space, each will be analyzed as a zero-length word.

This program has several deficiencies. The most important is that it will crash with a range value error if there is a word longer than 20 characters in the file. One solution is to make the type of `Word` extremely long. Some common lengths are 80, which is a standard line length on a screen, and 132, which is a standard line length on wide computer-printout paper.

Some deficiencies in Program 7.8

For such long arrays, it would be inconvenient to initialize the words with a string. It would be better to define a constant, `MaxLength`, and initialize each component in the words to ' ' with a `for` loop.

Even then, there is no guarantee that a file will not contain a longer word than you allocate. A better method is to test the value of `I` before updating `Word`. If `I` is greater than `MaxLength`, do not update. You would have to be content with saving a truncated version of the longest word. You could still continue to increment `I` and store the correct value of `LengthLongWord`.

Another deficiency you can see from the sample output is the inclusion of punctuation characters in a word. The period after "advanced" was counted as part of the word. You can eliminate this deficiency by testing whether `Ch` is a letter instead of testing whether it is the space character.

You may have recognized these two problems at the outset of the design. But sometimes it is easier to proceed with a simplified version of the problem and then modify your solution after you solve the simplified problem.

7.3 Two-Dimensional Arrays

Sometimes you need to store information not as a single list of values, but as a table of values. Tables have rows and columns. The Pascal data structure that corresponds to a table is a *two-dimensional array.*

Program 7.9

Program 7.9 declares `Matrix` to be a two-dimensional array. It shows how to input and output the values of `Matrix`.

The declaration

```
Matrix: array [1..10, 1..10] of real
```

shows two subrange indices, which is what makes the array two-dimensional. The first index numbers the rows and the second numbers the columns. `Matrix` contains storage for 100 values in 10 rows and 10 columns, although the program does not use all the storage.

Figure 7.8 shows how the cells in the `Matrix` are numbered. `Matrix [2, 3]` is the component in row two, column three. In general, `Matrix [I, J]` is the component in row I, column J.

Figure 7.8

The structure of the two-dimensional array, `Matrix`, in Program 7.7.

```
program MatrixInOut (DataFile, output);
   var
      Matrix:    array [1..10, 1..10] of real;
      NumRows:   integer;
      NumCols:   integer;
      I, J:      integer;
      DataFile: text;
   begin
   reset (DataFile);
   read (DataFile, NumRows, NumCols);
   for I := 1 to NumRows do
      for J := 1 to NumCols do
         read (DataFile, Matrix [I, J]);
   writeln ('The matrix:');
   for I := 1 to NumRows do
      begin
      for J := 1 to NumCols do
         write (Matrix [I, J]: 6: 1);
      writeln
      end
   end.
```

Program 7.9

A program with the input and output of a two-dimensional array of real values.

Input—DataFile

```
3   4
   12.0    8.0    6.0    4.0    3.0    5.0    7.0
    1.0    2.0   11.0    9.0   10.0
```

Output

```
The matrix:
  12.0    8.0    6.0    4.0
   3.0    5.0    7.0    1.0
   2.0   11.0    9.0   10.0
```

The program uses the count technique for input from a text file. It requires two integers to specify the data that follows, not a single NumItems integer. The number of values following the count is NumRows times NumCols. Nested for loops are typical in two-dimensional array processing.

You should trace this example by hand to make sure you understand how it works. Notice the last writeln statement in the program. If it were not there, all the values would be printed on the same line.

The same problem-solving technique of going from the specific to the general applies to two-dimensional arrays and one-dimensional arrays. Here are some illustrations. In each illustration, Matrix, NumRows, NumCols, I, and J are declared as in Program 7.9.

The Ethical and Legal Use of Software

Although the price-performance ratio of computing machinery often draws the headlines, and indeed makes it possible for students to consider buying a computer, it's the software that takes a bare-bones computer and turns it into a useful tool. At one moment, a computer can be a sophisticated word processing system on which you can do desktop publishing; then by swapping programs in the machine's memory, you can transform it into a programming environment; then you can turn the system into a payroll processor or a simulator of a supernova. The realm of applications for computers is limited only by the creative ability of programmers to construct software that fills some niche in our information-processing needs.

When investing in computing systems, whether for personal, academic, or business use, most buyers know to budget not only for the computer, monitor, and keyboard, but also for a printer, a modem, cables, and perhaps a maintenance contract. However, many neglect to consider the investment in software that will be required in order to adapt their machine to their particular needs. Unfortunately, many computer users participate in the unauthorized copying of software, under the impression that such actions "don't really hurt anyone, anyway."

But there are several reasons why we should not copy software without proper authorization. First and foremost, it is ethically wrong, as software represents a unique intellectual creation, just like an invention, a book, an article, or a graphic logo. The creative juices of our society might not flow quite so freely if we each had to fear having our ideas stolen from us—why bother to spend several years writing a computer program if you can't expect to sell it for a fair price in return for your efforts? If you've bought a computer program and are pleased with it, show it off to your friends and colleagues, and let them try it out on your machine. But don't just copy the program and distribute it. To do so would be to deprive the software's author of her fair return; in the long run, if too few copies of the software are legally sold, the author may go out of business, depriving you of the opportunity to benefit from new or improved versions of the software.

If ethics alone isn't enough, the long arm of the law is there as a backup. Software developers, threatened by the widespread practice of piracy, are putting the power of the law behind them in making a clear statement that software licensing is required. Copyright law in the U.S. and other countries protects computer software, either

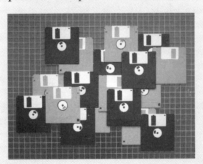

through the liberal interpretation of statutes for traditional printed media, or through new laws that explicitly refer to software and the media on which it is stored. Individuals and academic and business organizations have been successfully prosecuted for the illegal use of computer software. Computer-literate police officers may raid businesses or universities with search warrants, seize or erase illegal copies of software, and press charges.

Practically speaking, there are other reasons for obtaining your software legitimately. New software is shipped with a user's manual that describes how to install and use the software on your machine and how to take advantage of all its features. There is usually a registration card you can send in to the company so that you can receive automatic notices of updates for the software or purchase the documentation at a reduced cost. Often, free telephone support is provided so that you can have an expert talk you through a problem—this service may prevent you from losing valuable information. But such services are only available to registered owners of the software—software pirates have to wing it alone.

To obtain a copy of an EDUCOM brochure on this topic, contact your campus computing office or write to

EDUCOM
Software Initiative
P.O. Box 364
Princeton, NJ 08540

Printing a Column

Suppose you are given an integer variable, Col. The problem is to output all the components in that column. For example, if Col has the value of 2, the code should output

```
 8.0
 5.0
11.0
```

which are all the components in column two.

The specific output statements are

```
writeln (Matrix [1, 2])
writeln (Matrix [2, 2])
writeln (Matrix [3, 2])
```

where the format specification is omitted to keep things simple. In a for loop the statements are

```
for I := 1 to 3 do
   writeln (Matrix [I, 2])
```

for an array with values in three rows. Since the value of NumRows specifies how many rows of data are in the array, you must replace the 3 with NumRows. For a general column, you must replace the 2 with Col. Here is the code for printing the column.

```
for I := 1 to NumRows do
   writeln (Matrix [I, Col])
```

The code to print a column of a two-dimensional array

Finding the Largest in a Row

The second illustration involves finding the largest element in the row specified by the integer variable, Row. For example, if Row has the value 3, the code should give the value 11.0 to the real variable, Max.

The specific statements are

```
Max := Matrix [3, 1]
if Matrix [3, 2] > Max then
   Max := Matrix [3, 2]
if Matrix [3, 3] > Max then
   Max := Matrix [3, 3]
if Matrix [3, 4] > Max then
   Max := Matrix [3, 4]
```

after which Max has the maximum value of 11.0 from the third row. The corresponding for statement is

```
Max := Matrix [3, 1]
for J := 2 to 4 do
   if Matrix [3, J] > Max then
      Max := Matrix [3, J]
```

for an array with values in four columns. For `NumCols` in general, `J` in the `for` loop ranges from 2 to `NumCols`. And for a general row, the `for` loop is

```
Max := Matrix [Row, 1];
for J := 2 to NumCols do
   if Matrix [Row, J] > Max then
      Max := Matrix [Row, J]
```

The code to find the largest element in a row

Matrix Multiplication

The next illustration deals with matrix multiplication of two square matrices, A and B, with the product in C. A *square matrix* has an equal number of rows and columns. The integer variable `SideLength` will be the number of rows and columns in A, B, and C.

If A and B have the values

A				B		
1.0	3.0	−1.0		2.0	0.0	1.0
2.0	0.0	4.0		−2.0	3.0	2.0
1.0	−2.0	3.0		1.0	0.0	4.0

then the product, C should have the values

C		
−5.0	9.0	3.0
8.0	0.0	18.0
9.0	−6.0	9.0

With these values, `SideLength` is 3, since each array has three rows and three columns.

Each value of C comes from multiplying a row of A with a column of B. For example, the element in the second row and third column of C comes from multiplying the second row of A with the third column of B. You multiply a row with a column by multiplying corresponding components from left to right in the row and from top to bottom in the column. Then you add the products. This specific case is

```
2.0 * 1.0 + 0.0 * 2.0 + 4.0 * 4.0
```

which is 18.0. In general, the element in row I and column J of C comes from multiplying row I of A with column J of B.

Start with this specific case. For row two and column three of C, you need to compute

```
A[2,1] * B[1,3] + A[2,2] * B[2,3] + A[2,3] * B[3,3]
```

In a `for` loop, that is

```
Sum := 0.0;
for K := 1 to 3 do
   Sum := Sum + A [2, K] * B [K, 3];
C [2, 3] := Sum
```

where `Sum` is a real variable.

This code is for arrays with three rows and columns. For the more general case of `SideLength` rows and columns, `K` in the `for` statement ranges from 1 to `SideLength`. Also, this computation is for row two, column three. In the more general case of row `I` and column `J` the code is

```
Sum := 0.0;
for K := 1 to SideLength do
   Sum := Sum + A [I, K] * B [K, J];
C [I, J] := Sum
```

The code for matrix multiplication

This computation must be done for every row and column of `C`. So the final code for matrix multiplication is

```
for I := 1 to SideLength
   for J := 1 to SideLength
      begin
      Sum := 0.0;
      for K := 1 to SideLength do
         Sum := Sum + A [I, K] * B [K, J];
      C [I, J] := Sum
      end
```

Program 7.10

Pascal provides several ways to declare two-dimensional arrays. At first glance, `List` in Program 7.10 does not look like a two-dimensional array. Its declaration has only one subrange, `1..4`, not two.

In this program, `List` is an array of words. `List [4]` is the fourth word in the list, a packed array of `char`. `List [4] [2]` is the second letter in the packed array, a single `char`. Figure 7.9(a) shows the structure of `List` with this viewpoint.

With a slightly different viewpoint, you can consider `List` to be a two-dimensional array with four rows and three columns, as in Figure 7.9(b). In fact, you can write `List [4] [2]` in the last `writeln` statement as `List [4, 2]`. Similarly, you can write `Matrix [I, J]` in Program 7.9 as `Matrix [I] [J]`.

In Program 7.9, the type

```
array [1..10, 1..10] of real
```

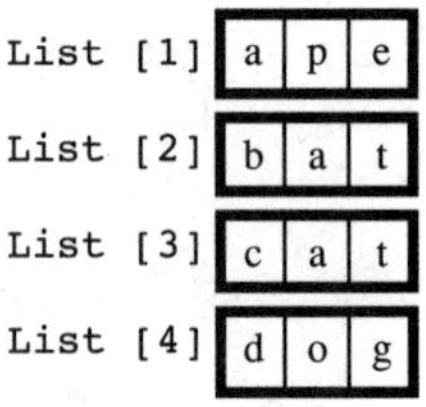
List [1]
a p e
List [2]
b a t
List [3]
c a t
List [4]
d o g

(a) An array of an array.

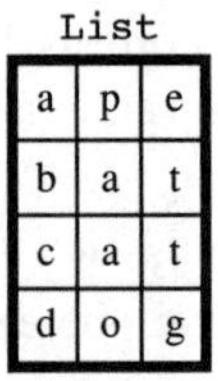
List
a p e
b a t
c a t
d o g

(b) A two-dimensional array.

Figure 7.9

Two different viewpoints of `List`.

```
program Words (output);
   type
      WordType = packed array [1..3] of char;
   var
      List: array [1..4] of WordType;
   begin
   List [1] := 'ape';
   List [2] := 'bat';
   List [3] := 'cat';
   List [4] := 'dog';
   writeln ('Third word = ', List [3]);
   writeln ('Fourth word, second letter = ', List [4] [2])
   end.
```

Program 7.10

A program declaring `List` to be
an array of an array.

Output

```
Third word = cat
Fourth word, second letter = o
```

is equivalent to the type

```
array [1..10] of array [1..10] of real
```

`Matrix` is an array of an array, just as `List` is.
   `List` does not have quite the same type as

```
packed array [1..4, 1..3] of char
```

however. This type is equivalent to

```
packed array [1..4] of packed array [1..3] of char
```

The characteristic of packed applies to both dimensions of the array. The type of
`List` is equivalent to

```
array [1..4] of packed array [1..3] of char
```

Only the second dimension is packed.

Program 7.11

Program 7.11 is an illustration of a useful two-dimensional array structure called a
string table. `GradeType`, `Grade`, and `GradeFile` are all defined as they were
in Program 7.4. `GradeType` is an enumerated type and `GradeFile` is a file of
`GradeType`. The program outputs the contents of `GradeFile`.

```
program GradePrint (GradeFile, output);
   type
      GradeType = (A, B, C, D, F, Cr, NC);
      Str2Type  = packed array [1..2] of char;
   var
      GradeFile: file of GradeType;
      StrTable:  array [GradeType] of Str2Type;
      Grade:     GradeType;
      Count:     integer;
   begin
   StrTable [A]  := 'A ';
   StrTable [B]  := 'B ';
   StrTable [C]  := 'C ';
   StrTable [D]  := 'D ';
   StrTable [F]  := 'F ';
   StrTable [Cr] := 'Cr';
   StrTable [NC] := 'NC';
   Count := 0;
   reset (GradeFile);
   while not eof (GradeFile) do
      begin
      read (GradeFile, Grade);
      write (StrTable [Grade]: 4);
      Count := Count + 1;
      if (Count mod 5) = 0 then
         writeln
      end
   end.
```

Program 7.11

A string table to output enumerated values.

Input—GradeFile (nontext)

C B F A B C Cr C B B D A C C A C Cr C

Output

```
C   B   F   A   B
C   Cr  C   B   B
D   A   C   C   A
C   Cr  C
```

The difficulty with enumerated values is that they cannot be output directly. The statement

write (Grade)

is illegal. Program 5.10 used one technique for outputting the contents of a file of enumerated values. It had a case statement with a writeln call in each case alternative. Program 7.11 is a more elegant solution, because it requires only one writeln call and no case statement.

The idea is to construct the two-dimensional array `StrTable`. The index of `StrTable` has type `GradeType`. That means there is a `StrTable [A]`, a `StrTable [B]`, and so on. Since `StrTable` is an array of `Str2Type`, each of these components has a two-character string value that can be output directly in a `writeln` call. Even though `write (Grade)` is illegal,

String tables to output enumerated values

```
write (StrTable [Grade])
```

is legal.

Another technique illustrated by this example is the output of a sequence of values in a set of rows instead of all in one column. The expression

```
(Count mod 5) = 0
```

Placing a stream of output values on separate rows

is true when `Count` is divisible by 5. Since `Count` increases by 1 each time through the loop, the expression will be true at every fifth execution. So after every fifth value is printed, the `writeln` statement positions the cursor at the beginning of the next line.

7.4 Searching and Sorting

Probably the most important algorithms in all of computer science are the searching and sorting algorithms. They are important because they are so common. Every time you look up a word in a dictionary or look up a phone number in a phone book, you are performing a *search*. Table entries in many business reports are in some kind of order. The post office wants bulk mailings to be in order by zip code. Putting data in order is performing a *sort*.

This section presents two basic search algorithms, the sequential search and the binary search. It presents an elementary sort algorithm, the selection sort.

In a search problem, you are given

- An array of values
- The number of values in the array
- A search value

The search problem

The algorithm must determine whether the array contains a value equal to the search value. If it does, the algorithm must compute the index of the array where the value is located.

For example, suppose you declare the following variables:

```
List:      array [1..100] of integer
NumItems:  integer
SearchNum: integer
Found:     boolean
I:         integer
```

Also, suppose that NumItems has the value 4, and the first four values in List are

50   20   70   60

If SearchNum has the value 70, then the search algorithm should set Found to true and I to 3, because List [3] has the value 70. If SearchNum has the value 40, the algorithm should set Found to false. It does not matter what value it gives to I, because List does not contain the value 40.

The Sequential Search

The sequential search algorithm starts at the first of the list. It compares SearchNum with List [1], then List [2], and so on until it either finds SearchNum in List or it gets to the end of the list. One version of the algorithm follows.

```
I := 1;
while (I <= NumItems) and (List [I] <> SearchNum) do
    I := I + 1;
Found := (I <= NumItems)
```

The first version of the sequential search algorithm

If you trace this algorithm with a value of 70 for SearchNum, you will see that I first gets 1. The while expression is true because 1 is less than 4, and 50 is not equal to SearchNum. When I gets 2, the while expression is true again, because 2 is less than 4 and 20 is not equal to SearchNum.

When I gets 3, however, the while expression is false, because List [3] equals SearchNum. The loop terminates, and Found gets true. The value of I is the index of List where SearchNum was found.

If you trace the algorithm with 40 for the value of SearchNum, I will get 1, then 2, then 3, then 4. When I is 4, the while expression will still be true, so I will get 5. Then the expression

```
(I <= NumItems) and (List [I] <> SearchNum)
```

will be evaluated with I having a value of 5.

At this point in the execution, a subtle problem occurs. The first part of the expression is false since I is greater than NumItems. Theoretically, the second part of the expression does not need to be evaluated. Regardless of whether it is true or false, the entire expression will be false because of the first part.

There are two evaluation techniques in this situation. One is called full evaluation, and the other is called short circuit evaluation. The steps of the *full evaluation technique* are

- Evaluate the first part.
- Evaluate the second part.
- Perform the AND operation.

The steps of the *short circuit evaluation* are

- Evaluate the first part.
- If it is false, skip the second part.
- Otherwise, evaluate the second part.

With full evaluation, both parts are evaluated, regardless of whether the first part is true or false.

The Pascal standard permits either evaluation technique. In this example, if the compiler uses short circuit evaluation, the second part of the expression

```
(List [I] <> SearchNum)
```

will not be evaluated, with `I` having the value 5. But if the compiler uses full evaluation, it will be evaluated.

The subtle problem referred to earlier is that `List [5]` has an undefined value, so you cannot predict what will happen. You may argue that it does not matter what `List [5]` contains, since the second part of the expression can be true or false without affecting the value of the entire expression. But that argument might not be valid. Some compilers put special initial values in the variables at the beginning of the program. These compilers would detect that you are making a comparison with an undefined value and would crash. You can fix this problem by setting

```
List [NumItems + 1] := 0
```

at the beginning of the algorithm.

How fast is this algorithm? That depends on several things, namely how many items are in the list, whether the list contains the value of `SearchNum`, and if it does contain `SearchNum`, where it is located. Because the performance depends on these various factors, three categories of performance are commonly specified. They are

- Best-case performance
- Worst-case performance
- Average performance

In this algorithm, the best case is when `List [1]` contains the same value as `SearchNum`. The worst case is when the value of `SearchNum` is not in the `List` at all. The average case is somewhat difficult to define since it depends on the probability that `SearchNum` will be in the list. We will not pursue the problem of determining the average performance of the search algorithms.

Search algorithms are usually evaluated by counting the number of comparisons necessary to find the search item. This algorithm makes two comparisons each time it evaluates the `while` expression. They are

```
I <= NumItems
```

and

```
List [I] <> SearchNum
```

In the best case, the `while` expression is true the first time, the body of the loop never executes, and the algorithm makes two comparisons. Let n equal the value of `NumItems`. In the worst case, the algorithm searches the entire list, evaluating the `while` expression $n + 1$ times. So it makes $2n + 2$ comparisons.

Therefore, the performance of this algorithm is

- Best case: 2 comparisons

- Worst case: $2n + 2$ comparisons

Performance of the first version of the sequential search algorithm

If you search a list of 1000 items, then in the best case you will make two comparisons and in the worst case you will make 2002 comparisons.

With a little thought, you can improve this sequential search algorithm substantially. Think about the `while` expression. Why do you need the comparison of `I` with `NumItems`? Because, if `SearchNum` is not in the list, `I` would keep getting bigger and the loop would not terminate. You would not need the first comparison if you knew that `SearchNum` was in the list. You can guarantee that it will be in the list if you put it there yourself, before starting the loop.

A better version of the sequential search algorithm follows. The algorithm puts the value of `SearchNum` at the end of the list to act as a sentinel, if necessary.

```
List [NumItems + 1] := SearchNum;
I := 1;
while List [I] <> SearchNum do
   I := I + 1;
Found := (I <= NumItems)
```

A better version of the sequential search algorithm

Figure 7.10 is a trace of the algorithm when the item searched is in the list. `I` never reaches `NumItems + 1`.

Figure 7.11 is a trace when the item is not in the list. This time, `I` reaches `NumItems + 1`, and the value of `SearchNum` acts like a sentinel.

How much better is this version of the sequential search? Counting the comparisons as in the analysis of the previous version gives the following performance figures:

- Best case: 1 comparison

- Worst case: $n + 1$ comparisons

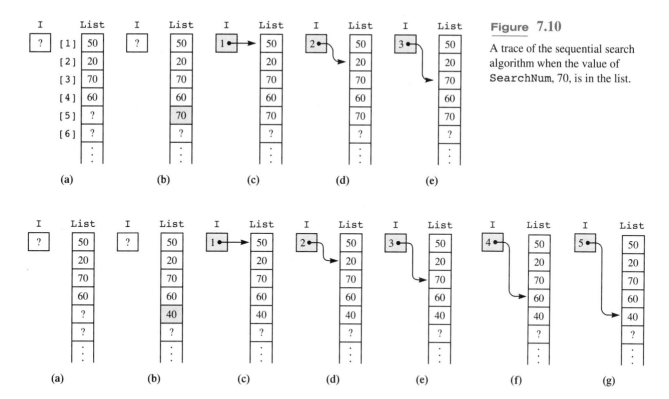

Figure 7.10

A trace of the sequential search algorithm when the value of `SearchNum`, 70, is in the list.

Figure 7.11

A trace of the sequential search algorithm when the value of `SearchNum`, 40, is not in the list.

If you search a list of 1000 items, in the best case you will make 1 comparison instead of 2 and in the worst case you will make 1001 comparisons instead of 2002. This version is substantially better than the first and is the one you should use whenever you need to do a sequential search.

▊ Program 7.12

In practice, you rarely will have to search for a numerical value in a single list of numbers. A more common need is to look up someone's name to retrieve additional information about the person. For example, you may want to search a list of names for a particular name to find the corresponding telephone number.

    The top level pseudocode outline of this problem is

The sequential search in practice

```
begin
```
Input the list of names and numbers.
Input the name to look up.
Look up the name in the list of names.
`if` *the name was in the list* `then`
    Output the corresponding number.
`else`
    Output a "no listing" message.
```
end
```

The first stepwise refinement pass for Program 7.12

Program 7.12 is a Pascal program that follows this outline. The sequential search algorithm is in the procedure `SeqSearch`.

```pascal
program LookUp (PhoneFile, input, output);
   const
      MaxEntries = 100;
   type
      NameType     = packed array [1..10] of char;
      NumType      = packed array [1..8] of char;
      NameLstType = array [1..MaxEntries] of NameType;
      NumLstType  = array [1..MaxEntries] of NumType;
   var
      PhoneFile:  text;
      NumEntries: integer;
      NameList:   NameLstType;
      NumberList: NumLstType;
      SearchName: NameType;
      Found:      boolean;
      Index:      integer;

   procedure GetNamesNumbers (var F:      text;
                              var NumEnt: integer;
                              var Names:  NameLstType;
                              var Nums:   NumLstType);
      var
         I, J: integer;
      begin
      readln (F, NumEnt);
      for I := 1 to NumEnt do
         begin
         for J := 1 to 10 do
            read (F, Names [I] [J]);
         for J := 1 to 8 do
            read (F, Nums [I] [J]);
         readln (F)
         end
      end;

   procedure GetString (var N: NameType);
      var
         I: integer;
      begin
      for I := 1 to 10 do
         if eoln (input) then
            N [I] := ' '
         else
            read (input, N [I]);
      readln (input)
      end;
```

Program 7.12

A program to look up a telephone number with the sequential search. It uses parallel arrays for the names and numbers.

```
        procedure SeqSearch (var Fnd:      boolean;            Program 7.12, continued
                             var I:        integer;
                                 NumEnt:   integer;
                             var Names:    NameLstType; {var for efficiency}
                                 SrchName: NameType);
      begin
      Names [NumEnt + 1] := SrchName;
      I := 1;
      while Names [I] <> SrchName do
         I := I + 1;
      Fnd := (I <> NumEnt + 1)
      end;

   begin
   reset (PhoneFile);
   GetNamesNumbers (PhoneFile, NumEntries, NameList, NumberList);
   write ('Enter name: ');
   GetString (SearchName);
   SeqSearch (Found, Index, NumEntries, NameList, SearchName);
   writeln;
   writeln ('Name: ', SearchName);
   if Found then
      writeln ('Number: ', NumberList [Index])
   else
      writeln ('Number: Not listed')
   end.
```

Input—PhoneFile

```
7
Pratt      242-1932
Hernandez  889-2505
Seymour    991-3800
Andrews    243-1056
Ward       123-4567
Jeffrey    765-4321
Packard    100-0000
```

Interactive Input/Output

```
Enter name: Andrews

Name: Andrews
Number: 243-1056
```

Interactive Input/Output

```
Enter name: Smith

Name: Smith
Number: Not listed
```

Program 7.12 uses the technique of *parallel arrays*. NameList is an array of words, and NumberList is an array of phone numbers. They are called parallel arrays because the number in a component of NumberList corresponds to the name in the same component of NameList. For example, the number in NumberList [4] is the phone number for the name in NameList [4]. The phone number for 'Andrews   ' is '243-1056'. Figure 7.12 shows the parallel arrays.

Parallel arrays

NameList		NumberList	
[1]	Pratt	[1]	242-1932
[2]	Hernandez	[2]	889-2505
[3]	Seymour	[3]	991-3800
[4]	Andrews	[4]	243-1056
[5]	Ward	[5]	123-4567
[6]	Jeffrey	[6]	765-4321
[7]	Packard	[7]	100-0000
[8]	?	[8]	?
	:		:

Figure 7.12

The parallel arrays of Program 7.12.

The main program calls procedure GetNamesNumbers to input the list of names and numbers into the parallel arrays. Input is with the count technique from the text file. All the parameters are called by reference, because the procedure changes the values of the actual parameters in the main program.

Then the main program prompts for the search name and calls procedure GetString, which is identical to procedure GetString in Program 7.7. It pads SearchName with spaces on the right.

The parameter list for procedure SeqSearch has NumEntries and SearchName called by value. The purpose of the procedure is not to change the values of these variables. The formal parameter Names could be called by value, but it is called by reference here for efficiency because of its large size. On the other hand, Found and Index are called by reference. Before calling the procedure, their values are undefined. The purpose of the procedure is to change these undefined values depending on the outcome of the search.

Procedure SeqSearch makes Found true or false. The main program tests Found to print the appropriate message. If Found is true it uses the value of I to print the number from the parallel array, NumberList.

The Binary Search

When you look up a word in a dictionary, you do not use the sequential search. If you want to look up the word *walrus*, you do not start at the front of the book and look sequentially from the first entry on. Instead, you use the fact that the words are in alphabetical order. You open the book to an arbitrary place and look at a word. If the word is greater than walrus, you know the word you are looking for is in the front part of the book. Otherwise it is in the back part.

This common idea is the basis of the binary search. To perform a binary search the list must be in order. The algorithm makes the initial selection at the midpoint of the list. After the first comparison, the algorithm knows which half of the list the item must be in.

The second comparison is at the midpoint of the proper half. After this comparison the algorithm knows which quarter of the list the item must be in.

The algorithm continues to split the known region in half until it finds the value or determines that it is not in the list. It gets the name "binary" from the fact that it divides the list into two equal parts with each comparison.

The variables for this algorithm are the same as those for the sequential search, except that three indices are necessary—`First`, `Mid`, and `Last`—instead of one index, `I`.

```
List:      array [1..100] of integer
NumItems:  integer
SearchNum: integer
Found:     boolean
First:     integer
Mid:       integer
Last:      integer
```

The variables `First` and `Last` will keep track of the boundaries of the list within which the search value must lie, if it is in the list at all. The algorithm initializes `First` to one and `Last` to `NumItems`. At the beginning of the loop, if `SearchNum` is in `List`, then

```
List [First] <= SearchNum <= List [Last]
```

will be true. It is the loop invariant.

The variable `Mid` will be the midpoint between `First` and `Last`. The algorithm compares `List [Mid]` with `SearchNum`. Depending on the test, it updates either `First` or `Last` such that the value is still between `List [First]` and `List [Last]`. When the algorithm terminates, `Mid` will be the index of the component of `List` that contains `SearchNum`. The binary search algorithm follows.

```
First := 1
Last := NumItems
Found := false
while (not Found) and (First <= Last) do
   begin
   Mid := (First + Last) div 2
   if SearchNum < List [Mid] then
      Last := Mid - 1
   else if SearchNum > List [Mid] then
      First := Mid + 1
   else
      Found := true
   end
```

The binary search algorithm

Figure 7.13 is a trace of the algorithm when the values of `List` are

10 30 40 50 60 70 90

and `SearchNum` is 40, a value in the list.

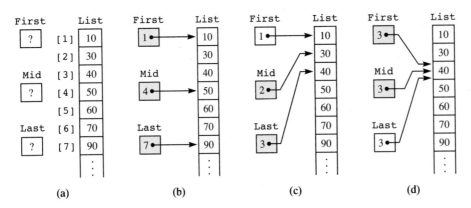

Figure 7.13

A trace of the binary search algorithm when the value of `SearchNum`, 40, is in the list.

The algorithm initializes `First` to 1 and `Last` to 7. `Mid` gets (1 + 7) div 2, which is 4, the midpoint between 1 and 7.

The `if` statement compares `SearchNum`, 40, with `List [Mid]`, 50. Since `SearchNum` is less than `List [Mid]`, the algorithm knows that the value cannot be in the bottom half of the list. So it updates `Last` to 1 less than `Mid`, which is 3. Notice how the loop invariant is still true. The search value, if it is in the list, must be between `List [1]` and `List [3]`.

The next time through the loop `Mid` gets 2, which is the midpoint between 1 and 3. After the comparison, `First` gets 3. The next time through the loop, `Mid` gets 3 also, and the loop terminates because `List [3]` has the same value as `SearchNum`.

Figure 7.14 is a trace with the same values as Figure 7.13 for `List`, but with a value of 80 for `SearchNum`, which is not in the list.

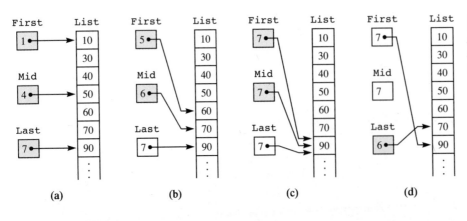

Figure 7.14

A trace of the binary search algorithm when the value of `SearchNum`, 80, is not in the list.

This time `First`, `Mid`, and `Last` eventually all get 7. Since `SearchNum`, 80, is less than `List [Mid]`, 90, the algorithm sets `Last` to `Mid - 1`, which is 6. In the figure, that causes `First` and `Last` to cross. Mathematically, `First > Last`, which causes the loop to terminate.

Does this algorithm look familiar? The bisection algorithm in Chapter 5 for finding the root of an equation was essentially a binary search. Figure 5.5 showed the variables `Left`, `Mid`, and `Right`, which correspond directly to `First`, `Mid`, and `Last`.

The difference is that the bisection algorithm searches for a real value on the continuous number line, while the binary search algorithm searches for a discrete value in an ordered array. The bisection algorithm updates the real variable `Mid` with

Comparison of the binary search with the bisection algorithm

```
Mid := (Left + Right) / 2.0
```

while the binary search algorithm updates the integer variable `Mid` with

```
Mid := (First + Last) div 2
```

How fast is this algorithm? As with the sequential search, that depends on several factors. The loop will terminate as soon as `SearchNum` equals `List [Mid]`. The best case is when they are equal the first time, which happens if the value is exactly in the middle of the list. The number of comparisons will be 4, assuming full evaluation of the `while` test.

The worst case is when the value is not in the list, both comparisons in the body of the `while` loop are made every time the body executes, and both comparisons in the `if` statements are made every time the body executes. That happens if `SearchNum` is always greater than `List [Mid]`. The worst case with the values of `List` that were just presented occurs with a value of 95 for `SearchNum`.

Each time the loop executes, it makes four comparisons. So the total number of comparisons is four times the number of times the loop executes. If `NumItems` has the value *n,* how many times will the loop execute?

The answer to that question is the same as the answer to the question, How many times must you cut an integer, *n,* in half to get to one? After all, each time the loop executes it eliminates half the possible locations for the value.

If you do not know the answer, you can use the problem-solving technique of going from the specific to the general. Let *t* equal the number of times. Here are some specific values of *n* and *t:*

$n = 16, t = 4$ times: 16   8   4   2   1
$n = 32, t = 5$ times: 32   16   8   4   2   1
$n = 64, t = 6$ times: 64   32   16   8   4   2   1

You can see that the general relationship between *n* and *t* is

$$n = 2^t$$

Size as a function of time

This relationship is approximately true even if *n* is not an exact power of 2. For example, if *n* is 40, the number of times you must halve it in order to get to 1 is either 5 or 6.

In mathematics, the logarithm to the base 10 is denoted log, and the logarithm to the base e is denoted ln. In computer science, logarithms are usually to the base 2. Rather than denote the logarithm to the base 2 with a different spelling, this book will denote it as log. Unless otherwise specified, log will mean logarithm to the base 2, not 10.

Logarithms in computer science are usually to the base 2.

The relationship between t and n can be written

$$t = \log n$$

Time as a function of size

by the definition of the logarithm. This is the number of times the loop executes in the worst case. Each time the loop executes, it makes 4 comparisons. So the number of comparisons is $4 \log n$.

Summarizing, the binary search has the following performance figures:

- Best case: 4 comparisons
- Worst case: $4 \log n$ comparisons

Performance of the binary search algorithm

The average case, however you define it, is somewhere between the best case and the worst case.

Figure 7.15 compares the binary search with the sequential search. It graphs the worst case number of comparisons for both algorithms as a function of n. If the number of items in the list is less than about 14, the sequential search is better than the binary search. But if the number of items is greater than 14, the binary search is better. For very large n, the binary search is much better. For example, if n is 1024, which is 2^{10}, the sequential search requires $n + 1 = 1025$ comparisons, but the binary search requires only $4(10) = 40$ comparisons. With a million items, the comparison is even more dramatic—about a million for the sequential search compared to 80 for the binary search!

This analysis produces the following guideline for selecting a search algorithm. If the number of items is less than about 10 or 20, use the sequential search. Otherwise use the binary search. The difference between the two algorithms in practice may not be noticeable even with 100 or so items. You may decide that the simpler code of the sequential search is better even with that number of items or more. Of course, you do not have a choice if the items are not in order. Then you cannot use the binary search.

This performance comparison is typical. For small amounts of data, a simple algorithm is best. But if you have large amounts of data to process, it pays to invest in a more complicated algorithm to speed up the processing. It is another example of a design tradeoff.

A design tradeoff

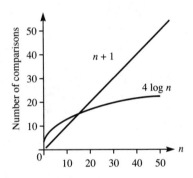

Figure 7.15

The worst case number of comparisons for the sequential search, $n + 1$, and the binary search, $4 \log n$.

The Selection Sort

Sort algorithms put lists of values in order. For example, if NumItems is 9 and the first 9 values of List are

The sort problem

7 3 8 2 1 4 9 5 6

then after the sort, the 9 values should be

1 2 3 4 5 6 7 8 9

The selection sort is based on the idea of finding the largest item in the list and putting it at the end. Then it finds the next largest and puts it next to the end. It continues finding the largest item in the top part of the list and putting it at the end of the top part until it gets to the top. Here is the first pass of the algorithm.

```
for N := NumItems downto 2 do
   begin
   Select the largest element from the top part
      of the list between List [1] and List [N].
   Put it in List [N].
   end
```

First pass of the selection sort

The first time the loop executes, N gets NumItems. So the largest element in the entire list is exchanged with the element at the bottom of the list.

The second time the loop executes, N gets NumItems - 1. So the largest element between List [1] and List [NumItems - 1] is exchanged with List [NumItems - 1]. At this point in the execution, the bottom two elements will be at their correct positions in the list.

Similarly, after the third execution of the loop the bottom three elements will be in their correct positions. The last time, N gets 2, after which the bottom N - 1 elements will be in their correct order. Therefore, the top one must be correct also.

The task for the second pass of the algorithm is to figure out how to put the largest element between List [1] and List [N] into List [N]. This is precisely the problem solved by procedure LargestLast in Section 7.1. Inserting this procedure call into the outer loop yields the following algorithm for the selection sort.

```
for N := NumItems downto 2 do
   LargestLast (List, N)
```

The selection sort algorithm

▣ Program 7.13

Program 7.13 is an implementation of the selection sort. Rather than call LargestLast, procedure SortList finds the location of the largest element directly and exchanges it with L [N].

Figure 7.16 is a trace of the outer loop of the selection sort algorithm. Figure 7.16(a) shows the original list. When N has the value 9 the first time the outer loop executes, the inner loop computes MaxIndex as 7, the index of the largest element between List [1] and List [9]. The algorithm exchanges List [9] with List [7].

Figure 7.16(b) shows the list after the first exchange. The second time the outer loop executes, MaxIndex is computed as 2, after which the algorithm exchanges List [8] with List [2]. At this point in the execution, the last two components are in order. The outer loop executes eight times, after which the entire list is in order.

How fast is the selection sort algorithm? Two criteria are common in the analysis of sort algorithms. One criterion counts the number of comparisons performed by the algorithm. The other counts the number of exchanges. In the selection sort, it is easier to count the number of comparisons.

```
program SelectionSort (DataFile, output);
   const
      MaxLength = 100;
   type
      ListType = array [1..MaxLength] of integer;
   var
      DataFile: text;
      List:     ListType;
      NumItems: integer;

   procedure GetList (var F:       text;
                      var NumItm: integer;
                      var L:       ListType);
      var
         I: integer;
      begin
      read (F, NumItm);
      for I := 1 to NumItm do
         read (F, L [I])
      end;

   procedure PutList (NumItm: integer; L: ListType);
      var
         I: integer;
      begin
      for I := 1 to NumItm do
         write (L [I]: 3);
      writeln
      end;

   procedure SortList (NumItm: integer; var L: ListType);
      var
         Temp:     integer;
         MaxIndex: integer;
         I, N:     integer;
      begin
      for N := NumItm downto 2 do
         begin
         MaxIndex := 1;
         for I := 2 to N do
            if L [I] > L [MaxIndex] then
               MaxIndex := I;
         Temp := L [N];
         L [N] := L [MaxIndex];
         L [MaxIndex] := Temp
         end
      end;
```

Program 7.13

Sorting a list of numbers with the selection sort algorithm.

Program 7.13, continued

```
begin
  reset (DataFile);
  GetList (DataFile, NumItems, List);
  writeln ('Original list:');
  PutList (NumItems, List);
  SortList (NumItems, List);
  writeln;
  writeln ('Sorted list:');
  PutList (NumItems, List)
end.
```

Input—DataFile

```
9
3  8  7  2  1  5  9  6  4
```

Output

```
Original list:
   3  8  7  2  1  5  9  6  4

Sorted list:
   1  2  3  4  5  6  7  8  9
```

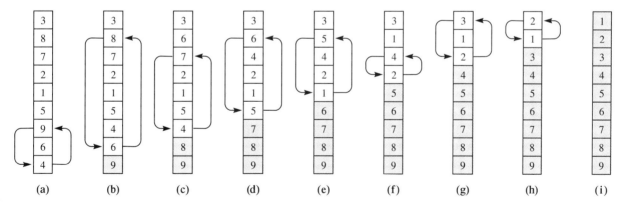

(a)   (b)   (c)   (d)   (e)   (f)   (g)   (h)   (i)

Figure 7.16

Eight executions of the outer loop of the selection sort. The shaded regions are the components of the array that are in order.

The inner loop makes one comparison each time it executes. So the number of comparisons is the number of times the inner loop executes. Let n be the value of NumItems. The first time the outer loop executes, the inner loop executes $n - 1$ times. The second time the outer loop executes, the inner loop executes one less time, which is $n - 2$. The third time the outer loop executes, the inner loop executes $n - 3$ times, and so on.

So the number of comparisons is

$$(n - 1) + (n - 2) + (n - 3) + \cdots + 3 + 2 + 1$$

which is the sum of the first $n - 1$ integers. You should recognize this problem from the statement execution count for the algorithm that prints a triangle in Section 5.5. Remember that the sum of the first m integers is $m(m + 1)/2$. So the sum of the first $n - 1$ integers is $(n - 1)(n - 1 + 1)/2$ or $n(n - 1)/2$, which is the number of comparisons the selection sort makes to sort n items.

Performance of the selection sort algorithm

Example 7.9 To sort 100 items requires $100(99)/2 = 4950$ comparisons. If you double the number of items to 200, the algorithm makes $200(199)/2 = 19,900$ comparisons. ∎

So doubling the number of items more than doubles the number of comparisons. Why? Because the number of comparisons is not linear in n. It is quadratic in n, since $n(n - 1)/2$ is the same as $(n^2 - n)/2$. That means doubling the number of items will approximately quadruple the number of comparisons. Four times 4950 is approximately 19,900.

Algorithm Complexity

Thus far, we have studied algorithms with three kinds of execution times, those proportional to log n, n, and n^2. Exercise 7.18 asks for a statement execution count of the matrix multiplication algorithm in Section 7.3. It has a doubly nested loop, and, as you may have guessed, its statement execution count is proportional to n^3 plus lower-order terms.

Computer scientists refer to an algorithm whose execution time is proportional to log n as an algorithm "with order log n complexity," or as an "order log n" algorithm. They abbreviate it with the O-notation as $O(\log n)$. Similarly, they call the other algorithms $O(n)$, $O(n^2)$, and $O(n^3)$.

The O-notation

The execution time of an algorithm that contains no loops is for all practical purposes independent of the data. Such algorithms are called "order one" algorithms, written $O(1)$.

This section concludes with a summary of techniques for estimating the execution time for algorithms with each of these orders. The problem is to estimate the execution time for one problem size, given the execution time for another size and the order of the algorithm. It is a generalization of the numerical estimates we have done in previous chapters.

The given time is usually for a smaller size. Typically, you test a program with a small data set and you want to estimate the time for a more realistic, larger set. We will assume that the size of the larger set for which the estimate is desired is r times the size of the set for which the execution time is known. T_1 will be the known time for the size n problem, and T_2 will be the time to estimate for the size rn problem.

Suppose the algorithm is $O(n)$. The time of execution is proportional to n plus a constant, say $an + b$ where a and b are constants. Setting up the usual ratio

Estimating run times for O(n) algorithms

$$\frac{T_1}{an + b} = \frac{T_2}{a(rn) + b}$$

Approximating the estimate by ignoring the low order b term gives $T_1/an = T_2/arn$ or $T_2 = rT_1$. Therefore, if you multiply the size of the problem by r, you multiply the execution time by r.

Example 7.10 Suppose an $O(n)$ algorithm requires 3 seconds to execute with 100 data values. How long will it take to execute with 250 values?

The ratio, r, is $250/100$, which is 2.5. So the execution time with the larger data set is $3(2.5)$, which is 7.5 seconds. ∎

Suppose the algorithm is $O(n^2)$. The time of execution is $an^2 + bn + c$ where a, b, and c are constants. This time the ratio is

Estimating run times for $O(n^2)$ algorithms

$$\frac{T_1}{an^2 + bn + c} = \frac{T_2}{a(rn)^2 + b(rn) + c}$$

Again approximating by ignoring the b and c terms, $T_1/an^2 = T_2/a(rn)^2$ or $T_2 = r^2T_1$. Therefore, if you multiply the size of the problem by r, you multiply the execution time by r^2.

Example 7.11 Suppose the algorithm of the previous example that required 3 seconds to execute with 100 data values is an $O(n^2)$ algorithm. How long will it take to execute with 250 values?

To execute with the larger data set requires $3(2.5)^2$, which is 19 seconds. ∎

A similar analysis will show that if you multiply the size of the problem for an $O(n^3)$ by r, the execution time will increase by a factor of r^3.

Estimating run times for $O(n^3)$ algorithms

An $O(\log n)$ algorithm requires $a \log n$ statement executions where a is a proportionality constant. The ratio is

$$\frac{T_1}{a \log n} = \frac{T_2}{a \log rn}$$

or $T_2 = T_1 (\log rn / \log n)$. Using the fact that the logarithm of a product is the sum of the logarithms,

Estimating run times for $O(\log n)$ algorithms

$$\frac{\log rn}{\log n} = \frac{\log n + \log r}{\log n} = 1 + \frac{\log r}{\log n}$$

These logarithms are to the base 2. The bad news is that most calculators do not have a base 2 log button. The good news is that you do not need one anyway. From mathematics, you know that the conversion formula from a base e logarithm to a base 2 logarithm is

$$\log x = 1.443 \ln x$$

See Exercise 7.25 if you are rusty on logarithmic conversions. Converting the base 2 logs gives the ratio

$$1 + \frac{\ln r}{\ln n}$$

where the logarithms are to the base *e*. Table 7.6 summarizes the estimation technique for each of these complexities.

Example 7.12 As in the previous examples, suppose an algorithm requires 3 seconds to execute with 100 data values. If the algorithm is $O(\log n)$, how long will it take to execute with 250 values?

The ratio of execution times is $1 + \ln 2.5/\ln 100$, which is 1.20. So the execution time with 250 data values is 3(1.20), or 3.6 seconds. That is much better than either the $O(n^2)$ algorithm, which took 19 seconds, or the $O(n)$ algorithm, which took 7.5 seconds. ■

Complexity	Multiply time by
$O(1)$	1
$O(\log n)$	$1 + \ln r/\ln n$
$O(n)$	r
$O(n^2)$	r^2
$O(n^3)$	r^3

Table 7.6

The effect on the execution time when you multiply the size of the problem by *r*.

7.5 Top-Down Design and Testing

We have looked at computer systems as a succession of levels of abstraction. A basic property of a level of abstraction is that a person can treat what is a collection of objects at one level as a single object at the next higher level.

The essence of abstraction

For example, even though a chair is a collection of parts—including upholstery, a cushion, legs, and a back—you normally treat it as one object. When you are tired you say, "I think I will sit on the chair." You do not say, "I think I will sit on the upholstery that is covering the cushion that is supported by the cross braces on top of the legs." You treat the collection of parts as one object, a chair.

The previous chapter presented functions and procedures as collections of Pascal statements. The collection of statements is *program abstraction*. A procedure lets you treat the sequence of operations performed by the collection of statements as one operation.

Program abstraction

This chapter has presented arrays as collections of values. The collection of values is *data abstraction*. An array lets you treat the collection of data values as one data object.

Data abstraction

Program `Rotate` of Program 7.3 illustrates both program abstraction and data abstraction. Figure 7.17 is its hierarchy diagram. The main program `Rotate` is at the higher level of abstraction. It calls procedures `GetList`, `PutList`, and

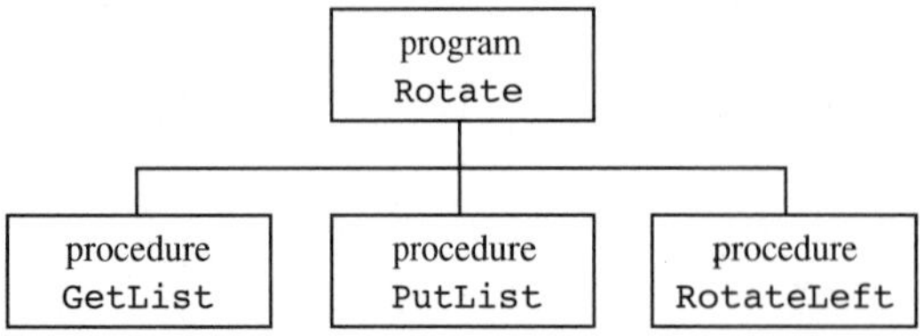

Figure 7.17

A hierarchy diagram of Program 7.3.

`RotateLeft`, which are at the lower level of abstraction.

Think of program `Rotate` as the president of a company. What viewpoint does he have of the procedures, which are the vice presidents, and of the data?

The main program consists of the president ordering the vice presidents to do what the president perceives as a single operation. For example, twice the president orders the vice president in charge of output to print the list on the screen. The president doesn't see the loop in the procedure that is necessary for performing the task. He thinks in terms of one list output operation. That is program abstraction.

Similarly, the president gives the entire list to each vice president so they can do their assigned tasks. The president does not think in terms of individual components of the list. Look at the variable declaration part of the main program. There is no integer, I, for accessing a particular component of List. The president thinks in terms of one list data object. That is data abstraction.

The effect of program and data abstraction at Level 6 is to create a more refined level structure in the system. Figure 7.18(a) shows the original level structure. Level 6, the high-order language level, is between Levels 7 and 5. Figure 7.18(b) shows the effect of program and data abstraction. When you design software with program and data abstraction, you split Level 6 into two levels, 6a and 6b. The same concepts that distinguish one level from another in the original system, say Level 7 and Level 6, distinguish the two new levels, 6a and 6b.

Each level has its own language. A statement in a language is an instruction the computer executes. Execution of a statement at Level 7 triggers the execution of many statements at Level 6.

For example, a word-search statement in a word processing application causes many Pascal statements to execute. The Level 7 users treat the search command as one statement. They do not need to know anything about the details of the language at Level 6. As far as they are concerned, the computer is executing a single search command. But Pascal programmers at Level 6 know better. They know that the single search command issued by users at Level 7 requires the execution of many Pascal statements at Level 6.

The same principle applies between Levels 6a and 6b. In Figure 7.17, procedure RotateLeft is a collection of primitive Pascal statements, such as the for statement and the assignment statement. They operate on the individual components of the array. They are the statements and the data at Level 6a.

But the language at Level 6b is not that detailed. Statements at Level 6b are the GetList statement, the PutList statement, and the RotateLeft statement. They operate on an entire list.

The statements in a language at one level should hide the irrelevant details of the language at the next lower level. The job of a designer at any particular level is to present a language, in other words a set of instructions and data objects, that are convenient for the user at the next higher level. The ultimate goal of designers at every level is to assist the person at the very top level to solve a problem. They do it by inventing languages at each level that hide irrelevant details of the level just below.

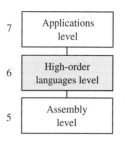

(a) The original level structure.

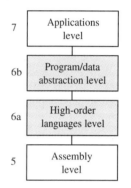

(b) Adding a level of abstraction.

Figure 7.18

Creating a more refined level structure in the system.

Hiding irrelevant detail

Top-Down Design

Data and program abstraction are the basis of a design technique called *top-down design*. It is especially appropriate when you are faced with a large programming project. The technique consists of three steps:

- Understand the problem.
- Subdivide the problem into modules.
- Write and test the modules top-down.

The three steps of top-down design

Top-down design and stepwise refinement share the philosophy of working from the more general and abstract to the more specific and detailed.

Your first job is to understand in detail what the program should do. If a user's guide will be produced with the program, it should be written first. Another way to make sure you understand the problem is to write down some sample input data and try to write down by hand what the corresponding output should be.

Understand the problem

Your next step is to break up the large problem into several smaller problems. The smaller problems are called *modules*. In this book, a module is either a main program, a function, or a procedure. (In the field of software design, a module sometimes has a slightly different meaning.)

Subdivide the problem into modules

Modules have two important characteristics:

- A module should be organized logically to do one specific task.
- A module should not be excessively long.

Two desirable characteristics of modules

Modules should be short so they will be easy to read and comprehend. Specifically, the control statements should not be nested more than about four to six levels deep. The executable statements should not occupy more than about one to two pages in a program listing.

After deciding on the subdivision of your program into modules, the next step is to write each module in Pascal. Top-down design now enters the picture. The top-down design principle is

- Always finish writing a module before you write any of the ones below it.

The top-down design principle

For example, in Figure 7.17, you should write program `Rotate` in complete detail first. Then you have your choice of three procedures to write next—either `GetList`, `PutList`, or `RotateLeft`.

A natural tendency is to write the bottom modules first then, when they are complete, to put them together into the module above. This design approach is called *bottom-up*.

Bottom-up versus top-down design

In practice, bottom-up design has proven to be inferior to top-down design. The reason is that as you write each module, you will discover that you must make certain changes in your plans. For example, as you progress you might find it more convenient to change the organization of a parameter list or change the way a module should be subdivided into smaller modules.

Furthermore, a small change in one module at a top level may require many changes in many modules at the bottom levels. If you discover a problem in a top-level module, it is much easier to correct it before the bottom modules have been written.

In bottom-up design, the bottom modules are frequently written with only a vague idea of how the parent modules will use them. Then, when the parent module is written, it is discovered that the bottom modules do not fit. That is, they do not perform the necessary task for the parent module in a convenient way.

Top-Down Testing

To verify that your program works correctly you must test it with sample input data and examine the output. Testing a large program only after it is completely written can be a problem. It would be better to test as you write. Then, any design problems that are discovered during the test can be corrected before they are compounded in further writing.

There are two solutions to the testing problem, depending on whether you design top-down or bottom-up. *Stubs* are for testing modules if you develop the program top-down. A stub is a group of `writeln` or assignment statements that simulate execution of a module for testing its calling module. *Drivers* are for testing modules if you develop the program bottom-up. A driver is a small main program for testing a module.

Stubs and drivers

Program 7.14

The top-down principle applied to Figure 7.17 says to write the main program `Rotate` before writing any of the procedures, `GetList`, `PutList`, or `RotateList`. How can you test the main program before you complete the procedures? Program 7.14 shows how to test the main program with testing stubs in the procedures.

The testing stubs are the statements in the procedure blocks. The stub for the `GetList` procedure is

```
writeln ('GetList called.');
L [1] := 1.0
```

The stub lets you compile and test the main program before completing the statements in `GetList`. It lets you postpone development of the lower level until you debug the higher level.

The purpose of procedure `GetList` is to input values from a file and give them to `List` in the main program. The assignment statement gives a value to just the first component of `L`. It simulates a read from the file, which should change the value of `List [1]` in the main program.

You must write the formal parameters as they will appear in the finished program. Otherwise, program `Rotate` will not compile and execute. But you do not need to write the local variable declaration parts of any of the procedures.

The output statements in the stubs are there to trace the execution. You can check the output of the program to verify that the main program called the procedures successfully. Since `1.00` appears in the output after `GetList` is called, you know that the parameter lists of `GetList` and `PutList` are correct. And since `2.00` appears after `RotateLeft` is called, you know its parameter list is set up

```
program Rotate (DataFile, output);
   const
      MaxLength = 100;
   type
      ListType = array [1..MaxLength] of real;
   var
      NumItems: integer;
      List:      ListType;
      DataFile: text;

   procedure GetList (var F:      text;
                      var L:      ListType;
                      var NumItm: integer);
      begin
      writeln ('GetList called.');
      L [1] := 1.0
      end;

   procedure PutList (L: ListType; NumItm: integer);
      begin
      write ('PutList called.  ');
      writeln (L [1]: 4: 2)
      end;

   procedure RotateLeft (var L: ListType; NumItm: integer);
      begin
      writeln ('RotateLeft called.');
      L [1] := 2.0
      end;

   begin
   GetList (DataFile, List, NumItems);
   PutList (List, NumItems);
   RotateLeft (List, NumItems);
   writeln;
   PutList (List, NumItems)
   end.
```

Program 7.14

A top-down test with stubs in the procedures. You can test the main program before you finish the procedures.

Input—DataFile

```
4
   5.0   -2.3   8.0   0.1
```

Output

```
GetList called.
PutList called.  1.00
RotateLeft called.

PutList called.  2.00
```

correctly. For example, had you mistakenly used call by value instead of call by reference for L in `RotateLeft`, the output would still be `1.00` instead of `2.00`.

This top-down testing technique is a powerful development tool. Suppose you finish the entire program before attempting to test it. Then when you test it you discover a bug. That bug could be in any one of your modules. On the other hand, if you test each module as you complete it, you can be relatively sure that any bugs that arise are in the single module you just wrote. Consequently, bugs are much easier to find and correct when you test as you write.

◻ Program 7.15

The following program is an example of top-down design and testing. The input for this problem is a text file such as this:

```
Hook       Captain    30.00    25.0
Pan        Peter      10.50    60.0
Darling    Wendy       8.50    45.0
Darling    John        6.50    20.0
Darling    Michael     1.50    10.0
Bell       Tinker     10.00    50.0
zzzzzzzzzz              0.00     0.0
```

Input for Program 7.15

Each line of the file contains a last name and a first name with 10 letters each, an hourly rate, and the number of hours worked in a week. The bottom line of the file is a sentinel.

The output is a report that lists the last name and first initial of each person and his or her wage, including the possibility of overtime. The total of all the wages appears at the bottom of the report.

```
----------------------
Name            Wages
----------------------
Hook       C     750.00
Pan        P     735.00
Darling    W     403.75
Darling    J     130.00
Darling    M      15.00
Bell       T     550.00
----------------------
Total:          2583.75
```

Output for Program 7.15

Here is a pseudocode outline of the problem:

```
begin
Output heading.
TotalWages := 0.00
Input first line.
```

The first pass of Program 7.15

```
while LastName <> Sentinel do
   begin
   Compute Wages
   Output detail line.
   TotalWages := TotalWages + Wages
   Input next line.
   end
Output footing, TotalWages
end
```

Now there are two ways to continue. The first is to use stepwise refinement, translating each statement into Pascal. This design approach would result in one large program without procedures or functions. This second is to use top-down design, dividing the problem into modules.

Stepwise refinement versus top-down design

From the pseudocode outline, it appears that the following modules will be helpful:

- **PutHeading** to output the heading of the report

- **GetLine** to get the next input line

- **CalcWage** to calculate the wage

- **PutFooting** to output the footing of the report

The top-down design principle states that we must write and debug the top module first. Program 7.15 shows the result.

```
program EmployeeWages (EmplFile, output);
   const
      Sentinel = 'zzzzzzzzzz';
   type
      Str10Type = packed array [1..10] of char;
   var
      LastName:    Str10Type;
      FirstName:   Str10Type;
      HourlyRate:  real;
      HoursWorked: real;
      Wages:       real;
      TotalWages:  real;
      EmplFile:    text;

   procedure PutHeading;
      begin
      writeln ('PutHeading called.')
      end;
```

Program 7.15

A top-down test with stubs in the function and procedures.

Program 7.15, continued

```
procedure GetLine (var F:              text;
                   var LName, FName:   Str10Type;
                   var HRate, HWorked: real);
   begin
   LName := 'Test      ';
   FName := 'Test      ';
   HRate := 0.00;
   HWorked := 0.0;
   writeln ('GetLine called.')
   end;

function CalcWage (HRate, HWorked: real): real;
   begin
   CalcWage := 1.00;
   writeln ('CalcWage called.')
   end;

procedure PutFooting (W: real);
   begin
   writeln ('PutFooting called.')
   end;

begin
reset (EmplFile);
PutHeading;
TotalWages := 0.00;
GetLine (EmplFile, LastName, FirstName, HourlyRate, HoursWorked);
while LastName <> Sentinel do
   begin
   Wages := CalcWage (HourlyRate, HoursWorked);
   writeln (LastName, FirstName [1]: 2, Wages: 8: 2);
   TotalWages := TotalWages + Wages;
   GetLine (EmplFile, LastName, FirstName, HourlyRate, HoursWorked);
   LastName := Sentinel
   end;
PutFooting (TotalWages)
end.
```

Input—EmplFile

See text.

Output

```
PutHeading called.
GetLine called.
CalcWage called.
Test       T    1.00
GetLine called.
PutFooting called.
```

In it, all the procedures called by the main program are declared, complete with formal parameter lists. Their bodies simply contain stubs that print a short message to verify they have been called properly by the top module.

The stub for procedure `GetLine` contains assignment statements. The purpose of `GetLine` is to get values from the file for the input variables. Furthermore, the test in the `while` loop assumes `LastName` has obtained a value from the file. The assignment statements in `GetLine` simulate the input operation so the `while` statement can be executed properly. Similarly, the assignment statement in the stub of function `CalcWage` simulates the calculation that it will eventually do in the finished program.

The main program contains one extraneous statement. The assignment statement that gives the sentinel value to `LastName` is necessary to keep the loop from repeating endlessly. It must be removed from the finished program.

Advantages of Top-Down Design

This example tests the top module. Writing the top module first forces you to define how all the procedures will fit together in the overall design. Avoiding the use of global variables forces you to decide on which information is necessary to pass through the parameter lists. But that is only possible if you have a clear idea of what the procedure needs to know to do its job. That is, writing the top module first forces you to think about your overall plan of attack.

Ensuring that the pieces fit together

Another benefit of top-down testing is that little code is wasted in the testing process. For example, suppose you decide to write the `PutFooting` module next. The only piece of code you need to discard is the single

Little wasted code

```
writeln ('PutFooting called.')
```

statement. You can insert the variable declaration part before the `begin`. And even the `begin` and `end` words will remain in the finished program.

What if you write the program bottom-up and want to test as you write? Say you write `PutFooting` first and want to test it before proceeding. You would need to write a short main program that calls `PutFooting`. A main program written for the sole purpose of testing a module is a driver. When you finally integrate the module into the program, you must discard the driver. You can see that much more unnecessary code is involved in writing a driver than in writing a stub.

SUMMARY

An array is a collection of values, each one of which must be the same type. You refer to the component of an array by supplying a value for a subscript, also called an index. A fixed length string is an array whose type is char. If the array of characters is packed, Pascal allows you to output its value, assign a string value, and compare for alphabetical order, all without a loop. A two-dimensional array contains two indices and can be visualized as a table of values organized into rows and columns.

The basic Pascal character-processing algorithm processes individual characters and lines from text files. It contains a nested loop, with the outer loop testing for the end of the file with `eof` and the inner loop testing for the end of a line with `eoln`. Character processing takes place within the inner loop, and line processing takes place within the outer loop.

In the search problem, you are given an array of values and a search value. The algorithm must determine whether the array contains a value equal to the search value. If it does, the algorithm must compute the index of the array where the value is located. The sequential search inspects the array values one after the other until it finds the search value. The worst-case statement execution count for the sequential search is proportional to n, the number of elements to search. The binary search is possible if the array is in order. It inspects the item in the middle of the array and eliminates half of the values in the array based on this one comparison. The worst-case statement execution count for the binary search is proportional to $n \log n$.

In the sort problem, you are given an array of unordered values. The algorithm must put them in order. The selection sort continually selects the largest element in the top part of the list and puts it at the bottom. The worst-case statement execution count for the selection sort is proportional to n^2.

Top-down design is a technique for software development that is based on levels of abstraction. A module is defined as a main program, a procedure, or a function. The top-down design principle can be stated as follows: Always finish writing a module before you write any of the ones below it. The principle implies that you must write the top-level main program first. A stub is a group of `writeln` or assignment statements that simulate execution of a module for testing its calling module.

EXERCISES

Section 7.1

1. Predict the output of Program 7.1 if the two loops are modified as follows:

*(a)
```
for I := 1 to 4 do
   read (DataFile, List [I]);
for I := 1 to 4 do
   write (List [I]: 6: 1)
```

*(b)
```
for I := 4 downto 1 do
   read (DataFile, List [I]);
for I := 1 to 4 do
   write (List [I]: 6: 1)
```

(c)
```
for I := 1 to 4 do
   read (DataFile, List [I]);
for I := 4 to 7 do
   write (List [I mod 4 + 1]: 6: 1)
```

(d)
```
for I := 4 to 7 do
   read (DataFile, List [I mod 4 + 1]);
for I := 1 to 4 do
   write (List [I]: 6: 1)
```

2. Suppose I and N are integers and V is an `array [1..10] of real` in the following code:

```
I := N;
while I >= 1 do
   begin
   write (V [I]: 5: 1);
   I := I - 2
   end
```

* (a) What is the output if N is 6 and the values of V are

     4.0   3.0   5.1   1.0   –7.0   8.5

(b) What is the output if N is 7 and the values of V are

     4.0   3.0   5.1   1.0   –7.0   8.5   2.0

3. If I is an integer and V is an array of integers, what is the output of the following code?

```
for I := 1 to 4 do
   V [I] := 2 * I;
for I := 4 downto 2 do
   V [I] := V [I - 1] + 1;
for I := 1 to 4 do
   write (V [I]: 3)
```

4. How many statements does procedure `RotateLeft` of Program 7.3 execute if the value of `NumItm` is *n*?

5. Your friend writes the following statements in procedure `RotateLeft` of Program 7.3.

```
for I := 1 to NumItm do
   if I = 1 then
       Temp := L [I]
   else
       L [I - 1] := L [I];
L [NumItm] := Temp
```

* (a) Does your friend's code work correctly? (b) How many statements execute if the value of `NumItm` is *n*? Compare this count with that of the previous exercise.

* 6. Your friend writes the following statements in procedure `RotateLeft` of Program 7.3. and renames the procedure `RotateRight`. If the program runs with the data of Program 7.3, what is the output?

```
Temp := L [NumItm];
for I := 1 to NumItm - 1 do
   L [I + 1] := L [I];
L [1] := Temp
```

7. Determine the statement execution count for both versions of procedure `Initialize` if the value of `NumItm` is *n*.

8. What would procedure `Reverse` do if you changed the `for` statement to

```
for I := NumItm downto 1 do
```

*9. Determine the statement execution count of program `GradeCount` in Program 7.4 if there are *n* grades in `GradeFile`.

10. Storage is allocated for how many real values with the following types?

   *(a) `array [0..6] of real`   (b) `array [-6..6] of real`

Section 7.2

11. Suppose `Word` is a `packed array [1..4] of char`. *(a) Is `read (Word)` a legal statement? *(b) Is `write (Word)` a legal statement? (c) Is `Word :='boat'` a legal statement? (d) Is `Word := 'bat'` a legal statement?

12. When a program begins execution, what is the value of `eoln (input)`?

13. *(a) In the ASCII character set, which is greater, 'cat' or 'Cat'? (b) Which is greater in the EBCDIC character set?

*14. Suppose `SomeFile` contains

```
aaaaa
bbbbb
ccccc
```

What is the total statement execution count for the basic Pascal character processing algorithm? Count *Perform character processing* and *Perform line processing* as individual statements.

15. Answer Exercise 14 as if `SomeFile` contains *m* lines with *n* characters in each line.

16. Answer Exercise 14 as if `SomeFile` contains *m* empty lines.

Section 7.3

17. Predict the output of Program 7.9 if the code is modified as follows:

   *(a)
```
read (DataFile, NumCols, NumRows);
for I := 1 to NumRows do
   for J := 1 to NumCols do
      read (DataFile, Matrix [I, J]);
for I := 1 to NumRows do
   begin
   for J := 1 to NumCols do
      write (Matrix [I, J]: 6: 1);
   writeln
   end
```

   (b)
```
read (DataFile, NumRows, NumCols);
for I := 1 to NumRows do
   for J := 1 to NumCols do
      read (DataFile, Matrix [I, J]);
for J := 1 to NumCols do
   begin
   for I := 1 to NumRows do
      write (Matrix [I, J]: 6: 1);
   writeln
   end
```

18. **(a)** How many statements does the code fragment for the matrix multiplication algorithm execute if the value of `SideLength` is 3? **(b)** How many statements execute if the value of `SideLength` is *n*? **(c)** If it takes 50 ms to execute with *n* = 25, how many seconds will it take to execute with *n* = 60?

Section 7.4

* 19. Suppose the value of `NumItm` in function `Maximum` (see p. 298) is *n*. **(a)** When does the best case occur? **(b)** What is the total statement execution count for this function in the best case? **(c)** When does the worst case occur? **(d)** What is the total statement execution count for this function in the worst case?

20. Suppose the value of `NumItm` in procedure `LargestLast` (see p. 300) is *n*. **(a)** When does the best case occur? **(b)** What is the total statement execution count for this procedure in the best case? **(c)** When does the worst case occur? **(d)** What is the total statement execution count for this procedure in the worst case?

21. `List` is an `array [1..5] of integer` and `I` is an integer. The following code is supposed to output the values up to but not including a value of –1, which may be in the list.

```
I := 1;
while (I <= 5) and (List [I] <> -1) do
    begin
    write (List [I]);
    I := I + 1
    end
```

* **(a)** What happens if the values in `List` are

   50   30   –1   0   0

and the compiler uses full evaluation? **(b)** What happens if the values in `List` are

   50   30   70   10   20

and the compiler uses full evaluation? **(c)** Answer part (a) if the compiler uses short circuit evaluation. **(d)** Answer part (b) if the compiler uses short circuit evaluation.

22. Trace the values of `First`, `Mid`, and `Last` in the binary search algorithm when the values of `List` are

   10   30   40   50   60   70   90

and the value of `SearchNum` is

* **(a)** 5   **(b)** 10   **(c)** 20
   (d) 50   **(e)** 90   **(f)** 95

23. Trace the execution of the outer loop of the selection sort algorithm as shown in Figure 7.16 with the following input.

* **(a)** 7   3   8   2   5   4   9   1   6
   (b) 9   8   7   6   5   4   3   2   1
   (c) 9   1   2   3   4   5   6   7   8
   (d) 2   3   4   5   6   7   8   9   1

24. A sorting algorithm is called *stable* if, when two items are identical, the items maintain the order after the sort that they had before the sort. For example, suppose you want to sort `NameList` as declared in Program 7.12, and there are two different Smith's in the array, one with index three and the other with index five. If a sort is stable, the final array will have the two Smith's adjacent with the Smith that had index three coming before the Smith that had index five. Is the selection sort in Program 7.13 stable? Explain.

25. Use the chain rule for logarithms

$$(\log_a b)(\log_b c) = \log_a c$$

to show that

$$\log x = 1.443 \ln x$$

where $\log x$ is the logarithm to the base 2 and $\ln x$ is the logarithm to the base e.

* 26. An algorithm requires 4 seconds to execute with 200 data values. How long does it take to execute with 1000 values (a) if the algorithm is $O(1)$, (b) if the algorithm is $O(\log n)$, (c) if the algorithm is $O(n)$, (d) if the algorithm is $O(n^2)$, and (e) if the algorithm is $O(n^3)$?

27. An algorithm requires 60 ms to execute with 300 data values. How long does it take to execute with 5000 values (a) if the algorithm is $O(1)$, (b) if the algorithm is $O(\log n)$, (c) if the algorithm is $O(n)$, (d) if the algorithm is $O(n^2)$, and (e) if the algorithm is $O(n^3)$?

PROBLEMS

Section 7.1

28. An input file contains an integer that indicates how many real numbers follow. Write a program that inputs the real numbers into an array and also does the following: outputs every other number starting with the first, outputs every other number starting with the second, outputs every negative number, and outputs how many negative numbers were in the list. Your one program should produce all the following output.

Sample Input

```
7

5.1   23.2   -6.2   1.0   -19.6   -13.0   4.8
```

Sample Output

```
Every other one from first:
    5.1    -6.2   -19.6     4.8

Every other one from second:
   23.2     1.0   -13.0

Every negative:
   -6.2   -19.6   -13.0

The list has 3 negative numbers.
```

29. Rewrite procedure `GetList` of Program 7.3 to input the data with the sentinel technique, assuming the sentinel value is greater than 1e30. Do not change the parameters of `GetList`. Test the program without making any other changes to any other code.

30. Rewrite procedure `GetList` of Program 7.3 to input the data from a nontext file of real values with the `eof` technique. Do not change the parameters of `GetList`. Test the program without making any other changes to any other code.

31. Write a procedure, `RotateRight`, with the same parameter list as `RotateLeft` in Program 7.3. Your procedure should rotate the numbers to the right instead of to the left. Test the procedure in a program similar to Program 7.3.

32. Modify procedure `RotateLeft` in Program 7.3 to rotate the items two places to the left instead of only one. For example, if `List` has the same initial values as in the example, its values after the procedure is called should be

    8.0   0.1   5.0   −2.3

Use only one `for` statement. Test the procedure in a program similar to Program 7.3.

33. Write procedure `Shuffle` with the same parameter list as `RotateLeft` in Program 7.3. The procedure should shuffle the values like a perfect shuffle of a card deck. Split the deck into two equal stacks and build the shuffled deck by alternately taking cards from the top of each stack. If the original list is

    1.0   2.0   3.0   4.0   5.0   6.0   7.0   8.0   9.0

then after the shuffle the list would be

    1.0   6.0   2.0   7.0   3.0   8.0   4.0   9.0   5.0

Test the procedure in a program similar to Program 7.3 with values from a file using the count technique. Do not include any output statements in `Shuffle`.

34. Write function `FirstOdd` with the same parameter list as function `Maximum` (see p. 298) except that `L` is an array of integers and `FirstOdd` has type integer. The function should return a value that is the first odd integer in the list, or zero if there are no odd integers. Test your function with interactive I/O. Do not use any input or output statements in the function.

35. Write procedure `InitOneZero` with the same parameter list as procedure `Initialize` (see p. 301) that sets the values of `L` to alternating ones and zeros. For example, if `NumItm` is 7, the values of `L` should be

    1   0   1   0   1   0   1

Test your procedure with interactive I/O, prompting the user for the number of values. Do not include any output statements in `InitOneZero`.

36. Write procedure `InitPairs` with the same parameter list as procedure `Initialize` (see p. 301) that sets the values of `L` to alternating pairs of ones and zeros. For example, if `NumItm` is 7, the values of `L` should be

    1   1   0   0   1   1   0

Test your procedure with interactive I/O, prompting the user for the number of values. Do not include any output statements in `InitPairs`.

37. Program 6.17 generated a random sequence of 15 integers between 1 and 10. With a seed of 853, the integers 1, 2, 3, 5, 7, and 8 each occurred twice and the integer 10 did not appear. Write a procedure

```
InitRandom (var L: ListType; NumItm, Seed: integer)
```

that puts random integer values between 1 and NumItm in the first NumItm components of L without any repeating values. Initialize the list with sequential integer values, then make one sweep through the list to exchange each component with another component chosen at random. For example, if NumItm is 7, initialize L to

    1 2 3 4 5 6 7

Then interchange L [1] with another component chosen at random, L [2] with another component chosen at random, and so on. Test your procedure with interactive I/O, prompting the user for the seed and the number of values. Do not include any output statements in InitRandom.

38. Write procedure Reverse (see p. 302) without the local variable, ListB. Exchange the first component with the last component in ListA. Then exchange the second with the next to last, and so on. Test your procedure with a program similar to Program 7.3 with data from a file using the count technique. Do not include any output statements in Reverse.

39. Declare

```
procedure Maximum (var Max, Occurs: integer;
                        L:          ListType;
                        NumItm:     integer)
```

which computes the maximum value and the number of times the value occurs in the array of integers, L. You should make only one pass through the array. Test your procedure with a program similar to Program 7.3 with data from a file using the count technique. Do not include any output statements in Maximum.

40. Write a program using the technique of Program 7.4 to count the number of each kind of animal in ZooFile as declared in Program 5.10. Declare an array of integers called AnimalCount whose indices have type AnimalType to tabulate the number of each kind of animal. Output the counts in a horizontal table as in Program 7.4.

41. Write a program whose input is a nontext file of real values. Declare Count to be an array [0..9] of integer. Use Count [I] to store the number of real values in the following intervals:

    Count [0] $x \le 10.0$
    Count [1] $10.0 \le x < 20.0$
    Count [2] $20.0 \le x < 30.0$
            .
            .
            .
    Count [8] $80.0 \le x < 90.0$
    Count [9] $90.0 \le x$

For a value, *x,* greater than or equal to 0.0 and less than 100.0, use the fact that trunc (x / 10.0) is the index of Count that should be incremented. Output the counts in bar chart form as in Program 6.6. (A bar chart of counts is called a *histogram.*)

Section 7.2

42. Write a program that asks the user to type a sequence of up to 40 characters. Output the sequence as it was typed, followed by the same sequence with any lowercase letters converted to uppercase letters. Do not try to convert a space or punctuation mark into an uppercase character. An example follows.

Sample Input/Output

```
Please type a string of characters: How much?

You typed: How much?
In uppercase it is: HOW MUCH?
```

43. Computer spelling checkers generally look for words in a dictionary that are close to a given misspelled word. Declare

```
type
    DiffType = (Equal, DiffByOne, DiffByMany);
```

```
function DiffWords (Wd1, Wd2: StrType): DiffType
```

where `StrType` is defined as in Program 7.7. `DiffWords` must return `Equal` if `Wd1` and `Wd2` are the same, `DiffByOne` if they differ by exactly one character, and `DiffByMany` if they differ by more than one character. Test your function with interactive I/O using procedure `GetString`.

44. In a variation on the previous problem, one word may differ from another word because it omits one letter. Declare

```
function DiffOmit (LongWd, ShortWd: StrType): boolean
```

which is true if `ShortWd` is identical to `LongWd`, except that it is missing one letter contained in `LongWd`. For example, the function should be true if `LongWd` is `'boat '` and `ShortWd` is `'bat '`. Test your function with interactive I/O using procedure `GetString`.

45. Procedure `GetString` in Program 7.7 pads unused trailing characters with spaces. You sometimes need to print the values of a packed array without the trailing spaces. For example, if array `Name` has 15 characters whose values are `'Tom Smith '`, the statement

```
writeln ('Hi ', Name, '.  How are you?')
```

will output

```
Hi Tom Smith    .  How are you?
```

Declare

```
procedure PutString (S: StrType)
```

which outputs all the characters of `S` except for the trailing spaces. Test your program with interactive I/O using procedure `GetString`. For example, the code fragment

```
write ('Hi ');
PutString (Name);
writeln ('.  How are you?')
```

should output

```
Hi Tom Smith.  How are you?
```

46. A palindrome is a word that is the same spelled backward or forward. For example, radar is a palindrome but bulb is not, because in reverse order it would be blub. Declare the function

```
IsPalindrome (S: StrType): boolean
```

to determine if S is a palindrome. Test it with interactive I/O using GetString. Assume the user will not enter any spaces within or before the word.

47. Remove the two deficiencies from Program 7.8 mentioned in the text. Store the truncated value of Word.

48. Declare Count to be an `array ['a'..'z'] of integer`. Use it to count the number of each letter from a text file. Convert any uppercase characters to lowercase for counting purposes. Do not count punctuation marks or digits. Output the counts in bar chart form as in Program 6.6.

49. Improve your solution to Problem 48 by scaling down the length of the bars if the longest one will not fit on a single line. Scale each bar such that the longest contains 50 asterisks.

50. Write a program to output the words from a text file on separate lines. Consider a word to be terminated by a space or the end of a line.

Sample Input

```
Here is
a sentence. Another
sentence.
```

Sample Output

```
Here
is
a
sentence.
Another
sentence.
```

51. Write a program that outputs a text file on the screen with all groups of two or more adjacent spaces collapsed into one space and with no leading spaces at the beginning of any line. Do not declare any arrays in your program.

Sample Input

```
   This     has
a lot         of
      spaces.
```

Sample Output

```
This has
a lot of
spaces.
```

52. Write a program to count the number of letters, words, and sentences in a text file. A letter can be uppercase or lowercase, but does not include any digits or punctuation marks. A single space or the end of a line follows each word. Assume that two or more adjacent spaces do not occur in the file, and there are no trailing spaces at the end of a line. A single period, question mark, or exclamation point follows each sentence. Output the average number of letters per word and words per sentence.

53. Using the same assumptions as in Problem 52, write a program that outputs each sentence on a separate line. For example, if the input is like that of Problem 50, the output should be

```
Here is a sentence.
Another sentence.
```

Assume that a sentence will not contain more than 80 characters.

54. Modify Problem 53 to allow for sentences that may be longer than 80 characters. Start each sentence on a new line. Continue a long sentence on the next line without a break in a word.

55. Using the same assumptions as in Problem 52, write a program that inputs a line length from the keyboard, and outputs the contents of a text file with each line as long as possible but not longer than the line length. Continue a long sentence on the next line without a break in a word. Continue each sentence on the same line as the previous sentence in general.

56. Modify Problem 55 to output the sentences right-justified.

57. Modify Problem 55 to output the sentences right and left justified. Insert spaces as evenly as possible between words to produce the right justification.

58. Write a program that outputs the contents of a file to the screen in double-double spaced format, with an extra space between each letter and an extra blank line between each line.

Sample Input

```
This is
double-double
spaced.
```

Sample Output

```
T h i s    i s

d o u b l e - d o u b l e

s p a c e d .
```

59. A secret code is formed by the following permutation of letters:

```
Plain:     a b c d e f g h i j k l m n o p q r s t u v w x y z
Encoded:   v e r u g c h i p y j b k l d w x a z n f o t q m s
```

For example, the plain message "hello" is encoded as "igbbd," with 'i' substituted for 'h', 'g' for 'e', and so on. Declare `Code` to be an `array ['a'..'z'] of char` and initialize it to

```
Code ['a'] := 'v';
Code ['b'] := 'e';
etc.
```

Ask the user to input a message and use the `Code` array to output the encoded message without an `if` or `case` statement. Convert all letters to lowercase before encoding and do not change any spaces, punctuation marks, or digits in the message.

Section 7.3

60. Write a program that inputs a two-dimensional array of real values from a text file with the count technique, and outputs the row sum of each row, the column sum of each column, and the grand total.

Sample Input

```
3   4
    4.0  -6.0    1.0    3.0
   -2.0   3.0    7.0    2.0
    1.0   0.0    4.0    5.0
```

Sample Output

```
                            Total
        4.0  -6.0    1.0    3.0     2.0
       -2.0   3.0    7.0    2.0    10.0
        1.0   0.0    4.0    5.0    10.0

Total   3.0  -3.0   12.0   10.0    22.0
```

61. Write a program to output the indices of the largest and smallest elements of a two-dimensional array of real values. For example, if the input is identical to that of Problem 60, the output should be

```
Largest element is in row 2, column 3.
Smallest element is in row 1, column 2.
```

62. Declare

```
procedure Normalize (var Mat:   MatType;
                          NormR: integer;
                          NumC:  integer)
```

where `MatType` is an `array [1..10, 1..10] of real`, `NormR` is a row in `Mat` to be normalized, and `NumC` is the number of columns in `Mat`. To normalize a row, divide every element in that row by the element in the row with the largest absolute value. For example, to normalize the first row of the matrix in Problem 60, you would call

```
Normalize (Matrix, 1, 4)
```

which would divide each element in the first row by −6.0, producing

```
   -0.667   1.000   -0.167   -0.500
   -2.000   3.000    7.000    2.000
    1.000   0.000    4.000    5.000
```

To normalize the second row, the procedure should divide each element in the second row by 7.0, producing

4.000	−6.000	1.000	3.000
−0.286	0.429	1.000	0.286
1.000	0.000	4.000	5.000

Test your procedure in a program that inputs the values from a file with the count technique and prompts the user for the row to normalize. Output the matrix before and after the normalization. Do not include any output statements in `Normalize`.

63. Declare

```
procedure SwapRow (var Mat:          MatType;
                       Row1, Row2: integer;
                       NumC:          integer)
```

where `Mat` and `NumC` have the same meaning as in Problem 62. The procedure should exchange `Row1` with `Row2` in the matrix. Test the procedure as specified in Problem 62.

64. Declare

```
procedure Transpose (var Mat:          MatType;
                         var NumR, NumC: integer)
```

where `Mat`, `NumR`, and `NumC` have the same meaning as in Problem 62. The procedure should transpose `Mat` and switch the values of `NumR` and `NumC`. To transpose a matrix, turn its columns into rows and its rows into columns. For example, the transpose of the matrix in Problem 60 is the following matrix with four rows and three columns.

4.0	−2.0	1.0
−6.0	3.0	0.0
1.0	7.0	4.0
3.0	2.0	5.0

Test the procedure as specified in Problem 62.

65. Write a program that inputs a list of less than 20 integers, each of which has a value less than 10, from a text file with the count technique. Output a vertical bar chart of their values.

Sample Input

```
6
2   5   8   7   3   1
```

Sample Output

```
                *
                *    *
                *    *
          *     *    *
          *     *    *
          *     *    *    *
     *    *     *    *    *
     *    *     *    *    *    *
    ----------------------
     2    5    8    7    3    1
```

Declare Chart to be an array of packed array of char as in Program 7.10. Initialize it to all spaces, then enter the appropriate asterisks for each data value. Output one line of the chart with a single writeln. It is not necessary to store the input in an array.

66. Generalize the random walk program of Problem 6.42. The drunk is in the center of a two-dimensional ledge. The probability is 1/4 that he will take a step to the left, 1/4 to the right, 1/4 up, and 1/4 down. If he takes a total of two steps to the right or down from his original location he will fall to the sidewalk below. Two steps to the left or up lets him fall to safety. Print a grid showing his position after each step. What follows is the output after the first step, assuming it was to the right.

Sample Input/Output

Enter seed: 172

```
(---------)
(         )
(         )
(    x    )
(         )
(         )
(---------)

(---------)
(         )
(         )
(       x )
(         )
(         )
(---------)
```

67. Generalize the program of Problem 6.43 to the two-dimensional walk of Problem 66. Compare the average number of steps for the one-dimensional walk with the average for the two-dimensional walk.

68. Declare a procedure

```
InitUnit (var Mat: MatType; NumR, NumC: integer)
```

where `MatType` is an `array [1..10, 1..10] of real`, NumR is the number of rows, and NumC is the number of columns in Mat. The procedure should initialize the matrix to all zeros, except for ones on the diagonal. For example, if NumR is 3 and NumC is 4, Mat should get

1.0	0.0	0.0	0.0
0.0	1.0	0.0	0.0
0.0	0.0	1.0	0.0

Test your procedure in a program that prompts the user for the number of rows and columns. Do not use any output statements in `InitUnit`.

69. Declare a procedure

    `InitBand (var Mat: MatType; NumR, NumC: integer)`

    where the meanings of the parameters are the same as in Problem 68. The procedure should initialize the matrix to all zeros, except for ones on the diagonal and elements immediately adjacent to the diagonal. For example, if NumR is 4 and NumC is 5, Mat should get

1.0	1.0	0.0	0.0	0.0
1.0	1.0	1.0	0.0	0.0
0.0	1.0	1.0	1.0	0.0
0.0	0.0	1.0	1.0	1.0

    Test your procedure as specified in Problem 68.

70. Generalize Problem 37 to a two-dimensional array.

Sample Input/Output

```
Number of rows: 3
Number of columns: 4
Seed: 529

 4   8   1  10
 7  12   3   5
11   2   9   6
```

The elements are random and nonrepeating.

71. Each integer of a two-dimensional array of integers represents the elevation at one point of some rugged terrain. A *local maximum* is a point whose integer value is greater than the values of its surrounding eight neighbors. For example, the integer array

20	30	30	43	53	72	83
41	40	53	61	77	95	99
42	62	90	85	71	87	88
30	60	70	50	49	56	58

has a local maximum at row three, column three because 90 is greater than 40, 53, 61, 62, 85, 60, 70, and 50. Values on the boarders, such as 99, are not candidates for local maxima. Note also that 95 is not a local maximum because 99 is greater than 95. Write a program that inputs a two-dimensional array of integers with the count technique, and outputs the location of all the local maxima, if any.

72. A *saddle point* is a point whose integer value is greater than its two neighbors' values in the same row but smaller than its two neighbors' values in the same column. A point can also be a saddle point if its integer value is smaller than its two neighbors' values in the same row but greater than its two neighbors' values in the same column. For example, the integer array

48	52	30	43	67
64	55	50	58	95
61	62	40	51	70
56	60	32	48	49

has a saddle point at row two, column three because 50 is greater than 30 and 40, but less than 55 and 58. Values on the borders are not candidates for saddle points. Write a program that inputs a two-dimensional array of integers with the count technique, and outputs the location of all the saddle points, if any.

73. Use the string table technique of Program 7.11 to output the contents of `ZooFile` as defined in Program 5.10. Output three animals per row.

74. Initialize an array of eight nouns to

    egg   cat   bird   wheel   chair   rug   floor   phone

and another array of eight verbs to

    sit   stand   walk   run   skip   lie   roll   talk

Use two-dimensional arrays such as `List` in Program 7.10. Write a program that asks the user to input a seed for a random number generator and outputs a sentence of the form

The *blank* should *blank* on the *blank*

where the first and last blanks are selected at random from the list of nouns and the second blank is selected at random from the list of verbs. Your program should not contain any `if` or `case` statements. Some sentences might make sense, such as

The bird   should sit   on the egg

but others will be nonsense, like

The cat   should skip on the phone

Section 7.4

75. Write a procedure

```
OddFirstSort (NumItm: integer; var L: ListType)
```

that rearranges the elements of a list of integers so all the odd integers are before all the even integers. To test it, write a program similar to Program 7.13, with input from a file using the count technique and with `OddFirstSort` taking the place of `SortList`.

76. Write a program to input values from `PhoneFile` into the parallel arrays `NameList` and `NumberList` as defined in Program 7.12. Sort the parallel arrays based on the values in `NameList`. For example, after the sort `NameList [1]` should be

Andrews, and `NumList [1]` should be 243-1056. Output the sorted names with the corresponding numbers next to them.

77. Modify Program 7.12 so that it uses the binary search instead of the sequential search. Assume the names are in order in `PhoneFile`.

78. The input for this problem is a text file that contains a number specifying how many integers follow. Write a program that inputs the list of up to 100 integers. Then output a list of those integers that occur more than once and the number of times each occurs. Hint: First sort the list. Also consider the possibility that the last item in the list might be duplicated. Considering that case, you may be able to simplify your code by appending an extra value after the last item of the list, similar to the technique of the sequential search.

Sample Input

```
17
  33  -2  25  25   3   7  -2  17  12  25
  33   8  17   2  17  20  25
```

Sample Output

```
-2 occurs  2 times
17 occurs  3 times
25 occurs  4 times
33 occurs  2 times
```

79. Modify procedure `SortList` in Program 7.13 so that it sorts with the largest element first.

80. Modify procedure `SortList` in Program 7.13 so that it moves the smallest element to `L [1]` on the first pass, the next larger to `L [2]` on the second pass, and so on.

81. Declare

```
procedure Compress (var L: ListType; var NumItm)
```

which removes duplicate integers from a sorted list of integers. For example, if `NumItm` is 12 and `L` is

```
  1  4  4  5  9  9  9  14  19  19  19  19
```

then `Compress` should change `L` to

```
  1  4  5  9  14  19
```

and `NumItm` to 6. Test it similarly to Program 7.13 with input from a file using the count technique and with `Compress` taking the place of `SortList`. Do not include any output statements in `Compress`.

82. Anagrams are words that use the same letters. For example, races and acres are anagrams, but car and cat are not. Declare

```
function Anagram (Wd1, Wd2: StrType): boolean
```

where `StrType` is defined as in Program 7.7, which determines if `Wd1` and `Wd2` are anagrams. Test your function with interactive I/O.

Section 7.5

83. Complete the module `GetLine` of Program 7.15. Do not complete any of the other modules except any that `GetLine` may call. Test the program with the stubs in the other modules.

84. This problem is to be done only after you have completed Problem 83. Finish writing the entire program, testing each module as you complete it.

85. Write a top-level module for the following problem. Compile and execute your top-level module with stubs for all of the called procedures and functions. Do not assume that lower modules will use global variables. Do not complete any of the lower modules. Draw a hierarchy chart.

    The problem is to input an array of integer values from a text file and determine whether the array is a *magic square*. A magic square is a square array of integers whose rows, columns, and diagonals all total the same value. For example,

8	1	6
3	5	7
4	9	2

    is a magic square whose total is 15.

86. Develop a top-level module according to the specifications of Problem 85. The problem is to convert a Roman numeral entered from the keyboard into a decimal number.

87. Develop a top-level module according to the specifications of Problem 85. The input for this problem is a text file containing an automotive parts list. The first line contains a description of the first part. The second line contains a part number (integer) followed by the cost (real value) for the first part. The third and fourth lines contain the same information for the second part, and so on. The last line contains a part number of 0000 as a sentinel.

Sample Input

```
Brake pads
1132   26.50
Radiator hose
8740    5.00
Fan belt
2381   12.25
Wiper blade
9028    8.00
Sentinel
0000    0.0
```

The problem is to ask the user to input part numbers and quantities for a purchase, look up the cost for each item, and output its description and the total bill.

Chapter

8

Structured Data Types

Remember that the collection of a group of objects is the first step toward abstraction. In previous chapters we learned that a procedure represents program abstraction because it is a collection of statements that can be treated as a single statement when called, and an array represents data abstraction because it is a collection of data values that can be treated as a single data object. This chapter continues to develop data abstraction with two more structured data types—records and sets. Both types are collections of data values that you can treat as a single data object.

Records and sets are collections of data values.

8.1   Record Structures

Like an array, a *record* is a collection of values into a single variable. But here the similarity ends. Each value of an array must be of the same type. For example, if `List` has the declaration

```
List: array [0..7] of real
```

then `List` is a collection of eight values. Each of those eight values must be a real number.

Records do not have that limitation. Different components of a record can have different types of values. A record might be a collection of eight values, but one of those eight might have type `real` while another might have type `char`. Each component of a record is called a *field*.

Components of records can have different types.

▢ Program 8.1

Program 8.1 illustrates how to declare and manipulate a record. The program has one variable called `SimpleRec` with type `record`. It has two parts, called `Ch` and `I`. `Ch` is of type `char` while `I` is of type `integer`.

373

```
program IntroRecord (output);
   var
      SimpleRec:
         record
         Ch: char;
         I:  integer
         end;
   begin
   SimpleRec.I := 13;
   SimpleRec.Ch := '%';
   SimpleRec.I := SimpleRec.I + 1;
   writeln ('SimpleRec.I = ', SimpleRec.I: 1);
   writeln ('SimpleRec.Ch = ', SimpleRec.Ch)
   end.
```

Program 8.1

Accessing a simple record.

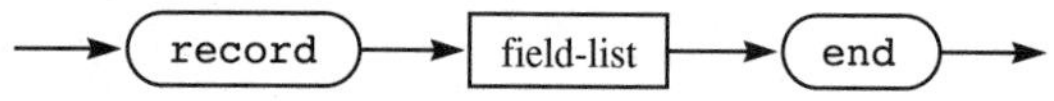

Output

```
SimpleRec.I = 14
SimpleRec.Ch = %
```

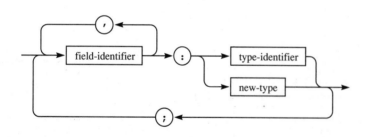

Figure 8.1

The syntax chart of a record type.

Figure 8.1 is the syntax chart of a record type. The word **record** is reserved. Each **record** must have a corresponding **end**.

The items between **record** and **end** comprise the field list. Figure 8.2 is the syntax chart for a field list. Records that contain a variant field list are called variant records, which will be discussed in Section 8.4.

The record in this example has a fixed field list. It is

```
Ch: char;
I:  integer
```

Figure 8.3 is the syntax chart of a fixed field list.

Figure 8.2

The syntax chart of a field list.

Figure 8.3

The syntax chart of a fixed field list.

Figure 8.4

The syntax chart of a field variable.

Compare this syntax chart with the chart for a variable declaration part, which was shown in Figure 2.14. They are identical in structure except for the reserved word `var` at the beginning of the variable declaration part. It looks like `Ch` is a variable with type `char` and `I` is a variable with type `integer`. `Ch` and `I` are not variable identifiers, however, but *field identifiers.*

In this program, `SimpleRec` is the variable. The component of a record variable is called a *field variable.* To reference a field variable, place a period between the variable name and a field identifier. For example, `SimpleRec.Ch` is the field variable corresponding to field `Ch` in the variable `SimpleRec`. The statement

```
SimpleRec.Ch := '%';
```

assigns the value '%' to the field variable. Figure 8.4 is the syntax chart for a field variable.

The assignment and output statements of Program 8.1 treat the field variables like ordinary variables. You can use field variables in expressions and assign values to them. You can output their values with `writeln` calls.

Figure 8.5 shows the structure of `SimpleRec`. Its first component contains a character value, its second component contains an integer value.

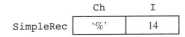

Figure 8.5

The structure of the record `SimpleRec` in Program 8.1.

Using Records

In most respects you can treat a field variable as you would any other variable. The only restriction is that you cannot use a field variable as a control variable in a `for` statement.

Field variables cannot be control variables in for statements.

Example **8.1**   Assuming `SimpleRec` is declared as in Program 8.1, the statement

```
for SimpleRec.I := 1 to 10 do
    Statement
```

is illegal because `SimpleRec.I` is a field variable.   ∎

A field identifier by itself does not name a variable, but rather the field of a variable. Therefore, you cannot use a field identifier alone as you would a variable.

A field is not a variable.

Example **8.2**   If `Ch` were a variable of type `char`, then the statement

```
Ch := '%'
```

would be legal. In Program 8.1, the field `Ch` has type `char`. But since `Ch` is not a variable, the statement would be illegal.   ∎

You will often have several lines of code that refer to field variables of the same record. Pascal provides the `with` statement so you can refer to the fields of the record without repeating the variable name. Figure 8.6 is the syntax chart of a `with` statement.

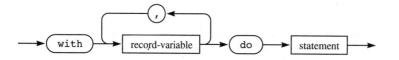

Figure 8.6

The syntax chart of a `with` statement.

Example **8.3**   You can write the statements in Program 8.1 as

```
with SimpleRec do
   begin
   I := 13;
   Ch := '%';
   I := I + 1;
   writeln ('SimpleRec.I = ', I: 1);
   writeln ('SimpleRec.Ch = ', Ch)
   end
```

When the compiler processes the identifier `I` in the statement `I := 13`, it realizes that it is contained in a `with` statement. It checks the field identifiers of `SimpleRec`. Since `SimpleRec` has a field identifier of `I`, the compiler knows to use the field variable `SimpleRec.I`. If `SimpleRec` did not have a field identifier of `I`, the compiler would check the variable declaration part of the program for a variable identifier of `I`.   ∎

Program 8.2

Records consolidate several related values into a single variable. This technique can help you design parameter lists for procedures and functions. Sometimes people avoid parameter lists because they need many variables to communicate between modules. Collecting the variables into a few records can shorten the parameter list considerably.

Program 8.2 performs the same computation as Program 6.9. In the original problem, procedure `CalcRect` had four parameters. In this program it has only two parameters.

This program illustrates the data abstraction possible with records. *Data abstraction with records* `DimenRec` is a record that holds the dimensions of the rectangle, while `SizeRec` holds the size of the rectangle. The program gives procedure `CalcRect` the

```
program Rectangle (input, output);
   type
      DimenType =
         record
         Width:  real;
         Height: real
         end;
      SizeType =
         record
         Area:  real;
         Perim: real
         end;
   var
      DimenRec: DimenType;
      SizeRec:  SizeType;

   procedure CalcRect (var SRec: SizeType; DRec: DimenType);
      begin
      with SRec, DRec do
         begin
         Area := Width * Height;
         Perim := 2.0 * (Width + Height)
         end
      end;

   begin
   write ('Enter width: ');
   readln (DimenRec.Width);
   write ('Enter height: ');
   readln (DimenRec.Height);
   CalcRect (SizeRec, DimenRec);
   writeln;
   writeln ('Area is ', SizeRec.Area: 3: 1);
   writeln ('Perimeter is ', SizeRec.Perim: 3: 1)
   end.
```

Program 8.2

Passing a record as a parameter. This program performs the same computation as Program 6.9.

Interactive Input/Output

```
Enter width: 5.0
Enter height: 4.0

Area is 20.0
Perimeter is 18.0
```

dimensions of the rectangle. The procedure computes the size from the dimensions. So DimenRec is called by value and SizeRec is called by reference. Each record is a collection of values that you can treat as a single object when you pass them as parameters.

■ **Program 8.3**

A file of records has all the advantages of a nontext file. It is smaller than a text file holding the same amount of information. The input/output operations are simpler to program and faster to execute as well. The only disadvantage is that you cannot manipulate a file of records with a text editor.

Program 8.3 is another version of the problem in Program 7.15. It consolidates all the information about an employee into the single record Empl. EmplFile is a nontext file of records. Like Program 7.15, this is the top level test in a top-down design.

Look how much simpler this version of the program is. Program 7.15 required procedure GetLine just to input a line of data from the text file. That was appropriate because the data included two string values and two real values. Each string value would require a for loop for input. But this version collects all that data into a single record. Pascal lets you treat that collection as a single object in the read call. You do not need a loop to input the data contained in a record. One read call inputs the entire collection. Figure 8.7 shows the structure of record Empl.

	LastName	FirstName	HourlyRate	HoursWorked
Empl	Hook	Captain	30.00	25.0

Figure 8.7

The structure of the record Empl in Program 8.3.

Another simplification comes from the fact that a file of records is nontext. Since the eof technique is preferred for nontext files, this version does not require a sentinel. Algorithms without sentinels are usually less error prone because you do not need to ensure that the sentinel test in the program corresponds to the sentinel value in the file.

```
program EmployeeWages (EmplFile, output);
   type
      Str10Type   = packed array [1..10] of char;
      EmplRecType =
         record
         LastName:    Str10Type;
         FirstName:   Str10Type;
         HourlyRate:  real;
         HoursWorked: real
         end;
   var
      Empl:       EmplRecType;
      Wages:      real;
      TotalWages: real;
      EmplFile:   file of EmplRecType;

   procedure PutHeading;
      begin
      writeln ('PutHeading called.')
      end;
```

Program 8.3

The top-level test of a program that processes a file of records.

Program 8.3, continued

```
function CalcWage (HRate, HWorked: real): real;
   begin
   CalcWage := 1.00;
   writeln ('CalcWage called.')
   end;

procedure PutFooting (W: real);
   begin
   writeln ('PutFooting called.')
   end;

begin
PutHeading;
TotalWages := 0.00;
reset (EmplFile);
while not eof (EmplFile) do
   begin
   read (EmplFile, Empl);
   Wages := CalcWage (Empl.HourlyRate, Empl.HoursWorked);
   writeln (Empl.LastName, Empl.FirstName [1]: 2, Wages: 8: 2);
   TotalWages := TotalWages + Wages
   end;
PutFooting (TotalWages)
end.
```

Input—EmplFile (nontext)

Hook	Captain	30.00	25.0
Pan	Peter	10.50	60.0
Darling	Wendy	8.50	45.0
Darling	John	6.50	20.0
Darling	Michael	1.50	10.0
Bell	Tinker	10.00	50.0

Output

```
PutHeading called.
CalcWage called.
Hook      C    1.00
CalcWage called.
Pan       P    1.00
CalcWage called.
Darling   W    1.00
CalcWage called.
Darling   J    1.00
CalcWage called.
Darling   M    1.00
CalcWage called.
Bell      T    1.00
PutFooting called.
```

8.2   ## Sequential File Processing

Sequential file-processing problems are an important class of problems in applications that store large amounts of data in files. Business applications typically require large amounts of personnel data, payroll data, inventory data, and so on. Some scientific applications also store large amounts of data in files, particularly experimental data.

Programs in previous chapters extracted data from files and put the output on the screen. Some of the programs also output the information to a file. But in those programs, the output file had a different structure from the input file.

Sequential file-processing algorithms have an input file and an output file. They differ from the previous algorithms because of the relationship between the input and output files. In sequential file processing, the output file is an updated version of the input file. Both files have the same structure. The purpose of the program is to create an output file whose structure is the same as the input file, but whose content is somehow modified.

Characteristics of sequential file-processing algorithms

Program 8.4

Program 8.4 solves a sequential file-processing problem. The input file is `OldEmplFile`, and the output file is `NewEmplFile`. Both have the same structure, since they are both files of `EmplRecType`. The file structures are identical to that of `EmplFile` in Program 8.3.

The purpose of the program is to delete one or more records from the file. `NewEmplFile` is identical to `OldEmplFile` except that a record has been deleted.

```
program DeleteRecord (input, output, OldEmplFile, NewEmplFile);
   type
      Str10Type  = packed array [1..10] of char;
      EmplRecType =
         record
         LastName:    Str10Type;
         FirstName:   Str10Type;
         HourlyRate:  real;
         HoursWorked: real
         end;
   var
      Empl:        EmplRecType;
      SearchName:  Str10Type;
      NumDeleted:  integer;
      OldEmplFile: file of EmplRecType;
      NewEmplFile: file of EmplRecType;
```

Program 8.4

A program to delete records from a file based on a search name.

Program 8.4, continued

```
procedure GetString (var S: Str10Type);
   {  This procedure gets a string value for S from  }
   {  the keyboard, padded with trailing spaces.      }
   var
      I: integer;
   begin
   for I := 1 to 10 do
      if eoln (input) then
         S [I] := ' '
      else
         read (input, S [I]);
   readln (input)
   end;


begin
write ('Enter last name of record to delete: ');
GetString (SearchName);
NumDeleted := 0;
reset (OldEmplFile);
rewrite (NewEmplFile);
while not eof (OldEmplFile) do
   begin
   read (OldEmplFile, Empl);
   if Empl.LastName <> SearchName then
      write (NewEmplFile, Empl)
   else
      NumDeleted := NumDeleted + 1
   end;
writeln ('Records deleted: ', NumDeleted: 1)
end.
```

Input—OldEmplFile (nontext)

Hook	Captain	30.00	25.0
Pan	Peter	10.50	60.0
Darling	Wendy	8.50	45.0
Darling	John	6.50	20.0
Darling	Michael	1.50	10.0
Bell	Tinker	10.00	50.0

Interactive Input/Output

```
Enter last name of record to delete: Pan
Records deleted: 1
```

Output—NewEmplFile (nontext)

Hook	Captain	30.00	25.0
Darling	Wendy	8.50	45.0
Darling	John	6.50	20.0
Darling	Michael	1.50	10.0
Bell	Tinker	10.00	50.0

Figure 8.8 is a system flowchart for this program. It shows the keyboard and OldEmplFile as input. NewEmplFile and the screen are output.

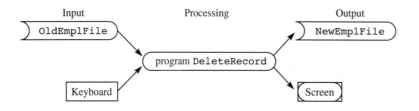

Input   Processing   Output

OldEmplFile

program DeleteRecord

NewEmplFile

Keyboard

Screen

Figure 8.8

The system flowchart for Program 8.4.

The program checks the name field of each record input from the file. If it is not identical to the name entered from the keyboard, the program writes the record to NewEmplFile. Otherwise it does not write it to NewEmplFile, in effect deleting the record. If no record has a LastName field equal to SearchName, no record is deleted. If LastNames match in more than one record, all of them are deleted.

Figure 8.9 shows the details of the data flow in the program. The values in the program variables correspond to the point of execution just after Wendy Darling's record has been written and just before John Darling's record has been read. You can think of the program as a filter. In the same way that a filter screens out particles from a liquid, the program screens out records from the input file whose name field matches SearchName.

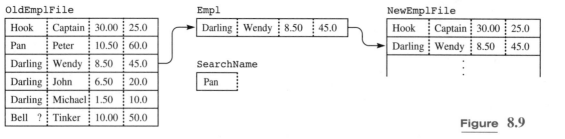

Input file   Program variables   Output file

OldEmplFile

Hook	Captain	30.00	25.0
Pan	Peter	10.50	60.0
Darling	Wendy	8.50	45.0
Darling	John	6.50	20.0
Darling	Michael	1.50	10.0
Bell ?	Tinker	10.00	50.0

Empl

| Darling | Wendy | 8.50 | 45.0 |

SearchName

| Pan |

NewEmplFile

| Hook | Captain | 30.00 | 25.0 |
| Darling | Wendy | 8.50 | 45.0 |

Figure 8.9

The data flow in Program 8.4.

After processing the data, you may not want the old version of the file. If not, you can delete it with an operating system command after you execute the program.

Typically, with sequential file processing it is necessary to maintain one updated file in your disk directory. Suppose you want the file to be named DataFile, and the program that updates the file creates a new file called NewDataFile. The steps you must follow to maintain one updated file are

- Run the sequential file-processing program, which creates `NewDataFile`. There are now two files in your directory—`DataFile` and `NewDataFile`.

- Delete `DataFile` from your file directory. There is now one file in your directory—`NewDataFile`.

- Change the name of `NewDataFile` to `DataFile`, which is now the updated version.

Some Pascal compilers let you write statements in your program to delete a file and change the name of a file. These features are useful but are not part of the standard language.

Program 8.5

Many variations of Program 8.4 are possible, depending on the filtering you want to do. You can add a record to the new file by inputting data from the keyboard for all the fields of the record variable and then writing the record to the new file. You could add records at the beginning of the file or at the end of the file.

Suppose you have two sorted sequential files of the same type. For example, they may be files of addresses sorted by zip code or files of customers sorted by last name. You want to merge them into one sorted file.

Figure 8.10 shows the system flowchart of Program 8.5. The inputs are two master files called `MasFileA` and `MasFileB`. The program `MergeTwoFiles` produces a single output file called `NewMasFile`, which contains all the records from both of the input files. `NewMasFile` is also sorted.

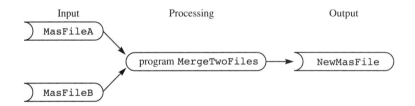

Input   Processing   Output

MasFileA → program MergeTwoFiles → NewMasFile

MasFileB

Figure 8.10

The system flowchart for Program 8.5.

The algorithm for performing the merge will use four variables—`MasRecA`, `MasRecB`, `NewMasRec`, and `LowKey`. Figure 8.11 (p. 385) shows these four variables along with the input and output files. The curved lines indicate data flow.

The main idea of the algorithm is to have `MasRecA` contain the most recent record from `MasFileA`, and `MasRecB` the most recent record from `MasFileB`. Then `LowKey` contains either the key field from `MasRecA` or the key field from `MasRecB`, whichever is smaller. The following is a pseudocode outline of the merge algorithm.

A pseudocode outline of the file-merge algorithm

```
begin
GetRec (MasFileA, MasRecA)
GetRec (MasFileB, MasRecB)
LowKey := minimum of MasRecA.Key and MasRecB.Key
{  Assert:                                                    }
{  1. LowKey has the minimum of MasRecA.Key and MasRecB.Key.  }
{  2. MasRecA has the next value from MasFileA to output.     }
{  3. MasRecB has the next value from MasFileB to output.     }
{  4. NewMasRec is empty.                                     }
while LowKey <> HighSentinel do
   begin
   if MasRecA.Key = LowKey then
      begin
      NewMasRec := MasRecA
      GetRec (MasFileA, MasRecA)
      end
   else
      begin
      NewMasRec := MasRecB
      GetRec (MasFileB, MasRecB)
      end
   write (NewMasFile, NewMasRec)
   LowKey := minimum of MasRecA.Key and MasRecB.Key
   end
write a sentinel record to NewsMasFile
end
```

A single while loop creates the new master file by writing NewMasRec to it. But where does NewMasRec get its value? If the key field from MasRecA equals LowKey, then MasRecA should appear before MasRecB in the new master file. In that case, NewMasRec will get its value from MasRecA. So the algorithm will write MasRecA to the new master file before it writes MasRecB. If the key field from MasRecB equals LowKey, then NewMasRec will get its value from MasRecB.

The remaining question is, How should the while loop terminate? Suppose the last record of each input file is a sentinel whose key value is larger than any other key value in the input file. For example, if the key field is of type packed array [1..10] of char, the sentinel value might be 'zzzzzzzzzz'.

As the while loop executes you will get to the end of one input file before the other. Say you get to the end of MasFileB first. When that happens the key field of MasRecB will contain 'zzzzzzzzzz', and LowKey must contain the key value of MasRecA. So the algorithm will write MasRecA to the new master file.

As the loop continues, it will eventually reach the end of MasFileA. Then the key field of MasRecA will contain 'zzzzzzzzzz'. At that point during execution, the key field of MasRecB will still contain 'zzzzzzzzzz'. So LowKey will get the minimum of these two, which is 'zzzzzzzzzz'. The while loop should terminate when LowKey contains the high sentinel value.

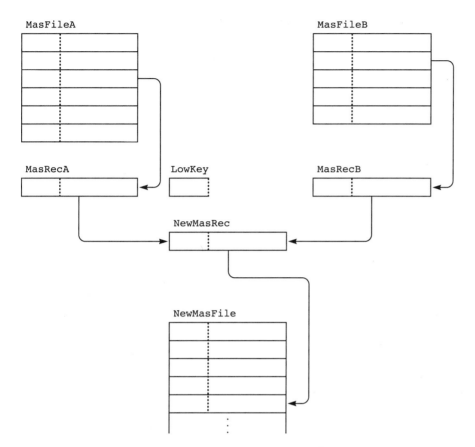

Figure **8.11**

The data flow in Program 8.5.

```
program MergeTwoFiles (MasFileA, MasFileB, NewMasFile);
   const
      HighSentinel = 'zzzzzzzzzz';
   type
      NameType    = packed array [1..10] of char;
      NumType     = packed array [1..8] of char;
      ListingType =
         record
         Name:   NameType; {  Name is the key.  }
         Number: NumType
         end;
      PhFileType = file of ListingType;
   var
      MasFileA:   PhFileType;
      MasFileB:   PhFileType;
      NewMasFile: PhFileType;
      MasRecA:    ListingType;
      MasRecB:    ListingType;
      NewMasRec:  ListingType;
      LowKey:     NameType;
```

Program 8.5

The file merge program.

```
procedure Min (var LowK: NameType; KeyA, KeyB: NameType);
   begin
   if KeyA < KeyB then
      LowK := KeyA
   else
      LowK := KeyB
   end;

procedure GetRec (var FileX: PhFileType; var RecX: ListingType);
   begin
   if eof (FileX) then
      RecX.Name := HighSentinel
   else
      read (FileX, RecX)
   end;


begin
reset (MasFileA);
reset (MasFileB);
rewrite (NewMasFile);
GetRec (MasFileA, MasRecA);
GetRec (MasFileB, MasRecB);
Min (LowKey, MasRecA.Name, MasRecB.Name);
{  Assert:                                                       }
{  1. LowKey has the minimum of MasRecA.Key and MasRecB.Key.     }
{  2. MasRecA has the next value from MasFileA to output.        }
{  3. MasRecB has the next value from MasFileB to output.        }
{  4. NewMasRec is empty.                                        }
while LowKey <> HighSentinel do
   begin
   if MasRecA.Name = LowKey then
      begin
      NewMasRec := MasRecA;
      GetRec (MasFileA, MasRecA)
      end
   else
      begin
      NewMasRec := MasRecB;
      GetRec (MasFileB, MasRecB)
      end;
   write (NewMasFile, NewMasRec);
   Min (LowKey, MasRecA.Name, MasRecB.Name)
   end
end.
```

Program 8.5, continued

Input—`MasFileA` (nontext)

Capablanca	349-0110
Kasparov	921-0375
Lasker	930-1881
Marshall	229-8762
Morphy	193-3320

Program 8.5, continued

Input—`MasFileB` (nontext)

Fine	298-1991
Fischer	220-1006
Karpov	231-3395
Korchnoi	311-0229
Spassky	993-4920
Tal	298-4478

Output—`NewMasFile` (nontext)

Capablanca	349-0110
Fine	298-1991
Fischer	220-1006
Karpov	231-3395
Kasparov	921-0375
Korchnoi	311-0229
Lasker	930-1881
Marshall	229-8762
Morphy	193-3320
Spassky	993-4920
Tal	298-4478

The four loop invariants are

Loop invariants for the file-merge algorithm

- `LowKey` has the minimum of `MasRecA.Key` and `MasRecB.Key`.
- `MasRecA` has the next value from `MasFileA` to output.
- `MasRecB` has the next value from `MasFileB` to output.
- `NewMasRec` is empty.

The first three statements of the algorithm make the invariants true just before the loop executes the first time. Inside the loop, the input statements keep the second and third invariants true. The output statement keeps the fourth invariant true. (After the output, even though `NewMasRec` still has values, the algorithm no longer uses them.) The minimization computation keeps the first invariant true.

Program 8.5 is the Pascal listing of the file merge algorithm. Procedure `Min` computes the minimum of the key values from `MasRecA` and `MasRecB`.

The algorithm assumed that the files contained high sentinel values. The logic of the main program in Program 8.5 makes the same assumption. But at the same time, procedure `GetRec` takes advantage of the `eof` feature for nontext file processing. The procedure simulates the sentinel record with an assignment statement. To the main program it appears that the file has a sentinel value, even though it does not.

The main program does not write a sentinel record to the new master file after the `while` loop terminates. The new master file has the same structure as the input files, that is, no sentinel value.

You should convince yourself that the program works correctly if either or both of the input files are empty.

Program 8.6

Another basic commercial data processing application is the sequential file update problem. Program 8.6 illustrates it for the situation of a master file maintained by the registrar's office at Your Local University (YLU).

The master file is a file of records. Each master record has the following three fields:

- *Social security number* packed array of `char`
- *Name* packed array of `char`
- *Class* enumerated

The enumerated values for class are `(Frosh, Soph, Jr, Sr, Grad, Blank)`. The records are sorted by social security number, which acts as the key field.

At the end of each semester, the class status of many students changes. Some students advance to a higher class. Some students drop out. Some freshmen and transfer students enter YLU. During the semester the registrar collects information about all these changes and stores it in a transaction file.

Each record of the transaction file has the following two fields:

- *Transaction kind* enumerated
- *Data* same as master record

The enumerated values for the transaction kind are `(Add, Change, Delete)`. The data field of the transaction record is another record with structure identical to a master record: that is, with three fields—social security number, name, and class. The transaction record is an example of a record nested inside a record. As in the master file, the transaction records are sorted by social security number, which acts as the key field.

The sequential file update problem is to modify the old master file based on the records of the transaction file, producing a new master file. We present a listing of a master file and a transaction file and the resulting new master file. Figure 8.12 is a system flowchart for the problem. The screen output is for error messages generated by incompatibilities between the transaction file and the old master file.

Figure 8.12

The system flowchart for Program 8.6.

Input—`OldMasFile` (nontext)

141-01-3957	Malone	Sr
163-33-3946	Hailey	Soph
215-04-2056	Wilkins	Frosh
224-89-1173	Fong	Grad
322-03-3844	Fernandez	Jr
378-45-5643	Wright	Sr
407-20-1036	Hobson	Sr
508-28-3311	McPherson	Grad
588-53-7633	Johnson	Soph
634-79-7724	Drake	Frosh
682-80-4138	Moore	Frosh
754-71-2887	Lavin	Jr
801-28-4133	Fiske	Soph
884-52-0851	Wu	Soph
907-14-9382	Campbell	Jr

Input—`TranFile` (nontext)

Change	163-33-3946		Jr
Change	215-04-2057		Jr
Add	310-26-5811	Alvarez	Frosh
Add	407-20-1036	Carter	Frosh
Delete	508-28-3311		
Delete	634-79-7723		
Add	701-00-6392	Sweetman	Soph
Change	701-00-6392		Jr
Change	701-00-6392		Sr
Add	850-63-0011	Jacobson	Jr
Change	850-63-0011		Sr
Delete	850-63-0011		

Output—`NewMasFile` (nontext)

141-01-3957	Malone	Sr
163-33-3946	Hailey	Jr
215-04-2056	Wilkins	Frosh
224-89-1173	Fong	Grad
310-26-5811	Alvarez	Frosh
322-03-3844	Fernandez	Jr
378-45-5643	Wright	Sr
407-20-1036	Hobson	Sr
588-53-7633	Johnson	Soph
634-79-7724	Drake	Frosh
682-80-4138	Moore	Frosh
701-00-6392	Sweetman	Sr
754-71-2887	Lavin	Jr
801-28-4133	Fiske	Soph
884-52-0851	Wu	Soph
907-14-9382	Campbell	Jr

Output—Screen

```
Error.  Attempt to change 215-04-2057
Error.  Attempt to add 407-20-1036
Error.  Attempt to delete 634-79-7723
```

What follows is an explanation of each transaction kind with examples from the sample input/output.

Add   The transaction record represents a new entering student. The algorithm should create a new master record, which contains the social security number, name, and class from the transaction record. In the sample transaction file, the record

Add   310-26-5811   Alvarez   Frosh

produces a record for Alvarez in the new master file. A possible problem with this transaction is if the record has a social security number identical to one in the old master file. The record

Add   407-20-1036   Carter   Frosh

is not added because Hobson's record has that number. This transaction generates an error message on the screen.

Change   The transaction record represents a student whose class status has changed. The algorithm should change the class field of the corresponding old master record to the one in the transaction record. It should ignore the `Name` field of the transaction record. In the sample transaction file, the record

Change   163-33-3946   Jr

changes Hailey's class from Sophomore to Junior. A problem could occur with this transaction if it attempts to change a nonexistent record. The transaction record

Change   215-04-2057   Jr

generates an error message on the screen because there is no record in the master file with that number.

Delete   The transaction record represents a student who has dropped out of YLU. The algorithm should delete the record in the old master file whose social security number matches that of the transaction record. It should ignore both the `Name` and `Class` fields of the transaction record. In the sample transaction file, the record

Delete   508-28-3311

removes McPherson's record from the master file. A problem could occur with this transaction if it attempts to delete a record that does not exist. The transaction record

Delete   634-79-7723

generates an error message on the screen because there is no master record with that social security number.

The sample input/output shows one more requirement of the problem. The registrar may receive several transactions for the same record. For example, the three records

Add	701-00-6392	Sweetman	Soph
Change	701-00-6392		Jr
Change	701-00-6392		Sr

in the transaction file represent adding Sweetman as a sophomore, changing his status to a junior, then changing it to a senior. The net result in the new master file is to add Sweetman as a senior. As another example, the three transaction records

Add	850-63-0011	Jacobson	Jr
Change	850-63-0011		Sr
Delete	850-63-0011		

should have no effect on the new master file. The algorithm should add, change, then delete a record for Jacobson. The net result in the new master file is to have no record for Jacobson. Neither of these sequences should generate any error messages on the screen.

The best solution to the sequential file update problem is known as the *balanced-line algorithm,* described by Edsger W. Dijkstra.[1] The version presented here is adapted from an article by Michael R. Levy.[2] Conceptually, the balanced-line algorithm is an extension of the file-merge algorithm in Program 8.5. As before, the main program has four variables—`MasRec`, `TranRec`, `NewMasRec`, and `LowKey`—that function exactly the way they did in the merge algorithm.

Now, however, a fifth variable called `NewMasPresent` is required, as Figure 8.13 (p. 393) shows. Its type is boolean. When values are transferred from `MasRec` to `NewMasRec`, then `NewMasPresent` gets true. When a record is added by an add transaction and values are transferred from `TranRec` to `NewMasRec`, then `NewMasPresent` gets true. But when `NewMasRec` is stored in the new master file, then `NewMasPresent` gets false. In other words, `NewMasPresent` indicates whether `NewMasRec` contains a current valid master record that has not yet been written to the new master file. The dotted lines that connect `NewMasPresent` with the three data flow lines in Figure 8.13 signify that the value of `NewMasPresent` depends on the data flow along those three paths.

The algorithm in pseudocode outline form follows. As in the merge algorithm, a single `while` loop that examines the value of `LowKey` controls the execution.

The balanced-line algorithm

1. Edsger W. Dijkstra, *A Discipline of Programming* (Englewood Cliffs, N.J.: Prentice-Hall, 1976).
2. Michael R. Levy, "Modularity and the Sequential File Update Problem," *Communications of the ACM*, 25 (June 1982): 362–67.

```
begin
NewMasPresent := false
GetMasRec (OldMasFile, MasRec)
GetTranRec (TransFile, TranRec)
LowKey := minimum of MasRec.Key and TranRec.Data.Key
{  Assert:                                          }
{  1. MasRec has the next master record             }
{  2. TranRec has the next transaction record       }
{  3. LowKey contains the smaller of their keys     }
{  4. NewMasPresent is false                        }
while LowKey <> HighSentinel do
   begin
   if MasRec.Key = LowKey then
      begin
      NewMasRec := MasRec
      NewMasPresent := true
      GetMasRec (OldMasFile, MasRec)
      end
   while TranRec.Data.Key = LowKey do
      begin
      Process transaction record, possibly
         modifying NewMasPresent
      GetTranRec (TransFile, TranRec)
      end
   if NewMasPresent then
      begin
      write (NewMasFile, NewMasRec)
      NewMasPresent := false
      end
   LowKey := minimum of MasRec.Key and TranRec.Data.Key
   end
end
```

A pseudocode outline of the balanced-line algorithm

The merge algorithm had a single `if` statement inside the `while` loop. The balanced line algorithm, however, has an `if` followed by a `while`, followed by another `if`.

The first `if` checks the necessity of sending `MasRec` to `NewMasRec`. Suppose the current `TranRec` is an add transaction, and the record should be inserted in the new master file before the current `MasRec`. In that case `MasRec` should not be sent to `NewMasRec`. `TranRec` should be sent to `NewMasRec` so it can be written to `NewMasFile`. The algorithm will not send `MasRec`, since `LowKey` will equal `TranRec.Key` instead of `MasRec.Key`.

The nested `while` continues to process transaction records as long as the key of `TranRec` matches `LowKey`. This is a `while` loop instead of an `if` statement because of the possibility of several consecutive transaction records with the same key.

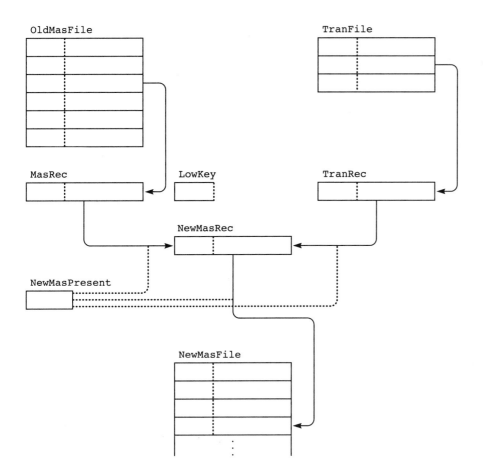

Figure 8.13

The data flow in Program 8.6.

The last `if` checks for the necessity of outputting `NewMasRec` to the new master file. Suppose `TranRec` is a delete transaction whose key matches the key of `NewMasRec`. The processing statement in the transaction loop will set `NewMasPresent` to false. Then this `if` statement will skip the output of `NewMasRec` to the new master file, deleting the record.

Table 8.1 is a high-level trace of the algorithm with the previous sample input/output. The trace identifies the records by name rather than number for readability. In the `TranRec` column, Ch stands for change. The trace shows the processing from the beginning to the completion of the first change transaction.

Lines 1–4 in the trace show the effect of the first four statements of the algorithm. They establish the four loop invariants:

- `MasRec` has the next master record.
- `TranRec` has the next transaction record.
- `LowKey` contains the smaller of their keys.
- `NewMasPresent` is false.

	MasRec	TranRec	LowKey	NewMasRec	NewMasPresent
	?	?	?	?	?
1.	?	?	?	?	false
2.	Malone	?	?	?	false
3.	Malone	Ch Hailey	?	?	false
4.	Malone	Ch Hailey	Malone's	?	false
5.	Malone	Ch Hailey	Malone's	Malone	false
6.	Malone	Ch Hailey	Malone's	Malone	true
7.	Hailey	Ch Hailey	Malone's	Malone	true
8.	Skip nested `while` loop				
9.	Send `NewMasRec` to `NewMasFile`				
10.	Hailey	Ch Hailey	Malone's	Malone	false
11.	Hailey	Ch Hailey	Hailey's	Malone	false
12.	Hailey	Ch Hailey	Hailey's	Hailey	false
13.	Hailey	Ch Hailey	Hailey's	Hailey	true
14.	Wilkin	Ch Hailey	Hailey's	Hailey	true
15.	Change `NewMasRec` with `TranRec` values				
16.	Wilkin	Ch 215-04	Hailey's	Hailey	true
17.	Send `NewMasRec` to `NewMasFile`				
18.	Wilkin	Ch 215-04	Hailey's	Hailey	false
19.	Wilkin	Ch 215-04	215-04's	Hailey	false

Table *8.1*

A trace of the first two executions of the outer loop of Program 8.6.

Lines 5–11 show the effect of one execution of the outer `while` loop. Malone's record is sent to `NewMasRec`, making `NewMasPresent` true. Hailey's master record immediately takes its place in `MasRec` on line 7. Line 9 sends Malone's record unchanged to the new master file, setting `NewMasPresent` to false in line 10. `LowKey` is updated in line 11.

The effect of the first execution of the outer loop is to send Malone's record unchanged to the new master file. Note how the loop invariants are not true in the middle of the `while` loop. For example, in line 7 `LowKey` is not the smaller of the keys in `MasRec` and `TranRec`. `LowKey` has Malone's key value, whereas `MasRec` and `TranRec` both have records for Hailey. But the algorithm establishes the loop invariants again at line 11.

Lines 12–19 show the effect of the second execution of the outer `while` loop. Hailey's record is sent to `NewMasRec`, making `NewMasPresent` true. Wilkins' master record immediately takes its place in `MasRec` on line 14. This time the inner `while` loop executes once, changing Hailey's values in `NewMasRec`. The next transaction record immediately takes the place of the old record in `TranRec`. Since its key is not equal to `LowKey`, the inner loop executes only once. Lines 17, 18, and 19 are identical in effect to lines 7, 8, and 9. Again, the algorithm establishes the four loop invariants.

The high-level traces of add and delete transactions are similar. You should work through some of the traces suggested in the exercises to make sure you understand how the algorithm works.

The loop invariants help show that the algorithm terminates properly. The outer loop terminates when `LowKey <> HighSentinel` is false, that is, when `LowKey` equals `HighSentinel`. But the only way that can be true by the loop invariants is if they both contain high-sentinel key values. Since `NewMasPresent` is false, we are guaranteed that the content of `NewMasRec` does not need to be written to `NewMasFile`.

Program 8.6 is the complete Pascal program of the balanced-line algorithm for the sequential file update problem. It shows the processing details of the inner `while` loop.

The program uses the same technique of simulating sentinels in the input files that the merge algorithm used. Both `GetMasRec` and `GetTranRec` test whether

Program 8.6

The sequential file update program.

```pascal
program FileUpdate (output, OldMasFile, TranFile, NewMasFile);
   const
      HighSentinel = '999-99-9999';
   type
      SSNumType  = packed array [1..11] of char;
      NameType   = packed array [1..15] of char;
      ClassType  = (Frosh, Soph, Jr, Sr, Grad, Blank);
      TranType   = (Add, Change, Delete);
      MasRecType =
         record
         Key:   SSNumType;
         Name:  NameType;
         Class: ClassType
         end;
      TranRecType =
         record
         Kind: TranType;
         Data: MasRecType
         end;
      TranFType = file of TranRecType;
      MasFType  = file of MasRecType;
   var
      OldMasFile:    MasFType;
      NewMasFile:    MasFType;
      TranFile:      TranFType;
      MasRec:        MasRecType;
      TranRec:       TranRecType;
      NewMasRec:     MasRecType;
      LowKey:        SSNumType;
      NewMasPresent: boolean;
```

Program 8.6, continued

```
procedure Min (var Low: SSNumType; KeyA, KeyB: SSNumType);
   begin
   if KeyA < KeyB then
      Low := KeyA
   else
      Low := KeyB
   end;

procedure GetTranRec (var TrFile: TranFType; var TrRec: TranRecType);
   begin
   if eof (TrFile) then
      TrRec.Data.Key := HighSentinel
   else
      read (TrFile, TrRec)
   end;

procedure GetMasRec (var MsFile: MasFType; var MsRec: MasRecType);
   begin
   if eof (MsFile) then
      MsRec.Key := HighSentinel
   else
      read (MsFile, MsRec)
   end;

procedure AddRec (TrRec:      TranRecType;
               var NewMsRec:  MasRecType;
               var NewMsPres: boolean);
   begin
   if NewMsPres then
      writeln ('Error.  Attempt to add ', TrRec.Data.Key)
   else
      begin
      NewMsRec := TrRec.Data;
      NewMsPres := true
      end
   end;

procedure ChangeRec (TrRec:      TranRecType;
                 var NewMsRec:  MasRecType;
                     NewMsPres: boolean);
   begin
   if NewMsPres then
      NewMsRec.Class := TrRec.Data.Class
   else
      writeln ('Error.  Attempt to change ', TrRec.Data.Key)
   end;
```

Program 8.6, continued

```
procedure DeleteRec (TrRec:      TranRecType;
                var NewMsPres: boolean);
   begin
   if NewMsPres then
      NewMsPres := false
   else
      writeln ('Error.  Attempt to delete ', TrRec.Data.Key)
   end;

begin {FileUpdate}
reset (OldMasFile);
reset (TranFile);
rewrite (NewMasFile);
NewMasPresent := false;
GetMasRec (OldMasFile, MasRec);
GetTranRec (TranFile, TranRec);
Min (LowKey, MasRec.Key, TranRec.Data.Key);
{  Assert:                                          }
{  1. MasRec has the next master record             }
{  2. TranRec has the next transaction record       }
{  3. LowKey contains the smaller of their keys      }
{  4. NewMasPresent is false                         }
while LowKey <> HighSentinel do
   begin
   if MasRec.Key = LowKey then
      begin
      NewMasRec := MasRec;
      NewMasPresent := true;
      GetMasRec (OldMasFile, MasRec)
      end;
   while TranRec.Data.Key = LowKey do
      begin
      case TranRec.Kind of
      Add:
         AddRec (TranRec, NewMasRec, NewMasPresent);
      Change:
         ChangeRec (TranRec, NewMasRec, NewMasPresent);
      Delete:
         DeleteRec (TranRec, NewMasPresent)
      end {case};
      GetTranRec (TranFile, TranRec)
      end;
   if NewMasPresent then
      begin
      write (NewMasFile, NewMasRec);
      NewMasPresent := false
      end;
   Min (LowKey, MasRec.Key, TranRec.Data.Key)
   end
end.
```

Input/Output

See text.

the file is empty. If it is, they give the high sentinel value to the record. Otherwise they read the record from the file.

Procedures `AddRec`, `ChangeRec`, and `DeleteRec` perform the processing in the transaction loop. Each one tests `NewMasPresent` for possible incompatibilities between `NewMasRec` and `TranRec`.

AddRec   The purpose of an *add transaction* is to insert the information from the transaction record into the new master file. Figure 8.13 shows that the data must flow along the data path from `TranRec` to `NewMasRec`, then from `NewMasRec` to `NewMasFile`.

If `NewMasPresent` is true when `AddRec` is called, the first `if` statement in the outer loop must have sent a record from `MasRec` to `NewMasRec`. That can only happen if the key for `TranRec` matches the key for `NewMasRec`, that is, if you are attempting to add a record with the same key as a record in the old master file.

Procedure `AddRec` tests `NewMasPresent`. If it is true, it issues the appropriate error message to the screen. If `NewMasPresent` is false, data can flow from `TranRec` to `NewMasRec` without colliding with any valid data already in `NewMasRec`. Procedure `AddRec` copies the `Key`, `Name`, and `Class` fields from `TranRec` to `NewMasRec`.

If there was no error, procedure `AddRec` must also set `NewMasPresent` to true for two reasons. First, the next transaction may be a change to the record just added. If so, procedure `ChangeRec` will need to know that `NewMasRec` contains valid data that can be changed. Second, if the next transaction is not a change to this record, the last `if` statement in the outer loop needs to know that `NewMasRec` contains valid data to be sent to `NewMasFile`.

ChangeRec   The purpose of a *change transaction* is to modify the value of the class field in a record that exists in the old master file. Like procedure `AddRec`, procedure `ChangeRec` tests `NewMasPresent` for a possible error condition. But unlike `AddRec`, if `NewMasPresent` is true, there is no error. If valid data is in `NewMasRec`, procedure `ChangeRec` modifies its class field. Otherwise, it issues an appropriate error message to the screen.

DeleteRec   The purpose of a *delete transaction* is to remove a record from the old master file. The key of the transaction record must match the key of a record in the old master file. Like procedure `ChangeRec`, there is no error if `NewMasPresent` is true. Procedure `DeleteRec` deletes the record by simply setting `NewMasPresent` to false. When the last `if` statement in the outer `while` loop executes, it will not write the data from `NewMasRec` to the new master file. The effect is to delete the record.

In practice, sequential file update problems can be much more complicated than this registrar's problem at YLU. There could be dozens of possible transactions, including payment to an account, change of address, and so on. But no matter how complicated the transaction, it must fall into one of three categories—add, change, or delete. The basic balanced-line algorithm remains unchanged. The only difference would be additional, perhaps more complicated, procedures in place of `ChangeRec`.

8.3 Arrays of Records

Figure 8.7 shows the structure of record `Empl`. The first two fields of the record are arrays. `Empl` is a record of arrays and real values. Pascal lets you reverse these roles of records and arrays. Not only can you build a record of arrays, you can also build an array of records.

Program 8.7

Program 8.7 shows how to declare and manipulate an array of records. In this example, the records are in the array.

`MemberType` is a record with two parts, `Name` and `Relation`. Figure 8.14 shows its structure. The value in `Name` is a 10-letter string. The value in `Relation` is enumerated—either Father, Mother, Son, or Daughter.

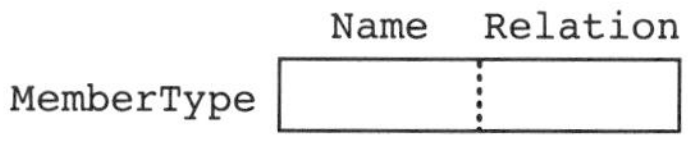

Figure 8.14

The structure of `MemberType` in Program 8.7.

`Family` is an array of four records whose structure is depicted in Figure 8.15. Each component of the array is a record of type `MemberType`. For example, `Family [2]` is a record with two parts, `Name` and `Relation`.

You would refer to elements in an array of records the same way you would refer to elements of arrays and records in general. Since `Family` is an array, `Family [2]` is the second component of the array. Since `Family [2]` is a record,

`Family [2].Relation`

is a field variable with enumerated type.

	Name	Relation
Family [1]	'Stan '	Father
Family [2]	'Ann '	Mother
Family [3]	'Elisa '	Daughter
Family [4]	'Tracey '	Daughter

Figure 8.15

The structure of array `Family` in Program 8.7.

`Family` is at the highest level of abstraction. One sequence from highest to lowest levels of data abstraction is the following:

`Family`	is an array of records.
`Family [2]`	is a record.
`Family [2].Relation`	is an enumerated field variable.

Another sequence is the following:

`Family`	is an array of records.
`Family [2]`	is a record.
`Family [2].Name`	is a packed array of `char`.
`Family [2].Name [3]`	is a `char`.

You can access the data at any level of abstraction.

```
program IntroArrayOfRecord (output);
   type
      MemberType =
         record
         Name:      packed array [1..10] of char;
         Relation: (Father, Mother, Son, Daughter)
         end;
   var
      Family:      array [1..4] of MemberType;
      NumFemales:  integer;
      NumChildren: integer;
      I:           integer;
   begin
   Family [1].Name := 'Stan      ';
   Family [1].Relation := Father;
   Family [2].Name := 'Ann       ';
   Family [2].Relation := Mother;
   Family [3].Name := 'Elisa     ';
   Family [3].Relation := Daughter;
   Family [4].Name := 'Tracey    ';
   Family [4].Relation := Daughter;
   NumFemales := 0;
   NumChildren := 0;
   for I := 1 to 4 do
      begin
      if (Family [I].Relation = Mother)
      or (Family [I].Relation = Daughter) then
         NumFemales := NumFemales + 1;
      if (Family [I].Relation = Son)
      or (Family [I].Relation = Daughter) then
         NumChildren := NumChildren + 1
      end;
   writeln ('There are ', NumFemales: 1, ' females.');
   writeln ('There are ', NumChildren: 1, ' children.')
   end.
```

Program 8.7

Accessing the components of an array of records.

Output

```
There are 3 females.
There are 2 children.
```

Example 8.4   The assignment

`Family [2].Name := 'Ann       '`

treats `Family [2].Name` as a single word at one level of abstraction. The assignment

`Family [2].Name [3] := 'n'`

treats the data at a lower level of abstraction.   ■

Modula-2: New and Improved Pascal

Why would Niklaus Wirth, the creator of Pascal, invent a second language, Modula-2, so close on the heels of the first? Unlike the development of a new laundry detergent, Wirth's development of a new language was not simply a case of marketing hype—Wirth deserves and receives credit for developing both languages.

Pascal was Wirth's elegant response to the top-heavy Algol-68 standard. The clean lines of Pascal were immediately attractive to programming language instructors and theorists who believed that it was time for the field of computer programming to admit the positive, structure-inducing influences of a well-ordered language. The predecessors of Pascal included FORTRAN and COBOL, in which unrestricted branching, or the goto command, often led to spaghetti code programs that were difficult to read and debug. The toolbox of natural structuring commands for controlling program loops and conditional expressions, together with Pascal's strong typing, made Pascal programs largely self-documenting and helped to make the waters of computer programming less murky.

If Pascal is so wonderful, what's all the hoopla about Modula-2? Is something fundamentally wrong with Pascal? Not really—Pascal is still a useful programming language that fills a niche in education and industry through its simplicity, elegance,

and efficiency. We should recall that the 1970s, the period in which Pascal became popular, was an exciting time in computing hardware developments. In the mid-1970s, the minicomputer appeared on the scene, replacing the huge mainframes and punch cards of the early 1970s. These minicomputers had increasingly user-friendly interfaces, including full-screen text editors, removable floppy diskettes, and dedicated printers. The seeds of what we now know as the workstation microcomputer were being sown.

After spending a sabbatical year as a visting researcher at Xerox PARC, a silicon valley think tank of innovative research and development, Wirth got excited about the new machines and their capabilities. He set to work on his design of the Lilith machine, a single-user computer that was to use a single programming language throughout.

Rather than write the low-level systems software in assembly language, Wirth preferred to take advantage of the high-level constructs available in Pascal. Yet he felt that it should be possible to hide the low-level system details from an applications programmer for the same reason that we want to be able to use a CD player without having to specify the geometrical coordinates of the starting and ending points of a song we want to hear. Wirth had previously

sketched an experimental language called Modula, an enhanced version of Pascal that better supported the software engineering task of splitting projects up into largely independent modules. He wanted modules to be capable of being separately compiled and tested, preserving data-hiding (or *data encapsulation*). Clean, well-specified interfaces would exist so that information sharing between modules would be accomplished only by explicit importing and exporting, not by obscure references to the innards of conceptually unrelated units.

Modula-2 represents the marriage of the best ideas in Pascal to the modularity concepts that arose from the theoretical investigations that went into Modula, driven by the fervor to build a practical machine with a powerful and consistent programming language throughout. By getting closer to the hardware, Modula-2 allows very precise control of a machine's resources for those who need it, yet simultaneously allows users to abstract implementation details away into separate modules, observing the maxim of good software engineering that everything should be in its own place. And since Modula-2 can do everything Pascal can, it is also a powerful high-level language for implementing diverse applications programs.

Program 8.8

Program 8.8 uses an array of records to represent a phone book. Here is a pseudocode outline of the main program:

```
begin
Input PhoneBook (including its length).
repeat
    Ask user for SearchName
    Look up SearchName in PhoneBook
    if SearchName in PhoneBook
        Output the number.
    else
        Output a "not found" message.
    Ask user if he wants to look up again
until user wants to stop.
end
```

```
program PhoneNumber (input, output, PhoneFile);
    const
        MaxBookLen = 50;
    type
        NameType   = packed array [1..10] of char;
        NumType    = packed array [1..8] of char;
        ListingType =
            record
            Name:   NameType;
            Number: NumType
            end;
        PhFileType = file of ListingType;
        BookType   = array [1..MaxBookLen] of ListingType;
    var
        PhoneFile:  PhFileType;
        SearchName: NameType;
        PhoneBook:  BookType;
        BookLen:    integer;
        Found:      boolean;
        Index:      integer;
        Response:   char;

    procedure LookUp (var Fnd:      boolean;
                      var Indx:     integer;
                          BkLen:    integer;
                      var PhBook:   BookType; {var for efficiency}
                          SrchName: NameType);
        begin
        writeln ('LookUp called.');
        Indx := 1;
        Fnd := true
        end;
```

Program 8.8

The top-level test of a program to look up the telephone number for a given name. The phone book is an array of records.

Program 8.8, continued

```
procedure GetBook (var PhFile: PhFileType;
                   var PhBook: BookType;
                   var BkLen:  integer);
   begin
   writeln ('GetBook called.');
   BkLen := 1;
   PhBook [1].Number := '000-0000'
   end;

procedure GetString (var S: NameType);
   {  This procedure gets a string value for S from  }
   {  the keyboard, padded with trailing spaces.     }
   var
      I: integer;
   begin
   for I := 1 to 10 do
      if eoln (input) then
         S [I] := ' '
      else
         read (input, S [I]);
   readln (input)
   end;

begin
GetBook (PhoneFile, PhoneBook, BookLen);
repeat
   write ('Enter name: ');
   GetString (SearchName);
   LookUp (Found, Index, BookLen, PhoneBook, SearchName);
   writeln ('Name: ', SearchName);
   if Found then
      writeln ('Number: ', PhoneBook [Index].Number)
   else
      writeln ('Number: Not listed');
   write ('Look up another number? (y or n): ');
   readln (Response);
   writeln
until not ((Response = 'Y') or (Response = 'y'))
end.
```

Input—`PhoneFile` (nontext)

Karpov	231-3395
Tal	298-4478
Fischer	220-1006
Korchnoi	311-0229
Fine	298-1991
Spassky	993-4920

Interactive Input/Output

```
GetBook called.
Enter name: Tal
LookUp called.
Name: Tal
Number: 000-0000
Look up another number? (y or n): y

Enter name: Jones
LookUp called.
Name: Jones
Number: 000-0000
Look up another number? (y or n): n
```

Program 8.8 is the top level of a top-down design of the program. Procedures
GetBook and LookUp have testing stubs.

Figure 8.16 shows the structure of PhoneBook, which is an array of records.
Compare this structure with Figure 7.11, which contained the same information but
in the form of parallel arrays.

	Name	Number
PhoneBook [1]	Karpov	231-3395
PhoneBook [2]	Tal	298-4478
PhoneBook [3]	Fischer	220-1006
PhoneBook [4]	Korchnoi	311-0229
PhoneBook [5]	Fine	298-1991
PhoneBook [6]	Spassky	993-4920
PhoneBook [7]	?	?

Figure 8.16

The structure of PhoneBook in
Programs 8.8 and 8.9.

The statements in procedure GetBook

```
writeln ('GetBook called.');
PhBook [1].Number := '000-0000'
```

are testing stubs. The purpose of the procedure is to input the records from the file
of records into the array of records. The procedure must count the number of
records input into the array. It should check that the number of records in the file
does not exceed the maximum size of the array. The stub simulates the input of
part of a single record into the first element of the array.

The statements in procedure `LookUp`

```
writeln ('LookUp called.');
Indx := 1;
Fnd := true
```

are also testing stubs. They simulate a search procedure that always finds the desired name in the first record of the phone book.

The test output is consistent with the stubs. Regardless of the search name entered by the user, the `LookUp` stub returns the index for the first record of the `PhoneBook` array. Completion of the procedures is left as an exercise.

Program 8.9

Program 8.9 is the top-level test of a program that inputs a phone book whose names are out of order. The program sorts the records by last name and prints out the book before and after the sort.

```
program PhoneSort (PhoneFile, output);
   const
      MaxBookLen = 50;
   type
      NameType    = packed array [1..10] of char;
      NumType     = packed array [1..8] of char;
      ListingType =
         record
         Name:   NameType;
         Number: NumType
         end;
      PhFileType = file of ListingType;
      BookType   = array [1..MaxBookLen] of ListingType;
   var
      PhoneFile: PhFileType;
      PhoneBook: BookType;
      BookLen:   integer;

   Procedure GetBook (var PhFile: PhFileType;
                      var PhBook: BookType;
                      var BkLen:  integer);
      begin
      writeln ('GetBook called.');
      PhBook [1].Name := 'Baker     ';
      PhBook [1].Number := '000-0000';
      PhBook [2].Name := 'Able      ';
      PhBook [2].Number := '000-0000';
      BkLen := 2
      end;
```

Program 8.9

The top-level test of a program to sort a phone book whose names are out of order.

Program 8.9, continued

```
procedure SortBook (var PhBook: BookType; BkLen: integer);
   begin
   writeln ('SortBook called.');
   writeln
   end;

procedure PrintBook (var PhBook: BookType; {var for efficiency}
                         BkLen:  integer);
   var
      I: integer;
   begin
   writeln ('Name          Number  ');
   writeln ('--------------------');
   for I := 1 to BkLen do
      writeln (PhBook [I].Name, PhBook [I].Number: 12);
   writeln
   end;

begin
GetBook (PhoneFile, PhoneBook, BookLen);
PrintBook (PhoneBook, BookLen);
SortBook (PhoneBook, BookLen);
PrintBook (PhoneBook, BookLen)
end.
```

Input—`PhoneFile` (nontext)

Karpov	231-3395
Tal	298-4478
Fischer	220-1006
Korchnoi	311-0229
Fine	298-1991
Spassky	993-4920

Output

```
GetBook called.
Name          Number
--------------------
Baker         000-0000
Able          000-0000


SortBook called.

Name          Number
--------------------
Baker         000-0000
Able          000-0000
```

The structure of `PhoneBook` in this program is identical to that of `PhoneBook` in the previous program, as Figure 8.16 shows.

The assignment statements in procedure `GetBook`

```
PhBook [1].Name := 'Baker     ';
PhBook [1].Number := '000-0000';
PhBook [2].Name := 'Able      ';
PhBook [2].Number := '000-0000';
BkLen := 2
```

simulate the input of two records from the file. They do not place the names in alphabetical order. In a top-down development, you could complete procedure `SortBook` next and test it before completing procedure `GetBook`. If it works, the two names will be output in order.

As in the previous example, procedure `GetBook` must count the number of records input into the array. It should check that the number of records in the file does not exceed the maximum size of the array.

In procedure `SortBook`, you can take advantage of the ability to treat a record as a single object. For example, the single statement

```
PhBook [I - 1] := PhBook [I]
```

moves both the `Name` and `Number` values of record `PhBook [I]` to record `PhBook [I - 1]`. The completion of procedures `GetBook` and `SortBook` is left as an exercise.

8.4 Variant Records

All the records considered thus far had fixed parts only. Sometimes the data you want to group into a single record does not have the same structure, however. For example, in a business application you may want to maintain a file of personnel records. Each record may contain a field for the employee's number, name, address, and job skills. If the job skills field indicates that the employee has clerical skills, then the fields that follow may indicate the kind of skills, such as whether the employee can type and, if so, how fast. If the job skills field indicates the employee has management experience, the following fields may indicate the type of management and the number of people managed.

The need for variant records

The structure of *variant records* depends on the value of the data in a field of the record. The field containing the value that the structure depends on is called the *tag field*. In the example just presented, the job skills field would be the tag field. The structure of the record would depend on whether the value in the tag field indicates clerical or managerial.

The tag field

◻ Program 8.10

Program 8.10 shows how to declare and manipulate a variant record. Figure 8.17 shows the structure of `ObjectType` as declared in the program. Figure 8.2, the syntax chart for a field list, shows that a field list can contain either a fixed field list, a variant field list, or both. `ObjectType` has both. `Color` is the fixed part, and the remainder of the record is the variant part.

The first field in the variant part, `Shape`, is the tag field. The program declares `Shape` to have `ShapeType`, which is enumerated. The two possible values of `Shape` are `Circle` and `Rectangle`. The value in the `Shape` field indicates which of the two variants will be used.

Figure 8.18 shows the values of the record variables. In `Obj1`, the value of `Shape` is `Rectangle`. In that case, the remainder of the variant field consists of `Width` and `Height`. In `Obj2`, the value of `Shape` is `Circle`. In that case, the remainder of the variant field consists of `Diameter`.

Figure 8.3 shows the syntax of a fixed field list. The fixed field list of `ObjectType` is

`Color: ColorType`

Figure 8.2 shows that it must be separated from the variant field list by a semicolon.

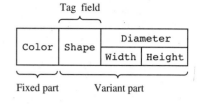

Figure 8.17

The structure of variant record `ObjectType` in Program 8.10. Each box contains its field identifier.

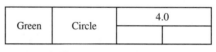

(a) The values in `Obj1`.   (b) The values in `Obj2`.

Figure 8.18

The values in the variant records in Program 8.10.

Figure 8.19 is the syntax chart of a variant field list. The variant field list of `ObjectType` is

```
case Shape: ShapeType of
Circle: (
    Diameter: real);
Rectangle: (
    Width:  real;
    Height: real)
```

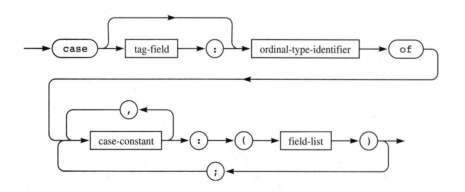

Figure 8.19

The syntax chart of a variant field list.

```
program IntroVariant (output);
   type
      ColorType  = (Red, Green, Blue);
      ShapeType  = (Circle, Rectangle);
      ObjectType =
         record
         Color: ColorType;
         case Shape: ShapeType of
         Circle: (
            Diameter: real);
         Rectangle: (
            Width:  real;
            Height: real)
         end;
   var
      Obj1, Obj2: ObjectType;
   begin
   Obj1.Color := Blue;
   Obj1.Shape := Rectangle;
   Obj1.Width := 2.1;
   Obj1.Height := 3.0;
   Obj2.Color := Green;
   Obj2.Shape := Circle;
   Obj2.Diameter := 4.0;
   writeln ('Obj1.Height = ', Obj1.Height: 3: 1);
   writeln ('Obj2.Diameter = ', Obj2.Diameter: 3: 1)
   end.
```

Program 8.10

A program to illustrate variant records.

Output

```
Obj1.Height = 3.0
Obj2.Diameter = 4.0
```

The fact that a field identifier is in a variant part of the record does not affect the way you refer to it. You refer to the `Color` field in the fixed part of `Obj1` as `Obj1.Color`. You refer to the `Width` field in the variant part of `Obj1` similarly as `Obj1.Width`.

One consequence of the uniformity of reference is the inability to use duplicate identifiers in different variations.

Example 8.5 You might wish to declare `Shape` to have the enumerated type (`Circle, Rectangle, Triangle`). Then you might want the variant field list to be

```
case Shape: ShapeType of
Circle: (
   Diameter: real);
Rectangle: (
   Width:  real;
   Height: real);
Triangle: (
   Base:   real;
   Height: real)
```

This field list would be illegal because `Height` is duplicated. If you write `Obj1.Height` in your program, the compiler would not know to which `Height` you are referring.   ■

This restriction, incidentally, does not apply to field identifiers in different records.

Example 8.6   Rather than nest a record in the transaction record of the sequential file update problem, you could define the record types as

```
type
   MasRecType =
      record
      Key:   SSNumType;
      Name:  NameType;
      Class: ClassType
      end;
   TranRecType =
      record
      Kind:  TranType;
      Key:   SSNumType;
      Name:  NameType;
      Class: ClassType
      end;
```

The assignment statements in procedure `AddRec` would be

```
NewMsRec.Key   := TrRec.Key;
NewMsRec.Name  := TrRec.Name;
NewMsRec.Class := TrRec.Class
```

There is no problem with duplicating a field identifier, for example `Key`, since the particular `Key` you refer to is qualified by the variable identifier—`NewMsRec` or `TrRec`.   ■

Program 8.11

Program 8.11 takes its input from a file of variant records. Each record has the same structure as the variant records in Program 8.10. Remember that the file is nontext. The input values shown after the program listing are misleading, because you cannot see the contents of a nontext file directly. The program outputs the color, shape, and area of each object.

Program 8.11

Processing a file of variant records.

```pascal
program ObjectAreas (ObjFile, output);
   const
      Pi = 3.1416;
   type
      ColorType  = (Red, Green, Blue);
      ShapeType  = (Circle, Rectangle);
      ObjectType =
         record
         Color: ColorType;
         case Shape: ShapeType of
         Circle: (
            Diameter: real);
         Rectangle: (
            Width:  real;
            Height: real)
         end;
   var
      ObjFile:  file of ObjectType;
      Object:   ObjectType;
      ColorStr: array [ColorType] of packed array [1..5] of char;
      ShapeStr: array [ShapeType] of packed array [1..9] of char;
      Area:     real;
   begin
   ColorStr [Red] := 'red  ';
   ColorStr [Green] := 'green';
   ColorStr [Blue] := 'blue ';
   ShapeStr [Circle] := 'circle   ';
   ShapeStr [Rectangle] := 'rectangle';
   writeln ('Color  Shape        Area');
   writeln ('------------------------');
   reset (ObjFile);
   while not eof (ObjFile) do
      begin
      read (ObjFile, Object);
      write (ColorStr [Object.Color], '  ');
      write (ShapeStr [Object.Shape]);
      case Object.Shape of
      Circle:
         Area := Pi * sqr (Object.Diameter) / 4.0;
      Rectangle:
         Area := Object.Width * Object.Height
      end {case};
      writeln (Area: 8: 2)
      end
   end.
```

Input—ObjFile (nontext)   Program 8.11, continued

red	circle	2.0	
green	circle	3.5	
green	rectangle	8.2	1.0
blue	rectangle	1.1	2.3
blue	circle	3.0	
red	rectangle	10.0	15.0
blue	circle	4.0	
red	circle	0.5	

Output

```
Color  Shape        Area
------------------------
red    circle        3.14
green  circle        9.62
green  rectangle     8.20
blue   rectangle     2.53
blue   circle        7.07
red    rectangle   150.00
blue   circle       12.57
red    circle        0.20
```

The program uses the string table technique to output the values of the enumerated field variables. `ColorStr` is an array of five-letter words to output the color, and `ShapeStr` is an array of nine-letter words to output the shape.

The computation of the area depends on the shape of the object. If the shape is a circle, the area is π times the square of the diameter divided by 4. If the shape is a rectangle, the area is the width times the height.

Note the similarity between the declaration of the variant record and the processing of the variant part with the `case` statement. The similarity is not accidental. Whenever you process information from a variant record, the `case` statement is usually the most appropriate control statement.

Declaration

```
case Shape: ShapeType of
Circle: (
   Diameter: real);
Rectangle: (
   Width:  real;
   Height: real)
```

Processing

```
case Object.Shape of
Circle:
   Area := ...  Object.Diameter ...
Rectangle:
   Area := Object.Width * Object.Height
end {case}
```

The similarity of structure between a variant field list and the case statement that processes it

Figure 8.19, the syntax chart for a variant field list, shows that the tag field is optional. You can omit the tag field when you do not need data within the record to tell you which variant to use.

The tag field is optional.

Example 8.7 Suppose you want to use the count technique with a file of records. Each record contains a real value for the hours worked and a real value for the hourly rate. But the first record should contain an integer value for the number of records that follows. An appropriate record type would be

```
record
case boolean of
true: (
   NumItems: integer);
false: (
   HoursWorked: real;
   HourlyRate:  real)
end
```

Figure 8.20 shows the structure of the record. It does not have a fixed field list, and the variant field list does not have a tag field. You do not need a tag field because you know that the first record input from the file contains a single integer, and the remaining records contain a pair of real values. You do not need a tag field to tell you which record is first. ∎

Variant records help to conserve memory. If Pascal did not provide for variant records, no processing power would be lost. The processing would just require more memory.

Example 8.8 You can also use the count technique with a nontext file of fixed records. Each record could have the following structure:

```
record
NumItems:    integer;
HoursWorked: real;
HourlyRate:  real
end
```

Each record would have enough memory for one integer and two real values. But most records in the file would use only the memory for the two real values. Only the first record would use the integer field, and it would not use the real fields. ∎

The variant record in Figure 8.20 shows the integer field overlapping the real fields. Those are not separate memory locations. They are the same memory locations that the program can interpret two different ways. In Figure 8.20, you cannot store an integer value and two real values. You can either store an integer value or you can store two real values.

The amount of memory allocated for a variant record is enough to store the longest variant. This declaration allocates enough memory for two real values, which is more than is necessary for one integer. The record that stores one integer value will have some unused memory.

Figure 8.18(a) shows values stored in one variant, and 8.18(b) shows a value in the other variant. Since memory for the variants is shared, you cannot have values in both variants simultaneously. However, you can put a value in one variant and later access the other variant. Even though Pascal compilers permit such accesses, the results are undefined because they will vary from one computer to the next.

NumItems	
HoursWorked	HourlyRate

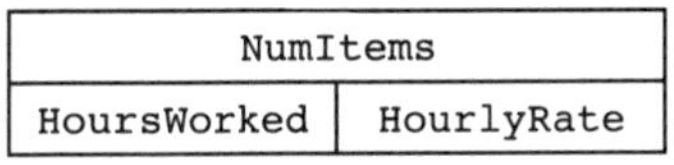

Figure 8.20

The structure of a variant record without a fixed part or a tag field.

Memory conservation with variant records

Variant fields share memory.

Accessing variant fields can produce undefined results.

Example 8.9 On one computer, variable X was declared to be a record as defined in Example 8.7 and the following code fragment was executed:

```
X.HoursWorked := 40.0;
X.HourlyRate := 10.00;
writeln ('X.NumItems = ', X.NumItems)
```

The output was

```
X.NumItems =      17184
```

However, if you perform the same processing on your computer, the integer value will probably be different. The particular value output depends on how the computer stores real values and integers in binary and is difficult to predict without delving into those details at the machine level. ∎

Nested variants

The syntax chart for a variant field list, Figure 8.19, shows that parentheses surround a field list. A field list can, however, consist of a fixed field list and/or a variant field list. You can put a variant field in a variant field. In other words, you can nest variant fields.

Example 8.10 Suppose that NameType, AddressType, and DateType have been previously defined. StatusType is enumerated with values (Annual, Associate).

```
record
Name:     NameType;
Address: AddressType;
case MemberStatus: StatusType of
Annual: (
   RenewDate: DateType);
Associate: (
   ContribDate: DateType;
   case HasLifeIns: boolean of
   true: (
      Amount: real);
   false: (
      SolicitDate: DateType))
end
```

Figure 8.21 shows the structure of the record.

The record represents information for a club member. A feature of the club is that it offers life insurance to all its associate members. If the associate member has life insurance, the record stores the amount. Otherwise it stores the last date insurance was solicited from the member. ∎

Name	Address	MemberStatus	RenewDate		
			ContribDate	HasLifeIns	Amount
					SolicitDate

Figure 8.21

A record with nested variants.

8.5 Sets

Like arrays and records, sets are collections of values. Sets are similar to arrays in that the elements of a set must all be of the same type. Unlike arrays, however, the values in a set are not ordered. You can access the third element of an array as a subscripted variable, but you cannot access the third element of a set. This section reviews the concept of sets in mathematics then shows how to declare and use set variables in Pascal.

Sets in Mathematics

A *set* is a collection of objects taken from some universal collection of objects. In mathematics notation, the collection is enclosed in set braces, and the order is irrelevant. The empty set is the set with no elements, denoted $\emptyset$.

Example 8.11   Suppose the universal set is the set of integers between 0 and 7. The universal set is denoted

$$\{0, 1, 2, 3, 4, 5, 6, 7\}$$

An example of a set whose elements are taken from the universal set is

$$A = \{0, 1, 2, 5\}$$

which can also be written, for example, as

$$A = \{0, 5, 1, 2\}$$

since the order is irrelevant. Another example of a set whose elements are from the same universal set is

$$B = \{1, 4, 5, 6\}$$

Figure 8.22 shows these sets as Venn diagrams. ∎

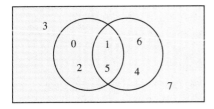

(a) The universal set.

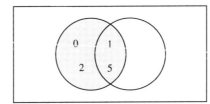

(b) Set A.

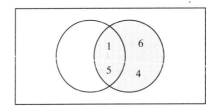

(c) Set B.

Figure 8.22

Some sets from the universal set $\{0, 1, 2, 3, 4, 5, 6, 7\}$.

Three common operations on sets are *union, intersection,* and *difference.* The union of sets A and B, denoted $A \cup B$ mathematically, is the set whose members are in either A or B or both. The intersection, $A \cap B$, is the set whose members are in both A and B. The difference, $A - B$, is the set of A's members that are not also in B. Another mathematical notation is $\in$, which means "is a member of."

Example 8.12 Assuming the same sets as in the previous example, the union of A and B is

$$A \cup B = \{0, 1, 2, 4, 5, 6\}$$

Notice that elements 1 and 5, which are in both A and B, are not duplicated in the union. Any element from the universal set is either in a given set once or it is not in the set. It cannot occur more than once. The intersection of A and B is

$$A \cap B = \{1, 5\}$$

since 1 and 5 are the only elements that are in both A and B. The difference of A and B is

$$A - B = \{0, 2\}$$

since 0 and 2 are the elements that are in A but not also in B. Figure 8.23 contains Venn diagrams that show these three set operations. The mathematical statement

$$2 \in A$$

means that 2 is an element of the set A. ∎

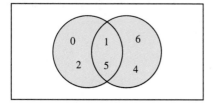

(a) The union, $A \cup B$.

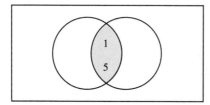

(b) The intersection, $A \cap B$.

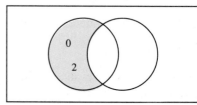

(c) The difference, $A - B$.

Figure 8.23

Three set operations as Venn diagrams.

Program 8.12

Set types in Pascal are built from other types using the set type constructor. The type constructors of Pascal include

The Pascal type constructors

- File
- Enumerated
- Subrange
- Array
- Record
- Set

For example, a record type is a type constructed from other types, as in Program 8.1 where the record is a collection of an integer and a character. Similarly, a set type is constructed by specifying the universal set from which the set variable will get its possible elements.

Program 8.12 shows how to declare and output set variables. SetX, SetY, and SetZ are variables of type set. Their values are computed from the three set

```pascal
program IntroSet (output);
   type
      SetType = set of 0..7;
   var
      SetX: SetType;
      SetY: SetType;
      SetZ: SetType;

   procedure PutSet (S: SetType);
      var
         I: integer;
      begin
      for I := 0 to 7 do
         if I in S then
            write (I: 3);
      writeln
      end;

   begin
   SetX := [0, 1, 2, 5] + [1, 4, 5, 6];
   SetY := [0, 1, 2, 5] * [1, 4, 5, 6];
   SetZ := [0, 1, 2, 5] - [1, 4, 5, 6];
   write ('Union:        ');
   PutSet (SetX);
   write ('Intersection:');
   PutSet (SetY);
   write ('Difference:  ');
   PutSet (SetZ);
   end.
```

Program 8.12

A program to introduce set variables.

Output

```
Union:        0  1  2  4  5  6
Intersection: 1  5
Difference:   0  2
```

operations illustrated by the previous example. The following discussion presents the syntax of Pascal sets using Program 8.12 as an example.

The type definition

```
SetType = set of 0..7
```

defines `SetType` to be a set of integers in the range `0..7`. The ordinal type `0..7` is called the base type of the set and corresponds to the universal set from which a variable of this type can get its elements. Figure 8.24 is the syntax chart for a set type. The object `0..7` is a new ordinal type.

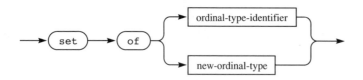

Figure 8.24

The syntax chart for a set type.

In Pascal, braces are used for comments and, therefore, cannot be used to enclose the elements of a set. Pascal uses square brackets instead. In the program, `[0, 1, 2, 5]` and `[1, 4, 5, 6]` are set constants, which correspond to the mathematical sets {0, 1, 2, 5} and {1, 4, 5, 6}. As in mathematics, the order of the elements is irrelevant, so the program will produce identical results if `[0, 1, 2, 5]` is replaced by `[0, 5, 1, 2]`. Figure 8.25 shows the syntax chart for a set constant.

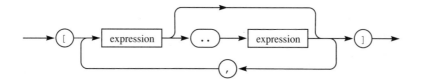

Figure 8.25

The syntax chart for a set constant.

In Program 8.12, `SetX` is computed as the union of the set constants, `SetY` as their intersection, and `SetZ` as their set difference. Pascal uses + for union, * for intersection, and – for set difference.

You cannot output the members of a set with a single `write` call. Instead, you must loop through all the values of the base type and test each one individually for membership in the set. In Program 8.12, procedure `PutSet` loops through all the values of the base set, `0..7`, testing if each one is in `S`. The Pascal operator `in` corresponds to the mathematical operator ∈. If an element is in the set, the `write` call outputs the element. A `write` call can output an integer value but not a set value.

The in operator

▭ Program 8.13

The base type in the previous program was a subrange of the integers. The base type can be any ordinal type, including enumerated. Program 8.13 processes data from a file of records. Each record has two fields. The first is a five-letter name, and the second is a set of enumerated values.

The purpose of the program is to determine the names of certain people who are free on the same days as the user. Each record in the input file contains the name of a person and the days of the week that person is free. The program outputs a table that lists the name of each person in the file and the free days that coincide with the set of days entered by the user.

The type definition part defines `DayType` to be enumerated with the seven values Sun, Mon, Tue, Wed, Thu, Fri, or Sat. It defines `DaySetType` to be a set of `DayType`. This definition is an example of using an ordinal type identifier as shown in Figure 8.24, the syntax chart for a set type. The variable declaration part declares `Day` as an enumerated variable and `UserPref` as a set variable.

Recall that the mathematical notation for the empty set is $\varnothing$. In Pascal, the empty set is written [ ]. The assignment statement

The empty set

```
UserPref := []
```

initializes `UserPref` to the empty set. The `for` statement

```
for Day := Sun to Sat do
```

executes the body of the loop seven times, once with Sun for the value of `Day`, once with Mon for the value of `Day`, and so on. Each time the loop executes, the program asks the user if `Day` is a free day. If the user responds in the affirmative, it adds the day to the `UserPref` set with the union operation.

```
UserPref := UserPref + [Day]
```

The `if` statement

```
if Response in ['y', 'Y'] then
```

is a handy use of the `in` operator, which can test for membership in a set constant as well as in a set variable. The constant `['y', 'Y']` is a set of characters, and `Response` is a character. Therefore, the boolean expression

```
Response in ['y', 'Y']
```

is legal. It is equivalent to the boolean expression

```
(Response = 'y') or (Response = 'Y')
```

It is important to distinguish between an enumerated type and a set of enumerated type. The plus sign signifies the union between two sets. The statement

```
UserPref := UserPref + Day
```

Program 8.13

Processing data from a file of
records containing sets. The base
type of the set is enumerated.

```
program Preference (DayFile, input, output);
   type
      DayType     = (Sun, Mon, Tue, Wed, Thu, Fri, Sat);
      DaySetType = set of DayType;
      NameType    = packed array [1..5] of char;
      CandType    =
         record
         Name: NameType;
         Days: DaySetType
         end;
      Str3Type     = packed array [1..3] of char;
      DayNamesType = array [Sun..Sat] of Str3Type;
   var
      DayFile:    file of CandType;
      Candidate:  CandType;
      UserPref:   DaySetType;
      CommonPref: DaySetType;
      DayNames:   DayNamesType;
      Day:        DayType;
      Response:   char;

   procedure Initialize (var DNames: DayNamesType);
      begin
      DNames [Sun] := 'Sun';
      DNames [Mon] := 'Mon';
      DNames [Tue] := 'Tue';
      DNames [Wed] := 'Wed';
      DNames [Thu] := 'Thu';
      DNames [Fri] := 'Fri';
      DNames [Sat] := 'Sat'
      end;

   procedure PutSet (DSet: DaySetType; DNames: DayNamesType);
      var
         D: DayType;
      begin
      for D := Sun to Sat do
         if D in DSet then
            write (DNames [D], ' ');
      writeln
      end;

   begin
   Initialize (DayNames);
   UserPref := [];
   for Day := Sun to Sat do
      begin
      write ('Are you free on ', DayNames [Day], '? (y or n): ');
      readln (Response);
      if Response in ['y', 'Y'] then
         UserPref := UserPref + [Day]
      end;
```

Program 8.13, continued

```
       writeln;
       write ('Your free days: ');
       PutSet (UserPref, DayNames);
       writeln ('--------------------');
       writeln ('Name   Days in common');
       writeln ('--------------------');
       reset (DayFile);
       while not eof (DayFile) do
          begin
          read (DayFile, Candidate);
          write (Candidate.Name, '  ');
          CommonPref := UserPref * Candidate.Days;
          PutSet (CommonPref, DayNames);
          end;
       writeln ('--------------------')
       end.
```

Input—`DayFile` (nontext)

David	[Sun, Wed, Thu, Fri]
Karin	[Wed, Thu]
TJ	[Sun, Mon, Tue, Wed, Thu, Fri, Sat]
Peter	[Fri]
Diane	[Sun, Tue, Thu, Sat]
Adam	[Mon, Wed, Fri]

Interactive Input/Output

```
Are you free on Sun? (y or n): y
Are you free on Mon? (y or n): y
Are you free on Tue? (y or n): n
Are you free on Wed? (y or n): n
Are you free on Thu? (y or n): y
Are you free on Fri? (y or n): n
Are you free on Sat? (y or n): y

Your free days: Sun Mon Thu Sat
--------------------
Name   Days in common
--------------------
David  Sun Thu
Karin  Thu
TJ     Sun Mon Thu Sat
Peter
Diane  Sun Thu Sat
Adam   Mon
--------------------
```

would not be a legal Pascal statement. `Day` has enumerated type, while `[Day]` is a set with one member. You must take the union of two sets. You cannot take the union of a set and an enumerated type.

Starting with the empty set, the `for` statement builds the values in the `UserPref` set as follows:

```
[]
[Sun]
[Sun, Mon]
[Sun, Mon, Thu]
[Sun, Mon, Thu, Sat]
```

Each time the `while` loop executes, it reads one record from the file into the `Candidate` record. The second field of the record, `Days`, has type `DaySetType` like `UserPref` has. The program computes the days in common between these two sets with the intersection operation.

```
CommonPref := UserPref * Candidate.Days;
```

As in Program 8.12, procedure `PutSet` outputs the values of the set. It requires the string table `DayNames` because an enumerated value cannot be output directly.

The Sieve of Eratosthenes

Eratosthenes (300 B.C.) devised a famous algorithm to calculate all the prime numbers that were less than a given number. The idea is to write down a list of integers beginning with 2. Start with the first number in the list, which is 2, and cross out every second number after it, which are 4, 6, 8, 10, 12, and so on. These numbers cannot be primes because they are divisible by 2.

Pick the next number not crossed out in the list, which is 3. It must be a prime because it is not divisible by any previous number. Cross out every third number after it, which are 6, 9, 12, 15, 18 and so on. These numbers cannot be primes because they are divisible by 3.

Pick the next number not crossed out in the list, which is 5, and cross out every fifth number after it. Keep picking the next number in the list not crossed out. It must be a prime. Cross out all multiples of it.

In the end, all the numbers crossed out are not prime and the numbers remaining in the list are prime. The algorithm is called the "sieve of Eratosthenes" because the list acts like a sieve, sifting out all the nonprime numbers and keeping the prime numbers. What follows is the Eratosthenes algorithm in the form of a procedure.

```
procedure Eratosthenes (var Sieve: SieveType);
   {  Assumes MaxNum is a constant integer and SieveType  }
   {  is defined to be a set of 2..MaxNum.                 }
   var
      Prime: integer;
      I:     integer;
      Step:  integer;
   begin
   Sieve := [2..MaxNum];
   Prime := 2;
   while sqr (Prime) <= MaxNum do
      begin
      I := 2 * Prime;
      Step := Prime;
      while I <= MaxNum do
         begin
         Sieve := Sieve - [I];
         I := I + Step
         end;
      {  Assert: Sieve contains a prime number > Prime  }
      repeat
         Prime := succ (Prime)
      until Prime in Sieve
      end
   end;
```

The procedure has one parameter, `Sieve`, called by reference. It is a set of integers in the range `2..MaxNum`, where `MaxNum` is a constant integer. After the procedure executes, the actual parameter corresponding to `Sieve` will contain all the prime numbers less than or equal to `MaxNum`.

The procedure initializes `Sieve` to its universal set and `Prime` to 2. Inside the loop, `I` gets 4, and `Step` gets 2. The inner `while` loop crosses out every second number in `Sieve` starting with 2. The set difference operation

```
Sieve := Sieve - [I]
```

performs the actual crossing out. It removes the element in the set `[I]` from `Sieve`. Table 8.2 shows a trace of `Prime` and `Sieve` in procedure Eratosthenes for a `MaxNum` of 37. Each × in the second row represents a member of `Sieve` removed by the set difference operation.

The nested `repeat` loop increments `Prime` by 1 until it finds the next integer still in `Sieve`, which is 3. The procedure then initializes `I` to 6. Since `Step` gets 3, the procedure removes every third number starting with 6.

The technique for crossing out the nonprimes is easy to understand. A more difficult concept is the termination condition for the outer `while` loop. The loop terminates when `Prime` gets 7, because 49 is greater than 37.

Prime	Sieve																	
?	2	3	4	5	6	7	8	9	10	11	12	13	14	15	16	17	18	19
2			×		×		×		×		×		×		×		×	
3					×			×			×			×			×	
5									×					×				
7	Terminate																	
Primes :	2	3		5		7				11		13				17		19

Prime	Sieve																	
?	20	21	22	23	24	25	26	27	28	29	30	31	32	33	34	35	36	37
2	×		×		×		×		×		×		×		×		×	
3		×			×			×			×			×			×	
5	×					×					×					×		
7	Terminate																	
Primes :				23						29		31						37

Table 8.2

A trace of `Prime` and `Sieve` in procedure `Eratosthenes`. MaxNum is 37.

The `while` loop can terminate when `sqr (Prime) > MaxNum` because factors come in pairs. For example, consider the number 36. The algorithm crosses it out when `Prime` is 2. That means 2 is a factor of 36. Specifically, 2(18) is 36. So 18 is also a factor of 36. Since the algorithm eliminates 36 with the factor of 2, it does not need to test it again with the factor of 18.

The number 36 was also eliminated when `Prime` was 3. Since 3(12) is 36, the algorithm does not need to test 36 with the factor of 12.

In the last step, 36 is eliminated when `Prime` is 6. Since 6(6) is 36, you no longer need to test 36 with potential factors greater than 6. You only need to test 36 for possible factors up to the square root of 36.

In general, you only need to test a possible prime number for factors up to the square root of that number. You know that 37 must be a prime even though you only test for factors up to the square root of 37. If there were a factor greater than the square root of 37, say x, it would be paired with a factor less than or equal to the square root of 37, say y, such that x times y is 37. But then 37 would have been crossed out with y.

Another concept more difficult to accept is the assertion

`Assert: Sieve contains a prime number > Prime`

How do you know when you increment `Prime` that there will be at least one more prime number left in `Sieve`?

The answer comes from a result in number theory that says there is always a prime between p and p^2 for any positive integer p. The test of the outer `while` loop guarantees that the square of `Prime` is less than `MaxNum`. Since the nested `while` loop cannot remove any prime numbers, `Sieve` must contain a prime number greater than the value of `Prime` just before the repeat loop.

Using Sets

One relation not illustrated by the previous programs is the subset relation. A set, *A*, is a subset of another set, *B*, if every element that is in *A* is also in *B*. In mathematical notation, $A \subseteq B$. In Pascal, the corresponding boolean expression is `A <= B`, or, equivalently, `B >= A`.

The subset relation

Example 8.13 Suppose A and B have `SetType` as defined in Program 8.12, with values

A = [3, 6]
B = [2, 3, 5, 6, 7]

then A is a subset of B, since every element in A is also in B. Statement 1 of the code fragment

```
if A <= B then
    Statement 1
```

would be executed with the above values for A and B. An equivalent code fragment is

```
if B >= A then
    Statement 1
```

Mathematically, two sets are equal if they contain the same elements. A more formal definition of equality is, "Set *A* equals set *B* if *A* is a subset of *B*, and *B* is a subset of *A*." The mathematical notation is = for set equality and ≠ for set inequality. In Pascal you can test for set equality with = and set inequality with <>. Table 8.3 summarizes the difference between mathematical set notation and Pascal set notation.

Mathematics	Pascal
$\{0, 1, 2, 5\}$	`[0, 1, 2, 5]`
$\varnothing$	`[]`
$A \cup B$	`A + B`
$A \cap B$	`A * B`
$A - B$	`A - B`
$A \subseteq B$	`A <= B`
$B \subseteq A$	`A >= B`
$A = B$	`A = B`
$A \neq B$	`A <> B`
$2 \in A$	`2 in A`

Table 8.3

The difference in set notation between mathematics and Pascal. *A* and *B* are sets.

Example 8.14 With the values for A and B as in the previous example, the code fragment

```
if A = B then
    Statement 1
```

will not execute Statement 1, since set A does not equal set B. The code fragment

```
if A <> B then
    Statement 1
```

will execute Statement 1.   ■

Figure 8.25, the syntax chart for a set constant, shows that you can use the double period notation within a set constant. Although this notation is identical to the notation for a subrange type, the two concepts are distinct and should not be confused.

The distinction between set elements and the subrange type with the double period notation

Example 8.15   You could write the assignment to SetX in Program 8.12 as

```
SetX := [0..2, 5] + [1, 4..6]
```

The set constant [0..2, 5] is equivalent to the constant [0, 1, 2, 5].   ■

Figure 8.25 also shows that you can write a set constant with an expression. This feature, however, is somewhat rare in practice.

Expressions in set constants

Example 8.16   The assignments are perfectly legal where I is an integer variable. If I has the value 2, SetX will get [4, 7] and SetY will get [0, 1, 2, 3].

```
SetX := [2 * I, 7];

SetY := [0..2 * I - 1]
```
                                                                                                              ■

A possible source of confusion is the difference between set constants and array subscripts. Pascal uses square brackets for both, but you must remember that they are different. The problem is compounded by the fact that the double period notation is used for subrange types that are common in array subscripts, and for set constants.

The distinction between set constants and array subscripts with the square bracket notation

Example 8.17   The type definition

```
SomeType = array [0..2, 6..9] of integer
```

defines SomeType to be a two-dimensional array of 12 integers. If A is a variable with type SomeType, the 12 subscripted variables are

```
A [0, 6]    A [0, 7]    A [0, 8]    A [0, 9]
A [1, 6]    A [1, 7]    A [1, 8]    A [1, 9]
A [2, 6]    A [2, 7]    A [2, 8]    A [2, 9]
```

That is quite different from A being a set. If A is a set of a subrange of integers, then

```
A := [0..2, 6..9]
```

gives the value [0, 1, 2, 6, 7, 8, 9] to A. The square brackets in the array definition do not have the same meaning as the square brackets in the set constant. ∎

The number of elements in a set is called the *cardinality* of the set. The cardinality of the set [0, 1, 2, 6, 7, 8, 9] is 7, since there are 7 elements in the set.

Cardinality

If there are n values in the ordinal base type, there are 2^n possible values of the corresponding set. For example, suppose ColorType is the enumerated type (Red, Yellow, Blue), and Mixture is a set of ColorType. The 8 possible values of Mixture are:

```
[ ]          [Red, Yellow]
[Red]        [Red, Blue]
[Yellow]     [Yellow, Blue]
[Blue]       [Red, Yellow, Blue]
```

Since there are 3 values of ColorType, there are 2^3 possible values of Mixture.

In mathematics terminology, the preceding list of possible values of Mixture is a set of sets called the *power set* of ColorType. If a base type has n values, the cardinality of the power set is 2^n.

The power set

SUMMARY

A record is a collection of values that may have different types. The parts of a record are called fields, which are named by field identifiers. To refer to part of a record, you use the variable name followed by the field identifier, with a period between them. Records are useful for consolidating values that need to be passed as parameters in parameter lists. A file of records is a nontext file that has all the general advantages of nontext files—namely, it is small, fast, and easy to use in programming I/O operations. A record may contain an array, and conversely, an array can have each element be a record.

In sequential file processing, the output file is an updated version of the input file. Both files have the same structure, which is usually a file of records. The file merge algorithm takes two ordered files and combines them into one file that is also ordered. The balanced-line algorithm combines an old master file with a transaction file to produce an updated master file.

Variant records are useful when the data you want to group into a single record does not have the same structure. A variant record contains a group of fields called the variant part that can store several different types. The tag field is the first field of the variant part and indicates the types of the values in the remainder of the variant part. As with most objects in Pascal, variants can be nested.

A type that is constructed from other types is called a type constructor. The type constructors of Pascal include file, enumerated, subrange, array, record, and set. A set is a collection of values, all of the same type and without regard to order. In Pascal, the operations on sets are the same as the common ones in mathematics, namely, union, intersection, set difference, subset, equality, inequality, and set membership. A famous algorithm that uses sets is the sieve of Eratosthenes, which computes prime numbers using the set difference operation in a nested loop.

EXERCISES

Section 8.1

1. How are arrays and records similar? How are they different?

2. State whether each of the following Pascal statements would be legal if placed in the main program of Program 8.1. For those that would be illegal, explain why.

```
*(a) Ch := 'B'
 (b) for I := 0 to 7 do
 (c) for SimpleRec.I := 0 to 7 do
```

3. Write the Pascal statements that would perform the following actions in the main program of Program 8.3. *(a) Multiply the hourly rate of `Empl` by 1.06. (b) Output the first name of `Empl`.

Section 8.2

*4. Suppose the record for Marshall in `MasFileA` of Program 8.5 is out of order between Capablanca and Kasparov. What will be the order of the records in `NewMasFile`?

5. What changes would you need to make to Program 8.5 if the files were in reverse alphabetical order and you wanted the new master file to be in reverse alphabetical order as well? Reverse order would have Morphy at the top of `MasFileA` and Capablanca at the bottom. The first record of `NewMasFile` would be Tal, and the last would be Capablanca.

6. In Program 8.5, suppose Lasker also appears in `MasFileB` with a phone number different from the one in `MasFileA`. Which Lasker will appear first in the output file?

*7. How many times does the outer loop of Program 8.6 execute with the input listed on page 389?

8. In Program 8.6, how many times does the outer loop execute? For each of the following possibilities, state whether the number described equals the number of outer-loop executions. If the numbers are equal, explain why. If the numbers are not equal, demonstrate this fact with a sample input/output. (a) The number of records in the old master file. (b) The number of records in the old master file plus the number of records in the transaction file. (c) The number of records in the old master file plus the number of records successfully added to the new master file. (d) The number of records in the new master file.

9. Write a high-level trace of Program 8.6 that corresponds to Table 8.1 for the following short input files. Begin the table assuming the first three statements have executed. That is, start your trace table at line 4.

* **(a)**

Input—OldMasFile (nontext)

215-04-2056	Wilkins	Frosh
224-89-1173	Fong	Grad

Input—TranFile (nontext)

Change	215-04-2057		Jr

(b)

Input—OldMasFile (nontext)

224-89-1173	Fong	Grad
322-03-3844	Fernandez	Jr

Input—TranFile (nontext)

Add	310-26-5811	Alvarez	Frosh

(c)

Input—OldMasFile (nontext)

378-45-5643	Wright	Sr
407-20-1036	Hobson	Sr

Input—TranFile (nontext)

Add	407-20-1036	Carter	Frosh

(d)

Input—OldMasFile (nontext)

508-28-3311	McPherson	Grad
588-53-7633	Johnson	Soph

Input—TranFile (nontext)

Delete	508-28-3311

(e)

Input—OldMasFile (nontext)

588-53-7633	Johnson	Soph
634-79-7724	Drake	Frosh

Input—TranFile (nontext)

Delete	634-79-7723

10. Suppose in Program 8.6 that the programmer mistakenly omits the `var` in front of `NewMsPres` in the formal parameter list of procedure `DeleteRec`. How does that affect `NewMasFile` for the input listed in the text?

Section 8.3

11. Suppose `MemberType` is defined as

```
record
FirstName: Str10Type;
LastName:  Str10Type;
Age:       integer
end
```

where `Str10Type` is a packed array of 10 characters, and `FamilyType` is defined as

```
record
Father:    MemberType;
Mother:    MemberType;
Son:       MemberType;
Daughter:  MemberType;
NumCars:   integer
end
```

If `Family` is a variable of type `FamilyType`, write the Pascal statements to perform the following actions: *(a) Increase the father's age by one. (b) Increase the number of cars by one. (c) Output the daughter's last name. (d) Test whether the son and the father have the same first name. (e) Test whether the mother and daughter have the same initials.

Section 8.4

*12. Write the type definition for the variant record diagramed in Figure 8.26. `AmtPledged` is real, and `Paid` is a boolean tag field. `AmtPaid` is a real applicable if `Paid` is true, and `NumNotices` is an integer applicable if `Paid` is false. Assuming `Entry` is a variable with this type, write the Pascal statements to perform the following actions: (a) Set `AmtPledged` to 0.0. (b) Set `Paid` to false. (c) Increment `NumNotices` by one. (d) If `Paid` is false, output a gentle message requesting payment for `NumNotices` of two or less and a more stern notice for `NumNotices` of more than two.

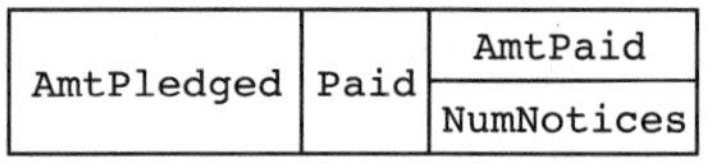

13. Write the type definition for the variant record diagramed in Figure 8.27. `Balance` is real, and `PastDue` is a boolean tag field. `NumNotices` is an integer, and `DateNotified` is a nested record, both of which are applicable when `PastDue` is true. `LastPymt` is a real, and `DatePaid` is a nested record, both of which are applicable when `PastDue` is false. Both date records consist of `Month`, `Day`, and `Year`, in that order, which are all integers. Assuming `Entry` is a variable with this type, write

AmtPledged	Paid	AmtPaid
		NumNotices

Figure 8.26

The variant record structure for Exercise 12.

Balance	PastDue	NumNotices	DateNotified
		LastPymt	DatePaid

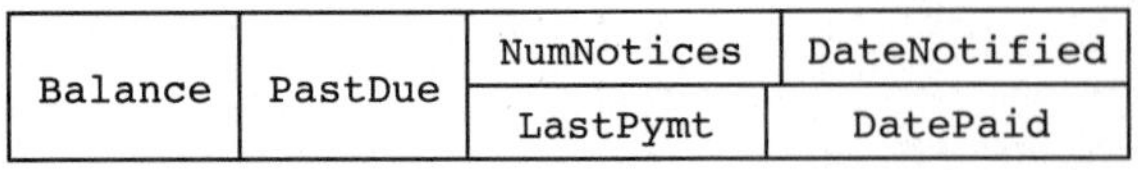

Figure 8.27

The variant record structure for Exercise 13.

the Pascal statements to perform the following actions: **(a)** Set `Balance` to 0.0. **(b)** Increase the month of `DateNotified` by one and then, if necessary because `Month` is 13, adjust the date properly. **(c)** Initialize all the integers of `DatePaid` to zero. **(d)** If `PastDue` is true, output `NumNotices`, otherwise output `LastPymt`.

14. Write the type definition for the record with nested variants diagramed in Figure 8.28. The boxes contain the field identifiers. `Name` is a packed array of 15 characters, and `Age` is an integer. `Position` is an enumerated tag field with the possible values (`Pitcher, Fielder`). The bottom variant in the figure is for `Fielder`. `FieldPosition` is enumerated with the possible values (`First, Second, Third, Short, Catch, Left, Center, Right`). `BatAbility` is enumerated with the possible values (`BatsRight, BatsLeft, Switch`). `BatAverage` is real. `PitchPosition` is another enumerated tag field with the possible values (`Start, Relief`). The top variant is for starting pitchers. `Starts, Wins, CompleteGames, Saves,` and `InningsPitched` are all integers.

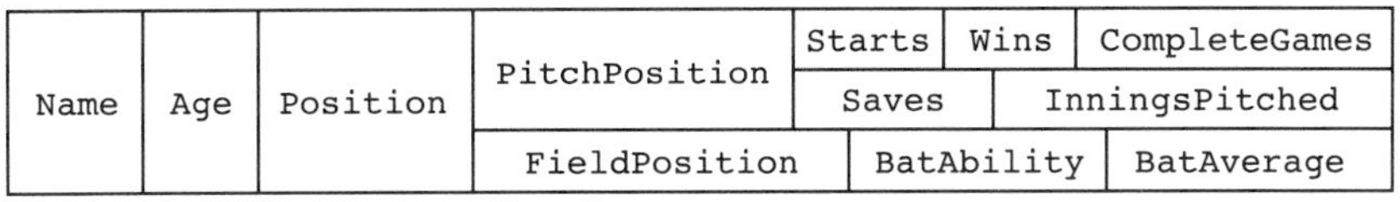

Name	Age	Position	PitchPosition	Starts	Wins	CompleteGames
				Saves		InningsPitched
			FieldPosition	BatAbility		BatAverage

Figure 8.28

The variant record structure for Exercise 14.

    Assuming `Player` is a variable with this type, write the Pascal statements to perform the following actions: *(a)** Increment `Age` by one. **(b)** Test if the player is a pitcher or a fielder. **(c)** Set `BatAbility` to `BatsRight`. **(d)** Use nested `case` statements to increment `Starts` by one if the player is a starting pitcher, increment `Saves` by one if he is a relief pitcher, or set `BatAverage` to .250 if he is a fielder.

Section 8.5

15. For `Pref` declared as `DaySetType` in Program 8.13, write Pascal statements to perform the following actions: *(a)** Set `Pref` to the empty set. *(b)** Set `Pref` to the universal set. **(c)** Set `Pref` to the set of all days except `Wed`. **(d)** Test if `Pref` is a subset of the days `Mon` through `Fri`.

16. Evaluate the following set expressions assuming A has the value $[0 .. 3]$ and B has the value $[2 .. 5]$. The base type is $0 .. 7$.

  *(a)** A + B   (b) A – B   *(c)** A * B
  (d) A = B   *(e)** A <= B   (f) A <= [4..7]
 *(g)** B <= [0..7]   (h) B <= [0, 2..5]

17. Two sets are *disjoint* if they have no elements in common. For example, {2, 4} and {0, 3, 5} are disjoint. Assuming `SetA` and `SetB` are set variables that have been given values earlier, write a Pascal code fragment that outputs a statement that tells whether the sets are disjoint.

18. The complement of a set, *A,* is the set of all elements from the universal set that are not in *A*. In Example 8.11, the complement of A is {3, 4, 6, 7}. Suppose `SetA` has type set of 0..`Largest` where `Largest` is a constant. Write a Pascal assignment statement that gives `SetB` the complement of the value of `SetA`.

Section 8.1

19. Complete Program 8.3.

20. Declare `TimeType` to be a record with three parts, each an integer subrange. `Hour` should be between 1 and 12 and `Min` and `Sec` between 0 and 59. **(a)** Write and test the top level of a program with the following procedures containing stubs: (1) Procedure `GetTime` to input the time from the keyboard, allowing only valid input. (2) Procedure `PutTime` to output the time with colons between the fields. (3) Procedure `AddTime` to add two times, with the result in a third time. (4) Procedure `SubTime` to compute the time interval between two times. The main program should ask for two times, and output their sum and difference. **(b)** Complete the program.

21. `RatNumType` is a record that stores rational numbers. Its two parts are `Num` and `Denom`, both integers, which stand for numerator and denominator. **(a)** Write and test the top level of a program with the following procedures containing stubs: (1) Procedure `GetRatNum` to input a rational number from the keyboard. (2) Procedure `PutRatNum` to output the rational number with a slash between the numerator and denominator. (3) Procedures `MulRatNum` and `DivRatNum` to multiply and divide two rational numbers, with the result in a third number. (4) Procedures `AddRatNum` and `SubRatNum` to add and subtract two rational numbers. (5) Procedure `Reduce` to reduce a rational number. If both the numerator and denominator are negative, this should make them both positive. If only the denominator is negative, this should make it positive and the numerator negative. Procedure `Reduce` should look for common factors in the numerator and denominator, and reduce the fraction if possible. **(b)** Complete the program.

22. `RankType` is enumerated with the possible values (`Deuce, Three, Four, Five, Six, Seven, Eight, Nine, Ten, Jack, Queen, King, Ace`). `SuitType` is enumerated with the possible values (`Heart, Club, Diamond, Spade`). `CardType` is a record with two parts, `Rank` and `Suit`. Write and test the top level of a program that reads five cards from a nontext file of `CardType`. Output the cards and the highest poker hand they represent.

From highest to lowest, the poker hands are as follows: royal flush (ace, king, queen, jack, ten of the same suit); straight flush (any five cards of the same suit in sequence); four of a kind (for example, four queens); full house (three of a kind and a pair); flush (five cards of the same suit not in sequence); straight (five cards in sequence but of mixed suits); three of a kind; two pairs; one pair.

Enumerate the 10 different kinds of poker hands (the 9 listed plus the possibility for none of the above) and write a function that takes 5 cards in its parameter list and returns the highest poker hand. Test the program with stubs in the lower modules.

23. An automobile record contains the following four parts: (1) `Model` is enumerated with the possible values (`Beetle, Jetta, Rabbit`). (2) `Year` is an integer subrange from 65 to 99. (3) `Color` is enumerated with possible values (`White, Black, Red, Blue`). (4) `Cost` is real. Write a program that asks the user to input a real price. Output a list of every record in a nontext file of records with a cost less than the price entered. Display all four fields of the record. Use the string table method to output the enumerated values.

Section 8.2

24. Modify Program 8.4 so that the new file is identical to the old file, except that in this case, the user has appended a group of new records to the end of the old file.

25. Modify Program 8.4 so that the new file is identical to the old file, except that in this case, the user has prefixed a group of new records to the front of the old file.

26. Modify Program 8.4 so that the new file is identical to the old file, except that in this case, the user has modified the record of his choice from the old file.

27. Suppose the old file in Program 8.4 stores records in alphabetical order by the last name. Modify the program so that the new file is identical to the old file except that in this case, the user has inserted a new record in the proper location so that alphabetical order is maintained. Make sure your program works if the key of the inserted record is less than the key of the first record in the file, or if it is greater than the key of the last record in the file.

28. Modify Program 8.5 to merge the three files `MasFileA`, `MasFileB`, and `MasFileC`, each one of which is in order, into `NewMasFile`, which also should be in order.

29. The Gas Glut Oil Company (GGOC) has a master file of all its credit card customers. Each record in the file contains

- The customer's credit card number (5 characters)
- The customer's name (20 characters)
- The current balance (real) owed on the account

The GGOC transaction file records contain

- The transaction type (enumerated)
- The customer's credit card number
- The customer's name
- The transaction amount (real)

The possible transaction values are (`Add, Delete, Payment, Purchase`). The actions to perform for each transaction are as follows: `Add`, which adds a new customer to the master file with a current balance of zero; `Delete`, which deletes a customer from the master file; `Payment`, which subtracts the transaction amount from the current balance; and `Purchase`, which adds the transaction amount to the current balance. Unlike Program 8.6, a transaction record does not contain a nested record.

   Both files are in order by credit card number. Write a program to update the GGOC master file and print a summary of the run on the screen. Include in the summary the number of new customers, the number of customers deleted, the total amount of payments, and the total amount of purchases. Use 'zzzzz' for the simulated high sentinel.

Section 8.3

30. Complete Program 8.8. Use the sequential search algorithm as in Program 7.12.

31. Complete Program 8.8. Use the binary search algorithm as described in Section 7.4 (see p. 337).

32. Complete Program 8.9. Use the selection sort algorithm as in Program 7.13.

33. `DateType` is a record with three integer fields—`Year`, `Month`, and `Day`. **(a)** Write the top level of a program to input dates from a file of `DateType` and output them in sorted order from the earliest date to the latest. Test your top level with stubs in the lower modules. **(b)** Complete the program.

34. **(a)** Write the top level for Problem 22 with the following two modifications. First, define `HandType` to be an array of five cards. Ask the user how many poker hands to deal with a maximum of seven hands. List the highest poker combination for each hand dealt. Second, do not get the input from a file of `CardType`. Instead, define `DeckType` to be an `array [1..52] of CardType`. Initialize a deck to the 52 cards (one for each possible combination of suit and rank). Ask the user to input a seed. Then use the technique of Problem 7.37 to randomize the array. Deal the cards in order from the randomized array. **(b)** Complete the program. You will find it useful for the function that evaluates the hand to first sort the five cards by rank.

35. **(a)** Write the top level of a program to play blackjack against the computer. Declare `CardType` as in Problem 22, and `DeckType` to be an `array [1..52] of CardType`. Initialize a deck to the 52 cards (one for each possible combination of suit and rank). Ask the user to input a seed. Then use the technique of Problem 7.37 to randomize the array. Deal the cards from the array. Play a series of games until the user wants to quit or you exhaust the deck.

    In blackjack, the dealer (the computer) deals each player two cards. The dealer keeps one card face down and the other face up. The object is to accumulate points as close as possible to 21 without exceeding 21. If you exceed 21, you automatically lose. Face cards (jack through king) count 10 points, and ace counts your choice of 1 or 11. Cards deuce through ten count their rank value. Note that `ord (Three)` is not 3, although it counts 3 points in blackjack.

    After the hand is dealt, the dealer asks you if you want another card. You may request as many as you want, one at a time. Then the dealer may take as many cards as he wants, one at a time. Program the dealer to refuse cards for himself when his hand totals 17 or more. The person closest to 21 without exceeding 21 wins.

    (b) Complete the program.

    (c) Play the game through 100 decks of cards. Practice memorizing the cards dealt to improve your odds of winning the games when the deck is low. Go to Las Vegas and demonstrate your newly acquired skill.

36. Modify Problem 34 to allow up to four players to play with the dealer.

Section 8.4

37. Modify `ShapeType` in Program 8.11 to have the enumerated values (`Circle`, `Square`, `Rectangle`, `Triangle`). Modify `ObjectType` to store one real value for the length of the side of a square, and three real values for the length of the sides of a triangle. Use the formula $\sqrt{s(s-a)(s-b)(s-c)}$ for the area of a triangle whose sides are of length a, b, and c, where s is half the perimeter.

38. A variant record in a file of records has the structure of Figure 8.26 for Exercise 12. Write a program to list the amount pledged and the number of notices for each record in the file that has a false value for `Paid`. Output the total amount at the bottom of the list.

39. A variant record in a file of records has the structure of Figure 8.27 for Exercise 13. Write a program to list the balance, last payment, and date paid for each record in the file that has a false value for `PastDue`. Output the total of the balances at the bottom of the list.

40. A variant record in a file of records has the structure of Figure 8.27 for Exercise 13. **(a)** Write the top level of a program to input `Balance`, `NumNotices`, and `DateNotified` fields from those records with a `PastDue` value of true into an array of records. Each record in the array should have only a fixed part with three fields. Sort the array by `Balance` from the largest to the smallest and output the sorted balances, number of notices, and dates on the screen. **(b)** Complete the program.

41. The variant records in a file of records have the structure of Figure 8.28 for Exercise 14. **(a)** Write a program to list the name and batting average for every fielder. **(b)** Write a program to list the name and number of complete games for every starting pitcher. **(c)** Write a program to list the name, position, and batting average of every switch hitter. Output the average of the batting averages for fielders.

42. Each record in a file of records is of type `ObjectType` as defined in Program 8.11. Write a program that asks the user to input a single character, R for red, B for blue, and G for green. If the user types R, then calculate and output the total area of all the red objects in the file. Do the same for B and G.

Section 8.5

43. Modify procedure `PutSet` in Program 8.12 to output the sets in mathematical set notation.

Sample Output

```
Union:          {0, 1, 2, 4, 5, 6}
Intersection:   {1, 5}
Difference:     {0, 2}
```

44. Modify Program 8.13 to output only those records for which the free days are a subset of the days entered by the user.

45. A file of automobile records has the same structure as in Problem 23. Write a program that declares three set variables for the model, year, and color of a prospective car. Input three sets of preferences from the customer and output all fields of those records whose attributes match the customer's preferences. For example, if the user indicates she is interested in a black or red 85 Rabbit, then output the model, year, color, and cost of all records that meet that criterion.

46. Use the basic Pascal character-processing algorithm to output a list of every character in a file that occurs at least once. Store the occurrence of each character detected as a set of `char`, and output the elements in the set at the conclusion of the file processing. Output 10 characters per line with a space between each character using the mod technique of Program 7.11.

47. Compilers have a maximum limit on the size of the base type of a set. Most limits are large enough to allow a set of `char`. Suppose you need a set of 0..359 to represent integer degree values, but your compiler does not allow sets that large. You can declare `DegSetType` to be a `packed array [0..359] of boolean` to implement the set. If `DegSet` has this type, then 20 is in the set if `DegSet [20]` is true. Otherwise, 20 is not in the set.

Implement the following functions and procedures for this large set.

```
function SetIn (I: integer; DSet: DegSetType): boolean
function Subset (DSetA, DSetB: DegSetType): boolean
function SetEqual (DSetA, DSetB: DegSetType): boolean
procedure Union (DSetA: DegSetType;
                 DSetB: DegSetType;
            var DSetC: DegSetType)
procedure Intersection (DSetA: DegSetType;
                        DSetB: DegSetType;
                   var DSetC: DegSetType)
procedure Difference (DSetA: DegSetType;
                      DSetB: DegSetType;
                 var DSetC: DegSetType)
```

SetIn should be true if I is in DSet. SubSet should be true if DSetA is a subset of DSetB. SetEqual should be true if DSetA equals DSetB. Union should make DSetC the union of DSetA and DSetB, and similarly for Intersection and Difference. Write a main program to test the functions and procedures with interactive I/O.

48. Write a program to output all the prime numbers less than 100 with procedure Eratosthenes.

Chapter

9

Recursion

This chapter completes our discussion of program and data abstraction by presenting the concept of an abstract data type. You will see the stack as an example of an abstract data type and its implementation as a data structure. Computers use stacks to translate so called infix expressions to postfix expressions and then to evaluate them. They also use the run-time stack to call functions and procedures. We will examine these terms in greater detail later in this chapter.

Recursion is an important programming technique that is only possible in Level 6 languages that have run-time stacks. A *recursive procedure* is a procedure that calls itself. Although this definition of a recursive procedure is simple to state, recursion is sometimes difficult to learn. The section on proof by mathematical induction will teach you how to think recursively before you learn how to program with recursion.

Definition of a recursive procedure

The chapter concludes with a presentation of recursive sort algorithms that are more efficient than the selection sort algorithm of Chapter 7.

9.1 General Stacks and Run-Time Stacks

A *stack* is also called a *last in, first out* (LIFO) list. It is a structure that stores values. Two operations access the values stored on a stack—*push* and *pop*. You can visualize a stack as a spring-loaded stack of dishes in a restaurant. When the busboy puts a clean dish on top of the stack, the weight of the dish pushes the stack. If he puts yet another dish on top, it will push down the stack a bit further. If a waitress needs a dish, she takes one from the top of the stack. In other words, the last dish put on the stack is the first one out when someone retrieves a dish.

The last in, first out (LIFO) nature of a stack

In abstract form, a stack is a list of values with the operations push for storage and pop for retrieval. Figure 9.1 shows a sequence of operations on a stack in abstract form. In the figure, the push operation places a value on the stack. x is a variable that is not a part of the stack. The pop operation gives the value to x from the top of the stack.

The figure shows the values 5.0, 2.0, and 4.0 pushed onto the stack. The first pop operation gives the value of 4.0 to x. Since 4.0 was the last value in, it is the first value out.

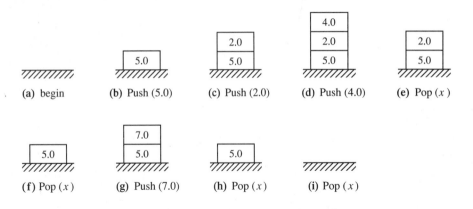

Figure 9.1

The sequence of the following operations on a stack.

begin
Push (5.0)
Push (2.0)
Push (4.0)
Pop (*x*)
Pop (*x*)
Push (7.0)
Pop (*x*)
Pop (*x*)
end

Figure 9.1(f) shows the stack partially empty, with only 5.0. Then 7.0 is pushed onto the stack. The next pop operation gives 7.0 to *x*. Since 7.0 was the last value in, it is the first value out.

Computer scientists define data types the way they define the stack—abstractly. The advantage of an abstract definition is that it allows you to investigate the properties of the data type mathematically. To be of practical use, however, you must program the abstract data type in a programming language. That is, you must implement it with a specific *data structure*.

A data structure is an implementation of an abstract type.

Program 9.1

Program 9.1 shows one way to implement a stack in Pascal. The stack consists of an array that stores the list of values and an integer that denotes the location in the array of the top of the stack.

Figure 9.2 (p. 440) is a trace of this example that corresponds directly to the trace in Figure 9.1. `Stack` is an array of real values indexed from 1 to 10. `Stack [1]` is the bottom of the stack. `Top` is an integer variable that the push and pop procedures use as an index to the stack array.

The program first initializes `Top` to 0. The first execution of `Push` increments `Top` to 1 and stores 5.0 at `Stack [Top]`, that is, at `Stack [1]`. The second execution of `Push` increments `Top` to 2 and stores 2.0 at `Stack [Top]`, that is, at `Stack [2]`. Similarly, the third execution of Push stores 4.0 at `Stack [3]`, incrementing `Top` in the process.

The first execution of `Pop` gives X the value of `Stack [3]` and then decrements `Top` to 2. Similarly, the second `Pop` gives 2.0 to X, decrementing `Top` in the process.

At any point of execution in the main program, the value of `Top` is the index of the component of the stack array that stores the item on top of the stack. In Figure 9.2(d), the value of `Top` is 3. The arrow pointing from `Top` to `Stack [3]` represents the fact that `Top` is a pointer to the top of the stack. Push increments `Top` first, then stores the item at `Stack [Top]`. Pop retrieves the item from `Stack [Top]`, then decrements `Top`.

```
program IntroStack (output);
   type
      StackType = array [1..10] of real;
   var
      Stack: StackType;
      Top:   integer;
      X:     real;

   procedure Push (Y: real; var S: StackType; var T: integer);
      begin
      T := T + 1;
      S [T] := Y
      end;

   procedure Pop (var Y: real; var S: StackType; var T: integer);
      begin
      Y := S [T];
      T := T - 1
      end;

   begin
   Top := 0;
   Push (5.0, Stack, Top);
   Push (2.0, Stack, Top);
   Push (4.0, Stack, Top);
   Pop (X, Stack, Top);
   write (X: 6: 1);
   Pop (X, Stack, Top);
   write (X: 6: 1);
   Push (7.0, Stack, Top);
   Pop (X, Stack, Top);
   write (X: 6: 1);
   Pop (X, Stack, Top);
   write (X: 6: 1)
   end.
```

Program 9.1

A Pascal implementation of a stack with an array.

Output

```
4.0    2.0    7.0    5.0
```

When the stack is empty, Top has the value 0. It points to no entry in the array. Figures 9.2(a) and (i) show the line from Top terminating in the dashed triangle symbol when Top is 0. That is the symbol for a pointer that points to nothing.

Figure 9.2(f) shows the values 2.0 and 4.0 still in the array, even though they have been popped off earlier. They are not visible in the corresponding Figure 9.1(f). Conceptually, the values are not on the stack. Actually, the values are still in

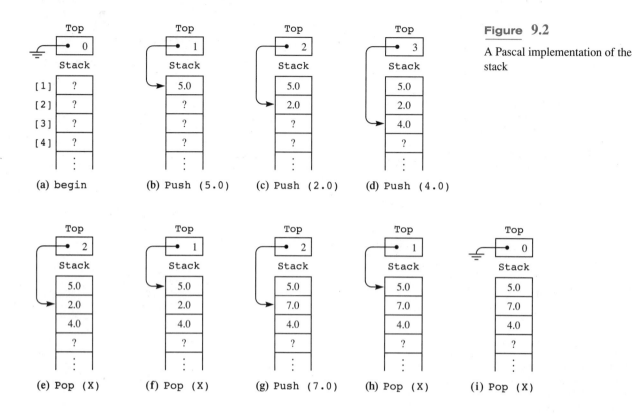

Figure 9.2

A Pascal implementation of the stack

the array. Values that exist in a data structure, but not in the concept of the abstract data type are called *garbage*. The values 2.0 and 4.0 in Figure 9.2(f) are garbage.

The definition of garbage

Garbage values exist in an implementation but are not intended to be used again. In Figure 9.2(f), 2.0 will never be used again. The next push overwrites it with 7.0. All three values in Figure 9.2(i)—5.0, 7.0, and 4.0—are garbage.

Abstract Data Types

The implementation of the stack in Program 9.1 has several deficiencies. One obvious deficiency is the possibility of a program crash because of a range error. If Top has the value 10 and you call Push, the program will crash trying to access Stack [11]. If Top has the value 0 and you call Pop, the program will crash trying to access Stack [0].

Deficiencies of Program 9.1

Another deficiency is more subtle, but perhaps more important. It concerns the view that the main program has of the stack. Figure 9.1 shows the conceptual picture of a stack. It is simply a structure for storing values with push and retrieving values with pop. Conceptually, it has no connection with an array. But the main program treats the stack as an array. It knows that Top is a variable with type integer that is used as an index in the Push and Pop procedures. So it must initialize Top to 0 and pass it to the procedures along with the array.

This arrangement for transmitting information between the main program and the procedures is not good. It means that the person writing the main program must think about the implementation of the stack, which is represented in Figure 9.2, as opposed to the concept of the stack, shown in Figure 9.1.

In this small example, the difficulty of programming with the implementation as opposed to the concept may not seem great. But in a large program with many different data types, the difficulty becomes severe. A fundamental goal in software design is to separate the concept of a data type from its implementation in a data structure.

Someone programming with an abstract data type should not be concerned with its internal representation. For example, the person writing the main program of Program 9.1 should be able to push and pop without worrying about indexes and arrays.

An *abstract data type* (ADT) lets you program with the abstract concept of the structure. A formal abstract data type has two parts:

- A collection of variables

Two parts of an abstract data type

- A set of operations on the variables

The collection of variables is *data abstraction*. The set of operations is *program abstraction*. An abstract data type brings together the concepts of program and data abstraction.

A stack is an example of an abstract data type. There are two types of variables in a stack ADT:

```
ValueType
StackType
```

`ValueType` is the type of each value stored in the stack. In Program 9.1, `ValueType` is real because the stack stored real values such as 5.0 and 2.0. `StackType` is the type of the stack itself.

The stack ADT has a set of five operations on the variables:

```
procedure Initialize (var S: StackType)
function Empty (S: StackType): boolean
procedure Push (Y: ValueType; var S: StackType)
procedure Pop (var Y: ValueType; var S: StackType)
function StackTop (S: StackType): ValueType
```

The stack ADT

`Initialize` lets the programmer initialize a stack without being concerned with its implementation details. `Empty` lets the programmer test whether the stack has no elements. `Push` and `Pop` have their usual meanings, but the programmer provides a single stack, as opposed to an array and index as in Program 9.1. `StackTop` lets the programmer access the value of the top element without popping it off the stack.

This collection of types and operations is a set of tools for the writer of the main program. If you initialize the stack at the beginning of the program with procedure `Initialize` and limit your accesses to the stack to this set of operations, you are guaranteed that your program will not crash. Furthermore, you can banish the idea of an array from your mind and think only about a stack.

Pascal provides *primitive* types and operations on them. For example, it provides the primitive type `char` and the operation `succ` on a variable of type `char`. `StackType` is not a Pascal primitive type. Pascal does not provide `Push`, `Empty`, or any of the other stack operations just mentioned. You must define the types and the operations yourself.

Primitive types versus programmer-defined types

Program 9.2

Program 9.2 shows an implementation of the stack ADT. The first line is labeled

```
{  data structure Stack  }
```

to emphasize that the listing does not comprise a complete Pascal program. Pascal does not let you compile a data structure without a calling program. The procedures in Program 9.2 were all tested with a driver and program heading not shown in the listing.

`StackType` is a record with two parts. The first part is the index, `Top`, that points to the component in the array that contains the top element in the stack. It is a subrange type whose lowest value can be 0. The second part is the array that stores the values. Its first element is `Body [1]`.

Procedure `Initialize` sets `Top` to 0. Function `Empty` is true if `Top` is 0. Otherwise `Empty` is false.

Procedures `Push` and `Pop` process the stack as in Program 9.1 with the important difference of testing for possible error conditions. If you call `Push` when `Top` equals `StackMax`, `Push` will not increment `Top` or store the value of `Y`. It will leave the array unchanged and output an error message. Similarly, procedure `Pop` will output an error message if you call it when `Top` is 0.

Function `StackTop` does not change the state of the stack, which is called by value. If the function tries to access the top of the stack when the stack is empty, the result is undefined, and an appropriate error message is output.

The data types and operations in Program 9.2 are fairly self-contained. None of the procedures or functions uses global variables. You can copy them into any program that needs a stack. You only need to change `StackMax` to a value appropriate for your computer memory size and `ValueType` to a type appropriate for your program. The only restriction on `ValueType` is that function `StackTop` will not work if `ValueType` is a record or an array, since functions cannot return structured types. If you want `ValueType` to be a structured type, you must rewrite `StackTop` as a procedure with a variable parameter.

Evaluating Postfix Expressions

Stacks are common in computer systems. One application of stacks is in the processing of arithmetic expressions. When you write a Pascal expression such as 3 + 5 in a program, the Pascal compiler must translate it to machine language at Level 3. Then the Level 3 program executes.

```
{  data structure Stack  }

const
   StackMax = 10;
type
   ValueType = real;
   StackType =
      record
      Top:  0..StackMax;
      Body: array [1..StackMax] of ValueType
      end;

procedure Initialize (var S: StackType);
   begin
   S.Top := 0
   end;

function Empty (S: StackType): boolean;
   begin
   Empty := (S.Top = 0)
   end;

procedure Push (Y: ValueType; var S: StackType);
   begin
   if S.Top < StackMax then
      begin
      S.Top := S.Top + 1;
      S.Body [S.Top] := Y
      end
   else
      writeln ('Error--stack overflow.')
   end;

procedure Pop (var Y: ValueType; var S: StackType);
   begin
   if S.Top > 0 then
      begin
      Y := S.Body [S.Top];
      S.Top := S.Top - 1
      end
   else
      writeln ('Error--stack underflow.')
   end;

function StackTop (S: StackType): ValueType;
   begin
   if S.Top > 0 then
      StackTop := S.Body [S.Top]
   else
      writeln ('Error--accessed top of empty stack.')
   end;
```

Program 9.2

An implementation of the stack abstract data type. The listing is not a complete Pascal program.

There are three kinds of arithmetic notation:

- *Infix*   3 + 5
- *Prefix* + 3 5
- *Postfix* 3 5 +

Infix notation is the notation you learned as a child. The plus operator is between the operands 3 and 5. In prefix notation, the operator precedes its operands, and in postfix notation, the operator follows its operands.

The expressions you write in a Pascal program are infix expressions. Unfortunately, infix expressions are difficult to evaluate when the program executes at Level 3. It is easier for the computer to evaluate a postfix expression. Pascal compilers convert infix expressions to postfix. Then, when the machine-language version of the program executes, it evaluates the postfix expression.

The evaluation of a postfix expression requires a stack of operands. The algorithm for evaluating a postfix expression is

- Scan the postfix expression from left to right.
- If you encounter an operand, push it onto the stack.
- If you encounter an operator, apply the operator to the top two operands of the stack. Replace the two operands with the result of the operation.
- After scanning the entire postfix expression, the stack should have one item, the value of the expression.

Example **9.1**   Here is a trace of the evaluation for the postfix expression

  1 6 + 5 2 − ×

In this trace, the bottom of the stack is on the left.

Stack	Expression
empty	1 6 + 5 2 − ×
1	6 + 5 2 − ×
1 6	+ 5 2 − ×
7	5 2 − ×
7 5	2 − ×
7 5 2	− ×
7 3	×
21	empty

The algorithm first pushes 1, then 6. It encounters the plus operator and applies it to 1 and 6, replacing them with 7 on the stack. It pushes 5 and 2, encounters the minus operator and replaces the 5 and 2 with their difference on the stack. Then it encounters the multiply operator. It applies it to 7 and 3, producing the final result of 21.   ∎

The algorithm in pseudocode follows. It uses the stack ADT with operations `Initialize`, `Push`, `Pop`, and `Empty`. The algorithm assumes the postfix expression is a sequence of the characters '+', '−', '*', 'd', 'm', '0', '1', '2', '3', ..., '9'. The operands are integers. Therefore, `ValueType` is integer in the data structure.

```
begin
Initialize (Stack)
Get Ch
while Ch <> Sentinel do
   begin
   if Ch is a digit character then
       Push (ord (Ch) - ord ('0'), Stack)
   else if Ch = '+' then
       Add
   else if Ch = '-' then
       Subtract
   else if Ch = '*' then
       Multiply
   else if Ch = 'd' then
       Div
   else if Ch = 'm' then
       Mod
   Get Ch
   end
Pop (X, Stack)
if Empty (Stack) then
   Output X
else
   Output "elements remain" error message.
end
```

A pseudocode description of the algorithm for evaluation of a postfix expression

To implement the algorithm in Pascal, you could use the data structure of Program 9.2. The algorithm assumes that an input operand is a one-character digit, and an input operator is a one-character symbol indicating the operation. The code necessary to perform an operation consists of two pop operations followed by a push of the result onto the stack. For example, the code for Add is

```
Pop (X, Stack);
Pop (Y, Stack);
Push (X + Y, Stack)
```

The code for the other operations is similar.

The while loop uses the sentinel technique to input the postfix expression one character at a time. In practice, the while loop and the Get Ch operation will depend on where the input comes from and what format it takes.

For example, if you want to input the postfix expression interactively from the keyboard on one line, you could use the following eoln technique:

```
Prompt for postfix expression
while not eoln (input) do
    begin
    read (Ch)
    Process Ch
    end
readln
```

With this technique, you replace both instances of Get Ch by one read (Ch). If the postfix expression is on one line in a file you could use the same technique, checking for eoln (SomeFile) and reading from the file.

If the input covers more than one line, then you must alter your approach accordingly. You could tell the user to type a symbol such as '%' at the end of the expression and use it as the sentinel. If the expression covers multiple lines in a file, you could use the basic character-processing algorithm that was presented in Section 7.2.

Another possibility arises when the postfix expression comes in a packed array of char, say Expr. Then, you might implement Get Ch as

```
I := I + 1;
Ch := Expr [I]
```

The algorithm ignores all characters other than the operators and operands. In particular, it lets you include any number of spaces anywhere in the input stream.

Translation from Infix to Postfix

A computer system must solve two basic problems to process an expression from a Pascal program. First, it must translate the infix expression to postfix, and second, it must evaluate the postfix expression at Level 3. The previous algorithm showed the evaluation of a postfix expression. The following discussion shows how to translate from infix to postfix.

Example 9.2 Five examples of infix expressions and their corresponding postfix expressions are

Infix	Postfix
2 + 3	2 3 +
2 × 5 + 3	2 5 × 3 +
2 + 5 × 3	2 5 3 × +
2 × 3 + 5 × 4	2 3 × 5 4 × +
2 + 3 × 5 + 4	2 3 5 × + 4 +

You can verify that they are equivalent by evaluating the postfix expression according to the evaluation algorithm. ∎

Two different postfix expressions can be equivalent to the same infix expression.

Example 9.3 The postfix expressions

   5 3 × 2 +

and

   2 5 3 × +

are both equivalent to the infix expression

   2 + 5 × 3

However, the operands of the first postfix expression (5, 3, 2) are in a different order from the operands of the infix expression (2, 5, 3). ∎

One property of the postfix expressions in Example 9.2 is that their operands are all in the same order as the operands of the equivalent infix expressions. The translation algorithm that follows has the same property.

One characteristic of infix that is not shared by postfix is the priority of the operators. In the infix expression 2 + 5 × 3, the multiplication is performed before the addition because multiplication has a higher priority than addition. In postfix, however, there is no operator priority. The order in which an operation is performed is determined strictly by the position of the operator in the postfix expression. That is one reason computers can evaluate postfix expressions more easily than infix expressions.

No operator priority in postfix expressions

In the translation of the preceding expressions from infix to postfix, only the placement of the operators is different. In fact, the multiplication operators occur before the addition operators, since multiplication has a higher priority than addition in the infix expression. An algorithm that translates from infix to postfix only needs to shift the operators to the right and possibly reorder them.

The following algorithm for translating an expression from infix to postfix uses a stack to temporarily store the operators until they can be inserted further to the right into the postfix expression.

- Scan the infix expression from left to right.

- If the item is an operand, move it directly to the postfix expression.

- If the item is an operator, compare it with the operator on top of the stack.

    If the operator on top of the stack has a priority lower than that of the item just encountered in the infix expression or if the stack is empty, push the item just encountered onto the stack.

    If the operator on top of the stack has a priority higher than or equal to that of the item just encountered in the infix expression, pop items off the stack. Place them in the postfix expression until either the priority of the top operator is less than the priority of the item or the stack is empty. Then push the item onto the stack.

- After the entire infix expression has been scanned, pop any remaining operators left on the stack and put them in the postfix expression.

The algorithm to translate from infix to postfix

Since the operands pass directly to the postfix expression, they will maintain their order. The algorithm allows an operator to be pushed onto the stack only if the stack top contains an operator of lower priority. Therefore, the stack will always have the operators with the highest priority near the top.

Example 9.4 Here is a trace of the translation process according to the previous algorithm:

Postfix output	Stack	Infix input
empty	empty	2 + 3 × 5 + 4
2	empty	+ 3 × 5 + 4
2	+	3 × 5 + 4
2 3	+	× 5 + 4
2 3	+ ×	5 + 4
2 3 5	+ ×	+ 4
2 3 5 ×	+	+ 4
2 3 5 × +	empty	+ 4
2 3 5 × +	+	4
2 3 5 × + 4	+	empty
2 3 5 × + 4 +	empty	empty

When the algorithm gets the multiplication operator, it compares it with the addition operator on top of the stack. Multiplication has a higher priority than addition. Therefore, it puts the multiplication operator on the stack. After it sends the 5 operand to the postfix expression, the multiplication operator follows it. So when you evaluate the postfix expression, you will multiply 3 by 5 before adding the result to 2.   ■

Another reason why postfix expressions are easier to evaluate than infix expressions is that postfix expressions have no parentheses. Infix expressions can have parentheses. When they do, all of the operations inside the parentheses must be performed before the operations outside.

Postfix expressions have no parentheses.

Converting an infix expression with parentheses is only slightly more complicated than converting an expression without parentheses.

Example 9.5   Here are some examples of infix expressions with parentheses and the corresponding postfix expressions:

Infix	Postfix
2 × (7 + 3)	2 7 3 + ×
2 × (7 + 3 × 4)	2 7 3 4 × + ×
2 × (7 × 3 + 4)	2 7 3 × 4 + ×
2 + (7 × 3 + 4)	2 7 3 × 4 + +
2 × (7 × (3 + 4) + 5)	2 7 3 4 + × 5 + ×

Again, the order of the operands is the same. You should evaluate these expressions to convince yourself that they are equivalent.   ■

When a left parenthesis is detected in the left to right scan, it marks the starting point of a substack within the main stack. It is as if a new expression is to be evaluated, the expression within the parentheses.

The algorithm pushes the left parenthesis onto the stack to mark the beginning of the substack. It converts the subexpression using the substack. When it encounters the matching right parenthesis, it pops the operators off the substack and places them in the postfix expression until it reaches the left parenthesis. It discards the pair of parentheses and continues converting.

Example 9.6   Here is an example of the translation process for an infix expression containing parentheses:

Postfix output	Stack	Infix input
empty	empty	2 × (7 + 3 × 4) + 6
2	empty	× (7 + 3 × 4) + 6
2	×	(7 + 3 × 4) + 6
2	× (	7 + 3 × 4) + 6
2 7	× (	+ 3 × 4) + 6
2 7	× (+	3 × 4) + 6
2 7 3	× (+	× 4) + 6
2 7 3	× (+ ×	4) + 6
2 7 3 4	× (+ ×	) + 6
2 7 3 4 ×	× (+	) + 6
2 7 3 4 × +	× (	) + 6
2 7 3 4 × +	×	+ 6
2 7 3 4 × + ×	empty	+ 6
2 7 3 4 × + ×	+	6
2 7 3 4 × + × 6	+	empty
2 7 3 4 × + × 6 +	empty	empty

When the algorithm encounters the left parenthesis, it simply pushes it onto the stack with the multiplication operator. It continues the conversion, placing the addition and multiplication operators on the stack. When it encounters the right parenthesis, the algorithm knows it is at the end of the subexpression between the two parentheses. It pops the multiplication and addition operators off the stack. Then the algorithm discards the pair of parentheses and continues the conversion. ∎

The algorithm for converting an infix expression to postfix appears on the next page. In the stack data structure, `ValueType` is `char`. The same considerations for Get Ch apply here as they do in the postfix evaluation algorithm.

This algorithm uses a clever technique reminiscent of the sequential search algorithm in Section 7.4. That algorithm installed the search value as a sentinel at the end of the list being searched.

This algorithm installs a sentinel operator on the stack that has priority lower than all the other operators. When the algorithm encounters an operator in the input stream, it does not need to perform a separate test for an empty stack. The first operator encountered in the input stream will have higher priority than the stack sentinel. It will therefore be pushed onto the stack. That is precisely what should happen if no stack sentinel is used and the stack is empty.

This is a useful design technique. Installing a sentinel with the right value can simplify the algorithm. You will recall that the same technique was used in the file merge and file update algorithms in Programs 8.5 and 8.6. In those programs, the existence of identical high sentinel values in the input files simplified the termination of the outer `while` loop.

```
begin
Initialize (Stack)
Push a stack sentinel with lowest priority.
Get Ch
while Ch <> input sentinel do
   begin
   if Ch is an operand then
      Output Ch
   else if Ch is an operator then
      begin
      while (Priority (StackTop (Stack)) >= Priority (Ch))
      and (StackTop (Stack) <> '(') do
         Pop and output operator from stack.
      Push (Ch, Stack)
      end
   else if Ch = '(' then
      Push (Ch, Stack)
   else if Ch = ')' then
      begin
      Pop and output operators until '(' is encountered.
      Pop the '(' and ignore it.
      end
   Get Ch
   end
Pop and output remaining operators.
end
```

A pseudocode description of the algorithm to translate from infix to postfix

The conversion algorithm requires one function not included in the stack data structure of Program 9.2:

```
function Priority (Operator: char): integer
```

should return priority values for the operators as listed in Table 9.1. The stack sentinel can be any character you choose.

The Run-Time Stack for Procedures

When you write a program that calls a procedure or a function, the computer allocates storage on a stack. It is called a *run-time stack* because the allocation takes place during program execution as opposed to program translation.

Table 6.3 showed how the computer allocates and deallocates storage for the formal parameter and local variables in Program 6.6. Figure 9.3 is a more detailed picture of this allocation process. In addition to the formal parameters and the local variables, the run-time stack stores the address of the statement after the calling statement. It needs this "return address" so the computer will know which state-

Operator	Priority
div	2 highest
mod	2
*	2
+	1
–	1
sentinel	0 lowest

Table 9.1

The operator priorities for the infix to postfix conversion algorithms.

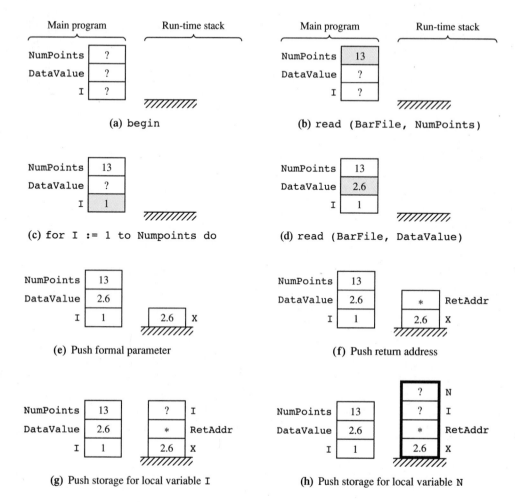

(a) begin

(b) read (BarFile, NumPoints)

(c) for I := 1 to Numpoints do

(d) read (BarFile, DataValue)

(e) Push formal parameter

(f) Push return address

(g) Push storage for local variable I

(h) Push storage for local variable N

ment in the calling program to execute after it executes the last statement in the procedure.

Allocation takes place on the run-time stack in the following order when you call a procedure:

- Push the actual parameters.
- Push the return address.
- Push storage for the local variables.

Figure 9.3(e) is the start of the allocation process for Program 6.6. The program pushes the value of DataValue for the formal parameter X. It pushes the return address in 9.3(f). In 9.3(g) and (h), it pushes the first local variable, I, then the second local variable, N. After the allocation process, the last local variable in the listing, N, is on top of the stack.

The collection of all the items pushed onto the run-time stack is called a *stack frame* or *activation record*. In Program 6.6, the stack frame consists of four

Figure 9.3

The run-time stack for Program 6.6. RetAddr stands for return address.

The allocation process for a procedure

The stack frame

items—X, the return address, I, and N. The return address indicated by the asterisk in the figure is the address of end in the if statement of the main program.

■ The Run-Time Stack
for Functions

The sequence of allocation steps with a function is the same as with a procedure except that storage must also be allocated for the value returned by the function. Allocation on the run-time stack for a function is in the following order:

The allocation process for a function

- Push storage for the returned value.

- Push the actual parameters.

- Push the return address.

- Push storage for the local variables.

Figure 9.4 shows the allocation process for the function in Program 6.2, which returned the factorial of the actual parameter.

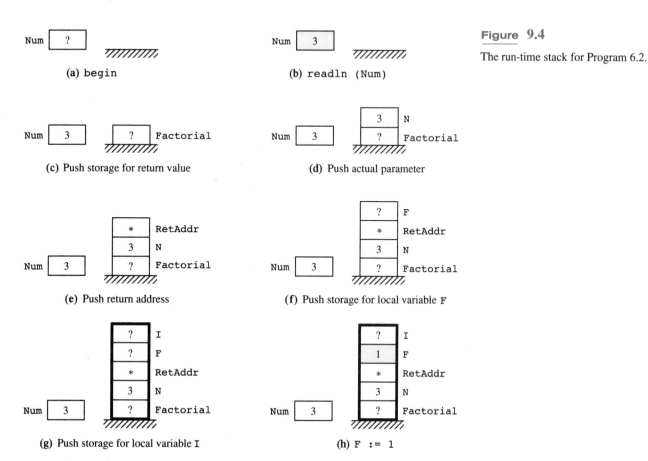

Figure 9.4

The run-time stack for Program 6.2.

(a) begin

(b) readln (Num)

(c) Push storage for return value

(d) Push actual parameter

(e) Push return address

(f) Push storage for local variable F

(g) Push storage for local variable I

(h) F := 1

Figure 9.4(c) shows storage for the returned value pushed first. Figure 9.4(d) shows the value of Num, 3, pushed for the formal parameter N. The return address is pushed in 9.4(e). Storage for local variables F and I are pushed in 9.4(f) and (g).

The stack frame for this function has five items. The return address indicated by the asterisk in the figure represents the address of the writeln statement in the main program. Remember that control returns from the function to the calling statement.

The Run-Time Stack for Reference Parameters

Program 6.13 had one procedure, Order3, that called another procedure, Swap. Figure 9.5 shows the allocation and deallocation sequence for that entire program.

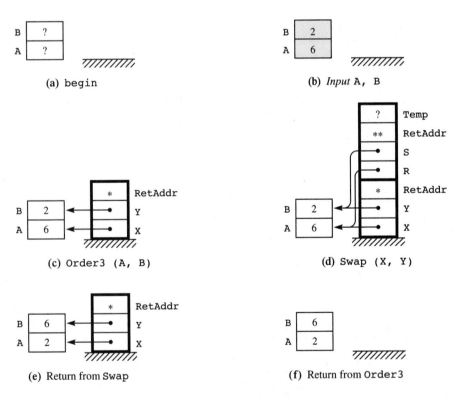

Figure *9.5*

The run-time stack for Program 6.13.

The stack frame for Order3 in Figure 9.5(c) has three items. The formal parameters, X and Y, are called by reference. The arrow pointing from X on the run-time stack to A in the main program indicates that X refers to A. Similarly, the arrow from Y to B indicates that Y refers to B.

The return address indicated by the single asterisk is the address of the writeln statement that follows the call to Order3 in the main program.

The stack frame for `Swap` in Figure 9.5(d) has four items. R refers to X, which refers to A. Therefore, R refers to A. The arrow pointing from R on the run-time stack points to A, as does the arrow from X. Similarly, the arrow from S points to B, as does the arrow from Y.

The return address indicated by the double asterisk is the address of the last statement in `Order3`.

The statements in `Swap` exchange the values of R and S. Since R refers to A and S refers to B, they exchange the values of A and B in the main program.

When a procedure terminates and it is time to deallocate its stack frame, the return address in the frame tells the computer which instruction to execute next. Figure 9.5(e) shows the return from procedure `Swap`, deallocating its stack frame. The return address in the stack frame for `Swap` tells the computer to execute the last statement in `Order3` after deallocation.

In Figure 9.5(f), the stack frame for `Order3` is deallocated. The return address in the stack frame for `Order3` tells the computer to execute the `writeln` statement in the main program after deallocation.

Since a stack is a LIFO structure, the last stack frame pushed onto the run-time stack will be the first one popped off at the completion of a procedure or function. The return address will, therefore, return control to the most recent calling procedure or function. This LIFO property of the run-time stack will be basic to your understanding of recursion in Section 9.3.

9.2   Proof by Mathematical Induction

Recursion is closely related to proof by mathematical induction. This section describes the induction proof technique. Mathematical induction will help you understand how recursion works and will give you a basis for designing error-free recursive software.

In a proof by induction you are given a formula containing an arbitrary variable, n. The problem is to prove that the formula is true for some infinite set of integer values of n. The range of values for n is usually $0, 1, 2, \ldots$, or $1, 2, 3, \ldots$ or some other infinite range of positive values. For example, you may wish to prove that the formula for the sum of the first n integers,

$$1 + 2 + \cdots + n = \tfrac{1}{2}n(n + 1)$$

is true for all the values, $n = 1, 2, 3, \ldots$.

It is usually easy to prove that the formula is true for one specific value of n. For example, you can substitute $n = 1$ into the previous formula and get

$$1 = \tfrac{1}{2}(1)(1 + 1)$$
$$1 = \tfrac{1}{2}(2)$$
$$1 = 1$$

which proves that the formula is true for a specific value of n.

Similarly, you could prove that the formula is true for $n = 2$ by direct substitution of that value:

$$1 + 2 = \tfrac{1}{2}(2)(2 + 1)$$

$$1 + 2 = (2 + 1)$$

$$3 = 3$$

You could also prove it true for $n = 3$, $n = 4$, and even $n = 100$, if you wanted, by direct substitution.

The problem is that you want to prove the formula is true for an infinite number of values of n. You may not have enough time before your homework assignment is due to substitute all those values directly! Fortunately, proof by mathematical induction lets you prove the formula true for an infinite number of values of n without an infinite number of direct substitutions.

Proof by mathematical induction is a four-step process:

- *Basis* Prove the formula is true for n_0, the smallest value of n, by direct substitution.

- *Inductive hypothesis* Assume the formula is true for an arbitrary $n = N$.

- *Induction* Prove, using the inductive hypothesis, that the formula must be true for $n = N + 1$.

- *Conclusion* From the basis step, the formula is true for the first value, n_0. Since the inductive hypothesis is true for $n = n_0$, the induction step implies that the formula must be true for $n = n_0 + 1$. But now the inductive hypothesis is true for $n = n_0 + 1$, so the induction step implies that the formula must be true for $n = n_0 + 2$. But now the inductive hypothesis is true for $n = n_0 + 2$, so the induction step implies that the formula must be true for $n = n_0 + 3$, and so on. The conclusion is that the formula must be true for all values of n greater than or equal to the first value, n_0.

The four steps in proof by mathematical induction

To prove a relationship using mathematical induction you must verify each of these four steps. The basis is usually a simple substitution step. The inductive hypothesis merely involves rewriting the relationship with n replaced by N. The induction step is the most difficult part, because you must transform the relationship from the hypothesis into a form that shows the relationship is true for $n = N + 1$. It is not always obvious how to do the transformation. The conclusion follows automatically from the first three steps.

Induction Proof of a Summation

Here is the proof by mathematical induction of the formula for the sum of the first n integers, $n = 1, 2, 3, \ldots$. We used this formula in Section 5.5 to count the number of statements executed in the algorithm to print a triangle and again in Section 7.4 to count the number of statements executed in the selection sort.

$$1 + 2 + \cdots + n = \tfrac{1}{2}n(n + 1)$$

Basis   The formula is true for $n = 1$ as shown previously.

Inductive Hypothesis   Assume the formula true for $n = N$. That is, assume that

$$1 + 2 + \cdots + N = \tfrac{1}{2}N(N+1)$$

Induction   Starting with the inductive hypothesis, you need to prove that the formula is true for $n = N + 1$. That is, you need to prove that

$$1 + 2 + \cdots + N + (N + 1) = \tfrac{1}{2}(N + 1)[(N + 1) + 1]$$

It is important in this part of the proof that you write down the relationship you need to show in the induction step, as we have just done. Remember, you need to show that this relationship follows from the inductive hypothesis. The clue is to ask yourself how these two relationships differ. In this problem, the left side of the relationship to prove is $(N + 1)$ more than the left side of the relationship in the inductive hypothesis. So, add $N + 1$ to both sides of the equation from the inductive hypothesis.

$$1 + 2 + \cdots + N + (N + 1) = (N + 1) + \tfrac{1}{2}N(N + 1)$$

Now, factor out the $(N + 1)$ on the right side

$$1 + 2 + \cdots + N + (N + 1) = (N + 1)(1 + \tfrac{1}{2}N)$$
$$= \tfrac{1}{2}(N + 1)(2 + N)$$
$$= \tfrac{1}{2}(N + 1)[(N + 1) + 1]$$

which is precisely the equation to prove.

Conclusion   The formula must be true for all n greater than or equal to 1.

In a proof by mathematical induction, it is helpful to write down all four steps, as in the previous proof. In the induction step, it is also helpful to write down the relationship that you are trying to prove with $n = N + 1$ before you prove it. That gives you a goal toward which you can work. But remember, in the proof you must start with the inductive hypothesis.

Induction Proof of an Inequality

The statement to be proved need not be a formula with an equality. Here is a proof by mathematical induction that

$$2^n > n$$

for all $n = 1, 2, 3, \ldots$.

Basis   The formula is true for $n = 1$ since $2^1 > 1$.

Inductive Hypothesis   Assume the formula true for $n = N$. That is, assume that

$$2^N > N$$

Induction   From the inductive hypothesis prove that the formula is true for $n = N + 1$. That is, from the inductive hypothesis prove that

$$2^{N+1} > N + 1$$

Again, the clue is to see how this relationship differs from the one in the inductive hypothesis. The left side of this relationship is two times the left side of the inductive hypothesis. So, to prove the induction step, first multiply both sides of the inductive hypotheses equation by 2.

$$2(2^N) > 2N$$

Combine the terms on the left.

$$2^{N+1} > 2N$$
$$= N + N$$
$$> N + 1$$

The last step follows since $N > 1$. That is, $N + N$ must be greater than or equal to $N + 1$ if N is greater than or equal to 1. It follows that

$$2^{N+1} > N + 1$$

which is what we were trying to prove.

Conclusion   By induction the statement must be true for all positive n values.

The two key features of proof by mathematical induction that apply to recursion are the basis step and the induction step. The basis serves as the starting point, and the induction assures you that if the statement for N is true, the statement for $N + 1$ must also be true. The main task in designing a recursive routine is to write the solution for the smallest case, corresponding to the basis step in mathematical induction. You then write the solution for $N + 1$ assuming that the solution for N is known, corresponding to the induction step.

9.3   Recursive Algorithms

Did you ever look up the definition of some unknown word in the dictionary only to discover that the dictionary defined it in terms of another unknown word? Then, when you looked up the second word, you discovered that it was defined in terms of the first word! That is an example of circular or indirect recursion.

The problem with the dictionary is that you did not know the meaning of the first word to begin with. Had the second word been defined in terms of a third word that you knew, you would have been satisfied.

In mathematics, a *recursive definition* of a function is a definition that uses the function itself. For example, suppose a function, $f(n)$, is defined as follows:

Recursive definitions in mathematics

$$f(n) = nf(n - 1)$$

You want to use this definition to determine $f(4)$, so you substitute 4 for n in the definition.

$$f(4) = 4f(3)$$

But now you do not know what $f(3)$ is. So you substitute 3 for n in the definition and get

$$f(3) = 3f(2)$$

Substituting this into the formula for $f(4)$ gives

$$f(4) = 4(3)f(2)$$

But now you do not know what $f(2)$ is. The definition tells you it is 2 times $f(1)$. So the formula for $f(4)$ becomes

$$f(4) = 4(3)(2)f(1)$$

You can see the problem with this definition. With nothing to stop the process, you will continue to compute $f(4)$ endlessly.

$$f(4) = 4(3)(2)(1)(0)(-1)(-2)(-3) \cdots$$

It is as if the dictionary gave you an endless string of definitions, each based on another unknown word.

To be complete, the definition must specify the value of $f(n)$ for a specific value of n. Then the preceding process will terminate, and you can compute $f(n)$ for any n.

Here is a complete recursive definition of $f(n)$:

$$f(n) = nf(n - 1) \qquad \text{for } n > 1$$
$$f(1) = 1$$

This definition says you can stop the previous process at $f(1)$. So $f(4)$ is

$$
\begin{aligned}
f(4) &= 4f(3) \\
&= 4(3)f(2) \\
&= 4(3)(2)f(1) \\
&= 4(3)(2)(1) \\
&= 24
\end{aligned}
$$

You should recognize this definition as the factorial function.

■ **Program 9.3**

A *recursive function* in Pascal is a function that calls itself. There is no special recursion statement with a new recursion syntax chart to learn. The method of storage allocation on the run-time stack is the same as with nonrecursive functions. The only difference is that a recursive function contains a statement that calls itself.

Recursive functions in Pascal

The function in Program 9.3 computes the factorial of a number recursively. It is a direct application of the recursive definition of $f(n)$, which was just shown.

```
program Factorial (input, output);
   var
      Num: integer;

   function Fact (N: integer): integer;
      begin
      if N = 1 then
         Fact := 1
      else
         Fact := N * Fact (N - 1)   {**}
      end;

   begin
   write ('Enter a small integer: ');
   readln (Num);
   writeln ('Its factorial is: ', Fact (Num): 1)   {*}
   end.
```

Program 9.3

A program to compute the factorial recursively.

Interactive Input/Output

```
Enter a small integer: 4
Its factorial is: 24
```

Figure 9.6 is a trace that shows the run-time stack. The first function call is from the main program. Figure 9.6(c) shows the stack frame for the first call. The return address is the single asterisk that represents the address of the `writeln` call in the main program.

The first statement in the function tests N for 1. Since the value of N is 4, the `else` part executes. But the statement in the else part

```
Fact := N * Fact (N - 1)   {**}
```

contains a call to function `Fact` on the right side of the assignment statement.

This is a recursive call, since it is a call to the function within the function itself. The same sequence of events happens as with any function call. A new stack frame is allocated as Figure 9.6(d) shows. The return address in the second stack

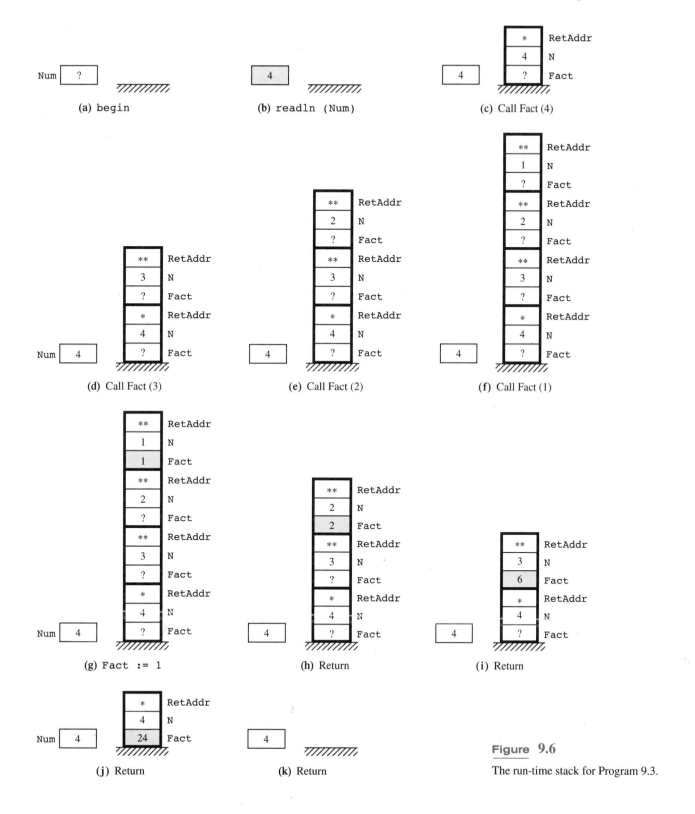

Figure 9.6

The run-time stack for Program 9.3.

frame is the address of the calling statement in the function, represented by the double asterisks.

The actual parameter is N – 1, whose value is 3, since the value of N in Figure 9.6(c) is 4. The formal parameter, N, is called by value. Therefore, the value of 3 is given to the formal parameter N in the top frame of Figure 9.6(d).

Figure 9.6(d) shows a curious situation that is typical of recursive calls. The program listing of Program 9.3 shows only one declaration of N in the formal parameter list of `Fact`. But Figure 9.6(d) shows two instances of N. The old instance of N has the value 4 from the main program. But the new instance of N has the value 3 from the recursive call.

Multiple instances of local variables and parameters

The computer suspends the old execution of the function and begins a new execution of the same function from its beginning. The first statement in the function tests N for 1. But which N? Figure 9.6(d) shows two N's on the run-time stack. The rule is that any reference to a local variable or formal parameter is to the one on the top stack frame. Since the value of N is 3, the `else` part executes.

But now the function makes another recursive call. It allocates a third stack frame as Figure 9.6(e) shows, then a fourth as Figure 9.6(f) shows. Each time, the newly allocated formal parameter gets a value one less than the old value of N because the function call is

```
Fact (N - 1)
```

Finally, in Figure 9.6(g), N has the value 1. The function gives 1 to the function variable `Fact`. It skips the `else` part and terminates. That triggers a return to the calling statement.

The same events transpire with a recursive return as with a nonrecursive return. `Fact` contains the returned value, and the return address tells which statement to execute next. In Figure 9.6(g), `Fact` is 1 and the return address is the calling statement in the function. The top frame is deallocated, and the calling statement

```
Fact := N * Fact (N - 1)   {**}
```

completes its execution. It multiplies its value of N, which is 2, by the value returned, which is 1, and assigns the result to `Fact`. So, `Fact` gets 2, as Figure 9.6(h) shows.

A similar sequence of events occurs on each return. Figures 9.6(i) and (j) show that the value returned from the second call is 6 and from the first call is 24.

Figure 9.7 shows the calling sequence for Program 9.3. The main program calls `Fact`. Then `Fact` calls itself three times. In this example, `Fact` is called a total of four times.

You see that the program computes the factorial of 4 the same way you would compute $f(4)$ from its recursive definition. You start by computing $f(4)$ as 4 times $f(3)$. Then you must suspend your computation of $f(4)$ to compute $f(3)$. After you get your result for $f(3)$, you can multiply it by 4 to get $f(4)$.

Similarly, the program must suspend its execution of the function to call the same function again. The run-time stack keeps track of the current values of the variables so they can be used when that instance of the function resumes.

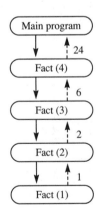

Figure 9.7

The calling sequence for Program 9.3. The solid arrows represent function calls. The dotted arrows represent returns. The value returned is next to each return arrow.

Thinking Recursively

You can take two different viewpoints when dealing with recursion—microscopic and macroscopic. Figure 9.6 illustrates the microscopic viewpoint and shows precisely what happens inside the computer during execution. It is the viewpoint that considers the details of the run-time stack during a trace of the program. The macroscopic viewpoint does not consider the individual trees. It considers the forest as a whole.

The microscopic and macroscopic viewpoints of recursion

You need to know the microscopic viewpoint to understand how Pascal implements recursion. The details of the run-time stack will be necessary when you study how recursion is implemented at Level 5. But to write a recursive function you should think macroscopically, not microscopically.

The most difficult aspect of writing a recursive function is the assumption that you can call the procedure that you are in the process of writing. To make that assumption, you must think macroscopically and forget about the run-time stack.

Proof by mathematical induction will help you think macroscopically. The two key elements of proof by induction are

- Establish the basis.
- Given the formula for N, prove it for $N + 1$.

Similarly, the two key elements of designing a recursive function are

The relation between proof by mathematical induction and recursion

- Compute the function for the basis.
- Assuming the function for $N - 1$, write it for N.

Imagine you are writing function `Fact`. You get to this point:

```
function Fact (N: integer): integer;
   begin
   if N = 1 then
      Fact := 1
   else
```

and wonder how to continue. You have computed the function for the basis, `N = 1`. But now you must assume that you can call function `Fact`, even though you have not finished writing `Fact`. You must assume that `Fact (N - 1)` will return the correct value for the factorial.

Here is where you must think macroscopically. If you start wondering how `Fact (N - 1)` will return the correct value, and if visions of stack frames begin dancing in your head, you are not thinking correctly. In proof by induction, you must assume the formula for `N`. Similarly, in writing `Fact`, you must assume you can call `Fact (N - 1)`, with no questions asked.

The importance of thinking macroscopically when you design a recursive function

Recursive programs are based on a divide and conquer strategy. It is appropriate when you can solve a large problem in terms of a smaller one. Each recursive call makes the problem smaller and smaller until the program reaches the smallest problem of all, the basis, which is simple to solve.

The divide and conquer strategy

Program 9.4

Here is another example of a recursive problem. Suppose `List` is an array of `N` integers. You want to find the sum of all `N` integers in the list recursively.

The first step is to formulate the solution of the large problem in terms of a smaller problem. If you knew how to find the sum of the first `N - 1` integers, you could simply add it to the `N`th integer in `List`. You would then have the sum of all `N` integers.

The next step is to design a function with the appropriate parameters. The function will compute the sum of `N` integers by calling itself to compute the sum of `N - 1` integers. So the parameter list must have a parameter that tells how many integers in the array to add. That should lead you to the following function head:

```
function Sum (A: ListType; N: integer): integer;
   {  Returns the sum of the elements of A  }
   {  between A [1] and A [N].              }
```

How do you establish the basis? That is simple. If `N` is 1, the function should add the sum of the elements between `A [1]` and `A [1]`. The sum of one element is just `A [1]`.

Now you can write

```
begin
if N = 1 then
   Sum := A [1]
else
```

Now think macroscopically. You can assume that `Sum (A, N - 1)` will return the sum of the first `N - 1` integers. Have faith. All you need to do is add that sum to `A [N]`. Program 9.4 shows the function in a finished program.

Even though you write the function without considering the microscopic view, you can still trace the run-time stack. Figure 9.8 shows the stack frames for the first two calls to `Sum`.

The stack frame consists of the value returned, `Sum`, the parameters, `A` and `N`, and the return address. Since there are no local variables, no storage for them is allocated on the run-time stack.

Since `A` is an array, it should be called by reference for efficiency. Each cell for `A` in the stack frames would be represented in the trace by an arrow that points to `List` in the main program, as in Figure 9.5. The savings in storage would be considerable, since the entire contents of the array are duplicated for each call in call by value.

```
program TotalIntegers (input, output);
   type
      ListType = array [1..4] of integer;
   var
      List: ListType;

   function Sum (A: ListType; N: integer): integer;
      {  Returns the sum of the elements of A  }
      {  between A [1] and A [N].              }
      begin
      if N = 1 then
         Sum := A [1]
      else
         Sum := A [N] + Sum (A, N - 1)   {**}
      end;

   begin
   write ('Enter four integers: ');
   readln (List [1], List [2], List [3], List [4]);
   writeln ('Their sum is: ', Sum (List, 4): 1)      {*}
   end.
```

Program 9.4

A recursive function that returns the sum of the first N numbers in an array.

Interactive Input/Output

```
Enter four integers: 3  2  6  4
Their sum is: 15
```

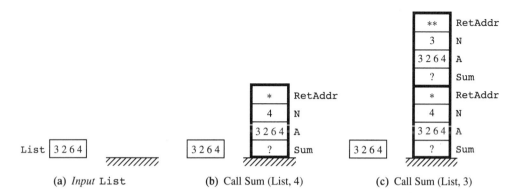

(a) *Input* List   (b) Call Sum (List, 4)   (c) Call Sum (List, 3)

Figure 9.8

The run-time stack for Program 9.4.

▢ Program 9.5

The next example of a recursive function has a more complex calling sequence. It is a function to compute the coefficient in the expansion of a binomial expression.

Consider the following expansions:

$$(x + y)^1 = x + y$$
$$(x + y)^2 = x^2 + 2xy + y^2$$
$$(x + y)^3 = x^3 + 3x^2y + 3xy^2 + y^3$$
$$(x + y)^4 = x^4 + 4x^3y + 6x^2y^2 + 4xy^3 + y^4$$

The coefficients of the terms are called *binomial coefficients*. If you write the coefficients without the terms, they form a triangle of values called *Pascal's triangle*. Figure 9.9 is Pascal's triangle for the coefficients up to the seventh power.

Power, n	Term number, k							
	0	1	2	3	4	5	6	7
1	1	1						
2	1	2	1					
3	1	3	3	1				
4	1	4	6	4	1			
5	1	5	10	10	5	1		
6	1	6	15	20	15	6	1	
7	1	7	21	35	35	21	7	1

Figure 9.9

Pascal's triangle of binomial coefficients.

You can see from Figure 9.9 that each coefficient is the sum of the coefficient immediately above and the coefficient above and to the left. For example, the binomial coefficient in row 5, column 2, which is 10, equals 4 plus 6. Six is above 10, and 4 is above and to the left.

Mathematically, the binomial coefficient $b(n, k)$ for power n and term k is

$$b(n, k) = b(n - 1, k) + b(n - 1, k - 1) \qquad \text{for } 0 \le k \le n$$

A recursive definition of the binomial coefficient

That is a recursive definition, since it defines the function $b(n, k)$ in terms of itself. You can also see that if k equals 0, or if n equals k, the value of the binomial coefficient is 1. Mathematically,

$$b(n, 0) = 1$$
$$b(k, k) = 1$$

which is the basis for the recursive function.

Program 9.5 computes the value of a binomial coefficient recursively. It is based directly on the recursive definition of $b(n, k)$.

Figure 9.10 (pp. 468–69) shows a trace of the run-time stack. Figures 9.10(b), (c), and (d) show the allocation of the first three stack frames. They represent calls

```
program Binomial (output);

    function BinomCoeff (N, K: integer): integer;
        var
            Y1, Y2: integer;
        begin
        if (K = 0) or (N = K) then
            BinomCoeff := 1
        else
            begin
            Y1 := BinomCoeff (N - 1, K);        {**}
            Y2 := BinomCoeff (N - 1, K - 1);   {***}
            BinomCoeff := Y1 + Y2
            end
        end;

    begin
    writeln ('BinomCoeff (3, 1) = ', BinomCoeff (3, 1): 1)   {*}
    end.
```

Program **9.5**

A recursive computation of the binomial coefficient.

Output

```
BinomCoeff (3, 1) = 3
```

to `BinomCoeff (3, 1)`, `BinomCoeff (2, 1)`, and `BinomCoeff (1, 1)`. The first stack frame has the return address of the calling program in the main program. The next two stack frames have the return address of the `Y1` assignment statement. The double asterisk represents that statement.

Figure 9.10(e) shows the return from `BinomCoeff (1, 1)`. `Y1` gets the value 1 returned by the function. Then the `Y2` assignment statement calls the function `BinomCoeff (1, 0)`. Figure 9.10(f) shows the run-time stack during execution of `BinomCoeff (1, 0)`. Each stack frame has a different return address.

The calling sequence for this program is different from the previous recursive programs. The other programs kept allocating stack frames until the run-time stack reached its maximum height. Then they kept deallocating stack frames until the run-time stack was empty.

This program allocates stack frames until the run-time stack reaches its maximum height. It does not deallocate stack frames until the run-time stack is empty, however. From Figure 9.10(d) to (e) it deallocates, but from 9.10(e) to (f) it allocates. From 9.10(f) to (g) to (h) it deallocates, but from 9.10(h) to (i) it allocates. Why?

Because this function has two recursive calls instead of one. If the basis step is true, the function makes no recursive call. But if the basis step is false, the function makes two recursive calls, one for `Y1` and one for `Y2`.

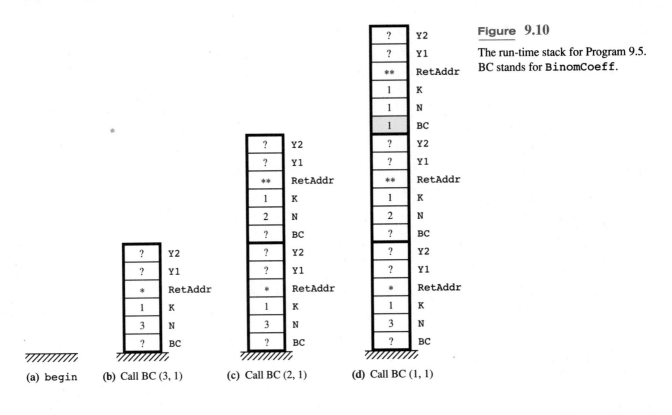

Figure **9.10**

The run-time stack for Program 9.5. BC stands for `BinomCoeff`.

(a) begin (b) Call BC (3, 1) (c) Call BC (2, 1) (d) Call BC (1, 1)

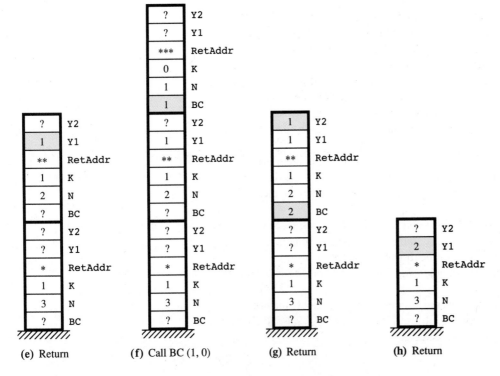

(e) Return (f) Call BC (1, 0) (g) Return (h) Return

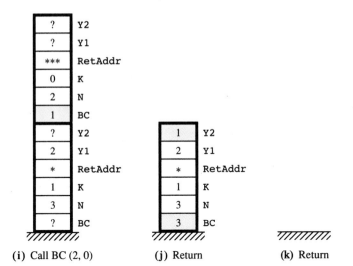

(i) Call BC (2, 0)   (j) Return   (k) Return

Figure 9.10, continued

Figure 9.11 shows the calling sequence for the program. Notice that it is in the shape of a tree. Each node of the tree represents a function call. Except for the main program, a node has either two children or no children, corresponding to two recursive calls or no recursive calls.

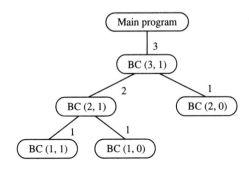

Figure 9.11

The call tree for Program 9.5.

Referring to Figure 9.11, the sequence of calls and returns is

Main program
Call   BC (3, 1)
Call   BC (2, 1)
Call   BC (1, 1)
Return to BC (2, 1)
Call   BC (1, 0)
Return to BC (2, 1)
Return to BC (3, 1)
Call   BC (2, 0)
Return to BC (3, 1)
Return to main program

The sequence of calls and returns in Program 9.5

You can visualize the order of execution on the call tree by imagining that the tree is a coastline in an ocean. A boat starts from the left side of the main program and sails along the coast, always keeping the shore to its left. The boat visits the nodes in the same order they are called and returned from. Figure 9.12 shows the visitation path.

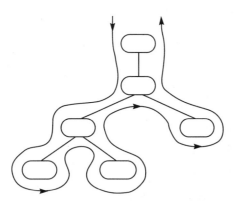

Figure 9.12

The order of execution of Program 9.5.

When analyzing a recursive program from a microscopic point of view, it is easier to construct the call tree before you construct the trace of the run-time stack. Once you have the tree, it is easy to see the behavior of the run-time stack. Every time the boat visits a lower node in the tree, the program allocates one stack frame. Every time the boat visits a higher node in the tree, the program deallocates one stack frame.

You can determine the maximum height of the run-time stack from the call tree. Just keep track of the net number of stack frames allocated when you get to the lowest node of the call tree. That will correspond to the maximum height of the run-time stack.

Drawing the call tree in the order of execution is not the easiest way. The previous execution sequence started

Main program
Call   BC (3, 1)
Call   BC (2, 1)
Call   BC (1, 1)
Return to BC (2, 1)

You should not draw the call tree in that order. It is easier to start with

Main program
Call BC (3, 1)

then recognize from the program listing that BC (3, 1) will call itself twice, BC (2, 1) once, and BC (2, 0) once. Then you can go back to BC (2, 1) and determine its children. In other words, determine all the children of a node before analyzing the deeper calls from any one of the children.

This is a "breadth first" construction of the tree as opposed to the "depth first" construction that follows the execution sequence. The problem with the depth-first construction arises when you return up several levels in a complicated call tree to some higher node. You might forget the state of execution the node is in and not be able to determine its next child node. If you determine all the children of a node at once, you no longer need to remember the state of execution of the node.

Constructing the call tree breadth first

Program 9.6

Program 9.6 (p. 473) has a recursive procedure instead of a function. It reverses the elements in an array of characters.

The procedure reverses the characters in the array Str between Str [I] and Str [J]. The main program wants to reverse the characters between 'B' and 's'. So it calls Reverse with 1 for I and 9 for J.

The procedure solves this problem by breaking it down into a smaller problem. Since 1 is less than 9, it knows the characters between 1 and 9 need to be reversed. So it switches Str [1] with Str [9] and calls itself recursively to switch all the characters between Str [2] and Str [8].

If I is ever greater than or equal to J, no switching is necessary and the procedure does nothing. Figure 9.13 shows the beginning of a trace of the run-time stack.

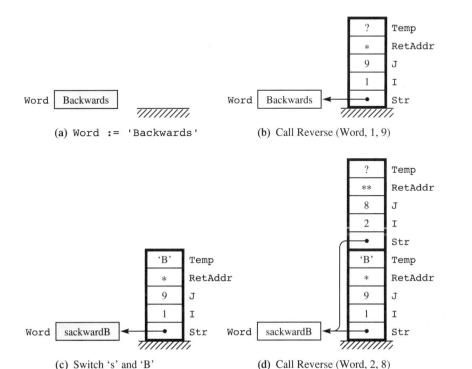

(a) Word := 'Backwards'

(b) Call Reverse (Word, 1, 9)

(c) Switch 's' and 'B'

(d) Call Reverse (Word, 2, 8)

Figure 9.13

The run-time stack for Program 9.6.

LISP: A Freewheeling, Functional Language

Though LISP is just as old as FOR-TRAN and COBOL, it is less well-known than these languages and less entrenched in the commercial computing world.

Developed at MIT during the late 1950s by John McCarthy, LISP (for List Processing) accommodated a programming need very different from that of traditional computing tasks. McCarthy and his students were interested in artificial intelligence (AI), that is, the capability of computer programs to demonstrate intelligence. In designing programs to model various aspects of intelligent behavior, McCarthy discovered that traditional programming languages were a little too "regular" for his needs. Although most programming languages are theoretically equivalent, so that a programmer should be able to get by with just one language, they are tailored to be used in a narrow range of applications. Claiming that theoretical equivalence should put a stop to the invention of new programming languages would be rather like telling the Wright brothers that walking, biking, or flying from point A to point B are identical because each method of transportation produces the same geometrical result.

The data-structuring abilities of traditional programming languages are well suited to dealing with consistently filled tables of data or to processing employee or customer records in which the information for a typical record is very similar in size and form to that of any other record. But AI programs often need to represent amorphous chunks of information

and respond dynamically to changing circumstances in the problem being modeled. An example of such a program is a concept-learning system. This system begins with a finite set of assumptions and can, over time, make more assumptions, act on them, evaluate which assumptions it's most certain about, discard facts that seem wrong, and invent new categories or ideas.

LISP is well suited to the ad hoc data structures and procedures that characterize the early work in AI. The fundamental data structure in LISP is the *atom,* which is a unit such as a number, phrase, or truth value. The next level of chunking takes us to the list, which may be empty or which may be arbitrarily long with heterogeneous members, including other lists. Procedures in LISP accept parameters, just as in Pascal; but unlike Pascal, which expects one-to-one matching of parameter values between the procedure call and the procedure definition, LISP accepts a list of values

John McCarthy.

for each parameter in the procedure definition. Because the structuring principle of LISP programs is the list, it's possible to pass a LISP program or procedure as a parameter to another program (or to itself). One way that this is accomplished is to follow a functional style of programming, in which a LISP function is a cross between the mathematical notion of function and other programming language notions of procedure. Thus, instead of the traditional mathematical notation, in which the operator is in between the operands and, we might write 2 + 3 to specify an addition of two values, in LISP we write (`plus 2 3`). If we want to add a list of values, we can simply list them all after the name of the function we want applied, for example, (`plus 2 3 5 6 4 9`).

Starting to sound a bit bizarre? The highly recursive nature of LISP, although confusing at first, is a very powerful programming tool. With LISP, programmers can write effective recursive programs that solve big problems by whittling them down into successively smaller versions of themselves until the problem almost goes away. Pascal and Modula-2 also support recursion, but in these languages data structuring is considerably more restrained, in the interest of software engineering principles. It's probably best to graduate to the less structured world of LISP only after first learning a more structured programming style. You may never need the capabilities of LISP, but it does provide a powerful programming tool for certain classes of problems.

```
program RecursiveReverse (output);
   type
      StrType = packed array [1..20] of char;
   var
      Word: StrType;

   procedure Reverse (var Str: StrType; I, J : integer);
      {  Reverses the characters in the array Str  }
      {  between Str [I] and Str [J].              }
      var
         Temp: char;
      begin
      if I < J then
         begin
         Temp := Str [I];
         Str [I] := Str [J];
         Str [J] := Temp;
         Reverse (Str, I + 1, J - 1)
         end                              {**}
      end;

   begin
   Word := 'Backwards           ';
   Reverse (Word, 1, 9);
   writeln (Word)                         {*}
   end.
```

Output

```
sdrawkcaB
```

Program 9.6

A recursive procedure to reverse the elements of an array.

In this program, `Str` must be called by reference because the procedure changes the values of the array in the actual parameter list. Even though there are multiple copies of `Str`, one in each stack frame, they all refer to `Word` in the main program.

Program 9.7

The next example has the most complex calling sequence yet. The problem is to print all the permutations of a set of characters. For example, the characters abcd have 24 permutations as follows:

abcd	bacd	cabd	dabc
abdc	badc	cadb	dacb
acbd	bcad	cbad	dbac
acdb	bcda	cbda	dbca
adbc	bdac	cdab	dcab
adcb	bdca	cdba	dcba

The 24 permutations of four characters

Program 9.7 must print all the permutations of any number of characters.

Remember, the key to a recursive solution is to solve the large problem assuming you already have the solution to a smaller problem. This problem is to print the permutations of the characters in some packed array of char, say A, between A [1] and A [4].

What can you assume? You can assume you have a procedure that will print all the permutations between A [2] and A [4]. For example, if you give the procedure the characters xabc, you can assume that it will print the following six permutations:

xabc   xacb   xbac   xbca   xcab   xcba

Look at the pattern of permutations for four characters. It is simply four groups of six permutations. Each group starts with one of the four characters and contains the six permutations of the remaining three characters. You can print the permutations of four characters as follows:

Make A [1] 'a'
Print permutations from A [2] to A [4]
Make A [1] 'b'
Print permutations from A [2] to A [4]
Make A [1] 'c'
Print permutations from A [2] to A [4]
Make A [1] 'd'
Print permutations from A [2] to A [4]

This is obviously a job for a loop. To make the first character of A each letter in turn, simply exchange it with each of the other characters.

```
for I := 1 to 4 do
   begin
   Exchange A [1] with A [I]
   Print permutations from A [2] to A [4]
   end
```

For this scheme to work, the procedure that prints the permutations cannot change any of the values in A. The array of characters must be called by value.

Starting with abcd, the loop exchanges 'a' with 'a' and prints the first group of six permutations starting with abcd. Then it exchanges 'a' with 'b' and prints the group of permutations starting with bacd. Then it exchanges 'b' with 'c' and prints the group of permutations starting with cabd. Then it exchanges 'c' with 'd' and prints the group of permutations starting with dabc.

In general, you want to be able to print the permutations between A [Left] and A [Right], where Left and Right are parameters. The loop generalizes to

```
for I := Left to Right do
   begin
   Exchange A [Left] with A [I]
   Print permutations from A [Left + 1] to A [Right]
   end
```

Program 9.7 shows the completed program with a print of the permutations of three letters.

Program **9.7**

A recursive procedure that prints the premutations of the elements in an array.

```pascal
program PrintPermutations (output);
   type
      StrType = packed array [1..10] of char;

   procedure Exchange (var B: StrType; I, J: integer);
      var
         Temp: char;
      begin
      Temp := B [I];
      B [I] := B [J];
      B [J] := Temp
      end;

   procedure Permute (A: StrType; Left, Right: integer);
      {  Prints all the permutations of A   }
      {  between A [Left] and A [Right].    }
      var
         I: integer;
      begin
      if Left = Right then
         writeln (A)
      else
         for I := Left to Right do
            begin
            Exchange (A, Left, I);
            Permute (A, Left + 1, Right)
            end
      end;

   begin
   Permute ('abc        ', 1, 3)
   end.
```

Output

```
abc
acb
bac
bca
cab
cba
```

Figure 9.14 shows the call tree for this example. The main program calls the procedure once with `Left` equals 1 and `Right` equals 3. The `for` loop executes three times. Each time it executes it makes a recursive call to itself. So the node below the main program has three children.

Each child has `Left` equals 2 and `Right` equals 3. Their `for` loops execute twice, so they each have two children.

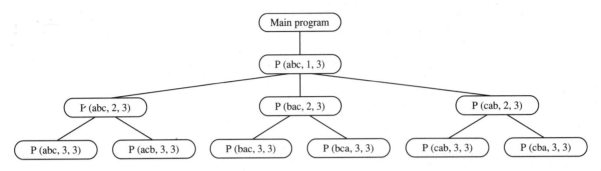

Figure 9.14

The call tree for Program 9.7.

The bottom nodes have `Left` equals 3 and `Right` equals 3. They have no children. They simply print the value they received in the array. The six leaves on the tree print the six permutations.

Towers of Hanoi

The Towers of Hanoi puzzle is a classic computer science problem that is conveniently solved by the recursive technique. The puzzle consists of three pegs and a set of disks with different diameters. The pegs are numbered 1, 2, and 3. Each disk has a hole at its center so that it can fit onto one of the pegs. The initial configuration of the puzzle consists of all the disks on one peg in a way that no disk rests directly on another disk with a smaller diameter. Figure 9.15 is the initial configuration for four disks.

The problem is to move all the disks from the starting peg to another peg under the following conditions:

- You may only move one disk at a time. It must be the top disk from one peg, which is moved to the top of another peg.

- You may not place one disk on another disk having a smaller diameter.

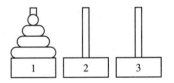

Figure 9.15

The Towers of Hanoi puzzle.

The procedure for solving this problem has three parameters, N, I, and J, where

- N is the number of disks to move
- I is the starting peg
- J is the goal peg

I and J are integers that identify the pegs. Given the values of I and J, you can calculate the intermediate peg, which is the one that is neither the starting peg nor the goal peg, as 6 − I − J. For example, if the starting peg is 1 and the goal peg is 3 then the intermediate peg is $6 - 1 - 3 = 2$.

To move the N disks from peg I to peg J, first check to see if N = 1. If it does, then simply move the one disk from peg I to peg J. But if it does not, then decompose the problem into several smaller parts.

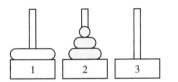

(a) Move three disks from peg 1 to peg 2.

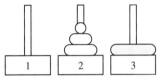

(b) Move one disk from peg 1 to peg 3.

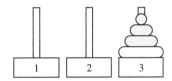

(c) Move three disks from peg 2 to peg 3.

Figure 9.16

The solution for moving four disks from peg 1 to peg 3 assuming you can move three disks from one peg to any other peg.

- Move `N` − 1 disks from peg `I` to the intermediate peg.
- Move one disk from peg `I` to peg `J`.
- Move `N` − 1 disks from the intermediate peg to peg `J`.

Figure 9.16 shows this decomposition for the problem of moving four disks from peg 1 to peg 3.

This procedure guarantees that a disk will not be placed on another disk with a smaller diameter, assuming that the original `N` disks are stacked correctly. Suppose, for example, that four disks are to be moved from peg 1 to peg 3 as in Figure 9.16. The procedure says that you should move the top three disks from peg 1 to peg 2, move the bottom disk from peg 1 to peg 3, and then move the three disks from peg 2 to peg 3.

In moving the top three disks from peg 1 to peg 2, you will leave the bottom disk on peg 1. Remember that it is the disk with the largest diameter, so any disk you place on it in the process of moving the other disks will be smaller.

In order to move the bottom disk from peg 1 to peg 3, peg 3 must be empty. You will not place the bottom disk on a smaller disk in this step either.

When you move the three disks from peg 2 to peg 3, you will place them on the largest disk, now on the bottom of peg 3. So the three disks will be placed on peg 3 correctly.

The procedure is recursive. In the first step, you must move three disks from peg 1 to peg 2. To do that, move two disks from peg 1 to peg 3, then one disk from peg 1 to peg 2, then two disks from peg 3 to peg 2. Figure 9.17 shows this sequence.

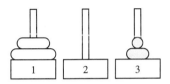

(a) Move two disks from peg 1 to peg 3.

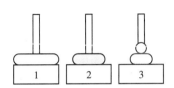

(b) Move one disk from peg 1 to peg 2.

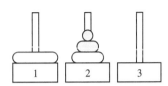

(c) Move two disks from peg 3 to peg 2.

Figure 9.17

The solution for moving three disks from peg 1 to peg 2 assuming you can move two disks from one peg to any other peg.

Using the previous reasoning, these steps will be carried out correctly. In the process of moving two disks from peg 1 to peg 3, you may place any of these two disks on the bottom two disks of peg 1 without fear of breaking the rules.

Eventually you will reduce the problem to the basis step where you only need to move one disk. But the solution with one disk is easy. Programming the solution to the Towers of Hanoi puzzle is left as a problem at the end of the chapter.

Mutual Recursion

Some problems are best solved by procedures that do not call themselves directly but that are recursive nonetheless. Suppose a main program calls procedure A, and procedure A contains a call to procedure B. If procedure B contains a call to procedure A, then A and B are mutually recursive. Even though procedure A does not call itself directly, it does call itself indirectly through procedure B.

There is nothing different about the implementation of mutual recursion compared to plain recursion. Stack frames are allocated on the run-time stack the same way, with parameters allocated first, followed by the return address, followed by local variables.

There is one slight problem in specifying mutually recursive procedures in a Pascal program, however. It arises from the fact that procedures must be declared before they are used.

If procedure A calls procedure B, the declaration of procedure B must appear before the declaration of procedure A in the listing. But, if procedure B calls procedure A, the declaration of procedure A must appear before the declaration of procedure B in the listing. The problem is that if each calls the other, each must appear before the other in the listing, an obvious impossibility.

For this situation, Pascal provides the *forward declaration*, which allows the programmer to write the first procedure heading without the block. In a forward declaration, you include the complete formal parameter list, but in place of the block, you put `forward`. After the forward declaration comes the declaration of the second procedure, followed by the block of the first procedure. You must repeat the procedure heading of the first procedure, but without the formal parameter list.

The forward declaration

Example   9.7   Here is an outline of the structure of the mutually recursive procedures A and B as just discussed:

```
const, type, var of main program

procedure A (X: SomeType);
    forward;

procedure B (Y: SomeOtherType);
    Block for B, including const, type, var, etc.

procedure A;
    Block for A, including const, type, var, etc.

begin {main program}
Executable statements of main program
end.
```

If B has a call to A, the compiler will be able to verify that the number and types of the actual parameters match the formal parameters of A scanned earlier in the forward declaration. If A has a call to B, the call will be in the block of A. The compiler will have scanned the declaration of B because it occurs before the block of A. ∎

Mutual recursion is rare in practice with one notable exception. Some compilers are based on a technique called *recursive descent*, which uses mutual recursion heavily. You can get an idea of why this is so by considering the structure of Pascal statements. It is possible to nest an `if` inside of a `while`, which is nested in turn inside of another `if`. A compiler that uses recursive descent has a procedure to translate `if` statements and another procedure to translate `while` statements. When the procedure that is translating the outer `if` statement encounters the `while` statement, it calls the procedure that translates `while` statements. But when that procedure encounters the nested `if` statement, it calls the statement that translates `if` statements; hence the mutual recursion. We will leave complete examples of mutual recursion to the problems following this chapter.

Mutual recursion in a recursive descent compiler

The Cost of Recursion

The selection of examples in this section was based on only one criterion—the ability of the example to illustrate recursion. You can see that recursive solutions require much storage for the run-time stack. It also takes time to allocate and deallocate the stack frames. Recursive solutions are expensive in both space and time.

If you can solve a problem easily without recursion, the nonrecursive solution will usually be better than the recursive solution. Program 6.2, the nonrecursive function to calculate the factorial, is certainly better than the recursive factorial function of Program 9.3. Both Program 9.4 to find the sum of the numbers in an array and Program 9.6 can easily be programmed nonrecursively with a loop.

The binomial coefficient $b(n, k)$ has a nonrecursive definition that based on factorials.

$$b(n, k) = \frac{n!}{k! \, (n - k)!}$$

If you compute the factorials nonrecursively, a program based on this definition may be more efficient than the corresponding recursive program. Here the choice is a little less clear, since the nonrecursive solution requires multiplication and division but the recursive solution requires only addition.

Some problems are recursive by nature and can only be solved nonrecursively with great difficulty. The problems of printing the permutations of N letters and solving the Towers of Hanoi puzzle are recursive by nature. You can try to solve them without recursion to see how difficult it would be. Quick sort, one of the best-known sorting algorithms, falls in this category also. It is much more difficult to program quick sort nonrecursively than recursively.

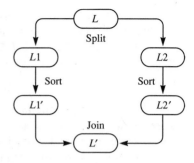

9.4 Sorting

The idea of a recursive solution is to solve a large problem assuming you have the same solution to a smaller problem. You can apply that idea to sorting.

Figure 9.18 shows the general approach. Suppose you have a list of elements, *L*. To sort the list, you split it into two sublists, *L*1 and *L*2. The sublists are each smaller than the original list, *L*.

The recursive idea lets you assume that you have the solution to the problem of sorting the smaller lists. So you would recursively sort *L*1, producing the sorted sublist *L*1′. Then you would recursively sort *L*2, producing the sorted sublist *L*2′.

The last step is to join the two sorted sublists, *L*1′ and *L*2′, into the final sorted list, *L*′.

Figure 9.18

The general sort algorithm.

Merge Sort and Quick Sort

There are two basic sort algorithms, which differ in the methods they use to perform the split and the join. The two are the *merge sort* algorithm and the *quick sort* algorithm, shown in Figure 9.19.

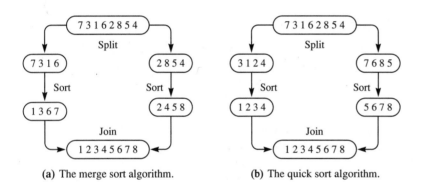

(a) The merge sort algorithm.   (b) The quick sort algorithm.

Figure 9.19

The two basic sort algorithms.

The figure shows the original unsorted list, *L*, as

7 3 1 6 2 8 5 4

for both algorithms. The final list for both is the sorted list, *L*′, which has eight values.

The merge sort algorithm performs a simple split. It takes *L*1 as the first half of the list and *L*2 as the second half of the list. It recursively sorts the sublists, producing the sorted sublist *L*1′ as

1 3 6 7

and the sorted sublist *L*2′ as

2 4 5 8

The last step is to merge these two sublists into a single sorted list, L'. You could perform the merge using the approach in the algorithm for merging two ordered files.

You can see that the split of L into $L1$ and $L2$ is easy. You simply take the left half of L as $L1$ and the right half as $L2$. On the other hand, the join is hard. It requires a loop to cycle through the sublists, selecting the smallest number at each step to place in the merged list.

The quick sort algorithm splits the original list, L, such that every element in the sublist $L1$ is less than every element in the sublist $L2$. The sublist $L1$ is

 3   1   2   4

and the sublist $L2$ is

 7   6   8   5

It sorts $L1$ recursively into the list $L1'$

 1   2   3   4

and $L2$ recursively into the list $L2'$

 5   6   7   8

Then it joins $L1'$ and $L2'$ into the final sorted list, L'.

You can see that the split of L into $L1$ and $L2$ is hard. It requires a loop that somehow compares the elements in the list with each other and moves the smaller elements to the left and the larger ones to the right. On the other hand, the join is easy. It does not require any further comparisons in a loop, the way the join in the merge sort does.

▨ Program 9.8

Figure 9.19(b) shows the ideal quick sort split. That figure had an original list, L, of eight items. The algorithm split L exactly in half, with four items in $L1$ and four in $L2$.

The *median value* of a list of items is that value, m, such that there are as many items less than m as greater than m. If you knew the median value, you could split the list exactly in half. Unfortunately, the only way to determine the median value is to sort the list and pick the middle item. But you need the median value to sort the list in the first place.

The only thing you can do in the face of this dilemma is to be satisfied with a less-than-ideal split. Program 9.8 is an implementation of the quick sort algorithm. It picks the middle item in the unsorted list and hopes it is close to the median value.

```pascal
program OrderQuick (NumFile, output);
   const
      MaxLength = 100;
   type
      ListType = array [1..MaxLength] of integer;
   var
      NumFile:  text;
      NumItems: integer;
      List:     ListType;
      I:        integer;

   procedure QuickSort (var A: ListType; Left, Right: integer);
      { Sorts the items of list A         }
      { between A [Left] and A [Right].  }
      var
         Temp: integer;
         Key:  integer;
         I, J: integer;
      begin
      I := Left;
      J := Right;
      Key := A [(Left + Right) div 2];
      repeat
         while A [I] < Key do
            I := I + 1;
         while Key < A [J] do
            J := J - 1;
         if I <= J then
            begin
            Temp := A [I];
            A [I] := A [J];
            A [J] := Temp;
            I := I + 1;
            J := J - 1
            end
      until I > J;
      { Assert:                                                    }
      { Every item between A [Left] and A [J] is less than  }
      { or equal to every item between A [I] and A [Right]. }
      if Left < J then
         QuickSort (A, Left, J);
      if I < Right then
         QuickSort (A, I, Right)
      end;
```

Program 9.8, continued

```
begin
reset (NumFile);
read (NumFile, NumItems);
for I := 1 to NumItems do
   begin
   read (NumFile, List [I]);
   write (List [I]: 4)
   end;
writeln;
QuickSort (List, 1, NumItems);
writeln;
for I := 1 to NumItems do
   write (List [I]: 4)
end.
```

Input—NumFile

```
10
90  20  80  50  40  10  95  60  30  70
```

Output

```
90  20  80  50  40  10  95  60  30  70

10  20  30  40  50  60  70  80  90  95
```

The value it picks is called the *key*. If the key is less than the true median, list *L*1 will contain fewer items than list *L*2. If the key is greater than the true median, *L*1 will contain more items.

You could be extremely unlucky and have the key be the smallest value in the list, in which case *L*1 will have only one value. Or if the key is the largest value, *L*2 will have only one value. On the other hand, you could be extremely lucky and have the key be the true median. You must be content to let the key be what it will be, and accept the average behavior of the algorithm.

Figure 9.20 is a trace of the first call to procedure QuickSort in Program 9.8. The main program calls the procedure with a value of 1 for Left and 10 for Right. As Figure 9.20(a) shows, QuickSort initializes I to Left and J to Right. It computes Key as 40.

The repeat loop splits the list into sublists *L*1 and *L*2. The two nested while loops increase I and decrease J until I finds the value 90, which is greater than Key, and J finds the value 30, which is less than Key. Since I is less than or equal to J, 90 is to the left of 30. So they need to be exchanged. Figure 9.20(c) shows the result of the exchange. Afterward, QuickSort increments I by 1 and decrements J by 1.

	[1]	[2]	[3]	[4]	[5]	[6]	[7]	[8]	[9]	[10]

(a) Left = 1
Right = 10
Key = 40

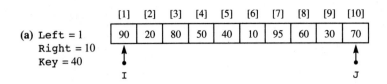

(b) Increase I
Decrease J

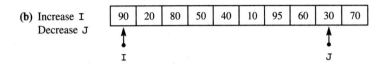

(c) Swap
I := I + 1
J := J - 1

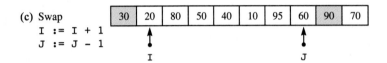

(d) Increase I
Decrease J

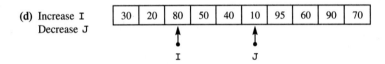

(e) Swap
I := I + 1
J := J - 1

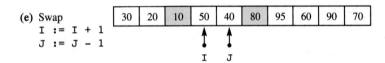

(f) Increase I
Decrease J

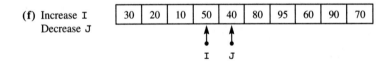

(g) Swap
I := I + 1
J := J - 1

(h) QS (1, 4)

(i) QS (5, 10)

Figure 9.20

A trace of the first call to
QuickSort in Program 9.8.

Since I is still to the left of J, the loop repeats. Figure 9.20(d) shows I increasing to find 80 and J decreasing to find 10. J skips over 60 and 95 because they are greater than Key.

I is still to the left of J. Figure 9.20(e) shows the exchange of 10 and 80, the increment of I, and the decrement of J.

From Figure 9.20(e) you can see that the loop invariant is

- Every element between A [Left] and A [I - 1] is less than or equal to every element between A [J + 1] and A [Right].

The loop invariant for QuickSort

In Figure 9.20(e), the loop invariant means that each of the values (30, 20, 10) is less than or equal to each of the values (80, 95, 60, 90, 70).

The initializing statements make the loop invariant true the first time. Since they initialize I to Left, there are no elements between A [Left] and A [Left - 1]. Since they initialize J to Right, there are no elements between A [Right + 1] and A [Right]. Since there are no elements in the left interval and no elements in the right interval, every element in the left interval is less than or equal to every element in the right interval.

The statements in the body of the repeat loop keep the invariant true. They increase I and/or decrease J, in effect widening the left and right intervals. When I finds a value greater than or equal to Key and J finds a value less than or equal to Key, you know that I's value is greater than or equal to J's value. The exchange keeps the invariant true.

Figure 9.20(g) shows the last exchange. QuickSort swaps 50 and 40. After it increments I and decrements J, I has the value 5 and J has the value 4. So J is to the left of I, and the loop terminates.

The assertion in the listing follows from the loop invariant and the termination condition. *L*1 is the sublist between A [Left] and A [J]. *L*2 is the sublist between A [I] and A [Right].

Figure 9.20(h) shows the result of the recursive call to QuickSort. The abbreviation QS (1, 4) stands for the procedure call

```
QuickSort (A, Left, J)
```

when Left has the value 1 and J has the value 4. Similarly, QS (5, 10) stands for the procedure call

```
QuickSort (A, I, Right)
```

when I has the value 5 and Right has the value 10.

Each recursive call to QuickSort splits a smaller list. The first recursive call splits the list

   30 20 10 40

with a Left of 1 and a Right of 4. The second recursive call splits the list

   50 80 95 60 90 70

with a Left of 5 and a Right of 10. Each of these executions produces a trace like that of Figure 9.20.

What is the structure of the call tree of `QuickSort`? The listing shows that the procedure makes either two, one, or no recursive calls, depending on the size of *L*1 and *L*2. Therefore, each node in the call tree will have two, one, or no children. For the values listed in Program 9.8, you would need to do a trace of the split at each call. If you do the traces, you will see that the call tree is structured as shown in Figure 9.21.

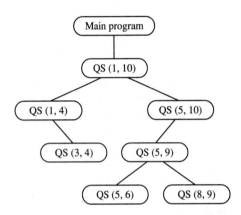

Figure 9.21

The call tree for `QuickSort` in Program 9.8.

The program makes a total of seven calls to `QuickSort`, including the call from the main program. The figure shows that QS (1, 4) splits the list of four elements into *L*1, with one element, and *L*2, with two elements. It does not call itself recursively for *L*1, but it does for *L*2. QS (5, 9) makes a more even split. Its list *L* has five items, from A [5] to A [9]. It splits it into sublist *L*1, from A [5] to A [6], and *L*2, from A [8] to A [9].

Using the technique of Figure 9.12, you can tell from the call tree that the order of calls and returns is as follows:

Call QS (1, 10)
Call QS (1, 4)
Call QS (3, 4)
Return
Return
Call QS (5, 10)
Call QS (5, 9)
Call QS (5, 6)
Return
Call QS (8, 9)
Return
Return
Return
Return

The calling sequence for Program 9.8

Program 9.9

Unlike the quick sort algorithm, merge sort splits *L* exactly in half every time. But it has a problem that quick sort does not have. To merge two parts of one list into a second list requires storage for the second list. To perform the merge you could allocate storage for the second list as a local array variable. You could merge the two sublists into the second list and then copy the second list back into the original.

Program 9.9 is a better implementation of the merge sort algorithm because it does not require extra storage for the second list or extra time for the copy operation. The program sorts an array of integers.

It stores each value in a record with two parts, `Value` and `Link`. The array to be sorted is an array of records. The algorithm does not exchange any records in the array. Instead, it alters the `Link` part of all the records in such a way that you can always determine the next higher number from the link field.

```
program OrderMerge (NumFile, output);
   const
      MaxLength = 100;
   type
      RecType =
         record
         Value: integer;
         Link:  integer
         end;
      ListType = array [1..MaxLength] of RecType;
   var
      NumFile:  text;
      NumItems: integer;
      List:     ListType;
      I:        integer;
      Start:    integer;

   procedure MergeSort (var A:    ListType;
                            Left:  integer;
                            Right: integer;
                        var Start: integer);
      { Sorts the list A between A [Left] and A [Right].      }
      { Sets Start to point to the smallest value between     }
      { A [Left] and A [Right].  A [Start].Link points to     }
      { the next larger value.  A [I].Link in general points  }
      { to the record whose Value part is the next larger     }
      { value than A [I].Value.                               }
      var
         Mid:        integer;
         LeftStart:  integer;
         RightStart: integer;
         I, J, K:    integer;
```

Program 9.9

The merge sort algorithm.

Chapter *9* *Recursion*

Program 9.9, continued

```
      begin
      if Left >= Right then
         Start := Left
      else
         begin
         Mid := (Left + Right) div 2;
         MergeSort (A, Left, Mid, LeftStart);
         MergeSort (A, Mid + 1, Right, RightStart);
         I := LeftStart;
         J := RightStart;
         K := MaxLength;    {  Temporary start of merged list.  }
         while (I <> 0) and (J <> 0) do
            if A [I].Value <= A [J].Value then
               begin
               A [K].Link := I;
               K := I;
               I := A [I].Link
               end
            else
               begin
               A [K].Link := J;
               K := J;
               J := A [J].Link
               end;
         if I = 0 then
            A [K].Link := J
         else
            A [K].Link := I;
         Start := A [MaxLength].Link
         end
      end;

begin
reset (NumFile);
read (NumFile, NumItems);
for I := 1 to NumItems do
   begin
   read (NumFile, List [I].Value);
   write (List [I].Value: 4);
   List [I].Link := 0
   end;
writeln;
MergeSort (List, 1, NumItems, Start);
writeln;
I := Start;
while I <> 0 do
   begin
   write (List [I].Value: 4);
   I := List [I].Link
   end
end.
```

Program 9.9, continued

Input—NumFile

```
10
90  20  80  50  40  10  95  60  30  70
```

Output

```
90  20  80  50  40  10  95  60  30  70

10  20  30  40  50  60  70  80  90  95
```

Figure 9.22(a) shows the array of records before the program calls procedure `MergeSort`. The main program sets the `Link` field of every record to 0 before the call.

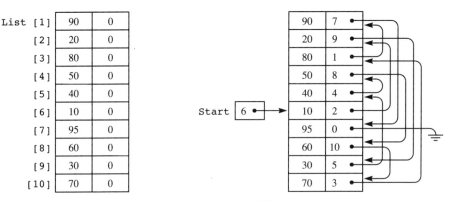

(a) Before the first `MergeSort` call. (b) After the top-level merge.

Figure 9.22

The result of a `MergeSort` call from the main program of Program 9.9.

Figure 9.22(b) shows the array of records after the call to `MergeSort`. The main program has an integer variable, `Start`. `MergeSort` sets `Start` to 6 because `List [6].Value` is the smallest item in the list. It sets `List [6].Link` to 2 because `List [2].Value` is the next larger item in the list. It sets `List [2].Link` to 9 because `List [9].Value` is the next larger item in the list, and so on.

For each record, `I`, `List [I].Link` is the index of the record whose value part is the next larger item in the list. The second field links each item to the next larger item. The record with the largest value, record 7 in this list, has a `Link` of 0. That link points to nothing at all, which the figure indicates by the dashed triangle.

The second `while` loop of the main program outputs the list in order. It initializes `I` to 6 and outputs `List [6].Value`. The assignment

```
I := List [I].Link
```

gives `I` the value 2. The next time through the loop the `write` call outputs `List [2].Value`. The loop continues to advance `I` through the linked list until it gets the value 0, when the loop terminates. Even though the program exchanged no values, the output is indistinguishable from the `QuickSort` program. In effect, the program sorted the list.

The main program calls `MergeSort` with a value of 1 for `Left` and 10 for `Right`. `MergeSort` splits the list in half with

```
Mid := (Left + Right) div 2
```

which gives 5 to `Mid`. It calls itself recursively to sort $L1$ as the list between A [1] and A [5], and $L2$ as the list between A [6] and A [10]. Figure 9.23 shows the list after these two recursive calls to `MergeSort`.

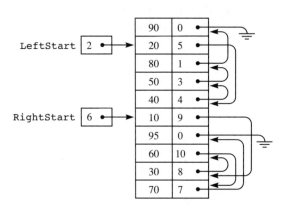

Figure 9.23

The list in the call to `MergeSort (A, 1, 10, Start)` after the recursive calls to `MergeSort (A, 1, 5, LeftStart)` and `MergeSort (A, 6, 10, RightStart)`.

The split was easy. The rest of `MergeSort`, that part in the `while` loop, is the join. Given the values for `LeftStart` and `RightStart`, which point to the start of two ordered linked lists, the problems is to alter their `Link` fields to make one ordered linked list with `Start` pointing to the smallest element. Figure 9.24 shows a trace of the join operation for two short linked lists.

Figure 9.24(b) shows I initialized to `LeftStart` and J initialized to `RightStart`. `MergeSort` initializes K to `MaxLength`. It assumes that the list does not use the entire array and that the last record is available for temporary storage. I will advance through the first list, and J will advance through the second list. K will advance through the merged list.

Each time the loop executes, it finds the next item from lists $L1$ and $L2$ to put in the merged list. It changes the link in the last record of the merged list to point to the newly merged item from $L1$ or $L2$. The newly merged item is taken off the sublist. At the conclusion of the loop, all the items will be in one merged list with no physical exchanges.

Figure 9.24(c) shows the operation after one loop execution. The statements

```
A [K].Link := I;
K := I;
I := A [I].Link
```

link the A [2] record into the new merged list and unlink it from the I list. Figures 9.24(d) and (e) show the same operation with both values from the J list.

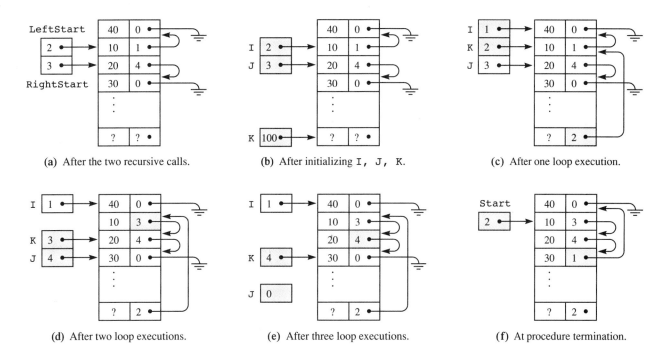

(a) After the two recursive calls. (b) After initializing I, J, K. (c) After one loop execution.

(d) After two loop executions. (e) After three loop executions. (f) At procedure termination.

Figure 9.24

A trace of the join operation in MergeSort for two short linked lists.

When the while loop gets to the end of one of the lists, you know that all the remaining links of the other sublist do not need changing. The last if statement links the tail of the other sublist to the end of the merged list, as Figure 9.24(f) shows.

Insertion Sort and Selection Sort

Both merge sort and quick sort are easier to program if the split operation takes only one element for *L2*. Figure 9.25 shows this special case.

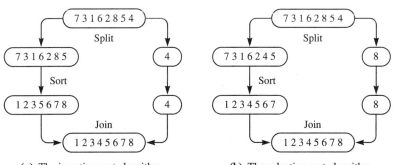

Figure 9.25

Sorting with a split of one element.

(a) The insertion sort algorithm. (b) The selection sort algorithm.

When *L2* has a single element, the merge sort algorithm simply picks the rightmost element in the list during the split operation. It sorts the sublist *L1*, but does not need to sort *L2* since *L2* has only one element. Then it joins *L1′* and *L2′* by inserting the single element from *L2′* into *L1′*. The insertion process requires a simple loop to shift the lower elements down one slot to make room for the element from *L2*. The merge sort with a split of one element is called the *insertion sort*.

When *L2* has a single element, the quick sort algorithm must select the largest value from *L* to put in *L2*. The selection process requires a simple loop to find the index of the largest value. After the index is computed, an exchange puts the largest value in *L2*. The algorithm sorts the sublist *L1*, but it does not need to sort *L2* since *L2* has only one element. The quick sort with a split of one element is called the *selection sort*.

You can program the selection and insertion sorts recursively or nonrecursively. Figure 9.26 is a nonrecursive trace of the single-element sort algorithms with the same original unsorted list, *L*, as in the previous figure. The shaded areas are those regions that are guaranteed to be in order after each pass of the algorithm.

The nonrecursive version of the insertion sort would begin by inserting 3 into the sublist

7

producing the sorted sublist

3   7

Then it would insert 1 into this list, producing the sorted sublist

1   3   7

and so on. The recursive version would begin by calling itself to sort

7   3   1   6   2   8   5

Then it would insert 4 into the sorted list.

Figure 9.26

Nonrecursive traces of the single element sort algorithms.

Initial list	7	3	1	6	2	8	5	4
Pass 1, insert 3	3	7	1	6	2	8	5	4
Pass 2, insert 1	1	3	7	6	2	8	5	4
Pass 3, insert 6	1	3	6	7	2	8	5	4
Pass 4, insert 2	1	2	3	6	7	8	5	4
Pass 5, insert 8	1	2	3	6	7	8	5	4
Pass 6, insert 5	1	2	3	5	6	7	8	4
Pass 7, insert 4	1	2	3	4	5	6	7	8

(a) The insertion sort algorithm.

Initial list	7	3	1	6	2	8	5	4
Pass 1, select 8	7	3	1	6	2	4	5	8
Pass 2, select 7	5	3	1	6	2	4	7	8
Pass 3, select 6	5	3	1	4	2	6	7	8
Pass 4, select 5	2	3	1	4	5	6	7	8
Pass 5, select 4	2	1	3	4	5	6	7	8
Pass 6, select 3	2	1	3	4	5	6	7	8
Pass 7, select 2	1	2	3	4	5	6	7	8

(b) The selection sort algorithm.

Program 7.13 was a nonrecursive implementation of the selection sort, which was traced in Figure 7.16. Figure 9.26(b) is also a trace of the nonrecursive selection sort, but with the same list as in Figure 9.26(a). The nonrecursive sort would begin by selecting 8 and exchanging it with the last element of the list. Then it would select 7 and exchange it with the penultimate element, and so on. The recursive version would select the 8 and exchange it with the last element of the list. Then it would call itself recursively to sort the first seven elements.

Figure 9.27 summarizes the four basic sort algorithms. Most sort algorithms fall into one of the two basic families, either merge sort or quick sort.

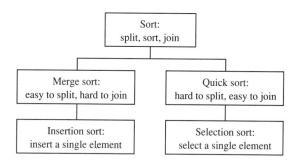

Figure 9.27

Summary of the sort algorithms.

Complexity of the Sort Algorithms

How fast are the sort algorithms that are described in this section? Remember from Section 7.4 that the selection sort is $O(n^2)$. The insertion sort is also $O(n^2)$. You can visualize in Figure 9.26 that each algorithm requires n passes through the list. Each pass requires a loop to do the insertion or selection. The doubly nested loops give the algorithms their $O(n^2)$ behavior.

How do `QuickSort` and `MergeSort` compare with the single-element sorts? In the best case with `QuickSort`, you divide the list in half each time. Figure 9.28 shows the call tree for `MergeSort` and the best case `QuickSort` for a 16-element list.

The list at the top level has 16 elements. The lists at the next lower recursive call have 8 elements. The lists at the next lower call have 4 elements, and the bottom level has 2-element lists.

A loop executes at each level. In `MergeSort`, the `while` loop performs the join. In `QuickSort`, the `repeat` loop performs the split. In both algorithms, the loop passes through the list comparing items. The number of comparisons equals the number of items in the list.

For example, the top level has a list of 16 items, and the algorithm makes 16 comparisons. The next level has lists with 8 items. The loops at this level make 8 comparisons each. Since there are 2 recursive calls at the second level, the total number of comparisons at this level is also 16.

Similarly, the number of comparisons at the next lower level is also 16. There are 4 lists, and each list requires 4 comparisons.

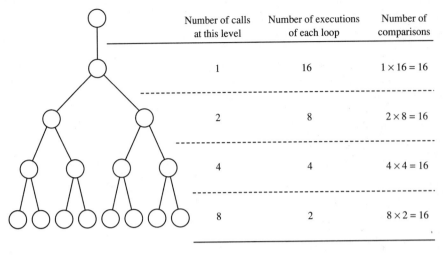

	Number of calls at this level	Number of executions of each loop	Number of comparisons
	1	16	$1 \times 16 = 16$
	2	8	$2 \times 8 = 16$
	4	4	$4 \times 4 = 16$
	8	2	$8 \times 2 = 16$
Total number of comparisons:			$4 \times 16 = 64$

Figure 9.28

The call tree for `MergeSort` and the best case `QuickSort` with a 16-element list.

In general, if the list has n elements, the algorithms make n comparisons at each level. So the total number of comparisons is n times the total number of levels.

How many levels are there for a list of n elements? The number of times you need to divide n in half to get it down to 1. You recognize this answer from the analysis of the binary search algorithm. It is log n. In Figure 9.28, the logarithm of 16 is 4, which corresponds to the 4 levels of recursive calls. The total number of comparisons is therefore 4 times 16, which is 64.

In general, the total number of comparisons is n times log n. `MergeSort` and the best-case `QuickSort` are $O(n \log n)$ algorithms. In the worst case, `QuickSort` is $O(n^2)$ because in that case it is equivalent to the selection sort. In practice, `QuickSort` is $O(n \log n)$ on the average.

The five orders encountered thus far, starting with the fastest, are

- $O(\log n)$ Example: the binary search
- $O(n)$ Example: the sequential search
- $O(n \log n)$ Example: the merge sort and quick sort
- $O(n^2)$ Example: the single-element sorts
- $O(n^3)$ Example: matrix multiplication

Five orders of complexity

If you are comparing two algorithms with different orders, the algorithm with an order farther down the list will be worse for large amounts of data, regardless of the coefficients. For example, an algorithm with a statement execution count of $5n$ log n will be faster than one with $2n^2$. Even though 5 is greater than 2, for large n the first expression will be smaller than the second. Another example of this behavior is Figure 7.15, which showed that 4 log n is better than $n + 1$ for large n, even though 4 is greater than 1.

On the other hand, the coefficients are important when you compare two algorithms with the same order. If one algorithm has a statement execution count of $5n$ log n, and the second has a count of $2n$ log n, the second algorithm will be faster.

Some algorithms, not encountered in this book, are even worse than $O(n^3)$. They are $O(2^n)$, and form a class of difficult problems that computer scientists have spent a great deal of time investigating. They are interesting problems that you will learn about if you take more advanced computer science courses.

SUMMARY

An abstract data type (ADT) is a collection of variables and a set of operations on the variables. A stack is an ADT that stores values with a last in, first out (LIFO) discipline. The operations on a stack include Push to store an item and Pop to retrieve an item. A stack can be implemented with an array and an integer that indicates the top of the stack. Stacks can be used to evaluate postfix expressions and to convert from infix to postfix expressions.

The LIFO nature of the run-time stack is required to implement function and procedure calls. The allocation process for a function is the following: push storage for the returned value, push the actual parameters, push the return address, push storage for the local variables. The allocation process for a procedure is identical except that storage for the returned value is not pushed. The stack frame consists of all the items pushed onto the run-time stack in one function or procedure call.

Proving a statement is true by mathematical induction involves a four-step process: basis, inductive hypothesis, induction, and conclusion. In the basis step, you prove that the statement is true for the smallest value of n. In the inductive hypothesis step, you assume the statement is true for an arbitrary $n = N$. In the induction step, you prove, using the inductive hypothesis, that the statement must be true for $n = N + 1$. The conclusion is that the statement must be true for all n greater than the smallest value.

A recursive procedure is one that calls itself. To avoid calling itself endlessly, a recursive procedure must have an if statement that serves as an escape hatch to stop the recursive calls. Two different viewpoints in thinking about recursion are the microscopic and the macroscopic viewpoints. The microscopic viewpoint considers the details of the run-time stack during execution. The macroscopic viewpoint is based on a higher level of abstraction and is related to proof by mathematical induction. The microscopic viewpoint is useful for analysis; the macroscopic viewpoint is useful for design.

The two families of sort algorithms are the merge sort family and the quick sort family. Each is based on the following operations: split list, sort sublists, and join sublists. With quick sorts, the split is hard and the join is easy. With merge sorts, the split is easy and the join is hard. Both sorts are programmed with recursion and are $O(n \log n)$ algorithms, where n is the number of elements to sort. The selection sort is a quick sort of one element, and the insertion sort is a merge sort of one element. Both of these algorithms are $O(n^2)$.

EXERCISES

Section 9.1

1. Evaluate the following postfix expressions.

*(a) 2 5 1 3 + − ×   (b) 2 5 1 + 3 − ×
*(c) 2 5 + 1 − 3 ×   (d) 1 1 1 1 1 1 − − − − −

2. Convert the following infix expressions to postfix.

   * (a) $a + b - c \times d$ (b) $x \times (z - y) / w$
   (c) $F - G \times (H + I \times J)$ (d) $p \times (q \times (r + s / t) + u) + v$

3. Trace the execution of the algorithm for converting the following infix expression to postfix. Show the contents of the stack at each step of the conversion as in Example 9.6.

   (a) $5 + 2 - 6 \times 4$ (b) $2 \times (3 + 4 \times 5 + 6)$

* 4. Draw the run-time stack for Program 6.1 just after the main program calls function `F` the second time.

5. Draw the run-time stack for Program 6.9 just before the return from procedure `CalcRect`.

Section 9.2

* 6. Prove by mathematical induction that the sum of the first n odd integers is

$$1 + 3 + 5 + \cdots + (2n - 1) = n^2$$

for values of $n = 1, 2, 3, \ldots$.

7. Prove by mathematical induction that the sum of the squares of the first n positive integers is

$$1 + 4 + 9 + \cdots + n^2 = \tfrac{1}{6}n(n + 1)(2n + 1)$$

for values of $n = 1, 2, 3, \ldots$.

8. Prove by mathematical induction that the sum of the squares of the first n odd integers is

$$1 + 9 + 25 + \cdots + (2n - 1)^2 = \tfrac{1}{3}n(2n - 1)(2n + 1)$$

for values of $n = 1, 2, 3, \ldots$.

* 9. Prove by mathematical induction that the sum of every fourth number starting with 2 is

$$2 + 6 + 10 + \cdots + (4n - 2) = 2n^2$$

for values of $n = 1, 2, 3, \ldots$.

10. Prove by mathematical induction that $2^{2n} - 1$ is divisible by 3 for $n \geq 1$.

11. Prove by mathematical induction that $2^n < n!$ for $n \geq 4$.

12. A square has two diagonals, and a pentagon has five diagonals. Suppose you have a polygon with n equal sides and diagonals between all possible pairs of corners. Can you determine how many diagonals it will have? *(a) Make a table of the number of diagonals a polygon has as a function of n for $n = 3, 4, 5, 6, 7, 8$. (b) Conjecture a formula for the number of diagonals for an n-sided polygon in general. (c) Prove the formula is valid by mathematical induction.

13. Show that the induction step is true in a proof by induction of

$$1 + 2 + 3 + \cdots + n = \tfrac{1}{8}(2n + 1)^2$$

Is the formula true for all positive n?

14. The Republic of Lower Slobovia has a postal service that only prints 5-cent and 9-cent stamps. Prove by mathematical induction that you can make up any postage of n cents with only 5-cent and 9-cent stamps for $n \geq 35$. Hint: For $n = N + 1$, consider two possible cases separately. Either the N-cent postage is made with only 5-cent stamps, or the N-cent postage has at least one 9-cent stamp.

Section 9.3

15. The function Sum in Program 9.4 is called for the first time by the main program. From the second time on it is called by itself. *(a) How many times is it called altogether? (b) Draw a picture of the main program variables and the run-time stack just after the function is called for the third time. You should have three stack frames. (c) Draw a picture of the main program variables and the run-time stack just before the return from the call of part (b). You should have three stack frames, but with different contents from part (b).

16. Draw the call tree, as in Figure 9.11, for the function BinomCoeff of Program 9.5 for the following call statements from the main program.

* (a) writeln (BinomCoeff (4, 1))
  (b) writeln (BinomCoeff (5, 1))
  (c) writeln (BinomCoeff (3, 2))
  (d) writeln (BinomCoeff (4, 4))
  (e) writeln (BinomCoeff (4, 2))

How many times is the procedure called? What is the maximum number of stack frames on the run-time stack during the execution? In what order does the program make the calls and returns?

17. For Exercise 16, draw the run-time stack as in Figure 9.10 just before the return from the following function calls.

* (a) BinomCoeff (2, 1)   (b) BinomCoeff (3, 1)
  (c) BinomCoeff (1, 0)   (d) BinomCoeff (4, 4)
  (e) BinomCoeff (2, 1)

In part (e), BinomCoeff (2, 1) is called twice. Draw the run-time stack just before the return from the second call of the function.

18. Draw the calling sequence for Program 9.6. How many times is procedure Reverse called? What is the maximum number of stack frames allocated on the run-time stack? Draw the run-time stack just after the third call to procedure Reverse.

19. Draw the call tree as in Figure 9.14 for procedure Permute of Program 9.7 for the following call statements from the main program.

* (a) Permute ('wxyz   ', 1, 4)
  (b) Permute ('wxyz   ', 2, 4)
  (c) Permute ('wxyz   ', 2, 3)
  (d) Permute ('wxyz   ', 3, 3)

How many times is the procedure called? What is the maximum number of stack frames on the run-time stack during the execution? In what order does the program make the calls and returns?

20. For Exercise 19, draw the run-time stack just after the following function calls.

   *(a) `Permute ('xwyz    ', 3, 4)`
   (b) `Permute ('wyzx    ', 4, 4)`
   (c) `Permute ('wyxz    ', 3, 3)`
   (d) `Permute ('wxyz    ', 3, 3)`

21. The mystery numbers are defined recursively as

   Myst (0) = 2
   Myst (1) = 1
   Myst (N) = 2 × Myst (N − 1) + 4 × Myst (N − 2)   for N > 1

   (a) Draw the calling sequence for Myst (4). (b) What is the value of Myst (4)?

22. Examine the Pascal program that follows. (a) Draw the run-time stack just after the procedure is called for the last time. (b) What is the output of the program?

```
program Main (output);
   type
      StrType = packed array [1..4] of char;
   var
      Str: StrType;

   procedure What (var Word: StrType; J: integer);
      begin
      if J > 2 then
         begin
         Word [J] := Word [5 - J];
         What (Word, J - 1)
         end
      end;

   begin
   Str := 'abcd';
   What (Str, 4);
   writeln (Str)
   end.
```

Section 9.4

23. Draw the ideal quick sort and merge sort traces corresponding to Figure 9.19 for the following lists:

   *(a) 4 7 5 2 3 8 1 6
   (b) 8 7 6 5 4 3 2 1
   (c) 8 1 2 3 4 5 6 7

*24. Work Exercise 23 for the single-element sorts of Figure 9.25.

*25. Work Exercise 23 for the nonrecursive single-element sorts of Figure 9.26.

26. Write the list of 10 integer values just after the following calls to `QuickSort` in Figure 9.21.

* **(a)** QS (1, 4)   **(b)** QS (3, 4)   **(c)** QS (5, 10)
    (d) QS (5, 9)   **(e)** QS (5, 6)   **(f)** QS (8, 9)

27. Draw the list and the elements that `J` and `I` point to corresponding to Figures 9.20(g), (h), and (i) for the initial lists that follow. Figure 9.20(g) represents the list just before the first recursive call to `QuickSort`.

* **(a)** 10   60   40   80   30   90   25   70   20   50
    (b) 10   20   25   30   40   50   60   70   80   90
    (c) 90   80   70   60   50   40   30   25   20   10
    (d) 80   90   50   50   50   50   50   50   10   20

28. Draw the `QuickSort` call tree as in Figure 9.21 for the following initial lists.

* **(a)** 30   70   40   20   **(b)** 80   40   20   90   70
    (c) 40   60   10   70   90   30   **(d)** 10   20   30   40   50   60   70
    (e) 70   60   50   40   30   20   10

 How many times is `QuickSort` called? What is the maximum number of stack frames on the run-time stack during the execution? In what order does the program make the calls and returns?

29. Draw the result of a `MergeSort` call corresponding to Figure 9.22 for the following lists of numbers.

* **(a)** 30   50   10   80   40   70   20   60
    (b) 10   20   30   40   50   60   70   80
    (c) 80   70   60   50   40   30   20   10

* 30. Work Exercise 29 for the two top-level recursive `MergeSort` calls corresponding to Figure 9.23.

31. What is the total number of comparisons for the merge sort and the best-case quick sort with the following number of elements?

* **(a)** 32   **(b)** 1024   **(c)** 65,536

 What is the maximum number of stack frames allocated at one time for each of the lists?

PROBLEMS

Section 9.1

32. Write a Pascal program to evaluate a postfix expression. Ask the user to input the postfix expression from the keyboard. You may assume that only single digit numbers will be input. Use the stack data structure of Program 9.2 and test for input errors.

Sample Input/Output

```
Enter postfix expression: 5 3 1 - 4 * +
Value: 13
```

33. Write a Pascal program to translate an infix expression to postfix. Ask the user to input the infix expression from the keyboard. You may assume that only single digit numbers will be input. Use the stack data structure of Program 9.2.

Sample Input/Output

```
Enter infix expression: 2*(7 + 3*4) + 6
Postfix expression: 2 7 3 4 * + * 6 +
```

34. Write a Pascal program to evaluate an infix expression. Ask the user to input the infix expression from the keyboard. First translate the expression to postfix, storing the intermediate postfix expression in an array of characters. Then evaluate the postfix expression. You may assume that only single digit numbers will be input.

    The problem with using the stack data structure of Program 9.2 is that `ValueType` should be `char` for translating but `integer` for evaluating. For your program you could duplicate all the procedures of the stack ADT with different element types for each case. Instead, make `ValueType` a variant record without a tag field that can store either a character or an integer. You will need to rewrite function `StackTop` as a procedure.

Sample Input/Output

```
Enter infix expression: 2*(7 + 3*4) + 6
Value: 44
```

Section 9.3

35. The Fibonacci sequence is

    0   1   1   2   3   5   8   13   21   · · ·

    Each Fibonacci number is the sum of the preceding two Fibonacci numbers. The sequence starts with the first two Fibonacci numbers, defined as

    $$\text{Fib}(0) = 0$$
    $$\text{Fib}(1) = 1$$
    $$\text{Fib}(N) = \text{Fib}(N - 1) + \text{Fib}(N - 2) \qquad \text{for } N > 1$$

    Write a program in Pascal that asks the user to input a small integer, N. Then use a recursive function to compute Fib (N) and output it. Draw the call tree for the following Fibonacci numbers.

    (a) Fib (3)
    (b) Fib (4)
    (c) Fib (5)

    For each of these calls, how many times is Fib called? What is the maximum number of stack frames allocated on the run-time stack?

36. Write a program in Pascal that prints the solution to the Towers of Hanoi puzzle. It should ask the user to input the number of disks in the puzzle, the peg on which all of the disks are placed initially, and the peg on which the disks are to be moved. Draw the call tree for the four-disk problem. How many times is your procedure called? What is the maximum number of stack frames on the run-time stack?

Sample Input/Output

```
How many disks do you want to move?   3
From which peg?   3
To which peg?   2

Move a disk from peg 3 to peg 2.
Move a disk from peg 3 to peg 1.
Move a disk from peg 2 to peg 1.
Move a disk from peg 3 to peg 2.
Move a disk from peg 1 to peg 3.
Move a disk from peg 1 to peg 2.
Move a disk from peg 3 to peg 2.
```

37. Write a recursive version of `RotateLeft` in Program 7.3. To rotate N items left, rotate the first $N - 1$ items left recursively, then exchange items $N - 1$ and N. For example, to rotate the five items

        5.0 –2.3 7.0 8.0 0.1

    to the left, recursively rotate the first four items to the left,

        –2.3 7.0 8.0 5.0 0.1

    then exchange items four and five.

        –2.3 7.0 8.0 0.1 5.0

    Do not use a loop.

38. Write a function

    ```
    Maximum (L: ListType; N: integer): integer
    ```

    that recursively finds the largest integer between `L [1]` and `L [N]`. Do not use a loop.

39. Write a recursive version of function `Palindrome` described in Problem 7.46. Do not use a loop.

40. Write a program to print all combinations of n letters taken r at a time. As opposed to permutations, the order of the elements in combinations is irrelevant. For example, the combinations of six letters taken four at a time are the possible sets of four letters from abcdef as follows:

abcd	bcde	cdef
abce	bcdf	
abcf	bcef	
abde	bdef	
abdf		
abef		
acde		
acdf		
acef		
adef		

The solution for selecting four letters from abcdef is to first output 'a' followed by the solution for selecting three letters from bcdef. Then output 'b' followed by the solution for selecting three letters from cdef. Then output 'c' followed by the solution for selecting three letters from def.

The following is the parameter list and the basis test for a procedure to output the combinations.

```
procedure Comb (A:            StrType;
                SelectNum:    integer;
                Left, Right: integer;
                PrintNum:     integer);
   {  Outputs all the combinations of SelectNum items   }
   {  taken between A [Left] and A [Right], printing    }
   {  the first PrintNum items.                          }
   var
      R, I: integer;
   begin
   if SelectNum = 1 then
      {  Supply the basis.   }
   else
      {  Supply the recursive calls.   }
   end
```

To produce the previous list of combinations, the main program called

```
Comb ('abcdef    ', 4, 1, 6, 4)
```

The top level recursive calls were

```
Comb ('abcdef    ', 3, 2, 6, 4)
Comb ('bcdefa    ', 3, 2, 5, 4)
Comb ('cdefab    ', 3, 2, 4, 4)
```

You will need a RotateLeft procedure for the recursive calls. Unlike the permutation program of Program 9.7, the basis also needs a loop. For example, the procedure call

```
Comb ('abcdef    ', 1, 4, 6, 4)
```

selects one item between A [4] and A [6] and prints all three combinations:

abcd
abce
abcf

Draw the call tree for this data set. How many times is your procedure called? What is the maximum number of stack frames on the run-time stack?

41. Write a program to print *n* selections of *m* letters with duplication. As opposed to the elements in combinations of Problem 40, the elements in selections can be duplicat-

ed. For example, the two selections of four letters with duplication from abcd are as follows:

aa	ba	ca	da
ab	bb	cb	db
ac	bc	cc	dc
ad	bd	cd	dd

The solution for selecting two letters from abcd is first to output 'a' followed by the solution for selecting one letter from abcd. Then output 'b' followed by the solution for selecting one letter from abcd. Next output 'c' followed by the solution for selecting one letter from abcd. Finally output 'd' followed by the solution for selecting one letter from abcd.

The following is the parameter list and the basis test for a procedure to output the combinations.

```
procedure Select (A:              StrType;
                   Left, Right: integer;
                   B:              StrType;
                   NumChars:    integer);
   {  Outputs all the selections of characters       }
   {  from the set of NumChars characters in B        }
   {  in the places between A [Left] and A [Right].  }
   var
      I: integer;
   begin
   if Left > Right then
      {  Supply the basis.  }
   else
      {  Supply the recursive calls.  }
   end;
```

To produce the previous list of selections, the main program called

```
Select ('          ', 1, 2, 'abcd      ', 4)
```

The top level recursive calls were

```
Select ('a          ', 2, 2, 'abcd      ', 4)
Select ('b          ', 2, 2, 'abcd      ', 4)
Select ('c          ', 2, 2, 'abcd      ', 4)
Select ('d          ', 2, 2, 'abcd      ', 4)
```

42. The determinant of an $n \times n$ matrix is defined recursively in terms of the determinants of $(n-1) \times (n-1)$ matrices. For example, the 3×3 determinant

$$\begin{vmatrix} 6 & 4 & 7 \\ 0 & 2 & 5 \\ 8 & 9 & 1 \end{vmatrix}$$

is defined recursively in terms of the 2×2 determinants as follows:

$$6 \begin{vmatrix} 2 & 5 \\ 9 & 1 \end{vmatrix} - 4 \begin{vmatrix} 0 & 5 \\ 8 & 1 \end{vmatrix} + 7 \begin{vmatrix} 0 & 2 \\ 8 & 9 \end{vmatrix}$$

In general, the coefficients that multiply the smaller determinants come from the first row of the larger determinant and alternate in sign starting with positive. Each smaller determinant comes from the larger one by eliminating the first row and the column of the coefficient. For example, the second determinant comes from eliminating the first row and the second column of the large determinant, because the coefficient, 4, is in the second column. The determinant of a 1×1 matrix is simply the value of the single element. Write a program that inputs a determinant of real values from a file with the count technique and outputs the value of the determinant. Assume the determinant will not be larger than 10×10. The following sample I/O is for the example just presented.

Sample Input

```
3
6.0   4.0   7.0   0.0   2.0   5.0   8.0   9.0   1.0
```

Sample Output

```
Determinant value:   -210.0
```

43. At the start of any particular day, a machine is either broken down or in operating condition. If the machine is broken at the start of day n, the probability is p that it will be successfully repaired and in operating condition at the start of day $(n + 1)$ and $(1 - p)$ that it will still be broken. If the machine is in operating condition at the start of day n, the probability is q that it will have a failure causing it to be broken down at the start of day $(n + 1)$ and $(1 - q)$ that it will still be in operating condition. At the start of day one, the machine is in operating condition.

The problem is to calculate the probability that the machine is in operating condition on day m. That state can occur in two ways, depending on its state the previous day. Either the machine was broken on the previous day and was repaired with probability p, or it was operating on the previous day and remained operating with probability $(1 - q)$. Mathematically,

Prob (Operating on day m)
   = p Prob (Broken on day $(m - 1)$) + $(1 - q)$ Prob (Operating on day $(m - 1)$)

Similarly

Prob (Broken on day m)
   = $(1 - p)$ Prob (Broken on day $(m - 1)$) + q Prob (Operating on day $(m - 1)$)

Notice that these two relationships are mutually recursive. What is the basis of the recursion?

(a) Declare `ProbOperate` and `ProbBroken`, two mutually recursive functions. Use them in a program that inputs the day, m, and probabilities, p and q, and outputs the probability that the machine is operating on day m. (b) Draw the call tree for $m = 3$. (c) Use your program to calculate the probability that the machine is operating on days $m = 1, 2, 3, 4, 5$ if $p = 0.4$ and $q = 0.2$. Plot your data. Experiment with different values of p and q and discuss your results.

Section 9.4

44. Write the recursive version of the insertion sort algorithm as shown in Figure 9.25(a).

45. Write the recursive version of the selection sort algorithm as shown in Figure 9.25(b).

46. Write the nonrecursive version of the insertion sort algorithm as shown in Figure 9.26(a).

47. Suppose an application uses the merge sort, but it needs to have the array elements physically in order, not just linked in order. Modify the main program of Program 9.9 to put the elements of `List` physically in order. Declare `TempList` to be `ListType`. After the call to `MergeSort`, copy the elements from `List` into `TempList` in physical order. Then set `List := TempList` and output `List` without using the `Link` field to verify that its elements are physically in order.

48. Write a version of the merge sort algorithm without links. Use a parameter list identical to the parameter list of procedure `QuickSort`. If `Left` is less than `Right`, make two recursive calls to `MergeSort`. Join the two sublists, $L1'$ and $L2'$, by copying them into a temporary local array of the same type as the array being sorted. Copy $L1'$ into the first part of the temporary array and install a high sentinel value in the next element. Immediately following the sentinel for $L1'$, copy $L2'$ into the temporary array and install a high sentinel value after it. Merge the two lists from the temporary array into the array to be sorted. Use the merge sort algorithm of Program 8.5 with a high key to control termination of the `while` loop.

Chapter

10

Dynamic Storage Allocation

The previous chapter showed how Pascal allocates storage on the run-time stack when a procedure is called. First, storage is allocated for the parameters, then for the return address, and finally for the local variables of the procedure. When the program returns from a procedure, it deallocates the storage.

Pascal also provides an alternate method for allocating and deallocating storage from main memory. It maintains a region in memory that is called the *heap*, which is separate from the stack. You do not control allocation and deallocation from the heap during procedure calls and returns. Instead, you allocate and deallocate from the heap with the help of pointer variables. Allocation that is not triggered automatically by procedure calls is called *dynamic storage allocation*.

The heap

Pointers are common building blocks for implementing abstract data types with data structures. This chapter presents the Pascal pointer type and shows how you can use pointers to implement the linked list and the binary tree abstract data types. It closes with a closer look at the Pascal `read` and `write` calls, which the compiler implements with file pointers.

10.1   Pointer Data Types

When you declare an array, you must declare it to be an array of some type. For example, you can declare an array of integers or an array of real values. Sets have the same property. When you declare a set variable, you must declare it to be a set of some base type. Pointers share this characteristic with arrays and sets. When you declare a pointer, you must declare that it points to some type.

A pointer must point to a specific type.

Another characteristic of arrays and sets is that they are collections of items. An `array [0..7] of real` is a collection of eight real values. A set of `0..7` is a collection of up to eight integers. Pointers do not share this characteristic with arrays and sets. When you declare a pointer in the variable declaration part, you are only declaring one item, not a collection of items.

A pointer is not a collection of items.

Figure 10.1 shows the relationships between the primitive Pascal types. The fact that sets and arrays are collections of items makes them structured types. As the figure shows, the pointer type is neither simple nor structured. It has its own category in the hierarchy chart of the primitive Pascal types.

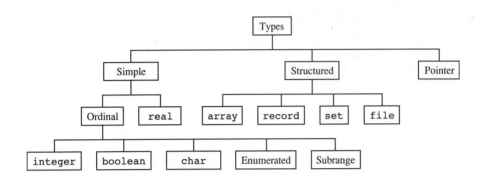

Figure 10.1

The Pascal data types.

Program 10.1

Program 10.1 illustrates the Pascal pointer type. The program declares A and B to be pointers.

```
program IntroPointer1 (output);
   var
      A: ^integer;
      B: ^real;
   begin
   new (A);
   A^ := 3;
   new (B);
   B^ := 5.7;
   writeln (A^: 3, B^: 6: 2);
   dispose (A);
   dispose (B)
   end.
```

Output

```
   3   5.70
```

Program 10.1

A program that illustrates the Pascal pointer type.

The variable declaration part declares A as a pointer to an integer and B as a pointer to a real number. Figure 10.2 shows the syntax chart for a pointer type. In the declaration of A and B in this program,

```
A: ^integer;
B: ^real
```

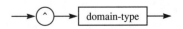

Figure 10.2

The syntax chart for a pointer type.

`integer` is the domain type for the pointer A, and `real` is the domain type for the pointer B.

The symbol ^ is called a *circumflex* or, colloquially, a *hat*. Some printers and screens show it as an upward pointing arrow ↑. You can read the statement `A^ := 3` as "A hat gets three."

A is not an integer. It is a pointer to an integer. When A acquires a value during execution of the program, that value will not be an integer. Instead, it will specify the memory location of where the integer is stored, somewhere in the heap. Similarly, B is not a real variable. It is a pointer to a location in memory where a real number is stored.

Figure 10.3 is a trace of the execution of Program 10.1. Figure 10.3(a) shows A and B at the start of execution. Like all variables, they have undefined values in the beginning.

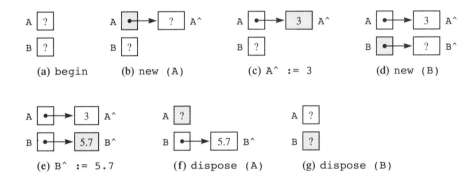

(a) begin   (b) new (A)   (c) A^ := 3   (d) new (B)

(e) B^ := 5.7   (f) dispose (A)   (g) dispose (B)

Figure 10.3

The trace of Program 10.1.

The first statement the program executes is

`new (A)`

The procedure **new** is a standard Pascal procedure that does two things:

- It allocates storage from the heap. Since A was previously declared to be a pointer to an integer, `new (A)` allocates enough memory to store a single integer.

- It assigns to A the location of this newly allocated storage. So A now points to the location of an integer.

Allocation with procedure new

Figure 10.3(b) indicates the effect of `new (A)`. The box adjacent to the A box represents the storage allocated from the heap. The arrow pointing from the A box to the newly allocated box represents the value that **new** assigns to A.

The next statement the program executes is

`A^ := 3`

Figure 10.3(c) shows the effect of the assignment. A^ is called an identified variable. It is the variable that was allocated from the heap with the new procedure. A points to A^. The type of A^ is integer, since the program declared A to be a pointer to an integer. This statement assigns the integer value 3 to the identified variable. Therefore, the memory location to which A points contains 3.

Figure 10.4 is the syntax chart for an identified variable. In the previous statement, A is a pointer variable and A^ is an identified variable.

The next statement,

```
new (B)
```

allocates storage from the heap as before. This time, however, B is a pointer to a real value. Therefore, new (B) allocates enough memory to contain a single real number. This newly allocated memory is referred to as B^. Also, new (B) sets the value of B to point to the newly allocated identified variable. Figure 10.3(d) shows the effect of new (B).

The statement

```
B^ := 5.7
```

assigns the real number 5.7 to the location to which B is pointing, as Figure 10.3(e) shows.

The output statement

```
writeln (A^: 3, B^: 6: 2)
```

puts the values of A^ and B^ on the screen. Since A^ is an integer, 3 is the field width. Since B^ is a real variable, 6 and 2 are the field width and number of places displayed past the decimal point.

Figure 10.3(f) shows the effect of

```
dispose (A)
```

The procedure dispose is a standard Pascal procedure that does two things:

- It deallocates storage back to the heap. In this case, dispose (A) returns A^ to the heap.
- It makes the value of its argument undefined. So now the value of A is undefined, and A^ is meaningless.

As with the standard procedure new, the argument of dispose must be a pointer. Figure 10.3(g) shows how dispose (B) deallocates B^.

When you write Pascal programs with pointer types, the placement of the pointer arrow ^ is crucial. Table 10.1 summarizes the variables in this example.

Notice that although A^ and B^ are variables, they are not declared in the variable declaration part. Instead, they are allocated dynamically with procedure new. A and B are also variables, but they are of pointer type and are declared as such in the variable declaration part.

Figure 10.4

The syntax chart for an identified variable.

Variable	Description
A	Not an integer, but a pointer to an integer
A^	An integer variable
B	Not a real but a pointer to a real
B^	A real variable

Table 10.1

The variables in Program 10.1.

Using Pointers

You can output identified variables, but you can never output a pointer variable.   *You cannot output a pointer.*

Example 10.1   The statement

```
write (A)
```

is illegal with A declared as in Program 10.1.   ∎

The only operations that are allowed on pointer data types are   *The legal pointer operations*

- := assignment
- = test for equality
- <> test for inequality

Specifically, you cannot test if one pointer is greater than another, and you cannot perform math on pointers.

Example 10.2   With A and B declared as in Program 10.1, the test

```
if A^ < B^ then
```

is legal, because you can test if an integer value is less than a real value. However, the test

```
if A < B then
```

is illegal because A and B are pointers.   ∎

Example 10.3   With A and B declared as in Program 10.1, the statement

```
A^ := A^ + 1
```

would be legal since A^ is an integer. On the other hand, the statement

```
A := A + 1
```

would be illegal, because you cannot add 1 to a pointer.   ∎

Program 10.2

Although you cannot perform arithmetic on pointer variables, you can assign one   *The effect of assigning pointers*
pointer to another. Since a pointer "points to" an object, if you give the pointer's value to a second pointer, the second pointer will point to the same object. Program 10.2 illustrates the effect of the assignment operation on pointers.

```
program IntroPointer2 (output);
   var
      A, B, C: ^integer;
   begin
   new (A);
   A^ := 5;
   new (B);
   B^ := 3;
   C := A;
   A := B;
   A^ := 2 + C^;
   writeln (A^: 3, B^: 3, C^: 3);
   dispose (A);
   dispose (C)
   end.
```

Program 10.2

The effect of the assignment operation on pointers.

Output

```
   7   7   5
```

The program allocates and assigns values to A^ and B^, as Figure 10.5(a–e) shows. These operations are similar to those of the previous program. Next, the statement

```
C := A
```

gives the value of A to C, as Figure 10.5(f) shows. A is a pointer. Therefore C will point to the same memory location to which A points. After the assignment, C also points to 5. Notice that the statement does not assign to C the value 5. It assigns to C the pointer to 5.

The statement

```
A := B
```

copies the B pointer into A. As in all assignment statements, the previous value of A is destroyed. A no longer points to 5, but to the same integer to which B points, namely 3.

The last assignment statement

```
A^ := 2 + C^
```

contains the + arithmetic operation. Since A^ and C^ are integer variables and not pointers, the statement is legal. It adds 2 to the integer to which C is pointing, 5, to get 7. The 7 is copied into the location to which A is pointing. As in all assignment statements, the original content of the memory location, 3, is destroyed.

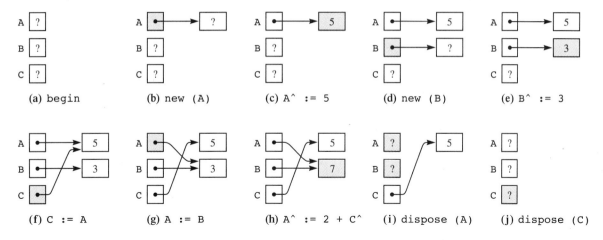

Figure 10.5

A trace of Program 10.2.

The output statement

```
writeln (A^ :3, B^:3, C^ :3)
```

produces

```
7   7   5
```

Since A and B now point to the same integer, 7, it is printed twice.

The deallocation statement

```
dispose (A)
```

returns to the heap the storage to which A points. Since A points to the cell containing 7, that cell goes back to the heap. A gets an undefined value. Figure 10.5(h) shows that B was also pointing to the same cell. Therefore, B gets an undefined value also, as Figure 10.5(i) shows. If you replace dispose (A) with dispose (B) in the program listing, the effect during execution would be the same.

The deallocation statement

```
dispose (C)
```

returns the cell containing 5 to the heap similarly.

10.2 Singly Linked Lists

In practice, you rarely use pointers in isolation. Instead you combine them with other variables into a record. Then the pointer part of the record can point to yet another record, linking the two records together.

Program 10.3

Program 10.3 constructs a linked list of three real numbers. Each record in the linked list has two parts, a `Value` part, which contains the value of a real number, and a `Link` part, which points to the next record in the linked list.

```
program IntroLinkedList (output);
   type
      PtrToCellType = ^CellType;
      CellType     =
         record
         Value: real;
         Link:  PtrToCellType
         end;
   var
      First: PtrToCellType;
      Last:  PtrToCellType;
      P:       PtrToCellType;
   begin
   {  Create linked list  }
   new (First);
   First^.Value := 7.3;
   new (P);
   P^.Value := 1.2;
   First^.Link := P;
   new (Last);
   Last^.Value := 4.5;
   P^.Link := Last;
   {  Output linked list  }
   P := First;
   write (P^.Value: 6: 1);
   P := P^.Link;
   write (P^.Value: 6: 1);
   P := P^.Link;
   write (P^.Value: 6: 1)
   end.
```

Program 10.3

A program that constructs a linked list of three real numbers.

Output

```
  7.3    1.2    4.5
```

In the type definition part,

```
PtrToCellType = ^CellType
```

defines `PtrToCellType` to be a pointer to `CellType`. Normally you cannot use an identifier before you define it. For example, if you define

```
OneType = array [0..15] of AnotherType
```

you must have previously defined `AnotherType`. This program, however, does not previously define `CellType`. Instead, it defines `CellType` after the definition of `PtrToCellType`.

Pascal permits you to define pointers to objects before you define the objects. That is fortunate in this program, because of the definition of `CellType`:

The "define before use" rule with pointers

```
record
Value: real;
Link:   PtrToCellType
end
```

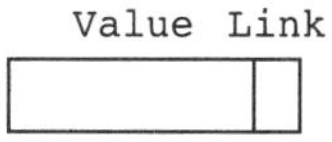

Figure 10.6 shows this structure. If you tried to define `PtrToCellType` after you defined `CellType`, you would still be in trouble. In `CellType`, you would be using `PtrToCellType` before you defined it.

You can understand why Pascal makes an exception to the "define before use" rule for pointers. The definition for `OneType` requires the compiler to determine the amount of storage required for a variable of type `OneType`. The compiler determines the storage requirement by multiplying the amount of storage required for `AnotherType` by 16. So it needs to know the amount of storage required by `AnotherType`. `AnotherType` must have been previously defined.

Similarly, the definition for `PtrToCellType` requires the compiler to determine the amount of storage required for a variable of type `PtrToCellType`. But the storage for `PtrToCellType` does not depend on how big `CellType` is. Regardless of how much storage `CellType` needs, `PtrToCellType` will require only as much storage as a single pointer. A pointer to a big object requires the same amount of storage as a pointer to a small object—namely, the amount of storage for one pointer.

Figure 10.7 is a trace of the first part of Program 10.3, which creates a linked list. The following is a description of each statement executed by the first part of the program (the letters in parentheses correspond to the parts of Figure 10.7).

(a) **begin**   At the beginning, the program allocates storage for the variables declared in the variable declaration part. The variables `First`, `Last`, and `P` are not records. They are pointers to records. Initially their values are undefined.

(b) **new (First)**   The procedure call `new (First)` does two things. It allocates enough storage from the heap for a record of type `CellType`. Then it changes the value of `First` to point to the record just allocated. It does not set the values within the record itself.

(c) **First^.Value := 7.3**   This statement assigns the value of 7.3 to a variable. You access the component of a record with the specification for the record, followed by a period, followed by a field identifier. The notation is consistent with the access notation for arrays of records. Here are the types of the variables involved in the assignment.

`First`	is a pointer to a record.
`First^`	is a record.
`First^.Value`	is a real.

Value Link

Figure 10.6

The structure of a record of type `CellType` in Program 10.3.

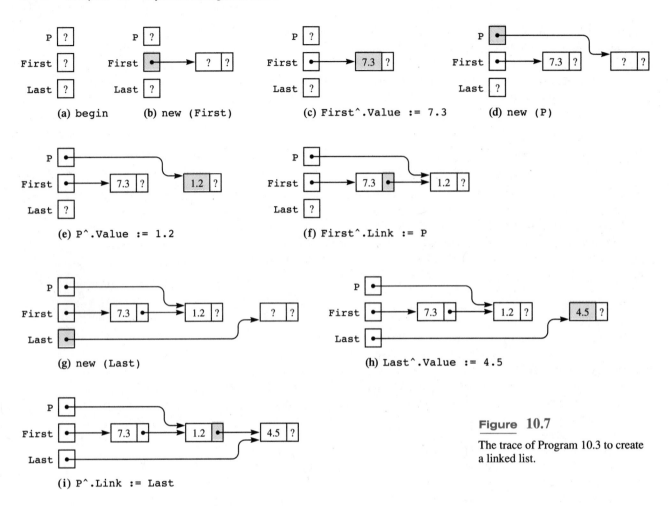

(a) begin   (b) new (First)

(c) First^.Value := 7.3   (d) new (P)

(e) P^.Value := 1.2   (f) First^.Link := P

(g) new (Last)   (h) Last^.Value := 4.5

(i) P^.Link := Last

Figure 10.7

The trace of Program 10.3 to create a linked list.

(d) **new (P)**   The procedure call **new (P)** allocates another record from the heap and sets P to point to the newly allocated record.

(e) **P^.Value := 1.2**   This statement assigns the value of 1.2 to a variable. It gives the value to the first part of the record that P points to.

(f) **First^.Link := P**   This assignment statement makes **First^.Link** point to the same thing that **P** points to, namely, the newly allocated record. This record is now linked to the previous record.

(g) **new (Last)**   The procedure call **new (Last)** allocates another record from the heap and sets **Last** to point to the newly allocated record.

(h) `Last^.Value := 1.2` This statement assigns the value of 1.2 to a variable. It gives the value to the first part of the record that `Last` points to.

(i) `P^.Link := Last` The variable `P^` is of type `record`. The variable `P^.Link` is the `Link` part of that record, which is a pointer. When it gets `Last`, it points to the same thing to which `Last` points. Since `Last` points to the newly allocated record, so does `P^.Link`.

Now the linked list is complete. The first record containing 7.3 in its value part is linked to the second record, which contains 1.2 in its value part. The second record is, in turn, linked to the third which contains 4.5 in its value part.

The last part of the program outputs the linked list. Figure 10.8 is a trace. Since the last part of the program does not access the pointer `Last`, the figure does not show it. The following is a description of each statement executed (the letters in parentheses correspond to the parts of Figure 10.8).

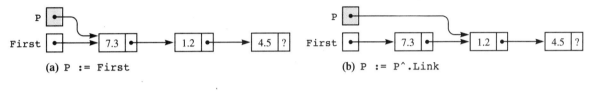

(a) P := First

(b) P := P^.Link

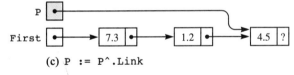

(c) P := P^.Link

Figure 10.8

The trace of Program 10.3 to output a linked list.

(a) `P := First` This assignment statement makes P point to the first record of the linked list. It is similar to an initializing statement. `P^.Value` is the value of the first record. The `write` call outputs `7.3`.

(b) `P := P^.Link` This statement advances P to the next record of the linked list. `P^.Value` is now the value of the second record. The `write` call outputs `1.2`.

(c) `P := P^.Link` This statement advances P to the next record of the linked list again. `P^.Value` is now the value of the last record. The `write` call outputs `4.5`.

This program allocated cells for the linked list with the standard procedure `new`, but it did not deallocate any of the cells with `dispose`. The operating system automatically deallocates all cells that the program leaves allocated at the termination of the program.

▨ Program 10.4

Program 10.3 created a linked list with three elements. Usually, you will not know how many elements a linked list will contain, since the length will depend on the input. Program 10.4 creates a linked list of an arbitrary number of words, then outputs the list.

The program declares `CellType` to be a record with two parts. A cell allocated dynamically in a linked structure is commonly called a *node*. As in the previous example, the second part is a link field for linking the node to the following node in the list. The `Value` field contains a five-letter word. This program links the words together to form an English sentence.

The main program calls procedure `GetList` to input the list from the keyboard. It calls procedure `PutList` to output the list on the screen. The only variable declared in the main program is `List`. Figure 10.9 shows the main program variable.

List ⬚ ?

    (a) Before the call to procedure
    GetList.

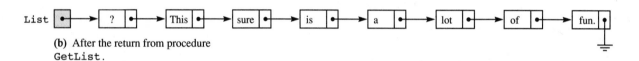

    (b) After the return from procedure
    GetList.

Figure 10.9

The linked list in the main program of Program 10.4.

When the main program begins execution, `List` is undefined. The program gives `List` to procedure `GetList`. `GetList` allocates storage for all the cells in the linked list and sets `List` to point to the first node in the list. Since `GetList` changes the value of `List`, it must call `List` by reference.

`List` points to a blank record, and the blank record points to the node that contains 'This ', the first word in the sentence. The blank record, called a *header cell*, simplifies the Pascal coding. Without the header cell, algorithms that process the linked list must test for an empty list and process it differently from a non-empty list. With the header cell, those algorithms can process both empty and non-empty lists with the same code.

Figure 10.9(b) shows the `Link` part of the last cell pointing to nothing. The dashed triangle attached to the `Link` part represents the pointer value `nil`. `nil` is a Pascal reserved word. Algorithms use it as a sentinel value to denote the end cells of linked data structures. Procedure `GetList` inserts `nil` in the `Link` part of the last cell of the list. Procedure `PutList` uses the sentinel value to detect the end of the list.

The pointer value nil

Figure 10.9 shows the basic difference between storage allocated from the runtime stack and storage allocated dynamically from the heap. If the nodes in the

```
program LinkedList (input, output);
   const
      StrLength = 5;
   type
      StrType       = packed array [1..StrLength] of char;
      PtrToCellType = ^CellType;
      ListType      = PtrToCellType;
      ValueType     = StrType;
      CellType =
         record
         Value: ValueType;
         Link:  PtrToCellType
         end;
   var
      List: ListType;

   procedure GetString (var S: StrType);
      var
         I: integer;
      begin
      for I := 1 to StrLength do
         if eoln (input) then
            S [I] := ' '
         else
            read (input, S [I]);
      readln (input)
      end;

   procedure GetList (var L: ListType);
      var
         Last: PtrToCellType;    {  Points to the last cell.  }
         P:    PtrToCellType;
         Word: ValueType;
      begin
      new (L);                   {  Create header cell.  }
      Last := L;
      Last^.Link := nil;
      write ('Enter word or <ret>: ');
      GetString (Word);
      while Word <> '     ' do { Create linked list.  }
         begin
         new (P);
         P^.Value := Word;
         P^.Link := nil;
         Last^.Link := P;        {  Link new cell to end of list.  }
         Last := P;              {  Set Last to point to new end.  }
         write ('Enter word or <ret>: ');
         GetString (Word)
         end
      end;
```

Program 10.4

Creation of a linked list of words. Procedure GetList creates the linked list, and procedure PutList outputs it.

Program 10.4, continued

```
procedure PutList (L: ListType);
   var
      P: PtrToCellType;
   begin
   P := L;
   while P^.Link <> nil do
      begin
      P := P^.Link;
      write (P^.Value)
      end
   end;

begin
GetList (List);
writeln;
PutList (List)
end.
```

Interactive Input/Output

```
Enter word or <ret>: This
Enter word or <ret>: sure
Enter word or <ret>: is
Enter word or <ret>: a
Enter word or <ret>: lot
Enter word or <ret>: of
Enter word or <ret>: fun.
Enter word or <ret>:

This sure is   a    lot  of   fun.
```

---

linked list were allocated on the run-time stack, they would be deallocated when the program returned from `GetList`. Since `GetList` allocates them with procedure new, the return from procedure `GetList` does not trigger their deallocation.

Figure 10.10 shows how procedure `GetList` allocates the nodes and links them together. `L` is the formal parameter that refers to `List` in the main program. `P` and `Last` are local variables. They are allocated on the run-time stack when the program calls `GetList` and are deallocated when the program returns.

The statements in Figures 10.10(a–c) establish the header cell. The statement new `(L)` allocates the cell, `Last := L` makes `Last` point to the newly allocated cell, and `Last^.Link := nil` installs the sentinel value in the link part of the cell. These three statements execute even if the user enters no words in the list. The empty list will have the header cell with `nil` in its `Link` part.

The statements in Figures 10.10(d–h) show the first execution of the `while` loop. The user types the word 'This '. Then, the procedure allocates a record for the word and attaches it to the header cell.

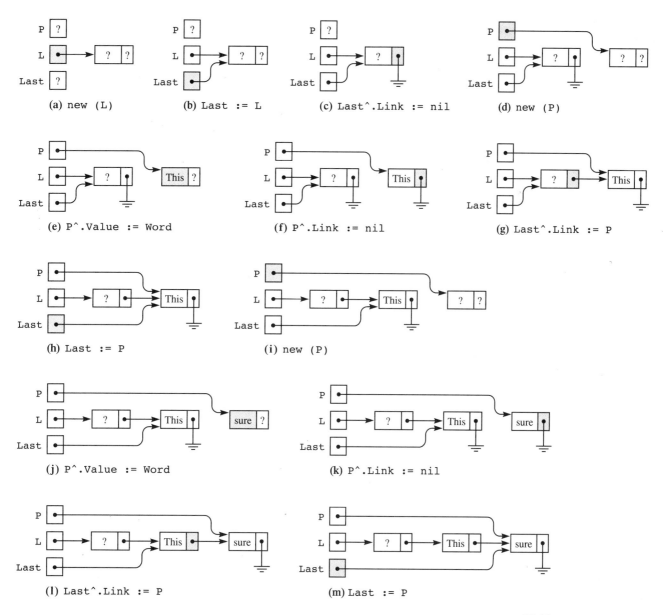

(a) new (L)

(b) Last := L

(c) Last^.Link := nil

(d) new (P)

(e) P^.Value := Word

(f) P^.Link := nil

(g) Last^.Link := P

(h) Last := P

(i) new (P)

(j) P^.Value := Word

(k) P^.Link := nil

(l) Last^.Link := P

(m) Last := P

Figure 10.10

A partial trace of procedure GetList in Program 10.4.

The statements in Figures 10.10(i–m) show the second execution of the while loop. The user types the word 'sure '. Next, the procedure allocates a record for that word and attaches it to the last cell of the list. The local pointer Last always points to the last cell in the list. The algorithm uses its value to link the newly allocated cell.

Procedure PutList outputs the list by initializing the local pointer P to point to the header cell. As long as the cell P points to is not the last cell in the list, P advances to the next cell and outputs its `Value` part. If the list is empty, the `while` loop does not execute and `PutList` outputs nothing. Note how the presence of the header cell eliminates any special code in `PutList` for dealing with the empty list.

■ The List Abstract Data Type

Remember that an abstract data type lets you program with the abstract concept of the type. The two parts of an abstract data type are

Data abstraction and program abstraction in an ADT

- A collection of variables
- A set of operations on the variables

These two parts represent data abstraction and program abstraction.

A list is an abstract data type. Variables in a list ADT have two types:

```
ValueType
ListType
```

In Program 10.3, `ValueType` was `real`, and in Program 10.4 it was `StrType`. `ValueType` is the type of each element in the list. In both programs `ListType` was `PtrToCellType`. Operations on the list ADT follow:

The list ADT

```
procedure GetList (var L: ListType)
procedure PutList (L: ListType)
procedure InsertBefore (var L:     ListType;
                            Srch:  ValueType;
                            Insrt: ValueType)
procedure InsertAfter (var L:     ListType;
                           Srch:  ValueType;
                           Insrt: ValueType)
procedure Delete (var L:    ListType;
                      Srch: ValueType)
```

`GetList` and `PutList` operate as in Program 10.4. You give `InsertBefore` and `InsertAfter` an item to search for and an item to insert. `InsertBefore` inserts the item in the list in front of `Srch`, and `InsertAfter` inserts it following `Srch`. `Delete` removes the cell from the list whose `Value` part contains `Srch`. The last three procedures do not affect the list if `Srch` is not in the list.

Inserting and deleting items from a linked list usually requires a local pointer, `P`, to advance through the list, and another local pointer, `Prev`, to follow it. `Prev` stands for *previous,* because it points to the cell that is previous to `P`. For example, Figure 10.11 shows the steps necessary to delete a node from a linked list.

In Figure 10.11(a) the procedure initializes `Prev` to the header node and `P` to the first node in the list.

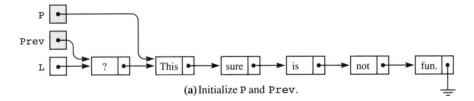

(a) Initialize P and Prev.

Figure 10.11

The action of procedure `Delete` when `Srch` has the value 'not'.

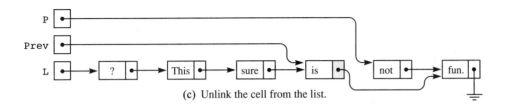

(b) Find the cell to delete.

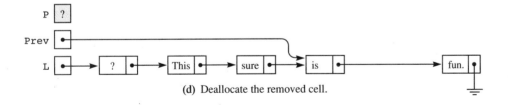

(c) Unlink the cell from the list.

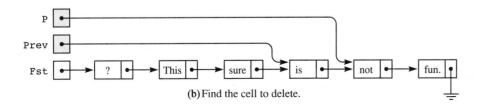

(d) Deallocate the removed cell.

Figure 10.11(b) shows the values of P and Prev when the procedure finds the node to delete. In this example, the procedure is to remove the node whose Value part is 'not '. As P advances through the list, Prev follows it. The statements to advance P and Prev by one node are

```
Prev := P;
P := P^.Link
```

When P points to the node to be removed, Prev points to the node before it.

Figure 10.11(c) shows how to remove the node from the list. The procedure merely changes the Link part of the preceding node as follows:

```
Prev^.Link := P^.Link
```

This statement shows why the procedure needs a pointer to follow P through the list. You need Prev to access the Link field of the node before the node to be deleted.

Figure 10.11(d) shows the deallocation of the removed node. You deallocate it with a call to procedure `dispose`. Programming procedure `Delete` is left as a problem.

Printing a Linked List in Reverse Order

The procedure that follows prints a list of words from a linked list in reverse order. The procedure is recursive. Printing a linked list in reverse order is easy if the list has no nodes. You simply do nothing but return to the calling statement. If the list has at least one node, you print recursively in reverse order the remainder of the list after the first node. Then you print the value of the first node.

```
procedure PrintReverse (L: ListType);
   begin
   if L <> nil then
      begin
      PrintReverse (L^.Link);
      write (L^.Value)        {**}
      end
   end
```

A recursive procedure to output a linked list in reverse order

With this procedure, the fact that there is a header node causes a slight complication. You must call the procedure with the actual parameter pointing to the node containing the first word. The call from the main program, therefore, must be

```
PrintReverse (List^.Link)
```

so that P will not point to the header node. This procedure call assumes that `List` is declared as in Program 10.4 and constructed with a header node as in procedure `GetList`.

Figure 10.12 is a snapshot of main memory during the execution of `PrintReverse`. It assumes that `GetList` was called with a user input of `this is fun`. The main program then called `PrintReverse` as shown above, and `PrintReverse` called itself recursively three times. The figure shows main memory just after the third recursive call.

There are a total of four stack frames on the run-time stack, one for each call. The single asterisk for the return address of the bottom frame is for the statement (not shown in any listing here) after the call from the main program. The other return addresses signify the `write` statement in `PrintReverse`.

`List` is declared in the main program and exists throughout the program's entire execution. The linked nodes that `List` points to are allocated dynamically

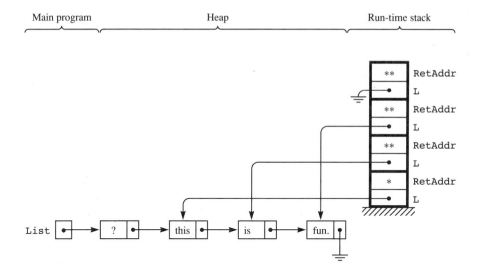

| Main program | Heap | Run-time stack |

Figure 10.12

Main memory during execution of `PrintReverse`.

in `GetList`. Since they are allocated from the heap, they retain their existence after the return from `GetList`. The pointers in the parameter list allocated on the stack frame come into existence with each call to `PrintReverse`.

On the first call to `PrintReverse`, `List` in the main program points to the header node, and the actual parameter, `L^.Link`, points to the 'this' node. On the last call to `PrintReverse`, the `L` in the calling procedure points to the 'fun' node, and the actual parameter, `L^.Link`, is `nil`. With each return from `PrintReverse`, a stack frame is deallocated, and the value of the node that `L` points to is printed. You can visualize from the figure that as the stack frames are deallocated, the list is printed in reverse order.

Stacks as Linked Lists

Remember that the five operations for the stack ADT are `Initialize`, `Empty`, `Push`, `Pop`, and `StackTop`. Program 9.2 showed how the types and operations could be implemented with a data structure that incorporated an array and the index of the top of the stack.

A major advantage of formulating abstract data types is that different implementations of them may be designed without affecting the way the operations are used in the main program. For example, it is possible to implement a stack with a linked list instead of with an array and index. The type definitions are shown in the following program fragment, together with a declaration of variable `Stack`, which has type `StackType`. The `ValueType` of `real` is appropriate for the abstract stack of Figure 9.1.

```
type
   ValueType     = real;
   PtrToCellType = ^CellType;
   StackType     = PtrToCellType;
   CellType =
      record
      Value: ValueType;
      Link:  PtrToCellType
      end;
var
   Stack: StackType;
```

Data structure for the stack
implemented with a linked list

To use this data structure you must reprogram the five operations described in Section 9.1. However, each operation will have the identical formal parameter list as specified in Program 9.2. From the point of view of the person writing the main program, the operations that use the stack as a linked list will be functionally equivalent to the operations that use the stack as an array.

Figure 10.13 shows the data structure for a stack implemented with a linked list. `Stack` is a pointer that points to the top of the stack.

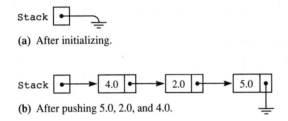

(a) After initializing.

(b) After pushing 5.0, 2.0, and 4.0.

Figure 10.13

Implementing a stack ADT with a linked list data structure.

Figure 10.13(a) shows the structure after executing `Initialize (Stack)` from the main program. The initializing procedure gives `Stack` a value of `nil`. Figure 10.13(b) shows the data structure after the main program executes.

```
Push (5.0, Stack);
Push (2.0, Stack);
Push (4.0, Stack);
```

This configuration corresponds to the abstract stack of Figure 9.1(d).

The code to implement the five stack operations for the linked-list implementation of a stack is left as a problem. The techniques are similar to those illustrated previously for other linked lists.

In programming the stack operations, it is more convenient to not use a header node. The `Initialize` procedure then merely sets S to `nil`.

To push a value onto the stack, you must first allocate a node from the heap with the new procedure,

```
new (P)
```

where P is a local variable in procedure Push. Next, store the value in the newly allocated node. Then link the node to the top of the stack with the statements

```
P^.Link := S;
```

which attaches the new node to the top of the stack, and

```
S := P
```

which makes S point to the new top of the stack.

To pop a value, you must test whether the stack is empty, and output an error message if it is. If the stack is not empty, you must give formal parameter Y the value part of the node that S points to. Then Stack must be made to point to the node next to the top, and the top node must be returned to the heap.

```
P := S;
S := S^.Link;
dispose (P);
```

Note that a local variable, P, is used to point to the top node before S advances to the next node. P then points to the node that needs to be returned to the heap.

Using Linked Lists

A common error message when processing linked data structures is the infamous *nil pointer reference*.

The nil pointer reference problem

Example 10.4   Suppose P is a pointer to a record with a Value and Link field. If P has the value nil, and your program tries to execute a statement such as

```
P^.Value := Word
```

your program will crash. P^ is normally a record, and P^.Value is normally the value part of that record. But since P is nil it does not point to anything, and P^ is meaningless. The system protests with the run-time error message, complaining that you are referring to something with P but that P is a nil pointer.   ■

Another problem to avoid when you program with linked structures is the *lost node*. Every node in Figure 10.10 has at least one pointer directed at it and can be accessed through the pointer by the program. A node with no pointers directed at it is lost and can never be accessed.

The lost node problem

Professional Responsibility

Beyond adhering to software copyright laws and not authoring computer viruses, computer scientists have less formal obligations to their profession and to society at large. Whether you become a freelance consultant or work in a large corporation, it's important to realize that being a computer scientist involves more than simply performing the technical role of understanding and controlling computers. Computer systems are seldom the end-in-themselves. Rather, they are designed and used for particular business or scientific operations intended to produce some sort of social benefit. This means that the work of a computer scientist has a direct effect on society and that she must consider the issue of professional responsibility.

Suppose a systems analyst has been hired to evaluate a business's inventory control system. During the systems analysis phase, the analyst studies the information flow in the organization by examining the current system—whether manual or automated—and trying to understand the ideal formal system. An experienced systems analyst will interview not only top-level management about their understanding and use of the current system, but also sales clerks, loading dock workers, and perhaps a few regular customers. A thorough interviewing process is necessary because an inventory control system includes not only lists of items in stock and orders processed against that stock, but also the nonformal agreements between managers and sales clerks. For example, a business may honor a favored customer's "hold" on a scarce stock item, even though new customers are willing to pay cash. In this case, the yellow Post-it note on the sales computer terminal that says "hold 10 widgets for J. Jones until November 16" is one of the information stores in the current system. The analyst who interviews even those who aren't management will discover the informal hold system and offer it as a formal feature of the new inventory management system that is to be designed and installed.

So where does professional responsibility come in? The analyst has been hired to design the best system possible within certain financial or time constraints. She must fulfill that goal, despite the fact that it might be easier in the short run to simply interview top-level managers, who may even resist her attempts to interview clerks and customers because they believe that the analyst is wasting time and padding the bill. But in the long run, the effectiveness of the new system will depend on how thoroughly the entire organization was studied, despite political pressure to take shortcuts.

Let's consider a more obvious example. If you are hired to design a commercial aircraft's avionics system for flight-control operations, what responsibilities do you have for future passengers' safety on those aircraft? Clearly, you are obligated to safeguard their lives, and as part of your design you should try to anticipate all possible situations the aircraft could get into. This includes building in backup and manual override facilities so that if a lightning strike knocks out the in-flight electrical power, the flight crew will have a chance to recover control of the aircraft. Similarly, when you are designing and laying out the cockpit information system, you should not place essential switches next to nonessential switches. This design principle prevents the pilot from turning the wrong mechanism on or off. For example, engine cut-off switches should not be placed too close to radio-control switches; this design feature prevents the pilot from accidentally shutting off the engines in flight. (A few years ago this design principle was violated on the Boeing 757/767 models, causing a passenger jet to fall several miles before the engines could be restarted. They have since been modified.)

Some professionals, such as doctors and civil engineers, are required to formally acknowledge their professional obligations to their customers and are legally liable for their work. Because computer science is a relatively young field, the legal accountability of software engineers and other computer science professionals is not yet entirely clear. It is difficult to assign blame for the failure of a 10,000-line program to a particular programmer or designer when a team of employees may have contributed to the project. But there is growing awareness that formal software engineering standards must be established and enforced. Independent of the legal ramifications, we clearly have a moral responsibility to behave professionally in our work.

Example 10.5 A simple example of losing a node is

```
new (P);
P := L
```

where P and L are declared as in Figure 10.10. The node allocated by new is lost because P, which used to be the only pointer to it, now points to something else. ∎

Example 10.6 Another example of losing a node assumes the linked list of Figure 10.9(b). If the main program executes

```
List := List^.Link
```

then the header node will be lost. It will be impossible to ever access the header node again. ∎

Lost nodes do not cause run-time errors. If you lose a node the program will not necessarily crash. Lost nodes represent storage allocated from the heap that can never be used again and, therefore, is simply wasted. Lost nodes are to data what dead code is to programs. There is no logical reason for you to ever write program statements that will lose nodes.

When a Pascal compiler checks your program statements for type compatibility, it uses the principle of *name equivalence* as opposed to *structure equivalence*. One of the more subtle syntax errors you can make comes from forgetting the distinction between these two.

Pascal uses name equivalence, not structure equivalence.

For two types to be equivalent, Pascal requires that they have the same name: that is, they must be name equivalent. It is possible for two types to have the same structure—to be structure equivalent—but not to be name equivalent. Remember that an anonymous type is a type that has not been given a name in the type definition part. The important point to remember is that two anonymous types are never name equivalent, even though they may be structure equivalent.

Anonymous types are not name equivalent.

Example 10.7 In Program 10.4, you may be tempted to dispense with the name PtrToCellType. Instead of declaring ListType as

```
PtrToCellType = ^CellType;
ListType      = PtrToCellType;
```

you might try simply

```
ListType = ^CellType;
```

in the main program type definition part, and

```
Last: ^CellType;
```

as the declaration of one of the local variables in GetList. If you do that, the compiler will protest that the assignment statement

```
Last := L
```

in `GetList` is a type conflict. Even though `Last` and `L` have the same type structure, their types are both anonymous, so they are not name equivalent.   ∎

Design Tradeoffs with Linked Lists

What are the advantages of using linked lists with pointers? You could do all the operations on the list data structure with arrays. `ListType` could be similar to `StackType` in the stack data structure. It could be a record with an `array [1..ListMax]` of `ValueType` and a current index that indicates how many items are in the list.

The linked implementation of lists has two advantages over the array implementation. The first advantage is the flexibility of dynamic storage allocation. With arrays you must allocate enough memory for the maximum problem size you expect to encounter. With dynamic storage allocation you always have the entire heap from which to allocate another element.

Flexible storage allocation

This advantage is particularly important in problems with many lists. Suppose you have three lists—A, B, and C. One time when you run the program, list A may have 10,000 elements, and lists B and C only a few. The next time, list B may have 10,000, and lists A and C only a few. If you implement the lists with arrays, you would need to allocate 10,000 elements for A, B, and C, for a total of 30,000 elements, to account for the possibility of any of the three lists having a maximum of 10,000 elements. Your computer would need storage for 30,000 elements to run the program.

But if you implement the lists with pointers, you do not need to declare the maximum size of each list. Your computer would need storage for only a few more than 10,000 elements regardless of which list used most of them. Using pointers, different lists use storage from the same heap. The net result is the linked list implementation can require less storage because of the flexibility of dynamic storage allocation from the heap.

The second advantage of a linked implementation is the speed of insertions and deletions in long lists. To delete item 50 in a 100-item array, A, requires you to shift A [51] to A [50], A [52] to A [51], A [53] to A [52], and so on. But to delete item 50 in a 100-item linked list only requires you to change the link field of item 49 to point to item 51. You need not make any shifts.

Speed of insertions and deletions

The disadvantage of linked lists is their sequential nature. The only way to access an element in the middle of a list is to start at the beginning and sequentially advance a pointer through all the intermediate nodes. Arrays, however, are random. You cannot do a binary search of a linked list because you cannot access the middle of the list in one step the way you can with an array.

The sequential nature of list accesses

10.3   Binary Trees

Figure 9.11, the call tree for function `BinomCoeff`, was a binary tree. It represented the calling sequence of the recursive function. Another binary tree was represented in Figure 9.21, the calling sequence for procedure `QuickSort`. Each node in these trees had either two, one, or no children.

The trees in those figures represented the trace of the function and procedure calls. They did not represent data structures. This section presents binary trees constructed from data. As with linked lists, pointer variables are the glue that connects the nodes of the structure.

The Binary Tree Abstract Data Type

Like stacks and lists, binary trees are structures that store values. From an abstract point of view, the two relevant types are

```
ValueType
TreeType
```

`ValueType` is the type of data stored in each node of the binary tree, and `TreeType` is the type of the tree itself. `ValueType` may be a single character, a numeric value, a record, or any other primitive or programmer-defined type, depending on the application of the tree.

The definition of an *abstract binary tree* is recursive. A binary tree is either empty or it is a node with two children, a left child and a right child, each of which is a binary subtree.

The definition of an abstract binary tree

Figure 10.14 illustrates this definition of an abstract binary tree for a tree that has `ValueType` of `integer`. The root of the tree is the node that contains 5. The leaves—6, 1, and 7—are those nodes whose left and right children are both empty.

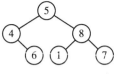

(a) The tree.   (b) Its left child.   (c) Its right child.

Figure 10.14

An abstract binary tree.

The structure in Figure 10.14(a) is a binary tree because its root, 5, has a left child that is a binary subtree, as shown in (b), and a right child that is a binary subtree, as shown in (c).

Figure 10.15 shows why the structure in Figure 10.14(b) is a binary tree. The root of this tree contains 4, its left child in Figure 10.15(b) is empty, and its right child, shown in 10.15(c), consists of a single node. You can see from this line of reasoning that each child of a node in the original structure of Figure 10.14(a) can be shown to be a binary tree. The basis of the definition is the fact that a binary tree can be empty.

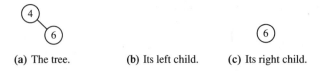

(a) The tree.   (b) Its left child.   (c) Its right child.

Figure **10.15**

Another abstract binary tree.

The values in the binary tree of Figure 10.14(a) have no particular order associated with them. This binary tree is said to be *unordered*. In practice, binary trees usually are ordered. In an *ordered* binary tree, every value in the left subtree of the root is less than or equal to the value of the root, and every value in the right subtree is greater than or equal to the value of the root. In addition, the left and right subtrees of the root must be ordered, which implies recursively that all the nodes must be ordered.

The definition of an ordered binary tree

Example **10.8**   In Figure 10.14(a), the fact that 1 is in the right subtree of root 5, shows that the tree is not ordered. Another node out of order is 6, which is in the left subtree of the root. ∎

Example **10.9**   The binary tree of Figure 10.16 is ordered. All the nodes in the left subtree of the root (20, 10, 30) are less than the root value, and all the nodes in the right subtree (60, 50) are greater than the root value. Furthermore, in the subtree with 20 as a root, 10 is less than 20, and 30 is greater than 20. Similarly, 50, the value in the left child of 60, is less than 60. ∎

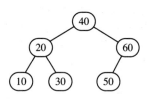

In their abstract form, binary trees are usually written on paper or displayed on the screen as two-dimensional drawings. It is frequently necessary, however, to output the values from the tree in a single list as opposed to a flat drawing. To print all the values requires a procedure that somehow travels around the tree, visiting the various nodes and outputting their values. Such a trip is called a *traversal*. Three common traversals of a binary tree are

Figure **10.16**

An ordered binary tree.

- Preorder traversal
- Inorder traversal
- Postorder traversal

Three common traversals of binary trees

The definition of each traversal is recursive and is related to the recursive nature of the definition of a binary tree.

The definition of a *preorder traversal* is

Preorder traversal

■ Visit the root.

■ Make a preorder traversal of the left subtree, if any.

■ Make a preorder traversal of the right subtree, if any.

This definition is recursive because the preorder traversal requires two other preorder traversals.

Figure 10.17(a) shows the preorder traversal of the binary tree of Figure 10.15. The line that enters from the upper left and exits to the upper right traces the path. The definition says to first visit the root, which the figure indicates by the solid box to the left of the root. Then do a preorder traversal of the subtree whose root is 20, followed by a preorder traversal of the subtree whose root is 60.

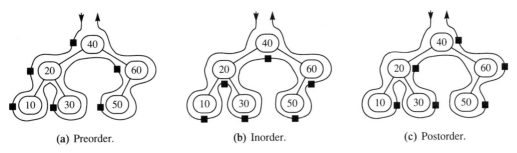

(a) Preorder.   (b) Inorder.   (c) Postorder.

Figure 10.17

The visits to the nodes in the tree-traversal algorithms.

Now apply the preorder traversal to the tree whose root is 20. First visit 20, then do a preorder traversal with 10 as the root, followed by a preorder traversal with 30 as the root. Similarly, the preorder traversal of the tree whose root is 60 consists of a visit to 60, followed by a visit to 50. The net result is

40 20 10 30 60 50

The definition of an *inorder traversal* is

Inorder traversal

■ Make an inorder traversal of the left subtree, if any.

■ Visit the root.

■ Make an inorder traversal of the right subtree, if any.

Figure 10.16(b) shows the corresponding inorder visitation on the same tree. This time the incoming path does not first visit the root. Instead, it waits until the left subtree has been traversed. Then the root is visited as indicated by the solid box on the path just under the root. After the root is visited, the path traverses the right subtree. The net result is

10 20 30 40 50 60

The definition of a *postorder traversal* is

- Make a postorder traversal of the left subtree, if any.
- Make a postorder traversal of the right subtree, if any.
- Visit the root.

Figure 10.16(c) shows the postorder traversal. The path does not show a visit to the root until both the left and right subtrees have been traversed. This time the output is

10   30   20   50   60   40

Remember that the tree in Figure 10.17 is an ordered binary tree. The example of an inorder traversal of an ordered binary tree showed that it outputs the values in order, as if they were sorted. In fact, one of the primary uses of binary trees is to maintain lists of elements in order.

Many operations are possible with a binary tree ADT, but the operations that follow are fundamental.

```
procedure Initialize (var T: TreeType)
function Empty (T: TreeType): boolean
function Leaf (T: TreeType): boolean
procedure PreOrder (T: TreeType)
procedure InOrder (T: TreeType)
procedure PostOrder (T: TreeType)
procedure Attach (Y: ValueType; var T: TreeType)
```

`Initialize` initializes a tree variable to an empty tree. `Empty` is true if `T` is an empty tree. `Leaf` is true if `T` is a leaf; that is, if both its left and right subtrees are empty. `PreOrder`, `InOrder`, and `PostOrder` visit the nodes of `T` as defined above.

Procedure `Attach` assumes that `T` is an ordered binary tree and attaches a new node with value `Y` to the tree, maintaining its ordered state. Figure 10.18 shows the structure of the abstract tree with the following sequence of procedure calls:

```
Initialize (Tree);
Attach (40, Tree);
Attach (20, Tree);
Attach (60, Tree);
Attach (50, Tree);
Attach (10, Tree);
Attach (30, Tree)
```

In each call to `Attach`, the newly created node takes the place of an empty left child or an empty right child of some node in the tree. The node that is attached becomes a leaf. If the node to which it is attached was previously a leaf, it becomes an internal node, that is, a node that is not a leaf.

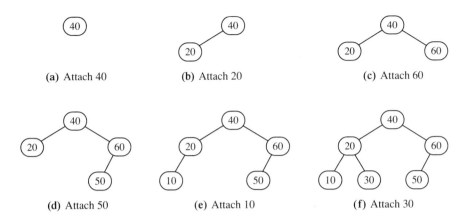

(a) Attach 40   **(b)** Attach 20   **(c)** Attach 60

(d) Attach 50   **(e)** Attach 10   **(f)** Attach 30

Figure 10.18

Constructing the ordered binary tree with procedure `Attach` of Program 10.5.

When a given value is attached to a given ordered binary tree, the attachment point is unique. For example, to attach 10 to the tree of Figure 10.18(d) it must take the place of the left child of 20. Placing 10 at any other available location would produce a tree that is not ordered.

Implementing Binary Trees

The previous discussion described some properties of abstract binary trees. To implement the operations requires you to define `TreeType`. One possibility is the following data structure:

Data structure for the binary tree implemented with pointers

```
PtrToCellType = ^CellType;
TreeType      = PtrToCellType;
CellType =
   record
   LeftChild:  TreeType;
   Value:      ValueType;
   RightChild: TreeType
   end;
```

Figure 10.19 shows the structure of `CellType`. The fields for `LeftChild` and `RightChild` contain pointers that link the child nodes to the parent node. `ValueType` must be defined previously to `CellType` and will depend on the particular application of the binary tree.

Figure 10.20 shows an abstract binary tree of integers with the corresponding linked implementation. Variable `Tree` has type `TreeType` and points to the root of the tree. The value field of the root contains 5. Its left child is a pointer to the cell that contains 4, and its right child is a pointer to the cell that contains 8.

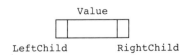

Figure 10.19

The structure of a record of type `CellType` in the implementation of a binary tree.

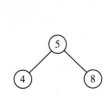

(a) The abstract binary tree.

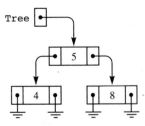

(b) The linked implementation of the binary tree.

Figure 10.20

An abstract binary tree and its implementation.

Here are the variables involved in the access to the left child:

`Tree`	is a pointer to a record.
`Tree^`	is a record.
`Tree^.LeftChild`	is a pointer to a record.
`Tree^.LeftChild^`	is a record.
`Tree^.LeftChild^.Value`	is an integer.

The notation is consistent. If `X` is a pointer to `Y`, then `X^` has the same type as `Y`.

Example 10.10 If `Tree` points to the root cell of the binary tree in Figure 10.20, then

`Tree^.RightChild^.Value`

is an integer with the value 8. The expression

`Tree^.LeftChild^.RightChild`

is a pointer with value `nil`, because it is the `RightChild` field of the cell with the value 4. ∎

▬ Program 10.5

Program 10.5 inputs unsorted integer values from a file and constructs an ordered binary tree with the values. It shows the specific implementation of procedures `Initialize`, `Attach`, and `InOrder`, which are operations of the binary tree ADT.

Notice in the main program that there are no references to the pointers or records that make up the cells of the tree. The main program refers only to variables with types `integer`, `text`, `ValueType`, and `TreeType`. As far as the person who wrote the main program is concerned, the pointers and records do not exist. Those details are hidden at a lower level of abstraction.

The main program initializes the binary tree and executes a loop that inputs values using the count technique. It processes each value by attaching it to the tree, maintaining the tree's ordered state. After attaching all the input values to the binary tree, the main program calls procedure `InOrder`, which makes an inorder transversal of the tree. Since the binary tree is ordered, the values are output in sorted order.

Procedure `Initialize` initializes the binary tree to an empty tree. Since `TreeType` is a pointer, empty trees are represented by a value of `nil` for the tree variable.

```
program OrderedBinaryTree (NumFile, output);
   type
      ValueType     = integer;
      PtrToCellType = ^CellType;
      TreeType      = PtrToCellType;
      CellType =
         record
         LeftChild:  TreeType;
         Value:      ValueType;
         RightChild: TreeType
         end;
   var
      Tree:     TreeType;
      NumFile:  text;
      NumItems: integer;
      Num:      ValueType;
      I:        integer;

   procedure Initialize (var T: TreeType);
      begin
      T := nil
      end;

   procedure InOrder (T: TreeType);
      begin
      if T <> nil then
         begin
         InOrder (T^.LeftChild);
         write (T^.Value: 4);
         InOrder (T^.RightChild)
         end
      end;
```

Program 10.5

A program that illustrates the construction of a binary tree.

Program 10.5, continued

```
procedure Attach (Y: ValueType; var T: TreeType);
   {  Creates a node with value Y and attaches it to the  }
   {  ordered binary tree T.                              }
   var
      Node: PtrToCellType;
      P:    PtrToCellType;
      Prev: PtrToCellType;
   begin
   new (Node);
   Node^.LeftChild := nil;  {  Create the new node.       }
   Node^.Value := Y;
   Node^.RightChild := nil;
   if T = nil then          {  The tree is empty, so      }
      T := Node             {     point T to the new node.}
   else                     {  The tree is not empty.     }
      begin
      P := T;               {  Find the insertion point.  }
      repeat
         Prev := P;
         if Node^.Value < P^.Value then
            P := P^.LeftChild
         else
            P := P^.RightChild
      until P = nil;                  {  Attach the node.  }
      if Node^.Value < Prev^.Value then
         Prev^.LeftChild := Node
      else
         Prev^.RightChild := Node
      end
   end;

begin
Initialize (Tree);
reset (NumFile);
read (NumFile, NumItems);
for I := 1 to NumItems do
   begin
   read (NumFile, Num);
   Attach (Num, Tree)
   end;
InOrder (Tree)
end.
```

Input—NumFile

```
6
40  20  60  50  10  30
```

Output

```
10  20  30  40  50  60
```

Procedure `Attach` first creates a new node by allocating a cell from the heap with `new (Node)`. After this procedure call, `Node` points to the newly allocated cell. The next three statements,

```
Node^.LeftChild := nil;
Node^.Value := Y;
Node^.RightChild := nil;
```

set `LeftChild` and `RightChild` of the new node to `nil` and `Value` to the value received from the main program. The new node is now ready to be attached to the binary tree.

The next statement in `Attach` tests whether the tree is empty. If the tree is empty, the procedure simply makes `T` point to the newly allocated node. Otherwise, the procedure must determine the insertion point for the new node. This test for the special case of an empty tree would be unnecessary if the tree were implemented with a header node. The code for the traversals would be much more complex with a header node than without one, however.

The technique to find the insertion point is similar to that in Figure 10.11(a) and (b), which shows how to search for the deletion point of a node in a linked list. In the linked list of Figure 10.11, `P` was initialized to the first node and advanced through the list by `P := P^.Link`. `Prev` was a pointer that followed `P` through the list. In `Attach` in Program 10.5, `P` is initialized to the tree pointer, `T`, and advances down the tree. The difference is that `P` in the linked list always advanced to the next node in the list, whereas `P` in `Attach` can advance to either the left child or the right child. To maintain the order of the tree, the node should be attached to the left subtree of `P^` if the value in `Node^` is less than the value in `P^`. `P` advances by `P := P^.LeftChild` or `P := P^.RightChild`, depending on the values in `Node^` and `P^`.

The `repeat` loop terminates with a value of `nil` for `P`. At that point `Prev`, which followed `P` down the tree, points to the node to which `Node^` should be attached. Again, a test must be made to determine whether `Node^` should be attached to the left or the right. When it should be attached to the left, the statement

```
Prev^.LeftChild := Node
```

attaches `Node^` by making the left child of `Prev^` point to the same thing that `Node` points to.

Procedure `InOrder` is a Pascal implementation of the inorder traversal. The pseudocode statement

Visit the root.

from the definition of an inorder traversal, is replaced in the code by

```
write (T^.Value: 4)
```

The placement of the output statement between the recursive calls guarantees that the procedure will print all the values in the left subtree of a node before the value of that node, and all the values in the right subtree after its value. Figure 10.17(b) shows the traversal path, with each solid square representing an execution of the `write` statement.

Since the binary tree is ordered, every number the procedure prints before a given number will be less than that number, and every number it prints after the number will be greater than that number. Therefore, the procedure also must print the numbers in order.

The ordered binary tree is one way to sort a list of elements. At each step of the algorithm, the next item is taken from the unsorted group and inserted into the ordered binary tree. It is another form of the insertion sort algorithm and belongs to the general merge sort family.

Inserting nodes into an ordered binary tree is faster than inserting them into an array. Consider Figure 9.26(a), which showed a trace of the insertion sort. In pass 6, the 5 was inserted into the front part of the array. That required values 8, 7, and 6 to all be shifted down one slot to make room for the 5. In the ordered binary tree, a new node is simply attached as a leaf, and nothing needs to be shifted.

Program 10.6

An interesting application of the tree-traversal algorithms is the processing of arithmetic expressions. The previous chapter showed how to translate an arithmetic expression from infix to postfix using a stack to store the operators. This section concludes with a program that inputs a prefix expression into a binary tree. Once the expression is stored in the tree, it can be output in prefix, infix, or postfix form.

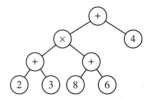

Figure 10.21

A binary tree representation for the arithmetic expression $(2 + 3) \times (8 + 6) + 4.$

Example 10.11   Figure 10.21 shows the binary tree representation of the infix arithmetic expression

$(2 + 3) \times (8 + 6) + 4$

If you traverse the tree with the `InOrder` procedure, you output the operands and operators in the order of the infix expression. If you traverse the tree with the `PostOrder` procedure, you output the operands and operators as

$2 \ 3 + 8 \ 6 + \times 4 +$

which is simply the corresponding postfix expression.   ∎

Example 10.12   The binary tree representation of an infix expression has no parentheses. Figure 10.22 is the binary tree representation of the infix expression

$2 + 3 \times (8 + 6) + 4$

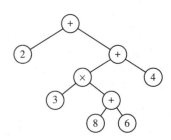

Figure 10.22

A binary tree representation for the arithmetic expression $2 + 3 \times (8 + 6) + 4.$

The order of the operands and operators is identical to the infix expression corresponding to Figure 10.21. But the placement of 3 as the left child of the multiply node in this figure indicates that 3 multiplies the quantity 8 plus 6. In Figure 10.21, the placement of the subtree as the left child of the multiply node indicates that the multiplier is the quantity 2 plus 3. The structure of the tree indicates the grouping rather than the explicit presence of parentheses.   ∎

Program 10.6 can create the binary trees shown in the previous examples. `ValueType` is `char`, which can store a single-digit character or a single-digit operator. Restricting the operands to single-digit integers is not realistic, but it keeps the program short. The input is also restricted to be error-free and to have no embedded spaces for simplicity. The sample I/O corresponds to the expression of Figure 10.21.

The input comes from `ExpressionFile`, which is a text file. The main program resets the file and then calls `Prefix`, which is a function. The function has type `TreeType` and takes the file as its parameter. Its purpose is to read the characters from the file, construct the corresponding tree for the arithmetic expression, and return the tree to `Tree` in the main program.

`Prefix` reads a character from the file and allocates a new node for it. The binary tree for an expression that consists of only one number is a tree with a single node. Therefore, if the character is a digit, the function returns a pointer to the single new node. This part of the procedure is the basis for the recursion.

If the character is not a digit, the function assumes it is an operator. The function calls itself recursively to get the tree to attach to its left child. It calls itself recursively again to get the tree to attach to its right child. Finally, the function returns the pointer to the node.

The `PostOrder` procedure is identical to the `InOrder` procedure of Program 10.5 except for the placement of the `write` statement. As in the abstract inorder algorithm presented earlier, the `write` statement, which corresponds to the visit statement, is after both recursive calls.

The binary trees described here store arithmetic expressions, but the idea applies to storing other structures as well. For example, a Pascal compiler must translate not only an expression, but an entire Pascal source program. In the same way that a sentence diagram shows the grammatical structure of a sentence, a

Program 10.6

Constructing a binary tree representation of an arithmetic expression.

```
program OrderedBinaryTree (ExpressionFile, output);
   type
      ValueType     = char;
      PtrToCellType = ^CellType;
      TreeType      = PtrToCellType;
      CellType =
         record
         LeftChild:  TreeType;
         Value:      ValueType;
         RightChild: TreeType
         end;
   var
      Tree:           TreeType;
      ExpressionFile: text;
```

Program 10.6, continued

```
procedure PostOrder (T: TreeType);
   begin
   if T <> nil then
      begin
      PostOrder (T^.LeftChild);
      PostOrder (T^.RightChild);
      write (T^.Value: 2)
      end
   end;

function Prefix (var F: text): TreeType;
   var
      Node: PtrToCellType;
      Ch:   char;
   begin
   read (F, Ch);
   new (Node);
   Node^.Value := Ch;
   if Ch in ['0'..'9'] then
      begin
      Node^.LeftChild := nil;
      Node^.RightChild := nil
      end
   else {assume operator}
      begin
      Node^.LeftChild := Prefix (F);
      Node^.RightChild := Prefix (F)
      end;
   Prefix := Node
   end;

begin
reset (ExpressionFile);
Tree := Prefix (ExpressionFile);
PostOrder (Tree)
end.
```

Input—ExpressionFile

```
+*+23+864
```

Output

```
 2  3  +  8  6  +  *  4  +
```

syntax tree shows the grammatical structure of a Pascal source program. Some compilers store the program internally in a syntax tree before producing the object code.

10.4 Input/Output Buffers

Every time you execute a `write` call or a `read` call, you transfer data between a variable in main memory and some peripheral device, often a disk file. When you declare a file, Pascal allocates an area in memory called a *buffer*. All the previous examples that used file I/O had buffers associated with the files. None of those examples accessed the buffers directly, however. They accessed them indirectly through the `read` and `write` calls.

Program 10.7

Pascal permits you to access the I/O buffers directly with pointers. Program 10.7 (p. 544), which performs the same computation as Program 5.2, illustrates output with a file buffer.

The program declares `AcctFile2` as a file of real values. It associates an output buffer with the file. The buffer is accessed as `AcctFile2^`. It is as if `AcctFile2` is a pointer to a real value.

This program differs from Program 5.2 only in that the output statement

```
write (AcctFile2, Num)
```

has been replaced by the two statements

```
AcctFile2^ := Num;
put (AcctFile2)
```

Procedure `put` is a standard Pascal procedure for output. It sends the contents of the file buffer to the file.

Figure 10.23 (p. 545) is the start of a trace of Program 10.7. `rewrite` prepares the file for output and establishes the output buffer `AcctFile^`. The `readln` call gets 54.00 from the keyboard.

The assignment statement

```
AcctFile2^ := Num
```

simply gives the value of `Num` to the output buffer. Then the procedure call

```
put (AcctFile2)
```

appends the value from the output buffer to the end of the file.

Program 10.7

Accessing the output buffer with a file pointer.

```
program MakeNonText (input, output, AcctFile2);
   var
      Num:       real;
      Response:  char;
      AcctFile2: file of real;
   begin
   rewrite (AcctFile2);
   write ('Enter a number? (y or n): ');
   readln (Response);
   while (Response = 'Y') or (Response = 'y') do
      begin
      write ('Type the number: ');
      readln (Num);
      AcctFile2^ := Num;
      put (AcctFile2);
      writeln;
      write ('Enter another number? (y or n): ');
      readln (Response)
      end
   end.
```

Intractive Input/Output

```
Enter a number? (y or n): y
Type the number: 54.00

Enter another number? (y or n): y
Type the number: 20.40

Enter another number? (y or n): y
Type the number: 76.50

Enter another number? (y or n): n
```

Output—`AcctFile2` (nontext)

54.00   20.40   76.50

The output buffer is an intermediate storage location between the variable whose value you wish to output and the file. You could dispense with the variable Num altogether and replace the statements

```
write ('Type the number: ');
readln (Num);
AcctFile2^ := Num;
put (AcctFile2)
```

with

```
write ('Type the number: ');
readln (AcctFile2^);
put (AcctFile2)
```

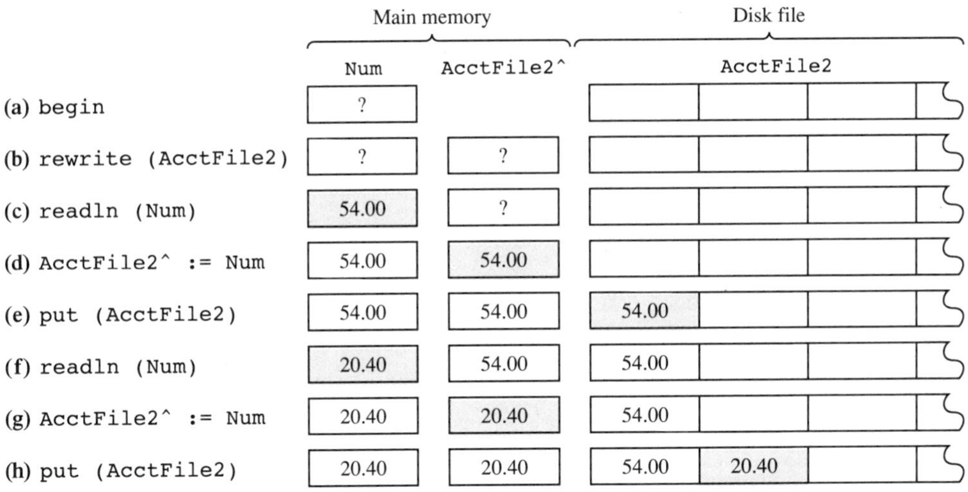

	Main memory		Disk file			
	Num	AcctFile2^	AcctFile2			
(a) begin	?					
(b) rewrite (AcctFile2)	?	?				
(c) readln (Num)	54.00	?				
(d) AcctFile2^ := Num	54.00	54.00				
(e) put (AcctFile2)	54.00	54.00	54.00			
(f) readln (Num)	20.40	54.00	54.00			
(g) AcctFile2^ := Num	20.40	20.40	54.00			
(h) put (AcctFile2)	20.40	20.40	54.00	20.40		

Figure 10.23

The start of a trace of Program 10.7.

Since AcctFile2 is similar to a pointer to a real value, you can use AcctFile2^ like any real variable.

In general, the write call

write (F, X)

where F is a file and X is any other type of variable, is equivalent to the two statements

```
F^ := X;
put (F)
```

The file buffer equivalent of the write call

The effect of put (F) is to send the value in F^ to file F.

Program 10.8

Program 10.8 performs the same computation as Program 5.3. It illustrates input with a file buffer.

As in the previous program, AcctFile2 is a file of real values with a buffer that is accessed as AcctFile2^. This program differs from Program 5.3 only in that the output statement

read (AcctFile2, Account)

has been replaced by the two statements

```
Account := AcctFile2^;
get (AcctFile2)
```

Procedure get is a standard Pascal procedure for input. It brings the next value from the file into the file buffer.

```
program TotalAccounts2 (AcctFile2, output);
    var
        Account:    real;
        Sum:        real;
        AcctFile2: file of real;
    begin
    reset (AcctFile2);
    Sum := 0.00;
    {  Assert: Sum is the sum of all the values  }
    {  input thus far.                           }
    while not eof (AcctFile2) do
        begin
        Account := AcctFile2^;
        get (AcctFile2);
        Sum := Sum + Account
        end;
    writeln ('Total is $', Sum :4: 2)
    end.
```

Program **10.8**

Accessing the input buffer with a file pointer.

Input—AcctFile2 (nontext)

54.00   20.40   76.50

Output

Total is $150.90

Figure 10.24 is the start of a trace of Program 10.8. `reset` prepares the file for input and establishes the input buffer `AcctFile2^`. Unlike the `rewrite` procedure call, `reset` does not leave `AcctFile2^` undefined. It fetches the first item from the file, anticipating the need for the first access later in the program. In effect, `reset` performs an automatic `get` `(AcctFile2)` call for the first item in the file.

Figure 10.24(c) shows the effect of assignment from the input buffer. Had the `reset` statement not fetched the first item in advance, you would need to execute the `get` call before the assignment from the buffer.

In general, the `read` call

```
read (F, X)
```

where F is a file and X is any other type of variable, is equivalent to the two statements

```
X := F^;
get (F)
```

The file buffer equivalent of the read call

The purpose for the "prefetch" with `reset` is speed of execution. It takes much more time to fetch a value from a disk than to process data in main memory. If the first value is prefetched, the variable `Account` can get its value from the

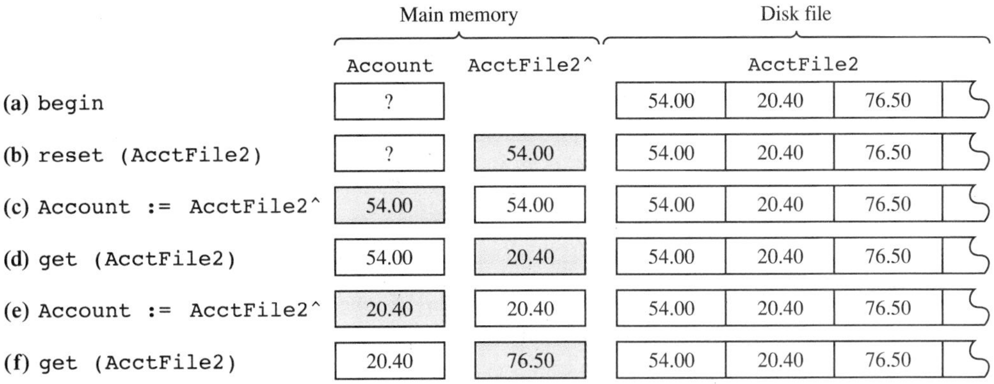

	Main memory		Disk file		
	Account	AcctFile2^	AcctFile2		
(a) begin	?		54.00	20.40	76.50
(b) reset (AcctFile2)	?	54.00	54.00	20.40	76.50
(c) Account := AcctFile2^	54.00	54.00	54.00	20.40	76.50
(d) get (AcctFile2)	54.00	20.40	54.00	20.40	76.50
(e) Account := AcctFile2^	20.40	20.40	54.00	20.40	76.50
(f) get (AcctFile2)	20.40	76.50	54.00	20.40	76.50

Figure 10.24

The start of a trace of Program 10.8.

buffer immediately. The **get** call initiates the next fetch from the disk. While the next fetch is occurring, the program can continue its processing of the values in main memory.

The next time the program needs a value from the file, it executes

```
Account := AcctFile2^
```

again. If the previous execution of **get** has completed, the program makes the assignment and continues without waiting. If the execution of **get** has not completed, the program must wait. Even if it must, however, the wait will be shorter than it would if the **get** call had not been executing simultaneously with the rest of the program.

This activity is a form of parallel processing. The processing of the data in main memory takes place at the same time, that is, in parallel with, the fetch from the file. The operating system coordinates the parallel executions. It prevents the assignment from the buffer variable until the **get** call has completed execution.

Although Pascal gives you the ability to access the I/O buffers directly, most programs do not. Sometimes using the buffer directly can save memory that wouldbe allocated for a program variable. The amount of memory saved is usually small, however. Some compilers do not even follow the Pascal standard in permitting direct access to the buffer. The absence of that option is no great loss.

SUMMARY

The heap is a region of main memory separate from the stack. A pointer variable points to a value in the heap. Values in the heap are not allocated, as are parameters and local variables, when a procedure is called. Instead, they are allocated with the **new** procedure and deallocated with the **dispose** procedure. The only operations that are allowed on pointer data types are assignment, test for equality, and test for inequality. The effect of assigning one pointer variable to a second pointer variable is to make the second pointer variable point to the same thing that the first variable points to.

Pointers are rarely used in isolation. They are usually contained in the field of a record and point to another record of the same type. A linked list is a linear sequence of such records. Linked lists can be used to implement stacks. The advantages of linked lists over arrays are flexibility of storage allocation and speed of insertions and deletions. It is possible to lose nodes in the heap. A lost node is to data what dead code is to program statements.

A binary tree ADT is either empty or a node with two children, a left child and a right child, each of which is a binary subtree. The three traversals of a binary tree are preorder, inorder, and postorder. An ordered binary tree has every value of the left subtree less than every value of the right subtree, for every node in the tree. An inorder traversal of an ordered binary tree outputs all the elements of the tree in order. A binary tree can be implemented with a collection of records, each of which has a pointer to the left child and a pointer to the right child.

Pascal maintains an input or output buffer for each file declared in the program. The file name is an identifier for a pointer variable that points to the buffer. A `write` statement is equivalent to an assignment to the file buffer followed by a call to the `put` procedure. A `read` statement is equivalent to an assignment from the file buffer followed by a call to the `get` procedure.

EXERCISES

Section 10.1

1. Suppose the variable declaration part of a Pascal program declares A, B, C, and D to be pointers to integers. What is the output of each of the following code fragments?

* (a)	(b)	(c)	(d)
new (A);	new (A);	new (A);	new (A);
new (B);	A^ := 7;	A^ := 9;	A^ := 2;
A^ := 5;	new (B);	B := A;	new (B);
B^ := 6;	B^ := 2;	A^ := B^ + A^;	B^ := 3;
A := B;	C := A;	*Output* A^, B^	C := A;
Output A^, B^	D := B;		A := B;
	A := B;		B := C;
	Output A^, B^		*Output* A^, B^
	Output C^, D^		

Section 1.2

2. Suppose P, Q, L, and Last are PtrToCellType as in Program 10.3 and have the values in Figure 10.25. Draw the figure after execution of the following instructions.

* (a)	(b)	(c)
Q := L;	Q := Q^.Link;	Q := Q^.Link^.Link;
P := Last	P := P^.Link	P := P^.Link^.Link

(d)	(e)
new (Q)	L^.Link := Q^.Link;
Q^.Link := L;	dispose (Q)
Q^.Value := 5.0;	
L := Q;	
Q := nil	

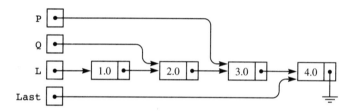

Figure 10.25

The linked list for Exercises 2, 3, and 4.

3. Suppose P, Q, L, and Last are PtrToCellType as in Program 10.3 and have the values in Figure 10.25. State whether each of the following instructions produces a nil pointer reference error. For those that do, explain why.

*(a)
```
P := nil;
P := P^.Link
```

(b)
```
P := P^.Link;
P := P^.Link
```

(c)
```
Last := Last^.Link;
Last := Last^.Link
```

4. Suppose P, Q, L, and Last are PtrToCellType as in Program 10.3 and have the values in Figure 10.25. State whether each of the following instructions produces a lost node. For those that do, explain why.

*(a) L := L^.Link   (b) Last := Last^.Link
(c) P := L   (d) L := P

5. Section 7.4 described the difference between full evaluation and short circuit evaluation. Suppose L, Last, P, and Word are declared as in procedure GetList of Program 10.4. The following loop is supposed to find the occurrence of Word in the linked list if it is present.

```
P := L;
while (P <> nil) and (P^.Value <> Word) do
    P := P^.Link
```

(a) Discuss the correctness of this loop, assuming the compiler uses the full evaluation technique. (b) Discuss the correctness of this loop, assuming it uses the short circuit evaluation technique.

Section 10.3

6. Draw the final ordered binary tree corresponding to Figure 10.18(f) for each of the following input files.

* (a) 50 30 80 60 40 20 10   (b) 50 30 80 60 40 10 20
(c) 50 60 70 80 10 20 30 40   (d) 10 20 30 40 50
(e) 50 40 30 20 10

*7. For each of the ordered binary trees of Exercise 6, write the preorder sequence.

*8. For each of the ordered binary trees of Exercise 6, write the postorder sequence.

9. Write the preorder, inorder, and postorder traversals for each binary tree in Figure 10.26.

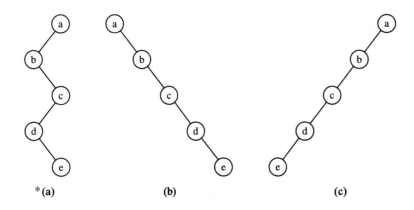

*(a)   (b)   (c)

Figure 10.26

The binary trees for Exercise 9.

10. An ordered binary tree contains a set of integers. Each of the following sequences is the preorder sequence. From the preorder sequence and the known inorder sequence, draw the ordered binary tree.

* (a) 40   20   60   (b) 60   40   20
  (c) 60   20   40   (d) 20   40   60   80
  (e) 60   30   10   80   70   90

* 11. Work Exercise 10, assuming the given lists are the postorder sequences.

12. Draw the binary tree representation of each of the following infix expressions.

(a) $2 + 3 \times 4$ (b) $(2 + 3) \times 4$
(c) $(2 + 3) \times (4 + 5)$ (d) $2 + 3 \times (4 + 5)$
(e) $((1 + 2) + 3) + 4$ (f) $1 + (2 + (3 + 4))$

PROBLEMS

Section 10.2

13. Write procedure `GetList` of Program 10.4 without the local variable `P`. Allocate the new node directly with

    `new (Last^.Link)`.

14. The input for this problem is a list of words in a text file. Each word is alone on one line and contains no more than eight characters. Rewrite procedure `GetList` in Program 10.4 to input the words from the text file (with the character-processing algo-

rithm of Section 7.2) into a linked list. Implement procedure `InsertBefore` as described in Section 10.2. Construct the linked list from the file and print it. Ask the user which word to insert and where to insert it, then print the list again. An empty file should produce an initially empty list, which should not crash the program. You must be able to insert before the first word.

Sample Input/Output

```
Now      is       the      time.
Word to insert: not
Insert before which word: the

Now      is       not      the      time.
```

Sample Input/Output

```
Now      is       the      time.
Word to insert: not
Insert before which word: all
That word is not in the list.

Now      is       the      time.
```

15. The input for this problem is identical to that of Problem 14. Implement procedure `InsertAfter` as described in Section 10.2. Construct the linked list from the file and print it. Ask the user which word to insert and where to insert it, then print the list again. An empty file should produce an initially empty list, which should not crash the program. You must be able to insert after the last word.

Sample Input/Output

```
Now      is       the      time.
Word to insert: not
Insert after which word: is

Now      is       not      the      time.
```

Sample Input/Output

```
Now      is       the      time.
Word to insert: not
Insert after which word: all
That word is not in the list.

Now      is       the      time.
```

16. The input for this problem is identical to that of Problem 14. Implement procedure `Delete` as described in Section 10.2. Repeatedly ask the user the word to be deleted from the list, delete the word, and print the list again.

Sample Input/Output

```
Now     is      the     time.
Delete which word? (<ret> to quit): the

Now     is      time.
Delete which word? (<ret> to quit): tame
That word is not in the list.

Now     is      time.
Delete which word? (<ret> to quit): time.

Now     is
Delete which word? (<ret> to quit):
```

17. Write

    `procedure Copy (ListA: ListType; var ListB: ListType)`

    to create a new list, ListB, which is a copy of ListA. Test it using GetList of Program 10.4 to get ListA, and Copy to copy ListA to ListB. Delete a node from ListA and output both lists with PutList to verify that ListB is a copy of the old ListA before the deletion.

18. Write

    `procedure CopyReverse (ListA: ListType; var ListB: ListType)`

    to create a new list, ListB, which is a copy of ListA in reverse order. Test it using GetList of Program 10.4 to get ListA, and CopyReverse to copy ListA to ListB. Output both lists with PutList to verify that ListB is the reverse of ListA.

19. For Problem 9.32, write the program to evaluate a postfix expression. Use the linked list data structure for the stack.

20. For Problem 9.33, write the program to translate an infix expression to postfix. Use the linked list data structure for the stack.

Section 10.3

21. Modify procedure InOrder in Program 10.5 to install the value into an array of integers instead of printing the value. Output the sorted array from the main program.

22. Write a function

    `Leaf (T: TreeType): boolean`

    that is true if T points to a leaf node in a tree. Modify InOrder in Program 10.5 to output only the leaves of the tree.

23. Write a procedure

    `StripLeaves (var T: TreeType)`

that deallocates all the leaves from binary tree T. Test it in the main program of Program 10.5 by printing the original inorder sequence, stripping the leaves, then printing the inorder sequence again. The following sample output is for the sample input in Program 10.5. `StripLeaves` should be based on a recursive traversal of the tree.

Sample Output

```
10  20  30  40  50  60
20  40  60
```

24. Write a traversal algorithm

```
procedure ReverseOrder (T: TreeType)
```

that outputs the values in a binary tree in the reverse of inorder. Test your procedure in the main program of Program 10.5.

25. Write

```
function NumNodes (T: TreeType): integer
```

that returns the number of nodes in binary tree T. Test your procedure in the main program of Program 10.5.

26. Write

```
function MaxDepth (T: TreeType): integer
```

that returns the maximum depth of the binary tree T. The definition of `MaxDepth` is recursive. If the tree is empty, the maximum depth is 0. Otherwise the maximum depth is 1 plus the larger of the maximum depth of the left and right subtrees. For example, the maximum depth of the tree in Figure 10.14(b) is 2 and in Figure 10.14(d) it is 3. Test your function in the main program of Program 10.5.

27. Problem 7.59 suggested one technique to generate a list of random numbers without duplicates. You can use a binary tree to solve the same problem. Modify procedure `Attach` in Program 10.5 to insert the values in the binary tree at random. Use a random number generator to decide whether P should advance to the left child or the right child with a 50% probability of either. Call the modified procedure from a `for` loop with a sequence of consecutive integer values. The random list may be output with any of the three traversal algorithms.

28. Parentheses are necessary for infix expressions and helpful for prefix and postfix expressions. The fully parenthesized expressions from the binary tree in Figure 10.20 are

```
Prefix:   ( + ( × ( + 2 3 ) ( + 8 6 ) ) 4 )
Infix:    ( ( ( 2 + 3 ) × ( 8 + 6 ) ) + 4 )
Postfix:  ( ( ( 2 3 + ) ( 8 6 + ) × ) 4 + )
```

Note that parentheses do not surround individual operands. Write a procedure that outputs the fully parenthesized expressions in the following formats:

(a) prefix   (b) infix   (c) postfix

Test your procedure from the main program in Program 10.6.

Chapter

11

Data Structures

Previous chapters introduced stacks, linked lists, and binary trees as abstract data types. You will recall that an abstract data type consists of a collection of variables and operations on those variables. A *data structure* is an implementation of the abstract data type that is constructed from the primitive types of some programming language. The abstract type is usually implemented as a record or a pointer to a record, and the operations are implemented as functions and procedures.

Definition of a data structure

It is possible to implement an abstract data type in several different ways. For example, a stack ADT could be implemented with an array and an integer that indicates the top of the stack. The stack could also be implemented with a linked list.

Remember that the theme of this book is the levels of abstraction in a computer system. We use Pascal, a Level 6 language, to demonstrate the separation of the concept of an abstract data type from its implementation in a data structure. This chapter continues to explore the concept of abstract data types and their implementation with data structures. We will examine variable-length strings, queues, and graphs, which are three of the more common abstract data types in computer science. As before, we will see that several different implementations are possible for a single type.

Separating an abstract data type from its implementation

This chapter contains no new Pascal features. It simply uses the Pascal we have already learned to implement the new types, which are at a higher level of abstraction than the primitive types of Pascal.

11.1 Variable-Length Strings

A common problem in text processing is to insert a person's name, which is arbitrary in length, into a sentence. A packed array of `char` always has a fixed number of characters. The variable declaration part determines the array length, which does not change for the duration of the program. That makes it difficult to output names because one may be short and the next one may be long.

Drawback of packed arrays of characters

555

Example 11.1 Suppose `Name` is a packed array of 15 characters, and you input a value of `Tom  Smith` using `GetString` from Program 7.7. The code fragment

```
write ('Hi ', Name, '.  How are you?')
```

will output

```
Hi Tom Smith       .  How are you?
```

instead of

```
Hi Tom Smith.  How are you?
```

The problem is that `GetString` pads the value of `Name` on the right with spaces, which are output along with the characters that the user entered from the keyboard for `Name`.   ∎

Packed arrays of characters have other drawbacks as well. For example, when processing text material you may need to extract a word from a sentence and replace it with another word. If the second word does not have the same number of characters as the first word, you would need to shift the characters in the array to accommodate the second word.

It would be convenient if you could use a single type that allowed you to store a string of any number of characters. Such a type is called a *variable-length string*. The operations available with this type are convenient for processing text, such as inserting one string into another string, extracting a substring from a string, and searching for a pattern in a string.

Most Pascal compilers provide a nonstandard variable-length string type with its associated operations. Unfortunately, each compiler has a different set of operations called by identifiers different from those of all other compilers. If you use this nonstandard feature in your compiler, your program will not be portable. If your program must be portable, then you can define your own variable-length string ADT in standard Pascal.

The String Abstract Data Type

As with the abstract data types discussed previously, a string ADT has two associated types:

```
ValueType
StringType
```

For most applications, `ValueType` will be `char`. That is, a string will be a string of characters. However, strings of other objects are possible simply by redefining

ValueType. For example, you may want to process strings of bits, in which case you could define ValueType as 0..1.

The operations that follow are typical for string ADTs. A description of each follows the code fragment. The fact that you can understand what each operation does without knowing how StringType is implemented shows the usefulness of abstract data types. The programmer who uses these functions and procedures as tools to solve a higher-level problem need not worry about the lower-level details of the StringType definition.

```
procedure Initialize (var S: StringType)
procedure GetString (var F: text; var S: StringType)
procedure PutString (var F: text; S: StringType)
function Length (S: StringType): integer
procedure Insert (var S:    StringType;
                      InS: StringType;
                      Pos: integer)
procedure Delete (var S:    StringType;
                      Pos: integer;
                      Len: integer)
procedure Substring (var Sub: StringType;
                      S:    StringType;
                      Pos: integer;
                      Len: integer)
function Match (Pat, S: StringType): integer
function GreaterThan (S1, S2: StringType): boolean
function Equal (S1, S2: StringType): boolean
function LessThan (S1, S2: StringType): boolean
```

The string ADT

Initialize initializes S to the empty string, whose length is zero. The procedure is useful in string-processing applications where you may construct a string from many other strings and you need to start the processing with an empty string.

Two procedures that provide input and output for variable-length strings are GetString and PutString respectively. Each is general purpose in that GetString's input can come from the keyboard or any text file and PutString's output can go to the screen or any text file. To get the input from the keyboard, simply pass input for the first parameter, F, in GetString. To send the output to the screen, simply pass output for the first parameter in PutString.

Procedures GetString and PutString

This GetString is not the same as the one in Program 7.7, which was for fixed-length packed arrays of characters. That procedure padded the value with trailing spaces after the user pressed <return>. This procedure maintains the length of the string so that, for example, if the user enters three characters followed by <return>, S will get a string of three characters with no padding necessary.

Example 11.2 If String has type StringType and the following code fragment executes:

```
write ('Enter your name: ');
GetString (input, Name);
write ('Hi ');
PutString (output, Name);
write ('.  How are you?')
```

the interactive I/O will be

```
Enter your name: Tom Smith
Hi Tom Smith.  How are you?
```

Since GetString and PutString are programmer defined, you do not have the option of omitting input or output in the actual parameter list, as you do with the read and write statements. ∎

Two variables, both with type StringType, can have two string values with different numbers of characters in each. Hence, each string value has its own length, which procedure GetString determines and function Length returns.

Function Length

Example 11.3 If Name has the same value as in Example 11.2, the statement

```
write ('Length = ', Length (Name): 1)
```

produces the output

```
Length = 9
```

because there are nine characters in Name. Notice that the embedded space counts as a character in the length. ∎

Insert inserts the string InS into string S at position Pos. If Pos is 0, InS is inserted before the first character of S. If Pos is Length (S), InS is inserted after the last character of S. If Pos is greater than Length (S) or less than 0, InS is not inserted at all.

Procedure Insert

Example 11.4 If Name has the same value as in Example 11.2 and Title has StringType with value 'Mr. ', then

```
Insert (Name, Title, 0)
```

will change Name to 'Mr. Tom Smith' and Length (Name) to 13. ∎

Example 11.5 If Name has the same value as in Example 11.2 and Middle has StringType with value 'Henry ', then

```
Insert (Name, Middle, 4)
```

will change Name to 'Tom Henry Smith' and Length (Name) to 15. ∎

Example 11.6 If Name has the same value as in Example 11.2 and Suffix has StringType with value ', Jr.', then

```
Insert (Name, Suffix, 9)
```

will change Name to 'Tom Smith, Jr.' and Length (Name) to 14. The procedure call

```
Insert (Name, Suffix, Length (Name))
```

has the same effect. ∎

Example 11.7 If Name and Suffix have the same values as in the previous example, then

```
Insert (Name, Suffix, 10)
```

will do nothing to Name, since 10 is greater than Length (Name). ∎

Delete deletes Len characters from string S starting at position Pos. If Pos is 1, the first Len characters are deleted. If Pos is greater than Length (S) or less than 1, nothing is deleted regardless of the value of Len. If Len is negative, the previous –Len characters starting at position Pos are deleted. If Len is so large that the procedure call would request deletion after the last character in S, the characters from Pos up to and including the last character in S are deleted.

Procedure Delete

Example 11.8 If Sentence has StringType with value 'now is not the time', which has length 19, the procedure call

```
Delete (Sentence, 8, 4)
```

will change the string to 'now is the time' with a new length of 15. The same value would be produced with the call

```
Delete (Sentence, 11, -4)
```

which deletes the previous four characters starting with the space after 'not'. ∎

Example 11.9 If Sentence has the same value as in Example 11.8, the procedure call

```
Delete (Sentence, 11, 100)
```

will change the string to 'now is not' with a new length of 10. By the same token, the procedure call

```
Delete (Sentence, 11, -100)
```

will change the string to 'the time' with a new length of 8. In both these cases, the magnitude of Len was so great as to specify deletion of characters beyond the end of Sentence. Such a call is legal and produces well-defined results. ∎

`Substring` extracts a partial string of length `Len` from `S` starting at position `Pos` and copies it into `Sub`. In general, the specifications for `Pos` and `Len` are the same as in procedure `Delete`. If `Pos` is greater than `Length (S)` or less than 1, `Sub` gets the empty string regardless of the value of `Len`. If `Len` is negative, the previous −`Len` characters starting at position `Pos` are extracted and the characters of `Sub` are in reverse order from the corresponding characters in `S`. If `Len` is so large that the procedure call would request extraction after the last character in `S`, the characters from `Pos` up to and including the last character in `S` are extracted.

Example 11.10 If `Sentence` has the same value as in Example 11.8 and `Word` has type `StringType`, the procedure call

```
Substring (Word, Sentence, 8, 3)
```

gives the value 'not' with length 3 to `Word`, and the call

```
Substring (Word, Sentence, 19, -4)
```

gives the value 'emit', which is 'time' spelled backwards, to `Word`. ∎

Example 11.11 If `Sentence` has the same value as in Example 11.8 and `Ending` has type `StringType`, the procedure call

```
Substring (Ending, Sentence, 12, 100)
```

gives the value 'the time' with length 8 to `Ending`. ∎

`Match` is a pattern-matching function that returns the position of the first occurrence of `Pat` in `S`. The value returned is the position of the first character in `S` of the substring that matches. If `Pat` does not occur in `S`, `Match` returns 0. If the length of `Pat` is greater than the length of `S` a match cannot occur, and `Match` will return 0. If `Pat` is the empty string, it matches `S` at position one regardless of the value of `S`.

Example 11.12 If `String` has type `StringType` with value 'This is a string of characters.' and `Pattern` has type `StringType` with value 'is', the statement

```
write ('Match = ', Match (Pattern, String): 1)
```

outputs

```
Match = 3
```

because the pattern matches 'is' in 'This'. If `Pattern` has value ' is' `Match` will return 5, the position of the space before 'is' in `String`. ∎

Since `StringType` is not a primitive Pascal type, you cannot compare values for alphabetical order as you can with packed arrays of characters. The three relational functions `GreaterThan`, `Equal`, and `LessThan` provide that capability. The empty string is less than all other strings.

Example 11.13 If `Word1`, `Word2`, and `Temp` have type `StringType`, the code fragment

```
if GreaterThan (Word1, Word2) then
   begin
   Temp := Word1;
   Word1 := Word2;
   Word2 := Temp
   end
```

puts `Word1` and `Word2` in alphabetical order. Compare this code fragment with Program 7.7, which does the same processing with packed arrays of characters. ∎

▭ **Program 11.1**

Several implementations are possible for variable-length strings. One common data structure uses a large array of characters with a special nonprintable character, usually `chr (0)`, as a sentinel. `GetString` appends the sentinel instead of padding with spaces, and `PutString` outputs individual characters from the beginning of the array until it detects the sentinel. Character values past the sentinel value in the array are unused.

Another sentinel technique is to store a variable-length string as a singly linked list with `nil` as the sentinel `Link` value. `GetString` allocates one node per character linking the nodes in the list, and `PutString` prints the list by advancing a local pointer variable down the list.

Program 11.1 shows another alternative. `StringType` is a record with two fields—`Len`, an integer that stores the length of the string, and `Str`, an array of characters that stores the string itself. Figure 11.1 shows the data structure for this implementation with a `StrMax` value of 12.

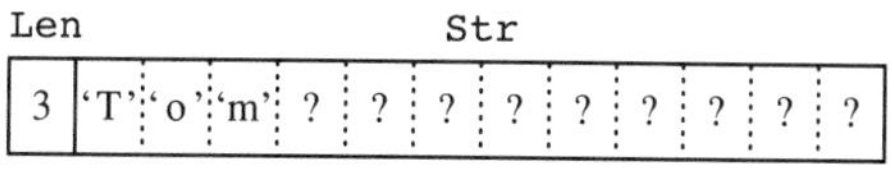

Figure 11.1

The data structure for `StringType` in Program 11.1.

The program implements procedures `GetString` and `PutString` and function `Match`. It asks the user to enter a string and then a pattern, then calls `Match` to see if the string contains the pattern.

`Match` uses two local variables, `I` and `J`, as indexes of the `Str` fields of `S` and `Pat`. `Start` is a local variable that stores the starting position in `S` of the substring to be tested for a match with `Pat`. Figure 11.2 shows a trace of `Match` when `Pat` has the value 'abc' and `S` has the value 'ababcd'.

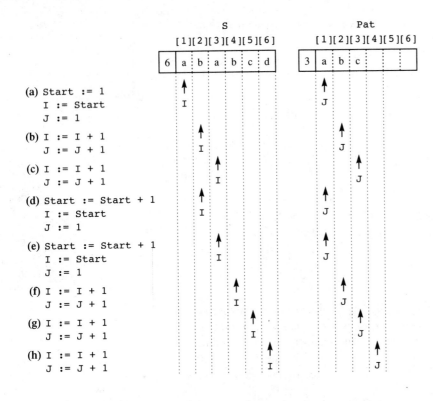

Figure 11.2

A trace of function `Match` when `Pat` is 'abc' and S is 'ababcd'.

The function initializes `Start`, `I`, and `J` to 1, as Figure 11.2(a) shows. Since the first 'a' in `Pat` equals the first 'a' in S, the function increments `I` and `J` by 1. Since the second character, 'b', in `Pat` equals the second character, 'b', in S, Figure 11.2(c) shows the indexes incremented by 1 again.

```
program StringTest (input, output);
   const
      StrMax = 80;
   type
      ValueType  = char;
      StringType =
         record
         Len: integer;
         Str: array [1..StrMax] of ValueType
         end;
   var
      String:  StringType;
      Pattern: StringType;
```

Program 11.1

An implementation of the string ADT.

```
function Match (Pat, S: StringType): integer;
   var
      Start: integer;
      I, J:  integer;
   begin
   Start := 1;
   I := Start;
   J := 1;
   while (I <= S.Len) and (J <= Pat.Len) do
      if S.Str [I] = Pat.Str [J] then  {  continue testing  }
         begin
         I := I + 1;
         J := J + 1
         end
      else                             {  start over  }
         begin
         Start := Start + 1;
         I := Start;
         J := 1
         end;
   if J > Pat.Len then  {  pattern found  }
      Match := Start
   else                 {  pattern not found  }
      Match := 0
   end;

procedure GetString (var F: text; var S: StringType);
   var
      I: integer;
   begin
   I := 1;
   while (I < StrMax) and (not eoln (F)) do
      begin
      read (F, S.Str [I]);
      I := I + 1
      end;
   S.Len := I - 1;
   readln (F)
   end;

procedure PutString (var F: text; S: StringType);
   var
      I: integer;
   begin
   for I := 1 to S.Len do
      write (F, S.Str [I])
   end;
```

Program 11.1, continued

```
begin
write ('Enter a string: ');
GetString (input, String);
write ('Enter a pattern: ');
GetString (input, Pattern);
write ('The pattern ''');
PutString (output, Pattern);
write (''' occurs at position ', Match (Pattern, String): 1)
end.
```

Program 11.1, continued

Interactive Input/Output

```
Enter a string: This is a string of characters.
Enter a pattern: is
The pattern 'is' occurs at position 3
```

Now the third character in `Pat` is 'c' and the third character in `S` is 'a'. Had the third character in `S` also been 'c', the function would have discovered the pattern at the beginning of `Str`. Since the pattern does not begin at the first character of `Str`, the algorithm must look for the pattern beginning at the second character of `Str`. The assignment

```
Start := Start + 1;
I := Start
```

backs up `I` to point to the second character of `S`. Figure 11.2(d) shows the effect of the updates on `I` and `J`.

The next comparison is with the first character of `Pat` and the second character of `S`. Since 'a' does not equal 'b', the same update as in the previous loop execution occurs, as Figure 11.2(e) shows. `I` gets 3, and the algorithm tries to match the pattern beginning at the third character of `S`.

Figures 11.2(f–h) are a result of the characters in `Pat`, beginning with the first, matching with the characters in `S`, beginning with the third. The algorithm increments `J` to 4, even though there are only three characters in `Pat`. However, it never tries to access the fourth character of `Pat`. Since the boolean expression

```
J > Pat.Len
```

is true, the function returns the value of `Start`, which is 3.

The loop will terminate under two conditions. Either `I` will be greater than `S.Len`, or `J` will be greater than `Pat.Len`. If `J` is greater than `Pat.Len`, the algorithm finds a match. Otherwise, the loop terminates because `I` is greater than `S.Len`. In that case, the algorithm runs out of characters in `S` before finding a match, and it returns 0.

Implementation of the string ADT operations not included in Program 11.1 is left to the problems at the end of the chapter.

String Processing with Files

`GetString` and `PutString` can perform I/O with files. To use `GetString` this way, the main program opens the file with `reset` and passes the opened file to the procedure. One call to `GetString` gives an entire line of characters from the file to `S`.

As you recall, in the basic Pascal character-processing algorithm (see Section 7.2), the outer loop tests `eof (SomeFile)` and executes once for each line in the file. The inner loop tests `eoln (SomeFile)` and executes once for each character.

Notice in Program 11.1 that `GetString` contains a `while` loop with an `eoln` test, followed by a `readln` statement outside the loop. The inner loop of the character-processing algorithm has the same structure. This similarity of `GetString` to the inner loop of the character-processing algorithm suggests that you can perform line processing from a file by placing `GetString` in the body of a `while` loop controlled by an `eof` test.

The following is the general string ADT line-processing algorithm, which corresponds to the character-processing algorithm. `Line` is a variable of type `StringType`, and `SomeFile` is a text file.

```
reset (SomeFile)
while not eof (SomeFile) do
   begin
   GetString (SomeFile, Line)
   Perform line processing.
   end
```

The general string ADT line-processing algorithm

The algorithm treats the file as a file of lines rather than a file of characters. Each time the loop executes, `Line` gets the next line in the file. You can use any of the string ADT operations with `Line` to perform the line processing. If `SomeFile` contains any empty lines, the corresponding `Line` will be the empty string with a length of zero.

An example of the string ADT line-processing algorithm is the following code, which echoes the contents of a file onto the screen. The line processing consists of simply calling `PutString` to send the line to the screen, followed by a `writeln` call.

```
reset (SomeFile);
while not eof (SomeFile) do
   begin
   GetString (SomeFile, Line);
   PutString (output, Line);
   writeln (output)
   end
```

An algorithm to echo a text file onto the screen

Missing Features

Although the variable-length string operations make string processing convenient for the programmer, they are missing some nice features that fixed-length strings have. One conspicuous disadvantage is the absence of variable-length string constants.

For example, if `Word` has type `StringType`, you cannot make the assignment

```
Word := 'Goodbye'
```

as you can in Program 7.6 where `Word` is a packed array of seven characters. You might try to implement the assignment with a procedure that you would call, such as

```
AssignStr (Word, 'Goodbye')
```

but the formal parameter that corresponds to 'Goodbye' would have to be a packed array of seven characters. In Pascal, there is no way that you can pass a string constant as a parameter unless the formal parameter is a packed array of characters that exactly matches the size of the actual parameter.

 Queues

A *queue* is also called a *first in, first out* (FIFO) list. It is similar to a stack in that it stores values in a list in the order it receives them, but different in that data is retrieved from the opposite end of the list. The two operations on a queue are *add* and *delete*, which correspond to push and pop for a stack. Sometimes, add is called *enqueue*, and delete is called *dequeue*.

The first in, first out nature of a queue

You can visualize a queue as a line of people at a ticket window. When another person comes to buy a ticket, she goes to the back of the line, corresponding to the add operation. When the clerk at the window can serve another person, he helps the person from the front of the line, corresponding to the delete operation. The first person to enter the queue is the first one to be served.

Figure 11.3 shows a sequence of operations on a queue in abstract form. It corresponds to the sequence in Figure 9.1 for a stack, but `Push` is replaced by `Add` and `Pop` is replaced by `Delete`.

In Figure 11.3, values 5.0, 2.0, and 4.0 are added to the queue. The first delete operation gives the value of 5.0 to *x*. Contrast this with the first pop operation in Figure 9.1, which gave 4.0 to *x*. In Figure 11.3 since 5.0 was the first value in, it is the first value out.

From an abstract point of view, a queue ADT has two types:

```
ValueType
QueueType
```

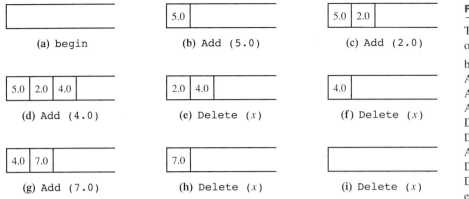

Figure 11.3

The sequence of the following operations on a queue:

begin
Add (5.0)
Add (2.0)
Add (4.0)
Delete (*x*)
Delete (*x*)
Add (7.0)
Delete (*x*)
Delete (*x*)
end

`ValueType` is the type of each element stored in the queue and is `real` in Figure 11.3. `QueueType` is the type of the queue itself. The operations on an abstract queue are as follows:

```
procedure Initialize (var Q: QueueType)
function Empty (Q: QueueType): boolean
procedure AddQ (Y: ValueType; var Q: QueueType)
procedure DeleteQ (var Y: ValueType; var Q: QueueType)
```

The queue ADT

`Initialize` initializes a queue to the empty queue. `Empty` is a function that returns true if Q is empty and false otherwise. `AddQ` adds an element, `Y`, to the rear of Q, and `DeleteQ` removes an element from the front of the queue and gives it to `Y`. `AddQ` and `DeleteQ` provide the first in, first out nature of the queue accesses.

Implementing Queues

Given the behavior of the abstract queue, how can you implement the operations in Pascal? A straightforward approach is to use an array as with the implementation of the stack in Program 9.2. For the stack, you need an integer variable, `Top`, that contains the index of the top of the stack. For the queue, you could have an integer variable, `Rear`, that contains the rear of the queue. Figure 11.4 shows an array with 10 elements that implements the queue ADT using this approach.

The elements in the array are indexed from 1 to 10. Figure 11.4(a) shows the contents of the array after three elements have been added. Adding an element to the queue is like pushing an element onto a stack. You increment `Rear` by 1 and use that value as the index of the array to store the element.

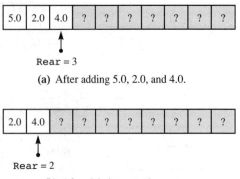

(a) After adding 5.0, 2.0, and 4.0.

(b) After deleting one element.

Figure 11.4

Implementation of a queue as an array with a fixed front. The shaded area is the unused portion of the array.

To delete an element, however, requires more work. If the front of the queue is fixed at index one of the array, then you must shift all the elements to the left when you delete an element. Figure 11.4(b) shows that elements 2.0 and 4.0 must be shifted to the left when 5.0 is deleted from the queue. If the queue has many elements, then many shifts will be required. The operation could be especially slow if `ValueType` is a large record.

To keep from shifting the elements during the delete operation, you could let the front of the queue float rather than remain fixed at index one. You could maintain a second integer variable called `Front` that stores the index of the array element just before the item in the front of the queue. Figure 11.5 depicts this implementation.

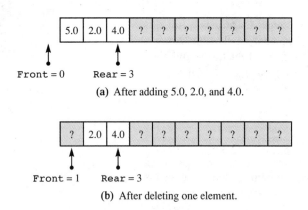

(a) After adding 5.0, 2.0, and 4.0.

(b) After deleting one element.

Figure 11.5

Implementation of a queue as an array with a floating front.

`Front` and `Rear` are each initialized to 0. You add an element as before, by incrementing `Rear` and using it as the index of the array to store the element. Figure 11.5(a) shows the array after adding 5.0, 2.0, and 4.0. To delete an element you simply increment `Front` by 1 and use it as the index to retrieve the element. Figure 11.5(b) shows the deletion of 5.0 from the front of the queue without shifting the 2.0 and 4.0. After the retrieval, the location to which `Front` points is considered garbage.

You can see from the figure that the occupied region of the array will gradually migrate to the right as elements are added and deleted. Eventually `Rear` will point to the rightmost location of the array, leaving the leftmost portion unoccupied. Then some provision must be made if another element is to be added, since there is room in the leftmost portion of the array.

One technique would be to shift the elements all the way to the left part of the array with `Front` equal to 0 and `Rear` equal to the number of elements currently stored. This approach is explored in the problems at the end of the chapter. It has an advantage over the implementation with the fixed front because it does not require nearly as many shifts. You only need to shift when `Rear` reaches the right end, and that shift can be done with a single loop.

Program 11.2

Although the implementation described previously is an improvement over the first one, we can do even better. Figure 11.6 shows an implementation of the queue that never requires shifting.

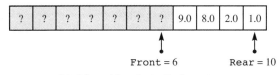

(a) After adding the tenth element.

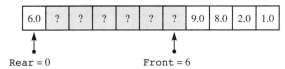

(b) After adding another element.

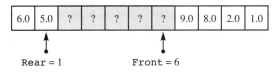

(c) After adding yet another element.

Figure 11.6

Implementation of a queue as a circular array.

Rather than index the array starting at 1, the array is indexed starting at 0. The figure shows an array with index type `0..10` rather than the `1..10` type in the previous figures. Figure 11.6(a) illustrates the elements of the queue when `Front` is 6 and `Rear` has reached the right end of the array with a value of 10.

To add an element, `Rear` is incremented by 1 modulo 11. In Figure 11.6(b), since 10 plus 1 is 11, and 11 modulo 11 is 0, `Rear` gets 0. So the 6.0 is stored at location 0. If 5.0 is subsequently added to the queue as shown in Figure 11.6(c), `Rear` gets 1 modulo 11, which is simply 1.

To delete an element, `Front` is also incremented by 1 modulo 11. As elements are deleted from the queue, `Front` will eventually get 10 and point to the right end of the array. Since `Front` is incremented modulo 11, its next value will be 0.

`Front` continually chases `Rear` with the occupied region of the array being that part to the right of `Front` and to the left of `Rear`. When either index gets to the end of the array, it wraps around to the beginning. Since you can visualize the end of the array connected to its beginning with this wrap-around feature, the array is often called a *circular array*.

Program 11.2 shows an implementation of the queue ADT as a circular array. The listing is not a complete program but was tested with a main program driver not shown.

`QueueMax` is a constant that sets the size of the array. `QueueType` is like `StackType` of Program 9.2 except that it has two index variables, `Front` and `Rear`, instead of one. `Body` is the array itself.

`Initialize` initializes the queue by setting `Front` and `Rear` both to 0. `Empty` detects an empty queue by testing whether `Front` equals `Rear`. You can imagine in Figure 11.6(a) that if the four elements are deleted, `Front` will increase from 6 to 10 and will equal `Rear`. Also, since `Front` equals `Rear` after initialization, the queue is initialized to the empty queue.

Before `AddQ` can add an item to the queue, it must test whether a location is available. For example, Figure 11.7 comes from Figure 11.6(c) by adding four more elements to the queue. It would appear that one more location is available for storage, namely `Body [6]`. However, if one more element is added to the array, `Rear` will increase by 1 and will be equal to `Front`. That is precisely the condition that `Empty` checks for when testing for an empty queue. This implementation requires that at least one vacant location in the array be unused so we can distinguish between an empty queue and a full queue.

Figure 11.7

A full queue in a circular array implementation.

`AddQ` therefore tests if a location is not available by

```
Q.Front = (Q.Rear + 1) mod (QueueMax + 1)
```

In Figure 11.7 this condition is true, because `Front` is 6 and `Rear` is 5. If the condition is false, `AddQ` increments `Rear` and installs the element.

`DeleteQ` tests whether the queue is empty before it attempts to delete the element. If the queue is not empty, it deletes the element by incrementing `Front` to access the element at the front of the queue.

```
{  data structure Queue                      }
{  Implemented with a circular array.   }

const
   QueueMax = 10;
type
   ValueType = integer;
   QueueType =
      record
      Front: integer;
      Rear:  integer;
      Body:  array [0..QueueMax] of ValueType
      end;

procedure Initialize (var Q: QueueType);
   begin
   Q.Front := 0;
   Q.Rear := 0
   end;

function Empty (Q: QueueType): boolean;
   begin
   Empty := (Q.Front = Q.Rear)
   end;

procedure AddQ (Y: ValueType; var Q: QueueType);
   begin
   if Q.Front = (Q.Rear + 1) mod (QueueMax + 1) then
      writeln ('Error--queue overflow')
   else
      begin
      Q.Rear := (Q.Rear + 1) mod (QueueMax + 1);
      Q.Body [Q.Rear] := Y
      end
   end;

procedure DeleteQ (var Y: ValueType; var Q: QueueType);
   begin
   if Q.Front = Q.Rear then
      writeln ('Error--queue underflow')
   else
      begin
      Q.Front := (Q.Front + 1) mod (QueueMax + 1);
      Y := Q.Body [Q.Front]
      end
   end;
```

Program 11.2

An implementation of the queue ADT with a circular array. The listing is not a complete Pascal program.

Program 11.3

An array is by no means the only way to implement the queue ADT. Program 11.3 implements it with a linked list. As before, this is not a complete Pascal program, but only the data structure part of a program.

```
{  data structure Queue              }
{  Implemented with a linked list.   }

type
   ValueType      = integer;
   PtrToCellType = ^CellType;
   QueueType =
      record
      Front: PtrToCellType;
      Rear:  PtrToCellType
      end;
   CellType =
      record
      Value: ValueType;
      Link:  PtrToCellType
      end;

procedure Initialize (var Q: QueueType);
   begin
   Q.Front := nil
   end;

function Empty (Q: QueueType): boolean;
   begin
   Empty := (Q.Front = nil)
   end;

procedure AddQ (Y: ValueType; var Q: QueueType);
   var
      P: PtrToCellType;
   begin
   new (P);
   P^.Value := Y;
   P^.Link := nil;
   if Q.Front = nil then  {  The queue was empty  }
      Q.Front := P
   else                   {  The queue was not empty  }
      Q.Rear^.Link := P;
   Q.Rear := P
   end;
```

Program 11.3

An implementation of the queue ADT with a linked list. The listing is not a complete Pascal program.

```
procedure DeleteQ (var Y: ValueType; var Q: QueueType);
   var
       P: PtrToCellType;
   begin
   if Q.Front = nil then
      writeln ('Error--queue underflow')
   else
      begin
      P := Q.Front;
      Y := P^.Value;
      Q.Front := P^.Link;
      dispose (P)
      end
   end;
```

Program 11.3, continued

The body of the queue is a linked list of records, each of which has a `Value` field and a `Link` field. The `Value` field stores the element in the queue, and the `Link` field points to the next node in the list. Figure 11.8 shows the data structure of the queue with four elements in it and corresponds to Figure 11.6(a) with the circular queue.

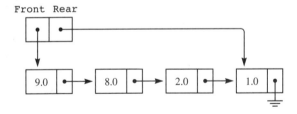

Figure 11.8

Implementing a queue ADT with a linked list data structure.

You could use a data structure identical to that of the stack, as in Figure 10.13, with `QueueType` a single pointer that points to the front of the queue. Deleting an element from the queue would be simple, since you would have direct access to the front node. But performing the add operation would require a local pointer variable to advance down the list to reach the node at the rear. The processing to do that would take time, $O(n)$, where n is the number of elements in the queue.

Making `QueueType` a record that contains pointers to both the front and rear of the queue decreases the processing time for the add operation to $O(1)$. This is another example of the fundamental space/time tradeoff in computer science. The extra storage—that is, more space—for pointer `Rear` in the data structure permits the operation to be executed faster—that is, less time. Storage space is being traded for speed.

The space/time tradeoff

`Initialize` gives `Front` the value `nil` and leaves `Rear` undefined. Since `Empty` returns true if `Front` is `nil`, the queue is initialized to the empty queue.

Issues of intelligence and cognition are extremely complex, and the study of artificial intelligence (AI) has several specialized branches. One branch is the development of expert systems. What is an expert system? Roughly, it is a computerized knowledge base and dialogue system that performs much like a human expert in a specialized field. AI has not been able to equal human intelligence, nor will it be able to anytime soon. But in sufficiently specialized areas, there are expert systems that can help to diagnose diseases, repair sophisticated equipment, invest stock portfolios, or configure complex computer systems.

The reasons for building expert systems are quite simple. It takes many years of training and experience for people to become experts, so they are very valuable. And when the human experts retire or die, their knowledge retires or dies with them. But an expert system, if properly constructed, represents a legacy of knowledge that can outlive its creators. Also, since most of us can't afford to keep a staff of specialized doctors for consultation or have Wall Street advisors attend to our daily banking needs, it would be desirable to have computer programs that simulate the behavior of such specialists.

In order to construct an expert system, a programmer has to have access to one or more experts willing to participate in the project. By interviewing the human expert on successive occasions, watching her at work, and encouraging her to review emerging prototypes of the expert system, the programmer comes up with an explicit description of the decision patterns being followed. But one difficulty in designing an expert system is to get the human expert to make explicit the rules she follows. Human experts often rely on intuitive patterns and experience-driven hunches, not just on formal rules. This makes it difficult to instruct the computer on how to mimic an expert's behavior.

Typically, expert knowledge is captured in the form of antecedent-consequent relations, or if-then rules. A stylized rule in the rule base for a nuclear reactor control system might read: `If core-temperature-rising and safety-threshold-temperature-exceeded then insert-all-control-rods-and-shut-down-reactor`. Of course, rule bases may contain hundreds or thousands of complex rules, and the behavior of the expert system as a whole depends on the dynamic cascading, or triggering, of rules at the time the system is actually used. Understanding and predicting the interactions of the different rules is one of the most difficult aspects of designing and debugging an expert system.

Two classic examples of a successful expert system are the Mycin and Xcon programs, which have taken years of development effort and are still in use today. Mycin is a medical diagnostic system developed at Stanford University. Intended for use as a physician's assistant and a desk reference, Mycin takes a patient's history, deduces likely diagnoses, and recommends treatments for infections of the blood. Mycin works in a *backward chaining* mode, starting from likely conclusions and working backward in an attempt to sustain the conclusions with supporting evidence.

Xcon, developed and used by Digital Equipment Corporation, is a *forward chaining* expert system. It accepts a customer's specifications for a minicomputer in terms of required disk access speeds, number of computer terminals desired, quality of printers to be attached, and so forth, then culls through the inventory of parts and engineering specifications to custom-configure a VAX computer. The primitive specifications trigger the firing of rules that sort out the hardware compatibilities and restrictions among the diverse components in the VAX family of hardware primitives; it works forward toward the conclusion—a complete specification, including wiring diagrams, of the computer to be constructed.

The construction of a successful expert system is a huge undertaking, usually requiring many years of work. But it takes more than just time and effort to achieve a successful system. For the time being, the field of application must be sufficiently regular and well-understood so that the human experts consulted can make their thought processes explicit enough to be encoded into rules for a computer to follow. Vaguely characterizable fields—where the human expert relies in part on intuition and hunches—will not yield useful expert systems, no matter how much effort is invested.

AddQ allocates a new node from the heap to store the value to be added to the queue. It sets the `Link` part of the newly allocated node to `nil`. If the queue was empty before the call to AddQ, the new node is at both the front and the rear of the queue, and AddQ sets both `Front` and `Rear` to point to the new node. If the queue was not empty, AddQ would link the new node to the rear with

```
Q.Rear^.Link := P
```

and would set `Rear` to point to the new node. Unlike the circular queue implementation of AddQ, this implementation assumes there will always be enough storage in the heap to allocate a new node and, therefore, does not check for a possible queue overflow.

DeleteQ checks whether the queue is empty before attempting to delete an element from the front. If the queue is not empty it sets `P` to point to the first node and advances `Front` to point to the second node with the statement

```
Q.Front := P^.Link;
```

It then returns the old front node to the heap with `dispose`.

You may have wondered why the `Link` field of the newly allocated node in AddQ was set to `nil`. Since the link field is changed anyway when another node is added to the rear, it may appear that initializing it to `nil` is unnecessary. Furthermore, the `nil` value is not used as a sentinel for an advancing pointer, since `Rear` will always point to the rear of the queue and an advancing pointer is never necessary.

Every time a node is deleted from the front, `Front` changes to point to the next node. To see why the `Link` field is initialized to `nil`, consider what happens when only one node is in the queue and DeleteQ is called. Figure 11.9 shows the details.

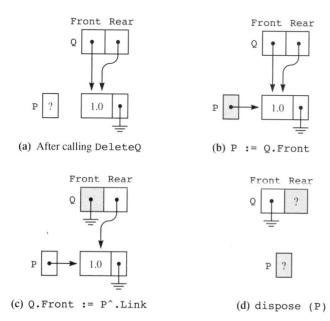

(a) After calling DeleteQ

(b) P := Q.Front

(c) Q.Front := P^.Link

(d) dispose (P)

Figure 11.9

Calling DeleteQ with a one-element queue.

In Figure 11.9(a), `DeleteQ` has been called and `P` has been allocated. There is only one node in the queue and, because of the initialization of the `Link` field in `AddQ`, its `Link` value is `nil`. In Figure 11.9(b), `P` points to the same thing that `Q.Front` points to. In (c), `Q.Front` points to the same thing that `P^.Link` points to. But `P^.Link` is `nil` because of the initialization, so `Q.Front` gets `nil` also. In (d), the node is deallocated, the queue is empty, and `Front` is `nil`, which is what it should be for an empty queue. The `Link` field is initialized in `AddQ` because of the test for the empty queue in `DeleteQ`.

11.3   Graphs

Figure 11.10(a) shows a section of the river Pregel and its bridges in 1736 in the town of Königsberg, Prussia. There was a fork in the river just past an island, which divided the land into four regions. Seven bridges crossed the river to connect the regions. The people of Königsberg wondered if it was possible, starting at any land region, to walk across each bridge just once and return to the same spot.

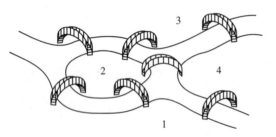

(a) The river Pregel and bridges in Königsberg.

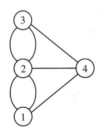

(b) Euler's multigraph representation.

Figure 11.10

The abstract representation of a physical system.

Although no one was able to devise such a path, no one knew if the path was impossible. A famous Swiss mathematician, Leonhard Euler (1707–1783), was able to prove that such a path was impossible. The key to his solution of the Königsberg bridge problem was to construct an abstract representation of the geography in the form of a *multigraph* shown in Figure 11.10(b). Each land region is represented as a numbered *vertex*, and each bridge is represented as an *edge* that connects two vertices.

The *degree* of a vertex is defined as the number of edges that connect the vertex with other vertices. For example, vertex 1 has degree 3 and vertex 2 has degree 5. Although we will not show it here, Euler was able to prove that such a path is possible if and only if the degree of every vertex in the multigraph is even.

Definition of degree

Euler's solution to the classical Königsberg bridge problem is the earliest known use of the graph abstract data type. Since then, graphs have been used to represent many diverse physical situations, including airline routes, circuit boards and the management of construction projects. In computer science, graphs are used to model computer system resources and computer networks.

A *graph* differs from a multigraph by restricting the number of edges between any two vertices to be at most one. Figure 11.10(b) is not a graph because it has two edges between vertices 1 and 2 and two edges between vertices 2 and 3. In a graph, two vertices are *adjacent* if an edge connects them.

Definition of adjacent vertices

Example 11.14 Figure 11.11(a) is a graph with 7 vertices and 10 edges. Vertex 1 has degree 3, and vertex 2 has degree 4. No pair of vertices is connected by more than one edge. ∎

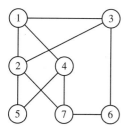
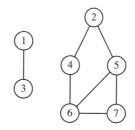

(a) A connected graph.

(b) An unconnected graph with two connected components.

Figure 11.11

Two abstract graphs.

Example 11.15 In Figure 11.11(a), vertex 7 is adjacent to vertex 2 because an edge connects those vertices. Vertex 3 is not adjacent to vertex 4, however, because there is no edge between those two vertices. ∎

A graph may be connected or unconnected. A connected graph is one that has a path from any vertex to any other vertex. An unconnected graph has at least one pair of vertices that are not connected by any path.

Connected and unconnected graphs

Example 11.16 Figure 11.11(a) is connected because any vertex can be reached from any other vertex. For example, you can reach vertex 5 from vertex 6 by the path

 6 7 4 5

and vertex 4 from vertex 1 by the path

 1 4

On the other hand, Figure 11.11(b) is not connected. Although you can get to vertex 2 from vertex 7 by the path

 7 6 4 2

there is at least one pair of vertices, for example 4 and 1, that have no connecting path. ∎

Abstract Graph Traversals

Remember that binary trees have three traversals—preorder, inorder, and post-order—that specify the order in which the nodes of the tree are visited. Graphs have two traversals called the *breadth-first search* and *depth-first search* that visit the vertices of the graph. Unlike binary tree traversals, the graph traversals are not unique. That is, a given graph may have more than one breadth-first search and more than one depth-first search. Figure 11.12 shows a connected graph that we will use to illustrate graph traversals.

A graph traversal can start at any vertex. Suppose you start a breadth-first search at vertex 2. Vertex 2 would be the first vertex visited as shown in Figure 11.13(a). All unvisited vertices adjacent to vertex 2 are visited next. In Figure 11.13(b), they are vertices 4, 1, and 5. The unvisited vertices adjacent to those vertices are visited next. Figure 11.13(c) shows that the unvisited vertices adjacent to 4, 1, and 5 are vertices 6, 3, 9, and 8. Each vertex in this group can be reached from the starting vertex by traversing two edges.

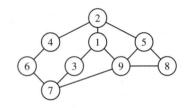

Figure 11.12

An abstract graph to illustrate graph traversals.

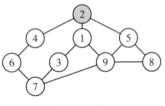

(a) Visit 2.

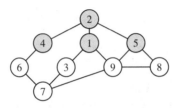

(b) Visit 4, 1, 5.

Figure 11.13

A breadth-first search of the graph of Figure 11.12 starting at vertex 2.

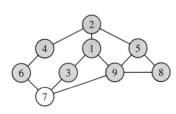

(c) Visit 6, 3, 9, 8.

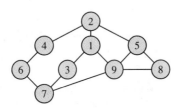

(d) Visit 7.

The process continues until no unvisited vertices are adjacent to the last group visited. Notice in Figure 11.13(d) that vertex 7 is the only vertex visited in the last step. It can be reached from the starting vertex by traversing three edges or more. Even though vertex 8 was visited in the previous step and it is adjacent to vertex 9, vertex 9 is not visited again because it was previously visited.

The order of the visits from this breadth-first search is

2 4 1 5 6 3 9 8 7

The order in which the group of adjacent nodes is visited at each step of the search is arbitrary. For example, the group of nodes 6, 3, 9, and 8 could be visited in any order. Another breadth-first search of the same graph is

   2 4 1 5 3 8 9 6 7

which also starts at vertex 2.

   You should not be misled by the drawing of the graph when you determine the group of adjacent nodes to visit during the next step. In Figure 11.12, suppose you start the breadth-first search from vertex 6. It is not immediately obvious that nodes 1, 5, and 8 are in the same group, but they are.

   Figure 11.14 shows the breadth-first search starting at vertex 6. Vertices 4 and 7 are adjacent to the starting vertex. Vertices 2, 3, and 9 can be reached from the starting vertex by traversing as few as two edges. Since vertices 1 and 5 are adjacent to vertex 2, and 8 is adjacent to 9, vertices 1, 5, and 8 are all in the same group. Each can be reached from the starting vertex by traversing three edges. The corresponding visitation order is

   6 4 7 2 3 9 1 5 8

which, as before, is not unique.

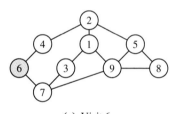

(a) Visit 6.

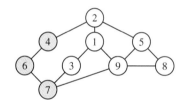

(b) Visit 4, 7.

(c) Visit 2, 3, 9.

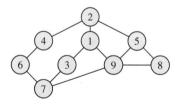

(d) Visit 1, 5, 8.

Figure 11.14

A breadth-first search of the graph of Figure 11.12 starting at vertex 6.

   The depth-first search is defined recursively. First the start vertex, v, is visited. Then any unvisited vertex, say w, adjacent to v is selected, and a depth-first search is started from w. When a vertex is reached that has no unvisited vertices adjacent to it, the process repeatedly backs up to the previously visited vertex until one is found that has an unvisited vertex, say *u,* adjacent to it. A depth-first search is started from vertex *u*. The process continues until no unvisited vertex can be reached from any of the visited vertices.

Figure 11.15 shows a depth-first search starting at vertex 2. In (a), vertex 1 is adjacent to 2, 9 is adjacent to 1, 8 is adjacent to 9, and 5 is adjacent to 8. Now there are no unvisited vertices adjacent to 5.

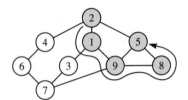

(a) Visit 2, 1, 9, 8, 5.

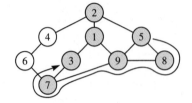

(b) Back up to 9. Visit 7, 3.

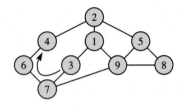

(c) Back up to 7. Visit 6, 4.

Figure 11.15

A depth-first search of the graph of Figure 11.12 starting at vertex 2.

Figure 11.15(b) shows that the process must back up to vertex 8, which has no unvisited vertices adjacent to it. It backs up again to vertex 9, which does have an unvisited vertex, 7, adjacent to it. The depth-first search starting at vertex 7 visits 7 and 3. Figure 11.15(c) shows the process backing up to 7, then visiting 6 and 4 to complete the search.

The visitation order is

   2 1 9 8 5 7 3 6 4

As with the breadth-first search, this order is not unique. The particular unvisited vertex adjacent to the last vertex visited is completely arbitrary. Another depth-first search starting from vertex 2 is

   2 1 3 7 6 4 9 8 5

In this traversal, when you arrive at vertex 4, you back up to 7, then traverse 9, 8, and 5.

Figure 11.16 shows a depth-first search starting from vertex 6. The visitation sequence is

   6 7 9 8 5 2 1 3 4

with one backup required from 3 to 2.

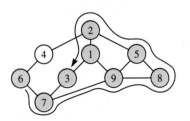

(a) Visit 6, 7, 9, 8, 5, 2, 1, 3.

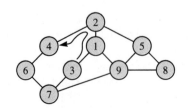

(b) Back up to 2. Visit 4.

Figure 11.16

A depth-first search of the graph of Figure 11.12 starting at vertex 6.

The Graph Abstract Data Type

In practice, the vertices of a graph are often fixed and denoted by integer values, as in the previous examples. Most applications do not store values in the vertices the way they are stored in the nodes of a binary tree or linked list. Instead, the pertinent information is contained in the structure of the graph, that is, in the way the vertices are connected by the edges. Consequently, the graph ADT does not have a `ValueType`. The operations of the graph ADT are as follows:

```
procedure Initialize (var G: GraphType; S: integer)
function SizeG (G: GraphType): integer
procedure AddEdge (var G: GraphType; V1, V2: integer)
procedure RemoveEdge (var G: GraphType; V1, V2: integer)
procedure DepthFirst (G: GraphType; StartV: integer)
procedure BreadthFirst (G: GraphType; StartV: integer)
procedure ConnectedComp (G: GraphType)
```

The graph ADT

`Initialize` initializes graph G to contain S vertices and no edges. S stands for size. `SizeG` returns the number of vertices that G contains. `AddEdge` adds a new edge to graph G that connects vertices V1 and V2. `RemoveEdge` removes an edge from the graph that connects V1 and V2. `DepthFirst` outputs a depth-first sequence of nodes starting from vertex `StartV`, and `BreadthFirst` outputs a breadth-first sequence. `ConnectedComp` outputs the connected components of graph G.

Example 11.17 If G is the graph shown in Figure 11.11(b), the output of `ConnectedComp` might be

```
Connected component:
  1   3
Connected component:
  2   4   5   6   7
```

The order of the vertices listed in each component is immaterial.   ∎

Program 11.4

One data structure for implementing a graph is called an *adjacency list*. It assumes that the vertices are numbered consecutively starting from 1. An array of pointers is maintained, one for each vertex, each of which points to a linked list of the vertices that are adjacent to the given vertex. Figure 11.17 shows the adjacency list representation of the graph in Figure 11.12.

The figure shows two arrays—`Visited`, an array of booleans, and `Body`, an array of pointers. The `Visited` array is for implementing the traversal algorithms, which will be described later. `Body` [1] is a pointer to a linked list whose nodes contain 9, 3, and 2. These values correspond to the fact that vertex 1 in

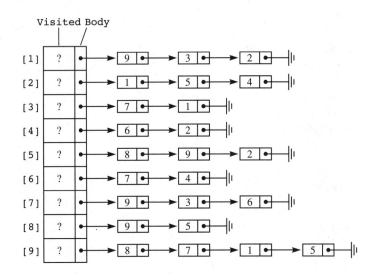

Figure 11.17

The adjacency list for the graph of Figure 11.12.

Figure 11.12 is adjacent to vertices 9, 3, and 2. Body [2] points to a linked list containing 1, 5, and 4, because vertex 2 is adjacent to vertices 1, 5, and 4 in the graph.

Note that the edge between vertices 1 and 2 in Figure 11.12 is represented by nodes in two linked lists in Figure 11.17, namely the node with 2 in the list of Body [1] and the node with 1 in the list of Body [2]. In general, there will be twice as many nodes in the linked lists as there are edges in the abstract graph. Figure 11.12 has 12 edges, while Figure 11.7 has 24 nodes in the linked lists.

Program 11.4 implements the graph ADT with an adjacency list data structure. It inputs the graph from a file using the count technique. The first two values are the number of vertices and edges, and the remaining values are the edges, represented by pairs of vertices that the edges connect.

The program implements Initialize, AddEdge, and DepthFirst. After reading in the graph, it asks the user for the starting vertex of the depth-first search, then prints the visitation sequence. The values in the sample input correspond to the graph of Figure 11.12 and the data structure of Figure 11.17. The visitation sequences correspond to Figures 11.15 and 11.16.

Initialize sets G.Size to the value given to formal parameter S from the main program. Then it sets the first S pointers in the Body array to nil, which signify empty lists corresponding to a graph with no edges.

AddEdge must allocate two nodes for the edge to be added—one in the list for Body [V1] and one in the list for Body [V2]. The order in which the nodes are inserted within each list is immaterial. So, to minimize execution time and code complexity, each node is simply linked to the front of the list. For example, the nodes in the list for Body [1] are 9, 3, and 2 because the corresponding edges appear in the input in the order of 2, 3, and 9 as follows:

··· 2   1 ···   1   3 ···   1   9

Program 11.4

An implementation of the graph
ADT with an adjacency list.

```
program DepthFirstSearch (GraphFile, input, output);
   const
      GraphMax = 20;
   type
      PtrToCellType = ^CellType;
      CellType =
         record
         Vertex: integer;
         Link:    PtrToCellType
         end;
      GraphType =
         record
         Size:     integer;
         Body:     array [1..GraphMax] of PtrToCellType;
         Visited: array [1..GraphMax] of boolean
         end;
   var
      GraphFile:     text;
      Graph:         GraphType;
      NumVerts:      integer;
      NumEdges:      integer;
      Vert1, Vert2: integer;
      StartVertex:  integer;
      I:             integer;

   procedure Initialize (var G: GraphType; S: integer);
      var
         I: integer;
      begin
      G.Size := S;
      for I := 1 to S do
         G.Body [I] := nil
      end;

   procedure AddEdge (var G: GraphType; V1, V2: integer);
      var
         P: PtrToCellType;
      begin
      new (P);
      P^.Vertex := V2;
      P^.Link := G.Body [V1];
      G.Body [V1] := P;
      new (P);
      P^.Vertex := V1;
      P^.Link := G.Body [V2];
      G.Body [V2] := P
      end;
```

Program 11.4, continued

```
procedure DFS (var G: GraphType; V: integer);
   var
      P: PtrToCellType;
   begin
   G.Visited [V] := true;
   write (V: 3);
   P := G.Body [V];
   while P <> nil do
      begin
      if not (G.Visited [P^.Vertex]) then
         DFS (G, P^.Vertex);
      P := P^.Link
      end
   end;

procedure DepthFirst (G: GraphType; StartV: integer);
   var
      I: integer;
   begin
   for I := 1 to G.Size do
      G.Visited [I] := false;
   DFS (G, StartV)
   end;

begin
reset (GraphFile);
read (GraphFile, NumVerts, NumEdges);
Initialize (Graph, NumVerts);
for I := 1 to NumEdges do
   begin
   read (GraphFile, Vert1, Vert2);
   AddEdge (Graph, Vert1, Vert2)
   end;
write ('Enter starting vertex: ');
readln (StartVertex);
write ('Depth first search: ');
DepthFirst (Graph, StartVertex)
end.
```

Input—GraphFile

```
9  12
2 4    2 5    2 1    5 9    4 6    1 3    5 8    1 9
6 7    3 7    9 7    8 9
```

Interactive Input/Output

```
Enter starting vertex: 2
Depth first search:    2  1  9  8  5  7  3  6  4
```

Interactive Input/Output

```
Enter starting vertex: 6
Depth first search:    6  7  9  8  5  2  1  3  4
```

`DepthFirst` implements a depth-first search. Since the search successively visits adjacent vertices until there is no adjacent vertex that has not been visited, the algorithm must mark the vertices as it visits them. The `Visited` array stores the marks as boolean values. If `Visited [I]` is false, then vertex `I` has not yet been visited.

`DepthFirst` uses procedure `DFS`, which stands for *depth-first search*, to perform the actual traversal. `DepthFirst` initializes the `Visited` array to contain a false value for every vertex in the graph, then it calls `DFS`. Figure 11.18 shows the data structure for a small graph after `Visited` is initialized and before the first call to DFS.

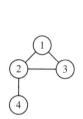

(a) The abstract graph.

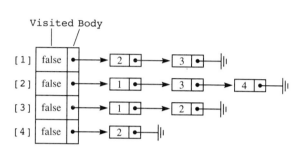

(b) The data structure before the first call to DFS .

Figure 11.18

The call to `DepthFirst` from the main program for a small graph.

The formal parameter list of `DFS` contains the graph, `G`, and its starting vertex, `V`, for the search. `G` is called by reference so the changes to `Visited` will be available upon return from a call. Assuming that the call from the main program gave a value of 1 to `StartV`, 1 is also passed to `V` on the first call to `DFS`.

In the abstract definition of a depth-first search, the starting vertex is visited. `DFS` therefore first visits `V` by marking

`G.Visited [V] := true`

and outputting `V`. Figure 11.19 shows a trace of the recursive calls to `DFS`. Since `V` has the value 1, Figure 11.19(a) shows that `G.Visited [1]` gets true.

In the abstract definition, any unvisited vertex, say *w*, adjacent to the start vertex is then selected, and a depth-first search is started from *w*. `DFS` implements the selection by initializing the local variable, `P`, to point to the first node in the linked list and advancing it down the list. When an unvisited vertex is encountered, which is detected by

`if not (G.Visited [P^.Vertex]) then`

`DFS` calls itself recursively.

In Figure 11.19(a), `P` points to the first node in the list, `G.Body [1]`. The `Vertex` field of the node contains 2, and, since `G.Visited [2]` is false, `DFS` calls itself, passing 2 to the formal parameter. Figure 11.19(b) shows the data structure after the call. After `G.Visited [2]` gets true, the newly allocated `P` points

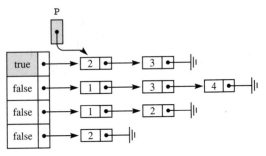

(a) Before the second call to DFS.

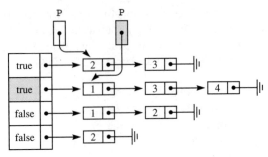

(b) After the second call, before the loop executes.

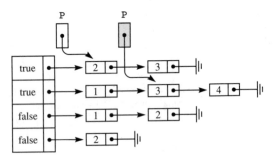

(c) Before the third call.

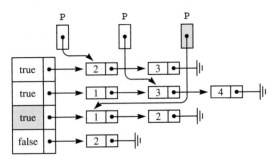

(d) After the third call, before the loop executes.

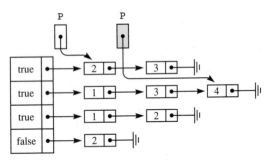

(e) Before the fourth call.

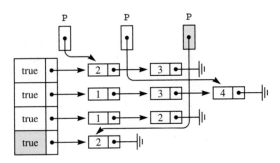

(f) After the fourth call, before the loop executes.

Figure 11.19

A trace of the recursive calls to DFS.

to the first node in list, G.Body [2]. As is usual with recursive calls, there is more than one instance of the local variable, P; in fact, there is one instance for each call. The P variables are allocated on the run-time stack.

The second P advances through its list, testing at each node whether the adjacent vertex has been visited. In Figure 11.19(b), P^.Vertex is 1, and vertex 1 has been visited. Therefore, P advances as shown in (c). This time P^.Vertex is 3, and vertex 3 has not yet been visited. So a third call is made, with 3 passed to formal parameter V. Figure 11.19(d) shows the data structure after the visit to vertex 3 and before the loop executes.

The third P now advances through its list. But the nodes in the list store vertices 1 and 2, both of which have been visited. So no recursive calls are made from this loop. P eventually gets nil, and control returns to the calling procedure. In the abstract definition of the depth-first search, the process repeatedly backs up to the previously visited vertex. In this procedure, the returns from the recursive calls implement the backup. Figure 11.19(e) shows the third P deallocated and the second P advancing from where it left off in (c).

In Figure 11.19(e), the node that P points to has a `Vertex` field of 4. Another call is made to DFS to visit vertex 4 as shown in (f). Not shown in the sequence of figures is the subsequent deallocation of the fourth P, deallocation of the second P, advance of the first P to the end of its list, and the deallocation of the first P.

Breadth-First Search

Unlike `DepthFirst`, `BreadthFirst` does not require another procedure such as `DFS`. Instead, it requires a local queue to store the vertices after they are visited. The algorithm in pseudocode format is as follows:

```
procedure BreadthFirst (G: GraphType; StartV: integer)
   var
      Queue: QueueType
      V, W:  integer
   begin
   Initialize G.Visited array to all false
   Initialize Queue to the empty queue
   Visit StartV
   Add StartV to Queue
   while  Queue is not empty do
      begin
      Delete V from Queue
      for all vertices W adjacent to V  do
         if vertex W is not visited then
             begin
             Visit W
             Add W to Queue
             end
      end
   end
```

An algorithm that implements a breadth-first search

Table 11.1 is a trace of the algorithm for the visitation sequence in Figure 11.13 and the corresponding adjacency list in Figure 11.17. It shows the queue with its front on the left. Each action from the algorithm is either a visit, add, or delete. As in `DepthFirst`, a visit to V is implemented by marking the `Visited` array and outputting the value of V.

Steps 1–3, which visit `StartV` and add it to the queue, occur outside the outer `while` loop. Step 4 reflects the first executable statement in the `while` loop and gives 2 to V. The inner loop examines all the vertices adjacent to 2, which are

Step	Action	Queue
1		empty
2	Visit 2	empty
3	Add 2	2
4	Delete 2	empty
5	Visit 1	empty
6	Add 1	1
7	Visit 5	1
8	Add 5	1 5
9	Visit 4	1 5
10	Add 4	1 5 4
11	Delete 1	5 4
12	Visit 9	5 4
13	Add 9	5 4 9
14	Visit 3	5 4 9
15	Add 3	5 4 9 3
16	Delete 5	4 9 3
17	Visit 8	4 9 3
18	Add 8	4 9 3 8
19	Delete 4	9 3 8
20	Visit 6	9 3 8
21	Add 6	9 3 8 6
22	Delete 9	3 8 6
23	Visit 7	3 8 6
24	Add 7	3 8 6 7
25	Delete 3	8 6 7
26	Delete 8	6 7
27	Delete 6	7
28	Delete 7	empty

Table 11.1

A trace of the breadth-first search algorithm for the graph of Figure 11.13.

1, 5, and 4. Since none of them are visited, the condition of the `if` statement is always true. Steps 5–10 visit each and add it to the queue.

Step 11 shows the effect of the first executable statement in the `while` loop again. This time vertex 1 is deleted and vertices 9 and 3 are visited and added, as shown in steps 12–15.

Similarly, step 16 deletes vertex 5, and steps 17 and 18 visit the node adjacent to vertex 5 that has not yet been visited, which is vertex 8, and add it to the queue. The first in, first out nature of the queue is necessary for the vertices to be visited in the proper order. At step 16, if you delete vertex 3 from the rear of the queue (instead of 5 from the front) and visit the vertices adjacent to 3, you will visit vertex 7 before vertex 8.

Steps 19–24 show the remainder of the visits. When all the vertices have been visited, the condition of the `if` statement will always be false, and no vertices will be added to the queue. The first executable statement in the outer `while` loop deletes the remaining vertices, as reflected in steps 25–28.

If you implement the graph with an adjacency list as in Program 11.4, the inner loop should not be a Pascal `for` statement. Instead, the vertices adjacent to `V` should be obtained by advancing a local pointer down the linked list as in `DFS`. The Pascal implementation of `BreadthFirst` is left as a problem at the end of this chapter.

It is interesting that the difference between the depth-first search and the breadth-first search is tied to the difference between the stack, which is a last in, first out structure, and the queue, which is a first in, first out structure. The depth-first search uses the run-time stack to back up to the most recently visited vertex. The breadth-first search uses the queue to store together the groups of vertices that are visited at the same level from the start vertex.

Connected Components

Once you implement the graph traversal algorithms, the procedure to output the connected components is straightforward. The idea is to initialize the `Visited` array to all false, and to traverse the graph starting at vertex 1. Then you check the remaining vertices to see if any were not visited by the traversal. Vertices that were not visited cannot be connected to those previously visited. To output another connected component, you would select an unvisited vertex and do another traversal using it as the starting vertex. Details are in the following algorithm:

```
procedure ConnectedComp (G: GraphType)
   var
      I: integer
   begin
   Initialize G.Visited array to all false
   for I := 1 to G.Size do
      if vertex I is not visited then
         begin
         Output connected component heading.
         DFS (G, I)
         end
   end
```

An algorithm that outputs the connected components of a graph

This algorithm selects an unvisited vertex by simply examining every vertex in a `for` statement. All vertices must be visited once at the termination of the loop, so all the connected components will be output.

The code shows a call to `DFS` to do the actual traversal, but a breadth-first search would function just as well. However, you could not simply call `BreadthFirst` as presented in place of `DFS`, because `BreadthFirst` would reinitialize the `Visited` array.

Adjacency Matrix Implementation

Another common implementation of a graph is called the *adjacency matrix*. The idea is to maintain a two-dimensional array of integers, each of which is 0 or 1. If row I and column J of the array contains 1, there is an edge between vertex I and vertex J. A value of 0 indicates no edge between vertices I and J. The declarations that follow define the data structure.

```
const
   GraphMax = 20;
type
   GraphType =
      record
      Size:    integer;
      Body:    array [1..GraphMax, 1..GraphMax] of 0..1;
      Visited: array [1..GraphMax] of boolean
      end;
```

Data structure for the graph implemented with an adjacency matrix

An example of an adjacency matrix is the following array, which represents the graph in Figure 11.12. The 1 in row 8, column 5 represents the edge between vertices 8 and 5 in the graph. The matrix is symmetric. That is, the element in row I, column J equals the element in row J, column I.

	1	2	3	4	5	6	7	8	9
1	0	1	1	0	0	0	0	0	1
2	1	0	0	1	1	0	0	0	0
3	1	0	0	0	0	0	1	0	0
4	0	1	0	0	0	1	0	0	0
5	0	1	0	0	0	0	0	1	1
6	0	0	0	1	0	0	1	0	0
7	0	0	1	0	0	1	0	0	1
8	0	0	0	0	1	0	0	0	1
9	1	0	0	0	1	0	1	1	0

Adjacency matrix for the graph of Figure 11.12

All the operations of the graph ADT can be implemented using this representation of the graph. The question naturally arises as to which representation is better—the adjacency list or the adjacency matrix. To a certain extent, the answer depends on the problem to be solved. Some problems, not described here, are easier to solve with an array implementation than with a list representation.

In a graph with n vertices and m edges, the array representation requires n^2 elements, $2m$ of which are 1 and the rest 0. On the other hand, the list representation requires only n elements in the one-dimensional array of pointers and $2m$ nodes in the linked lists. Even though the list representation requires additional storage for the `Link` fields, the array representation frequently requires more storage for problems where n is large and there are few edges in the graph.

Storage requirements for different implementations of the graph ADT

The fundamental space/time tradeoff may apply here. Frequently, with the list representation a problem can be solved using less storage, but with a slower execution time than the array representation would require.

SUMMARY

A data structure is an implementation of an abstract data type. A variable-length string is an abstract data type that includes operations to search for a pattern in a string, insert and delete substrings within a string, and test two strings for alphabetical order. A variable-length string can be implemented in standard Pascal by a record with two fields containing the number of characters in the string, followed by an array of the characters. The general string line-processing algorithm corresponds to the basic Pascal character-processing algorithm, but is at a higher level of abstraction and does not require a nested loop.

A queue is a first in, first out (FIFO) list of values. The operations on a queue include `AddQ` to add an element to the queue and `DeleteQ` to remove an element from the queue. One possible implementation of a queue is with a circular array. The data structure includes two index variables, one for the front of the queue and one for the rear. The array is called circular because the end of the array is connected to the beginning of the array conceptually with the `mod` operator. Another implementation is with a linked list. The data structure contains two pointer variables, instead of two integer index variables, to point to the front and rear of the queue.

As an ADT, a graph is a set of vertices and a set of edges, each one of which connects two vertices. Two vertices are adjacent if there is an edge that connects them. A connected graph is one for which there is a path from any vertex to any other vertex. Operations on a graph include depth-first search, breadth-first search, and testing for connectivity. One possible implementation of a graph is with an adjacency list. It consists of an array of pointers, one for each vertex in the graph. Each pointer points to a linked list of nodes, each node of which contains a vertex adjacent to the vertex corresponding to the array pointer. Another implementation of a graph is with an adjacency matrix. This matrix is two-dimensional with a 1 in row i and column j if there is an edge between vertex i and vertex j in the graph, and a 0 otherwise.

EXERCISES

Section 11.1

1. Suppose `String1` and `String2` are variable-length strings of type `StringType` with values 'abcdefg' and 'def' respectively. What does each of the following functions return?

* (a) Length (String1)
  (b) Match (String1, String2)
  (c) Match (String2, String1)
  (d) GreaterThan (String1, String2)

2. Assuming the values for String1 and String2 in Exercise 1, what does each of the following procedures do?

* (a) Delete (String1, 2, 3)
* (b) Insert (String1, String2, 2)
  (c) Insert (String2, String1, 2)
  (d) Substring (String2, String1, 2, 5)
  (e) Substring (String2, String1, 2, 10)
  (f) Substring (String2, String1, 5, -4)

3. If String is a variable-length string of type StringType with value 'goodbye' and I is an integer variable, what is the output of each of the following code fragments?

* (a)
```
for I := 1 to 7 do
   begin
   PutString (String);
   Delete (String, 1, 1)
   end
```

(b)
```
for I := 1 to 7 do
   begin
   PutString (String);
   Delete (String, Length (String), 1)
   end
```

4. Suppose Sentence and Reverse both have type StringType. Write a single procedure call using only the operations of the string ADT described in the text that gives Reverse the same string of characters as in Sentence, but in reverse order.

5. In function Match, suppose that Pat has the 5 characters 'abcab' and S has the 10 characters 'abababcabc'. *(a) How many times does the following statement in the body of the while loop execute?

```
I := I + 1
```

(b) How many times does the following statement in the body of the while loop execute?

```
Start := Start + 1
```

(c) How many times does the while loop execute?

6. In function Match, suppose that Pat.Len has the value 5 and S.Len has the value 10. In the worst case, how many times will the body of the while loop execute? That is, what is the maximum number of executions possible? Write down values for Pat and S that will cause the loop to execute the maximum number of times.

7. Work Exercise 6 for the general case of *m* for Pat.Len and *n* for S.Len.

Section 11.2

8. Suppose procedure Initialize in Program 11.2 sets Q.Front and Q.Rear both to QueueMax instead of to zero. Will the implementation work correctly? Explain.

*9. In the circular array implementation of a queue, suppose Body is declared as

```
array [0..QueueMax] of ValueType
```

and QueueMax has the value *n*. How many values can be stored in the queue?

10. Suppose a queue contains the four values

    9.0   3.0   4.0   1.0

    with 9.0 at the front and 1.0 at the rear. **(a)** In the linked list implementation, sketch the data structure before the procedure is called and after each executable statement in the procedure if `AddQ` is called to add 7.0 to the queue. **(b)** Do the same if `DeleteQ` is called to delete an element from the queue.

Section 11.3

*11. Is it possible to draw Figure 11.20 starting at one point and returning to the original point without lifting your pencil from the paper? Explain.

12. Figure 11.21 represents five rooms connected to each other and to the outside by doors. **(a)** Draw the multigraph that represents this physical situation. **(b)** Is it possible to start at one spot, go through each door exactly once, and return to the original spot? Explain.

13. ***(a)** In the graph of Figure 11.12, how many different breadth-first searches are there starting at vertex 2? **(b)** How many are there starting at vertex 6?

14. Write the visitation sequence of a depth-first search that does not require a backup for the graph of Figure 11.12 starting at vertex 6.

15. You can consider a binary tree to be a graph with a vertex representing each node in the tree and an edge connecting each node with its parent. With this interpretation, do the following: **(a)** Draw the adjacency list representation of the binary tree of Figure 10.14(a). **(b)** Draw the adjacency matrix representation of the binary tree of Figure 10.14(a). **(c)** Explain whether it is possible for a breadth-first search or a depth-first search of the binary tree represented as a graph to produce the same visitation sequence as a preorder, inorder, or postorder traversal.

16. Suppose that `DepthFirst` in Program 11.4 executes the depth-first search of Figure 11.15. ***(a)** What is the maximum number of stack frames on the run-time stack? **(b)** Draw the call tree.

17. Suppose that `DepthFirst` in Program 11.4 executes the depth-first search of Figure 11.16. **(a)** What is the maximum number of stack frames on the run-time stack? **(b)** Draw the call tree.

18. In the adjacency list implementation of the graph ADT, suppose `GraphType` contains a single array of records as follows:

```
GraphRecType =
   record
   EdgeList: PtrToCellType;
   Visited:  boolean
   end;
GraphType =
   record
   Size: integer;
   Body: array [1..GraphMax] of GraphRecType
   end;
```

Write procedure `DFS` with this definition of `GraphType`.

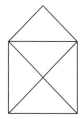

Figure 11.20

The drawing for Exercise 11.

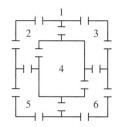

Figure 11.21

The five rooms for Exercise 12.

19. Suppose a pointer requires as much storage as an integer, and you want to represent a graph with 10 vertices. *(a) How many edges can the graph include before the list representation takes more storage than the array representation? (b) Repeat the problem for a graph with 100 vertices.

Section 11.1

20. Implement the following functions and procedures that operate on the string ADT as described in the text. Test your implementation in a main program similar to Program 11.1.

    (a) procedure Initialize   (b) function Length
    (c) procedure Insert   (d) procedure Delete
    (e) procedure Substring   (f) function GreaterThan
    (g) function Equal   (h) function LessThan

21. Implement the string ADT as an array with the null sentinel value chr (0). Do not include an integer field for the length. Implement the following functions and procedures as described in the text. Test your implementation in a main program similar to Program 11.1.

    (a) procedure Initialize   (b) procedure GetString
    (c) procedure PutString   (d) function Length
    (e) procedure Insert   (f) procedure Delete
    (g) procedure Substring   (h) function Match
    (i) function GreaterThan   (j) function Equal
    (k) function LessThan

22. Implement the string ADT as a singly linked list with one character per node. Do not include an integer field for the length. Implement the following functions and procedures as described in the text. Test your implementation in a main program similar to Program 11.1.

    (a) procedure Initialize   (b) procedure GetString
    (c) procedure PutString   (d) function Length
    (e) procedure Insert   (f) procedure Delete
    (g) procedure Substring   (h) function Match
    (i) function GreaterThan   (j) function Equal
    (k) function LessThan

23. Use the general string-ADT-processing algorithm to count the number of empty lines in a file. Use only the string ADT operations described in the text.

24. Use the general string-ADT-processing algorithm to count the number of characters in a file. Use only the string ADT operations described in the text.

25. Write a new procedure for the variable-length string ADT called MatchLast, which has the same parameter list as Match but matches the last occurrence of the pattern in the string. Test your implementation in a main program similar to Program 11.1.

26. A company wants to send out "personalized" form letters in which the recipient's name is inserted throughout the letter. The first line of a form-letter file contains a string of

characters that are to be substituted in the remaining lines of the file. Another file contains a list of names, one on each line. Write a program that outputs to the screen copies of the letter for each person on the mailing list with the correct names inserted. Use only the string ADT operations described in the text. Assume each name will occur no more than once on a line.

Sample Input—`FormLetterFile`

```
***
Dear ***,

As a person who needs to stay well informed, you cannot
afford to be without a subscription to the Daily News.
If you subscribe, as you walk down the street people will
say, "There goes ***, the best-informed person in town."
Please ***, send us your subscription to the Daily News
right away.
```

Sample Input—`NameFile`

```
Tom
Aristotle
John
```

27. Write a program that reads a positive number interactively as a variable-length string and formats it into a string as follows:

Format 210732 as `$2,107.32`

Format 67150 as `$671.50`

Format 4 as `$0.04`

There must be two digits following the decimal point and at least one digit preceding the decimal point. The dollar sign is next to the first nonzero digit, or next to the leading zero if the integer input is less than 100. Use only the string ADT operations described in the text.

Sample Input/Output

```
Enter unformatted number: 210732
Formatted: $2,107.32
```

Section 11.2

28. Write a driver program to test the implementation of the queue ADT **(a)** as a circular array in Program 11.2, and **(b)** as a linked list in Program 11.3. The program should initialize the queue then repeatedly give the user the choice of testing whether the queue is empty, adding to the queue, or deleting from the queue. Output the value of each element deleted. Use any `ValueType` of your own choosing, but indicate its type in the prompt.

29. Implement the queue ADT as a noncircular array with a floating front. Have `AddQ` test whether there is room in the array on the right of `Rear` to add the element. If not, test whether there is room in the left part of the array to add the element. If there is, shift

the elements to the beginning of the array using one loop and complete the add operation. Test your implementation with a main program as described in Problem 28.

30. Implement the queue ADT as a linked list, with `QueueType` a single pointer that points to the front of the list as described for the stack implementation in Section 10.2. In `AddQ`, find the rear of the queue by advancing a local pointer down the list. Test your implementation with a main program as described in Problem 28.

Section 11.3

31. Modify Program 11.4, which outputs a depth-first search, by using the adjacency matrix implementation of the graph ADT.

32. Implement procedure `RemoveEdge` to remove an edge from a graph. Test your implementation with a program that inputs a graph as in Program 11.4. Then repeatedly give the user the choice of adding an edge to the graph, removing an edge from the graph, or performing a depth-first search of the graph starting from any vertex. **(a)** Use the adjacency list implementation of the graph ADT. **(b)** Use the adjacency matrix implementation of the graph ADT.

33. Add error checking to procedures `AddEdge` and `RemoveEdge` in Problem 32. Each vertex in an edge must be between 1 and the largest vertex of the graph. You cannot add an edge to a graph that already contains the edge. You cannot remove an edge from a graph that does not contain the edge. If an error condition exists, output an appropriate error message and do not alter the graph. **(a)** Use the adjacency list implementation of the graph ADT. **(b)** Use the adjacency matrix implementation of the graph ADT.

34. The following function returns the degree of vertex V in graph G.

```
function Degree (G: GraphType; V: integer): integer
```

Write the function in Pascal. Test your implementation with a main program as described in Problem 32. **(a)** Use the adjacency list implementation of the graph ADT. **(b)** Use the adjacency matrix implementation of the graph ADT.

35. Implement `BreadthFirst` in a main program similar to Program 11.4. Use a circular array to implement the queue of vertices. **(a)** Use the adjacency list implementation of the graph. **(b)** Use the adjacency matrix implementation of the graph.

36. Implement `ConnectedComp` in a main program similar to Program 11.4. Modify your procedure to output not only the vertices of each component, but also the number of connected components. The sample output is for the abstract graph of Figure 11.11(b). **(a)** Use the adjacency list implementation of the graph. **(b)** Use the adjacency matrix implementation of the graph. **(c)** Use a breadth-first search for the traversal in conjunction with the adjacency list implementation of the graph.

Sample Output

```
Connected component:
   1   3
Connected component:
   2   4   6   5   7
Number of connected components: 2
```

Standard Pascal Syntax

This appendix contains all the syntax charts from the text. The diagrams are ordered top-down, beginning with the syntax chart for a complete Pascal program. Each syntax chart contains a reference to the figure number and page number in the text where an example and description of the diagram can be found. Also included here is the syntax chart for an expression, which was not included in the text.

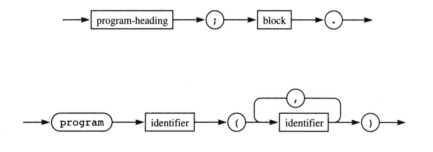

Figure A.1

The syntax chart for a program. (See Figure 2.8, p. 42.)

Figure A.2

The syntax chart for a program heading. (See Figure 2.9, p. 42.)

The block is the basic structural unit of a Pascal program. Figure A.3 shows the structure of a block. It consists of an optional constant definition part, type definition part, variable definition part, procedure declaration part, any number of procedure and/or function declaration parts, and a required compound statement. The compound statement contains the executable statements of the block.

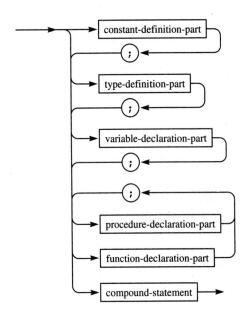

Figure A.3

The syntax chart for a block. (See Figure 2.10, p. 42.)

The constant definition part is defined in terms of identifiers, strings, unsigned numbers, and constant identifiers. Strings are sequences of characters enclosed in apostrophes, as described on page 40. Unsigned numbers are reals and integers, as defined in Figures A.40 and A.41.

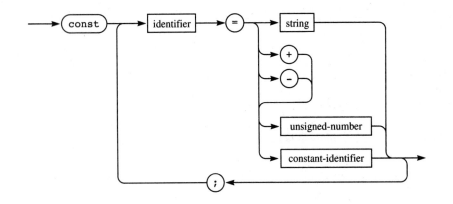

Figure A.4

The syntax chart for a constant definition part. (See Figure 3.9, p. 90.)

The type definition part is defined in terms of type identifiers, enumerated types, subrange types, pointer types, and structured types. The structured types are file type, array type, record type, and set type. The ordinal types included in the definition of the array type are integer, boolean, character, and subrange. The classification of all the Pascal types is shown in Figure 5.12 on page 185.

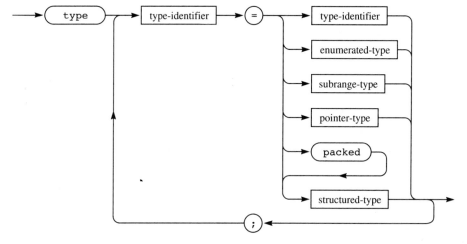

Figure A.5

The syntax chart for a type definition part. (See Figure 15.13, p. 186.)

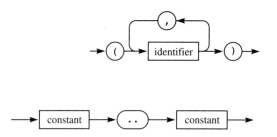

Figure A.6

The syntax chart for an enumerated type. (See Figure 5.14, p. 186.)

Figure A.7

The syntax chart for a subrange type. (See Figure 5.17, p. 193.)

A pointer type is defined in terms of a domain type, which is a type identifier.

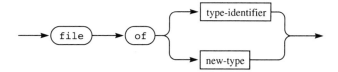

Figure A.8

The syntax chart for a pointer type. (See Figure 10.2, p. 508.)

The structured types are all defined in terms of type identifiers and new types. New types are the type constructors listed on page 185.

Figure A.9

The syntax chart for a file type. (See Figure 4.2, p. 134.)

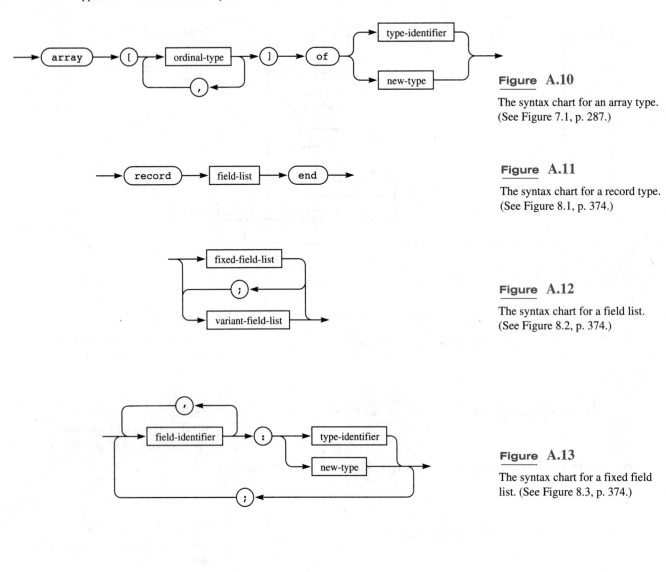

Figure A.10

The syntax chart for an array type. (See Figure 7.1, p. 287.)

Figure A.11

The syntax chart for a record type. (See Figure 8.1, p. 374.)

Figure A.12

The syntax chart for a field list. (See Figure 8.2, p. 374.)

Figure A.13

The syntax chart for a fixed field list. (See Figure 8.3, p. 374.)

Figure A.14

The syntax chart for a variant field list. (See Figure 8.19, p. 408.)

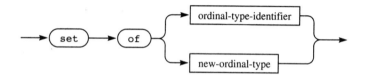

Figure A.15

The syntax chart for a set type. (See Figure 8.24, p. 418.)

The variable declaration part is defined in terms of identifiers, type identifiers, and new types.

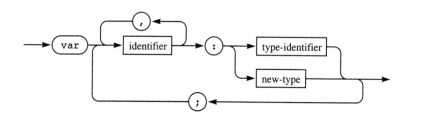

Figure A.16

The syntax chart for a variable declaration part. (See Figure 2.14, p. 50.)

The function declaration part is defined in terms of the function heading and the block. This is a recursive definition of the block, since it was defined in Figure A.3.

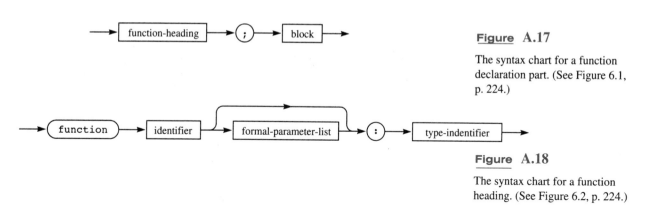

Figure A.17

The syntax chart for a function declaration part. (See Figure 6.1, p. 224.)

Figure A.18

The syntax chart for a function heading. (See Figure 6.2, p. 224.)

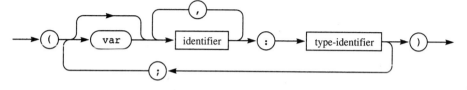

Figure A.19

The syntax chart for a formal parameter list. (See Figure 6.3, p. 226.)

The procedure declaration part is defined in terms of the procedure heading and the block. The definition of the formal parameter list for a procedure, referred to in Figure A.21, is identical to that for functions, as shown in Figure A.19.

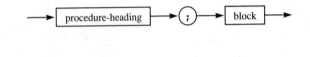

Figure A.20

The syntax chart for a procedure declaration part. (See Figure 6.6, p. 235.)

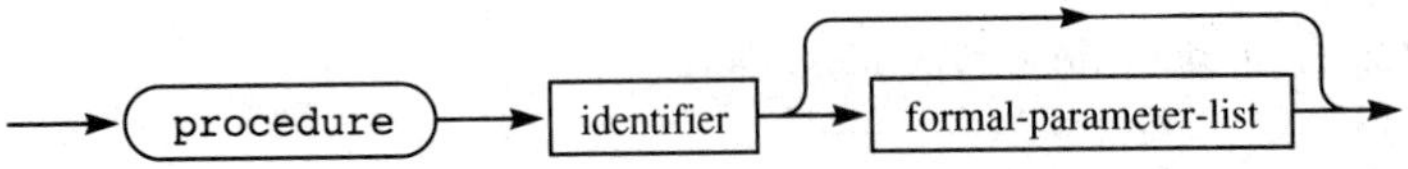

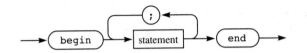

Figure A.21

The syntax chart for a procedure heading. (See Figure 6.7, p. 236.)

The compound statement is the basis of the executable statements in a block and is the structure by which two or more statements are placed in the body of a structured statement.

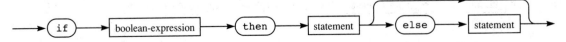

Figure A.22

The syntax chart for a compound statement. (See Figure 2.11, p. 43.)

The classification of all the Pascal statements is shown in Figure 5.11 on page 184. The `readln` call and `writeln` call are special cases of the procedure call.

Figure A.23

The syntax chart for an assignment statement. (See Figure 2.15, p. 51.)

Figure A.24

The syntax chart for an `if` statement. (See Figure 3.4, p. 86.)

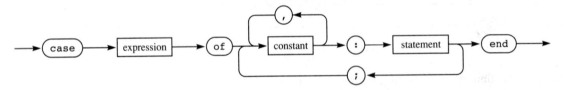

Figure A.25

The syntax chart for a `case` statement. (See Figure 3.16, p. 110.)

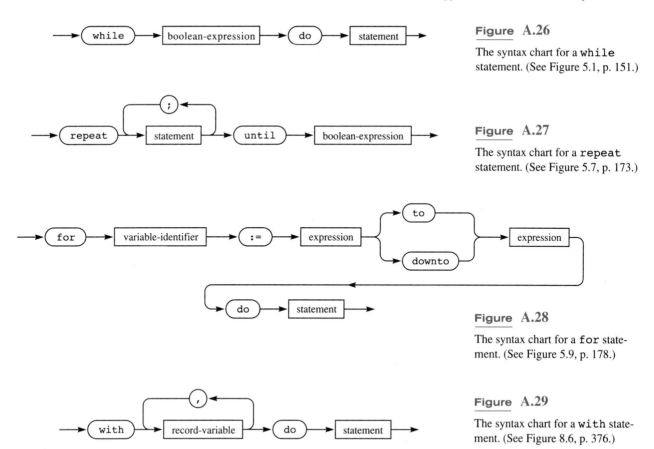

Figure A.26

The syntax chart for a `while` statement. (See Figure 5.1, p. 151.)

Figure A.27

The syntax chart for a `repeat` statement. (See Figure 5.7, p. 173.)

Figure A.28

The syntax chart for a `for` statement. (See Figure 5.9, p. 178.)

Figure A.29

The syntax chart for a `with` statement. (See Figure 8.6, p. 376.)

A procedure call is a Pascal statement. A function call, however, is not a statement but occurs in an expression. The definition of the actual parameter list for a function, referred to in Figure A.39, is identical to that for procedures, as shown in Figure A.31.

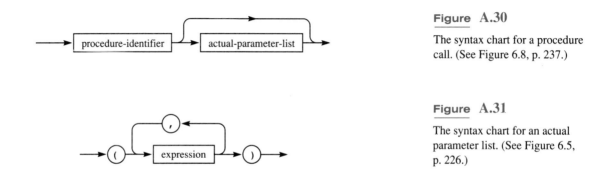

Figure A.30

The syntax chart for a procedure call. (See Figure 6.8, p. 237.)

Figure A.31

The syntax chart for an actual parameter list. (See Figure 6.5, p. 226.)

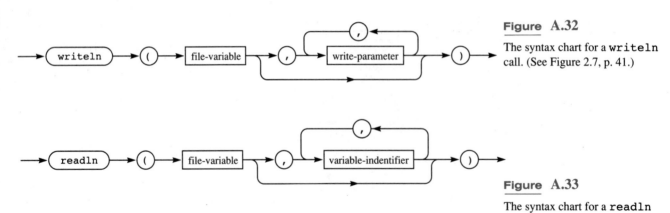

Figure A.32

The syntax chart for a `writeln` call. (See Figure 2.7, p. 41.)

Figure A.33

The syntax chart for a `readln` call. (See Figure 2.20, p. 60.)

The syntax chart for an expression was not given in the text. It is shown here in Figure A.34 and is defined in terms of a simple expression. A simple expression is defined in terms of a term, which is defined in terms of a factor. The boolean expressions referred to in previous figures are included in the general definition of an expression. See pages 67–83 for a discussion of real, integer, mixed, character, and boolean expressions. See pages 417–27 for a discussion of set expressions.

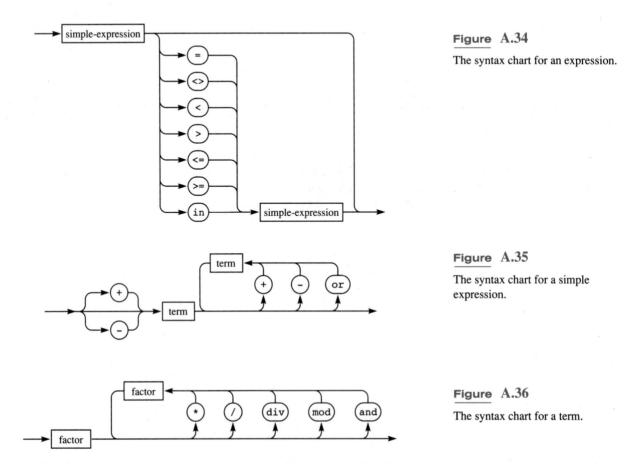

Figure A.34

The syntax chart for an expression.

Figure A.35

The syntax chart for a simple expression.

Figure A.36

The syntax chart for a term.

25

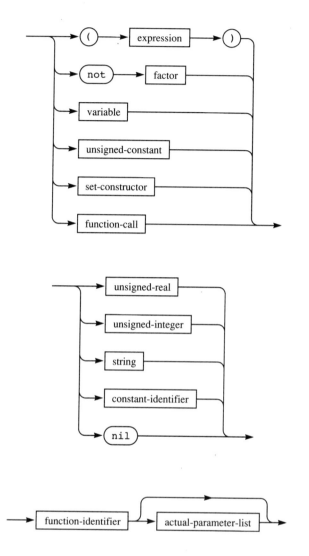

Figure A.37

The syntax chart for a factor.

Figure A.38

The syntax chart for an unsigned constant.

Figure A.39

The syntax chart for a function call. (See Figure 6.4, p. 226.)

The text defines signed reals and integers. This appendix defines unsigned reals and integers. Any leading signs come from the definition of a simple expression.

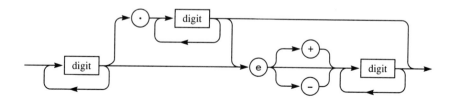

Figure A.40

The syntax chart for an unsigned real. (Similar to Figure 2.17, p. 55.)

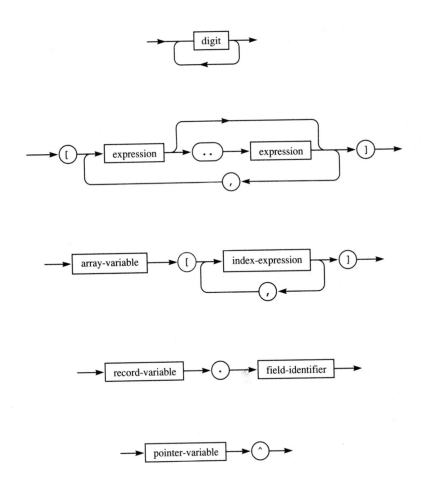

Figure A.41

The syntax chart for an unsigned integer. (Similar to Figure 2.18, p. 57.)

Figure A.42

The syntax chart for a set constant. (See Figure 8.25, p. 418.)

Figure A.43

The syntax chart for an indexed variable. (See Figure 7.2, p. 287.)

Figure A.44

The syntax chart for a field variable. (See Figure 8.4, p. 375.)

Figure A.45

The syntax chart for an identified variable. (See Figure 10.4, p. 510.)

Identifiers are used to name programs, constants, types, enumerated values, fields, functions, procedures, and variables.

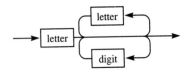

Figure A.46

The syntax chart for an identifier. (See Figure 2.4, p. 39.)

Solutions to Selected Exercises

Chapter 1

2. **(a)** 11,110 not counting Khan

3. **(a)**

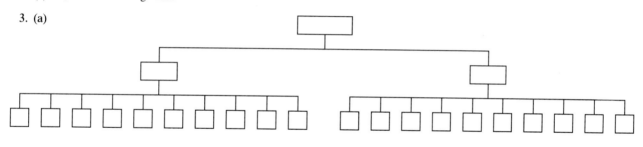

4. **(a)** See figure **(b)** 31

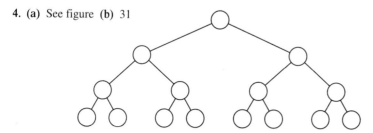

5. 0.4 bits per second

7. **(a)** 55 or 56, depending on whether you use the computer science value of K **(b)** 2

9. **(a)** 153,600 **(b)** 19,200 bytes, which is about 19.2 Kbytes

12. **(a)** 18.5 hours

16. **Temp5**

F.Name	F.Major	F.State
Ron	Math	OR

Temp6

S.Name	S.Class	S.Major	S.State
Beth	Soph	Hist	TX
Allison	Soph	Math	AZ

17. (a)
```
select Sor where S.Name = Beth giving Temp
project Temp over S.State giving Result
```

Chapter 2

1. (a) Valid (b) Not valid, contains a space (c) Not valid, reserved word (d) Not valid, contains a space (e) Not valid, begins with a digit (f) Not valid, contains a nonalphanumeric character (g) Not valid, contains a nonalphanumeric character (h) Valid

3. The semicolon in the program heading should be after (output). The single apostrophe in it's should be duplicated.

5. ```
The company's name is Gigantic Ant Control.
Their business is
controlling ants.
```

7. ```
xoo
oxo
oox
oxo
xoo
oxo
oox
oxo
```

9. (a) No

10. (a) | −396.784|

(b) | −396.78|

(c) | −396.8|

(d) | −397.|

(e) | −396.8|

(f) |−3.968e 02|

Chapter 3

1. (a) 2.5 (b) 2.5 (c) 2 (d) Illegal, div requires integer operands (e) 1 (f) Illegal, mod requires integer operands (g) 9 (h) 8 (i) 6.8 (j) 6 (k) 9 (l) 9.0 (m) 4.0 (n) 4.0 (o) 0.0 (p) 2.718 (q) 4.7

3. (a)

I	J	X
?	?	?
18	2	4.5
19		42.5

4. (a) 'D' (b) 'Y' (c) '3' (d) '8' (e) 2 (f) 'A' (g) 41 (h) 'd'

6. (a) false (b) false (c) true

8. (a) true

9. Hint: Here is the first table:

p	q	p AND q	NOT (p AND q)
true	true	true	false
true	false	false	true
false	true	false	true
false	false	false	true

12. (a) if Ch <= 'z' then

13. (a)

Hours	Rate	Wages
?	?	?
36.0	4.75	171.0

Output

Total Wages are $171.00

15. (a)

Fare	NumFlights	Response	Qualified
?	?	?	?
100.00	9	'N'	false

Output

You do not qualify for discount.

17. (a)

19. (a)
Statement 1;
if *Condition 1* then
    Statement 2
else
    Statement 3;
Statement 4;
Statement 5

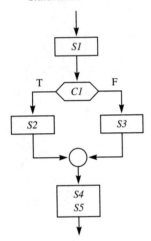

21. (a)

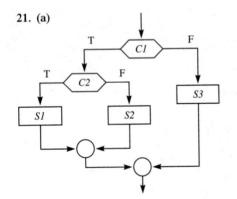

22. (a)
if *Condition 1* then
    if *Condition 2* then
        Statement 1
    else
        Statement 2

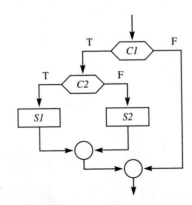

25.
```
if Age >= 65 then
    write (output, 'Social Security')
  else if Age >= 18 then
    write (output, 'Taxable')
  else
    write (output, 'Exempt')
```

27. (a) 4 (b) No output (c) 10

28. (a) 5

30. (a)
```
if Num < 23 then
    if Num >= 15 then
        {  Assert: 15 <= Num < 23}
        Statement 1
    else
        {  Assert: Num < 15}
        Statement 2
  else
      {  Assert: Num >= 23}
      Statement 3
```

31. (a)
```
if Num < 70 then
    if Num >= 80 then
        {  Dead code}
        Statement 1
    else
        {  Assert: Num < 70}
        Statement 2
  else
      {  Assert: Num >= 70}
      Statement 3
```

32.
```
case I of
    2, 5:     Statement 1;
    3:        Statement 2;
    1, 4, 6: Statement 3
  end {case}
```

Chapter 4

1.

	I	J	K
(a)	2	8	6
(b)	2	8	6
(c)	2	8	1
(d)	2	1	3
(e)	2	1	3
(f)	1	3	5
(g)	2	8	6
(h)	6	8	?

3. ```
begin
    Input BDay, BMonth, BYear
    Input TDay, TMonth, TYear
    if TMonth < BMonth then
        {No birthday yet this year.}
        Output TYear - BYear - 1
    else if TMonth > BMonth then
        {Birthday already this year}
        Output TYear - BYear
    else if TDay < BDay then
        {No birthday yet this month}
        Output TYear - BYear - 1
    else
        {Birthday already this month}
        Output TYear - BYear
end
```

## Chapter 5

1. (a)

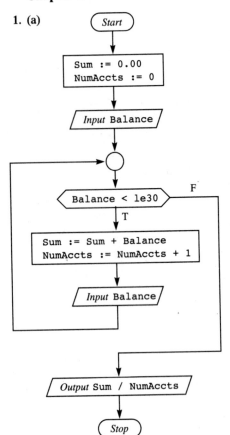
```

(b)

Sum	NumAccts	Balance
?	?	?
0.00	0	100.00
100.00	1	200.00
300.00	2	15.00
315.00	3	2e 30

3.

Left	FLeft	Mid	FMid	Right	Tolerance
?	?	?	?	?	?
1.0	-1.0	1.5	-0.625	2.0	0.3
1.5	-0.625	1.75	0.359	1.75	

6. (a)

A	Sum
?	?
5	0
6	5
7	11
8	18
9	26

The output is 26.

7. **(a)** (1) 52 (2) 100 (3) 100 (4) 25

9. **(a)** If the file is empty, `reset` will make `eof (SomeFile)` true, and `read` will try to read past the end of the file. The program will crash.

11.

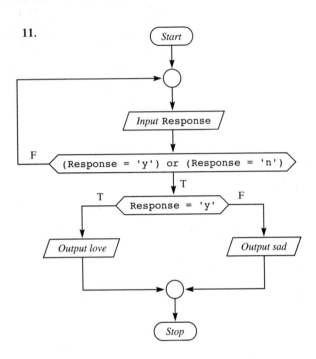

15. (a)

A	Sum
~~?~~	~~?~~
~~5~~	~~0~~
~~6~~	~~5~~
~~7~~	~~11~~
~~8~~	~~18~~
~~9~~	~~26~~
10	35

The output is 35.

16. (a) (1) 52 (2) 102 (3) 102 (4) 26

18.
```
repeat
     write ('Type an integer: ');
     readln (A)
until (A < 2) or (A >= 15)
```

20. (a)

Num	Sum	I
?	?	?
10	0	5
	5	6
	11	7
	18	8
	26	9
	35	10
	45	?

The output is 45.

22. (a)

Num	Sum	I
?	?	?
5	0	10
	10	9
	19	8
	27	7
	34	6
	40	5
	45	?

The output is 45.

25. (a) Apr

29. (a) 23

30. (a) 41

Chapter 6

1. (a) 6 (b) 18

2. (a)

Output
___

10
5

(b)

Output

```
10
10
```

4. **(a)** Legal **(b)** Illegal because there is only one actual parameter but two formal parameters **(c)** Legal **(d)** Legal because of the automatic conversion from integer to real **(e)** Illegal because the actual parameter 7.0 must be a variable in call by reference **(f)** Illegal because the actual parameter 7 must be a variable in call by reference

Chapter 7

1. (a)

Output

```
    1.6    2.3  -1.0    5.1
```

(b)

Output

```
    5.1  -1.0    2.3    1.6
```

2. (a)

Output

```
    8.5   1.0   3.0
```

5. (a) Yes, it works correctly, but see part **(b)**.

6. This modification does not rotate the elements to the right.

Output

```
    0.1    5.0    5.0    5.0
```

9. $3n + 34$

10. (a) 7

11. (a) Illegal because you cannot input a packed array without a loop **(b)** Legal

13. (a) 'cat' is greater

14. 59

17. (a)

Output

```
The matrix:
    12.0    8.0    6.0
     4.0    3.0    5.0
     7.0    1.0    2.0
    11.0    9.0   10.0
```

19. **(a)** The best case occurs when the `if` statement is always false, which happens if the first element is the largest one in the array. **(b)** $2n + 1$ **(c)** The worst case occurs when the `if` statement is always true, which happens if the array is in increasing order. **(d)** $3n$

21. **(a)** If the compiler uses full evaluation, the output is 50 30 as it should be, and the program does not crash.

22. **(a)**

First	Mid	Last	Found
~~?~~	~~?~~	~~2~~	~~?~~
1	~~4~~	~~7~~	false
	~~2~~	~~3~~	
	1	~~1~~	
		0	

23. **(a)**

```
7  7  7  6  4  4  2  2  1
3  3  3  3  3  3  3  1  2
8  8  1  1  1  1  1  3  3
2  2  2  2  2  2  4  4  4
5  5  5  5  5  5  5  5  5
4  4  4  4  6  6  6  6  6
9  6  6  7  7  7  7  7  7
1  1  8  8  8  8  8  8  8
6  9  9  9  9  9  9  9  9
```

26. **(a)** 4 seconds **(b)** 5.2 seconds **(c)** 20 seconds **(d)** 1 minute, 40 seconds **(e)** 8 minutes, 20 seconds

Chapter 8

2. **(a)** Illegal because `Ch` is a field identifier and not a variable

3. **(a)** `Empl.HourlyRate := Empl.HourlyRate * 1.06`

4. Capablanca
   Fine
   Fischer
   Karpov
   Korchnoi
   Marshall
   Kasparov
   Lasker
   Morphy
   Spassky
   Tal

7. 17 times

9. (a)

MasRec	TranRec	LowKey	NewMasRec	NewMasPresent
~~Wilkins'~~	Ch 2057's	~~Wilkins'~~	?	~~false~~
Fong's			Wilkins'	~~true~~
Skip nested while	—			
		2057's		false
Skip first if	—			

Issue error message, tried to change nonexistent record

11. (a) `Family.Father.Age := Family.Father.Age + 1`

12. ```
record
  AmtPledged: real;
  case Paid: boolean of
  true: (
     AmtPaid: real);
  false: (
     NumNotices: integer)
end
```

(a) `Entry.AmtPledged := 0.0`
(b) `Entry.Paid := false`
(c) `Entry.NumNotices := Entry.NumNotices + 1`
(d)
```
if not Entry.Paid then
    if NumNotices <= 2 then
        writeln ('Please note that your payment is past due.')
    else
        writeln ('Pay now, or else.')
```

14. (a) `Player.Age := Player.Age + 1`

15. (a) `Pref := []` (b) `Pref := [Sun..Sat]`

16. (a) `[0..5]` (c) `[2, 3]` (e) false (g) true

## Chapter 9

1. (a) 2 (c) 18

2. (a) $a \ b + c \ d \times -$

4.
```

6. Basis: $1 = 1^2$ is true.

   Hypothesis: $1 + 3 + 5 + \cdots + (2N - 1) = N^2$

   Induction: Add $(2N + 1)$ to both sides of the hypothesis equation.

$$1 + 3 + 5 + \cdots + (2N - 1) + (2N + 1) = N^2 + (2N + 1)$$
$$= (N + 1)^2$$

   Conclusion: True for all $n = 1, 2, 3, \ldots$

9. Hint: Add $(4N + 2)$ to both sides of the hypothesis equation.

12. (a) Number of sides: 3   4   5   6   7   8

          Number of diagonals: 0   2   5   9   14   20

15. (a) Four times

16. (a) Called seven times. Maximum of four stack frames. Calling order:

Main program
Call   BC (4, 1)
Call   BC (3, 1)
Call   BC (2, 1)
Call   BC (1, 1)
Return to   BC (2, 1)
Call   BC (1, 0)
Return to   BC (2, 1)
Return to   BC (3, 1)
Call   BC (2, 0)
Return to   BC (3, 1)
Return to   BC (4, 1)
Call   BC (4, 0)
Return to   BC (4, 1)
Return to main program

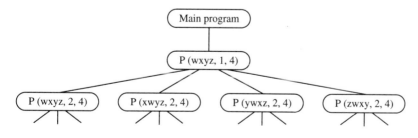

17. (a) See figure in margin.

19. (a) Called 41 times. Maximum of four stack frames. Only the top few levels of the call tree are shown. The calling sequence can be determined from the complete tree.

20. (a) See figure in margin.

Stack figure for Exercise 17(a):

1	Y2
1	Y1
**	RetAddr
1	K
2	N
2	BC
?	Y2
?	Y1
**	RetAddr
1	K
3	N
?	BC
?	Y2
?	Y1
*	RetAddr
1	K
4	N
?	BC

Figure for Exercise 17(a).

Stack figure for Exercise 20(a):

?	I
**	RetAddr
4	Right
3	Left
xwyz	A
1	I
**	RetAddr
4	Right
2	Left
xwyz	A
2	I
*	RetAddr
4	Right
1	Left
xwyz	A

Figure for Exercise 20(a).

23. (a)

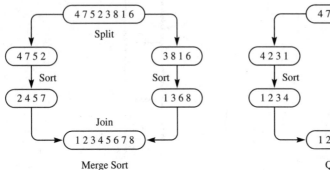

Merge Sort   Quick Sort

24. (a)

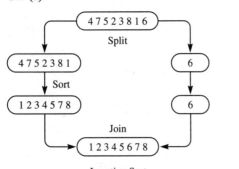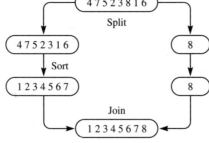

Insertion Sort   Selection Sort

25. (a) Insertion sort:

Initial:	4	7	5	2	3	8	1	6
Pass 1, insert 7:	4	7	5	2	3	8	1	6
Pass 2, insert 5:	4	5	7	2	3	8	1	6

etc.

Selection sort:

Initial:	4	7	5	2	3	8	1	6
Pass 1, select 8:	4	7	5	2	3	6	1	8
Pass 2, select 7:	4	1	5	2	3	6	7	8

etc.

26. (a) 30   20   10   40   50   80   95   60   90   70

27. (a) The key is 30.

Before QS (1, 4):	10	20	25	30	80	90	40	70	60	50
After QS (1, 4):	10	20	25	30	80	90	40	70	60	50
After QS (5, 10):	10	20	25	30	40	50	60	70	80	90

28. (a) QuickSort is called twice, including the call from the main program. There is a maximum number of two stack frames on the run-time stack. Calling order:

Main program
Call   QS (1, 3)
Call   QS (2, 3)
Return to   QS (2, 3)
Return to   QS (1, 3)
Return to main program

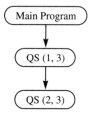

29. (a)

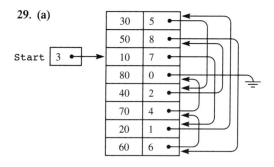

30. (a)

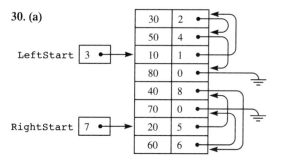

31. (a) 160

Chapter 10

1. (a) The output is 6   6.

2. (a)

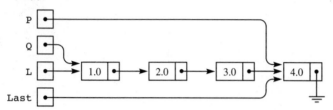

3. (a) These instructions do produce a `nil` pointer reference error since P is set to `nil`, then used to reference a cell.

4. (a) This instruction does produce a lost node. L will point to the cell containing 2.0 and nothing will point to the cell containing 1.0, which will be lost.

6. (a)

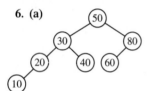

7. (a) 50   30   20   10   40   80   60

8. (a) 10   20   40   30   60   80   50

9. (a) Preorder: a   b   c   d   e
  Inorder: b   d   e   c   a
  Postorder: e   d   c   b   a

10. (a)

11. (a)

Chapter 11

1. (a) 7

2. (a) Changes `String1` to 'aefg' (b) Changes `String1` to 'adefbcdefg'

3. (a)
```
goodbye
oodbye
odbye
dbye
bye
ye
e
```

5. (a) Nine times. Note that J equals 6, not 5, when the loop terminates.

9. Although there are $n + 1$ elements in the array, only n elements can be stored.

11. It is impossible because there is a vertex with degree 3, which is odd.

13. (a) 1!3!4!1!, which is 144

16. (a) 6

19. (a) The array representation would require $10^2 = 100$ cells of memory. The list representation would require 98 cells with 22 edges and 104 cells with 23 edges. For less than 23 edges, therefore, the list representation requires less storage than the array representation.

Index